The Business of Sports

The Business of Sports provides a comprehensive foundation of the economic, organizational, legal, and political components of the sports industry. Geared for U.S. and international-based professionals and students in the journalism, communication and business fields, this text introduces readers to the ever-increasing complexity of an industry that is in constant flux. Now in its third edition, the volume continues to offer a wealth of statistics and case studies, updated with the newest developments in sports industry, including the many changes in international sports and the role of analytics in decision making and tax rules that have a major effect on athletes and teams.

Mark Conrad is Associate Professor of Law and Ethics at Fordham University's Gabelli School of Business Administration, where he is also the director of the Sports Business Program. He has been a commentator on sports law and business issues for leading newspapers, broadcast media and online services and has spoken at a number of leading universities. Before entering academia, Prof. Conrad worked as a legal journalist. In addition to a law degree, he received a Master's degree from Columbia University's Graduate School of Journalism. He is a member of the New York and District of Columbia bars and lives in New York City.

D1089451

Routledge Communication Series
Jennings Bryant/Dolf Zillmann, Series Editors

Selected Titles Include

Media Management, A Casebook Approach, 5th Edition
Hollifield et al.

Classroom Communication and Diversity
Enhancing Instructional Practice, 3rd Edition
Powell et al.

Crisis Communications
A Casebook Approach, 5th Edition
Fearn-Banks

The Media Handbook
A Complete Guide to Advertising Media Selection, Planning, Research, and Buying, 6th Edition
Katz

The Dynamics of Persuasion
Communication and Attitudes in the 21st Century, 6th Edition
Perloff

The Business of Sports
Off the Field, in the Office, on the News

Third Edition

Mark Conrad

Routledge
Taylor & Francis Group

NEW YORK AND LONDON

Third edition published 2017
by Routledge
711 Third Avenue, New York, NY 10017

and by Routledge
2 Park Square, Milton Park, Abingdon, Oxon, OX14 4RN

Routledge is an imprint of the Taylor & Francis Group, an informa business

© 2017 Taylor & Francis

First edition published by Lawrence Erlbaum Associates Inc. 2006
Second edition published by Routledge 2011

Library of Congress Cataloging-in-Publication Data
Names: Conrad, Mark, 1958–
Title: The business of sports : off the field, in the office, on the news / Mark Conrad.
Description: Third edition. | New York, NY : Routledge, 2017. | Series: Routledge communication series | Includes bibliographical references and index.
Identifiers: LCCN 2016039404 (print) | LCCN 2016039849 (ebook) | ISBN 9781138913196 (hardback) | ISBN 9781138913202 (pbk.) | ISBN 9781315691572 (ebook)
Subjects: LCSH: Sports—Economic aspects. | Sports administration. | Sports journalism.
Classification: LCC GV716 .C665 2017 (print) | LCC GV716 (ebook) | DDC 796.06/8—dc23
LC record available at https://lccn.loc.gov/2016039404

ISBN: 978-1-138-91319-6 (hbk)
ISBN: 978-1-138-91320-2 (pbk)
ISBN: 978-1-315-69157-2 (ebk)

Typeset in Sabon
by Apex CoVantage, LLC

To Kaz and Josh, the stars of my home team, and to my parents, who brought me into the big leagues

Contents

Preface to the First Edition

Professional and amateur sports occupy a prominent place in society as a dynamic and visible entertainment business with worldwide reach. The numbers of spectators, viewers and participants run into the billions. Millions of people read the sports pages of a newspaper, buy a sports-oriented magazine, watch the sports segment of a newscast, subscribe to a cable service offering sports programming, or listen to or call in to a "sports talk" radio station.

At one time, sports coverage was quite simply scores, standings and star performances. However, the continuing popularity and increased complexity of the sports landscape require that sports journalists possess a background on issues more fundamental than mere knowledge of the game. The sports industry is a multibillion-dollar business that involves many unique and complicated issues—issues that often beg to be discussed and analyzed in an objective and systematic way. Think of the amount of coverage the labor controversies receive, for example. Other issues also abound, including contract rights, free agency, amateur eligibility, drug testing, franchise relocation, stadium construction and athlete and spectator injuries. There are also the questions of intellectual property rights, racial and gender discrimination and the use and power of agents and financial advisors. Even seemingly arcane matters such as league governance, calculation of team revenues, salary cap restraints and taxation of athletes' salaries result in greater discussion and coverage.

Many seasoned journalists do an excellent job covering the business of sports. But others—not only writers and broadcasters, but also many sports talk hosts—do not. Misstatements of facts, improbable assumptions and other evidence of a lack of understanding occur all too frequently. For students of journalism and communications (and younger practitioners of the craft), this text is a primer to the business of sports and provides a guide to give students and newly minted sports writers, producers and broadcasters a basic knowledge of the sports business.

This text covers many facets of the business. I focus on what I think constitute the main issues of importance to young journalists: professional, amateur and international sports structure and governance; contract and labor issues; and stadium economics. Agents, intellectual property, testing for performance-enhancing drugs, personal injury and media issues are also covered, although in shorter chapters. Some readers may be surprised at the paucity of discussion of criminal activity by athletes. Because most criminal cases against athletes involve actions outside of the athletic activity, the issues are no different for an athlete than for a nonathlete. The trials of O. J. Simpson and the charges against Kobe Bryant do not directly bear on the sports business, and there are many sources for learning about the criminal justice system.

Many readers will notice that a great deal of the subject matter is complex and very detailed. Topics such as salary caps and stadium revenues are difficult by nature, but are crucial to a knowledge of the business of sports.

I wish to thank all who contributed to this book—my graduate assistants Hannah Amoah, Benjamin Berlin, Jacob Preiserwicz, Paul Rudewick, Lisa Brubaker, Alyona Teeter, Anide Jean, Hanna Minkin, Jeffrey Franco, Jeff Li, Parandzem Gharibian and Samuel I. Mok. I also want to thank my colleagues Priti Doshi, Esq.; Marianne Reilly, Associate Athletic Director, Fordham University; and Bob Pockrass, Associate Editor of *NASCAR Scene* for all their help. Finally I want to express my gratitude to Acquisitions Editor Linda Bathgate and Senior Production Editor Marianna Vertullo for their patience, encouragement and guidance. Similar thanks go to Kirsten Kite, who went beyond the call of duty in creating the indices that appear in the book.

Preface to the Second Edition

Often second editions of academic texts do not require much content change from that of the prior editions. However, the changes in the sports business landscape over the last half-decade necessitated considerable revisions in this text. Professional sports leagues have new owners and, in some cases, new commissioners. Franchise values continue to increase, despite the economic downturn of the late 2000s. Collective bargaining agreements that were freshly minted in 2006 expire in 2011, with the possibility of labor unrest in any or all of the four major league sports. Drug testing (better termed testing for performance-enhancing drugs [PEDs]) became a cause célèbre in the halls of Congress, which resulted in greater testing regimens, but a feeling that the authorities must play catch-up with the pharmacologists who, in the laboratory trenches, develop new forms of PEDs and their masking agents. Sports endorsement contracts have become even more sophisticated. Salaries for in-demand coaches continue their spiral. Intellectual property issues involving dissemination of team logos and player names into newer technological formats provide fascinating property issues, but bedevil the courts, which have to apply more traditional laws to new electronic media.

The 2008 and 2010 Olympics are now history. The National Collegiate Athletic Association (NCAA) continues to face pressure to ease some of its bedrock amateurism rules. Sports injuries receive greater attention in the wake of the high-profile cases of former NFL players disabled by the effects of concussions received during their playing days. The increasing utilization of social media, such as Twitter, and blogging limits privacy as never before, but expands and changes the scope of intellectual property rights.

All this necessitated a new edition of the book. More comprehensive and more up to date, the second edition of *The Business of Sports: A Primer for Journalists* includes more discussion about international sports (including a description of the "promotion/relegation" system found in much of world soccer), labor agreements, and the interconnection between sports leagues and antitrust law. New media—including creations such as

Twitter—that did not exist in 2005 and the increased prevalence of Internet streaming of sports events are covered. A major change is an enhanced treatment of ethical issues in sports. Found in almost every chapter, the goal of the "ethical issues" segment is to alert readers of the ethical consequences of a policy or rule, or lack thereof. Ethical issues often pose not answers but questions, which result in debate and discussion. Finally, on a more technical matter, many of the references found in the first edition were websites that no longer exist. Those found to be inaccessible were eliminated and replaced by updated websites.

During my one-year-plus time in revamping the old text into the new edition, I have been assisted by two of my graduate assistants. Thanks go to Patrick Harrington, an undergraduate student at Fordham University's College of Business, who displayed a keen sensitivity for proofreading and identified some inconsistencies in the text. Yao Huang deserves major league kudos for his hard work in this endeavor. Yao was absolutely indispensable in fact checking, perusing the various collective bargaining agreements and updating references. Without him, this project would not be done.

Preface to the Third Edition

In the last half-decade, the landscape of sports continues to evolve and new and ever more complex business issues come to the fore. That evolution services as a backdrop for this new edition, which constitutes a major rewrite of this book. Because of the greater focus and interest in the business applications of this dynamic industry, it was decided to expand its scope to those studying the business of sport. This is not to slight the professional journalists and journalism and communications students who were the intended audience for the first two editions. However, the increased content in this new edition—focusing on more familiar organizational, management, marketing, financial and legal structures, with new developments in analytics, tax and media that are driving the sports industry—will appeal to those working or aiming to work in the sports industry, as well as those who plan to cover that industry.

Profound changes mark the time between this edition and the prior one. In the last six years, team valuations continue to increase, sometimes dramatically. Relative labor peace reigns among the major sports leagues. Revenues continue to increase, spurred by consistently rising media rights fees and the creation and dissemination of content in new platforms. New or refurbished facilities continue to open. More sophisticated marketing, often through social media, has driven fan interest in innovative ways. Soccer has become a major sport in the United States, and more and more Americans are watching international leagues. The Olympics continues to be the marquee event in the international sports, but one that has become so large that the host city model may be impractical. Other international sports organizations have reeled from corruption and lack of transparency. Fédération Internationale de Football Association (FIFA), the governing body for international soccer, has been the subject of scorn and criminal indictment of leading members, resulting in the need for urgent reform and greater transparency. At the time of this writing, the International Association of Athletics Federations (IAAF), the international track and field federation, has been embarrassed by admissions of doping by leading athletes, mainly from Russia.

The greater awareness of head injuries and the resulting mental and physical damage have spawned litigation and charges that leagues and teams have failed to adequately protect athletes. The collegiate sports rubric, characterized by the near-monolithic control of the NCAA, is on the verge of change—or even collapse. The possibility of collegiate athletes being compensated is ever more likely, and the rise of the uber-conferences and postseason playoffs will change big-time college football.

A greater push toward legalized sports gambling propelled by the hope of harvesting some of the millions of dollars in illicit wagers is causing states to contest the federal government's effective ban on the practice. Also, states have been more aggressive in creating tax rules in an attempt to collect revenues from athletes who come from out of town to practice and compete in that location.

Race continues to play a role in athletics, as it does in society—both in the United States and abroad. Attitudes of various stakeholders—owners, managers, players, fans, media—continue to shape what is a subject fraught with long-standing grievances and present controversy. Gender equity continues to navigate between the needs and expectations of historically unrepresented genders and athletic programs squeezed by tight budgets. In addition, the increasingly vocal rights of transgender athletes will undoubtedly be a growing part of this equation.

In recent years, sports decision making has become more and more analytics based. The increase in the use of statistical information and metrics to predict player and team success has become a standard, even in sports outside of baseball.

Finally, the continued technological changes have fueled innovations in the way sports media deals are crafted—from streaming on the Internet to the powerful effect of social media. Rights fees continue to increase, in part because of the evolution of "TV everywhere" agreements, which cover both traditional and newer forms of content platforms. The effect of greater media convergence and governmental policies also may shape broadcast, cable and online sports for years to come.

All of these events necessitated a new edition of this text. As noted in the beginning, this edition will have an expanded focus. Readers may notice that the title has been changed. This book is intended to appeal not only to communications students, but also business students and sports management students. There will more discussion of marketing and finance. The "Ethical Issues" component, well received in the last edition, will be expanded. A new feature will be proposed assignments concluding most of the chapters. These assignments are really case studies intended to stimulate thought and focus on some of the cutting-edge questions one finds in the sports industry.

As noted earlier, the new edition involved a major overhaul of the previous edition. During this process, I have been assisted by very able and dedicated graduate and undergraduate assistants. Thanks go to Corina Tse, an undergraduate student at Fordham University's Gabelli School of Business, who displayed a maturity and professionalism way beyond her years; Oren Rafii, a JD/MBA student at Gabelli and at Fordham Law School, who was able to utilize his considerable research skills to tackle difficult areas of revision; Douglas DiMedio, also a JD/MBA student who helped greatly in the analytics chapter and meticulously caught inconsistencies in other chapters; and Yaquien Liu, who proofread through the many pages of chapters in this edition. Many thanks to all. Could not have done it without you!

In sum, I hope you will use the text as a general reference for a subject of endless fascination.

Mark Conrad
July 2016

Introduction
What Makes Sports a Unique Business?

In 2014 over 73 million people attended Major League Baseball games in the United States and Canada. The numbers for National Basketball Association (NBA), National Hockey League (NHL), National Football League (NFL), and Major League Soccer (MLS) contests in the United States and Canada were 22 million, 17 million, 21.4 million and 6.1 million, respectively. Another 82 million attended college football and basketball games. Such numbers define sports as a premier entertainment business. Evolving over the last century from a mom-and-pop–style enterprise into a dynamic economic juggernaut of high revenues, lucrative compensation and high visibility, professional and amateur sports are not only watched, but financed, broadcast and streamed domestically and around the world. For anyone seeking to study sports, its business structure is just as salient as the runs, touchdowns, baskets and goals.

Yet the sports business defies easy categorization. Unlike manufacturing, it does not focus on the production of goods. Unlike real estate, it does not center on the buying and selling of land. Unlike accounting or law, it does not involve licensed professionals charging fees for advice and counsel. But an industry it is, evolving into multifaceted enterprises with tentacles reaching far beyond its original objective.

The sports business displays similarities to the entertainment industry. At first glance one may wince at this characterization, but sports possess characteristics akin to film, theater and music. They all provide a form of leisure—a diversion from the daily stresses of life, albeit a passionate one. People pay to attend sports exhibitions by choice, not by governmental fiat or financial necessity.

With sports, as in other aspects of entertainment, the focus often centers on the *person*, not the property. Professional athletes (and more and more collegiate athletes) engage in personal services. Star athletes, like star actors and musicians, command tremendous public recognition often covered by media thirsty for every angle of their professional and personal lives. Athletes are frequently public figures, which means that the media have a de facto license to report on their athletic and nonathletic activities. And these performers are often far better known than the owners who pay them.

As in the case of entertainers, agents represent professional athletes. Although differences exist, their basic role is the same: negotiating employment contracts and marketing their clients. As shown later in this book, agents not only engage in face-to-face negotiations, but also have to sell the image of the athlete to the public, much like an agent representing a film or music star. Additionally, both athletes and entertainers work under the rules of their respective unions. For example, film actors often have to operate under the rules negotiated by the Screen Actors' Guild and Hollywood studios. Similarly, football players have to operate under the agreements negotiated between the NFL Players Association (NFLPA) and the NFL. In the amateur world, fame (but not fortune) greets the top National Collegiate Athletic Association (NCAA) athletes in football and in men's and, increasingly, women's basketball. Often better known than the valedictorians of their classes, these top players bring considerable publicity and revenues to the institutions they attend in terms of ticket sales, broadcast revenues and merchandising. Note the term *revenues*, not profits. In most collegiate athletic programs, costs outpace revenue, and therefore the programs lose money.

As in the case of entertainers, athletes' careers and fortunes ride a roller coaster of highs and lows. A famous movie star makes three bad films, diminishing or possibly ending his or her career. An athlete in the midst of his second consecutive disappointing season will incur the wrath of the fans and may be released on completion of his contract (or during the contract, as is often the case with the NFL). On the other hand, an unsung third-string player may lead teammates to a championship and be forever immortalized.

Unlike entertainers, who have received compensation for their work for centuries, athletes and athletic organizations traditionally embraced the ideal of "amateurism." In the nineteenth century, sports activities were largely the domain of wealthy men who participated in polo, yachting and tennis (Thorne, Wright, & Jones, 2001). The twentieth century brought viability to "professionals" in sports, and the result has been a dramatic increase in the economic effects of sports exhibitions, which by the end of the century generated nearly $400 billion annually in the United States through corporate sponsorship, stadium construction, licensing, apparel, equipment, media investments and spectator expenditures (Thorne, Wright, & Jones, 2001, citing Burton, 1999; Hunter & Mayo, 1999). Amateur sporting events such as the NCAA tournaments and college bowl games also have been revenue raisers.

Contrary to the pieties of certain sports writers of yore, sports have been a business longer than some care to admit. Today, the industry is simply a bigger one. The increased popularity and complexities of the sports universe have resulted in the expansion and growing sophistication of the business side to include issues such as intellectual property, stadium construction and business governance. Revenue streams have diversified. For example, until the advent of modern broadcasting, gate receipts were virtually the only revenue stream for sports. In the last ninety years, revenues from radio, then television, then cable, satellite and, more recently, the Internet have brought billions of dollars to the pockets of team owners, athletes, colleges, conferences and amateur organizations. Sports marketing has therefore evolved into an important specialty, as merchandise sales, sponsorships and naming rights command an important base in producing revenues and branding the sport.

The ownership of sports franchises has changed greatly. In the early twentieth century, owners of baseball teams often had a reputation of being "penny-ante" businessmen just one stop on the right side of the law (Fetter, 2003). Today, some of the largest corporations and wealthiest individuals own franchises, which are often the crown jewel of their financial portfolios. And some of the players achieve wealth matching or exceeding the level of successful corporate chief executive officers.

All of these considerations result in a complex economic and regulatory structure, with a vast array of rules and a full slate of constituencies that have to be satisfied. Leagues, team owners, coaches, players, colleges, amateur athletic associations, unions, agents and the Olympic personnel are just some of the stakeholders in the business of sports.

The growing internationalization of sports has spawned a great awareness and scrutiny of international sports organizations. The scandals surrounding members of FIFA, soccer's governing body and its regional federations in 2015 and 2016, coupled with the corruption by international and certain domestic federations overseeing track and field involving performance-enhancing drugs, which occurred at the same time, demonstrated the need for more oversight and regulation for some of the most high-profile sports in the world.

What Makes Sports a Unique Industry?

United States and Canada—A Cartel Structure

In a market-driven economy, the goal of a typical business is to achieve success by direct competition with others. Whether the business is automobiles or appliances, most consumers consider buying a product from a number of firms that manufacture or sell that item, and their decision to purchase is based on factors such as needs, quality, brand reputation and/or price. The same can be said for choosing service professionals. One may choose a physician or a lawyer from a number of practitioners based on references, training, professional manner and insurance coverage.

This traditional competitive structure is not found in professional sports leagues in the United States and Canada.

First and foremost, the competition is limited not by circumstance, but by intention. Almost every American-based sports organization's structure restricts competition. In the professional sphere, the leagues limit the number of competitors by awarding exclusive franchises in different markets, so consumer choice is inherently limited. With a few exceptions, one team occupies that particular market. In doing so, leagues create a limited market and operate as a cartel. In certain respects, this is analogous to the market control demonstrated by the Organization of the Petroleum Exporting Countries (OPEC) in the 1970s and 1980s. In both cases, membership is limited and the product is controlled. OPEC countries may have controlled the production, distribution and sale of oil in an attempt to dominate the market. Similarly, sports leagues regulate which teams may compete, where they can compete, the number of players on a team and the sharing of certain revenues. But by no means does this discourage athletic competition. In fact, there is direct, and often intense, competition among the teams in a given league, even resulting in rancor between the owners. The desired goal of the franchise (and the hope of fans) is to win a championship. If a team has the resources and the will, its owner will sometimes acquire expensive free-agent players to increase its chances of success. In the past, a strong rivalry developed between teams that had significant financial resources, such as the Boston Red Sox and the New York Yankees, and both teams have spent lavishly on players not only to win championships, but to outperform their rivals.

Yet, on another level, these teams cooperate in very important matters, such as labor negotiations, broadcasting, merchandising and revenue sharing. The result is a hybrid identity. The team sells itself as both a local franchise and a representative of the league. As shown later, differences exist among the major leagues regarding the sharing of revenues and salary controls, but the basic organizational plan remains the same. This competition versus cooperation dichotomy is explained in more detail in Chapter 1.

Many of the controversies that have bedeviled sports leagues involve the balance of power between the respective leagues' central offices and the individual team owners. Centralized league control of independent franchises has existed in its present form for almost a century. Major League Baseball created the position of commissioner to run the league's affairs, which has since been adopted by other professional and amateur sports leagues. The commissioner is a de facto chief executive officer of the respective sport, empowered to regulate league policy, setting disciplinary standards for players and other employees and, in more recent years, often spearheading labor negotiations with the league's players association.

The interplay of a centralized authority with competing independently owned teams has created tension between the players, team owners and the league commissioners. The courts have had a role in attempting to resolve these disputes because the unique nature of professional sports league structure has raised antitrust law concerns (with Major League Baseball being the notable exception due to its exemption from antitrust laws).

The specter of antitrust lurks through much of the legal regime of professional and even amateur sports. Courts have been asked to determine the anticompetitive impact of league and organization decisions for the last half-century. As will be discussed in later chapters, these antitrust challenges involve complex legal applications and, at times, inconsistent legal conclusions.

Because of the often extensive and expensive litigation, an alternative known as a "single-entity" league was created about two decades ago. This is discussed in more detail in Chapter 1. Simply put, in a pure single-entity league, no independent owners exist. Rather, the league owns and operates the teams in a single corporation. There may be some advantages in this scheme, particularly in salary control, but there are structural disadvantages as well. For reasons discussed later, the allure of single-entity leagues has diminished, as these leagues either folded outright or were transformed into a more traditional league or a hybrid.

Another alternative is the approach that has governed many non-U.S. professional soccer leagues. This system, known as "promotion and relegation," also discussed in Chapter 1, creates a system in which teams are promoted to higher divisions or demoted to lower levels of competition based on success (Ziegler, 2009). Promotion and relegation leagues result in more fluidity and fewer antitrust issues, but the system may weaken the marketability and economic value of individual teams. Therefore, this approach has not caught on in the United States.

In nonprofessional sports, the NCAA is the body that legislates, adjudicates and enforces the rules for collegiate sports for most four-year colleges in the United States. The NCAA has de facto control over the great majority of collegiate athletics and produces a tome-like manual of bylaws to ensure that college athletes conform to the organization's definition of "amateur." The enforcement powers of these organizations are considerable, although in recent years regional athletic conferences have assumed greater powers with regard to athletic rules and regulations. Also, some of the NCAA's policies have been successfully challenged in the courts. More discussion is found in Chapter 3.

International Sports

As will be explained in more detail in Chapter 4, the international sports governance system derives from nineteenth- and early twentieth-century notions of amateur sports. Today, a top-to-bottom governance system exists with regard to organizations that control their particular sports. There are exclusive international bodies, aided by domestic affiliates, that govern various team and individual sports. The International Skating Union regulates competitive figure skating, and U.S. Figure Skating is its domestic counterpart. A figure skater performs under the rules of U.S. Figure Skating, which is under the jurisdiction of its international parent, the International Skating Union. The International Association of Athletics Federations (IAAF) and USA Track have a similar relationship with track and field competitions.

Often, bureaucratic power struggles erupt. Tensions may occur between individual schools and the NCAA or between international organizations and their national counterparts over a wide array of issues, including eligibility and drug-testing policies. Until recently, dispute mechanisms were scattershot or nonexistent. Transparency and resulting ethical dilemmas have resulted in governance scandals involving FIFA and other organizations.

Areas of Exclusivity

The primary focus of most sports organizations and leagues is on franchising and income-producing possibilities. Many concepts have been implemented with those goals in mind—some through internal development and others by sheer circumstance and technological evolution. The following is a brief overview of some of the more pertinent operational considerations.

EXCLUSIVE FRANCHISING AUTHORITY

In the United States professional leagues, in order to admit new franchises (the official term for a team), an affirmative vote of the other team owners is needed. Usually, a high percentage (known in corporate law parlance as a maxi-majority) of owners in the league must approve any new franchise. For example, in Major League Baseball, that requirement is a three-quarter majority vote (Major League Constitution, Article V, sec. 2(b)(1)). Most leagues will screen the applications for new franchises to ensure a good fit within the league. In the National Hockey League, for example, the commissioner and team owners (or an appointed committee) scrutinize the finances and investigate the backgrounds of the applicants under a "due diligence" standard to ensure they display proper "good character" before approving them (*In re Dewey Ranch Holdings*, 2009).

MARKETING AND LICENSING CONTROL

Each of the professional leagues engages in marketing its product by concluding league-wide merchandising and sponsorship agreements (often with the respective players' unions' approval and participation). Major League Baseball, the NFL, NBA and NHL have created separate departments to control the licensing of its intellectual property, which includes trademarks, copyrighted materials and the likenesses of its athletes. As is explained in Chapter 14, although differences exist, the basic agreement is that sales revenues from items containing league and team logos and players' names and likenesses are divided among all the teams and the players. Such rights amount to billions of dollars in respective leagues' coffers. In addition, individual teams have their own marketing departments, often involving more localized sponsorship agreements with vendors. Although certain products have league-wide exclusivity, there are some product areas reserved for individual teams, such as deals with local food companies or auto dealers. Similar powers exist in the NCAA, but they are not as encompassing and have been subject to legal challenges, as noted in Chapter 3. Member schools and athletic conferences retain rights involving licensing and merchandising.

Often, the leagues, as representatives of their teams, conclude agreements with vendors to license the names of their member teams to apparel and shoe firms and companies making collectables, such as trading cards and bobblehead dolls.

BROADCASTING

In professional sports, the determination and division of broadcasting rights varies from league to league, but all of the major leagues have the power to negotiate exclusive broadcasting, cablecasting, mobility, satellite and, increasingly, Internet video streaming agreements. The scope and amount of these rights differ considerably among the leagues. In Major League Baseball, local broadcasting and cable rights are independently negotiated and the revenues they generate are not shared by other teams. This results in considerable disparity in revenue streams, as major market teams such as the New York Yankees and Boston Red Sox receive far more revenue than the Pittsburgh Pirates. However, the league retains "national rights," such as a game of the week and the postseason competition, as part of the national package. With minor exceptions, the teams do share these league-wide revenues equally. In contrast, the NFL's broadcasting and cable agreements give the league far more control. The result has been less dominance by large-market franchises. The NCAA and international sports organizations also negotiate agreements with various broadcasters, cablecasters and Internet providers. However, the type and scope of these agreements vary. The NCAA contracts to broadcast its championship games in every sport except the highest division of football, which, as a result of a 1984 Supreme Court ruling, is controlled by the athletic conferences. For example, the NCAA has a contract with

CBS and Turner Broadcasting to broadcast men's "March Madness" basketball tournament games. Conferences such as the Southeastern Conference negotiate such rights on behalf of the member schools. In rare instances, an "independent" (non-conference-based) school, such as Notre Dame, may establish its own broadcasting arrangement (in this case with NBC).

International sports organizations, such as the International Olympic Committee (IOC), negotiate television contracts with broadcasters all over the world. The IOC selected NBC as its exclusive broadcaster in the United States through 2032. As a long-standing rights holder for the Summer and Winter Games, NBC broadcast and video-streamed the 2012 Summer Games in London, the 2014 Sochi Winter Games and the 2016 Rio Summer Games. These contracts include considerable rights fees, given the elite nature of the Olympics. Such sums—$775 million for the 2014 Sochi Winter Games and $1.23 billion for the 2016 Rio Summer Games—give considerable financial heft to the Olympic movement. Similar powers, albeit less ubiquitous, exist in the international governing bodies of particular sports to broadcast world championship events.

CLOSE RELATIONSHIPS WITH GOVERNMENT

Nearly every professional sports team is privately owned. Yet, despite the private ownership, franchises become an extension of their communities. Often the team, and even the league, may negotiate with cities and counties for help in the building of new sports facilities. In many cases, governments have established a regimen of financial incentives to prevent teams from relocating.

During the last large-scale stadium-building boom of the 1990s and early 2000s, this largess by governments cut across party lines. Politicians who considered themselves fiscal conservatives and were loath to increase general spending nonetheless supported significant public expenditures—through authorization of bonds and even tax increases—to help pay for the construction of new stadiums and arenas (Keating, 1997; Malkin, 2001). Additionally, funds for highway access and other "indirect" support were approved. And, as we see in Chapter 8, favorable lease terms between the stadium owner (in many cases a local or county government or a governmental authority) are frequently negotiated. However, the use of governmental support for new sports facilities has been controversial. Voters have been increasingly skeptical about approving public monies for such projects and the related highway construction. For example, in 2011, voters in Nassau County, New York, rejected funding a $400 million overhaul of the New York Islanders' hockey arena. Shortly afterward, the team announced it would move from the county and play its games in Brooklyn, New York (WNYC, 2012).

RESTRICTIONS ON PLAYER SALARIES AND MOVEMENT

Every sports league, including minor leagues, has significant salary controls in place. Although there is no question that elite professional athletes from the major sports leagues command high salaries, the salary structure and right to seek similar employment from another team are far more restricted than those found in most industries. It is a myth that all professional athletes have the freedom to work for whatever team they wish. In fact, only a small class of "free agents" fit into this category. Many younger athletes are restricted from signing contracts with rival teams once their obligations terminate, due to their relative lack of seniority. These restrictions derive from the terms of the collective bargaining agreements negotiated between the leagues and the players' unions.

Until the mid-1970s, player restrictions were so absolute that the athletes were virtually indentured servants of their teams. The only way they could join another team in the league was by a trade, a breach of contract or a contractual release by the team. Not surprisingly, that "reserve" system artificially reduced salaries. However, as explained in Chapter 6, the players' associations agreed to keep some of these restrictions in place.

EXCLUSIVE RIGHT TO RENT OR OWN STADIUMS OR ARENAS

As noted earlier, a boom in stadium and arena construction occurred over the last two decades. Municipalities and counties would assist in funding a facility in the hope of either keeping an existing team or luring a franchise from out of town. For teams, the stakes were high. If a team cannot own or lease the stadium on favorable terms, this can severely hurt the team's balance sheet.

The negotiation of stadium agreements is one function that is retained by a particular franchise, rather than a league. Sometimes the franchise will own the stadium outright, such as in the case of the San Francisco Giants. More often, the team will sign an agreement to have exclusive rights to use the stadium for a stipulated period. These agreements are often very specific, with the team typically receiving a percentage of parking fees, advertisements and concessions. We discuss the terms of a stadium deal in Chapter 8.

QUASI-PUBLIC NATURE

Despite private ownership, sports franchises take on the character of their locale and become part of the community. The effect on the community psyche when a team departs to a new city can be profound. Some say that Brooklyn never recovered from the day the Dodgers moved to Los Angeles—and that was in 1957!

The same can be said about certain college football and basketball teams. They have been the "face" of their respective institutions and generate passion not only from students and alumni, but also from members of their communities. The strong loyalties shown by fans of the University of Alabama and their rival Auburn University demonstrate this point.

Although it is true that a major employer in a town or small city may take on a similar persona, there is a significant difference. For decades, Kodak, in Rochester, New York, employed a large number of local workers and dominated the economic and civic landscape of the community (Eaton, 2000). A professional sports team does not have this same impact. Employees of a team include the players (many of whom do not live in the area in the off-season), managerial and coaching staff, front-office staff and stadium or arena personnel (such as security guards and vendors). Based on the numbers, a sports franchise hardly qualifies as the dominant business in the area.

FINALLY . . . FAN LOYALTY

The factors just discussed derive from an overlooked aspect of the sports business: the loyalty of the fan. The sports fan is an odd consumer, often fiercely loyal and passionate. Once a person becomes bonded with a particular sports team—professional or collegiate—the connection often becomes extremely powerful and very long term. And the brand loyalty of the team transcends its success.

Let's look at an example. If a consumer purchased a product that turned out to be of lower quality than he or she expected, most likely that person would abandon allegiance to that firm and would purchase the product made by a rival company. Imagine that consumer, after purchasing a poorly made car requiring many unsuccessful repairs, buying a new car of the same brand! Not very likely. But, in sports, many fans often will continue to support their poorly performing teams. Why would these souls spend their hard-earned dollars year after year to subsidize a team that has been less than top quality? Despite unpopular strikes and lockouts, fans have often come back to root for their teams after play is resumed. Talk of fan unions and of boycotts of particular sports or teams has generally come to nothing.

Dan Wann, a psychologist at Murray State University, studied this phenomenon and found that team devotion can provide a number of positive feelings in a person, all of which help rationalize the seemingly irrational fan loyalty concept. They include:

- Entertainment: Watching a game is a form of leisure.
- Escape: You can't yell at your boss. You shouldn't yell at your spouse. You can, and will, yell at the team you root for.

- "Eustress": The pleasurable combination of euphoria and stress, alternating between the euphoria felt when a player homers in the first inning and the stress resulting when that same player strikes out later in the game.
- Aesthetic: You appreciate the grace and precision of a well-turned double play.
- Family: Attending a game with family members or friends is a bonding experience.
- Self-esteem: Your team wins, therefore you win.
- Group affiliation: The other fans at the ballpark also want the team to win, validating your own affinity for the team.

(King, 2004)

The dissemination of sports through traditional and new media has created a greater following among existing fans and a potential base for more enthusiasts. At one time, the only way one could view a sporting event was by attending it in person. Gate attendance was the predominant source of revenue. With the advent and utilization of radio, then television, cable, satellite and Internet, greater opportunities to follow the team or athlete allow more people to become fans, with the ability to view the event from a more comfortable venue.

Team loyalty continues even if a fan moves to a different part of the country because of the availability of information and broadcasts about the team. Out-of-market fans are able to purchase digital cable, satellite or online packages enabling them to watch their respective teams. It also results in greater revenue to the team, its athletes (assuming they are professionals) and the particular league or organization.

Projected to grow $145 billion between 2010 and 2015, the sports industry has long been one of the fastest-growing sectors of the global economy (Belzer, 2014). However, some have argued that it could be a victim of its own success, because the business models that have propelled that growth have not radically changed. Unlike comparative industries, sports have somehow managed sustained growth while lacking any fundamental innovation to the business models that fuel it. However, although these models have not changed, they are evolving in sophistication and technological prowess, resulting in continued (and expanded) profitability. Examples include changes in the scope of media rights deals, sponsorships and the tweaking of the definition of amateurism in collegiate sports. The industry has been expanding with newer distribution models, more competitive pricing and more international scope. This leads to a unique, often (but not always) profitable industry, a fascinating business for those interested in working it, covering it or analyzing it. I hope that the following chapters prove this point.

References

Belzer, J. (2014, July 24). How RSE Ventures Is Revolutionizing Business As We Know It. Forbes.com. Retrieved October 20, 2016, from http://www.forbes.com/sites/jasonbelzer/2014/07/24/how-rse-ventures-is-revolutionizing-business-as-we-know-it/#10097d737ca2

Burton, R. (1999, December 19). From heart to stern: The shaping of an industry over a century. *New York Times*, sec. 8, p. 11.

Eaton, L. (2000, June 6). A city, once smug, is redefined; Company town becomes a town of tiny companies. *New York Times*. Retrieved August 21, 2009, from http://www.nytimes.com/2000/06/06/nyregion/a-city-once-smug-is-redefined-company-town-becomes-a-town-of-tiny-companies.html?pagewanted=1

Fetter, H. (2003). *Taking on the Yankees: Winning and losing in the business of baseball.* New York: W. W. Norton, pp. 28–29.

Hunter, R., & Mayo, A. (1999, July–September). The business of sport. *The Mid-Atlantic Journal of Business, 35,* 75–76.

In re Dewey Ranch Hockey, LLC, 406 B.R. 30 (Bankr. D. Ariz. 2009) (No. 2:09-bk-09488-RTBP) (quoting NHL BYLAWS § 35). NHL Bylaws, Sections 35.1.

Keating, R. J. (1997, March–April). We wuz robbed!: The subsidized stadium scam. *Policy Review (Heritage Foundation), 82,* 54–57.

King, B. (2004, March 1). What makes fans tick? *Street and Smith's Sports Business Journal,* p. 25.

Major League Constitution, Article V, sec. 2(b)(1), 2000.

Malkin, M. (2001, April 4). Bush's baseball tax fetish. *Capitalism Magazine.* Retrieved June 14, 2005, from http://www.capmag.com/article.asp?id=446

Thorne, D., Wright, L. B., & Jones, S. A. (2001). The impact of sports marketing relationships and antitrust issues in the United States. *Journal of Public Policy & Marketing, 20*(1), 73.

WNYC.com (2012, October 24). New York Islanders will move to Brooklyn. Retrieved September 25, 2015, from http://www.wnyc.org/story/245934-new-york-islanders-will-move-brooklyn/

Ziegler, M. (2009). Outside U.S., Pads would face relegation. *San Diego Times-Union.* Retrieved July 20, 2009, from http://www3.signonsandiego.com/stories/2009/jul/19/1s19relegate23335-outside-us-pads-would-face-releg/?uniontrib

1 The Structure of Professional Team Sports

Professional sports governance in the United States is based on a closed, but united, system of independently owned franchises that operates as cooperative venture which displays the characteristics of an economic cartel. Created in the early and middle years of the last century, these sports leagues control the operations of their respective sports and create an organizational decision-making structure, providing governance on issues as varied as player and owner discipline, revenue control, dissemination of marketing and media revenues and expansion and relocation of league franchises. A general knowledge of the structure and power of professional sports organizations is imperative for anyone interested in working in or writing about the professional sports industry in the United States and Canada.

All professional sports leagues and their member teams are privately owned entities. Their internal rules and regulations are generally immune from governmental scrutiny. Because the leagues and, particularly, their teams (with a few exceptions) do not sell shares on a public stock exchange, no public release of financial records and no standardized auditing procedures are required under U.S. securities laws. Hence, team owners have considerable latitude in running their business, subject only to the guidelines and constraints of the league's rules and regulation. There is no requirement that a team owner must put the best product on the field, and examples exist of unsuccessful yet profitable teams. One example is the National Basketball Association's (NBA's) New York Knicks, who have not won a championship since 1973 and have had generally poor records from 2000 to 2016. However, although the team has generally languished in performance, it has ranked highly on the balance sheet. According to *Forbes Magazine*, in 2016 the Knicks were worth $3 billion, which ranked the team as the most valuable NBA franchise. The 2016 Cleveland Cavaliers, the NBA champion that seasonally ranked twelfth, is worth $1.1 billion (Forbes.com, 2016).

League membership rules and requirements constitute the most important check on a team owner's powers. As pointed out in the introduction, professional sports leagues possess many unique attributes. Their characteristics not only differ from other types of businesses, but even from amateur sports organizations, whose attributes and complexities are discussed in Chapters 3 and 4.

The Professional Leagues

Traditional professional sports leagues, such as Major League Baseball (MLB), the National Football League (NFL), the National Basketball Association (NBA) and the National Hockey League (NHL), have both cooperative and competitive operational characteristics. While individual teams compete for athletic success, their respective leagues lack a pure free-market competitive structure because each restricts free and open competition in a number of ways. The leagues have the inherent power to limit the number of competitors by awarding exclusive franchises in different markets. With a few exceptions, it is one team to a market. As noted in the introduction, each league operates as a cartel, much like the Organization of the Petroleum Exporting Countries (OPEC), as membership is limited and the product controlled. OPEC countries have controlled the production levels of oil in attempts to control the market. Sports leagues control the numbers of teams, their locations and the numbers of players on a team. League policies foster cooperation among all teams by their sharing of certain revenues, league-wide merchandising and a unified negotiation strategy with players' unions. For a team to be a part of the league means cooperation—and subservience—to league policies.

League control of independently owned franchises has existed in its present form for almost a century. In 1920, Major League Baseball became the first "modern" league, with the creation of the office of the commissioner to run the league's affairs. As the chief executive officer (CEO) of baseball, the commissioner was empowered to set league policy, control discipline and, in more recent years, spearhead labor negotiations with the players.

On the whole, the major professional sports leagues in the United States have been successful in developing their respective sports, creating an exclusivity that resulted in ever-increasing franchise values, and have increasingly developed an international presence.

The league system, however, is not perfect. Many of the controversies that have bedeviled sports leagues involve the balance of power between the central office and the team owners. Although players (through their respective players' associations) and leagues have concluded collective bargaining agreements for decades, tensions have also existed between players and management. The courts have, at times, been forced to resolve such issues because the singular control mechanisms by the leagues have raised antitrust law concerns (except in the case of Major League Baseball, which has been exempt from application of antitrust law, a subject covered in more detail in Chapter 6). Economic disparity has also caused concerns. In the past, tensions between larger and smaller market teams have occurred due to the unequal revenues generated between teams in cities such as New York and Los Angeles and their counterparts in Kansas City and Oakland. However, in recent years, league-wide revenue sharing (with or without salary caps) has eased those tensions (Vrooman, 2009). Another issue was the lack of competitiveness as certain teams dominated their respective league, causing some teams, like the New York Yankees or the NBA's Boston Celtics, to win consecutive championships, while other teams frequently occupy the bottom rung of the ladder. As a result of an improved revenue-sharing system, the Kansas City Royals won their first World Series in thirty years in 2015. However, some economists remain unconvinced that baseball, in particular, has achieved substantial competitive balance (Zepfel, 2015). In the 1990s, because of the threat and ultimate expense of antitrust litigation, some newer leagues utilized an alternative model of governance known as a "single entity" league. Simply put, in a pure single-entity league, no independent owners exist. Rather, the league owns the teams in a single for-profit corporation, and those who run the teams are shareholders of that corporation. As will be discussed later, the result has been decidedly mixed.

The Major Stakeholders in a Traditional League Structure

The Commissioner

As noted earlier, all major sports leagues in the United States and Canada are headed by a commissioner. In a traditional league structure, a commissioner is assigned to take ultimate responsibility for league matters. This results in considerable power being bestowed on one individual. The creation of the position was the result of a gambling scandal that shook the foundations of baseball.

As many baseball fans know, eight players from the 1919 Chicago White Sox were accused, but never convicted, of accepting money to "throw" the World Series. As a morality tale, the story of players such as "Shoeless Joe Jackson" betraying the fans has been retold countless times. However, the "Black Sox" scandal was not the only reason for a drastic change of governance. At the time, baseball was run by a three-member "National Commission," consisting of the presidents of the National League and American League and a third party, usually a team owner. In reality, the American League president, Byron Bancroft "Ban" Johnson, exercised the most power. The tripartite system was widely disliked, and many found this scandal an excuse to end the system and replace it with a more centralized authority (MLB.com, n.d.).

In November 1920, Kenesaw Mountain Landis, a federal judge who ruled in favor of what is now known as Major League Baseball in an antitrust case a few years earlier, was unanimously selected as commissioner by the owners. On January 12, 1921, Landis told a meeting of club owners that he had agreed to accept the position upon the clear understanding that the owners had sought "an authority . . . outside of your own business, and that a part of that authority would be a control over whatever and whoever had to do with baseball" (*Finley v. Kuhn*, 1978). Empowered to investigate "any act, transaction or practice suspected to be detrimental to the best interests of baseball," Landis (and future commissioners) had authority to summon individuals, order the production of documents and "determine, after investigation, what preventive, remedial or punitive action is appropriate in the premises, and to take such action either against Major League Clubs or individuals, as the case may be" (MLB Constitution, Article II, Sec. 2(c)). Despite some minor differences in language among the leagues, this "best interests of the sport" clause has been a bedrock section of the NFL, NBA and NHL league constitutions as well. In the NFL, the commissioner has the disciplinary authority over "conduct detrimental to the welfare of the League or professional football" (NFL Constitution, Article 8, sec. 8.13(A)). The NBA gives the commissioner the authority to suspend or fine any player, owner, team employee or referee guilty of conduct "that is prejudicial or detrimental to the Association" (NBA Constitution, Article 35), whereas in the NHL's document conduct "dishonorable, prejudicial to, or against the welfare of the League" deserves sanction (NHL Constitution and Bylaws, sec. 17). The structure gives the commissioner the right to be a judge and jury in investigating alleged transgressions among owners, officials and administrators. Presently, in the case of player discipline, in each of these leagues, such decisions can be appealed, often to an independent arbitrator (except in the NFL), but many of these appeals processes cannot be utilized when the fine or suspension is less than a designated amount or time (NBA Collective Bargaining Agreement, sec. XXXI, 2011).

Before the rise of players' unions and collective bargaining agreements, a commissioner's power was considered almost limitless. One court decision described the aforementioned Landis's mandate as that of a "plenipotentate" (*Milwaukee American Ass'n v. Landis*, 1931), and during Landis's term (1920–44) he indeed ruled with an iron hand. He meted out discipline, sometimes ruthlessly, to maintain what he considered the integrity of the sport. That meant fining, suspending and even banning players and owners for transgressions, which included gambling and other criminal activity. He even suspended Babe Ruth for the first six weeks of the 1922 season when Ruth violated the prohibition of "barnstorming" (Ambrose, 2008).

More recently, however, the unilateral power of commissioners to punish players has been limited, primarily because of mandatory grievance arbitration procedures found in collective bargaining agreements of some, but not all, of the major leagues. What makes these provisions noteworthy is not only the right of a player to take certain disciplinary matters to an independent arbitrator, but the standard—known as "just cause"—that the arbitrator uses to determine whether the punishment is justified. "Just cause" is a fairly high standard, which requires that substantial evidence exists for the commissioner's determination and that the resulting penalty is reasonable under the circumstances. In effect, "just cause" results in giving the arbitrator the power to provide an independent check on the commissioner's power (*Enterprise Wire Co. v. Enterprise Independent Union*, 1966).

Even with these limitations, the disciplinary power of a commissioner is not to be taken for granted. For infractions and violations of policy during competition, the commissioner (or someone in the commissioner's office) can impose fines and suspensions. Although limited by labor agreements, the commissioner still can mete out punishment. For Major League Baseball teams, the fines are limited to a maximum of $2 million, whereas owners, officers and employees have a cap at $500,000. Fine limitations on players are determined by the active agreement with the MLB Players Association (MLB Constitution, Article II, sec. 3(a)). Regarding player discipline, Major League Baseball and the NBA have a grievance arbitration system in effect whereby a neutral party adjudicates the dispute if the player appeals the ruling. In the NFL, the commissioner can suspend players without pay for a period he deems appropriate and also can fine them up to $500,000 (NFL Constitution, Article VIII, sec. 8.13). However, nearly all appeals are decided by hearing officers that are solely appointed by Goodell himself (the commissioner), thus giving him broader power compared to his contemporaries (NFL–NFLPA CBA, Article 46, sec. 3(a)).

Because the owners elect commissioners, the commissioners frequently (although not always) serve as representatives of ownership interests. Often commissioners will work with an owners' management committee or board of governors. This committee may consist of representatives of all the teams or a smaller group. Although the commissioner has the disciplinary authority and often the final say on governance matters, the owners' committee will often control decisions involving franchise relocation or the granting of new franchises. In those matters, the commissioner will take a back seat. Depending on the league, the management committee may control labor negotiations (as is the case in Major League Baseball) or the commissioner may spearhead them (as in the NBA).

Yet many think that the commissioner is a lackey of the owners. That view is simplistic and inaccurate. The commissioner's role is more than just a cheerleader or shill for the owners because that person is the face of the league and must convince the public that he or she acts in the *league's* best interests—which sometimes may be counter to owners' parochial interests. The example of the NBA's Adam Silver fining the then-owner of the Los Angeles Clippers and forcing a sale of the team will be discussed later in this chapter. But that is not the only case. Each of the major league commissioners can and has fined and suspended owners. In 1990, the Yankees' George Steinbrenner was suspended for two years by MLB commissioner Fay Vincent for paying a known gambler $40,000 for information about the Yankees' player Dave Winfield (Weiler & Roberts, 2004, p. 33). A few years later, the owner of the Cincinnati Reds was suspended for her comments on minorities and a professed admiration for Hitler (Macnow, 1993).

Typically, the commissioner runs a central "operations" office, which may include such duties as scheduling; hiring officials; marketing the league; controlling the intellectual property of the teams; negotiating nationwide broadcast, and cable and new media agreements; dealing with minor leagues (the case in baseball); engaging in political lobbying; and interacting with other sports leagues or international sports governing bodies, particularly regarding Olympic eligibility (Cozzillio, Levinstein, Dimino, & Feldman, 2007).

Commissioners are well paid for their services. In 2013, baseball's then-commissioner Bud Selig received compensation of over $22 million (Badenhausen, 2012), the NFL's Roger Goodell was paid $44.2 million (Kaplan, 2014a). In short, establishing policy, marketing the sport and building cohesion among the owners and players rank as the principal duties of a commissioner.

The Teams

The teams (known officially as "franchises") that constitute a traditional league are its backbone. Particular markets are awarded franchises based on a vote of league owners through an application process. Also, in rare situations, teams can be dissolved or folded either by the team terminating operations outright or by two teams merging their operations. An example of the latter occurred in 1978 when the NHL's Cleveland Barons ceased operations and merged with the then-Minnesota North Stars (Ohio History Central, n.d.).

Traditional league sports franchises are classified as joint ventures, which unite under the umbrella of the league. Although the methods of calculation differ in each league, certain revenues are shared, whereas others are kept by the team. Examples of unshared revenues include fees from local broadcasting rights (more limited in the NFL than in the other traditional leagues), parking, concessions, club seating and luxury boxes. Given the autonomy of the traditional league structure, individual teams employ their own personnel—athletes and management—who are paid by that team, rather than by the league itself. Team responsibilities include negotiating stadium leases and local television and radio broadcast rights, engaging in local marketing efforts, selling individual and season tickets and leasing luxury box seating. Teams also provide their own marketing and promotional personnel, and their roles differ from their marketing and media counterparts in the league office.

Because teams are independently owned in the traditional leagues, they can be bought and sold (with league approval) as the case of a general business. And despite the economic ups and downs, team values have consistently increased over the last thirty years. Since the last edition of this book, the prices realized have skyrocketed. In 2012 the Los Angeles Dodgers sold for $2 billion (and the price included Dodger Stadium); in 2014, the NBA's Los Angeles Clippers sold for $2 billion (despite being a secondary tenant in the Staples Center), and the Milwaukee Bucks sold for $550 million.

Most significantly, teams control the product they put on display. The team administrators—which include the owners, general managers and coaching staffs—assemble a group of athletes in the hopes of on-field performance success. This includes drafting, trading, promoting or releasing them. And like the commissioners, owners have the right to suspend, fine and even terminate players for breach of contract or for conduct detrimental to their team, and in some cases, as punishment for petty offenses. A player for the Cleveland Browns was fined $1,701 (the maximum then allowed under the collective bargaining agreement) because he failed to pay for a $3 bottle of water he'd consumed at a hotel while the team was on the road (Cooper, 2009). Fines for tardiness have also been levied, such as when Johnny Manziel and other rookies of the Cleveland Browns were fined for arriving a few minutes late to a team meeting. (Mortensen, 2014). The age of social media has presented a slew of opportunities for athletes to engage in finable behavior. While playing for the San Diego Chargers, Antonio Cromartie took to Twitter to complain about the food at the team's training camp. They forced him to pay $2,500 for the online post (Rosenthal, 2009).

The Owners

In most traditional sports leagues, a team owner can be an individual, corporation, limited partnership or limited liability company (LLC). In the past, individuals owned most teams, and in some cases that ownership would become a family business. Over time, these families would become synonymous with their franchises. The best example of this is the Steinbrenner family, who has owned the New York Yankees since 1973. More recently though, corporations and LLCs have acquired most ownership interests, and the number of familyowned franchises is diminishing. Yet some still remain, including the Yankees and the Pittsburgh Steelers (who have been owned by the Rooney family since the team's inception in 1933).

Each league has its own system of selecting team owners, and a league may impose restrictions on certain types of ownership structures. For instance, the NFL prohibits publicly traded corporations from ownership by way of requiring the names and addresses of all persons who own any interest in the entity—something that would practically be impossible to achieve for publicly traded firms (NFL Constitution and Bylaws, Art. III, sec. 3.3(A)(1)). The NFL did make an exception to this rule for the Green Bay Packers, who have been owned by a publicly held nonprofit corporation since 1923. The NFL also bars its team owners from owning any professional sports team in a different city (NFL Constitution and Bylaws, 1997 Resolution FC-3). Other limitations include a minimum percentage (currently 10 percent) of an NFL team that a lead owner (or general partner) needs (Kaplan, 2009).

Some individual owners bear the mark of longevity—Connie Mack with the Philadelphia Athletics (1901–54) and George Halas of the Chicago Bears (1920–83) come to mind. Others have been family dynasties, such as the Griffithses (Washington Senators, Minnesota Twins, 1919–84) and the Maras (New York Giants, 1925–present). Certain individuals, such as the late George Steinbrenner, have been intimately involved in team operations, whereas others have been less conspicuous. Even celebrities have taken the ownership route. In past years, Bing Crosby owned small portions of two baseball teams, and Bob Hope once owned 11 percent of the Los Angeles Rams and a part of the Cleveland Indians (Downey, 2003). In 2004, Jon Bon Jovi became a part-owner of the Philadelphia Soul of the now-defunct Arena Football League, and Jay-Z became a minority owner of the then–New Jersey Nets (he ultimately sold his interest in 2013). Presently, former NBA star Magic Johnson has an ownership interest in the Dodgers, Will Smith and his wife Jada Pinkett Smith are minority owners of the Philadelphia 76ers and the Miami Dolphins ownership group includes Gloria Estefan, Serena and Venus Williams and Sarah, the Duchess of York (popularly known as "Fergie").

Often, a managing partner–limited partner relationship exists among many sports franchises. An example of this would be Fenway Sports Group, L.P. ("FSG"), the parent company that owns the Boston Red Sox, EPL team Liverpool F.C., an auto-racing team, multiple stadiums, sports television networks and more. The FSG principal owner is John Henry with 40 percent of the ownership interests. The rest of the ownership group holds varying levels of minority interest (Kelso, 2011).

Limited partners usually invest a sum of money, hoping for a profitable return, but do not take an active part in the management of the team. But these investors often invest for the joy (or ego) of having an ownership stake in a major or minor league professional team, as well as for the profit potential. In some cases, limited partners get experience seeing the operations of a franchise, leading them to become managing partners of a team in the future. The aforementioned John Henry, the principal owner of the Boston Red Sox, once owned a small piece of the New York Yankees (Nethery, 2004).

Team sales and purchases are relatively infrequent in the major leagues. For a prospective purchaser of a team, the rules can be intricate and potentially time consuming. Although the purchaser (or, very often, purchasers) will own the franchise outright, that purchaser or group has to go through a vetting process known as "due diligence." Often the financial health of the purchaser or group is examined by the league. Because professional sports teams have become so expensive, each of the leagues has rules as to ownership stakes. At one time, the NFL required the controlling owner to have 51 percent of the team. More recently, that number was decreased to 30 percent (20 percent for family-owned teams). The NBA requires the controlling owner to have at least 15 percent of the equity value of the franchise. The league also limits the number of individuals who can have an ownership stake in a franchise to twenty-five, and each of the minority stakeholders must own at least 1 percent of the team. The NHL and Major League Baseball have no such restrictions (Sports Business Journal, 2015). Often the ownership group will form what is known as a limited liability partnership ("LLP") as the legal entity.

The Players

The one group that traditionally has had little influence in professional sports governance is the players. As employees, they occupy positions, not as management, but as paid workers performing services for their teams. Until forty years ago, they had little leverage in the negotiation of their contracts, primarily on account of onerous rules such as baseball's reserve clause that depressed wages.

Since that time, the players have made significant improvements in their compensation and have been active in asserting their rights through the labor-management negotiations. The number of strikes and lockouts and resulting favorable agreements with management attest to their power. Yet, even today, the player's role in the management and operations of the league remains minimal.

The Players' Associations

The major reason for the players' growing influence has been the presence of players' associations. Such worker unions, organized under the nation's labor laws, give these athletes the power to elect representatives and collectively bargain with team owners. As will be discussed in Chapter 6, players' unions have resulted in significant wage increases and the development of various forms of free agency to give certain players the right to choose the team of their liking. They have also spawned bidding wars for highly prized free agents. Additionally, grievance arbitration procedures have restricted the potential for subjective and overly harsh determinations by commissioners.

Agents

Before player unionization, when athletes had little bargaining leverage, the need for agent representation was minimal. However, with the dawn of free agency and salary arbitration, athletes sought agents in their contract negotiations, endorsements and financial management. The major league players' associations require agents to be certified with the respective unions and limit the amount of compensation received to a stipulated percentage. As discussed in Chapter 7, agents also serve as the representative of the athlete to the media and often must attempt to craft the athlete's image in times when the athlete commits some transgression or engages in a controversial act, although higher-profile athletes often hire public relations managers specifically for this role. Financial advisors are also required to be certified by the NFL Players' Association.

Municipalities and Counties

Sports facilities are costly, and financing structures for new facilities often involve cities, counties and/or states. Although total public funding for sports venues is relatively rare today, it is far more frequent that some financial assistance—whether it is in building roadways, public transportation, bond issuances and tax abatements—involves government. Hence, local and state governments constitute an important stakeholder in professional sports. More specific treatment of the funding methods is found in Chapter 8, but suffice it to say that the support of elected leaders (and, by extension, the public) is important to the survival of a team in that area. The lack of such governmental support has been a reason for team relocations, such as the New York Islanders' move away from Nassau County, New York, as mentioned in the book's introduction.

The Media—Old and New

Sports and the media have a symbiotic relationship. The media publicize the athlete, team, league or other organization and in many cases pay considerable rights fees to broadcast or otherwise distribute sports content. The media gain by obtaining more viewers and listeners, which helps their bottom line. Without the role of the media, professional and college sports would not attain their present scope and power.

Sports have been disseminated via "traditional" and "new" media formats. Traditional media include print, broadcast, cable and satellite, and the business model is tried and true. Broadcast and cable services pay the bulk of the media rights fees received by teams and the leagues for the right to broadcast game content. Additionally, cable sports networks, most notably ESPN, have a specialized twenty-four-hour all-sports niche carrying news and highlights as well as play-by-play content. Sports-oriented radio stations may also broadcast games, but more often, saturate the airwaves with on-air hosts and audience discussions (including second-guessing and criticism) about athletes and teams. And more and more print articles and a few broadcast/cable programs are devoted to the business of sport.

"New" media, such as the Internet, differs from the more traditional forms because individuals have more unfettered control over content. Websites, blogs and social media contribute a huge variety of information—informative, entertaining, outrageous and sometimes unfair—keeping sports in the consciousness of millions of fans and adding to the headaches of owners, managers, coaches and athletes. As is the case with politicians and entertainers, this has resulted in a diminution of an athlete's privacy, discussed in more detail in Chapter 15.

However, with more Internet streaming rights negotiated by marquee leagues and teams, the more traditional "rights-fee" model is taking shape online and through mobile phone apps. These so-called "over the top" or "360" deals will become more prevalent as media convergence between broadcast, cable and online keeps evolving. Mobile telephony is opening up more avenues for teams to connect to fans, either by streaming or by mobile apps, but there is still substantial room for growth in the revenue that can be realized from it (Goss, 2014).

Cooperation versus Competition

As we noted earlier, the four major traditional professional sports leagues offer a system that features elements of cooperation as well as competition. Because of this hybrid arrangement, these professional leagues constitute unique businesses. One court aptly described the conflict by noting:

> [Sports leagues have] problems which no other business has. The ordinary business makes every effort to sell as much of its product or services as it can. In the course of doing this it may and often does put many of its competitors out of business. The ordinary businessman is not troubled by the knowledge that he is doing so well that his competitors are being driven out of business.

Professional teams in a league, however, must not compete too well with each other in a business way . . . [i]t is unwise for all the teams to compete as hard as they can against each other in a business way. If all the teams should compete [this way], the stronger teams would be likely to drive the weaker ones into financial failure. If this should happen not only would the weaker teams fail, but eventually the whole league, both the weaker and the stronger teams, would fail, because without a league, no team can operate profitably.

(*United States v. NFL*, 1953)

This structure has raised an important legal question concerning the antitrust liability of traditional sports leagues. The issue centers on whether they act as "single entities" or as "joint ventures." If leagues determine their policies through a single, concerted decision-making process, then they are unitary bodies, known as single entities, and their policies are immune from the most important antitrust laws. If, however, the league is composed of a group of team owners who make policy based on their personal and sometimes competing economic interests, then such decisions are subject to antitrust challenge. The subject of scholarly debate over the last few decades, the U.S. Supreme Court finally answered that question in 2010, concluding that the NFL, despite its centralized decision making, does not confer single-entity status. Therefore, the NFL's—and a number of the NBA's and NHL's—policies have been subject to section 1 of the Sherman Act, discussed later in the chapter (*American Needle v. NFL*, 2010).

With this in mind, let us look at the areas of cooperation.

Salary Structure

No league has an entirely open market in which every player is a free agent with the freedom to jump from one team to another. Every league engages in salary control, and the nature of the restrictions varies from league to league. In the NBA, NFL and, most recently, NHL, a salary cap structure prohibits "richer" teams from gaining competitive advantage by signing high-caliber players. Major League Baseball, lacking a salary cap system, employs a luxury tax method to control salary growth.

Equitable Draft

Each of the leagues employs a draft system for choosing players. Usually the poorest-performing teams have the right to select the most talented rookie players. That draft pick is an exclusive one for the team. In the NBA and the NHL, the draft replaced a territorial system whereby players living within a stipulated territory became the property of the team that played in that area—a system that produced skewed results. Far more talented young hockey players skated in the province of Quebec than in the Chicago area, giving the Montreal Canadiens greater quality than the Blackhawks. This could be one reason why the Canadiens won more Stanley Cups—particularly in the 1940s and 1950s—than any other team. However, in part due to the equalization shown in the draft system, the Canadiens have not dominated the sports as they did in the past.

Sharing of Merchandising Monies

Each of the leagues has a subsidiary involving the sale of league-licensed merchandising. Generally, revenues are shared equally among teams and players. The subject is discussed in more detail in Chapter 14.

Sharing of Gate Receipts

Often the sharing of monies from ticket sales between teams in a given league is limited. The NFL has the most equitable sharing, 60 to 40 percent, with the home team receiving the larger amount and the rest shared among the other thirty-one teams. In the NBA, the home team retains 94 percent of the gate, with the league receiving the other 6 percent (Quirk & Fort, 1997; Easton & Rockerbee, 2002) (NBA Constitution & Bylaws, Art. 31(b)).

Sharing of Revenues from National Broadcasting and Cable, Satellite and Internet Streaming Contracts

The amount of broadcasting revenues shared between teams in a particular league varies. This NFL revenue-sharing model, as noted earlier, was conceived in the early 1960s and became a brilliant success (Fisher, 2004). The other leagues do share some revenue league-wide, although not to the extent of the NFL. Revenue-sharing systems are discussed in more detail in Chapter 15.

Restrictions on Franchise Relocation

Each of the major leagues has limitations on the movement of franchises. Permission must be given by a vote of the other team owners, often in a so-called "maxi-majority" number, such as two-thirds or 75 percent. Because of legal challenges to team relocations in the 1980s, most team moves have not been seriously contested.

Rules to Approve Ownership Changes and League Expansion

Each league permits ownership changes and the creation of new franchises only by approval of the existing franchise owners. Criteria may differ, but usually it is a maxi-majority vote (e.g., three-quarters) of the owners. However, there have been legal challenges in instances when relocations have been blocked (*Los Angeles Memorial Coliseum v. NFL*, 1984) and the threat of litigation by the losing owners hovers over a respective league.

Fostering Competition

The traditional league structure also fosters competition among the franchises. The reasons are as follows.

Autonomy in Individual Team Operations

As noted earlier in this chapter, each owner has considerable discretion in operating his or her team. Team owners have the right to hire and fire personnel, usually without league interference, and can acquire and trade players. If the team has enough money, an owner contracts with talented, and in many cases expensive, free-agent players (although within applicable salary constraints and taxes, depending on the league). The teams can market their brand to their particular community in efforts to sell tickets and gain favorable publicity. They also negotiate local broadcasting and cablecasting agreements. Additionally, since Major League Baseball, the NBA, NFL and NHL allow owners to keep a portion of their revenues, the owners have the right to utilize those funds (or, in some cases, not) to their benefit. Owners also have the right (with constraints) to sell or move their team and negotiate a stadium lease or even build their own facility.

These traditional leagues normally do not micromanage the owner in terms of personnel decisions, facility deals and local broadcasting agreements. Often, the team mirrors the spirit of the community it represents, with all the hometown pride and competitive juices aimed against teams from rival cities. Some fierce rivalries exist; in addition to the New York Yankees and the Boston Red Sox mentioned earlier, there are the Chicago Bears and Green Bay Packers and the Boston Bruins and Montreal Canadiens.

Drawbacks

Although the traditional league system remains a mainstay of professional sports in the United States and Canada, it has drawbacks, as noted next.

Disparity of Revenues and Payrolls

Allowing teams to keep a large portion of their revenue produces franchises with unequal financial resources. At one time, the disparity was relatively minor because gate attendance served as the single most important revenue stream. Since the advent of television, the skew has become greater, as fees paid for broadcast and cable rights vary greatly between large and small markets. As a general rule, owners in lucrative markets have more opportunities to field a successful team than those in smaller, less revenue-friendly areas.

However, a common misperception is that high revenue streams guarantee success. With more sophisticated methods of tracking athletic performance through improved conditioning and analytics, general managers have been bucking that stereotype. Examples abound of rich franchises spending money foolishly, especially in MLB where there is no real limit to what an owner can shell out. In 2014, two of the three highest payrolls in baseball belonged to the Yankees and Philadelphia Phillies, yet neither team made the postseason. Before achieving victory in the 2016 World Series, the Chicago Cubs participated in the post-season once between 2003 and 2015, despite ranking among the top ten teams in payroll eight times—twice in the top three.

The Specter of Antitrust Litigation

Individual owners, players and players' unions have used antitrust theory to institute lawsuits challenging many league policies and determinations over the last three decades.

Stripped to its essentials, section 1 of the Sherman Anti-Trust Act, the basic statute on the subject, prohibits agreements in interstate commerce between two or more parties that "unreasonably restrain trade." That means that if two or more entities (say, the large automobile manufacturers) get together and agree to limit sales of their cars to specific regions in the United States, that agreement could be an unreasonable and illegal restraint of trade. Two key issues must be determined: first, is the "relevant market" adversely affected and, if so, does the anticompetitive policy involve "two or more" entities (*Levine v. Central Florida Medical Affiliates, Inc.*, 1996)? Once those issues are determined, then the plaintiff can prove that the defendant's behavior either had an actual detrimental effect on competition or the potential for genuine effects of competition (*Indiana Federation of Dentists v. FTC*, 1976). Let's examine a hypothetical situation. League X has a franchise, the Alpha Athletes. The franchise wishes to move from Alpha, where it has played for sixty years, to the bustling new community of Beta, 500 miles away. The league requires a three-quarters vote of the owners to permit the move. Only two-thirds approve. If League X is a traditional sports league, the issue becomes whether a Sherman Act violation occurs. Assuming that it controls the relevant market for the appropriate sports, then the issue is whether the league is a unitary entity or a confederation of two or more groups of owners. As noted earlier, the Supreme Court concluded that traditional sports leagues are not considered single entities, but a group of joint venturers (*American Needle v. NFL*, 2010), so potentially this activity could unreasonably restrain the right of the team to move its operations. In so ruling, the court rejected the arguments by the league and some scholars that the antitrust liability involving the NFL, NBA and NHL resulted in the weakening of league power (Roberts, 1984, 1988). As will be explained in Chapter 6, Major League Baseball is not subject to this standard because it was fortunate enough to gain an antitrust exemption in place due to a 1922 Supreme Court ruling (*Federal Baseball Club v. National League*, 1922).

Past antitrust challenges involved different aspects of league decision making, such as prohibitions of team relocations, age restrictions on athletes and the imposition of labor rules. As we will see, even if the antitrust laws apply, the leagues do have various defenses they can utilize, and in most cases from the 1980s, they have been victorious. However, the time and cost of such litigation can be long and prohibitive.

Labor Issues

Each of the major leagues has suffered through strikes or lockouts with their players' unions over the last twenty years. These actions often resulted in bad publicity, and in some cases, a decrease in attendance after settlement. For example, Major League Baseball's attendance dropped 20 percent in the season after the 1994 strike (Sandomir, 2002). Traditional leagues cannot simply impose salary caps and other controls on compensation because of collective bargaining rules, and, even if no union exists, such acts could run afoul of the antitrust laws.

Alternatives to the Traditional Sports League

One Alternative: The Single-Entity Model

In the 1990s, newly created sports leagues eschewed the traditional system in favor of a far more centralized one. In a single-entity league, owners own stock in the league, which would be a for-profit corporation. The principal common feature of all single-entity leagues is one central entity with which all players in the league contract and which in turn allocates those players to the teams. Such a league consists of investors who buy shares in the league, rather than owning a particular team in the league. These investors, in return for their investment, have the right to operate individual teams but have limited autonomy in doing so. The focus is primarily on local promotions and marketing.

The most notable leagues to adopt single-entity systems are Major League Soccer (MLS) and (initially) the Women's National Basketball Association (WNBA). Others have included the Major Indoor Lacrosse League, the Continental Basketball Association and the now-defunct Women's United Soccer Association and American Basketball League (Lebowitz, 1997).

A key advantage is direct and centralized management resulting in quick decisions. Other advantages of a pure single-entity league include the following.

Unilaterally Imposed Salary Minimums and Maximums

The league may impose salary caps unless the players unionize and engage in collective bargaining negotiations. In a single-entity league, the directors can decide on salary restraints by fiat and do not have to worry about conflicting ownership interests, such as big-market versus small-market rivalries. If the players organize a union, the negotiations with the players can, theoretically, be smoother for the same reason.

"Pure" Sharing of Profits

As stated earlier in the chapter, no traditional league shares all team profits. On the other hand, a single-entity league shares all profits and expenses equally, regardless of the size of the market.

Competitive Parity

Because of the salary structure and the control of player trades, it is less likely that one or two "rich" teams dominate the sport and skew competitive balance.

Ease of Team Relocation

If a team is not profitable, it affects every owner, and relocation is easier. The league directors can decide to move the team, with little objection from the investor running the team.

Ease of Franchise Expansion

If the league feels that a viable business opportunity exists, it can create a new franchise far more quickly than in a traditional league. No owner is needed, and fees from ticket sales, stadium deals and broadcast agreements can be drawn into the coffers of the league for all the investors to share.

No Antitrust Problems, as the League Is One Business Entity

This is probably the single biggest reason for the implementation of this model. A pure single-entity league prevents most time-consuming and expensive antitrust litigation.

Although there are a number of benefits, the existing single-entity leagues have some significant structural problems as well, which have made it less attractive as a viable alternative to the traditional league. These include the following.

Lack of Owner Autonomy to Make Innovative, Locally Oriented Decisions

Because each investor is a shareholder in the league, the autonomy to make such decisions with regard to team personnel, salary structure and overall management is severely compromised. All major decisions come from the league office, even if they involve mundane matters that would not occupy the time of a traditional league office. This may stifle creativity and limit the ability of franchises to make decisions based on the particular aspects of their given markets.

Restrictions on Sale and Relocation

Owners of teams in traditional leagues have sold or relocated their teams for a potential improvement in business opportunity. A single-entity league can easily block the sale of an investors' stock and can prevent the movement of an existing team.

Less Incentive to Improve the Product

The goal of many owners in a traditional league is to produce a winning team, even a dynasty. In the case of a single-entity league, a dominant team or two may hurt the league, and the investors may take steps to weaken the team by forcing player trades to preserve parity for other teams. That kind of action may anger fans of the dominant team and create a backlash. In such a structure, the owner-investors may not have as much of a "winning attitude." Partly because of the problems just described, "single-entity" leagues have not produced great successes and few, if any, leagues precisely follow this exact model. Instead of "pure" single-entity leagues, MLS and the WNBA were originally hybrids, primarily because of the difficulties in finding investors to support an organization in which their individual rights are limited.

Examples of Partial Single-Entity Leagues

Women's National Basketball Association

The WNBA, though formed in 1997, was not the first women's professional league, nor even the first women's professional basketball league (the long-defunct American Basketball League has that distinction). At its founding, the then eight-team league had the advantage of the publicity and the marketing juggernaut of its venerable brother, the NBA. The WNBA's original business plan tried to use the NBA's large number of season ticket holders to its advantage by trying to sell itself to that audience.

That marketing did not prove successful. Only 10 percent of its fan base came from NBA ticket holders. Rather, it centered on women aged eighteen through forty-nine years and their children, particularly their daughters (Heath, 2003)—far different from the male-dominated NBA audience. The WNBA was originally conceived as a pure single-entity league. Each of the eight original WNBA teams was located in cities that had an existing NBA franchise. All twenty-nine NBA teams owned an equal share of the women's league and shared in the WNBA's costs and losses. The league was run by a board of governors representing the investors, and the teams were operated by their respective local NBA franchises. As in the case of MLS, the advantage was the unitary policy that resulted in salary restrictions and centralized control over all operations.

By 2002, the WNBA's board of governors, faced with stagnant or declining attendance and lack of profitability, was forced to significantly change the league's structure. The board eliminated the single-entity organization and allowed individual owners to buy teams and assume the financial risk. One important reason for the change was the potential value increase of the franchises. If the WNBA became a traditional league, an incentive would exist for an owner to sustain short-term losses to make the team competitive so that team's value would increase. In 2003, the Mohegan Tribe, owners of the Mohegan Sun casino, purchased the Orlando Miracle for $5 million and moved the team to Connecticut (Cavanaugh, 2003). This marked the abandonment of two core principles from the league's founding: no independently owned teams, and franchises must be paired with NBA counterparts—single-entity concepts that were considered to be stunting the league's growth.

As of 2016, the WNBA had twelve teams, down from sixteen in 2002, six of which remain owned by NBA teams. In recent years, attendance has been modest, as have television ratings. NBA officials have admitted that the WNBA has not progressed as far as was hoped when it founded. NBA Commissioner Adam Silver stated, "As much as we've done in lending the league our name," he said, "the people who have been in the sports business for a long time, and I'm one of them, historically underestimated the marketing it takes to launch a new property" (Sandomir, 2016). Whereas the NBA receives $2.6 billion in annual television revenues, the WNBA garners $25 million annually. Even converting the league to a traditional model did not ensure success.

Although the traditional league possesses elements of a cartel, the single-entity league displays an idealistic, but often impractical, cooperation model. Also, the creation of an organizational structure whose primary purpose provides a legal defense against antitrust lawsuits does not necessarily result in economic success. It will be interesting to see how future leagues organize and whether MLS continues its present system. MLS is discussed later in the chapter.

Leagues that Failed

The sports business is littered with the remains of leagues created that could not attain economic success and ultimately folded. The Women's United Soccer Association (WUSA) began with high hopes in 2001, seeking to capitalize on the success of the 1999 Women's World Cup in the United States as the first professional women's league. However, it folded two years later because of lack of fan support and corporate sponsorships, along with a failure to control expenses. More recently, Women's Professional Soccer, or WPS, opened its doors in 2009, but it was less successful and was dissolved in 2012 (Sports Business Daily, 2013).

A Second Alternative: Promotion and Relegation

Although issues involving international sports will be covered in Chapter 4, soccer (known to most of the world as "football") has produced a very different organizational system than those in either the traditional or single-entity leagues discussed. The differences are twofold. First, like other international sports, soccer is governed by FIFA, an international governing body for the sport. National leagues are covered by bodies such as the Football Association (FA), the English domestic equivalent, which existed before the birth of professional leagues. So, unlike the NFL, which acts as both a governing body and a professional league, in international football, the domestic leagues and teams are subservient to the policies crafted by the separate governing body (Szymanski, 2009). Second, these soccer leagues use a "promotion and relegation" system whereby the success of the team is a prerequisite for its level of competition. Successful teams in a "second division" can be promoted to a "first division," whereas unsuccessful first division teams face demotion to the lower tier. This approach creates a fluid system whereby, unlike a traditional U.S. league, no team automatically retains its position in the league irrespective of quality of play. For example, in England, there are four main professional divisions and, over a twenty-year period, 95 percent of the teams experienced promotion or relegation (Szymanski, 2009).

Although highly unlikely, if a particular sports league in the United States adopts a promotion/relegation system, certain advantages accrue. First, with teams going up and down the various tiers, poorly performing teams have a strong incentive to produce a better product. Revenue streams for broadcasting rights would likely be significantly reduced in a second division from that of a top division, and a team in this position would lose significant resale value, as well as prestige. Additionally, the teams in danger of being relegated (meaning the teams that are in the last two or three places in a respective league) would play meaningful games late in the season. Instead of the empty seats often found in stadiums during baseball games between the bottom two teams in September, attendance could be far healthier as these teams battle to stay in their respective division.

Also, a promotion/relegation system would not restrict franchises in the same way as traditional leagues because the number of teams competing in a given market would be greater. For example, say that in a given city there are teams in each of three or four divisions. With promotion and relegation, it is possible that more than one team may be in the first division. The number and the identity of the teams in a particular division would be subject to change.

The ebb and flow of team promotion and relegation makes such a league impervious to antitrust lawsuits, because this is no closed market. This results in a more open competition and permits, at least in theory, a team from a very small market to conceivably jump to a top-tier division. Conversely, a large-market team can jump to a lower division. There is no market restraint.

However, there would result a radical rethinking of the traditional U.S. league approach. As inferred from the prior paragraph, the relative ease of promotion or relegation means that different teams are in a particular division from year to year. The league's structure would be more fluid and there would be less control over franchise issues and less territorial exclusivity. The general financial health of particular teams could vary greatly because of uncertainties over which division they occupy in a given season. Yet, this venerable system does provide for an intriguing alternative to the traditional league system, and the day may come when a new league or maybe a series of minor or developmental leagues may consolidate to try it in the United States. Given its international popularity, those in the sports business should familiarize themselves with this league alternative.

A Short Summary of the Four Traditional Major Leagues

National Football League

By popularity and revenue generation, the NFL, established in 1920, has become the most dominant of the four major leagues in the United States (Rovell, 2014). Its management structure center consists of an executive committee composed of one representative (often the owner) of each club and the commissioner, elected by the executive committee. Although the executive committee has more general decision-making powers, the commissioner wields considerable influence in the decisions of the committee (NFL Constitution and Bylaws, Art. VI, sec. 1). The commissioner (presently Roger Goodell) possesses disciplinary powers, dispute resolution and decision-making authority, including the power to appoint other officers and committees (NFL Constitution and Bylaws, Article VIII, 2006). Notably, the commissioner possesses considerable power to impose disciplinary action and render disciplinary punishment. Presently, the NFL commissioner is the only major league CEO that has the power to settle disputes between players and teams. Instead of an independent third party (as required under other leagues' collective bargaining agreements), the commissioner retains that authority and his decision cannot be appealed (NFL Constitution and Bylaws, Article VIII, Sec. 8.3). Other powers include suspension and banishment for life from involvement in the NFL (NFL Constitution and Bylaws, Article VIII, Sec. 8.13, 2006).

The creation or sale of a franchise requires a positive vote of at least three-quarters, or twenty of the owners, whichever is greater (NFL Constitution and Bylaws, Article III, Sec. 3.3(C), 2006). The NFL permits ownership of teams by corporations, individuals or partnerships, but limits the "home territory" of a team to a seventy-five-mile radius, with certain limited exceptions, such as the San Francisco Bay Area, which each have two teams (NFL Constitution and Bylaws, Article IV, Sec. 4.1, 2006). Presently, the NFL contains thirty-two teams, the most among U.S. professional sports leagues, yet it has the most centralized operations of them all. Notably, the league split $7.2 billion between those teams during the 2014–15 season in its revenue-sharing arrangement, which is far greater than the other leagues (Petchesky, 2015). The large majority of that revenue comes from national broadcast agreements negotiated by the league. The idea came in the early 1960s from the then–Cleveland Browns' then-owner Art Modell, who convinced owners George Halas (Chicago Bears), Dan Reeves (Los Angeles Rams) and Jack Mara (New York Giants) to join a proposed revenue-sharing plan and give up the ability to independently negotiate TV rights. The shared television rights ensured competitive balance and helped the league create a profitable and equitable relationship between the central office and the team owners.

The revenue sharing also applies to gate receipts. Currently, 40 percent of the gate receipts from NFL games go into a pool that is divided equally among the teams (NFL Constitution and Bylaws, Article XIX, Sec. 19.1(A), 2006). However, unshared revenues from luxury box seating, stadium naming rights and stadium signage have created greater economic disparity among the member teams. Franchises with new stadiums tend to receive more of such income than older venues. The revenue gap between NFL teams has grown from $10 million in the late 1990s to more than $300 million in 2013 (Ozanian, 2014).

As of 2016, the NFL remains the premier sports league in the United States. According to an Associated Press-GfK poll conducted in 2014, 49 percent of Americans consider themselves fans of professional football, although this number represents a slight decline from the same poll conducted one year prior (AP, 2014). Revenue reached $13 billion in 2016 (Belzer, 2016). However, after increasing 5 percent from 1999 to 2008, attendance has become flat from 2010 to 2014. Still, 17 million fans attended NFL games in 2013, nearly 97 percent of stadium capacity.

Present commissioner Roger Goodell, selected in 2006, assumed his position after a period of sustained labor peace. He has had a rockier experience with NFL players than his predecessor, Paul Tagliabue. A lockout of the players occurred in 2011, but after almost half a year and a favorable court ruling later, the players and the league signed on to a new, long-term collective bargaining agreement. But more controversial has been its disciplinary policies and the perception of inconsistent and improper use of his powers. Shortly after assuming his position, Goodell enacted and enforced a players' "personal conduct" policy in light of a number of highly publicized transgressions involving NFL players. Under this policy, the commissioner has the power to suspend indefinitely any player who engages in violent or criminal behavior. That means a player may be sanctioned even if he is not convicted of a crime (Edelman, 2009). As one commentator noted: "Goodell has definitely defined himself as being a bigger sheriff than any other previous commissioner" (Sports Business Daily, 2009). More recently, he was criticized for displaying a lax attitude toward domestic violence issues and then inconsistently applying a higher level of punishment for it. For example, after suspending then-Baltimore Ravens running back Ray Rice for two games, he amended the personal conduct policy to require a minimum suspension of six games for such acts (Farmer, 2014). The change in policy may have resulted, at least in part, from the emergence of an explicit video of the act. After seeing it, Goodell increased Rice's penalty retroactively to six games, claiming that the player was not cooperative. That punishment was reversed by an arbitrator appointed by Goodell (*Matter of Ray Rice*, 2014).

Another controversial incident occurred when Minnesota Vikings Adrian Peterson was arrested for child abuse. After a plea deal, he was suspended for the rest of the season, a decision upheld by an arbitrator, but later vacated by a federal trial court (*National Football League Players Association (Peterson) v. NFL*, 2015). However, a federal appeals court reinstated the arbitrator's ruling (*National Football League Players Association (Peterson) v. NFL*, 2016).

A third, and probably most publicized, controversy involved allegations that the New England Patriots deflated their footballs to an air pressure under the required level during an AFC Championship game in 2015. The allegations centered on the team's star quarterback, Tom Brady. Upon hearing of the alleged deflation of the footballs, the NFL authorized a noted law firm to conduct an investigation, and the report concluded that "it was more probable than not" that Brady was aware of the deflation of the footballs (which gives the quarterback undue advantage). Commissioner Goodell suspended him for the first four games of the 2015–16 season and fined the team. Brady and the NFL Players' Association appealed to Goodell (who under the terms of the collective bargaining agreement can hear the appeal), who, not surprisingly, upheld the determination. The matter then went to the courts. The NFL sought to have a judge uphold the arbitration, while Brady and the NFL Players Association sought to vacate it, largely on procedural grounds, arguing that the league engaged in a manifestly unfair proceeding with lack of adequate notice of all information and a punishment that went beyond that of an ordinary rules violation. Notably, the trial judge did not take a position as to whether Brady was "guilty" of violating the rules involving football pressure, but that his side did not have access to all the information and that the suspension was beyond the scope of the NFL's rules (*NFL Management Council v. NFLPA*, 2015). However, an appeals court, in a divided opinion, reversed the trial court and concluded that the commissioner's determination and punishment were not improper and were not fundamentally unfair, but rather, were within the powers given to the commissioner under the collective bargaining agreement between the NFL and its players association (*NFL Management Council v. NFLPA*, 2016). After unsuccessfully seeking a hearing in front of the entire panel of the appeals court judges, Brady conceded defeat and intended to serve his suspension (Reyes, 2016).

On one level, the end of the Brady litigation is a victory for the NFL and the scope of authority of a league commissioner under the terms of the respective collective bargaining agreement. No one won this case in the court of public opinion. The NFL Players Association lost because it negotiated such a broad level of power to the commissioner; the New England Patriots owner Robert Kraft lost a power struggle with Roger Goodell; the Patriots, through their personnel, were deemed to have violated rules of the sport by deflating the footballs; Brady lost, had to serve the suspension and had his stellar reputation tarnished. The NFL also lost because it fought for a system where the commissioner was the judge and jury, and it served to antagonize relations with its players (not only in the Brady case). It is likely that the NFLPA will press for a more neutral grievance arbitration procedure in the next round of collective bargaining negotiations.

Ethical Issue: New Orleans Saints "Bounties"

In 2012, it was revealed that a number of New Orleans Saints' players and coaches had been illegally pooling money and using it for incentives since 2009. Specifically, players were paid "bonuses" for certain achievements during games, including injuring or "knocking out" opposing players—the equivalent of a bounty. As a result, Goodell disciplined several members of the team and coaching staff for "conduct detrimental to the league." Defensive Coordinator Greg Williams, the creator and primary instigator of the scheme, was banned from the league indefinitely. Three other coaches and four players were suspended anywhere from three games to the entire 2012 season—the latter being issued to Sean Payton, the Saints' head coach (ESPN, 2012a; ESPN, 2012b).

All parties later appealed their suspensions, with the exception of Williams. Whereas the coaches' suspensions were upheld, all four players' suspensions were vacated by former NFL commissioner Paul Tagliabue, who was assigned by Goodell to handle the appeals process. Tagliabue affirmed Goodell's factual findings that the players acted improperly by participating in the program, but he felt there was insufficient evidence to assign these suspensions due to the "contaminat[ion] by the coaches and others in the Saints' organization" (Iyer, 2012).

Does the arbitrator's reversal of Goodell's determination undermine the commissioner's authority to adequately punish wrongdoers? What effect does this ruling have on the ability of a league commissioner to exact punishment?

Ethical Issue: The Bullying Case

Shortly after the Saints' incident, Goodell was forced to confront a different type of ethical issue. Instead of physical abuse aimed at opponents, this involved mental and emotional abuse aimed at a teammate.

Jonathan Martin was an offensive tackle for the Miami Dolphins. On October 30, 2013, while a member of the Dolphins, reports surfaced that he suddenly left the team facilities two days prior due to emotional reasons. It was discovered that he had been a victim of team bullying since his arrival as a rookie, primarily led by teammate Richie Incognito. Martin could no longer withstand the crude verbal harassments and decided that he would rather sit out the season than face it any longer (Jackson, 2014).

More details came to the public light, and the Dolphins responded by suspending Incognito for the remainder of the season. The NFL launched its own investigation, concluding that the repeated targeted harassment by Incognito and others contributed to Martin's departure from the team (Rosenthal, 2014). Despite these findings, the league could not institute its own punishment of Incognito due to the collective bargaining agreement, which only permits "one penalty" (Florio, 2014). The questions resulting from this incident are complex—more so than the media reported. First, what exactly is bullying? Its definition can vary. Second, were the actions of the players part of a long-standing culture of bonding rituals—as vulgar, tasteless and offensive as they were—that have been done in the past, even though it would violate codes of conduct and social norms found in a normal employment relationship?

The investigation and report, conducted and drafted by a prominent law firm, did note that Martin responded to the other players in, at times, equally offensive terms, but concluded he was a victim nonetheless. Does this serve as a defense to the conduct alleged? Should the NFL (or any league) craft a specific definition as to what kind of conduct constitutes "bullying"?

National Basketball Association

Like the NFL, the NBA is a traditional league with independent teams under the leadership of a commissioner. Although the NBA controls a considerable amount of revenues, local teams retain considerable freedom to make their own local media deals, a feature somewhat different from the more centralized revenue structure of the NFL.

Each entity or person seeking an NBA franchise or wishing to buy an existing team must be approved by the affirmative vote of no fewer than three-fourths of the members represented by a board of governors (essentially the owners or their representatives) (NBA Constitution and Bylaws, Article 4(d)).

A three-fourths majority is also required to transfer a membership to another entity (NBA Constitution and Bylaws, Article 5(f)). Commissioner Adam Silver has similar, but not identical, powers to the NFL's Goodell. But a key difference involves player discipline. The NBA commissioner does not have the discretion that the NFL's Goodell has in disciplining players because of limitations found in their respective collective bargaining agreements. In the NBA, for example, the commissioner's disciplinary actions for off-the-court conduct are reviewable by a neutral arbitrator (NBA Collective Bargaining Agreement, Article XXXI).

Like the NFL, the NBA has made quantum leaps in exposure and profitability over the last 30 years. The NBA transformed from a league of twenty-three teams, some of which were on the brink of bankruptcy, in the early 1980s to a thirty-team juggernaut with worldwide popularity. One of the reasons for the turnaround was the emergence of superstar players such as Michael Jordan, Larry Bird and Erwin "Magic" Johnson in the 1980s; Shaquille O'Neal and Tim Duncan in the 1990s; and even more recently, LeBron James. But another reason for its success was the thirty-year tenure of its former commissioner, David Stern. In 2004, one commentator remarked that, in leading the NBA, "[David] Stern has single-handedly done more as commissioner of the NBA over a [then] 20-year tenure than any other top executive in sports history" (Rovell, 2004). At the time of his retirement, one commentator stated, "David Stern has ruled the NBA for 30 years with a velvet glove, iron fist, breathtaking intellect, inexhaustible work ethic, a personal sense of right and wrong, and a love for basketball" (Mahoney, 2014). Stern took over a league with declining attendance, few recognizable stars and red ink, as seventeen of the twenty-three teams reported financial losses. Fan apathy had grown rampant. Many believed that the league was too "Black," and drug use was common, even among some marquee players (Schneider-Mayerson, 2010). As late as 1981, NBA Finals games aired on tape delay. During collective bargaining with the players in 1983, the league claimed $118 million in revenue for the previous season, about $5 million per team. It also said that financially unstable franchises in Kansas City, San Diego and elsewhere collectively owed former players as much as $90 million in deferred pay (Sports Business Daily, 2014).

Stern proved to be a very adept marketer who increased brand recognition, utilized the star power of Jordan and others and created an international fan base. Under his watch, he started licensing the NBA brand and took the league and its marketing international. He made exposure of the NBA in China a priority. In addition, Stern pioneered the use of the salary cap, a method to control player salaries by tying them to league revenues. This idea, since adopted in varying degrees by the NHL and the NFL, has become central in controlling player costs and has been a central tenet in labor relations between the players' association and the respective league. As of 2015, only Major League Baseball does not utilize such a system, which will be examined in detail in Chapter 6.

During Stern's tenure, the average franchise value increased from $17 million in 1984 to $634 million in 2014, with the New York Knicks reaching a record valuation of $3.2 billion that year (Forbes.com, 2016). Gross revenues from licensed products increased from a mere $10 million in 1984 to over $5.5 billion thirty years later. Overall annual league revenues increased from $118 million to $4.6 billion in 2014 (Badenhausen, 2014a), and U.S. television rights bring in $930 million annually, which is up over 250 percent from the prior broadcasting deal. That fee will increase substantially starting in the 2016–17 season to an astounding $2.6 billion per season as part of an extended media rights agreement (ESPN.com, 2016).

Stern was known as a powerful manager who did not hesitate to impose disciplinary sanctions for in-game conduct that he felt was detrimental to his sport. Following one of the most infamous incidents in NBA history, Stern showed just how much disciplinary muscle he had. In 2004 he suspended Indiana Pacers players Ron Artest (season-long), Stephen Jackson (thirty games) and Jermaine O'Neal (twenty-five games) for participation in a melee that involved both opposing players and fans during a game with the Detroit Pistons in the Pistons' home arena. This brawl received considerable coverage, and the severity of the penalties resulted in players' union protests (McCallum, 2004). When announcing the suspensions to the public, Stern quipped "it was unanimous, one to nothing," highlighting the power he has over such incidents (ESPN, 2004).

The commissioner also has the authority to fine owners, and Stern utilized it when he saw fit. Dallas Mavericks owner Mark Cuban was penalized almost $2 million in fines over thirteen years, mostly for criticizing referees. As one owner put it: "[H]e was very effective at being the sheriff" (Boudway, 2014).

In February 2014, Adam Silver, Stern's deputy, assumed the commissioner's position. He was put to the test very early in his tenure.

Case Study: The Donald Sterling Saga

In 2014, Donald Sterling, the principal owner of the NBA's Los Angeles Clippers, was secretly recorded by an alleged girlfriend making racially offensive statements about African Americans. The tape, illegally recorded under California law, as it was done without the consent of Mr. Sterling, was disseminated to TMZ.com, a gossip website, and uploaded. It went viral, and the consequence of his statements put the new NBA commissioner Adam Silver to a supreme test of governance.

After verifying the voice on the recordings as that of Sterling, Silver announced that he would fine Sterling $2.5 million and ban him from the NBA for life, which forced him to sell the team. Although some have said that Sterling did nothing illegal, and in fact the recordings were illegal, that does not prevent the league from taking action, as long as the justification and sanctions are within the NBA's constitution and bylaws. Because the NBA is a private organization, it has far greater discretion than the state does in issuing penalties.

The NBA justified Silver's actions under Article 13(d) of the league's constitution, which states that an owner cannot "fail or refuse to fulfill its contractual obligations to the Association, its Members, Players, or any other third party in such a way as to affect the Association or its Members adversely," and provides for the termination of an owner who violates this provision. It even granted the Clippers co-owner and Sterling's estranged spouse, Rochelle, the right to sell the franchise (which was in a trust in both of their names). Sterling, who was known as an aggressive litigator against the NBA in the 1980s, challenged this action. Despite this, his wife, as trustee, was able to sell the team in August 2014 to Steve Ballmer, a former principal at Microsoft, for $2 billion—three times the value estimated by Forbes (Brown, 2014).

This saga raises a number of ethical questions. Have racially insensitive statements been made by other NBA owners behind closed doors with no sanctions due to the fact they were not recorded? If so, is the league engaging in a double standard? An even more difficult issue is whether the same result would occur if Sterling made offensive and crude statements against, say, Native Americans, given that few, if any, Native Americans play in the NBA, as opposed to about three-quarters of the players being African American. Did the fears of labor unrest play a role? Should an elderly owner who was diagnosed with dementia lose his business over admittedly offensive and insensitive statements? Did the lack of success of his team through much of Sterling's tenure and the reports of lack of congeniality with other owners play a part in this decision by Commissioner Silver? Finally, did Silver and the other owners read Article 13 too broadly? There is no evidence that he, as owner of the Clippers, failed to follow his contractual obligations. There have been reports that Sterling signed "moral and ethical" contracts with the league (Zilgitt, 2014), but even if that was not the case, is there a "social contract" on how owners should behave?

Conversely, can it be argued that Sterling (and his estranged spouse Rochelle) are the big winners here? Had this scandal not occurred and Sterling wished to sell the team, he and his wife could have received less based on the estimated team valuation. So, aside from the embarrassment and a $2.5 million fine, Sterling came out with a windfall. Is this an ethically desirable result? If the NBA constitution gives the commissioner unfettered powers to impose whatever fines he wishes, would it be possible that a percentage of the sale go to the league in the form of damages?

Yet another issue involves the economics of the NBA itself. Did Silver and the NBA look into the effect that Sterling's continued ownership of the team could have on its bottom line, business reputation and marketing? If that is so, then owners can open themselves up to sanction simply for controversial viewpoints and political allegiances. If players and fans disagree with those views and threaten to stop playing or boycott games, could the league take similar action?

In any event, Silver received high marks for his leadership and helped burnish his legacy early in this tenure.

The National Hockey League

Founded in 1917, the NHL has traditionally been considered the "fourth league" because it has had more difficulty gaining widespread appeal.

However, since the lockout of 2012, it is on the upswing with increased popularity and revenues.

Until 1967, the NHL contained just six franchises but in the last forty years, it has expanded rapidly to reach the present total of thirty teams. In the 1990s, a number of franchises moved or were awarded to untraditional Sun Belt markets, such as Dallas, Phoenix and Atlanta. Some of the "Sun Belt" teams thrived, whereas others like the Phoenix Coyotes and Atlanta Thrashers did not. The NHL had to take control over the Phoenix team in 2011 until it found new owners in 2013. The Atlanta franchise ultimately moved to Winnipeg, which, ironically, was where the Coyotes franchise had moved from in 1996. Gary Bettman was selected as the first NHL commissioner in 1993. Before him were a series of presidents that did not have the kinds of powers inherent in the other league commissioners. A protégé of David Stern, Bettman came to the NHL from the NBA. As of 2015, he is the longest-tenured commissioner of the four major sports. Much of his tenure has been marked by labor disputes: the league and its players endured the loss of an entire season in 2004–05, and additional, but shorter, lockouts occurred in 1995 and 2012. Despite predictions of loss of fan support the NHL has had a renaissance. Although public interest has not reached the levels of the other major leagues, the league has been able to secure considerably more lucrative broadcast rights in both the United States and Canada. After the last lockout, the league rebounded impressively with 2013–14 revenues estimated to be $3.7 billion. Team valuation continues to increase. As of 2015, the NHL team with the highest franchise value was the New York Rangers, at $1.2 billion (Ozanian, 2015). The league instituted a salary cap system similar to that of the NBA after the 2005 lockout, and it was further refined after the 2012 lockout (Ozanian & Badenhausen, 2008). The NHL remains the most "tribal" of the big four leagues, as 80 percent of its revenues come from local (nonshared) sources, like tickets, luxury seating, advertising and television (Ozanian, 2015). In 2016, the league approved its first expansion franchise in over fifteen years, granting Las Vegas a team, starting with the 2017–18 season. It would be the first major league sports franchise in that city.

Like the NBA, the NHL has increased its marketing campaign in both North America and internationally. Starting in 1998, the league permitted its players to play in the Winter Olympics to further its brand. However, unlike the NBA, the NHL actually has to put its season on hold for two weeks because of the timing of the games. Because the league and team owners lose revenue for this downtime and derive no direct economic benefit from participation from the International Olympic Committee or the International Ice Hockey Federation, the international federation for the sport, many owners are reluctant to permit their players to participate in the Olympics. Additionally, participation in an intense competition can increase the risk of player injury. For these reasons as of 2016, it has not been decided whether NHL players will compete in the 2018 games in Pyeongchang, South Korea.

Major League Baseball

Thirty teams make up Major League Baseball. Unlike the other sports, Major League Baseball's roots derive from a unification of two independent entities: the National League and the American League. In 1903 the two leagues agreed to operate simultaneously as major baseball leagues, and each year, their respective champions would play one another for the World Series. The two leagues remained separate legal entities until 2000, when they officially merged. For decades, its governing documents were akin to articles of confederation, rather than a unitary constitution found in the other major sports. Before the mid-1990s, each of the leagues had its own president and staff. In a shift toward centralization, the league presidents were eliminated and instead there is now a vice-president and an executive council.

The Major League Baseball Agreement dates from 1876, when it was created as the National League Constitution. It took its current general form—and name—in 2000. It gives the commissioner "executive responsibility" for labor relations and maintains the power to take actions deemed detrimental to the sport (MLB Constitution, Art. II, Sec. 2).

Like their counterparts in other leagues, baseball owners retain significant voting rights in league matters. To approve an expansion, a three-fourths majority of all member clubs in the league seeking expansion and a majority of clubs in the nonexpanding league are required. The same ratios are required for the movement of a team. The owners also define the appropriate "home territory" for a particular team. For example, the Los Angeles Dodgers' and the Los Angeles Angels' territory includes Orange, Ventura and Los Angeles counties.

Bud Selig, a former owner of the Milwaukee Brewers, became acting commissioner in 1992 (and commissioner in 1998) after the forced resignation of Fay Vincent. Selig was the first commissioner with a direct ownership interest, but he transferred the ownership interest to his daughter before assuming office to avoid potential conflicts. He retired shortly after the 2014 season and was replaced by Robert Manfred, who took office in 2015.

Like Bettman of the NHL, Selig's early tenure was marked by labor disputes, culminating in a 1994 strike that resulted in the cancellation of the postseason. In the following years he was plagued by the highly publicized use of performance-enhancing drugs by some key players, resulting in amendments to the collective bargaining agreement between the league and the Major League Baseball Players' Association that stiffened penalties for violations. The climax was the suspension of New York Yankees' third baseman Alex Rodriguez for the 2014 season.

Yet, Selig can be credited for leading an era of greater profitability, better organization and labor peace. With the opening of many new ballparks, coupled with a sophisticated and very highly regarded new media division, Major League Baseball Advanced Media ("MLBAM"), revenue streams have increased significantly under Selig's tenure (MLB. com, 2013). However, some of that success has been tarnished by the lax standards in policing the use of performance-enhancing substances, which may have helped players increase their prowess and resulted in the breaking of some long-cherished records, such as the single-season and career home run records (Wilbon, 2004). Major League Baseball has also expanded its international marketing. Its seasons have begun with at least one series of games outside North America, and it has launched its World Baseball Classic—an international baseball tournament allowing countries to compete for the title (similar to the World Cup of soccer).

Despite the sport's fractious beginnings, today's MLB owners think of themselves as a part of a unified league and have shared revenues, particularly by means of a tax system, that penalizes heavy spending teams. It also shares its merchandising and national broadcasting and cable rights.

In part due to its long-standing exemption from antitrust laws, Major League Baseball teams exercise control over affiliated minor league teams in a manner that could be illegal if done by other sports (Weiler & Roberts, 2004, p. 172). Baseball teams negotiate affiliation agreements with such teams, which serve as feeders for talented players going to the Major League club. Yet the minor leagues have constitutions and bylaws that delegate decision-making authority to a board of directors and the minor league's president. Some decisions, however, require ratification by Major League Baseball. For example, all proposed franchise sales and transfers of minor league teams must be registered with the commissioner, who in certain instances can reject a sale or transfer if it is deemed "not in the best interests of baseball." The commissioner must also approve any grant of protected territory to a minor league club (Rosner & Shropshire, 2004).

Minor League Baseball

Minor league teams are divided into five primary classifications: rookie, short-season Class A, full-season Class A, Class AA (Double-A) and Class AAA (Triple-A), with the latter being considered the highest level. Each Major League franchise has associated minor league teams in these classifications, and the Major League club has significant control over their respective rosters. Generally, players advance from Class A to Triple-A based on performance and the Major League franchise's desire to bring that player to the Major League team (this would be referred to as a player being "called up"). It is also used for rehabilitation games for professional players returning from injury. Players on a Major League team who are not performing well may also be sent to the minor league team (demoted or "sent down") so that they do not have to be released completely and can be called back up at any time. However, minor league teams are not owned by their Major League counterparts. There are independent owners who buy, sell, move and market their respective teams and own or lease their facilities.

Some minor league teams are "independent," meaning that they do not have any affiliation with Major League Baseball clubs. A relatively recent development starting in the 1990s, as of 2016, there are eight such leagues currently operating, seven of which operate during the traditional baseball season and one operating during the winter months. Because they are not affiliated with a major league club, the independent league team owners are responsible for all costs. These teams tend to be very frugal. For example, the Frontier League caps a team's salary at $75,000 a season, with individual player salaries capped at $1,600 a month. To attract audiences these leagues may sign veteran Major League Baseball players who are at the end of their careers or engage in various kinds of publicity stunts. For example, one team utilized a trained pig to deliver baseballs to the umpires (Beaton, 2015).

Minor League Baseball attendance was strong in 2013. The nineteen leagues and 243 clubs drew 41,553,781 patrons. The average crowd in a game was 4,040 (Kronheim, 2014).

Major League Soccer

For two decades, Major League Soccer (MLS) has been the "major" soccer league operating in the United States. Although some consider MLS a second-tier league as compared with the elite European leagues, it has been successful in expanding interest in the sport in the United States. Since 1999, its commissioner has been Don Garber.

The structure of MLS is different from that of the traditional leagues. It was founded at a time when newer leagues were formed as "single-entity" leagues. Rather than a consortium of independent owners acting together, a single-entity league is organized as a unitary organization. The primary advantage of a single-entity league was easier governance and protection from the threat of antitrust litigation. The mechanics of a pure single-entity league were discussed earlier in the chapter. This structure serves as a shield against the use of antitrust lawsuits by owners and players and creates a more economically competitive landscape than the traditional league.

Although it displays many characteristics of such a league, MLS has really become a hybrid or quasi-single entity. When the league was conceived, its creators sought true single-entity status by soliciting investors (called "investor-operators") to become shareholders in the league, and the league would oversee all policies and would centrally control all earned revenues (Weiler & Roberts, 2004, p. 214). MLS revenues would pay all costs incurred by each team for players, staff, stadium leases and travel. Any profits would be distributed as dividends to the investor-operators, similar to the way a standard corporation operates.

Ultimately, the idea proved unsuccessful in attracting the required amount of capital needed to fund the league. An altered business model resulted, combining elements of a pure single-entity and a more traditional league. As of 2016, there are twenty owner-investors and twenty teams. This may change, as the league plans to add four more teams by 2018. Originally the league was not able to attract enough investors for a one-to-one owner-to-team ratio, resulting in owners owning multiple teams in the league. For example, at one time Anschutz Entertainment Group (AEG) owned as many as six teams. But as of 2016, each owner-investor has only one team.

Despite the semi-autonomous nature of the majority of teams, the MLS system does retain a very centralized approach. All investors are represented on the MLS management committee, the functional equivalent of a board of directors. The management committee hires, fires and trades players. It owns all MLS trademarks and copyrights, executes all stadium leases and controls all radio broadcast rights, advertising and sponsorship agreements. The investor-operators, however, are responsible for negotiating local sponsorship and broadcast agreements for their own teams.

After years of losses, the quality and profitability of MLS have been increasing recently. The interest in soccer has grown in the last decade to the point that for those ages 12 to 17, soccer is just as popular as baseball (Bennett, 2014). MLS has been able to unilaterally impose salary restraints, a course of action upheld by two federal courts, which rejected antitrust challenges to this policy (*Fraser v. Major League Soccer*, 2000, 2002). More recently, its players have become unionized, and salary restrictions are a part of recent collective bargaining agreements. In 2013, per-game attendance averaged 18,594 league-wide (Oshan, 2013).

In the last decade, more and more soccer-specific stadiums have been built, replacing the converted football fields that have been the norm. As of 2014, there are thirteen soccer-specific stadiums used, and more coming in the ensuing years (Bushnell, 2016).

A key difference between MLS and the four traditional major leagues is that the NBA, NFL, NHL and Major League Baseball do not have any competing leagues on the same level of quality. MLS, on the other hand, must compete with the elite international leagues, like the English Premier League (EPL), whose games are broadcast and streamed in the United States. Despite the increase in quality of play, many conclude that the MLS teams are not the same caliber as teams such as Manchester United, Arsenal or FC Barcelona of the La Liga.

A number of reasons are advanced for the rise in interest in soccer. The first is the growing number of youngsters playing the sport. In recent years, soccer has become the most-played sport among six-, seven- and eight-year-olds, according to the Sports and Fitness Industry Association (*Sports Business Journal*, 2014). A second reason is the rising Latino population, which now comprises 17 percent of the total U.S. population. Often coming from countries with rich soccer traditions, many have carried that interest to the MLS and other leagues like the North American Soccer League. The outpouring of interest that germinated from the 1994 World Cup held in the United States is also a factor. MLS was created in part to secure that successful bid (Baxter, 2014). Also, soccer's demographic is a young one, and video games such as FIFA's soccer has reached this audience (Badenhausen, 2014b). A final consideration has been the success of the U.S. women's soccer team, which has won three World Cups since 1999 (despite the fact that efforts to create and sustain a professional league have been difficult).

Although all of the major U.S. leagues discussed in this chapter have differences in the structure and control of their respective teams, the one constant has been that the team valuation has consistency increased, climbing to what one correspondent called "once unthought-of levels" (Kaplan, 2014b).

Chapter Assignment: Creating a New Domestic Sports League

Due to the success of Title IX (the law that prohibits discrimination on the basis of sex in educational institutions that receive federal funding), women's sports have become an important component of most colleges. Although professional sports opportunities are available for male baseball teams, there has not been a sustained professional women's softball league.

A professional women's softball league, it is thought, could be economically viable and expose audiences in the United States and Canada as both an alternative to Major League Baseball and to publicize the sport of softball. Also, a women's' league could serve as a role model for women and girls interested in playing softball on the amateur and collegiate level and could also be of interest to a male audience (fathers and those who may find women's softball an interesting spectator sport).

About fifteen individuals and corporations have expressed interest in creating such a league, tentatively called the WSLA (Women's'

Softball League of North America). It would include initial franchises in Long Island, New York; Providence, Rhode Island; Rockford, Illinois; St. Louis, Missouri; and Bloomfield Hills, Michigan. Major League Baseball has expressed no interest in this venture, although the owners of three unidentified teams have expressed initial interest, but nothing more than that. Nor has UA Softball, the governing body for Olympic softball competition. The interested groups include individual Americans, as well as corporations that make softball equipment and Internet start-ups. YouTube has also been interested as a sponsor and may be willing to pay for exclusive streaming rights to certain games.

There is much discussion as to what kind of league to create and the rights and obligations of the league and its teams. You (an individual or a group) have been consulted as an expert to assist in the formation.

You are to create a presentation entitled "A Proposed Framework" for the creation for the WSLA. The areas you are to cover in this agreement are the ownership structure of the league, franchising procedures, rules on franchise relocation, rules on expansion, player salaries (note that at this time there is no union) player draft, merchandising control, broadcasting (TV, radio, cable, new media) and any other points you deem important. You are not to consider the actual rules of the sport.

Each individual or group will make an oral presentation outlining these and other issues you wish to include. The presentations will be about twenty to thirty minutes in length. Based on what you have read in this chapter, try to anticipate the kinds of questions asked by your professor and fellow students when preparing your presentation.

In preparing for the presentations, you may use whatever sources you wish to aid you. However, it is imperative to include all of the sources utilized in preparing this presentation. It may be an option for the professor to ask for an outline before the presentation so that he or she can provide guidance and feedback.

References

Ambrose, R. (2008). The NFL makes it rain: Through strict enforcement of its conduct policy, the NHL protects its integrity, wealth, and popularity. *William Mitchell Law Review*, 34, 1070, 1081.

American Needle v. NFL, 130 S. Ct. 2201 (2010).

Associated Press (2014, January 25). Poll: 49 percent are pro football fans. *ESPN*. Retrieved September 11, 2014, from http://espn.go.com/nfl/story/_/id/10350802/poll-indicates-49-percent-americans-pro-football-fans

Badenhausen, K. (2012, January 13). Bud Selig's golden age of baseball. *Forbes*. Retrieved October 1, 2014, from http://www.forbes.com/sites/kurtbadenhausen/2012/01/13/bud-seligs-golden-age-of-baseball/

Badenhausen, K. (2014a, January 22). As Stern says goodbye, Knicks, Lakers set records as NBA's most valuable teams. *Forbes*. Retrieved September 20, 2014, from http://www.forbes.com/sites/kurtbadenhausen/2014/01/22/as-stern-says-goodbye-knicks-lakers-set-records-as-nbas-most-valuable-teams/

Badenhausen, K. (2014b, July 7). EA Sports' FIFA video game helps fuel interest in the World Cup. *Forbes*. Retrieved September 30, 2014, from http://www.forbes.com/sites/kurtbadenhausen/2014/07/13/ea-sports-fifa-video-game-helps-fuel-interest-in-the-world-cup/

Baxter, K. (2014, May 31). World Cup in 1994 gave U.S. soccer the kick in the pants it needed. *Los Angeles Times*. Retrieved September 30, 2014, from http://www.latimes.com/sports/soccer/la-sp-us-world-cup-mls-20140601-story.html

Beaton, A. (2015, August 24). How independent baseball teams make money. Or don't. *The Wall Street Journal*. Retrieved March 17, 2016, from http://www.wsj.com/articles/how-independent-baseball-teams-make-money-or-dont-1440381696

Belzer, J. (2016, Feb. 29). Thanks to Roger Goodell, NFL revenues projected to surpass $13 billion in 2016. *Forbes.com*. Retrieved June 1, 2016, from http://www.forbes.com/sites/jasonbelzer/2016/02/29/thanks-to-roger-goodell-nfl-revenues-projected-to-surpass-13-billion-in-2016/#5817fb5d3278

Bennett, R. (2014, March 7). MLS equals MLB in popularity with kids. *ESPNFC.com*. Retrieved March 4, 2016, from http://www.espnfc.us/major-league-soccer/story/1740529/mls-catches-mlb-in-popularity-with-kids-says-espn-poll

Boudway, I. (2014, January 16). He's got next: David Stern passes the NBA to Adam Silver. *Bloomberg Businessweek*. Retrieved September 20, 2014, from http://www.businessweek.com/articles/2014–01–16/david-sterns-seamless-handover-to-new-nba-commissioner-adam-silver

Brown, M. (2014, August 8). $2 billion sale of Los Angeles Clippers to Steve Ballmer now official. *Forbes*. Retrieved September 20, 2014, from http://www.forbes.com/sites/maurybrown/2014/08/12/2-billion-sale-of-los-angeles-clippers-to-steve-ballmer-now-official/

Bushnell, H., 2016, August 26). How soccer-specific stadiums have (and haven't) transformed MLS. Yahoo Sports. Retrieved October 22, 2016, from http://sports.yahoo.com/news/how-soccer-specific-stadiums-have-and-havent-transformed-mls-111337263.html

Cavanaugh, J. (2003, January 28). Mohegan Tribe to own W.N.B.A. team in Connecticut. *The New York Times*. Retrieved October 3, 2014, from http://www.nytimes.com/2003/01/28/sports/pro-basketball-mohegan-tribe-to-own-wnba-team-in-connecticut.html

Chicago Professional Sports Limited Partnership v. NBA ("Bulls II"), 95 F.3d 593 (7th Cir. 1996).

Cooper, J. (2009, September 19). Report: Mangini fines player over bottle of water. *NFL Fanhouse*. Retrieved February 21, 2010, from http://nfl.fanhouse.com/2009/09/19/report-mangini-slams-browns-player-for-using-the-minibar/

Cozzillio, M., Levinstein, M., Dimino, J., & Feldman, G. (2007). *Sports law*. Durham, NC: Carolina Academic Press, p. 20.

The Daily Hits 20: Remembering the XFL and Other Leagues that Have Come and Gone (2013, December 20). *Sports Business Daily*. Retrieved from http://www.sportsbusinessdaily.com/Daily/Issues/2013/12/10/Anniversary-Special-Issue/Leagues-Come-Gone.aspx

Downey, M. (2003, July 29). Hope's legacy goes beyond making sport. *Chicago Tribune*, p. 1.

Easton, S., & Rockerbee, D. (2002). Revenue sharing, conjectures and scarce talent in a sports league model. Retrieved February 21, 2010, from http://129.3.20.41/eps/io/papers/0303/0303010.pdf

Edelman, M. (2009). Are commissioner suspensions really any different from illegal group boycotts? Analyzing whether the NFL personal conduct policy illegally restrains trade. *Catholic University Law Review*, *58*, 631.

Enterprise Wire Co. v. Enterprise Independent Union (1966). 46 LA 359. (Arbitrator Daugherty).

ESPN (2004, November 22). Suspensions without pay, won't be staggered. Retrieved September 20, 2014, from http://sports.espn.go.com/nba/news/story?id=1928540

ESPN (2012a, March 22). Sean Payton of New Orleans Saints banned one year for bounties. Retrieved September 15, 2014, from http://espn.go.com/nfl/story/_/id/7718136/sean-payton-new-orleans-saints-banned-one-year-bounties

ESPN (2012b, May 3). NFL bans four players for New Orleans Saints' bounty roles. Retrieved September 15, 2014, from http://espn.go.com/nfl/story/_/id/7881761/nfl-bans-four-players-new-orleans-saints-bounty-roles

ESPN (2016, February 14). NBA extends television deals. *ESPN.com*. Retrieved June 1, 2016, from http://espn.go.com/nba/story/_/id/11652297/nba-extends-television-deals-espn-tnt

Farmer, S. (2014, November 28). Ray Rice wins suspension appeal, deals rare upset to NFL authority. *Los Angeles Times*. Retrieved November 1, 2015, from http://www.latimes.com/sports/sportsnow/la-sp-sn-ray-rice-appeal-20141128-story.html

Finley v. Kuhn, 569 F.2d 527 (7th Cir. 1978).

Fisher, E. (2004, February 22). NFL to re-examine successful revenue-sharing plan. *Washington Times*, p. C05.

Florio, M. (2014, February 17). NFL may not be able to discipline Incognito. *NBC Sports*. Retrieved September 15, 2014, from http://profootballtalk.nbcsports.com/2014/02/17/nfl-may-not-be-able-to-discipline-incognito/

Forbes.com (2016). NBA Team values. Retrieved July 2, 2016, from http://www.forbes.com/sites/forbespr/2016/01/20/forbes-releases-18th-annual-nba-team-valuations/#72571206e3e5

Fraser v. Major League Soccer, 97 F. Supp. 2d 130 (D. Mass, 2000), affirmed 284 F.3d 47 (1st Cir. 2002).

Goss, B. (2014, January 23). Sports teams' mobile apps are leaving money on the touchscreen. *Huffington Post*. Retrieved October 2, 2014, from http://www.huffingtonpost.com/benjamin-d-goss-edd/sports-teams-mobile-apps-_b_4214493.html

Heath, T. (2003, April 1). WUSA, WNBA's plan: To market, to market; Timing, new audiences key to success. *Washington Post*, p. D01.

Indiana Federation of Dentists v. FTC (1976) 476 U.S. at 460–61.

Iyer, V. (2012, December 11). Saints bounty scandal: Suspensions vacated by Paul Tagliabue. *Sporting News*. Retrieved September 15, 2014, from http://www. sportingnews.com/nfl/story/2012–12–11/saints-bounty-scandal-suspensions-news-penalties-punishment-ruling-case-update

Jackson, B. (2014, February 15). A timeline of the Jonathan Martin bullying scandal. *Miami Herald*. Retrieved September 15, 2014, from http://www. miamiherald.com/2014/02/15/3936500/a-timeline-of-the-jonathan-martin. html

Kaplan, D. (2009, October 26). NFL pares ownership rule. *Sports Business Journal*, p. 1.

Kaplan, D. (2014a, February 14). Roger Goodell's NFL compensation exceeds $44M in 12-month period. *Street & Smith's Sportsbusiness Daily*. Retrieved October 1, 2014, from http://www.sportsbusinessdaily.com/Daily/Closing-Bell/2014/02/14/Goodell.aspx

Kaplan, D. (2014b, October 27). Team valuations reflect hot market. *Street & Smith's Sportsbusiness Daily*. Retrieved November 1, 2014, from http://www. sportsbusinessdaily.com/Journal/Issues/2014/10/27/Franchises/Franchise-valuations.aspx?utm_campaign=ET10&utm_source=sbsnewsletter&utm_medium=email

Kelso, P. (2011, April 12). New York Times confirmed as second largest shareholder in Liverpool football club. *The Telegraph*. Retrieved October 2, 2014, from http://www.telegraph.co.uk/sport/football/teams/liverpool/8446713/New-York-Times-confirmed-as-second-largest-shareholder-in-Liverpool-football-club.html

Kronheim, D. (2014). Minor League Baseball 2013 attendance analysis. Number Tamer. Retrieved October 12, 2016, from http://numbertamer.com/files/2013_Prelim_notes-Revised_1_.pdf.

Lebowitz, L. (1997, April 20). Sports Inc. Leagues are forming as "single entities" where decision and profits are shared by all owners. *Ft. Lauderdale Sun-Sentinel*, p. 1F.

Levine v. Central Florida Medical Affiliates, Inc. (1996) 72 F.3d 1538 (11th Cir.).

Los Angeles Memorial Coliseum Commission v. NFL, 726 F.2d 1381 (9th Cir. 1984).

Macnow, G. (1993, February 4). Reds owner is suspended 1 year, fined the penalty: $25,000. Marge Schott will still pay the bills. But she won't be able to run the team. *Philadelphia Inquirer*. Retrieved October 1, 2014, from http://articles. philly.com/1993–02–04/sports/25955938_1_cincinnati-reds-owner-marge-schott-inappropriate-language

Mahoney, B. (2014, January 31). Remembering what Stern did, and how he did it. *Associated Press*. Retrieved September 20, 2014, from http://bigstory.ap. org/article/remembering-what-stern-did-and-how-he-did-it

Major League Baseball Constitution, Article II, sec. 2. (2005). Retrieved March 5, 2015, from http://www.ipmall.info/hosted_resources/SportsEntLaw_Institute/League%20Constitutions%20&%20Bylaws/MLConsititutionJune2005Update.pdf

Major League Baseball Constitution, Article II, sec. 3. (2005). Retrieved March 5, 2015, from http://www.ipmall.info/hosted_resources/SportsEntLaw_Institute/

League%20Constitutions%20&%20Bylaws/MLConsititutionJune2005 Update.pdf

Matter of Ray Rice (2014, November 28). ESPN.com. Retrieved February 12, 2015, from http://espn.go.com/pdf/2014/1128/141128_rice-summary.pdf

McCallum, J. (2004, November 29). The ugliest game. *Sports Illustrated*, p. 44.

Milwaukee American Ass'n v. Landis, 49 F.2d 298 (N.D. Illinois, 1931).

MLB.com (n.d.). The commissionership: A historical perspective. Retrieved March 4, 2016, from http://mlb.mlb.com/mlb/history/mlb_history_people.jsp? story=com

MLB.com (2013, September 26). Growth of MLB under Selig as commissioner. Retrieved September 25, 2014, from http://m.mlb.com/news/article/61836384/

Mortensen, C. (2014, August 14). Johnny Manziel late to team meeting. *ESPN*. Retrieved October 2, 2014, from http://espn.go.com/nfl/story/_/id/11355064/ johnny-manziel-tardiness-cleveland-browns-handled-internally

National Football League Players Association (Peterson) v. NFL (2015). 88 F. Supp. 3d 84 (D. Minn. 2015).

NBA CBA (2005). Retrieved August 2, 2010, from http://www.nbpa.org/sites/ default/files/ARTICLE%20XXXI.pdf

NBA Constitution and Bylaws, Article 35 (2010). Retrieved April 1, 2010, from http://basketball.about.com/od/history/a/nba-gun-policy.htm

NBA—NBPA Collective Bargaining Agreement (2011). Retrieved March 1, 2016, from http://www.nba.com/media/CBA101.pdf

Nethery, R. (2004, September 27–October 3). Limited partnership, unlimited goals—Investors in pro teams spend big for a small piece of the action. *Street & Smith's Sports Business Journal*, p. 19.

NFL Constitution and Bylaws, 1997 Resolution FC-3 (1997). Retrieved March, 1, 2016, from http://static.nfl.com/static/content//public/static/html/careers/ pdf/co_.pdf

NFL Constitution and Bylaws, Art. III, sec. 3.3(1) (2006). Retrieved April 1, 2010, from http://static.nfl.com/static/content//public/static/html/careers/pdf/co_.pdf

NFL Constitution and Bylaws, Art. IV, sec. 1 (2006). Retrieved April 1, 2010, from http://static.nfl.com/static/content//public/static/html/careers/pdf/co_.pdf

NFL Constitution and Bylaws, Art. VI, sec. 1 (2006). Retrieved April 1, 2010, from http://static.nfl.com/static/content//public/static/html/careers/pdf/co_.pdf

NFL Constitution and Bylaws, Art. VIII, sec. 8.13 (2006). Retrieved April 1, 2010, from http://static.nfl.com/static/content//public/static/html/careers/pdf/co_.pdf

NFL Constitution and Bylaws, Art. VIII, sec. 8.13 (2006). Retrieved April 1, 2010, from http://static.nfl.com/static/content//public/static/html/careers/pdf/co_.pdf

NFL Constitution and Bylaws, Art. XIX, sec. 19.1 (2006). Retrieved April 1, 2010, from http://static.nfl.com/static/content//public/static/html/careers/pdf/co_.pdf

NFL Management Council v. NFL Players' Association, 125 F.Supp.3d 449 (SDNY, 2015).

NFL Management Council v. NFL Players' Association, 2016 WL 1619883 (2d Cir. 2016).

NFL–NFLPA Collective Bargaining Agreement, Art. 46, sec. 3(a) (2005). Retrieved March 1, 2010, from http://images.nflplayers.com/mediaResources/files/PDFs/ General/NFL%20COLLECTIVE%20BARGAINING%20AGREEMENT% 202006%20-%202012.pdf

NHL Constitution and Bylaws, section 17 (n.d.). Retrieved March 6, 2016, from http://democrats.judiciary.house.gov/sites/democrats.judiciary.house.gov/files/NHLByLaw17.pdf

Office of the Comm'r of Baseball v. Markell, 579 F. 3d 293 (3d Cir. 2009).

Ohio History Central (n.d.). Cleveland Barons. Retrieved February 19, 2010, from http://www.ohiohistorycentral.org/entry.php?rec=2434

Oshan, J. (2013, October 31). MLS attendance down in 2013, but only slightly off 2012's record high. *SB Nation*. Retrieved September 30, 2014, from http://www.sbnation.com/soccer/2013/10/31/5047982/mls-attendance-2013-report

Ozanian, J., & Badenhausen, K. (2008, October 29). The business of hockey. *Forbes*. Retrieved August 15, 2009, from http://www.forbes.com/2008/10/29/nhl-team-values-biz-sports-nhl08_cz_mo_kb_1029intro.html

Ozanian, M. (2014, August 20). The NFL's most valuable teams. *Forbes*. Retrieved September 11, 2014, from http://www.forbes.com/sites/mikeozanian/2014/08/20/the-nfls-most-valuable-teams/

Ozanian, M. (2015, November 24). The NHL's most valuable teams. *Forbes*. Retrieved May 5, 2016, from http://www.forbes.com/sites/mikeozanian/2015/11/24/the-nhls-most-valuable-teams-2/#2170bdae3920

Petchesky, B. (2015, July 21). The NFL split $7.2 billion in revenue sharing last year. *Deadspin*. Retrieved June 1, 2016, from http://deadspin.com/the-nfl-split-7–2-billion-in-revenue-sharing-last-year-1719217695

Quirk, J., & Fort, R. (1997). *Paydirt: The business of professional team sports*. Princeton, NJ: Princeton University Press, p. 101.

Reyes, L. (2016, July 15). Tom Brady announces he won't fight Deflategate suspension further in court. *USA Today*. Retrieved July 16, 2016, from http://www.usatoday.com/story/sports/nfl/patriots/2016/07/15/tom-brady-deflategate-suspension-new-england/87134710/

Roberts, G. R. (1984). Sports leagues and the Sherman Act: The use and abuse of Section 1 to regulate restraints in intra-league rivalry. *UCLA Law Review, 32*, 219, 241 n. 72.

Roberts, G. R. (1988). The evolving confusion of professional sports antitrust, the rule of reason, and the doctrine of ancillary restraints. *Southern California Law Review, 61*, 943, 954 n. 34.

Rosenthal, G. (2009, August 4). Chargers fine Cromartie for Twitter complaint. *NBC Sports*. Retrieved October 2, 2014, from http://profootballtalk.nbcsports.com/2009/08/04/source-chargers-fine-cromartie-for-twitter-complaint/

Rosenthal, G. (2014, February 14). Summary of Ted Wells report on Miami Dolphins. NFL.com. Retrieved October 20 2016, from http://www.nfl.com/news/story/0ap2000000325899/article/summary-of-ted-wells-report-on-miami-dolphins

Rosner, S., & Shropshire, K. (2004). *The business of sports*. Sudbury, MA: Jones & Bartlett, p. 336.

Rovell, D. (2004, January 22). How Stern showed NBA the money. *ESPN.com*. Retrieved March 31, 2010, from http://sports.espn.go.com/nba/columns/story?id=1714434

Rovell, D. (2014, January 26). NFL most popular for 30th year in row. *ESPN.com*. Retrieved March 17, 2016, from http://espn.go.com/nfl/story/_/id/10354114/harris-poll-nfl-most-popular-mlb-2nd

Sandomir, R. (2002, October 1). Biggest drop for attendance in major leagues since the 1995 season. *New York Times*. Retrieved February 22, 2010, from http://www.nytimes.com/2002/10/01/sports/baseball-biggest-drop-for-attendance-in-major-leagues-since-the-1995-season.html?pagewanted=1

Sandomir, R. (2016, May 28). After two decades, W.N.B.A. still struggling for relevance. *New York Times*. Retrieved May 31, 2016, from http://www.nytimes.com/2016/05/28/sports/basketball/after-two-decades-wnba-still-struggling-for-relevance.html

Schneider-Mayerson, M. (2010). "Too Black": Race in the "Dark Ages" of the National Basketball Association. *The International Journal of Sport & Society*, 1(1), 223–233.

Sports Business Daily (2009). Roger Goodell puts stamp on NFL with personal conduct policy, citing Mortensen, Chris, "Beyond the Lines," ESPN, 7/8/09. Retrieved August 28, 2009, from http://www.sportsbusinessdaily.com/article/131602

Sports Business Journal (2014, June 2). Tracking soccer participation. Retrieved September 30, 2014, from http://www.sportsbusinessdaily.com/Journal/Issues/2014/06/02/In-Depth/Participation.aspx

Sports Business Journal (2015, May 25). Who's in charge? Retrieved May 1, 2016, from http://www.sportsbusinessdaily.com/Journal/Issues/2015/05/25/Leagues-and-Governing-Bodies/NFL-trust.aspx

Szymanski, S. (2009). *Playbooks and checkbooks: An introduction to the economics of modern sports*. Princeton, NJ: Princeton University Press, pp. 56–58.

United States v. NFL, 116 F. Supp. 319 (1953).

Vrooman, J. (2009). Theory of the perfect game: Competitive balance in monopoly sports leagues. *Review of Industrial Organization*, 34, 5–44. Retrieved March 1, 2016, from http://www.vanderbilt.edu/econ/faculty/Vrooman/vrooman-rio-sports-special.pdf

Weiler, P. C., & Roberts, G. R. (2004). *Sports and the law* (3rd ed.). St. Paul, MN: West.

Weinbach, J. (2006, September 28). Major League Soccer to sell ad space on jerseys. *Pittsburgh Post-Gazette*. Retrieved February 26, 2010, from http://www.post-gazette.com/pg/06271/725842-28.stm

Wilbon, M. (2004, December 4). Tarnished records deserve an asterisk. *The Washington Post*, p. D10.

Women's Basketball Online.com (n.d.). WNBA attendance. Retrieved February 25, 2010, from http://www.womensbasketballonline.com/wnba/wnbattendance.html

Zepfel, E. (2015, February 13). Have MLB's efforts to preserve competitive balance done enough? *Harvard Sports Analytics Collective*. Retrieved March 1, 2016, from http://harvardsportsanalysis.org/2015/02/have-mlbs-efforts-to-preserve-competitive-balance-done-enough/

Zilgitt, J. (2014, May 7). Donald Sterling signed moral, ethical contracts with NBA. *USA Today*. Retrieved August 1, 2015, from http://www.usatoday.com/story/sports/nba/clippers/2014/05/07/donald-sterling-agreement-owners-racism-lifetime-ban-los-angeles/8814969/

2   The Structure of Individual Sports

The business operations of individual sports differ greatly from the league structures discussed in Chapter 1. Sometimes secretive and even Byzantine, an individual sport's decision-making, compensation, sponsorships and tournament characteristics are not always easy to gauge. There may be seemingly peculiar rules on qualifications, rankings, control (or lack thereof) of tournaments and discipline. The niche interests of these sports, plus the previously mentioned intricacies, may be reasons why individual sports governance does not receive the same amount of coverage and scrutiny as that of the major team sports.

At one time, major individual sport competitions were limited to amateur athletes. A "golf professional" meant someone who worked at a country club, usually teaching or coaching, rather than a top-notch competitor. Tennis "pros" were allowed to compete in certain tournaments, but not the major events, like Wimbledon. By the 1960s, this began to change as golf and tennis, for example, entered the "open era" with prize money awarded. No longer was winning a major tournament just a matter of prestige, it became a contest for dollars as well.

To gain an understanding of the organizational structure of individual sports, it is crucial to understand the basic characteristics of individual sports competition and the nature of the organizations created to regulate it.

Tournaments and Tours

In the world of individual sports the central mode of competition is a "tournament" or "event." Although a team-based league such as the NBA schedules and controls all matches, preseason games and playoff series, individual sports events are often conceived and promoted by independent owners or presenters with the backing of one or more sponsors. Frequently the event presenters create the event, obtain a venue (if they do not own a facility) and offer prize money to entice individual athletes to compete. The presenter is responsible for the event's ticketing, parking and security and receives revenue derived from those activities, as well as concessions, sales of licensed products and, in many cases, broadcasting rights.

Sponsorships are central to event presentation because the fees paid help defray the costs. The types of sponsorships vary, ranging from expensive naming rights to more modest promotions such as sponsored entertainment and the right to demonstrate a product during the event. From the point of view of the naming rights holder (usually a business), the sponsorship offers opportunities to publicize the brand, communicate with current and future customers and generate goodwill. Sponsors utilize a full range of marketing techniques, including advertising, personal selling, sales promotion and public/community relations.

Sponsorships are often divided into two categories: primary (or presenting) sponsors and secondary sponsors. The primary sponsor often makes a long-term financial commitment to the event and sometimes receives a stipulated percentage of the gross revenues. That sponsor will often have "title rights" to the event. An example would be the "Buick Classic" golf tournament. Sometimes the term *primary* is eschewed in favor of *presenting sponsor*, which also receives title rights.

Although primary sponsors play a crucial role, secondary sponsors may also be solicited, especially if the tournament has a track record of success. Sometimes known as "official sponsors," secondary sponsors may be entitled to some (although a more modest) percentage of revenues, but more often exposure is key. Although primary or presenting sponsors pay for the "title sponsor" association with the event, the secondary sponsors would pay lower fees or even no fees at all. A secondary sponsor may rather provide free lodging, transportation or clothing. In recent years, the number and types of sponsorship categories have expanded, resulting in more complex deals. Although Chapter 5 discusses the specifics of a sponsorship agreement in more detail, here is an example of a typical sponsorship setup:

Example: The 2016 BNP Paribas Open, Indian Wells, California (tennis)

Title Sponsor

- BNP Paribas

Premiere Sponsors

- Rolex
- Indian Wells, California

- Emirates Air
- Audi
- Masino
- Esurance
- Fila
- Xerox
- Steve Furgal's International Tennis Tours
- Oracle
- Michelob Ultra
- Head
- Penn

Champion Sponsors

- Jeffrey Scott Fine Magnetics
- TW Tennis Warehouse
- Moet & Chandon Champagne
- USANA Health Sciences

There is also a category listing "Contributory Sponsors"

Although these organizations do not normally disclose details of the various agreements and compensation, it is safe to say that the higher the level of sponsorship, the greater the cost and the greater the exposure. More discussion on sponsorship agreements is found in Chapter 5.

Unlike a professional team sport whose events remain under its league's control, most organized individual sports lack the same level of direct control from their governing body. Individual sports events can be rather diffuse, where sponsors retain considerable control to market the event. However, individual sports do have governing bodies that set rules for the operation of the sports and eligibility requirements for competition. The degree of control of these bodies varies from sport to sport. Examples include the National Association for Stock Car Auto Racing (NASCAR), the Professional Golfers' Association Tour (PGA Tour) and the Women's Tennis Association (WTA). Yet, they often have sanctioning power that requires any independent tournament to comply with basic requirements to allow member athletes to compete. For example, the rules of the PGA Tour require that a player have a "tour card" to play in tour events and must maintain a certain number of wins or a certain ranking to maintain eligibility (Gregory, n.d.). Without that sanction from the governing body, attracting quality athletes may prove difficult for sponsors.

In an attempt to gain more control over what could be a series of disparate events, some nonleague sports organizations attempt to establish a "tour" or a "series." This is done by NASCAR with its Sprint Cup Series. An integrated series of thirty-six races increases the brand identification of the organization and creates fan excitement by assigning a point system to drivers based on their success in the various events. Such a tour gives the organization more control over eligibility by imposing a ranking system and control over scheduling so that the tour events are in a certain sequence.

Individual Sports Athletes Are Not Employees

Athletes who compete in tournaments sanctioned by the organization are independent contractors, not employees. That means that participating athletes do not work for NASCAR, the PGA Tour or the United States Tennis Association (USTA), and unlike their counterparts in the NFL or the NBA, these individual athletes must absorb the considerable expenses of training, travel and lodging.

This financial responsibility imposes hardships. Touring costs are high, and a young or lower-ranked athlete must pay those costs (travel, hotel or equipment) out of his or her own pocket or through a sponsor. On the other hand, top-ranked individual athletes often have endorsement agreements that give them the financial means to travel, and the costs of equipment and clothing are paid for by the endorsing company (Noer, 2012).

The method of compensation differs between team athletes and individual athletes. Team athletes, as employees, are paid based on a contract individually negotiated and (where a union is involved) subject to the collective bargaining agreement between the players' union and the particular league. Whether the team wins or loses, the player receives a paycheck, with taxes deducted. If the player has a guaranteed contract (as many professional team athletes do), the salary must be paid even if the athlete is injured while engaging in competition or in training. As an independent contractor, the individual athlete receives prize money based on his or her success in the tournament. Fees are generally calculated by the tournament's producer or, in the case of a tour, with input from the sanctioning organization.

In addition to the success-based payment system, individual sport athletes may receive appearance fees. Defined as a sum of money to entice an athlete to come and play at a tournament, appearance fees have had an "under-the-table" quality. Often unpublicized by the tournament presenter or the sanctioning organization, appearance fees may, in some minds, negate an incentive to win and can be a vehicle to cement connections with event sponsors. (Sirak, 2012).

On the other hand, valid business reasons exist for a presenter to pay appearance fees. The participation of a top-ranked athlete in a tournament often stimulates public interest, resulting in increased publicity, media exposure and ticket sales. For example, if a presenter pays $200,000 for an athlete to appear but that results in a $500,000 increase in revenues, the appearance fee results in a very profitable return. This also lays the groundwork for the continuation of the tournament in the future and the possibility that more top-quality athletes may participate (without the need for appearance fees) (Cozzillio & Levinstein, 2007).

Scheduling

A team player plays a set schedule of games per season. His or her unexplained and unjustified failure to do so results in a penalty by the team. Individual athletes, on the other hand, make their own schedules. They are not required to play in every tournament in a given season. Although most individual sports bodies require participation in a specified number of matches to maintain ranking, the number varies. In the Women's Tennis Association (WTA), it is three tournaments, unless the player earns sufficient points in one (WTA Official Rulebook, 2014). For men's tennis, which is governed in the Association of Tennis Professionals (ATP), there are thirteen mandatory tournaments (ATP Official Rulebook, 2016). In golf, the PGA does not have its own ranking system, but instead takes the rankings from an independent entity known as the World Golf Rankings. The standard set forth by this organization requires a minimum of forty tournaments over the previous two years to calculate a player's ranking score (Official World Golf Ranking, 2013). Strategizing on the number and type of events to compete in can be important, especially with veterans who do not want to risk injury. For example, Serena Williams competed in twenty events in 2015 (ESPN, 2015).

Rankings

As noted earlier, individual athletes are ranked. Ranking systems vary from sport to sport but, because individual sports lack a "playoff" structure, ranking is the only way to assess the success of a particular athlete. The ranking system quantifies the athlete's success, thereby creating fan interest in a particularly successful athlete. Ranking also serves to retain competitive spirit and to increase athlete winnings in competition and/or endorsement deals. It is more effective to give that player a number one ranking than just saying that the player is "great" or the "best." Ranking gives the player a validation of his or her success.

Rank has an important effect on endorsement contracts. If an athlete maintains a particularly high ranking, the endorsement agreement often mandates that the athlete receive a bonus or extension of the contract, or both. Additionally, it results in greater demand for that athlete by owners and tournament presenters, with the possibility of large appearance fees (when allowed).

The ranking system, however, is far from perfect and often subjective. The ATP (the men's tennis tour), for example, has a ranking system that does not "penalize" a player if he does not play well. A player's ATP ranking is based on the total points he accrued in nineteen tournaments, including the four "Grand Slam" tournaments, eight mandatory top-tier ATP "World Tour Masters 1000" tournaments and the Barclays ATP World Tour Finals. In addition, the best six results from a number of other ATP tournaments are included (ATP Official Rulebook, Sec. 9.03 (2016)). The system helps a player who won or placed well in tournaments. Thus, a skewed result occurs because a top player's early elimination in two of fifteen tournaments played in a given season does not negatively affect his ranking. Significantly, for presenters and sponsors, the ATP's ranking system encourages male players to play more tournaments without threat to their rank and resulting endorsement deals. In professional golf, the PGA Tour and Ladies Professional Golf Association (LPGA) both have the winnings, scores, and positions of major players available at http://www.pgatour.com/players.html (PGA Tour) and http://www.lpga.com/golf-players/players.aspx (LPGA). The ATP has the rankings of every male player available at http://www.atpworldtour.com/Rankings/Singles.aspx. Rankings for the top female players are found at http://www.wtatennis.com/singles-rankings. For NASCAR, the Sprint Cup standings can be found at http://www.nascar.com/en_us/sprint-cup-series/standings.html.

Examples of Individual Sports Governing Bodies

Although many such organizations exist, we focus on the organizational structure for three well-known professional individual sports: automobile racing, tennis and golf. Governing bodies for individual sports that are more internationally and traditionally amateur based are found in Chapter 4. As you read through the following examples, note the considerable differences in their organizations.

National Association for Stock Car Auto Racing

The organizational structure of NASCAR, the central organization overseeing stock car racing in the United States, is unique because one family has dominated the organization since its inception in 1947. Although not a league composed of team owners, NASCAR operates like one. NASCAR makes the rules, sanctions races, disciplines racers and car owners and negotiates sponsorships and broadcasting contracts.

William Henry Getty "Bill" France, Sr., brought together racing promoters throughout the southeastern region of the United States and created a unified organization in an attempt to "legitimize" the sport, which had a sordid reputation derived from the days of dirt track racing by rum runners. France was a racer and understood the need for an organization to establish rules of competition and meet the needs of drivers, car owners and track owners (Hangstrom, 1998).

For much of its history, NASCAR has achieved phenomenal success, in large part due to France and other family members who have guided the organization over the last half-century. The sport moved from dirt tracks to paved state-of-the-art racetracks located throughout the United States. Presently, NASCAR operates on a ten-month season from February through November, sanctioning approximately 1500 races at over 100 tracks across thirty-nine states and Canada annually. The competitive divisions of NASCAR are divided into a number of different racing series, including the Sprint Cup Series (the best known), the Nationwide Series and the Camping World Truck Series. NASCAR estimates that there are over 75 million fans of the sport (Nascar.com, 2014).

The Sprint Cup Series currently consists of thirty-six sanctioned points races. At the conclusion of each race, the drivers and teams earn points based on their finishing position, and at the end of the season, the driver with the most cumulative points based on the full season and a final ten-race section called the "Chase for the Sprint Cup" is crowned the NASCAR Sprint Cup Champion. Purse monies are awarded in each race with additional bonus monies for final point standings (Pockrass, 2012).

NASCAR conducts Sprint Cup races at twenty-three racetracks, each of which is located in the United States. As noted later, two entities (Speedway Motorsports, Inc., and the International Speedway Corporation, or ISC) own and operate twenty tracks that host thirty-one of the thirty-six races that compromise the Sprint Cup schedule.

There has been some controversy over the centralized control of racetracks. NASCAR created the ISC, an affiliated company that owns multiple racetracks, in 1953. Over the years, the ISC has raised funds through public offerings of its shares, which it has used to finance the acquisition and development of additional racing facilities, but the France family retains control and has made all major decisions for the company. As of 2014, over 50 percent of all Sprint Cup races are held at racetracks owned at least in part by the ISC. The relationship between NASCAR, the ISC and other independent racetracks spawned one unsuccessful lawsuit involving attacking NASCAR's control on antitrust grounds (*Kentucky Speedway, LLC v. NASCAR*, 2009).

NASCAR expanded the reach of the sport from a regional one to a nationally recognized brand with lucrative television contracts. Part of this success came from the changing demographics of NASCAR's audience from a regionally based, white, male, working-class grouping to a more family-based and nationwide one. According to a study conducted in 2012 by Scarborough research, NASCAR fans are 3 percent more likely than the general American population to have a household income of $75,000 or more (Anderson, 2012). This is a far cry from the early days when the fan base primarily consisted of farmers and bootleggers (Cokley, 2001).

In 2003 Brian France became chairman and chief executive officer. NASCAR's five-member board remains solidly under the control of members of the family. This arrangement is unusual, as there are few sports organizations that maintain such family control.

NASCAR utilizes a complicated point system to determine success. The winner of a NASCAR race pockets 43 points. Each subsequent place earns one point less (for example, second and third place finish with 42 and 41 points, respectively) with last place (forty-third) receiving one point. In addition to the 43 points, the winning driver receives 3 bonus points. Any driver who led any lap during the race receives one total bonus point (not one per lap), and the driver who led the most laps receives an additional one point. Similar point totals are awarded to owners. Racing fees and bonuses are based on a complex formula that factors in performance, past performance and bonuses. This point system was instituted starting with the 2011 season (NASCAR, 2011).

In recent years, NASCAR's popularity has waned. The economic downturn of 2008–10 hurt NASCAR in terms of sponsorships and attendance, resulting in decreases in race winnings (Tuckman, 2015). However, NASCAR's present television deal—at $8.2 billion over ten years, and shared with Fox and NBC, was a 40 percent increase from the previous broadcasting contract. NASCAR allocates approximately 65 percent of those revenues to the tracks, 25 percent to the teams and retains 10 percent for itself.

The mixed financial success of NASCAR during those years may have been instrumental in attempts to increase the value of race teams. In 2014, a union of nine team owners representing twenty-five cars in NASCAR's premier Sprint Cup Series formed the Race Team Alliance (RTA) in an attempt to increase the equity value of its members and pursue deals (such as with the daily fantasy sports site "DraftKings") that NASCAR would traditionally avoid. The following year that number grew to fifteen owners.

In 2016, NASCAR created a new "charter system" intended to decrease the number of Sprint Cup racing cars and create a system de facto franchising based on cars that have run full time in the circuit. Those who receive these charters—which require a stipulated fee—are guaranteed starting spots and a certain level of income. The charters could be transferred or sold (Stern, 2016). Other characteristics of the charter plan include auditing of NASCAR's income, a greater role of team owners in NASCAR governance and the right of team owners to negotiate digital rights deals (with 30 percent going to the racetracks and 10 percent to NASCAR).

Tennis

In contrast to the centralized power of NASCAR, the structure of tennis is quite the opposite. "Tennis is the only major professional sport in this country that does not have a governing body solely dedicated to the sport," said Arlen Kantarian, then–chief executive of professional tennis at the USTA, as quoted in the *Sports Business Journal* (Kaplan, 2001). One might think the USTA would be that body, but in reality it possesses relatively little power in professional tennis. The USTA owns and runs the U.S. Open, the leading U.S. tennis tournament, and one of the four "Grand Slam" events. It also organizes and manages grassroots tennis programs and oversees the selection of the U.S. team in the Davis and Fed cups. The USTA also runs a "professional circuit" for the development of professional players, allowing these players to gain the experience and ranking points necessary to qualify for the Grand Slams.

The limited powers of the USTA result in a professional tennis structure consisting of a hodgepodge of various organizations with different jurisdictions. Players' groups, tournament owners and sponsors exercise control. Companies such as IMG and Octagon frequently own tournaments, and at the same time represent players, as well as sit on the tour boards.

In addition to the USTA, tournament owners and tournament presenters, separate governing bodies exist that represent men's and women's tennis players. The ATP World Tour is the governing body for men's tennis. It sanctions about seventy events and works to protect the interests of male players. Essentially, it sets rules regarding prize money and tournament qualification. It also allows representatives of management companies to sit on its board of directors. The ATP World Tour permits and encourages the use of appearance fees, a practice that has drawn criticism.

The Women's Tennis Association (WTA) is the women's counterpart. Similar to the ATP in structure, the WTA sanctions about sixty events. Although the WTA had title sponsors in the past, as of 2016 it lacks such a lead sponsor.

The ATP, like the WTA, is a hybrid of labor and management under one roof: the tournaments and players each get three board votes, with the tour president holding the seventh and potentially tie-breaking vote.

In addition, there is the International Tennis Federation, which oversees the four Grand Slam events and organizes a number of international competitions, often focusing on team events, such as the Davis Cup (ITFTennis.com, n.d.). The international component of tennis is discussed in more detail in Chapter 4.

Sensing the need for more presence in the tennis landscape, the USTA controls a six-week tennis season known as the "U.S. Open Series," currently sponsored by Emirates Air. It includes a series of ATP and WTA Tour professional tournaments in North America leading up to and linked to the U.S. Open. Players who win the most in the series earn points and arrive at the U.S. Open with a chance to earn up to $1 million in bonus prize money. In 2014, Serena Williams and Novak Djokovic each set the record for the largest tennis payout by winning the U.S. Open and collecting the $1 million bonus prize, totaling $3.6 million (Emirates US Open Series, 2014).

To add to the mix, whereas the USTA runs the U.S. Open, other organizations govern the three remaining Grand Slam events: Wimbledon, the French Open and the Australian Open. Wimbledon, which takes place in London, is hosted by the Lawn Tennis Association, or LTA. This is the UK equivalent of the USTA. Other countries have similar organizations that govern their local tennis tournaments. The International Tennis Federation, the international governing body of the sport, is also a stakeholder and oversees each of these regional organizations in large international competitions.

As of 2016, the total prize money for the four Grand Slam events ranged from $29 million (French Open) to $42 million (both Wimbledon and the U.S. Open). The Australian Open totaled $31 million (Total Sportek, 2015).

Golf—A Detailed Examination of the PGA Tour

The PGA Tour should not be confused with the Professional Golf Association (PGA). The PGA, founded in 1916, has served as an umbrella organization for the sport, consisting of teaching professionals who promote the game to people of all ages and skill levels. The PGA Tour, once a part of the PGA but independent since 1968, is a trade association that represents professional male golfers, who play more than 100 "official-money" tournaments. The PGA Tour split from the PGA so that the players could gain more control of their financial benefits and tournament schedule (Gabriel, 2001).

Tour players compete on one of three levels: the PGA Tour is for the very best players, whereas the Champions Tour consists of players over 50, and the Web.com Tour is for players not quite on the level of the PGA Tour. Although the PGA is less involved in professional competitions, it still sponsors four major golf events—the Ryder Cup, the PGA Championship, the Senior PGA Championship and the PGA Grand Slam of Golf, among others. The PGA Tour's organizational structure consists of a "Tour Policy Board" which consists of four independent directors, four players and a director from the PGA. It also has a "Player Advisory Council" of sixteen members.

The PGA Tour negotiates television agreements and title sponsorships. It also must approve the particular golf course for an event. Revenue streams consist of the tour's marketing partners, television rights fees, supporting businesses and title sponsorships. Revenues derived are used for prize money, player pensions and charitable contributions. Like many sports organizations, the PGA Tour controls its web content and has phone apps. It contains exclusive video content, live tournament video, highlights, some original programming, live scoring and statistics. As of 2016, it had a partnership with Yahoo!, which delivers tour-specific content beyond the PGA's website (Dudley, 2016).

In 1994, Timothy Finchem became the PGA Tour's third commissioner. The next year he undertook a restructuring program designed to strengthen its competitions (which are the PGA Tour's core business) and expand the PGA Tour's international scope. In 2011, the tour signed a nine-year broadcasting contract with CBS, NBC and the Golf Channel. The structure is unusual. The networks are paying enough to the tour that it, in turn, can fund 62 percent of the purse each week. The remaining 38 percent comes from the title sponsor of the particular event. A portion of that goes to the respective network as guaranteed advertising buys (Harig, 2011).

From the late 1990s to 2010, the tour has had one superstar, Tiger Woods. Woods boosted TV ratings and increased public interest in the game. Tournaments became media events. However, his highly publicized marital problems in 2009 and a decline in the quality of his game due to injuries diminished the exposure of the sport (Shipnuck, 2016).

Internationally, a number of countries have tours similar to that of the PGA Tour, such as the Canadian Tour and the Japan Tour, whereas other countries have regionalized their tournament governance into regional organizations like the European and Asian Tours, respectively. In 1996, these tours entered into the International Federation of PGA Tours, which sponsors international events such as the Bridgestone Invitational and the Cadillac Championship. In additional, a "World Golf Championship" was launched in 2000, which features players from around the world competing against one another in varied formats (worldgolfchampionships. com, n.d.).

The LPGA serves as the umbrella organization for women's competitive golf. Despite a talented pool of players, the LPGA does not command the popularity or the sponsorship of its male counterpart, and therefore obtains only a fraction of the prize money of the PGA Tour. The group also lacks a comprehensive network television contract and receives a fee only from the tournament sponsors. Most of the LPGA's media deals involve splitting of profits, rather than a predetermined amount up front (Cassidy, 2001). In recent years, the LPGA has sponsored or cosponsored more international events, and many of its top stars are players from outside the United States. In recent years, its total prize money has increased to $56 million in 2014 from $41 million in 2010 (Smith, 2014).

Chapter Assignment

A group of darts enthusiasts wishes to start an association to organize competitions for those interested in professional competition. The idea behind the "Darts Association of America" would be to arrange competitions, come up with a system of prize money for winners, find sponsors and garner publicity for the sport. Although the organization has been created, there is no organized system for competitions, locations, sponsorships or standards. To be viable, the group must raise $3 million. Working in small groups, please come up with a business plan for the group, focusing on the following:

1 Attracting sponsors—who would be likely sponsors?
2 Would it be better to have one overriding sponsor or a number of sponsors in various categories?
3 What kinds of locations would be best for competitions?
4 What seating capacities would be ideal?
5 What kind of media deals could be considered?
6 How would a season's competitions be structured?
7 How would prize money be determined?
8 Eligibility rules for competitors?

This assignment can be a group assignment or an individual one. It requires preparing a presentation for twenty to thirty minutes outlining these and any other issues the group would think is important. Additionally, it requires an accompanying paper detailing some of the points raised in the presentation. Outside sources may be used, but must be cited in both the paper and in the presentation.

References

Anderson, R. (2012, March 8). Statistical report offers a beyond-the-stereotype look at NASCAR fans. *Las Vegas Sun*. Retrieved October 16, 2014, from http://www.lasvegassun.com/news/2012/mar/08/statistical-report-offers-beyond—stereotype-look-/

ATP Official Rulebook (2016). Sec. 9.03. Retrieved June 8, 2016, from http://www.atpworldtour.com/en/corporate/rulebook

atpworldtour.com, (2010). ATP rankings, frequency asked questions. Retrieved August 10, 2010, from http://www.atpworldtour.com/Rankings/Rankings-FAQ.aspx

Cassidy, H. (2001, January 22). LPGA's Durkin focused on new messaging. *Brandweek*, p. 58.

Cokley, M. A. (2001). In the fast lane to big bucks: The growth of NASCAR. *Sports Law Journal*, 8, 67.

Cozzillio, M., & Levinstein, M. (2007). *Sports law*. Durham, NC: Carolina Academic Press, pp. 46–50.

Dudley, G. (2016, February 12). Yahoo and PGA Tour announce content collaboration. *Sportspro.com*. Retrieved March 8, 2016, from http://www.sportspro media.com/news/yahoo_and_pga_tour_announce_content_collaboration

Emirates US Open Series (ND). Bonus challenge. Retrieved October 16, 2014, from http://www.emiratesusopenseries.com/Standings/Bonus_Challenge/

ESPN (2015). Serena Williams tournament results. Retrieved March 8, 2016, from http://espn.go.com/tennis/player/results/_/id/394/year/2015/serena-williams

Gabriel, M. (2001). *The Professional Golfers' Association Tour: A history*. Jefferson, NC: McFarland.

Gregory, J. (n.d.). What are the requirements for a PGA Tour card? *Golflink.com*. Retrieved May 2, 2015, from http://www.golflink.com/facts_8066_what-requirements-pga-tour-card.html

Hangstrom, R. G. (1998). *The NASCAR way: The business that drives the sport*. New York: John Wiley & Sons.

Harig, B. (2011, September 7). PGA hitting green with new TV contracts. *ESPN. com*. Retrieved January 4, 2016, from http://espn.go.com/golf/story/_/id/6939104/pga-tour-hitting-green-new-tv-contracts

International Federation of PGA Tours (n.d.). *Worldgolfchampionships.com*. Retrieved March 6, 2016, from http://www.worldgolfchampionships.com/internationalfederation.html

Kaplan, D. (2001, August 27). Can tennis mend its fractured world? Sports Business Journal. Retrieved October 20, 2016, from http://www.sportsbusinessdaily.com/Journal/Issues/2001/08/20010827/Special-Report/Can-Tennis-Mend-Its-Fractured-World.aspx

Kentucky Speedway, LLC v. NASCAR, 588 F.3d 908 (6th Cir. 2009).

Nascar.com (2011, January 27). Changes for 2011 include emphasis on winning, simpler points. Retrieved October 16, 2014, from http://www.nascar.com/en_us/news-media/articles/2011/01/27/nascar-rules-changes.html

Nascar.com (2014, January 1). NASCAR racing statistics. Retrieved October 16, 2014, from http://www.statisticbrain.com/nascar-racing-statistics/

Noer, M. (2012, February 8). On the edge: Money, life and loneliness on the fringe of the PGA Tour. *Forbes*. Retrieved October 16, 2014, from http://www.forbes.com/sites/michaelnoer/2012/02/08/ben-martin-pga-tour/

Official World Golf Ranking (2013, January 1). How the ranking system works. Retrieved October 16, 2014, from http://www.owgr.com/about

Pockrass, B. (2012, December 5). NASCAR's highest paid drivers make their money from a variety of sources. *Sporting News*. Retrieved October 16, 2014, from http://www.sportingnews.com/nascar/story/2012–12–04/nascar-highest-paid-drivers-salaries-race-earnings-dale-earnhardt-jr-jeff-gordon

Shipnuck, A. (2016, March 29). What Happened to Tiger Woods? It's the Most Vexing Question in Sports. Gold.com. Retrieved October 21, 2016, from http://www.golf.com/tour-and-news/what-happened-tiger-woods-it-remains-most-vexing-question-sports

Sirak, R. (2012, July 10). Golf's dirty little screen. *Golf Digest*. Retrieved April 2, 2015, from http://www.golfdigest.com/golf-tours-news/2012–07/golf-appearance-fees-sirak-0710

Smith, M. (2014, January 6). The front 9: Issues to watch in golf in 2014. *Sports Business Journal.* Retrieved March 6, 2016, from http://www.sportsbusiness daily.com/Journal/Issues/2014/01/06/In-Depth/Front-9.aspx?hl=LPGA%20 total%20prize%20money&sc=0

Stern, A. (2016, January 4). NASCAR, teams closer on charter system. *Sports Business Journal.* Retrieved March 8, 2016, from http://www.sportsbusiness daily.com/Journal/Issues/2016/01/04/Leagues-and-Governing-Bodies/ NASCAR-medallions.aspx?hl=Nascar%20charter%20system%20and%20 stern&sc=0

Totalsportek (2015, June 29). Highest prize money in tennis grand slams. Retrieved May 28, 2016, from http://www.totalsportek.com/money/highest-prize-money-in-tennis-grand-slams/

Tuckman, R. (2015, February 23). What has happened to the once high-flying sport of NASCAR? *Forbes.com.* Retrieved March 8, 2016, from http://www. forbes.com/sites/roberttuchman/2015/02/23/what-has-happened-to-the-once-high-flying-sport-of-nascar/#a3582c45c0b7

USTA (ND). USTA National Open Hard Court Championships. Retrieved October 16, 2014, from http://tennislink.usta.com/tournaments/TournamentHome/ Tournament.aspx?T=138230

WTA Official Rulebook (2014). Sec. XIV(A)(2)(a)). Retrieved May 1, 2015, from http://www.wtatennis.com/SEWTATour-Archive/Archive/AboutTheTour/ rules2014.pdf

3 The Structure of College and High School Sports

Since the last edition of this book, there has been a sea change in the governance of collegiate sports. The sixty-year system of "student-athletes"—a unique classification that classifies college students as amateurs and significantly restricts compensation for those athletic activities—has come under sustained attack, both in the courts of law and in the court of public opinion. With ever-increasing revenues derived from a few "big-time" sports such as football and men's (and increasingly women's) basketball, the long-standing policy and the powers of the National Collegiate Athletic Association (NCAA) to regulate are in the throes of change and may well be weakened in the next few years. Yet some of the tenets of college athletics remain as true today as they were sixty years ago, at the dawn of the NCAA's modern governance system. Many, if not most, four-year institutions of higher education have sports programs allowing intercollegiate competition, and the great majority of them are NCAA members.

Often, these colleges and universities place considerable importance on their sports programs because a school with a successful program gains a number of tangible benefits. One benefit is the sheer joy of victory. Winning boosts the morale of team members and their school, and a cohesive school spirit and camaraderie often result. As a result, economic benefits may also accrue, as athletic success leads to the branding of the school as a top competitor to a potentially nationwide audience. The resulting national attention raises awareness of a school's educational programs and, ideally, expands the pool of potential applicants.

A frequently cited example is Boston College, a respected Jesuit institution. In 1984, the Boston College quarterback Doug Flutie won the Heisman Trophy and the national championship on a late "Hail Mary" pass. The following year, applications to Boston College increased 25 percent. This result became known as the "Flutie effect." More recently, quarterback Johnny Manziel, the Heisman Trophy–winning quarterback of the Texas A&M team, probably cost the school about $120,000 in scholarships during the three years that he was at A&M, but his high profile and success may have contributed to a $300 million increase (for a total of

$740 million) in donations to the institution. One study commissioned by the university valued the team's exposure as Mr. Manziel passed and rushed his way to a Heisman Trophy in the last two months of his first season at $37 million (Schwartz & Eder, 2014).

However, some have questioned the existence of the "Flutie effect." A survey of the general public by *The Chronicle of Higher Education* concluded that, among twenty-one goals for colleges, "playing athletics for the entertainment of the community" was found to be the least important. Other goals, such as preparing students to be future leaders and presenting cultural events, were deemed more important. Only 35 percent of respondents said sports were "somewhat" or "very important" for colleges (Scruggs, 2003). However, more recently, a study confirmed the connection, finding that applications increased by 17.7 percent depending on the success of the football and men's basketball teams (Silverthorne, 2013).

Collegiate athletics are revenue generating, but not often profitable, for the schools served. In terms of revenue, the University of Texas attained the top spot in 2014–15 academic year, producing about $180 million in revenue. This was followed by Ohio State University with $170.9 million and the University of Alabama reaching just over $150 million (Solomon, 2015).

However, it is a major misconception that most collegiate programs garner net profits. Athletics expenses outpaced revenues in schools of what is now known as the Football Bowl Subdivision (formerly known as Division I-A), the top division in the collegiate system, throughout the 1990s and early 2000s, even among conferences that compete in the lucrative bowl games played to national television audiences. The study noted that only the Southeastern Conference (SEC) schools averaged a profit from 1993 to 2002 (Sylwester, 2004). More recently, a study noted that of the 123 Football Bowl Subdivision programs, only 20 programs reported positive net revenues for the 2013 fiscal year. According to the study, of the 103 schools that lost money, the median deficit was $14.9 million. Furthermore, all athletic departments outside of the Football Bowl Subdivision operated at a deficit. In other words, only 20 of the 1083 college sports programs in the nation reported profits from their athletic programs (Madsen, 2014).

As noted, the NCAA is the umbrella body governing and regulating collegiate sports. However, with thousands of schools and dozens of sports, the regulatory structure of collegiate sports is more complex and more controversial. Consisting of more than 1200 four-year institutions, the NCAA develops guidelines and standards for athletic eligibility in each of three divisions, known as Divisions I, II and III. As of the 2015–16 school year, there were 347 Division I schools, 300 Division II schools and 443 Division III schools. That means that the great majority of four-year institutions are not in the top division, and many do not even offer athletic scholarships. And what is overlooked in the debate over the merits of NCAA policies is that it governs many different sports, not just the few that result in high revenues. Soccer, swimming, ice hockey, field hockey, tennis, golf, crew and lacrosse are just a few of the sports covered by the NCAA umbrella and suffice it to say, these sports do not bring in revenues in any great degree. Even in the relatively rare case where football revenues exceed costs, the costs of maintaining an athletic department offering many sports for participation rely on subsidies. As a result, most colleges and universities rely on what the NCAA calls "allocated revenue." This includes direct and indirect support from general funds, student fees and government appropriations. In other words, most colleges subsidize their athletics programs, sometimes to startling degrees (Suggs, 2012).

The NCAA's mission statement represents an idealistic purpose of collegiate athletics. It emphasizes the association's "belief and commitment to: [t]he college model of athletics in which students participate as an avocation, balancing their academic, social and athletics experiences." It exhorts student-athletes to perform at the highest level of integrity, to pursue excellence in both academics and athletics and to encourage diversity and respect philosophical difference and institutional autonomy (NCAA Core Values, 2015).

Essentially, the NCAA system creates a social contract: "student-athletes" participate in intercollegiate sports, receive an education and often (but not always) receive a partial or full scholarship to an institution. In return for these benefits, student-athletes are bound to accept a series of restrictions to maintain their "student-athlete" status. For many of the 460,000 student-athletes involved, this system works well. For college students talented enough to play a sport on a competitive level, the opportunity to play intercollegiate sports (often with an accompanying scholarship), under fine coaches and in up-to-date facilities, coupled with the opportunity to receive an education, is a wonderful experience. The difficulty—and at times, the corruption—found in the system involve student-athletes at a minority of schools in a very small number of sports. But these scandals have occurred in the big-revenue sports which make the headlines.

The NCAA is not the only vehicle for governance of student athletics. Most colleges and universities are part of independent conferences and play competitively against teams in those conferences. The conferences can institute their own regulations as to academics, eligibility and compensation. With the increasingly lucrative media deals negotiated, major (or "power") conferences are dictating the debate over collegiate athletics, particularly in the FBS football. As will be discussed later in this chapter, the rise of the power of the major conferences poses challenges for the NCAA and intriguing issues for the future of college athletics.

Institutional Control

The NCAA was formed in 1906, as a result of President Theodore Roosevelt's concern over the high number of injuries and deaths in college football. The NCAA is not a governmental agency, despite the fact that public universities are part of its membership. The NCAA's nongovernmental status weighs significantly in the organization's procedures and gives it considerable latitude in enforcement.

The organization seeks to "maintain intercollegiate athletics as an integral part of the education program and the athlete as an integral part of the student body" (NCAA Division I Manual—August Version, 2014, sec. 1.3.1). Its principal goals are to promote intercollegiate athletics, administer national championships and maintain integrity and standards of fair play.

Many regulations are listed in the manual—limitations on payments to athletes, minimum eligibility requirements and academic standing and prohibitions on prior professional arrangements, to name just a few. However, there is one overriding objective to the NCAA system: institutional control. In other words, in what ways does the college or university create an atmosphere to comply with NCAA requirements and prevent transgressions from occurring? When there is a breakdown in such control—through poor reporting or lack of oversight—the NCAA metes out significant punishment.

Although the NCAA employs a relatively small number of personnel to enforce its complex rules, it is neither a police force nor a district attorney's office. Institution control mandates that member institutions report violations, and failure to report results in even greater punishment based on its internal rules and regulations. An NCAA institution must conduct a self-study to provide university faculty, staff and students, as well as the public, with a transparent view of its operations. The period ranges from ten years (Division I) to five years (Divisions II and III) (NCAA Division I Manual—August Version, 2014, sec. 6.3.1; NCAA Division II Manual—August Version, 2014, sec. 6.3.1; NCAA Division III Manual—August Version, 2014, sec. 6.3.1). The study includes the governance of the institutions and the roles of the president, athletic director and compliance officers and issues of fiscal responsibility, academic rules and gender equity.

Problems often occur when institutional control breaks down.

Case Studies: The St. Bonaventure and University of Miami Cases

A particularly sad example of the breakdown of institutional control occurred at St. Bonaventure University, a respected institution located near Buffalo, New York. In 2004, the NCAA placed the school on three-year probation for violations in the men's basketball program, specifically concluding that the stiff punishment was justified by the breakdown of institutional control. The direct violation focused on the eligibility of a particular men's basketball player who transferred to St. Bonaventure after spending two years at a junior college. The student came to the university after receiving a "Certificate of Welding," a designation that clearly did not meet the requirements for academic eligibility under the NCAA's rules.

This violation was serious enough, but the conduct of the then-president and an assistant men's basketball coach made the situation far worse. The assistant coach communicated directly with the president (who happened to be his father) and convinced the president that the student was eligible, despite advice to the contrary from the athletic director. Compounding the problem, the institution changed the grade of the student-athlete from an "incomplete" to a "withdrawal" in a particular class taken during the student-athlete's first term at St. Bonaventure so that he remained eligible to travel to "away" games. (The university had a policy denying such travel for those with "incomplete" grades under its institutional policy.) The violation occurred after the president's son asked his father to "request" that the vice-president for academic affairs reconsider his initial decision on a strict withdrawal date deadline.

The result of this hubris was three years of probation (from 2003 to 2006), no postseason competition in either the 2003 NCAA tournament or the Atlantic 10 Tournament (the conference St. Bonaventure belongs to), limitations on recruitment and developing a new system of governance during the probationary period.

The NCAA found it "extremely troubling that a university president would assert independent interpretive authority with regard to NCAA legislation despite the repeated advice of the Athletic Director. Such lack of judgment . . . [was] at the root of why this case occurred" (Infractions case: St. Bonaventure University, 2004). As a result, the president, the athletic director and the entire basketball coaching staff resigned. Even though the athletic director objected to the policy, it was concluded that he did not take enough steps to prevent it. This case serves as an example of the need for adequate institutional control: an effective structure must be in place to avoid transgressions and to resolve them effectively when they occur. If the NCAA has to take unilateral action, the severity of the penalties and sanctions increases.

Do you think that the penalty fit the transgression? If you were the president of the college, how would you have handled the matter once you found out that the student was improperly admitted?

More recently, the wrongdoings of the University of Miami demonstrated clear weaknesses in the NCAA's enforcement mechanism. In 2013, the NCAA Infractions Committee issued a report outlining what it stated were major violations of NCAA rules in failing to control athletic boosters with regard to the university's football and basketball programs. The booster gained access to the athletic department first as a booster, then made inroads with assistant coaches and student-athletes. He not only gave players cash, but also hosted parties for student-athletes and recruits at his home, on his yacht, at local bowling alleys and in strip clubs (Adelson, 2013). Because the university instituted a "self-reported" ban on bowl competition, Miami lost nine football scholarships and three men's basketball scholarships over three seasons.

However, the NCAA was embarrassed by its own investigation tactics. It paid the lawyer of that very booster (who was convicted of running a Ponzi scheme) to provide information related to the booster's involvement with the university's student-athletes. This questionable decision resulted in the exodus of the head of infractions and many experienced investigators (Forde, 2013).

These cases highlight the importance of the role of a college or university's athletic director. The athletic director controls the athletic department budget, which often ranges in the tens of millions of dollars annually. Construction of new facilities, fund-raising efforts, Title IX compliance and a thorough knowledge of NCAA rules are under the aegis of the athletic director and his or her staff. Athletic directors appoint staff, which generally consists of an NCAA compliance specialist, marketing personnel, coaches, assistant coaches (in some cases) and trainers. But the athletic director's role in running large departments calls for greater management skills than purely athletic ones, and an ideal athletic director must possess knowledge of finance, marketing and fund-raising. He or she must interact with upper administration such as the president of the school and the board of trustees. The athletic director must possess skills necessary to answer questions posed by the media. Some have even perused Internet chat rooms to quell rumors and criticisms of the athletic program of their particular college or university (Lee, 2004; Belzer, 2013).

The NCAA posits these questions for a prospective athletic director:

1 Is he or she comfortable being directly accountable to the president of the institution, even when things go wrong?
2 Can he or she develop organizational and communication skills to keep supervisors informed about all aspects of athletics department operations?
3 Does he or she understand and respect the role of the faculty athletics representative?
4 Does he or she value counsel and oversight from an athletics advisory board?

5 Is he or she willing to commit to finding and reporting secondary violations within your athletics program (in addition to major infractions)?

6 If he or she is not already familiar with NCAA legislation, how does the person plan to learn it?

(NCAA.org, n.d.)

In 2016, Baylor University was found to lack institutional control after it was revealed that university officials and coaches were aware of sexual assault allegations involving members of the school's football team and failed to pursue disciplinary action. A report by an outside law firm commissioned by the university concluded that both the football program and athletics department leadership failed to identify and respond to a pattern of sexual violence by a football player, failed to take action in response to reports of a sexual assault by multiple football players and failed to take action in response to a report of dating violence (Baylor University Board of Regents, Findings of Fact, 2016).

As a result, the football coach was dismissed and the president of the university was demoted and then ultimately resigned from that position. The athletic director was placed on probation, but not fired (SportsdayDFW.com, 2016). However, he ultimately resigned.

Governance System

The NCAA's governance emanates from an association-wide executive committee, consisting of twelve members from Division I schools and two members each from Division II and III institutions. Composed of college or university presidents, the executive committee is charged with ensuring that each division operates consistently with the basic purposes, fundamental policies and general principles of the association (NCAA Division I Manual—October Version, 2014, sec. 4.1). In sum, the executive committee is the NCAA's highest-ranking governance body. In fact, in October 2014, the NCAA Executive Committee voted to change its name to the NCAA Board of Governors as part of a proposal designed to clarify the role of the committee and affirm its strategic purpose amid the changing landscape of college sports (Hendrickson, 2014).

Additionally, considerable powers are given to committees governing the various divisions. Although committees representing Division II and III schools serve important roles, we focus here on Division I's intradivisional governance system. The Division I Board of Directors has eighteen members. Directly below is the Division I Leadership Council, an advisory body to the Division I Board of Directors. It identifies issues important to the future of Division I and offers its expertise in defining appropriate action items. Committees on such policy issues as minority opportunities, ethical conduct and women's athletics and a student-athlete advisory committee report to the Leadership Council.

The NCAA has a considerable number of committees, cabinets and task forces governing the wide gamut of activities. Its bureaucratic structure would rival that of any international sports federation or, for that matter, a state or local government. Two of the most important are the Committee on Infractions, composed of individuals from NCAA member institutions, and the Management Council, a day-to-day operating arm of the NCAA, with final approval for all decisions being up to the board of directors. (Although we are focusing just on Division I, it should be noted that the other divisions have their own infractions committees.) Other Division I committees include a student-athlete advisory committee, made up of student-athletes "assembled to provide insight on the student-athlete experience," and men's and women's basketball issues committees (About SAAC, n.d.).

Divisions

As noted earlier, the NCAA consists of three divisions. The criteria for a school's membership in the appropriate division include the number of sports the school sponsors, the average attendance for home games and the number of home games played. College football is further subdivided into Football Bowl Subdivision or FBS (formerly Division I-A), Football Championship Subdivision or FCS (formerly Division I-AA) and Division I nonfootball schools (formerly known as Division I-AAA), which do not compete in college football. The requirements for division membership are intricate, but a basic outline follows.

Division I schools are required to sponsor a minimum of seven men's teams and seven women's teams (or six men's teams and eight women's teams), all of which are required to play 100 percent of the minimum number of contests against Division I opponents—anything over the minimum number of games has to be 50 percent Division I. Men's and women's basketball teams have to play all but two games against Division I teams; men must play one-third of all their contests in the home arena. Division I schools must meet certain financial aid requirements (Divisional Differences and the History of Multidivision Classification, n.d.).

Division II schools must sponsor five men's and five women's sports (or four for men and six for women). Football teams and men's and women's basketball teams must play at least 50 percent of their games against Division I or II opponents. For sports other than football and basketball there are no scheduling requirements. Division III schools are required to sponsor five men's and five women's sports. There are no financial aid requirements (Divisional Differences and the History of Multidivision Classification, n.d.).

For admission into the Football Bowl Subdivision (the former Division I-A) teams have to meet minimum attendance requirements (average 15,000 people in actual or paid attendance per home game) once in a rolling two-year period (NCAA Division I Manual—August Version, 2014, sec. 20.9.9.3). NCAA Football Championship Subdivision teams do not need to meet minimum attendance requirements. A school must provide an average of 90 percent of the maximum number of football scholarships allowed over a rolling two-year period (NCAA Division I Manual—August Version, 2014, sec. 20.9.9.4).

Additionally, each school must play at least five home games each season against another FBS opponent, must sponsor at least sixteen varsity sports—two more than the normal Division I minimum, with a minimum of six men's sports and eight women's sports—and must offer a minimum of 200 athletic scholarships or offer $4 million in athletic financial aid.

Presently, the FBS includes schools from eleven athletic conferences and seven nonaffiliated schools (so-called "independent schools" such as Notre Dame). Schools align themselves into conferences to operate more efficiently.

Division I Enforcement

The NCAA employs a "membership services" staff, which works with schools to help interpret rules. The enforcement staff has the power to investigate complaints based on information received from self-reporting by the school or other methods of information gathering (Enforcement Process: Investigations, n.d.). It has the responsibility to gather "basic information" regarding possible violations and, in doing so, may contact individuals to solicit information. If the enforcement staff has developed "reasonably reliable" information indicating that an institution has been in violation of the association's governing legislation that requires further in-person investigation, the enforcement staff shall provide a written notice of inquiry to the enforcement staff's chief executive officer. If the investigation uncovers significant information concerning a possible major violation, the institution will be notified. To the extent possible, the notice of inquiry also shall contain the following information:

- The involved sport
- The approximate time period during which the alleged violations occurred
- The identity of involved individuals
- An approximate time frame for the investigation
- A statement requesting that the individuals associated with the institution not discuss the case prior to interviews by the enforcement staff and institution, except for consultation with legal counsel or reasonable campus communications not intended to impede the investigation of the allegations

Hearings by the infractions committee of the appropriate division (I, II or III) then occur. The Division I Committee on Infractions currently has ten members, composed of seven individuals from NCAA member institutions and three from the general public. Members have been attorneys, professors, conference commissioners and athletic department officials (NCAA Committees, n.d.). The infractions committee has the authority to determine what findings (if any) should be made and what (if any) penalties should be imposed upon a member institution. This committee meets up to six times per year, and committee members serve three-year terms, for a maximum of nine years (NCAA Committees, n.d.).

The duties of this committee include determining the merits of complaints filed with the NCAA, charging members with the failure to maintain academic or athletics standards required for membership, determining facts related to alleged violations, making findings of violations of NCAA rules, imposing appropriate penalties on member institutions found to be involved in major violations and carrying out any other duties directly related to the administration of the enforcement program. In the past, the NCAA differentiates between "major" and "secondary" violations in assessing punishment. For secondary violations, a hearing is often waived.

Similar to an administrative hearing or arbitration procedure, each side presents its case in front of the entire committee. After the hearing, the committee issues a report summarizing its findings and the recommended penalties (if any) (NCAA Division I Manual—August Version, 2014, sec. 19.4–19.5). The aggrieved party may appeal to an infractions appeals committee. However, this committee does not operate like a court of law. As Michael Rogers, who represented Baylor University in one hearing, stated: "[O]ne misconception is that a [committee on infractions hearing] is like a trial we would see in our judicial system." Says Rogers, "It is very different." In an interview in 2010, the chairperson referred to the process as "quasi-judicial" and "in a way like arbitration" and similar to an "administrative hearing" (Dohrmann, 2010).

In 2014, the NCAA revised its penalty structure to replace the traditional "Major" and "Secondary" classification of violations. The goal of the revised structure is to create a more nuanced method of determining improper behavior (NCAA Division I Manual—2015, sec, 19.1). The new tiers include Level I: Severe Breach of Conduct, Level II: Significant Breach of Conduct, Level III: Breach of Conduct and Level IV: Incidental Issues.

The most severe penalty is the repeat-violator legislation (so-called "death penalty"), applicable if a major rules violation occurs within five years of another major violation. The second major case (or Level I, II or III case after 2015) does not have to be in the same sport as the earlier case to affect the second sport (NCAA Division I Manual, August Version, 2014, sec. 19.9.3). The result: termination of the school's program in that sport for two years. The most famous instance where the NCAA instituted this punishment to a Division I institution occurred against Southern Methodist University in 1987.

Other penalties for repeat violators of legislation include:

- Prohibition of some or all outside competition in the sport involved in the last major violation for one or two seasons
- Prohibition of all coaching staff members in that sport from involvement directly or indirectly in any coaching activities at the institution during that period
- Elimination of all initial grants-in-aid and recruiting activities in the sport involved in the last major violation in question for a two-year period
- All institutional staff members serving on the NCAA Presidents Cabinet Council, executive committee or other committees of the association resign their positions

(NCAA Division I Manual, 2014 August, sec. 19.5.2, 2014)

The recent enforcement standards explicitly provide that a head coach is responsible for the actions of his or her assistant coaches and other administrators who report directly to that coach (NCAA Division I Manual, 2015, sec. 11.1.2.1). As a consequence, if any member of a coach's staff commits an infraction, he or she will be subject to significant suspensions.

Although many have criticized past NCAA enforcement as too broad and lacking in adequate due process (Nocera, 2015), others, such as conference officials, have criticized the system as inadequate due to lack of adequate staffing and funding, lacking in the power to subpoena individuals (Griffin, 2014).

Legal Status of NCAA Policies

The NCAA is a private organization, not a governmental agency or an organization with direct connections to a governmental agency. Because of its private status, it is not obligated to observe constitutional requirements of due process in its enforcement procedures (*NCAA v. Tarkanian*, 1988). Therefore, it can fashion a system of discipline and enforcement less stringent than that of a government agency and does not have to fear lawsuits for alleged violations of due process or other constitutional rights.

However, despite its nongovernmental nature, the NCAA can and has been sued. The major lawsuits focused on alleged anticompetitive activities under antitrust laws. The U.S. Supreme Court rejected NCAA claims that it was exempt from liability under the Sherman Act, the bedrock U.S. antitrust statute that bars agreements by two or more entities that engage in restraining trade (*NCAA v. Board of Regents of the University of Oklahoma*, 1984, Sherman Anti-trust Law, sec. 1). The result of that case was that the NCAA lost control of Division I-A (now FBS) football. In another case, a court concluded that the NCAA's policy of limiting compensation for certain part-time coaches violated antitrust laws and the organization had to pay $65 million in a settlement (*Law v. NCAA*, 1998).

A more recent antitrust case may be the most significant and may result in the end of the NCAA's blanket prohibitions of student compensation. In 2014, a federal judge concluded that the NCAA, and by extension its member schools, engaged in antitrust violations when it mandated that students agree to license their names and likenesses to the NCAA and their schools (*O'Bannon v. NCAA*, 2014). The judge even proposed ways to permit compensation by lump-sum fees for the use of their images. However, in 2015, a federal appeals court negated the compensation scheme proposed by the trial judge, although it concluded that the antitrust laws apply (*O'Bannon v. NCAA*, 2015). As of the summer of 2016, the case remains in litigation.

Due to the growing pressure to ease the rigidity of the student-athletes rules and the lack of student-athlete participation in the NCAA governance, the NCAA changed its governance structure for Division I in 2014. The final model establishes a twenty-four-member board of directors that grants considerable representation to the major conferences. The twenty-four members would consist of the five presidents from the five major conferences (Atlantic Coast Conference, Big Ten Conference, Big 12 Conference, Pacific 12 Conference and Southeastern Conference) and five presidents from the remaining five Football Bowl Subdivision Conferences (American Athletic Conference, Conference-USA, Mid-American Conference, Mountain West Conference and Sun Belt Conference).

Other members include five presidents from the Football Championship Subdivision, five presidents from Division I schools without football and representatives from faculty and a campus senior female representative (Hosick, 2014).

The board would have a weighted vote, giving the representatives of the five major conferences almost 40 percent of the vote. Coupled with the other five FBS conference presidents, a solid majority of the votes (about 56 percent) would be in the hands of the conferences, which could liberalize the student-athlete compensation rules if they wished. In addition, an eight-member "council" is responsible for day-to-day operations of Division I. It includes two seats for student-athletes, two for faculty and four for commissioners. However, there is also a subgroup focusing on athletes, consisting mainly of athletic directors (Tracy, 2014).

The Rules

The substantive rules are contained in the NCAA's *Manuals*, which can be either purchased or downloaded from the NCAA's website (www.ncaa.org).

Written like a statutory code, the Division I manual, for example, has thirty-three separate articles and many accompanying sections and subsections.

Like federal or state laws, the manual has its minute details, and many use those as examples when criticizing the NCAA. For example, one clause requires laundry labels on a school uniform to be no more than 2¼ square inches within a four-sided geometrical shape (i.e., rectangle, square, parallelogram) (NCAA Division I Manual—August Version, 2014, sec. 12.5.4.1). Criticisms may be valid but, before totally assailing the organization, note that many sections of the bylaws contain important standards applicable to many different sports, not just the "big-time" ones. We summarize some of the key provisions in the Division I manual, as Division I schools are most frequently covered. Because the manual is over 500 pages, the following summary will give readers a basic idea of the key provisions.

Amateurism

Article 12 of the NCAA's Division I manual discusses the requirement that all student-athletes must be amateurs. The NCAA has held to a traditional definition of amateurism, one that prohibits most forms of compensation for services. The concept dates back to the nineteenth century, when upper-class gentlemen had the time and means to participate in sporting events for the pleasure of doing so. The manual notes that an athlete becomes ineligible to play for his or her school if that athlete "directly or indirectly" receives pay "in any form in that sport" (NCAA Division I Manual—August Version, 2014, sec. 12.1.2). The section further prohibits receipt of any compensation from a professional sports organization and even bars playing for a professional team without compensation (NCAA Division I Manual—August Version, 2014, sec. 12.2.2.1). The proscription extends to contracting with an agent or signing a contract with a professional team while playing at school.

Traditionally, the major exception to the no-compensation requirement was the athletic scholarship that some student-athletes received as consideration for attending the school. But other exceptions exist, although more limited. An individual may receive "actual and necessary" expenses from a professional sports organization to attend an academy, camp or clinic, provided that no NCAA institution or conference owns or operates the academy, camp or clinic and no camp participant is above the age of fifteen. Basketball players may accept actual and necessary travel and room-and-board expenses from a professional sports organization to attend that organization's predraft basketball camp (NCAA Division I Manual—August Version, 2014, sec. 12.2.1.3.1). But as of 2015, under the revised rules, the appropriate athletic conferences have amended the compensation rules to cover the "full costs" of attendance such as transportation and miscellaneous expenses (Terlep, 2015).

In many cases, a player who enters a professional league draft loses NCAA eligibility (NCAA Division I Manual—August Version, 2014, sec. 12.2.4.2). However, there are some important exceptions to this rule. A student-athlete playing basketball may enter the NBA or other professional league draft. If the player is not drafted, he or she may seek to return to intercollegiate participation within thirty days after the draft date. A similar rule is in effect regarding FBS and FCS football. An enrolled student-athlete (as opposed to a prospective student-athlete) in FBS or FCS football may enter the National Football League draft one time during his collegiate career without jeopardizing eligibility in that sport, provided the student-athlete is not drafted by any team in that league and the student-athlete declares his intention to resume intercollegiate participation within seventy-two hours following the National Football League draft declaration date (NCAA Division I Manual—August Version, 2014, secs. 12.2.4.2.1 and 12.2.4.2.3).

For those who have criticized the strict application of the amateurism rules, two particularly egregious examples were cited. The first stated that if a student was a professional athlete in one sport but wished to compete as a student-athlete in another sport, he could neither receive an athletic scholarship nor accept any compensation from the professional team or companies seeking endorsement deals (NCAA Division I Manual, 2009, sec. 12.1.2). More recently, the NCAA amended that rule. As of 2014, if a student is a professional athlete in one sport but wishes to compete as a student-athlete in another sport, he may receive institutional financial assistance in the second sport (NCAA Division I Manual—August Version, 2014, sec. 15.3.1.4). This may be a response to a situation that occurred when Jeremy Bloom, a successful mogul skier, sought student-athlete status to play football at the University of Colorado. As a condition, he was forced to give up endorsement opportunities based on his success as a participant in a very different sport (Bloom, 2003).

Agents

The NCAA and its member schools do not look with favor on sports agent solicitation of student-athletes. Vulnerability to possible exploitation serves as the official reason, but cynics can point to the loss of a talent pool as well. Whatever the motive, the NCAA manual states that

> an individual shall be ineligible for participation in an intercollegiate sport if he or she ever has agreed (orally or in writing) to be represented by an agent for the purpose of marketing his or her athletic ability or reputation in that sport.

Further, an agency contract not specifically limited in writing to a sport or particular sports shall be deemed applicable to all sports, and the individual shall be ineligible to participate in any sport (NCAA Division I Manual, 2014—August Version, sec. 12.3.1). Additionally:

> an individual shall be ineligible if he or she *or his or her relatives or friends* [emphasis added] accepts transportation or other benefits from: any person who represents any individual in the marketing of his or her athletic ability, or an agent.

This is the case even if the agent has indicated that he or she has no interest in representing the student-athlete in the marketing of his or her athletic ability or reputation and does not represent individuals in the student-athlete's sport (NCAA Division I Manual, 2014—August Version, sec. 12.3.1.2).

The NCAA also prohibits student-athletes from using "legal advisors" in contract negotiations with professional teams and forbids these advisors to "make contact" with the pro team that had drafted the athlete (NCAA Division I Manual, 2014—August Version, sec. 12.3.2.1). This poses a particular problem in baseball, where college players are frequently drafted. These strict rules limiting an agent's duties have been challenged in court by Andy Oliver, an all-American pitcher at Oklahoma State University, who was rendered ineligible to compete for violating the "no agent" rule just hours before a scheduled appearance in a regional playoff game. The NCAA ultimately settled for a considerable sum just before trial (Mullen, 2009). The role of agents in general is discussed further in Chapter 7.

Recruiting

Intricate and *limiting* characterizes the rules regarding the recruitment of student-athletes by member schools. Intended to equalize recruitment opportunities, the rules prevent wealthier schools, possessing the resources to wine and dine prospective student-athletes, from monopolizing the top talent. However, beneath this noble basis rests the nitty-gritty of the recruiting standards.

These rules cover such issues as restrictions on times and number of trips and places of recruitment. The following serves as an example of the minutiae found in Article 13 of the bylaws. High school prospects cannot be contacted before July 1 following the student's junior year (NCAA Division I Manual, 2014—August Version, sec. 13.1.1.1). Similar rules apply to telephone calls made by authorized staff members of the school's athletic department. The frequency of the calls cannot be more than once per week (NCAA Division I Manual—August Version, 2014, sec. 13.1.3.1). For FBS and FCS football, the contact may be made in May of the junior year and then again in September of the senior year. Time exceptions also exist for men's and women's basketball (NCAA Division I Manual, 2014 secs. 13.1.3.1.4 and 13.1.3.1.7).

Entertainment expenses must be "reasonable" and only for on-campus recruits. A member institution may pay the prospect's actual round-trip transport costs for his or her official visit to its campus, provided a direct route between the prospect's home and the institution's campus is used. There is a limitation of one sponsored visit to each school per prospect. However, with the exception for prospective men's or women's basketball players, a prospect may visit a member institution's campus at his or her own expense an unlimited number of times (NCAA Division I Manual—August Version, 2014, sec. 13.7.1). The Division I Manual also notes the time periods permissible for recruiting in a given sport (NCAA Division I Manual—August Version, 2014, sec. 13.1.4). Bowing to the increasing ubiquitous social media technology, the NCAA has allowed, for example, allowing colleges to start recruiting student-athletes via Snapchat (Patterson, 2014).

Academic Requirements

In the past, the debate surrounding academic criteria for student-athletes' admission and eligibility has been a battleground between those who feel that standards are too minimal and need tightening and those who feel that increasing standards unfairly discriminates against many of those students who lack skills on account of their socioeconomic circumstances. The claim—rejected by one federal court (*Cureton v. NCAA*, 1999)—has been that an "adverse impact" results because a higher percentage of African American student athletes come from backgrounds in which educational opportunities are lacking and therefore have greater difficulties in maintaining the minimums.

To be eligible to represent an institution in intercollegiate athletics competition, a student-athlete must be enrolled in at least a minimum full-time program of studies, be in "good academic standing" and maintain progress toward a baccalaureate or equivalent degree. Note the lack of a graduation requirement. The rules require only that the student-athlete be "making progress" toward a degree at a prescribed schedule. Note that these standards are *minimums*. Particular conferences and individual schools often impose higher admission and matriculation standards.

For Division I schools, entering freshmen must have successfully completed a high school core curriculum of at least sixteen academic "core" courses, including:

- Four years of English
- Three years of math (at the level of Algebra I or higher)

- Two years of natural or physical science
- One extra year of English, math or natural or physical science
- Two years of social science
- Four years of additional academic courses in any of the previous areas or foreign language, computer science, philosophy or nondoctrinal religion

(NCAA Division I Manual—August Version, 2014, sec. 14.3.1.1)

Division II schools require completion of fourteen core classes in a similar breakdown:

- Three years of English
- Two years of math (at the level of Algebra I or higher)
- Two years of natural or physical science
- Three extra years of English, math or natural or physical science
- Two years of social science
- Four years of additional academic courses in any of the previous areas or foreign language, computer science, philosophy or nondoctrinal religion

(NCAA Division II Manual—August Version, 2014, sec. 14.3.1.1)

In addition to the core course requirement, the NCAA requires minimum SAT (Scholastic Aptitude Test) or ACT (American College Test) scores. Because of the past debate over the wisdom of these tests and the adverse impact they may have on certain minority group applicants, the NCAA concluded that a sliding-scale approach worked best, featuring a combination of high school grade point average and corresponding test scores to give a greater academic picture of an application. As of 2016, for Division I schools, the scale ranges from a 2.3 grade point average (GPA) in sixteen core courses for a student to be eligible to compete in the first year of college. The scale is similar to those in the past. For example, a student with a 2.3 GPA must score a 900 on the combined reading and math SAT or a 75 on the ACT exams. If a student has a 3.0 GPA, those scores are 620 and 52, respectively. If a 3.5 GPA is attained, the scores drop to 420 and 39. Note that these are NCAA minimums (NCAA Eligibility Center, 2015). The institutions and the conferences can have higher requirements, and the schools often do.

Once the student is admitted, the NCAA requires adequate "progress" toward a degree to maintain eligibility. The requirements are backended (NCAA Division I Manual—August Version, 2014, sec. 14.4.3.2). After two years, a student-athlete must have completed 40 percent of the school's requirements for graduation. At the end of three years, student-athletes must have completed 60 percent, and by the end of four years the figure is 80 percent (NCAA Division I Manual—August Version, 2014, sec. 14.4.3.2).

A student-athlete must maintain a GPA that places the individual in good academic standing, as established by the institution. The NCAA requires that the student-athlete maintain a GPA of at least 90 percent of the school's minimum in the sophomore year, 95 percent in the third year and 100 percent in the fourth and fifth years (NCAA Division I Manual—August Version, 2014, sec. 14.4.3.3).

The NCAA also requires disclosure of the graduation rates among student-athletes. Failure to disclose a graduation-rate survey may disqualify a team or individual from competing in an NCAA championship (NCAA Division I Manual—August Version, 2014, sec. 18.4.2.2.1).

Transfers

To prevent students from soliciting schools and to prevent schools from trying to steal away talented athletes from other schools, the NCAA has devised rules that prohibit transfer students from playing on a team for one year (NCAA Division I Manual—August Version, 2014, sec. 14.5.1) and limiting transfer of students from two-year (or junior) colleges, with the exception of a student who had maintained a 2.0 GPA with twelve credits per semester (NCAA Division I Manual—August Version, 2014, sec. 14.5.4.1). A significant exception occurs where the student transfers from a school after the discontinuance of his or her athletic program. So student X, a member of the men's swim team at a particular Division I school that discontinued intercollegiate swimming, may transfer to another Division I school and need not sit out the year (NCAA Division I Manual—August Version, 2014, sec. 14.5.4.6.1).

Financial Aid

Division I schools may offer financial aid, in the name of an athletic scholarship, to student-athletes. Under the NCAA Division I bylaws, "financial aid" includes scholarships, grants, tuition waivers and loans (NCAA Division I Manual, 2009, sec. 15.02.4.1). The maximum amount allowed (known as "grant-in-aid") has traditionally covered tuition, fees, room and board and required course-related books (NCAA Division I Manual, 2009, sec. 15.02.5). If the student received anything above this amount, the student is ineligible to compete in intercollegiate athletics. However, as noted earlier in this chapter, the rules were somewhat liberalized in 2015 to include the "full cost" of grant-in-aid, which was expanded to include "other expenses related to attendance at the institution up to the cost of attendance" (NCAA Division I Manual, 2015, sec. 15.02.5).

Additionally, the NCAA liberalized the rules regarding earnings from a student-athlete's on- or off-campus employment. Such earnings are exempt, without limitation, and not counted in determining a student-athlete's full grant-in-aid or in the institution's financial aid limitations. This exemption applies only if the student-athlete's compensation is *not* based on the reputation, fame or following of that athlete and the student-athlete's compensation is at the "going rate" for that locality for similar services (NCAA Division I Manual, 2009, sec. 15.2.7).

Financial aid may be reduced or canceled if the student loses eligibility (NCAA Division I Manual, 2009, sec. 15.3.4.2). The bylaws limit the number of scholarships available, depending on the sport (NCAA Division I Manual, 2009, sec. 15.5.3). Additional awards, benefits and expenses to student athletes are severely restricted under NCAA rules. These monies, defined as allowance beyond the NCAA maximum amounts, result in the student-athlete's ineligibility for intercollegiate competition.

Of particular interest is the prohibition on so-called "extra benefit" awards. Defined as compensation from the school or representative of the institution's athletic interests to provide the student-athlete or his or her relatives or friends with a benefit not expressly authorized by NCAA legislation (NCAA Division I Manual, 2015, sec. 16.11.1.1), such benefits include discounts and credits on purchases (such as airline tickets) or services (laundry), telephone cards, credit cards and entertainment services such as movie tickets and the use of a car. Even a car ride home with a coach or staff member is prohibited in most instances (even if the student-athlete reimburses the costs of gas) (NCAA Division I Manual, 2015, secs. 16.11.2.2.1–16.11.2.2.3).

Student-athletes may not receive cash or cash-equivalent awards, such as gift certificates, merchandise or services (NCAA Division I Manual, 2015, sec. 16.1.1.2). One minor exception: as of 2015, a maximum of $325 can be disbursed for winning a conference and $415 for a national championship (NCAA Division I Manual, 2015, sec. 16.1.4.2).

Regarding noncash goods, the NCAA permits housing and meal costs to be paid by the school. Certain preseason practice expenses and meals incidental to competition are permitted (NCAA Division I Manual, 2015, sec. 16.5.2). Also, the school covers travel costs for trips to road games. As of 2015, a per diem award of $30/day is allowed for student-athletes at NCAA championship tournaments (NCAA Division I Manual, 2015, sec. 16.8.1.1). Also, a student-athlete may request additional financial aid (with no obligation to repay such aid) from a fund established pursuant to a special financial need program approved by the NCAA Management Council. The institution may provide reasonable local transport in conjunction with financial assistance approved under this program (NCAA Division I Manual, 2015, sec. 16.12.2).

Practice Dates

The bylaws provide a detailed listing of the prescribed dates and range of practice sessions for various NCAA sports. Practice dates are limited to particular times of the year, and violations of such schedules can result in sanctions for the school. The schedules are found in Article 17 of the NCAA Division I bylaws.

The Role of Coaches

Professional athletic coaches have specific goals: to employ strategies and skills to motivate athletes to win games. Collegiate coaches have more varied duties and more constraints under the NCAA system. They must be familiar with the NCAA bylaws, particularly restrictions on practice time and recruiting. Also, they have to build a rapport with the student-athlete, sometimes becoming an educator, role model and even surrogate parent. Often these young people, some away from home for the first time, go through a major life transition. College coaches "mold" these student-athletes, and their guidance may help or hinder their maturity.

College coaches also spend a great deal of their time recruiting. The NCAA allows football and basketball coaches to travel a total of forty days over two periods of time during a year. Coaches of other sports may travel to recruit during the whole year, except for specified "dead periods" (interview with Marianne Reilly, assistant athletic coordinator, Fordham University, Bronx, NY, March 15, 2004). Spotting talent, traveling and interviewing are very important aspects of the job. In professional sports, general managers, not coaches, usually do these tasks.

Athletic Conferences

In addition to the NCAA, the organizational structure of intercollegiate athletics includes conferences. Conferences serve as "mini-leagues" in which collegiate teams compete. Although there is no mandate that a college or university join a conference (Notre Dame football is one example of an "independent" school), the overwhelming majority of colleges and universities do. Schools gain a variety of benefits from conference membership.

In recent years, the gulf between the "haves" and "have nots" among the respective conferences has grown to a point where it is acknowledged that five of the conferences involving Division I schools are considered "power" conferences. But many of the smaller conferences have signed television contracts, which provide exposure to their member schools. Scheduling is easier with conference membership because of the designated number of competitors. Many, if not most, conferences hold championship tournaments, giving teams more exposure and potentially more revenues, and winning a conference championship usually gives that team the opportunity to compete in the NCAA championship competition. For example, in 2014, thirty-one conferences received revenues from the NCAA basketball tournament.

The five major conferences and their participating schools are listed below.

Atlantic Coast Conference (ACC)

- Boston College (Eagles)
- Clemson University (Tigers)
- Duke University (Blue Devils)
- Florida State University (Seminoles)
- Georgia Tech University (Yellow Jackets)
- University of Louisville (Cardinals)
- University of Miami (Hurricanes)
- University of North Carolina (Tar Heels)
- North Carolina State University (Wolfpack)
- University of Notre Dame (Fighting Irish)
- University of Pittsburgh (Panthers)
- Syracuse University (Orange)
- University of Virginia (Cavaliers)
- Virginia Tech (Hokies)
- Wake Forest University (Demon Deacons)

The Atlantic Coast Conference was founded in 1953 and had seven members until 1978, when Georgia Tech was admitted. With the addition of Florida State in 1991, the ACC expanded to nine members. Since then, Miami and Virginia Tech joined in 2004 and Boston College in 2005.

The Big Ten Conference

Eastern Division

- Indiana University (Hoosiers)
- University of Maryland (Terrapins)
- University of Michigan (Wolverines)
- Michigan State University (Spartans)
- Ohio State University (Buckeyes)
- Pennsylvania State University (Nittany Lions)
- Rutgers University (Scarlet Knights)

Western Division

- University of Illinois (Fighting Illini)
- University of Iowa (Hawkeyes)
- University of Minnesota (Golden Gophers)
- University of Nebraska (Cornhuskers)
- Northwestern University (Wildcats)
- Purdue University (Boilermakers)
- University of Wisconsin (Badgers)

Formed in 1896, this conference is the oldest and predates the establishment of the NCAA. It created eligibility rules that became the basis of the NCAA's amateurism standard. This venerable conference's institutions sponsor more than 250 athletic programs (www.BigTen.org). The inclusion of two Eastern U.S. schools in 2014 broadened the scope of the conference, as Rutgers, located in Highland Park, New Jersey, and Maryland, in College Park, Maryland, and opened the New York–Metropolitan area and the Baltimore–Washington, D.C. markets to competitions.

The Big 12 Conference

- Baylor University (Bears)
- Iowa State University (Cyclones)
- University of Kansas (Jayhawks)
- Kansas State University (Wildcats)
- University of Oklahoma (Sooners)
- Oklahoma State University (Cowboys)
- University of Texas (Longhorns)
- Texas Tech (Red Raiders)
- Texas Christian University (Horned Frogs)
- West Virginia University (Mountaineers)

The Big 12 is a relatively young organization, begun in 1994, when the former Big Eight Conference joined with four Texas schools that had been members of the Southwest Conference, which had just disbanded. Since 2011 four of the original schools have left—Nebraska, Texas A&M, University of Colorado and University of Missouri. With ten members, it is the only "power" conference that does not host a championship game, although a 2016 NCAA rules change would permit a football championship game if the conference wishes. It also has an agreement with the Southeastern Conference to host a joint postseason college football game between the respective champions of each conference (the Sugar Bowl). At this time of this writing, the conference is considering adding two or four schools.

Pac-12 Conference (Formerly Pac-10)

- University of Arizona (Wildcats)
- Arizona State University (Sun Devils)
- University of California Berkeley (Golden Bears)
- University of California at Los Angeles (Bruins)
- University of Colorado, Boulder (Buffaloes)
- University of Oregon (Ducks)
- Oregon State University (Beavers)
- University of Southern California (Trojans)
- Stanford University (Cardinal)
- University of Utah (Utes)
- University of Washington (Huskies)
- Washington State University (Cougars)

Not surprisingly, the Pac-12 schools reside in the west and northwest. Originally known as the "Pac-10," its roots date to 1915. Renamed in 2013 after the inclusion of the Universities of Colorado and Utah, the Pac-12 has won more NCAA national championships than any other conference (Pac-12.com). The top three schools with the most NCAA championships—UCLA, Stanford and the University of Southern California—belong to the Pac-12.

Southeastern Conference

The teams in this now fourteen-school conference are divided into two groups: the Eastern and Western divisions.

Eastern Division

- University of Florida (Gators)
- University of Georgia (Bulldogs)
- University of Kentucky (Wildcats)
- University of Missouri (Tigers)
- University of South Carolina (Gamecocks)
- University of Tennessee (Volunteers)
- Vanderbilt University (Commodores)

Western Division

- University of Alabama (Crimson Tide)
- University of Arkansas (Razorbacks)
- Auburn University (Tigers)
- Louisiana State University (Tigers)

- Mississippi State University (Bulldogs)
- University of Mississippi ("Ole Miss") (Rebels)
- Texas A&M (Aggies)

The Southeastern Conference (SEC), founded in 1933, has had relatively few changes in its roster over the years. Unlike the Big 12 Conference, a football championship game is needed to determine the conference winner. The SEC is a huge money maker. Since 2010, its television contract with CBS has brought in over $50 million per year and will continue to do so until 2024. Starting in 2014, its newly signed television contract with ESPN and ABC will bring in an additional $300 million per year until 2034. In other words, the SEC will collect over $350 million annually from its network partners over the next ten years (Ourand, 2014).

In addition to the "big five" conferences listed here, the NCAA FBS includes six other major conferences that are not guaranteed bids for a football bowl game. They include the American Athletic, Conference USA, FBS Independents, Mid-American, Mountain West and Sun Belt. There are also numerous other athletic conferences that do much the same. As we will see, conference affiliation plays a major role in determining whether a school can compete in the NCAA playoffs (for other sports besides FBS football) or a major bowl game or playoff (for FBS football).

Championships

The NCAA has conducted national championships in various sports since 1921 and currently administers eighty-nine championships in twenty-three sports for its member institutions (NCAA, 2015). The top team in each conference is invited to participate, along with selected other teams. The chosen teams compete against each other in single-game elimination contests until there are two teams left. Those two teams compete for the championship (Hales, 2003).

As noted earlier, the exception is top-tier football. Although the NCAA sponsors football championships in its FCS (formerly Division I-AA) and Divisions II and III, it does not control those of the FBS teams. For decades, a long-standing system of independent bowls invites specific teams to play in postseason games. Because the bowl system has generated considerable controversy, it was changed dramatically in the 2014 season to a four-team playoff system to determine a national champion. This approach has brought added brand value to the respective universities—and considerable revenues due to the lucrative television deal signed with ESPN.

Although the playoff system is limited to four teams (as of 2016), there is talk about expanding it in part because of difficulty in choosing those four teams, which are picked by a thirteen-person selection committee consisting of individuals with experience as coaches, student athletes, administrators, journalists and sitting directors of athletics. Selection committee members first review any data they find relevant to making a decision and then vote to produce a group decision (Selection Committee FAQs, n.d.). Though the selection committee process is meant to be as transparent as possible, the committee's evaluations can fluctuate from week to week based on a team's full body of work and strength of opponents, leaving would-be contenders outside the final playoff field (Culpepper, 2014).

FBS (Formally Division I-A) College Football Bowl Games— Pre-Bowl Championship Series

The bowl system dates back decades, and over the years different bowl games have been created and disbanded (Klein, 2013). Currently there are about thirty-nine postseason bowls. Even with the playoff system, which is geared toward a few top bowl games, other bowl games continue to be viable and are represented by fine collegiate teams.

Bowls began as a method to attract tourists to warm-weather climates between Christmas and New Year's Day (Hales, 2003). In more recent years, bowl game administrators have become more market savvy. The major bowls enjoy financial success, which has spawned sponsorship agreements from various businesses. Today, just about every bowl has a sponsor that makes payments to the bowl organization for permission to advertise using bowl logos and other trademarks. Examples are Tostitos for the Fiesta Bowl and Citigroup for the Rose Bowl (Associated Press, 2014).

Initially, each bowl negotiated participation agreements with individual teams. Eventually, some of these agreements gave way to multiyear contracts with particular conferences for a specifically ranked team from that conference. For example, the champions of both the Pac-10 and the Big Ten were obligated to participate in the Rose Bowl (McCarthy, 1991).

The Bowl Championship Series

The present playoff series replaced a "BCS," or Bowl Champion Series, that existed in one form or another for twenty years.

The final iteration of the bowl game arrangement began in 1998 with the creation of the BCS, which consisted of the champions of the six most dominant conferences at the time. The top two teams in the final BCS standings (derived from a computer ranking by the BCS) play in the national championship game.

However, this prior system (and even the present playoff system) presented greater difficulties for teams in the other BCS conferences. Top conferences received automatic berths for their championship teams to the select bowl games, whereas other conference champion teams had to out-rank those from the power conferences (Collegefootballpoll.com, 2013).

Although the old BCS system has been lucrative, as it resulted in a $730 million contract with ABC over eight years, the playoff system is a greater money maker, fueled by a $5.64 billion, twelve-year broadcasting agreement with ESPN (Hinnen, 2012).

High School Interscholastic Sports

In 2014, about 7.8 million youngsters, or one in two students, partici-pated in competitive school athletics (NFHS News, 2014). Governance of these competitions also exists, but without an NCAA-like national organi-zation. Rather, the system is more diffuse, with differing governing bodies regulating local, school district or independent youth league competitions.

Statewide interscholastic associations administer high school sports programs and run state championship tournaments. Committees consist-ing of coaches, administrators and parents often set eligibility rules. With laws prohibiting discrimination against students with disabilities, these committees have to draft rules with the goal of inclusion or face potential lawsuits. What makes this issue problematic is the complexity of enforce-ment provisions of laws such as the Americans with Disabilities Act. The interplay of laws and regulations and interscholastic athletics becomes important, more than in the case of the NCAA. Unlike the NCAA, which is considered a private organization, most state interscholastic associa-tions are considered "state actors," which means that they can be sued by member schools and by athletes, alleging constitutional violations (*Brent-wood Academy v. TSSAA*, 2001).

Another important issue is liability for injury. The associations (and their local affiliates) have (or should have) drafted risk management pro-cedures to prevent injuries and minimize risk of injury-producing events during competition. Chapter 11 provides more discussion on this issue. However, the increasing awareness of the effects of concussions has led to greater pressure for high school athletic associations to exercise a higher standard of care, often utilizing litigation (*Conine v. Schmidt*, 2015).

Interscholastic athletes learn teamwork and discipline, but rarely do they see athletic glory. According to the NCAA, fewer than one in thirty-five, or approximately 2.9 percent, of high school senior boys playing interscholastic basketball will go on to play men's basketball at an NCAA member institution. Fewer than one in seventy-five, or approximately 1.3 percent, of NCAA male senior basketball players will get drafted by an NBA team. Therefore, approximately 3 in 10,000, or approxi-mately 0.03 percent, of high school senior boys playing interscholastic basketball will eventually be drafted by an NBA team. The same can be said of football. About 5.8 percent, or approximately one in seventeen, of all high school senior boys playing interscholastic football will go on to play football at an NCAA member institution. About 2.0 percent, or approximately one in fifty, of NCAA senior football players will get drafted by an NFL team. Approximately 9 in 10,000, or approximately 0.09 percent, of high school senior boys playing interscholastic football will eventually be drafted by an NFL team (Langley, 2006).

Ethical Question: Should NCAA Student-Athletes Be Paid?

Some argue that Division I players should be paid outright for their services (Sanderson & Siegfried, 2015). On one level, the idea has appeal. Because big-time college athletes—notably those in football and men's and women's basketball—may earn direct or indirect revenues for the school due to fan attendance, more lucrative broadcasting and cable contracts and the sale of their names and likenesses on merchandise, why should they not receive compensation for their services beyond the scholarship? Specifically, advocates point to the fourteen-year, $10.8 billion contract between the NCAA, CBS Sports and Turner Broadcasting and the twelve-year, $7.3 billion contract for the NCAA College Football Playoff and six associated bowl games and the evolution of the economic clout of the five "power" conferences. Others point to the possible illegality of the current system under antitrust laws. Under legal assault in recent years, the NCAA may find itself on the losing end of ruling that makes the current system void, or the NCAA may settle the case and create some kind of compensation model.

One way is to treat student-athletes as employees, permitting them to unionize. This argument was made by a group that wanted to represent Northwestern University football players under the labor laws. In 2014, a regional director for the National Labor Relations Board (NLRB) concluded that the student-athletes were "employees" based on the amount of hours they worked and that their scholarships were tied to their performance; therefore, they were "covered" under the National Labor Relations Act (*Northwestern University and CAPA*, 2014). However, on appeal, the NLRB reversed the ruling on procedural grounds, but did not address the underlying question of college athletes as employees (Northwestern University and CAPA, 2015).

But in terms of compensation, would a free-market system of pay for play work? Would it only permit a few star players paid for a few top colleges to alter the competitive landscape to the point where the top programs would be de facto professional teams and would dominate the collegiate sports landscape?

Other ideas are not as drastic. Would college football or basketball players receive modest compensation based on a more equitable division? If so, should it be deferred until a certain amount of time? Should the NCAA simply liberalize the rules to permit students to share compensation from the use of their names and likenesses (similar to merchandising division in the professional leagues)? Or the other hand, should the NCAA get out of the business of regulating big-time college sports and leave it to the conferences, which have their pots of money from broadcasting contracts?

One intriguing idea has been proposed that would create a pool, coming from 25 percent of all broadcast revenues, into an amount earmarked for scholarship athletes in all sports. Money to cover the full cost of attendance would be paid on an annual basis to the athletes. But if monies were left over, it would be held in trust in each athlete's name, payable when the athlete leaves school (King & Smith, 2013). The amount of that scholarship the athlete could receive may grow in the future as the broadcast revenue continues to grow.

All of these pay-based models have drawbacks. If a student is an employee, then he or she could be terminated based on stipulations in his or her respective contract. The goal of committing to a scholarship for one to four years would be nullified. So imagine if a starting quarterback had four bad games. Could he be fired?

Another issue would be taxation. Income received by a student-athlete as an employee is taxable under federal and state law. This would involve student-athletes losing some of their income and forcing them to file tax returns. Depending on the respective income, taxes could reduce the take-home amount due to federal taxes (with brackets ranging from 10 percent to 39.6 percent as of 2016) and many state taxes (which could add up to an additional 10 percent or even more in a few states).

Would a payment system result in financial limitation for non–revenue-generating programs (which make up the bulk of the college sports played)? Would some compensation for players from the revenue-generating sports dry up funds for others? There could be serious issues involving U.S. laws and regulations guaranteeing equal opportunities for underrepresented genders, the so-called Title IX standards. If funding shortfalls disproportionally affect women's sports (by far the underrepresented gender), litigation will ensue. Or, would non–revenue-generating men's sports such as swimming or baseball have to face cuts in scholarships or outright elimination?

Another idea is permitting athletes to sign professional team contracts while still eligible to play collegiate sports. However, this has risks. Say star player X of the basketball team enters the NBA draft at the end of his junior year and is chosen. However, the player decides to complete his senior year and play on the college team in order to finish his degree. Injury concerns could limit effectiveness on that team. The same result may occur if the player signs with an agent but continues to play (another reform discussed). The agent may also have qualms about the risk of injury and may hint that the player "go easy."

Conference realignment based on the revenues generated (or potentially generated) by a particular school's athletic department has resulted in the increased prominence of the five "power" conferences. Going one step further, one writer proposed a "for-profit" system that would compete with the NCAA (Staples, 2010). However, such an idea—or other profit-based systems—would greatly affect the mission of collegiate sports as a part of one's educational experience.

The rise of so-called "big-time" programs raises a societal question of whether athletics should be cast further away from the mission of a college or university. Blue-ribbon panels have been convened to make changes in the system in the hope of preventing college sports from spinning out of control. One commentator concluded that

> [c]hasing after sports revenue and athletic prestige, schools admit more and more athletes, in the process sapping resources from the schools' academic mission and send the message to young people that sports is the best way to get into college.
>
> (Just, 2002)

The system, according to the authors, leads to students who are Balkanized from the rest of the student body and who consistently perform more poorly.

Some have proposed a permanent split of the "Big 5 Conferences" from the NCAA—at least for basketball and football (Katz, 2015). Those conferences would end the "amateurism" requirement and could craft compensation schemes for their athletes. However, the other 1100 NCAA schools (the great majority of which lose money on their athletic programs) would adhere to the amateurism standard. Student-athletes would simply be students, just like students who participate in other extracurricular activities like band or entrepreneur club. There would be no special rules for those students who partake in athletics and, therefore, the NCAA manual could be sharply reduced from its almost 400 pages (Katz, 2015).

Going even further, should the NCAA be abolished? Could college sports govern themselves? Of all the criticism of the NCAA, few have advocated a laissez-faire system, as it would produce a free-agency free-for-all, whereby the biggest and richest schools could simply attract the best talent and perpetuate a system of haves versus have-nots. Could colleges and universities self-police their programs? Or would it be up to the conferences or even law enforcement to police transgressions (whatever they are defined to be)?

As this book is being written, a lawsuit challenging the entire NCAA amateurism structure as an illegal boycott under the antitrust laws was filed by prominent antitrust and sports lawyer Jeffrey Kessler (*Jenkins v. NCAA*, 2014) seeking an injunction to end all restrictions on player compensation. Will this lawsuit be successful? Will it spur the NCAA to change? Only time will tell.

In any event, the slow professionalization of college athletes may be upon us.

Chapter Assignment

In looking at the changing framework for student-athletes, what is the best way to balance the educational goals of collegiate athletes with the realities of big-time college sports in a relatively small number of the nation's colleges and universities with nationally ranked athletic programs? A major think tank has commissioned you to think of and draft a plan that involves reforms of collegiate athletics from the five "Power Conferences." The plan is to address the following points:

1 Maintaining a quality education with appropriate standards for admission and retention.
2 Creating a method to calculate scholarships based on the "true cost" of education.
3 Creating a system of increasing injury protections and provide insurance for catastrophic, lifelong injuries.
4 Proposing restrictions on outside income by college or university athletes and, if so, how and when. Or, eliminating all restrictions on outside income.
5 Addressing the question of whether the NCAA should continue to exist. If not, what should replace it?
6 Looking at how non–revenue-generating sports would fare under this system.
7 Determining the appropriate manner to consider gender issues that have to be addressed if student-athletes are compensated. (You may want to refer to Chapter 13 for more information.)
8 Discussing any restrictions on coaches' compensation.

References

About SAAC (n.d.). Retrieved January 23, 2015, from http://www.ncaa.org/student-athletes/about-saac

Adelson, A. (2013, Oct. 23). No bowl ban for Miami Hurricanes. *ESPN.com*. Retrieved November 15, 2014, from http://espn.go.com/college-sports/story/_/id/9861775/miami-hurricanes-avoid-bowl-ban-lose-nine-scholarships-part-ncaa-sanctions

Associated Press (2014, December 19). Sponsors pay big bucks to join college bowl games. *Nytimes.com*. Retrieved January 28, 2015, from www.nytimes.com/aponline/2014/12/19/us/ap-us-college-bowls-name-game.html

Baylor University Board of Regents, Findings of Fact (Executive Summary) (2016). Retrieved May 27, 2016, from http://www.baylor.edu/rtsv/doc.php/266596.pdf

Belzer, J. (2013, September 23). What the changing landscape of college athletics means for new athletic director hires. *Forbes.com*. Retrieved January 23, 2015, from http://www.forbes.com/sites/jasonbelzer/2013/09/23/what-the-changing-landscape-of-college-athletics-means-for-new-athletic-director-hires/

Bloom, J. (2003, August 1). Show us the money. *Nytimes.com*. Retrieved January 26, 2015, from http://www.nytimes.com/2003/08/01/opinion/show-us-the-money.html

Brentwood Academy v. Tennessee Secondary School Athletic Association, 531 U.S. 288 (2001).

Collegefootballpoll.com (2013, May 9). BCS automatic qualification, at-large eligibility and selection procedures, 2011–2014 games. Retrieved January 27, 2015, from http://www.collegefootballpoll.com/bcs_selection_procedures.html

Conine v. Schmidt, (2015, September 14). Amended complaint 15-L-105. Retrieved December 28, 2015, from http://www.siprut.com/assets/Conine-Amended-Complaint.pdf

Culpepper, C. (2014, December 7). College Football Playoff field set but controversy lingers with Ohio State in, TCU snubbed. *Thewashingtonpost.com*. Retrieved January 27, 2015, from http://www.washingtonpost.com/news/sports/wp/2014/12/07/college-football-playoff-field-set-ohio-state-in-tcu-snubbed/

Cureton v. NCAA, 198 F.3d 107 (3d Cir. 1999).

Divisional Differences and the History of Multidivision Classification (n.d.). Retrieved January 23, 2015, from http://www.ncaa.org/about/who-we-are/membership/divisional-differences-and-history-multidivision-classification

Dohrmann, G. (2010, February 18). An inside look at the NCAA's secretive Committee on Infractions. *Si.com*. Retrieved March 15, 2010, from http://sportsillustrated.cnn.com/2010/writers/george_dohrmann/02/17/usc.coi

Enforcement Process: Investigations (n.d.). Retrieved January 23, 2015, from http://www.ncaa.org/enforcement/enforcement-process-investigations

Forde, P. (2013, October 22). Miami "wins" investigation battle with NCAA, but nobody should feel good about result. *Yahoo Sports*. Retrieved January 15, 2015, from http://sports.yahoo.com/news/ncaaf—miami-investigation-ncaa-12-scholarship-penalty-182331365.html

Griffin, T. (2014, July 22). Bowlsby rips NCAA's enforcement efforts. *San Antonio Express-News*. Retrieved December 27, 2014, from http://www.expressnews.com/sports/colleges/article/Bowlsby-rips-NCAA-s-enforcement-powers-5636917.php

Hales, M. (2003). The antitrust issues of NCAA college football within the Bowl championship series. *Sports Law Journal*, 10, 97.

Hendrickson, B. (2014, October 31). Executive committee changes name, clarifies role. *NCAA.org*. Retrieved January 23, 2015, from http://www.ncaa.org/about/resources/media-center/news/executive-committee-changes-name-clarifies-role

Hinnen, J. (2012, November 21). ESPN reaches 12-year deal to air college football playoffs. *cbssports.com*. Retrieved December 28, 2015, from http://www.cbssports.com/collegefootball/eye-on-college-football/21083689/espn-reaches-12year-deal-to-air-college-football-playoffs

Hosick, M. (2014, August 7). NCAA adopts new Division I structure, NCAA.org. Retrieved December 27, 2015, from http://www.ncaa.org/about/resources/media-center/news/board-adopts-new-division-i-structure

Infractions case: St. Bonaventure University (2004, May 1). *NCAA News.* Retrieved April 1, 2010, from http://web1.ncaa.org/web_files/NCAANews Archive/2004/Division+I/infractions%2Bcase_%2Bst.html

Jenkins v. NCAA (2014, March 17). Plaintiffs' complaint. Retrieved December 28, 2015, from http://a.espncdn.com/pdf/2014/0317/NCAA_lawsuit.pdf

Just, R. (2002, March 11). Can the next NCAA president reform college sports? *The American Prospect,* p. 15 [citing Robert Brown, an economist at California State University–San Marcos, from a 1990 study].

Katz, R. (2015, November 5). To preserve "amateurism," NCAA should separate power five schools. *Forbes.* Retrieved January 30, 2016, from http://www.forbes.com/sites/danielfisher/2015/11/05/to-preserve-amateurism-ncaa-should-separate-power-five-schools/4/#6fef94363622

King, B., & Smith, M. (2013, December 2–8). A pay-for-play model. *Sports Business Daily.* Retrieved December 15, 2014, from http://www.sportsbusinessdaily.com/Journal/Issues/2013/12/02/In-Depth/Main-story.aspx?hl=A%20Pay-for%3Dplay%20model&sc=0

Klein, C. (2013, January 1). A brief history of college bowl games. *History.com.* Retrieved January 27, 2015, from www.history.com/news/a-brief-history-of-college-bowl-games

Langley, C. (2006, May 10). Estimated probability of competing in athletics beyond the high school interscholastic level. *Summit-academy.com.* Retrieved March 18, 2010, from http://www.summit-academy.com/HighSchool/educational%20planning/College%20bound%20athletes/Estimated%20Probability%20of%20Competing%20in%20Athletics.pdfLaw v. NCAA, 134 F.3d 1010 (10th Cir. 1998).

Law v. NCAA, 134 F.3d 1438 (10th Cir. 1998).

Lee, J. (2004, June). Old school, new school—The role of the athletic director changes with the times. *Street & Smith's Sports Business Journal,* p. 23.

Madsen, N. (2014, December 22). Jim Moran says only 20 colleges make a profit from sports. *Politifact.com.* Retrieved January 23, 2015, from http://www.politifact.com/virginia/statements/2014/dec/22/jim-moran/moran-says-only-20-colleges-make-profit-sports/

McCarthy, M. J. (1991, April 24). Keeping careful score on sports tie-ins. *Wall Street Journal,* p. B1.

Mullen, J. (2009, October 6). Andy Oliver settles with NCAA prior to scheduled trial. *Sports Business Daily.* Retrieved May 10, 2010, from http://www.sportsbusinessdaily.com/article/133846

NCAA (n.d.). Institutional control—So you want to be an AD, Retrived January 23, 2015, from http://www.ncaa.org/about/institutional-control

NCAA (2015). What we do—Championships. Retrieved January 27, 2015, from http://www.ncaa.org/about/what-we-do/championships

NCAA Committee on Infractions (n.d.). Retrieved March 15, 2010, from http://web1.ncaa.org/committees/committees_roster.jsp?CommitteeName=1INFRACTION

NCAA Committees (n.d.). Title. Retrieved October 18, 2009, from https://www.ncaa.org/wps/ncaa?key=/ncaa/NCAA/Legislation+and+Governance/Committees/

NCAA Core Values (2015). Retrieved January 23, 2015, from http://www.ncaa.org/about/ncaa-core-purpose-and-values

NCAA Division I Committee on Infractions (n.d.). Retrieved April 5, 2010, from http://www.ncaa.org/wps/portal/ncaahome?WCM_GLOBAL_CONTEXT=/ncaa/ncaa/legislation+and+governance/committees/division+i/infractions/index.html

NCAA Division I Manual (2009). Various sections. Retrieved February 2010, from http://www.ncaapublications.com/productdownloads/D110.pdf

NCAA Division I Manual 2015 (2015). Bylaws, various sections. Retrieved March 17, 2016, from http://www.ncaapublications.com/productdownloads/D116.pdf

NCAA Division I Manual—August Version (2014). Bylaws, various sections. Retrieved January 23, 2015, from http://www.ncaapublications.com/productdownloads/D115.pdf

NCAA Division I Manual—October Version (2014). Bylaws, various sections. Retrieved January 23, 2015, from http://www.ncaapublications.com/productdownloads/D115OCT.pdf

NCAA Division II Manual—August Version (2014). Bylaws, various sections. Retrieved January 23, 2015, from http://www.ncaapublications.com/productdownloads/D215.pdf

NCAA Division III Manual—August Version (2014). Retrieved January 23, 2015, from http://www.ncaapublications.com/productdownloads/D315.pdf

NCAA Eligibility Center Quick Reference Guide (n.d.). Retrieved December 27, 2015, from http://fs.ncaa.org/Docs/eligibility_center/Quick_Reference_Sheet.pdf

NCAA v. Board of Regents of the University of Oklahoma, 468 U.S. 85 (1984).

NCAA v. Tarkanian, 488 U.S. 179 (1988).

NFHS News (2014, October 30). High school participation increases for 25th consecutive year. *NFHS.org*. Retrieved January 28, 2015, from www.nfhs.org/articles/high-school-participation-increases-for-25th-consecutive-year/

Nocera, J. (2015, December 25). Jerry Tarkanian and Walter Byers: Adversaries who left mark on N.C.A.A.. *The New York Times*. Retrieved December 27, 2015, from http://www.nytimes.com/2015/12/26/sports/ncaabasketball/jerry-tarkanian-and-walter-byers-adversaries-who-left-mark-on-ncaa.html?smtyp=cur

Northwestern University and College Athletes Players Assn (2014, March 26). Case 13-RC-121359. Retrieved January 15, 2015, from https://www.nlrb.gov/news-outreach/news-story/nlrb-director-region-13-issues-decision-northwestern-university-athletes

Northwestern University and College Athletes Players Assn (2015, August 17), Case 13-RC-121359. Retrieved December 28, 2015, from https://www.nlrb.gov/news-outreach/news-story/board-unanimously-decides-decline-jurisdiction-northwestern-case

O'Bannon v. NCAA, 7 F. Supp. 3d 955 (N.D. Ca. 2014).

O'Bannon v. NCAA, 802 F. 3d 1049 (9th Cir. 2015).

Ourand, J. (2014, November 3). With major media rights deals done, how will networks grow revenue? *Sports Business Daily*. Retrieved January 27, 2015, from www.sportsbusinessdaily.com/Journal/Issues/2014/11/03/In-Depth/Networks-main.aspx

Pac-12 National Champions. Pac-12.com. Retrieved March 18, 2016, from http://pac-12.com/content/pac-12-national-championships

Patterson, C. (2014, February 11). NCAA recognizes Snapchat as communication tool for recruiting. *CBSsports.com*. Retrieved January 26, 2015, from www.cbssports.com/collegefootball/eye-on-college-football/24439413/ncaa-recognizes-snapchat-as-communication-tool-for-recruiting

Sanderson, A., & Siegfried, J. (Winter 2015). The case for paying college athletes. *Journal of Economic Perspectives, 29*, 115–138. Retrieved December 28, 2015, from http://pubs.aeaweb.org/doi/pdfplus/10.1257/jep.29.1.115

Schwartz, S., & Eder, S. (2014, March 27). College athletes aim to put price on "priceless". *Nytimes.com*. Retrieved January 27, 2015, from http://www.nytimes.com/2014/03/28/sports/ncaafootball/college-athletes-aim-to-put-price-on-priceless.html?hp&_r=1

Scruggs, W. (2003, May 3). Sports as the university's "front porch"? The public is skeptical. *Chronicles*, p. 17.

Selection Committee FAQs (n.d.). Retrieved January 27, 2015, from www.collegefootballplayoff.com/selection-committee-faqs

Silverthorne, S. (2013, April 29). The Flutie Effect: How athletic success boosts college applications. *Forbes.com*. Retrieved January 22, 2015, from http://www.forbes.com/sites/hbsworkingknowledge/2013/04/29/the-flutie-effect-how-athletic-success-boosts-college-applications/

Solomon, J. (2015, Dec. 15). Inside college sports: SEC, Bit Ten dominate 100m revenue club. Retrieved December 18, 2015, from http://www.cbssports.com/collegefootball/writer/jon-solomon/25417211/inside-college-sports-sec-big-ten-dominate-100m-revenue-club

SportsdayDFW.com (2016, May 26). Baylor doesn't fire athletic director amid scandal. Retrieved May 28, 2016, from http://sportsday.dallasnews.com/collegesports/collegesports/2016/05/26/baylor-fire-athletic-director-amid-scandal

Staples, A. (2010, February 17). Time for full-blown conference realignment. *SI.com*. Retrieved February 18, 2010, from http://sportsillustrated.cnn.com/2010/writers/andy_staples/02/16/conference-realignment/1.html

Suggs, D. W. (2012, April 4). Myth: College sports are a cash cow. *Presidency*. Retrieved January 23, 2014, from http://www.acenet.edu/the-presidency/columns-and-features/Pages/Myth-College-Sports-Are-a-Cash-Cow.aspx

Sylwester, M. (2004, April 16). Athletics expenses gobble up revenues. *USA Today*, p. 19C.

Terlep, S. (2015, January 17). NCAA to allow big sports schools to offer full cost-of-attendance scholarships. *The Wall Street Journal*. Retrieved July 2, 2016, from http://www.wsj.com/articles/ncaa-to-allow-big-sports-schools-to-offer-full-cost-of-attendance-scholarships-1421542833

Tracy, M. (2014, August 7). N.C.A.A. votes to give richest conferences more autonomy. Retrieved December 27, 2015, from http://www.ncaa.org/about/resources/media-center/news/board-adopts-new-division-i-structure

4   The International Sports System

Until quite recently, international sports and the resulting competitions have not received the kind of exposure that baseball, football and basketball have in the United States, except for certain cyclical events such as the Olympics, which garner huge coverage. Events such as regional or even international championship tournaments have not enjoyed the public interest and the journalistic scrutiny of the domestic major leagues or college sports. Unfortunately, the lack of interest means that the organizational structure and the resulting issues arising from questions such as eligibility, use of performance-enhancing drugs (PEDs), match fixing and rights and compensation of athletes are relatively unknown to many in the U.S. sports business. However, this is changing, as more issues are being reported (notably in international soccer) and there is greater coverage of international events on American broadcast outlets (Lenskyj, 1998). And more and more colleges and university sports programs have created curriculum featuring international sports issues.

As private entities that "reside" outside of the United States, international sports organizations (known as "federations") are not subject to any legal requirements and obligations under U.S. law. Their structure is more bureaucratic than which is found in the U.S. sports leagues, but somewhat closer to the NCAA system described in the previous chapter.

In the past, the leaders of these international federations could demonstrate a combination of tremendous power and sheer pettiness to a startling degree. Witness this example: Primo Nebiolo (an Italian national), the then-president of track and field's international federation, arranged with Italian field judges to add almost one-half meter to the long jump of an Italian competitor in the 1987 World Track and Field Championship (which conveniently took place in Rome) so that this competitor could win a bronze medal ahead of an American. This stunt was apparently concocted in retaliation for what the Italians thought was a bad call against the Italian competitors at the prior year's world championship (held in Indianapolis). A videotape inadvertently running evidenced the tampering, and the federation was forced, over the great resistance of its president, to strip the bronze medal from the Italian competitor (Weiler & Roberts, 2004, p. 1067).

In essence, international sports are governed by a system created at an earlier time for a different clientele. Based on the notion that only amateurs compete in international events for the glory of their sport and country, the structure remains quite different from the professional leagues found in the United States. This system is replete with multiple layers of governing organizations and complicated and sometimes arbitrary rules of authority. Operating in relative secrecy, these organizations, to put it diplomatically, have been lacking in transparency.

In the last decade, controversies involving international sports governance have become more public. Allegations of corruption, notably payments by governments or individuals to secure international events, have generated headlines. The terms and powers of the leadership of certain organizations also raise questions of proper succession and fair elections. Relations between international federations and their domestic affiliates sometimes have been frayed. Fan racism and hooliganism has reared its head in certain international matches.

The fallout from this has had some positive effect, but as of 2016, it is too early to tell if some of the major organizations will engage in lasting change. In response to unfavorable reports of bribery of Olympic officials and event judges, some international athletic organizations, such as the International Olympic Committee (IOC) and the International Skating Union (ISU), have changed their structure, eligibility rules and scoring systems in competitions. Others, such as FIFA, the governing body for international football (soccer), have not (as of 2016), resulting in full-blown scandals involving charges of racketeering and fraud.

The international sports paradigm, which is often perplexing, falls into several categories and levels of power. At the apex sits the IOC, the umbrella organization for the Olympic movement. Under the IOC, each country participating in an Olympic Games competition (known as an "Olympiad") has a national Olympic committee (NOC). For those cities who seek the Olympic Games, an organizing committee is created. In addition, international athletic federations regulate particular sports. Although not directly part of the Olympic organization, they wield considerable power. Finally, there are domestic organizations affiliated with the international federations, known as national governing bodies (NGBs). The jurisdiction and powers of these entities create an interlocking relationship that sometimes becomes tangled.

Let's use the sport of figure skating as an example to illustrate. Although the IOC is the international body overseeing the Olympics, the United States Olympic Committee (USOC) is the national Olympic committee. The International Skating Union (ISU) is the international federation, and U.S. Figure Skating and U.S. Speed Skating are the NGBs. The respective federation and domestic governing body has a role in regulating the sport, choosing Olympic athletes and regulating both international and Olympic competition.

The ISU is fairly typical of the makeup of an international sporting federation. There is a president; vice-presidents for the figure skating and speedskating branches; committees handling discipline, technical matters, medical issues and development; and a group of honorary members (ISU. org, 2016). A detailed discussion of the organizational structure of certain international federations is found later in the chapter.

The International Olympic Committee

Background

From modest beginnings as a revival of an ancient Greek tradition, the Olympics have become one of the most glamorous events on the world stage and possibly the most prestigious brand in sports (Bitting, 1998). As a consequence, it is viewed by billions of people.

The Olympic Games are governed by the IOC, the best-known and most powerful body in international sports. Headquartered in Lausanne, Switzerland, the IOC is a nonprofit, nongovernmental entity that serves as caretaker of the modern Olympics. Founded in 1894 by the French educator Baron Pierre de Coubertin, the IOC's original mandate was to revive the ancient Greek Games. According to IOC rules, the organization grants rights to stage quadrennial Summer and Winter Games. Since 1994, the Summer and Winter Games alternate every two years. For example, the 2014 Winter Games were held in Sochi, Russia, and the 2016 games took place in Rio de Janeiro, Brazil. Pyeongchang, South Korea, is the site of the 2018 Winter Games, and Tokyo will hold the 2020 Summer Games.

The IOC serves three major functions. First, it is an umbrella organization for the various domestic affiliates known as national Olympic committees (NOCs). Second, it interacts with the international sports federations, which control particular sports and are discussed in more detail later in the chapter. Third, the IOC owns and controls the intellectual property rights, such as copyrights, trademarks and other intangible properties associated with the Olympic Games. These include such familiar symbols as the five interlocking rings, the Olympic motto ("citius, altius, fortius," which translates to "swifter, higher, stronger") and the flame (Masteralexis, Barr, & Hums, 1998).

Although the IOC is a nongovernmental organization, the Olympic Charter, the IOC's governing document, states that any person or organization involved with the Olympic movement "shall accept the supreme authority of the IOC and shall be bound by its Rules and submit to its jurisdiction," thereby creating a powerful mandate for compliance. The IOC is a United Nations–like organization governing the premier event in international sports competition, but inherently more powerful. The United Nations is a confederation of nation-states that try to achieve world cooperation, but often exhibit national self-interest in the debates involving political and security questions. The secretary-general, the UN's equivalent of a chief executive officer, cannot impose his or her values unilaterally. The IOC, on the other hand, has traditionally selected strong-willed individuals to serve as presidents, aided by a compliant board often made up of allies of that president. The IOC president traditionally carries the authority vested in professional league commissioners but is not subject to checks and balances of constituencies such as players' unions (because none exist) or general public scrutiny. One commentator said, "Although the IOC cannot compel governmental compliance, the Olympic Charter reflects current international practice and is thus almost as binding as the law itself" (Ansley, 1995).

This last point marks a key difference between a major international sports organization like the IOC and American professional leagues. The IOC and other international sports organizations take a more holistic (or, if one wishes to be cynical, a self-aggrandizing) attitude, whereas the professional leagues approach their respective sports as a part of an entertainment business. For example, the Olympics are considered "movements," whereas the U.S. leagues are considered businesses providing sports events to millions of people.

As will be noted, the cities that host an Olympic Games take considerable risks. They are responsible for facility construction, financing and general logistics, but only receive a percentage of the broadcast rights secured by the IOC. For the IOC, the broadcast rights fees continue to increase. The majority of the IOC's budget comes from the rights fees for the Summer Games, which include NBC's U.S. television rights fees of $1.226 billion for 2016 and $1.418 billion for the 2020 games (Associated Press, 2011). For example, for the 2008 Beijing Games, the IOC earned $1.7 billion in rights fees; for 2012 in London, it increased to $2.6 billion, with $1.1 billion from NBC. About 20 percent of that money went to national Olympic committees.

Currently, the 106 active members of the IOC meet at least once a year. The members elect a president for an eight-year term, renewable for one additional period of four years, and also elect an executive board whose members serve four-year terms. IOC members include fifteen active Olympic athletes elected by their peers at the Olympic Games. Another fifteen members come from international federations, fifteen from the national Olympic committees, and seventy others are individual, nonaffiliated members (Olympic Charter, 2015, Chapter 2, Rule 16–1). The mandatory retirement age for IOC members, including the president, is seventy. After the expiration of former president Jacques Rogge's term in 2013, the IOC voted to approve Thomas Bach as his successor.

The executive board, consisting of the IOC president, four vice-presidents, and ten other members, is the backbone of IOC governance, akin to a board of directors in a corporation (Olympic Charter, 2015, Chapter 2, Rule 19–1). The board assumes the "ultimate responsibility" for the administration of the IOC by managing the IOC's finances, preparing annual reports, conducting the procedure for acceptance and selection of candidates for the organization of the Olympic Games and enacting "all regulations necessary" to ensure the proper implementation of the Olympic Charter and the organization of the Olympic Games (Olympic Charter, 2015, Chapter 2, Rule 19–3).

Marketing the Event

The Olympic Games are awarded to different cities, so a different organization must plan each event. Known as an "Olympic organizing committee," it controls the facility construction, living arrangements, transportation and media services. The committee must also "sell" the event to the public. If the particular Olympics are successful, then the resulting favorable publicity promotes tourism and leaves that city with new facilities for sports and other functions for future years. In one sense, Olympics preparations become an urban renewal project.

The "selling" of the event is crucial because the host city keeps about 95 percent of the revenue from ticket sales, but, as noted earlier, obtains little from the lucrative broadcast rights and corporate sponsorships, the major sources of income. Certain cities hosted successful Games—Los Angeles in 1984, Barcelona in 1992, Sydney in 2000 and Salt Lake City in 2002. Others were a financial or political disaster, such as Montreal's Games in 1976, which almost bankrupted the city and the province of Quebec. The Munich Olympics in 1972 were marred by the murder of eleven Israeli athletes by Palestinian terrorists. Moscow's Games in 1980 were hurt by the boycott by the United States and other nations protesting the Soviet invasion of Afghanistan. The more recent 2014 Winter Games at Sochi resulted in an astounding total cost of over $50 billion (Panja, 2014). The cost—far more than any other Winter or Summer Games, resulted in a general reluctance of cities to bid for the 2022 Games, which Beijing won in a close vote over Almaty, Kazakhstan.

In the post-9/11 environment, host cities have to pay far more for security than in the past. As noted earlier, the costs for the 2008 Beijing Summer Games and the 2014 Sochi Winter Games greatly surpassed any other Games, and the increase in security costs factored into these amounts. For example, the security cost for the Sydney games in 2000 was $200 million. That jumped to $1.5 billion in Athens. For the Beijing Summer Games, that figure jumped to $6.5 billion, which included 300,000 video cameras and 100,000 antiterrorism squad members (Magnier, 2008). For the London Summer Games, security costs were estimated at $1.6 billion, including $862 million in expenses to secure the venues and other sensitive sites (Associated Press, 2011). The security costs for the Sochi Winter Olympics jumped to about $3 billion, a figure including the installation of 1400 video cameras across the city (Bushuev, 2014). Brazil deployed a security force of 85,000 in Rio, which was more than double the number used in London (Dow Jones Business News, 2016; Kaiser & Jacobs, 2016). Although the Rio Games did not have any terrorist incidents, street crime was a major concern. During the games, an Olympic official and several athletes were mugged at gunpoint (Kaiser & Jacobs, 2016).

Because of the prestige of the event, the IOC has been highly successful in attracting blue-chip sponsors, who pay large sums to attain the designation of "Top Olympic Sponsor." The fees for "Top Olympic Partner" ("TOP") increased to $200 million per sponsor, a doubling from the previous amount (Mickle, 2014a). The TOP level runs for four years, and as of 2015 it includes well-known brands such as Coca-Cola, General Electric, McDonald's, Panasonic, Procter & Gamble, Samsung and Visa. These revenues help clear the IOC's balance sheet (Mickle, 2014a).

Although several levels exist, these top-level sponsors receive exclusive marketing rights and opportunities within their designated product category and can exercise these rights on a worldwide basis (Olympic. org, 2010). These sponsors may develop marketing programs with the IOC, the national Olympic committees and the Olympic sites' organizing committees.

As part of their sponsorship, these companies receive rights to use Olympic trademarks, showcase their products at Olympic locations and are protected from ambush marketing (a technique whereby competitors attempt to market their products near the official Olympic sites). A discussion of these rules and requirements is found in Chapter 14.

Broadcast Rights

Broadcast rights bring substantial sums to the IOC and fees to the host cities. For example, NBC has paid $4.38 billion and $7.65 billion for the rights to broadcast the 2016 to 2020 Games (Sandomir, 2011) and the 2022 to 2032 Games (Olympic.org, 2014), respectively. Hosting the Olympic Games may bring positive publicity to the host city, but often results in considerable costs and controversy. Some cities, such as Montreal, Barcelona and Sydney, took years to pay the costs of hosting the Games (Merron, 2003; Crouse, 1998), whereas others, such as Salt Lake City, ended up with a small profit (Abrahamson, 2002). The Athens Games were estimated to cost Greek taxpayers over $11 billion (BBC News, 2004), but the 2008 Beijing Olympics, despite a price tag of $42 billion, reportedly earned a slight profit of $16 million (*China Sports Review*, 2009) as did the 2012 London Games (London Organising Committee, 2013). The 2014 Winter Games at Sochi cost over $50 billion, eclipsing Beijing's $40 billion as the costliest Olympics ever held (Yaffa, 2014).

The Scandals

The procedures for selecting host cities for the Olympic Games have received considerable attention in the wake of past scandals involving the selection process. Responding to improper conduct revealed during the bidding for the 2002 Winter Olympics in Salt Lake City, the present IOC structure reflects the changes implemented after a pattern of improper conduct between IOC members and the local organizing committee was revealed in 2002. Nine IOC members were censured and four others resigned due to the payoffs by the organizing committee to those IOC officials (Longman & Thomas, 1999).

As a result, in 1999 the IOC voted to ban all-expenses-paid visits to cities bidding for the Olympics. Also, as part of those reforms, the IOC established a new ethics watchdog, made up of three IOC delegates and five independent members (Shipley, 1999). Other changes include the abolishment of visits by IOC members to candidate cities, and, notably for journalists, the release of financial reports on the sources and uses of the Olympic movement's income, an important window into the fiscal policies of the IOC.

Yet, the political intrigue in the selection of host cities continues. Rumors of political considerations in the selection of Beijing have been alleged (ABC News, 2008). It has been suggested that Chicago's surprising first-round elimination from the 2016 Summer Games bid was due to poor relations between the IOC and the United States Olympic Committee and the fact that many Europeans voted for Madrid (considered a weaker candidate) in deference to the former IOC head Juan Antonio Samaranch, who, in either a poignant ode or a calculated political gambit (depending on one's point of view), stated: "I am very near the end of my time. I ask you to consider granting my country the honor and the duty of hosting the Olympic and Paralympic Games in 2016" (Futterman, Moffett, & Belkin, 2009).

Economic and political stability are also factors. For example, for 2020, the IOC unsurprisingly accepted Tokyo's bid over Madrid and Istanbul. Tokyo was considered a "safe" choice given the high unemployment and economic recession in Spain and the political instability and turmoil in Turkey's regional area (Longman & Fackler 2013). It may turn out that Tokyo is not as "safe" a bid. As of the end of 2016, costs increased to four times the bid amount, and the city is seeking cheaper venues for some of the events. Also, the proposed Olympic stadium was replaced with a less costly version (Armstrong & Yamaguchi, 2016).

Despite the controversies and the changes, the IOC's considerable power remains largely intact and is felt by national Olympic committees, international sports federations and domestic affiliates of those sports federations.

Professionalism

At one time, only amateur athletes were eligible to compete in the Olympic Games, disqualifying anyone who received any compensation for his or her athletic pursuits. Jim Thorpe, one of the great all-around athletes of his time, won the gold medal in the decathlon at the 1912 Summer Games in Stockholm. When it was discovered that Thorpe played semi-professional baseball, the IOC stripped him of his medal (Flatter, 2007).

The strict amateur policy dates from the advent of the modern Olympic Games. In the nineteenth and early twentieth centuries, working-class people did not have the time for or access to sports facilities. The amateurism requirement limited competition to the wealthy, because the average laborer could not afford to train, travel and compete. The rigid adherence to amateurism later became hypocritical when Communist states used it to great advantage. During the Cold War, athletes from Soviet-bloc countries often had government or military positions, but devoted much, if not all, of their time to training and competing in athletic events. For example, many Olympic ice hockey players were members of the Soviet Central Army team. They worked in the military, but, of course, never served in any infantry position. The United States and other non-Communist countries accused the Soviets and other Soviet-bloc nations of de facto compensation of their athletes. In response, the Soviets alleged that the United States college system, whereby athletes often received full scholarships, was also a type of compensation.

The IOC relaxed the strict amateur standard in 1986. Presently, professional athletes are permitted to compete under rules stipulated by the particular sport's international federation. Amateurism versus professionalism has not been a controversial Olympic issue since that time.

Dispute Resolution

Arbitration is the IOC's preferred method of dispute resolution and, since 1994, all Olympic disputes (and many disputes involving international athletic federations) fall under the jurisdiction of the Court of Arbitration for Sport (CAS), an arbitration panel formed by the IOC. When an athlete signs the entry form into the Olympics, he or she consents to the court's jurisdiction to arbitrate disputes arising during the Games. When a dispute occurs, an application is submitted to the CAS and the arbitration panel is required to render a written decision within twenty-four hours. The ruling is final and binding and may not be appealed or challenged (CAS Arbitration Rules for the Olympic Games, 2012, Article 21). The CAS procedure applies even if the athlete participates in a sport whose international federation has its own arbitration system for resolving disputes because the IOC's rules take precedence.

Generally, two types of disputes may be submitted to the CAS. The first focuses on contractual issues involving teams, players and sponsors. Disciplinary cases represent the second group of disputes submitted to the CAS, of which a large number are doping related. In addition to doping cases, the CAS is called upon to rule on various disciplinary cases, such as in-game violence and abuse of officials (CAS Bulletin, 2015, Page 7).

No matter where the arbitrations are held, they are governed by the CAS rules, which state that arbitrators base their decisions on the Olympic Charter and "general principles of law" (CAS Arbitration Rules for the Olympic Games, 2012, Article 17).

Ethical Issue: Does Hosting the Olympics Actually Pay Off?

Hosting an Olympic Games is high risk with a possible high reward. Cities have been able to leverage the Olympics as a way to improve their infrastructure and create a positive image that could potentially increase tourism and reputational capital. For some cities, this worked very well. Tokyo in 1964 brought the city (and, by extension, Japan) goodwill and was proof of the nation's development less than two decades from defeat and destruction after World War II. Seoul (in 1988) showed a dynamic city in a country transitioning to a democratically elected state. However, for others, as noted earlier, the Olympics were a financial and political disaster. The image of Munich in 1972 is forever scarred by the terrorist killings of Israeli athletes mentioned earlier. Montreal in 1976 was saddled with billions in debt after the games. More recently, the Sochi games were marked by huge cost and major controversies involving gender rights and drug testing violations. In 2009, Rio, then riding on an economic wave, won the right to host the 2016 Olympics, but since then, it has endured economic hardship and an impeachment of its president. Coming at the heels of the expenses from the 2014 World Cup, one had to wonder how the city (and Brazil) could undertake such a challenge. Past Olympics also have left cities with "white elephant" infrastructure, such as hulking stadia rarely used in Athens (Bloor, 2014) and Beijing (SINA. com, 2012), which resulted in the deterioration of their Olympic facilities in the years after the event.

Although projects like new highways and public transportation are part and parcel of many Olympics, many economists are skeptical about the general economic uplift resulting from the Olympics. Some tourists may not want to go near a city during an Olympic Games period, and some residents may want to leave, not wanting to put up with the inconveniences. Britain received about 5 percent fewer foreign visitors in August 2012 than it did in the same month the previous year. As one sports writer noted, "[I]t's misleading to calculate how much money is spent in a city during the Olympics. A fair comparison requires some estimate of how much would have been spent without them" (Applebaum, 2014).

Should the International Olympic Committee change its policy regarding host cities? Should there be one or two "permanent" locations to host the Games? Should cities bid as a group to avoid excessive costs?

National Olympic Committees

Each nation competing in the Olympics must have a "national Olympic committee" or NOC. The NOCs "shall be the sole authorities responsible for the representation of their respective countries at the Olympic Games as well as at other events held under the patronage of the IOC" (Bitting, 1998) (sec. 27, Olympic Charter, 2014). Presently, 205 NOCs promote the principles of the Olympics at a national level and are committed to the development of athletes in their respective countries. In the United States, the NOC is the United States Olympic Committee.

Sometimes an uneasy relationship exists between the International Olympic Committee, the national Olympic committees and their respective governments. In 2013, the IOC president Thomas Bach spoke about the need for governments to protect the autonomy of sports organizations and the need for sports organizations to conduct their business by "demonstrating good governance" (Carpenter, 2013). In some cases, the IOC has taken the steps of suspending NOCs for alleged governmental interference in their operations. This happened in India, Sri Lanka and Egypt.

An IOC suspension of a particular NOC means that athletes from that country cannot compete under the flag of their country, but only under the Olympic flag. Suspension also results in the stripping of financial support by the IOC. It can take some time to get back into the good graces of the IOC. The Indian Olympic Association's December 2012 suspension over alleged corruption, for example, lasted fourteen months and was lifted during the Sochi Olympics, which was the first time in Olympic history that such a reinstatement was issued during competition (Independent, 2014).

Yet, this kind of super-governmental authority of the IOC may have benefits and can serve as a check on human rights abuses by particular governments. The Olympic Charter guarantees that engaging in sports is a human right and every individual must have the possibility of participating without discrimination of any kind (Olympic Charter, sec. 1. 4, 2014).

Ethical Issue: The Sochi Olympics

The 2014 Sochi Winter Olympics was arguably the "most geopolitically charged" Olympic Games in recent years due to environmental and economic concerns, threats of terror attacks and social unrest (Friedman, 2014). For many, especially in the West, the Russian government's stance on gay rights, however, caused particular controversy. In June 2013, the Russian parliament unanimously passed a bill into effect that prohibits the spreading of "propaganda of non-traditional sexual relations" among minors (Elder, 2013). The legislation allowed the government to detain foreigners for up to fifteen days, issue fines of up to 100,000 rubles and deport violators. The law also imposed fines on Russian citizens who disseminate "homosexual propaganda" through the media or Internet, while organizations faced a ninety-day period of closure in addition to fines of up to 1 million rubles. Russian President Vladimir Putin signed the law into effect later that month, inciting anger and criticism from rights activists and Western governments (Malkin, 2013).

Gay rights protests were held in major cities across the globe in the days leading up to Sochi's Opening Ceremony in hopes of persuading Olympic sponsors to issue public statements against the Russian government and its discriminatory laws. Many rights activists argued that the Russian legislation was contrary to the goals of the Olympic movement and the Olympic spirit. Marie Campbell, a director at the LGBT rights organization "All Out," expressed the rationale behind these protests by stating that the discrimination in Russia cannot be ignored and that "these anti-gay laws are preventing the Olympic values being lived and enjoyed by millions of people" (BBC.com, 2014).

Many corporations, including non-Olympic and Olympic sponsors, contributed to the advocacy of gay rights through antidiscrimination statements and advertising. For example, USOC sponsor AT&T condemned the Russian law in a blog post on its corporate website and stated "we support LGBT equality globally and we condemn violence, discrimination, and harassment targeted against LGBT individuals everywhere" (The Associated Press, 2014). Google utilized its homepage to express its support by incorporating a doodle of athletes performing winter sports with a rainbow-colored backdrop, which was representative of the rainbow gay pride flag and linked to search results for the Olympic Charter. Beneath its search bar, Google also displayed the Olympic Charter's fourth principle in its entirety:

> The practice of sport is a human right. Every individual must have the possibility of practicing sport, without discrimination of any kind and in the Olympic spirit, which requires mutual understanding with a spirit of friendship, solidarity and fair play.
>
> (Guynn, 2014)

The Coca-Cola Company, who has sponsored the Olympic movement since 1928, did not explicitly make a statement on the Russian law; however, the company did re-air one of its Super Bowl commercials during the opening ceremonies that celebrates American diversity and features two gay dads (Socarides, 2014).

As a result of this controversy, the IOC has since added an antidiscrimination clause to its contracts with future host cities. This clause was first introduced to the three bidders of the 2022 Winter Olympics—Norway, Almaty and Beijing—in September 2014 and states "any form of discrimination with regard to a country or a person on grounds of race, religion, politics, gender or otherwise is incompatible with belonging to the Olympic movement" (Gibson, 2014b). Andre Banks, cofounder of All Out, was a key proponent for such a provision and stated that the IOC's clause is a "significant step in ensuring the protection of both citizens and athletes around the world" (Rhodan, 2014).

Do you think that these actions are adequate to avoid future antigay laws and discriminatory policies by potential host nations? Or should the IOC do more? Conversely, should the IOC and its supporters be less public in their efforts to ensure that gay athletes and gay people in general are protected?

A related issue involves the rights of transgender athletes. What protections should they have? Should that include competing as their desired sex? With the rise of transgender awareness in the United States and some other countries, the eligibility issues may be an increasingly important subject in future years.

Ethical Issue: The Russian Olympic Drug Scandal and the Rio Olympics

Chapter 12 outlines the wholesale violation of performance-enhancing drug testing protocols by Russian sports officials in the 2014 Sochi Olympics to manipulate the results of those tests by tampering with the samples. Consequently, athletes who were doping could not be caught. Once this leaked, the International Olympic Committee was thrust in the position of having to decide whether to ban the entire Russian team on the eve of the Rio Olympics (the Russian track and field athletes were banned by the international track federation, as noted later in this chapter). Banning a large nation like Russia with a tradition of Olympic medal success would have been an extraordinary action. Although the IOC concluded that the "presumption of taint" on the part of Russian athletes existed, it assigned the respective international federations the task of scrutinizing hundreds of athletes less than two weeks before the start of the games. Some of these federations had close ties with Russia (Ruiz, 2016). Although the Russian team was depleted, many Russian athletes did compete in Rio.

Do you think that the IOC should have decided on the ban or at least made the determination on a case-by-case basis, rather than compelling the federations to engage in this task? What are the long-range implications for the integrity of the Olympic Games in the wake of this decision?

The United States Olympic Committee

History

Created in 1896, the year of the first modern Olympic Games, the USOC is a nonprofit corporation unique among national Olympic committees. Unlike other NOCs, which are government funded, the USOC obtains the majority of its funding from public donations and corporate sponsorships.

Throughout most of its history, the USOC had surprisingly little power. Unlike many countries whose Olympic committees are government arms, the USOC is, at best, only quasi-governmental. As the "coordinating body" over all amateur athletic activity within the United States, it has exclusive jurisdiction over "all matters pertaining to the United States' participation in the Olympic Games" and is the "ultimate authority with respect to United States' representation in the Olympic Games" (*Foschi v. United States Swimming, Inc.*, 1996). The USOC has the authority to recognize a national governing body for any amateur sport. Although this sounds like a powerful mandate, for many years the USOC was subordinate to powerful amateur athletic organizations. According to one commentator, the USOC was little more than a travel agency that sent athletes to the Olympic sites every four years (De Varona, 2003).

While other countries were developing coordinated Olympic programs, the USOC was embroiled in jurisdictional problems throughout the 1950s and early 1960s. Three competing amateur sports organizations fought over athlete eligibility. First was the Amateur Athletic Union (AAU), which at the time was the national governing body for ten Olympic sports. Second was the school/college sports community. Finally, a number of non–AAU-affiliated independent national governing bodies that did not have school/college participation in their sports sought consideration in Olympic team selection. As a result, the selection of the best athletes was haphazard, and, to make matters worse, no dispute resolution mechanism existed to solve or address these problems.

In the mid-1970s, President Gerald Ford formed a commission to present recommendations for revising the organization of Olympic sports, resolving disputes and improving ways to finance Olympic sports in America. No disagreement surfaced on the central issue: the USOC had to be changed dramatically. Acting on the commission's recommendations, Congress passed the Amateur Sports Act of 1978 (now the Ted Stevens Olympic and Amateur Sports Act), which mandated the USOC as the one entity responsible for coordinating all Olympic athletic activity (Ted Stevens Olympic and Amateur Sports Act, 36 USC, sec. 220504).

United States Olympic Committee Structure

A key goal of the 1978 Amateur Sports Act was to strengthen the USOC. Unfortunately, the result served as a case study in bad policy making because the law did not create a practical structure. A bloated policy board and executive committee with confusing reporting structures set the stage for frequent disputes. Two uncoordinated chains of command occurred, with some members reporting to the USOC president and others reporting to the chief executive officer (CEO).

The law "suggested" that the USOC president, a twenty-three-member executive committee, and a 125-member board set policies for the organization. Yet the CEO and his or her paid staff implemented the policies while also raising money. The president and CEO often fought over control and the use of that money. This created a revolving door of CEOs and presidents. From 1978 to 2003, the USOC had thirteen CEOs and eleven presidents (Scott, 2004).

In 2003, responding to political pressures and bad publicity, the USOC agreed to eliminate twenty members of the executive committee and reduce the 125-member board to eleven. The board now consists of six directors who have no USOC ties, three NGB representatives and three athlete representatives (USOC Bylaws, 2015). In addition, the board will include two to three U.S. IOC members with limited voting power of one vote each.

Powers

The Amateur Sports Act of 1978 mandated that the USOC was responsible for coordinating international sporting events for the U.S. NGBs (Ted Stevens Olympic and Amateur Sports Act, 36 USC sec. 220504). The USOC was allowed to recognize one national governing body per sport, eliminating the earlier jurisdictional overlaps between different organizations claiming to represent the same sport. Once recognized, all the selected NGBs were required to report to the USOC. Although not a government agency, the USOC became a "quasi-governmental" organization because the law mandated that it periodically report to Congress. However, Congress does not oversee the USOC on a day-to-day basis, leaving the USOC largely unchecked, but that could change if the USOC does not resolve its problems.

To make matters worse, relations between the USOC and IOC became particularly fraught, which may have contributed to the failure of the bid by the city of Chicago to host the 2016 Summer Games (which ultimately went to Rio). Relations between the USOC and IOC became tense after the USOC intended to create an Olympic television network without the approval of the IOC. Also, many IOC members felt that the USOC's share of global sponsorships and TV rights was excessive at 20 percent and 12.75 percent, respectively, and that the contract ought to be renegotiated (Associated Press, 2012).

A revised revenue-sharing agreement made in 2012 has been attributed as the catalyst for the improved relationship between the IOC and USOC. The new contract, which will become effective in 2020, reportedly reduced the USOC's TV rights and sponsorship revenue shares to 7 and 10 percent, respectively. After the contract was announced, Anita DeFrantz, who is a U.S. IOC member and USOC board member, expressed her belief that the new contract signifies that "there is no longer any barrier (to a [U.S.] bid) or bad will" (Associated Press, 2012). The resulting goodwill from the renegotiated revenue deal has since translated into a more hands-on involvement from USOC officials with IOC matters.

USOC Chairman Larry Probst's nomination in July 2013 and eventual confirmation for membership to the IOC signified "a thaw in the chilly relationship" between the two parties (Pilon, 2013). Probst has also become chairman of the IOC's press commission, and USOC CEO Scott Blackmun was appointed a member of the IOC's marketing commission. Perhaps the most significant evidence of the repaired relationship under Probst and Blackmun's leadership was the USOC's involvement in the most recent negotiations between NBC and the IOC, which resulted in a $7.65 billion extension with NBC for rights to the 2022–32 Olympic Games (Mickle, 2014b).

Resolution of Disputes

Because of court orders preventing the USOC from taking action against the figure skater Tonya Harding for her alleged role in the assault against Nancy Kerrigan in January 1994, Congress amended the Amateur Sports Act in 1998 to strengthen the USOC's arbitration system. Under the amendments, a court may generally not impose any injunction against the USOC within twenty-one days of the beginning of a major competition. The amendments also established the office of an ombudsman, who, among other powers, may seek to mediate disputes (Ted Stevens Olympic and Amateur Sports Act, 36 USC, sec. 220509).

In 2004, the USOC adopted new bylaws covering the rights of athletes, coaches, trainers, managers or other officials seeking participation in the conduct of international amateur athletic competitions (USOC Bylaws, sec. 9.1). Aggrieved parties may submit their claims to arbitration within six months of the alleged denial of rights (USOC Bylaws sec. 9.10).

Sponsorships

USOC partners receive marketing rights to the U.S. Olympic team and commercial access to the USA five-ring logo and Olympic themes, terminology and imagery for use in sponsor marketing programs. This level of sponsorship is limited to the United States and is not a part of the IOC's international sponsorship program. Several levels of sponsorship exist. The top two are "partner level" and "sponsor level" companies, which have access to the previously mentioned items and the rights to list the year in which they first became Olympic sponsors or partners. Since the 2012 Summer Olympics, the USOC has signed four new sponsors through the Rio Olympics, including Dick's Sporting Goods, Airweave, USG and the J.M. Smucker Company (Fischer, 2016a). Additionally, the USOC has signed two new sponsors through the 2020 Olympics—Hershey Co. in 2015 for an undisclosed amount and MilkPep in 2016 for $8 to $10 million (Fischer, 2016b). As of 2015, companies who are seeking a sponsor-level partnership with the USOC are expected to pay between $1 and $3 million annually (Fischer, 2015). Other "partners" as of 2016 include Coca-Cola, General Electric, McDonald's and Visa, and "sponsors" include Liberty Mutual Insurance, Nike and United Airlines (USOC, 2016).

International Federations

International federations are the worldwide governing bodies of various sports subject only to the limitations of the Olympic Charter. A federation's responsibilities include conducting international competitions, detailing eligibility rules, choosing judges and referees for competitions (including the Olympic Games), organizing world championships and resolving technical issues in their sport. By their nature the international federations have a more centralized decision-making structure. Often powerful and sometimes autocratic presidents or CEOs have led international federations.

In order to receive and maintain recognition from the IOC, international federations must agree to comply with the Olympic Charter and other IOC criteria. The federations are officially recognized upon approval by the IOC executive board. Like the IOC, for many decades, most international federations limited membership to amateur athletes. Most, if not all, now allow professionals to compete. Athlete challenges to international federation rulings on disputes are heard by the Court of Arbitration for Sport, which handles similar appeals involving Olympic athletes.

FIFA, the federation that controls international soccer, and the IAAF, which runs track and field, are two of the most well-known international federations. However, there are many more, and a list of the international federations for each international sport recognized by the IOC, along with their websites, is found at the end of this chapter.

National Governing Bodies

Each international federation has a corresponding national governing body. An NGB is an organization in charge of running the sport in a given country. The particular international federation generally recognizes one domestic body as an NGB. The NGBs set eligibility standards for domestic participation in the sport, such as age limitations and professionalism. They also conduct competitions for selecting teams to participate in international competitions organized under the aegis of the international federation or the IOC. National governing bodies must abide by the rules of their corresponding international federation, as well as those of the IOC. Yet conflicts between the international federations and the NGBs have arisen in recent years regarding arbitration rules.

The United States Olympic Committee's bylaws outline the duties of NGBs in the United States. They include establishing written procedures to select athletes, coaches and team leaders for the Olympic, Pan American and Paralympic Games teams; selecting site(s) and date(s) to qualify for the Olympic, Pan American and Paralympic Games teams; recommending a training plan for Olympic, Pan American and Paralympic Games team members; establishing programs for the development of its sport; and preparing the requirements of its sport for submission to the USOC for apparel, supplies, equipment, training services and transportation to service the Olympic, Pan American and Paralympic teams (USOC Bylaws, sec. 8). The NGBs also must participate in the international federation activities of their sport and carry out those responsibilities required by the international federations. In the United States, the Ted Stevens Olympic and Amateur Sports Act requires that NGBs "agree to submit to binding arbitration . . . the opportunity of any amateur athlete . . . to participate in amateur athletic competition, upon demand of the corporation or any aggrieved amateur athlete" (36 USC, sec. 220522(a)(4)(B)(2003).

We next examine the structures of the international federations and national governing bodies representing track and field, figure skating and swimming.

Examples of International Federations and National Governing Bodies

Track and Field

International Federation—International Association of Athletics Federations (IAAF)

First established in 1912, the IAAF governs racing, walking and other track and field events. In 1982, the sport moved away from its traditional "amateur" eligibility to the present rules allowing professionals to compete in its events. For example, the IAAF now offers prize money for its competitions based on a points system, as well as additional bonuses for outstanding performances such as breaking world records. The organization has procured increased financing from areas such as corporate sponsorship—a departure from merely collecting membership fees.

Headquartered in Monaco, the IAAF has 214 affiliated NGBs. The IAAF Council, the central body administering all IAAF affairs, includes the president, treasurer, four vice-presidents, six representatives and fifteen individual members. Six committees and eight commissions assist the council. Council members are elected for four years, with the exception of the general secretary, who is appointed by the council (IAAF Constitution, 2012, Article 6).

In 2015 and 2016, allegations of widespread doping by Russian competitors, coupled with allegation of bribery by leaders of the IAAF, rocked the world of international sports. The World Anti-Doping Agency's November 2015 report revealed that "the acceptance of cheating at all levels is widespread and of long standing" within the international federation and that the 2012 London Olympics were "sabotaged" by athletes belonging to the Russian Athletics Federation (ARAF) (Webb, 2015). Many ARAF athletes won numerous Olympic medals during the 2012 Games after their drug abuse had been effectively covered up by seemingly negative reissued results by a laboratory in Moscow. As a result of these state-sponsored doping accusations, the ARAF was suspended from international competition, and three senior IAAF officials—Papa Massata Diack (son of former IAAF President Lamine Diack), Valentin Balakhnichev and Alexei Melnikov—received lifetime bans for engaging in beyond unethical behavior, including "blackmailing athletes and covering up positive drug tests" (Ziegler, 2016). Even more drastic was the IAAF's ban on participation in the Rio Olympics for all Russian track and field athletes, except for those who can prove they were "not tainted" because they have been outside the country and subject to rigorous testing—they could individually petition to compete (Ruiz, 2016).

Michael Johnson, a former American sprinter who won four Olympic gold medals, said that he believed the IAAF needed to be "completely restructured" and that this scandal is "absolutely worse" compared to that of FIFA (BBC.com, 2016). World Anti-Doping Agency (WADA) officials added that the leadership council in which IAAF President Sebastian Coe served on "could not have been unaware of the extent of doping and the non-enforcement of applicable doping rules" that has plagued the IAAF's reputation (Papenfuss, 2016).

Many of the IAAF's sponsors have terminated sponsorship deals with the federation after the allegations surfaced. In 2016, Adidas reportedly informed the IAAF of its decision to terminate its eleven-year sponsorship deal four years early because of the doping scandal (Daly & Roan 2016). The IAAF is expected to lose nearly $30 million over the next four years as a result of Adidas' severance of ties. As of the summer of 2016, no specific plans to reorganize the IAAF have been announced.

NGB—USA Track & Field (USATF)

The USATF is the IAAF NOG in the United States. It inherited that role from the old Amateur Athletic Union (AAU), which dated from 1878. The AAU governed track and field until 1979, when the Amateur Sports Act decreed that the AAU could no longer hold international franchises for more than one sport. The officers and members of the USATF board, the chairs of all the committees and twelve delegates from each association are permitted to vote at meetings. In addition, it requires that 20 percent of the delegates be athletes. Since the mid-1980s, USATF events have been open to professionals. The USATF has fifty-seven regional associations (USA Track & Field Bylaws 2010, Article 7). Disputes between athletes and the USATF are first submitted to an appellate tribunal. If one party wishes a further appeal, the CAS assumes jurisdiction. Its rulings are final.

In the past, the USATF has suffered organizational and economic difficulties. Track and field lacks consistent popularity, which makes finding sponsors difficult. As a result, the organization has limited economic resources to stage competitions and otherwise promote the sport. Even worse, the USATF has been embroiled in controversy over its drug-testing rules. The IOC criticized the USATF for permitting the sprinter Jerome Young to run in the 2000 Sydney Olympics after having tested positive in the prior year for a banned steroid (Abrahamson, 2003).

In a not-so-veiled criticism of USATF governance, in 2003 the USOC's board voted unanimously to mandate that USATF update its bylaws, improve its financial reporting and improve its coordination with the United States Anti-Doping Agency (the agency now in charge of drug testing). Things did not improve, and in 2008 the USOC once again urged USATF to reform its organization structure and threatened to eliminate funding and even to decertify the body. Ultimately, major governance changes were adopted reducing the board of directors from thirty-one to fifteen members and giving the CEO greater powers (Mickle, 2008). More recently, USATF President Stephanie Hightower drew criticism over her appointment of "political allies and friends" to positions in the organization. One of the appointees was suspended by the Amateur Athletic Union for her "extravagant expenditures" (Reid, 2015).

Swimming

International Federation—Fédération Internationale de Natation Amateur (FINA)

FINA governs competitive swimming and other aquatic sports, including water polo, diving and synchronized swimming at the international level. The national body governing swimming in any country is eligible for membership in FINA.

FINA's central governing group, known as "the bureau," consists of seventeen members: the president, honorary secretary, honorary treasurer, five vice-presidents and nine additional members. Its duties are to encourage development of swimming throughout the world, to ensure uniformity of rules and to adopt rules for the control of competitions, as well as many other functions. The bureau is elected by the General Congress (FINA Constitution, Article 17.3).

As is typical in many international federations, FINA has an intricate organizational structure. The General Congress, the highest authority of FINA, has the power to decide upon all matters arising in FINA. The Technical Congress decides on all technical matters concerning the sports under FINA's jurisdiction. Both congresses meet once a year. The bureau's powers include interpreting and enforcing FINA rules, deciding on bylaws and, not insignificantly, making decisions in case of "emergency" (FINA Constitution, Article 17.14).

In the past, FINA had its share of problems, most notably allegations of performance-enhancing drug use. This issue was at the forefront in the 1990s, when the Chinese swim team suddenly started dominating in a sport where it had previously made modest showings. Despite various protests, FINA claimed that doping was limited to individual Chinese athletes, but rejected the claim that it was part of a systematic pattern of abuse by the Chinese Swimming Federation. During the Asian Games in 1994, seven female Chinese swimmers tested positive for anabolic steroids and were suspended for two years by the Chinese Swimming Federation. These test results created widespread suspicion of team-wide doping, especially given the meteoric rise in the Olympic medal count. During the 1988 Seoul Summer Games, the female swimmers took home three silver medals and one bronze. In the 1992 Barcelona Olympics, they captured four golds, five silvers and one bronze. In response to the growing concern over this problem, FINA joined the World Anti-Doping Agency and adopted its drug-testing standards.

More recently, FINA adopted new regulations to ban the use of so-called "techno" or "super swimsuits," those made of "non-permeable materials," which helped break many world records in the 2008 Beijing Olympics. These swimsuits incorporated plastics and rubberized material to enhance the ability of the athlete to be buoyant. Starting in 2010, the rules require swimsuits to be made of fabric (IBN Sports, 2009). An interesting question is whether the records set during the period of use of the "super swimsuits" will continue to be acknowledged as official or not. At this time, FINA has not nullified past records that were set by athletes who wore the "super swimsuits" made of polyurethane (Barrow, 2012). FINA embraced professionalism in the mid-1980s.

NGB—USA Swimming, USA Diving, USA Synchro

FINA has affiliations with several U.S. national organizations, including USA Swimming, Inc., USA Water Polo, USA Diving, USA Synchro and U.S. Masters Swimming. Unlike areas of sports such as track and field, in which one organization governs all the various sports within its domain, aquatics have individual organizations for each particular sport.

Soccer (Known Internationally as Football)

International Federation—FIFA

In recent years, the Fédération Internationale de Football Associations, or FIFA, has become a poster child for corruption and lack of transparency. The organization runs the most popular sport in the world and has leveraged its brand and its World Cup tournament into a huge money machine. FIFA generates billions in revenue, driven by TV and sponsorship rights for hosting the World Cup, the most popular single sporting event in the world (Harrison, 2015). It is estimated that more than 3 billion people watched the 2014 World Cup in Brazil (FIFA.com, 2015). FIFA earned $5.7 billion in revenue between 2010 and 2014 and earned a $2.6 billion profit for FIFA. Ticket sales for the 2014 event reached over $500 million. Its top-line sponsors included Coca-Cola, Hyundai, Emirates Airways, Sony and Visa, who paid a cumulative total of $1.7 billion between 2011 and 2014. Some of those revenues were used on "infrastructure, sporting facilities, equipment and education" during that period. However, FIFA was generous to its executives. The top thirteen earned a cumulative total of $40 million in 2014 (Harrison, 2015).

Like just about every international sports organization, FIFA is not based in the United States or other large industrial nation. Rather, it is a Swiss entity, governed by the rules of Swiss law. Until recently, oversight was noticeably less rigorous than would be found in the United States. And that could be just one reason why FIFA has been plagued with major corruption allegations resulting in a major scandal in 2014 and 2015. Although still evolving as of this writing, the allegations show, as we will see, a shocking lack of transparency between the organization and a number of its regional confederations and in the way it solicited winning bids for World Cup.

The organization is headed by a president, elected for a four-year term and a twenty-two-member board, composed of members from various soccer federations. However, the real power was in the hands of Sepp Blatter, who has led the organization from 1998 to 2015 and the heads of the regional confederations covering Europe (known as UEFA), Asia (AFC), North and Central America and the Caribbean (CONCACAF), South America (CONMEBOL) and Africa (CAF), many of whose directors wield considerable power within FIFA. Some of the corruption charges center on the activities of these confederations.

Although rumors of corruption—in the nature of payoffs—have circulated for years, the official beginning of the scandal came in 2015, when Swiss authorities arrested several top FIFA officials based on warrants issued by the U.S. Department of Justice under an indictment charging fourteen people, many affiliated with FIFA, on corruption activities dating for almost a quarter-century before. The impetus for these charges came in previously sealed guilty pleas by an American who served on the FIFA executive committee (Ruiz and Mather, 2015). Just a few weeks later, Blatter (who was not indicted at that time) was re-elected to a fifth term as FIFA president. In an act of imperiousness, he declared, "For the next four years, I will be in command of this boat called FIFA . . . and we will bring it back on shore" (Ruiz and Mather, 2015). Just weeks later, Blatter promised to resign his position, but did not set a specific date. In December 2015, FIFA's Independent Ethics Committee announced that Blatter and Michel Platini, FIFA vice-president and UEFA president, had been banned from "all football related activities (administrative, sports or any other) on a national and international level . . . [effective] immediately" (de Menezes, 2015). The FIFA Appeal Committee upheld the Independent Ethics Committee's decision to ban Blatter and Platini over "a conflict of interest in a 2 million Swiss franc payment deal made to Platini"; however, the Appeal Committee reduced the suspensions from eight to six years (ESPN Staff, 2016).

The allegations center on bank transactions involving tainted monies through U.S. banks. Some of those assets stem from the controversial bids by Russia and Qatar to host the 2018 and 2022 Men's World Cup tournaments. In particular, there was much discussion and media coverage involving how Qatar, a small but oil-rich Middle Eastern nation, was able to win the bid over the United States (which hosted the men's World Cup in 1994). In 2014, accusations of payoffs through "slush funds" by Qatari officials to FIFA voting members were first reported. The "dozens of payments" totaled more than $5 million, according to one report, and were intended to buy support for the bid (Blake & Calvert, 2014).

The payments allegedly went to the presidents of thirty African soccer associations and to bank accounts controlled by Jack Warner, a former FIFA vice-president from Trinidad and Tobago who led CONCACAF as president from 1990 to 2011. It was further reported that fourteen of the twenty-two FIFA executive committee members ultimately ignored their organization's technical report—which highlighted the potential health risk to players, officials and spectators and described Qatar's plans as "high risk" (Gibson, 2014a). Although it is too early to say whether FIFA will be overhauled and significantly reformed, one result of alleged corruption is that Switzerland tightened its laws overseeing the conduct of international sports organizations. One law increases the scrutiny of top executives of FIFA and other organizations such as the IOC (also headquartered in Switzerland) in regard to bank transactions, as they would have to ensure that funds deposited in Swiss banks are not of "suspicious origin." The other law would make FIFA and other sports bodies subject to new EU-based money-laundering laws (Bart, 2014). In 2016, Gianni Infantino, a soccer official from UEFA (the European federation), was elected FIFA president, pledging reforms. As of the time of the writing, it is too early to say whether any meaningful reforms will be implemented.

International federations tend to be bloated in their organization, with many different committees or honorary committees. How much work they do depends on the organization and their respective powers. FIFA's committees include a bureaucrat's dream: in addition to the FIFA Congress (where all representatives vote), there are more than twenty-five standing committees, including such seemingly overlapping entities as a Committee on Fair Play and Social Responsibility and a Governance Committee, a Media Committee and a Marketing and TV Committee, a Football Committee and a Committee for Club Football. Each committee has a chair and a deputy chair and about six to twelve members. Other committees include those for medical issues, legal issues, discipline, women's football and player status (FIFA.com, n.d.).

Other Soccer Bodies

Professional soccer generates billions of dollars through its national leagues as well as international tournaments. Consequently, it is structured as a pyramid, from amateur and school organizations to top-level leagues. Those top leagues, known as Premier Leagues in many countries, allow teams to grant lucrative compensation for star players, but also certain restrictions on where they can play. One major difference between professional soccer outside the United States and the traditional U.S. sports leagues is that soccer lacks formal players' unions to negotiate collective bargaining agreements outlining basic terms and conditions of employment. Instead, international soccer players have attempted to utilize the courts and arbitral panels to make such rules. It should be noted, however, that players in MLS, the main soccer league in the United States, are unionized and work under a collective bargaining agreement.

The judicial approach has resulted in some success for European soccer players. In 1995, the European Court of Justice concluded that Jean-Marc Bosman, a player from a top-division Belgian club, entertained offers from other teams, much like a free agent would in the United States. However, the team, like many in European soccer, required a "transfer fee" if Bosman signed with another team, effectively limiting his options. To make matters worse, his team refused to permit him to leave the team and reduced his wages. Bosman challenged the transfer fee rule (and a rule that limited the number of foreign players on a team's roster), arguing that it violated Art. 39 of the European Community Treaty (now Art. 45 of the Treaty on the Functioning of the European Community), which prohibited discrimination by restricting the free movement of works (*Union Royale Belge v. Bosman*, 1995). The court ruled in favor of Bosman, but noted that clubs had an interest in preserving players who they recruited and trained, but concluded the compensation and foreign nation rules were too restricted under the treaty. This ruling was affirmed in more recent rulings (*Lehtonen v. Fédération Royale Belge des Sociétés de Basket-ball (Belgian Royal Federation of Basketball Clubs—FRBSB)*, 2000) and ultimately encapsulated in the EU-wide Treaty of Lisbon, which came into force in 2009 (Kehrli, 2014).

Despite the scandals at FIFA, soccer continues to produce revenues. The European football market is predicted to generate up to $30 billion in revenue in 2016–17, an $8 billion increase from the comparative amounts in 2011–12 (Deloitte, 2016).

Fair Play Rules

The player transfer rules are a method of talent and salary control, as the transfer fee would be a method to control free-agent players from moving to richer teams and more lucrative contracts. After the transfer rules were litigated in Bosman and other cases, European soccer created the "Financial Fair Play" Rules, an alternative method of controlling team spending. Whereas the U.S. sports leagues have either utilized a tax system when a team's player compensation extends beyond a certain point (as found in Major League Baseball) or a salary cap system where compensation is based on a stipulated sum compromising the cap on revenues that could be spent (found in the NFL, NHL and NBA in various forms), European soccer adopted a different approach to prevent high-power teams such as Manchester United or Real Madrid from outspending other teams for top players. The Financial Fair Play Regulations came into force in 2011 and were amended in 2015 (Uefa.org, 2015). The goal is what the confederation calls "responsible spending" by its member teams "for the long-term benefit of football" (Schaerlaeckens, 2012).

In 2014, Manchester City accepted an $84 million fine for violating the rules. Manchester City was the premier league champion that year after spending £1 billion ($1.68 billion) The club's settlement with UEFA's regulatory body in charge of financial control also included a ban on wage increases for a period of one year (Rumsby, 2014).

Ethical Issue: Corruption in International Sports

Match-Fixing Example: Tennis

Professional tennis became one of the first sports to introduce an anti-gambling corruption organization by establishing its Tennis Integrity Unit (TIU) in September 2008. Match-fixing allegations first rocked the tennis world in 2007, when Nikolay Davydenko, ranked fourth in the world at the time, was investigated for "allegedly fixing his August 2, 2007, match at the Prokom Open against Martin Arguello, ranked 87th" (Ehresman, 2014). The International Tennis Federation (ITF), Association of Tennis Professionals (ATP), Women's Tennis Association (WTA) and the Grand Slam Board created this joint initiative in order to protect and maintain the reputation and "integrity of the sport for all stakeholders and fans around the world" (Tennis Integrity Unit, n.d.). Many fans and sports industry professionals have since criticized the TIU for its lack of transparency, because the organization's policies do not allow the TIU to publicly comment on investigations with the exception of confirming "an outcome [of an investigation] that results in a disciplinary action being taken" (Tennis Integrity Unit, n.d.). Players who are found to have violated provisions of the Uniform Anti-Corruption Programme will face sanctions, including a $250,000 fine in addition to the monetary value of prize winnings and compensation related to the offense, or a lifetime ban from participation in any event sanctioned by any governing body of tennis. In 2016, the Italian Tennis Federation suspended three players for periods of twelve to eighteen months for match fixing, which included "benefiting from illegal gambling" and "other sports corruption" (Reuters, 2016).

The TIU faced more scrutiny in 2016, when a BBC/Buzzfeed News report was released highlighting "evidence of widespread suspected match-fixing at the top level of tennis" (Cox, 2016). The report revealed the news organizations obtained files that prove there are sixteen players, who either are currently or were previously ranked in the top fifty, that "have been repeatedly flagged to the TIU over suspicions they have thrown matches" over the past ten years and "were allowed to continue competing" (Cox, 2016). Although some of these players include Grand Slam title winners, the BBC and Buzzfeed News ultimately chose not to divulge the names of the suspected players because the news organizations are unable to definitively determine whether they have personally taken part in match fixing "without access to their phone, bank and computer records" (Cox, 2016).

As a result of the intensified scrutiny, the TIU has since adopted more transparent policies regarding public knowledge of its anticorruption efforts, including quarterly reports on its findings. In April 2016, the TIU revealed that there were forty-eight matches flagged by betting companies for suspicious betting patterns compared to thirty-one matches during the same period in the preceding year. The integrity unit, however, noted that these alerts are not concrete evidence of match fixing, as unusual activity patterns could also be caused by a variety of reasons, including player fitness, fatigue and form, as well as playing conditions and incorrect odds betting (Rothenburg, 2016). Additionally, tennis officials established an independent review board to examine and provide recommendations for the TIU's governance, structure, resources and ability to increase transparency without potentially compromising open investigations (Clarey, 2016).

Do you think these efforts are enough? Do you think that professional tennis should be dependent on gambling firms (sports gambling is legal in the UK) to aid match-fixing investigations? Or should governments be more proactive, utilizing criminal laws to combat the problem?

General Corruption

The match-fixing issue described earlier is one type of corruption, focused on the players and the competition. There is, however, a category of sports corruption based on the governance of the authorities designated to run and control the sports. Bribery of officials to secure sites for competition or to obtain broadcasting arrangements would be examples of this kind of corruption. Because many of these organizations lack the transparency and the kind of media scrutiny, any transgressions may be hidden from the public. In addition, adequate laws to prevent such activities may be lacking in many countries or, if they exist, are not adequately enforced.

U.S. anticorruption laws tend to be more encompassing in terms of prohibited activity and in terms of jurisdiction. A single banking transaction with ill-gotten gains involving a U.S. bank can be enough for foreign nationals to be charged and tried in U.S. courts on a variety of charges, including racketeering, conspiracy, money laundering and wire fraud (*U.S. v. Webb*, 2015). Under the Foreign Corrupt Practices Act, it may be possible to charge sports federation officials with bribery. Although the law applies to "government" officials, it could apply to officials of state-run national governing bodies or federations (Koehler, 2015). Growing U.S. involvement in international sports corruption coincides with greater scrutiny by public interest organizations. But it points to some glaring problems in international sports administration, some of which were discussed earlier in the chapter. In 2016, Transparency International, a global anticorruption organization, released a report outlining the systematic problems of international sports and the need for major reform in the system. The report's executive summary encapsulates the inherent problems found in the federation system: too much autonomy and too little governmental and public scrutiny (transparency.org, 2016).

The report notes:

> Sport is also organised on the historic principle of autonomy, however, and sports organisations—whether international organisations, regional confederations or national associations—are subsequently afforded 'non-profit' or 'nongovernmental organisation' status in most jurisdictions. This allows them to operate without any effective external oversight (or interference, depending on perspective). The statutes of most sports associations therefore require that reforms are initiated and approved by the same individuals who will be most directly affected by them. It stands to reason, then, that the murkiest sports will be the most resistant to self-incrimination and change.
>
> Even the corporate structures of sport are largely archaic. The administration of sport is often overseen by ex-athletes with little prior experience in management, operating through very linear hierarchical organisational models. While these models may have worked in the past, many international sports organisations (ISOs), regional confederations and national sports organisations (NSOs) have simply not kept pace with the huge commercial growth of the sector, and have even chosen not to adapt in order to protect certain self-interests, including high salaries, bonuses and virtually limitless tenures. Finally, this insular environment is facilitated by the countries that host these organisations, such as Switzerland and the United Arab Emirates, which traditionally afford favourable legal status and generous tax breaks in order to attract and keep ISOs resident.

The report recommends the following changes:

In Terms of Governance

- Heads of international sports organizations should be elected by an open vote of members.
- Executive decision makers should be elected rather than appointed.
- There should be a clear separation between the administrative and commercial operations of all international and national sports organizations.

- Decision-making bodies should contain at least one independent executive member.
- The gender balance of decision-making bodies should at least reflect the gender balance of participation in the respective sport as a whole.
- All ISO heads and decision-making body members should be bound by fixed terms, with mandatory gaps in service before being eligible for re-election.
- ISOs should put in place internal governance committees, presided over by an independent nonexecutive or lead director on governance issues to provide ongoing external oversight of sport organizational decisions.
- Sports organizations should establish independent ethics commissions/ethics advisors, with effective oversight and disciplinary authority related to codes of conduct and ethics guidelines.
- The IOC, in consultation with all relevant stakeholders, should give serious consideration to the creation of an independent global anti-corruption agency for sport.

To Aid Transparency

- Sports organizations should establish cultures of transparency so that good work is not just done, but is seen to be done. Access to information policies should be integrated and promoted.
- The publication of ISO finances—expenditures, revenues and disbursements—should go far beyond minimum legal requirements in host countries so as to meet public expectations.
- Sports organizations should adhere to strict disclosure requirements, including financial reporting, and adequately communicate their activities to their internal stakeholders and the general public through accessible open data platforms.
- International and national sports organizations should publish the pay scales, as well as the salaries and costs, of senior executives/members of the executive committee, remuneration for board members, etc.
- The disbursement of funding to national member associations should be contingent on the receipt of annual financial accounts and activity reports to be made available to the public via their national websites and searchable on the websites of ISOs (Transparency.org, 2016).

Do you think these proposals go far enough? Or do they interfere too much with the internal governance of sports organizations? Do they help or harm various constituencies, such as athletes, sponsors, fans and broadcasters? Would the disclosure rules cause undue difficulty and make it difficult to recruit those who wish to work for these organizations?

The Internationalization of the U.S.-Based Major Sports Leagues

Major League Baseball

Major League Baseball International (MLBI) is the league's division tasked with creating opportunities for the "worldwide growth of baseball, and the promotion of Major League Baseball through special events, broadcasting, market development, licensing and sponsorship initiatives" (MLB.com, n.d.). MLBI retransmits game telecasts in seventeen different languages across 233 countries and territories. MLBI has worked with league and club executives to host international games, including exhibition and opening day games. For example, the Arizona Diamondbacks and Los Angeles Dodgers opened the 2014 regular season in Australia, and the San Diego Padres and Houston Astros played two exhibition games in Mexico City in March 2016. Major League Baseball Commissioner Rob Manfred hopes to arrange for regular season games played in London as early as 2017 at Olympic Stadium (Cwik, 2016).

NFL

Although football is a very U.S.-centered sport, the NFL has tried to foster interest in the sport beyond North America. Realizing that there is "a business opportunity that raises the ceiling for the league's growth beyond what can happen in the U.S." (Vrentas, 2015), the league has broadcast partners in 234 countries and territories and has played some games outside its shores. The most successful and well known of its global initiatives is the UK International Series, which was first introduced in 2007 and is credited to have increased the UK fan base to more than 13 million people as well as the UK's Super Bowl audience by 75 percent (NFL.com, 2015). Six teams were featured in the 2016 series, with regular season games in London and Mexico City.

The league's presence has also expanded into Canada and China, with league offices established there besides those in the UK and Mexico. In 2016, NFL executives revealed plans to explore having a regular season in Beijing or Shanghai as early as 2018 (Belson, 2016). The NFL could also consider the growing interest in Russia when discussing further expansion, as a Repucom report found that "13.3 percent of Russians are fans of the NFL" which translates to 10.38 million fans as of 2015 and a 5.3 percent growth from 2014 (Evans, 2015).

NBA

The NBA has found global success in promoting basketball with a reach across 230 countries and territories through its international entities, including NBA China, NBA Europe, NBA India and NBA Latin America. The NBA's commitment to internationalizing the sport goes back four decades. It first established an international presence with an exhibition game in 1978 in Tel Aviv, Israel, where the Maccabi Tel Aviv beat the Washington Bullets 98–87 (NBA.com, 2016). The NBA has worked with its global entities throughout the years to host exhibition, preseason and regular season games in major international cities, including Tokyo, Paris, Mexico City, London, Istanbul, Shanghai, Beijing, Barcelona and Madrid.

The league first introduced the "NBA Global Games" in 2013, a series of five to eight preseason and one to two regular season games played in international cities. NBA Commissioner Adam Silver has revealed expansion plans across Asia, particularly in China, India and South Korea. These plans include "promoting the sport through after-school programs" in India and expanding NBA apparel in South Korea (Sin, 2014). The league and NBA China announced plans in 2012 to develop the NBA Center near Beijing, which will feature "a restaurant, merchandise store, fitness center and multiple full-size basketball courts" (Sin, 2014). Despite a large international presence with its global business units and the "Global Games," the NBA does not have any immediate plans to further expand regular season play (Aschburner, 2016).

NHL

The NHL has had a higher percentage of non–North American players than other North American leagues and has sought to capitalize on the popularity of the sport in a number of European countries. In 2016, it relaunched the World Cup of Hockey focused on internationalizing hockey under the NHL brand. The World Cup of Hockey, first introduced in 1996, is a two-week tournament organized by the NHL and the NHL Players' Association, where the preliminary round is played in a round robin format. In addition to the United States and Canada, participating teams hailed from the Czech Republic, Finland, Russia and Sweden (NHL Public Relations, 2015).

Helpful Websites

International Archery Federation (FITA): www.archery.org

International Association of Athletics Federations (IAAF), the international federation for track and field: www.iaaf.org

International Basketball Federation (FIBA): www.fiba.com

International Bobsleigh & Tobogganing Federation (FIBT): www.ibsf.org

International Boxing Association (AIBA): www.aiba.org

International Cycling Union (UCI): www.uci.ch

International Federation for Equestrian Sports (FEI): www.fei.org

International Federation of Rowing Associations (FISA): www.fisa.org

International Fencing Federation (FIE): www.fie.ch

International Gymnastics Federation: www.fig-gymnastics.com

International Ice Hockey Federation: www.iihf.com

International Judo Federation (IJF): www.ijf.org

International Olympic Committee: www.olympic.org

International Paralympic Committee: www.paralympic.org

International Skating Union (ISU): www.isu.org

International Swimming Federation (FINA): www.fina.org

International Tennis Federation (ITF): www.itftennis.com

International Volleyball Federation (FIVB): www.fivb.ch

International Weightlifting Federation: www.iwf.net

Royal and Ancient Golf Club of St. Andrews: www.randa.org

World Baseball Softball Confederation: www.wbsc.org

US Paralympics: www.teamusa.org/US-Paralympics

US Speedskating: www.teamusa.org/US-Speedskating

USA Archery: www.usarchery.org/

USA Basketball: www.usabasketball.com

USA Bobsled & Skeleton: www.usbsf.com

USA Boxing: www.usaboxing.org

USA Cycling, Inc.: www.usacycling.org

USA Gymnastics: www.usagym.com

USA Hockey: www.usahockey.com

USA Judo: www.usjudo.org

USA Swimming: www.usaswimming.org

USA Track & Field: www.usatf.org

USA Volleyball: www.usavolleyball.org

USA Weightlifting Federation: www.usaweightlifting.org

United States Equestrian Federation: www.usef.org

United States Fencing Association: www.usfencing.org

United States Figure Skating: www.usfsa.org

United States Golf Association: www.usga.org

United States Olympic Committee: www.teamusa.org

United States Rowing Association: www.usrowing.org

United States Tennis Association: www.usta.com

Chapter Assignment 1: Expansion a U.S. League Team in Europe

On the economic upswing after a period of labor unrest, the National Hockey League has generated more revenues than at any time in its history. Many of its franchises are benefiting from more lucrative media rights agreements in the United States and Canada and the general financial health of its franchises. The excitement of the Stanley Cup playoffs has generated more interest in nontraditional markets and the NHL board of governors is seriously considering expansion.

Assume that after a series of expansion over the last ten years, the NHL concluded that markets in North America were tapped. However, given the interest in ice hockey in Europe due in part to the growth of European Leagues and the Russian KHL and the greater number of NHL games broadcast, there is an opportunity to extend the NHL brand to the European locales.

The league's marketing department has issued a report recommending that the league and its owners look to two European markets for possible expansion. Given that the most recent expansions (in Las Vegas) raised $500 million each in expansion fees from owners who made billions in technology, the marketing department concludes that the two franchises in Europe could fetch even more money.

After months of research, the owners met and issued a call for potential franchises in the following European cities: Vienna, Prague, Berlin and Moscow. The advantages for the league would be exposure to markets in areas of hockey interest, which could cultivate greater interest in the NHL brand on the continent, which could result in increased merchandise sales and increased broadcast rights fees. The downside would be extra expense for travel for the North American teams while they play in Europe and the same for the European teams playing games in North America.

The NHL board of governors is quite interested in this idea. It would mark the first time that a North American professional sports league would have franchises in Europe. However, there are a number of business and legal hurdles to overcome.

Groups or individuals will draft a report of approximately eight to ten pages double-spaced outlining all of the major issues involved in such a franchise expansion. They could include issues such as an analysis of the competitor leagues in those countries, the economic viability of the existing franchises, the availability of arenas to play in those cities and whether players can be recruited from teams in other leagues and what contractual restrictions exist.

Chapter Assignment 2: Reimaging an International Sports Federation

The World Federation of Eating ("WFE") is the governing body for competitive eating contests. Such contests are held all over the world. The organization has national governing bodies in over fifty countries. Although it is not part of the Olympic movement, it does have world championships every two years, with prize money that derives from a group of sponsors. The organization hosts tournaments in various weight classifications and is divided by sex.

The WFE has been led for two decades by Blat Seppler, who has run the organization with an iron hand. Although there is a board of directors, Seppler picked each of the members personally. The WFE Congress is composed of fifty-five delegates, one from each member country. Under Article V of the organization's constitution, each delegate gets one vote. In reality, Seppler has been able to "persuade" delegates from certain countries by using the organization's sponsorship money to give "gifts" to their competitive eating program. He has been re-elected by large margins and was serving his sixth four-year term when he was forced to resign after he and the entire board were indicted by U.S. authorities on charges of money laundering, wire fraud and other alleged criminal activities.

The WFE's Congress has elected an acting president who is the former attorney general of the United States and board members who are new to the sport. With the blessing of the Congress, the acting president and the new board have announced a "major strategic plan" to restructure the organization—from top to bottom. No one and no division could be spared. The goal is to create an organization that is legal, transparent and represents the best of competitive eating. The powers of the president and others are open to change. In other words, everything is on the table.

You are to create a new governing structure for the WFE. You will propose changes (or you may keep aspects of the present structure) involving such issues as elections of officials and the nature, duties and power of the WFE officials, any legislative body, its powers and its representatives. Terms of office and election procedures can also be included. You can discuss athlete representation (if any), changes in bidding procedures for future world championships, allocations of resources between the WFE and the national governing bodies, the negotiations and the rights of sponsors and a code of ethics or general ethical procedures in the conduct of the WFE officials and representatives. Financial disclosure and other transparency rules can also be proposed.

The project consists of a PowerPoint presentation that should last thirty to forty minutes. You may want to look at the websites of various international sports federations as a guide. All works use in preparation of the presentation must be cited, and a bibliography page or pages should be appended at the end of the presentation.

References

ABC News (2008, October 20). Ex-China sports official tells of Olympic deals. Retrieved April 14, 2010, from http://abcnews.go.com/Sports/wireStory?id=8870799

Abrahamson, A. (2002, April 24). Salt Lake Winter Games turn a profit. *Los Angeles Times*. Retrieved April 10, 2010, from http://articles.latimes.com/2002/apr/24/sports/sp-usoc24

Abrahamson, A. (2003, December 2). Steroid secrecy upsets IOC; U.S. track officials haven't explained why gold medalist Young was cleared to run in 2000 Games despite a positive test, Olympic chief says. *Los Angeles Times*, p. D1.

Ansley, C. C. (1995). International athletic dispute resolution: Tarnishing the Olympic dream. *Arizona Journal of International Comparative Law*, 12, 277, 290.

Applebaum, B. (2014, August 5). Does hosting the Olympics actually pay off? *The New York Times*. Retrieved February 10, 2016, from http://www.nytimes.com/2014/08/10/magazine/does-hosting-the-olympics-actually-pay-off.html

Armstrong, J. & Yamaguchi, M. (2016, October 3). Another case against the Olympics: 2020 Tokyo Games see skyrocketing costs. Salon.com, Retrieved October 14, 2016, from http://www.salon.com/2016/10/03/a-look-at-rising-costs-for-the-tokyo-2020-olympics/

Aschburner, S. (2016, January 14). Silver: Time zones, miles still hurdle to expanding NBA Euro presence. Retrieved May 8, 2016, from http://hangtime.blogs.nba.com/2016/01/14/silver-time-zones-miles-still-hurdles-to-expanding-nba-euro-presence/

Associated Press (2011, June 7). NBC retains Olympic TV rights. *ESPN.com*. Retrieved April 6, 2016, from espn.go.com/olympics/news/story?id=6634886

Associated Press (2012, May 24). IOC, USOC finalize revenue deal. *ESPN.com*. Retrieved April 6, 2016, from http://espn.go.com/olympics/story/_/id/7967000/ioc-usoc-resolve-differences-revenues

Associated Press (2014, February 5). USOC sponsor AT&T condemns Russia's antigay law. *USA Today*. Retrieved April 20, 2016, from http://www.usatoday.com/story/sports/olympics/sochi/2014/02/05/att-usoc-sponsor-condemns-russia-anti-gay-law/5220131/

Barrow, J. (2012, July 25). Why ban full-body Olympic swimsuits? A scientist explains polyurethane. *The Daily Beast*. Retrieved April 6, 2016, from http://www.thedailybeast.com/articles/2012/07/25/why-ban-full-body-olympics-swimsuits-a-scientist-explains-polyurethane.html

Bart, K. (2014, December 7). Swiss to increase oversight of FIFA, other sports bodies. *Reuters*. Retrieved February 10, 2016, from http://uk.reuters.com/article/uk-soccer-fifa-switzerland-idUKKCN0JJ1IQ20141205

BBC.com (2014, February 5). Sochi 2014: Gay rights protests target Russia's games. Retrieved April 20, 2016, from http://www.bbc.com/news/world-europe-26043872

BBC.com (2016, January 19). IAAF scandal worse than Fifa's, says US great Michael Johnson. Retrieved April 8, 2016, from http://www.bbc.com/sport/athletics/35348906

BBC News (2004). Green Olympic bill doubles. Retrieved January 5, 2005, from http://news.bbc.co.uk/2/hi/business/4007429.stm

Belson, K. (2016, March 21). NFL aims to play regular-season game in China. *The New York Times*. Retrieved May 5, 2016, from http://www.nytimes.com/2016/03/22/sports/football/nfl-china-roundup.html?_r=0

Bitting, M. R. (1998). Mandatory binding arbitration for Olympic athletes: Is the process better or worse for "job security"? *Florida State University Law Review*, 25, 655.

Blake, H, & Calvert, J. (2014, June 3). Qatar's dirty player. *The Australian*. Retrieved October 21, 2016, from http://www.theaustralian.com.au/news/world/qatars-dirty-player/story-fnb64oi6-1226940629992

Bloor, S. (2014, August 13). Abandoned Athens Olympic 2004 venues, 10 years on—In pictures. *The Guardian*. Retrieved April 6, 2016, from http://www.theguardian.com/sport/gallery/2014/aug/13/abandoned-athens-olympic-2004-venues-10-years-on-in-pictures

Bushuev, M. (2014, January 7). Security at all costs in Sochi. Retrieved April 3, 2016, from http://www.dw.com/en/security-at-all-costs-in-sochi/a-17343797

Carpenter, K. (2013, December 23). IOC, national governments and the autonomy of sport: An uneasy relationship *Law in Sport*. Retrieved October 20, 2016, from http://www.lawinsport.com/blog/kevin-carpenter/item/ioc-national-governments-and-the-autonomy-of-sport-an-uneasy-relationship

China Sports Review (2009, March 7). Beijing Olympics made $16 million profit? Retrieved March 21, 2010, from http://www.chinasportsreview.com/2009/03/07/beijing-olympics-made-16-million-profit/

Clarey, C. (2016, January 26). Tennis announces review of anticorruption efforts. *The New York Times*. Retrieved May 1, 2016, from http://www.nytimes.com/2016/01/27/sports/tennis/tennis-plans-new-measures-to-fight-match-fixing.html

Court of Arbitration for Sport (2012). Arbitration rules for the Olympic Games. Retrieved April 6, 2016, from http://www.tas-cas.org/fileadmin/user_upload/CAS_adhoc_rules_Olympic_Games_London_2012.pdf

Court of Arbitration for Sport (2015). CAS bulletin. Retrieved April 6, 2016, from http://www.tas-cas.org/fileadmin/user_upload/Bulletin_2015_1_internet3.pdf

Cox, S. (2016, January 18). Tennis match fixing: Evidence of suspected match-fixing revealed. *BBC.com*. Retrieved May 5, 2016, from http://www.bbc.com/sport/tennis/35319202

Crouse, K. (1998, February 6). Saving grace; Kwan puts sparkle back into women's figure skating. *Los Angeles Daily News*. Retrieved August 10, 2010, from http://www.thefreelibrary.com/SAVING+GRACE%3B+KWAN+PUTS+SPARKLE+BACK+INTO+WOMEN'S+FIGURE+SKATING-a083810163

Cwik, C. (2016, January 26). "MLB looking to play regular season games in London by 2017". *Yahoo Sports*. Retrieved May 8, 2016, from http://sports.yahoo.com/blogs/mlb-big-league-stew/mlb-looking-to-play-regular-season-games-in-london-by-2017–204819820.html

Daly, M., & Roan, D. (2016, January 25). Adidas to end IAAF sponsorship deal early in wake of doping crisis. *BBC.com*. Retrieved April 8, 2016, from http://www.bbc.com/sport/athletics/35385415

Deloitte.com (2016). European football scores $30 billion. Retrieved May 19, 2016, from http://www2.deloitte.com/global/en/pages/technology-media-and-telecommunications/articles/tmt-pred16-media-european-football-scores-30billion.html

De Menezes, J. (2015, December 21). Sepp Blatter and Michel Platini banned: FIFA and UEFA presidents to appeal eight-year bans from football. *Independent*. Retrieved April 2, 2016, from http://www.independent.co.uk/sport/football/international/sepp-blatter-banned-from-fifa-for-eight-years-michel-platini-a6781151.html

De Varona, D. (2003, February 13). United States Olympic Committee Reform. Hearing before the Committee on Commerce, Science and Transportation, U.S. Senate. 108th Congress, 1st Session, p. 20. Retrieved May 11, 2010, from http://books.google.com/books?id=6Up7IrwLzpoC&pg=PA20&lpg=PA20&dq=USOC+was+little+more+than+a+travel+agent&source=bl&ots=rQNtiTzwWn&sig=EL1mmLogcGM4Rz2-zOy4aUQ1FT8&hl=en&ei=QBzsS6GkE4H58AaP5OyLBQ&sa=X&oi=book_result&ct=result&resnum=5&ved=0CB4Q6AEwBA#v=onepage&q&f=false

Dow Jones Business News (2016, April 1). Head of security force resigns ahead of Rio Olympics. *Nasdaq.com.* Retrieved April 3, 2016, from http://www. nasdaq.com/article/head-of-security-force-resigns-ahead-of-rio-olympics-20160401–00551

Ehresman, C. (2014, November 26). Match-fixing and corruption in professional tennis. *NYSBar.com.* Retrieved May 5, 2016, from http://nysbar.com/blogs/ EASL/2014/11/match-fixing_and_corruption_in.html

Elder, M. (2013, June 11). Russia passes law banning gay "propaganda". *The Guardian.* Retrieved April 20, 2016, from http://www.theguardian.com/ world/2013/jun/11/russia-law-banning-gay-propaganda

ESPN Staff (2016, February 24). Sepp Blatter, Michel Platini bans reduced to 6 years by FIFA. Retrieved April 2, 2016, from http://www.espnfc.us/blog/ fifa/243/post/2814374/fifa-cuts-sepp-blatter-and-michel-platini-bans-to-6-years

Evans, S. (2015, January 28). Russia, China lead global growth in NFL interest says study. *Reuters.com.* Retrieved May 5, 2016, from http://www.reuters. com/article/uk-nfl-international-growth-idUSKBN0L120D20150128

Executive Board, International Olympic Committee (n.d.). Retrieved April 10, 2010, from http://www.olympic.org/en/content/The-IOC/Commissions/ Executive-Board/

Fédération Internationale de Natation (FINA) Constitution (2015). Retrieved April 6, 2016, from https://www.fina.org/sites/default/files/fina_constitution. pdf FIFA.com

Fédération Internationale de Natation (FINA) Constitution (2015, December 16). 2014 FIFA World Cup reached 3.2 billion viewers, one billion watched final. Retrieved April 2, 2016, from http://www.fifa.com/worldcup/news/y=2015/ m=12/news=2014-fifa-world-cuptm-reached-3-2-billion-viewers-one-billion-watched--2745519.html

FIFA.com (n.d.). Committees. Retrieved June 1, 2016, from http://www.fifa.com/ about-fifa/committees/index.html

Fischer, B. (2015, October 14). Sealed with a kiss: Hershey Co. signs deal to sponsor USOC through '20 Tokyo Games. *Sports Business Daily.* Retrieved April 6, 2016, from http://www.sportsbusinessdaily.com/Daily/Issues/2015/10/14/ Marketing-and-Sponsorship/Hershey-USOC.aspx

Fischer, B. (2016a, January 4). Amid strong sales, challenges await USOC. *Sports Business Journal.* Retrieved April 6, 2016, from http://www.sports businessdaily.com/Journal/Issues/2016/01/04/Olympics/USOC.aspx

Fischer, B. (2016b, January 18). USOC crafts deal for MilkPEP. *Sports Business Journal.* Retrieved April 6, 2016, from http://www.sportsbusinessdaily.com/ Journal/Issues/2016/01/18/Olympics/USOC-MilkPEP.aspx

Flatter, J. (2007). Thorpe preceded Deion, Bo. SportsCentury biography. *ESPN Classic.* Retrieved April 14, 2010, from http://espn.go.com/classic/biography/s/ thorpe_jim.htmlFoschi v. United States Swimming, Inc. 916 F. Supp. 232, 240 (E.D.N.Y. 1966).

Foschi v. United States Swimming, Inc., 916 F. Supp. 232 (E.D.N.Y. 1996).

Friedman, U. (2014, January 28). How Sochi became the gay Olympics. *The Atlantic.* Retrieved April 20, 2016, from http://www.theatlantic.com/ international/archive/2014/01/how-sochi-became-the-gay-olympics/283398/

Futterman, M., Moffett, M., & Belkin, B. (2009, October 5). Rio throws Chicago for a loop. *The Wall Street Journal*. Retrieved April 14, 2010, from http://online.wsj.com/article/SB125446379425258861.html

Gibson, O. (2014a, January 8). Winter 2022 World Cup in Qatar was inevitable from the start. Retrieved February 10, 2016, from http://www.theguardian.com/football/blog/2014/jan/08/world-cup-2022-qatar-winter-fifa

Gibson, O. (2014b, September 25). Olympic anti-discrimination clause introduced after Sochi gay rights row. Retrieved April 20, 2016, from http://www.theguardian.com/sport/2014/sep/25/olympic-anti-discrimination-clause-sochi-gay-rights-row

Guynn, J. (2014, February 6). Google takes stand against anti-gay law at Sochi Winter Olympics. *Los Angeles Times*. Retrieved April 20, 2016, from http://articles.latimes.com/2014/feb/06/business/la-fi-tn-google-takes-stand-against-antigay-law-at-sochi-winter-olympics-20140206

Harrison, V. (2015, May 27). How FIFA makes its billions. CNNMoney.com. Retrieved October 20, 2015, from http://money.cnn.com/2015/05/27/news/fifa-corruption-profit/

IBN Sports (2009, August 1). New swimsuit rules valid from January [2010]. Retrieved April 14, 2010, from http://ibnlive.in.com/news/new-swimsuit-rules-valid-from-january-fina/98337-5.html

Independent (UK) (2014, February 11). IOC lift ban on Indian Olympic Association after 14-month suspension for corruption. Retrieved March 27, 2016, from http://www.independent.co.uk/sport/olympics/ioc-lift-ban-on-indian-olympic-association-after-14-month-suspension-for-corruption-9120538.html

International Association of Athletics Federation (IAAF) Constitution (2012, October 24). Retrieved April 6, 2016, from http://www.iaaf.org/about-iaaf/documents/constitution

International Skating Union, Constitution and General Regulations 2016 (2016). Retrieved October 20, 2016, from http://static.isu.org/media/1017/constitution-and-general-regulations-2016.pdf Kaiser, A and Jacobs, A. (2016, Aug. 7). Security Force of 85,000 Fills Rio, Unsettling Rights Activists. *The New York Times*, retrieved October 14, 2016, from http://www.nytimes.com/2016/08/08/world/americas/rio-olympics-crime.html

Kehrli, K. (2014). The unspecified specificity of sport: A proposed solution to the European Court of Justice's treatment of the specificity of sport. *Brooklyn Journal of International Law*, 39, 403.

Koehler, M. (2015). Non profits and the FCPA. *FCPA Professor*. Retrieved May 19, 2016, from http://www.fcpaprofessor.com/non-profits-and-the-fcpa

Lehtonen v. Fédération Royale Belge des Sociétés de Basket-ball (Belgian Royal Federation of Basketball Clubs—FRBSB (2000). Case C-176/96, European Court of Justice. Retrieved May 15, 2016, from http://www.biicl.org/files/1883_c-176-96.pdf

Lenskyj, H. (1998). "Inside sport" or "On the margins?" Australian women and the sport media. *International Review for the Sociology of Sport*, 33(1), 19–32.

London 2012 Olympics Report (2013). Retrieved May 1, 2016, from http://www.olympic.org/Documents/Games_London_2012/London_Reports/LOCOG_FINAL_ANNUAL_REPORT_Mar2013.PDF

Longman, J., & Fackler, M. (2013, September 7). For 2020 Olympics, IOC picks Tokyo, considered safe choice. *New York Times*. Retrieved March 27, 2016, from http://www.nytimes.com/2013/09/08/sports/olympics/tokyo-wins-bid-for-2020-olympics.html?module=ArrowsNav&contentCollection=Sports&action=keypress&region=FixedLeft&pgtype=article

Longman, J., & Thomas, J. (1999, February 9). Report details lavish spending in Salt Lake's bid to win Games. *New York Times*, p. A1.

Magnier, M. (2008, August 7). Many eyes will watch visitors. *Los Angeles Times*. Retrieved April 11, 2010, from http://articles.latimes.com/2008/aug/07/world/fg-snoop7

Malkin, B. (2013, June 30). Vladimir Putin signs anti-gay propaganda bill. *The Telegraph*. Retrieved April 20, 2016, from http://www.telegraph.co.uk/news/worldnews/europe/russia/10151790/Vladimir-Putin-signs-anti-gay-propaganda-bill.html

Masteralexis, L. P., Barr, C. A., & Hums, M. A. (1998). *Principles and practice of sport management*. Gaithersburg, MD: Aspen, p. 221.

Merron, J. (2003, April 22). Montreal's house of horrors. Retrieved April 14, 2010, from http://a.espncdn.com/mlb/s/2003/0422/1542254.html

Michaelis, V. (2003, October 20). USOC hopes to take note of change. *USA Today*, p. 13C.

Mickle, T. (2008, December 4). USATF approves bylaws; Size of BOD to be cut by more than half. *Sports Business Daily*. Retrieved October 22, 2009, from http://www.sportsbusinessdaily.com/article/126019

Mickle, T. (2014a, February 28). IOC Reprices TOP deals at $200 million. *Sports Business Daily*. Retrieved October 1, 2015, from http://www.sportsbusinessdaily.com/SB-Blogs/On-The-Ground/2014/02/SochiSiteTOPprice.aspx

Mickle, T. (2014b, May 12). Improved USOC-IOC relationship on display. *Sports Business Journal*. Retrieved April 7, 2016, from http://www.sportsbusinessdaily.com/Journal/Issues/2014/05/12/Olympics/USOC-NBC-side.aspx

MLB International (n.d.) Retrieved October 20, 2016, from http://mlb.mlb.com/mlb/international/

NBA.com (2016). History of the NBA Global Games. Retrieved May 8, 2016, from http://www.nba.com/global/games2013/all-time-international-game-list-printable.html

NFL.com (2015, November 25). 2016 UK International Series schedule announced. Retrieved May 5, 2016, from http://www.nfl.com/news/story/0ap3000000587776/article/2016-uk-international-series-schedule-announced

NHL Public Relations (2015, September 9). 2016 World Cup of Hockey schedule announced. Retrieved May 5, 2016, from https://www.nhl.com/news/2016-world-cup-of-hockey-schedule-announced/c-778411

Olympic.org (2010). Olympic sponsorships. Retrieved May 1, 2010, from http://www.olympic.org/en/content/The-IOC/Sponsoring/Sponsorship/?Tab=1

Olympic.org (2014, May 7). IOC awards Olympic Games broadcast rights to NBCUniversal through to 2032. Retrieved March 27, 2016, from http://www.olympic.org/news/ioc-awards-olympic-games-broadcast-rights-to-nbcuniversal-through-to-2032/230995

Olympic Charter (2014). Retrieved October 20, 2016, from https://stillmed. olympic.org/Documents/olympic_charter_en.pdf

Olympic Charter (2015). Retrieved October 20, 2016, from https://stillmed. olympic.org/Documents/olympic_charter_en.pdf

Panja, T. (2014, October 30). Sochi Olympics $51 billion price tag deters host cities. *Bloomberg*. Retrieved March 27, 2016, from http://www.bloomberg. com/news/articles/2014–10–30/sochi-olympics-51-billion-price-tag-deters-host-cities

Papenfuss, M. (2016, January 25). Adidas "to end sponsorship" of IAAF over doping and corruption scandal. *International Business Times*. Retrieved April 8, 2016, from http://www.ibtimes.co.uk/adidas-end-sponsorship-iaaf-over-doping-corruption-scandal-1539828

Pilon, M. (2013, July 2). Nomination of Probst indicated thaw in USOC-IOC relations. *The New York Times*. Retrieved April 7, 2016, from http://www. nytimes.com/2013/07/03/sports/olympics/nomination-of-probst-indicates-thaw-in-usoc-ioc-relations.html?_r=0

Reid, S. (2015, December 1). USTAF President draws scrutiny for appointing committee member suspended by AAU. *The Orange County Register*. Retrieved April 6, 2016, from http://www.ocregister.com/articles/beamon-694449-brown-usatf.html

Reuters (2016, July 20). Three Italians banned and fined for match-fixing. Retrieved July 21, 2016, from http://uk.reuters.com/article/uk-tennis-matchfixing-cecchinato-idUKKCN1001QR

Rhodan, M. (2014, September 24). Olympic Committee adds anti-discrimination clause for host cities. *Time*. Retrieved April 20, 2016, from http://time. com/3427596/olympic-committee-host-discrimination/

Rothenburg, B. (2016, April 22). Tennis's integrity unit says flagged matches rise. *The New York Times*. Retrieved May 1, 2016, from http://www.nytimes. com/2016/04/23/sports/tennis/integrity-unit-says-flagged-matches-rise.html

Ruiz, R. (2016, June 17). Russia's track and field team barred from Rio Olympics. *The New York Times*. Retrieved July 2016, from http://www.nytimes. com/2016/06/18/sports/olympics/russia-barred-rio-summer-olympics-doping. html

Ruiz, R and Mather, V. (2015, September 25). The FIFA Scandal: What's Happened, and What's to Come. The New York Times. Retrieved October 20, 2016, from http://www.nytimes.com/2015/09/26/sports/soccer/the-fifa-scandal-whats-happened-and-whats-to-come.html

Rumsby, B. (2014, May 16). Manchester City accept world-record £50m fine for breach of Uefa Financial Fair Play rules. Retrieved May 19, 2016, from http:// www.telegraph.co.uk/sport/football/teams/manchester-city/10837079/ Manchester-City-accept-world-record-50m-fine-for-breach-of-Uefa-Financial-Fair-Play-rules.html

Sandomir, R. (2011, June 7). NBC wins U.S. television rights to four more Olympics. *New York Times*. Retrieved March 27, 2016, from http://www.nytimes. com/2011/06/08/sports/nbc-wins-tv-rights-to-next-four-olympics.html

Schaerlaeckens, L. (2012, January 4). Will FFP save football from itself? *ESPN. com*. Retrieved April 20, 2016, from http://espn.go.com/sports/soccer/news/_/ id/7355528/soccer-financial-fair-play-end-football-reckless-spending

Scott, M. S. (2004, January). Lloyd Ward: Victim or villain? *Black Enterprise*, Section BE Exclusive, p. 60.

Shipley, A. (1999, May 4). IOC retains right to conduct probes: Ethics panel declines to take over task. *Washington Post*, p. D01.

Sin, B. (2014, March 14). NBA looks to Asia for next growth spurt. *The New York Times*. Retrieved May 8, 2016, from http://www.nytimes.com/2014/03/15/business/international/nba-looks-to-asia-for-next-growth-spurt.html?_r=1

SINA.com (2012, April 11). Beijing's deserted Olympic sites. Retrieved April 6, 2016, from http://english.sina.com/life/p/2012/0410/456869.html

Socarides, R. (2014, February 10). Gay rights at Sochi, round one. *The New Yorker*. Retrieved April 20, 2016, from http://www.newyorker.com/business/currency/gay-rights-at-sochi-round-one

Ted Stevens Olympic and Amateur Sports Act, 36 U.S.C. (2010). Retrieved April 14, 2010, from http://videos.usoc.org/legal/TedStevens.pdf

Tennis Integrity Unit (n.d.). About Us: The Tennis Integrity Unit and Tennis Integrity Unit Remit. Retrieved May 1, 2016, from www.tennisintegrityunit.com/about-us/

Transparency.org (2016, February 16). Global Corruption Report: Sport (Executive Summary). Retrieved May 19, 2016, from https://www.transparency.org/whatwedo/publication/global_corruption_report_sport

UEFA.org (2015, June 30). Club Licensing and FFP Regulations approved. Retrieved April 20, 2016, from http://www.uefa.org/about-uefa/executive-committee/news/newsid=2262293.html

Union Royale Belge v. Bosman, [1995] ECR I-4921.

United States Olympic Committee Bylaws (2015). Retrieved April 6, 2016, from http://www.teamusa.org/~/media/Legal/2015-By-laws-APPROVED-12–15–15.pdf?la=en

U.S. v. Webb et al, (2015, May 20), Indictment.15 CR 0252(RJD)(RML). Retrieved May 19, 2016, from https://www.justice.gov/opa/file/450211/download

USA Track & Field Bylaws (2010). Retrieved October 24, 2009, from http://www.usatf.org/about/governance/2009/09_Governance.pdf

Vrentas, J. (2015, July 24). The NFL's future in Europe. *MMQB.si.com*. Retrieved May 5, 2016, from http://mmqb.si.com/mmqb/2015/07/24/nfl-future-europe

Webb, J. (2015, November 9). "A deeply rooted culture of cheating": IAAF corruption scandal worse than FIFA. *Forbes.com*. Retrieved April 8, 2016, from http://www.forbes.com/sites/jwebb/2015/11/09/a-deeply-rooted-culture-of-cheating-iaaf-corruption-scandal-worse-than-fifa/#1d2cfbc3706f

Weiler, P., & Roberts, G. (2004). *Sports law: Text, cases and problems* (3rd ed.). St. Paul, MN: West Group, p. 1067.

Yaffa, J. (2014, January 20). The waste and corruption of Vladimir Putin's 2014 Winter Olympics. *Bloomberg News*. Retrieved October 1, 2015, from http://www.bloomberg.com/bw/articles/2014–01–02/the-2014-winter-olympics-in-sochi-cost-51-billion

Ziegler, M. (2016, January 7). Three IAAF officials receive lifetime bans for doping cover-up . . . including son of former president Lamine Diack. *The Daily Mail*. Retrieved April 8, 2016, from http://www.dailymail.co.uk/sport/sportsnews/article-3388707/Three-IAAF-officials-receive-lifetime-bans-doping-cover-including-son-former-president-Lamine-Diack.html

5   Sports Contracts

Contracts are fundamental to the sports business. These documents determine the rights and obligations of the athletes, coaches, general managers and the organizations that employ them. They also outline the responsibilities of owners and users of stadiums and state the duties of sponsors, to name just a few examples.

Unlike other industries, contract issues involving sports have certain unique characteristics. Individual player contracts are subject to the labor agreements negotiated between players' unions and their leagues (also a type of contract) and to the salary control mechanisms found in many of those labor–management agreements. Additionally, sports contracts contain particular duties and prohibitions not normally found in a standard business contract.

Top-level professional athletes earn princely sums. In 2014, the average salary of a Major League Baseball player was $3.8 million. For an NFL player, it was slightly over $2 million, for NBA players, $4.9 million and for NHL players, $2.8 million (Badenhausen, 2015).

Even more telling is the total compensation, including earnings from salaries, appearances, endorsements and sponsorships paid to the few marquee athletes. *Fortune* and *Sports Illustrated* annually list the fifty highest-paid American athletes. The calculations take into account base salaries, winnings (for individual athletes), endorsements and appearance fees. For 2014, boxer Floyd Mayweather ($105 million) and NBA stars LeBron James ($57 million) and Kobe Bryant ($50 million) topped the list (Roberts, 2014).

It has become routine for many fans to question the contracts signed by professional athletes. Although these salaries are generous, even excessive to some, it must be emphasized that professional athletes constitute elite talent. The numbers tell the story. Hundreds of thousands of youngsters play basketball, but there are only about 440 active players in the NBA (Player Index, n.d.). The same can be said of athletes in almost every other sport, including individual sports such as golf and tennis. The owners and general managers who negotiate contracts with the athlete or his or her agent base their offers on the skills of the athlete, as well as leadership ability, fan popularity and, of course, the potential for that athlete to increase the club's success. True, many cases of bad deals exist. Teams like the New York Yankees were saddled with expensive, long-term contracts that left them little financial room to maneuver and improve the rest of their roster. Third baseman Alex Rodriguez signed a ten-year $275 million contract extension at a time when his skills were eroding and the only relief the team had was a one-year hiatus where they did not have to pay him because of his suspension for violating baseball's drug policy (Blum, 2015). But often the bad deals look bad in hindsight. At the time they are made, the contracts may seem perfectly sensible.

Athletes rarely breach their contracts. The risks are too great from a legal, business and public relations point of view. Legally, penalties in the form of damages and even injunctions issued by courts are possible (*Central New York Basketball v. Barnett*, 1961). From a business perspective, such an action weakens the credibility of the player and effectively limits his or her options to sign with another team in the particular league. It creates ill will on the part of the team and its fans. Additionally, the move makes very little sense in this era of free agency, as an athlete attaining that status may simply pursue alternatives with other teams once his or her contract expires. Finally, a team inducing an athlete to breach will be dealt with harshly by the commissioner of the league under the "best interests of the sport" power in the league constitution, as discussed in Chapter 1.

Knowledge of the basics of these agreements is crucial in understanding the parameters of the terms of an athlete's agreement. The mechanics of contract making are simple. Both parties make binding promises involving the exchange of a sum of money, services or property. The terms of the agreement must be legal, and the parties must have the mental capacity to contract. This means attaining a certain age (usually eighteen years) and understanding the nature and consequences of the agreement they make. As a practical matter, the terms of a contract should be as definite and specific as possible. Otherwise, a court must interpret the contract for the parties.

It is best to view sports contracts as a variant of entertainment contracts. In both cases, talent performing personal services is the centerpiece of the contract. Unlike commercial contracts involving mass-produced goods, in an agreement involving talent (in this case, the sports-oriented talent), one party agrees to perform certain specified tasks at a level of expertise that may not be easily replaceable.

Before players unionized, general managers often imposed contracts on them because the players had little bargaining position. Professional athletes lacked free-agency rights and were not represented by agents. Additionally, such agreements were interpreted in unusual ways. Until the mid-1970s, most players signed one-year contracts, which contained a unique form of option clause, known as a "reserve clause," essentially binding the player to the team for his entire playing career. These onerous clauses were eliminated through collective bargaining, arbitration or court rulings, as discussed in Chapter 6.

Contracts Involving Team Sports Athletes

Presently, each of the major sports leagues (Major League Baseball, NFL, NBA, NHL, Major League Soccer) has unionized players and collective bargaining agreements (CBAs) between the union and the respective league. The CBAs standardize many of the items found in an individual player's contract, such as grievance and salary arbitrations and performance-enhancing substances. Salaries and ranges of salaries, and minimums, especially for rookies but also for veterans, are regulated by the CBAs, which is discussed in more detail in Chapter 6.

Bonus provisions often serve as a key component, especially in coaches' contracts and endorsement agreements between athletes and products. Examples include rewards for winning a championship or making it to a playoff round. Also, bonuses for certain individual achievements (1500 yards rushing, forty stolen bases, scoring fifty goals) are not uncommon, or, in the case of coaches, for winning a certain number of games and/or a conference championship. Winning a Grand Slam in tennis can result in a bonus payment to a player under an endorsement contract.

A final unique aspect of team athlete contracts is that they are conditioned on the approval of the commissioner of the respective league, even though the athlete is employed by a particular team and both parties agreed to the terms. Despite the fact that the parties—the team and the player—have concluded an agreement, the commissioner of the league retains the power to void the document if it is deemed contrary to the "best interests of the sport."

Contracts Involving Individual Sports Athletes

Contracts involving individual competitors offer different issues. Professional golfers, tennis players and boxers, for example, are not employees. Rather, they are independent contractors—in essence, people competing for prizes in competition. Although a team athlete is paid a salary whether his or her team wins or loses, individual athletes sign a participation contract with stipulated winnings if they attain a certain level of success at that event. However, some athletes get paid "appearance fees" for simply participating in the event, often in an attempt to attract public interest (described in more detail in Chapter 2).

There are other key differences between a team athlete and an individual competitor. In order to qualify to participate in an event, an individual athlete must demonstrate evidence of past success or a sports-wide ranking level based on a system like the Association of Tennis Professionals (ATP) in tennis. Also, athletes (or their sponsors) must pay expenses such as for transport, housing and equipment, in contrast to team athletes, whose expenses, including transport, lodging and meal allowances, are paid by their team.

Key Clauses in a League–Player Contract

The contracts negotiated by professional athletes and their teams are in standardized form. Samples can be found on various websites, such as NBPA.com (the website of the NBA players' union). Similarities in the provisions among each of the major league contracts outweigh their differences. A basic examination of the major provisions in a typical players' contract follows.

Salary

Often, an athlete receives a base salary, sometimes coupled with performance bonuses (as permitted under the respective CBA). Bonuses will be contingent on surpassing a stipulated level in such statistics as field goal percentage, rebounds or, in the case of an NBA contract, points per game. Additionally, bonuses for being picked for an All-Star team or winning awards such as the "most valuable player" title will be factored (Greenberg & Gray, 1998).

Guaranteed status: Many players' contracts "guarantee" payment of salary for the term of the agreement. This means that, barring very limited circumstances, the player gets paid, even if his or her play deteriorates or even if the player suffers a career-ending injury. Very few employees in other businesses have such contractual power. For teams, it adds to the risk of signing a player to a long-term contract. The use of such contracts varies from league to league. In Major League Baseball, many, if not most, player contracts are guaranteed, negating many of the standard grounds for termination. In the NFL, the practice is far less frequent. Instead, it is the signing bonus that is guaranteed, although in some cases marquee players have also been able to negotiate guaranteed salary clauses or escape clauses allowing them to reopen the contract in the event that their salary does not place them within a specified number of top-paid players in that position (Sando, 2013).

Services

This clause states what is required of the player. In the NBA agreement, the player is required to participate in training camp, team practices, exhibition games, regular season games, All-Star events, playoff games and certain stipulated promotional activities (NBA Uniform Player Contract, 2015, sec. 2). A player cannot simply "feel like" not playing in the All-Star game. Likewise, unexplained absences from practices, games and promotional events also violate this clause. Rarely does a team terminate a player based on individual violations, but the team can (and often does) impose fines on the player.

Conduct

This provision permits clubs to terminate players for certain improper conduct. An example is Paragraph 7(b)(1) of Major League Baseball's uniform players' contract, which states that a club may terminate a contract if the player should "fail, refuse or neglect to conform his personal conduct to the standards of good citizenship and good sportsmanship" (Major League Baseball Basic Agreement, 2012–16, Schedule A, sec. 7(b)). To alleviate the potential for overly harsh punishment (which can include fines and/or suspensions), the determination may be challenged by the player in front of an independent arbitrator in some of the leagues under their respective collective bargaining agreements.

Examples of such actions include public criticism by a player of a team coach, owner, league or referees. Even political statements and commentary may be deemed a violation. Because the player works for a private organization, the U.S. Constitution's First Amendment protection against laws abridging freedom of speech does not apply and such a clause, although possibly unfair, is not illegal.

Most professional player contracts include a clause prohibiting a player from betting or attempting to bet on any league contest. The NBA's standard contract, for example, specifically states that the commissioner has the sole authority to suspend the player or expel the player from the league (NBA Uniform Player Contract, 2015, sec. 5(e)). In contrast to the player's general right to challenge a determination of misconduct, a determination of gambling is not appealable. That distinction demonstrates the importance of a "no-tolerance" policy on gambling.

Physical Condition

All agreements mandate that players must be in "good physical condition" throughout the season. Often the failure to maintain such a level of playing condition, in the opinion of the team doctor, gives the team the right to suspend the player until he or she becomes so conditioned, again in the opinion of the physician. The player's salary will be reduced accordingly for the time suspended. If, however, the player is injured while playing, the player will retain his or her salary during that injury period.

Prohibited Substances

The professional sports leagues address the issue of substance abuse. The NBA has a detailed set of provisions regarding substance abuse by players, and a player's failure to adhere to those conditions will result in suspension and possible termination of the agreement. The issue of substance testing, particularly in regard to performance-enhancing drugs, and how it is handled differ among the leagues, individual sports and Olympic sports, and is discussed in detail in Chapter 12.

"Unique" Skills

All major league contracts contain a clause, such as that found in the NBA contracts, which state that all league players "have extraordinary and unique skills and abilities, such that a team can seek the remedy of injunction (as noted earlier) from a judge or arbitrator" (NBA Uniform Player Contract, 2015, sec. 9). This is an attempt to "force" a court or arbitrator to treat a breach of contract with an injunction. However, it does not necessarily mean that a court or arbitrator will impose this remedy. As mentioned earlier, this remedy is discretionary.

Assignment (Player Trades)

In the overwhelming majority of cases, a player's contract permits assigning (the official term for trading) that player to another team. Note that the right to trade players is unique to the world of sports. In no other area of employment does it exist. Although some elite athletes have no-trade clauses or trade clauses limited to specific teams, teams do not like to have this right restricted.

Other Athletic Activities

A team invests considerable money, benefits and resources in its athletes, and it does not want its players engaging in conduct likely to cause injury or that may detract from his or her focus on the sport. This clause prohibits a player from engaging in "other sports [that] may impair or destroy his [or her] ability and skill as a player" (NBA Uniform Player Contract, 2015, sec. 9). Often written team consent is required for the player to engage in sports endangering his or her health or safety, notably boxing, wrestling, sky diving, baseball, football, hockey and off-season basketball. However, allowed sports often include amateur golf, tennis, handball, swimming, hiking, softball and volleyball.

Promotional Activities

Although individuals have commercial rights in their names, voices and likenesses, this clause allows the league or team to take photos and video of the player for use in promotional and publicity purposes. Often the player is restricted from participating in radio or television programs or sponsoring commercial products without the consent of the team. This section also requires the player to be available for media interviews (NBA Uniform Player Contract, 2015, sec. 13).

Group License

Each of the leagues has a licensing division, and this clause states that a player consents to have his or her image used and shares in royalties generated from that image. The great majority of players in the major leagues consent to this, although there are some opt-out provisions. Chapter 14 details the licensing system.

Termination

Although rare, this provision gives a team the right to terminate a player's contract if the player fails to act with "good moral character" and good sportsmanship. In the NBA's player contract, termination may occur if the player commits "a significant and inexcusable physical attack against any official or employee of the team or the NBA (other than another player), or any person in attendance at any NBA game or event" (NBA Uniform Player Contract, 2015, sec. 16(a)(ii)). The team must consider "the totality of the circumstances" in making its decision.

Coaches' Contracts

Collegiate Coaching

Professional and college coaches often negotiate agreements covering many more subjects than simple compensation. The college coach is required to be not only an instructor, but also a fund-raiser, recruiter, academic coordinator, public figure, budget director, television and radio personality and whatever else the university's athletic director or president may direct the coach to do in the best interest of the university's athletic program (Greenberg & Gray, 1998). Specifically, college coaches must address issues such as student graduation rates, prevention of criminal conduct and NCAA rules enforcement. Even winning may not guarantee job security for a college coach. If game attendance has decreased and the university's alumni simply do not like the coach's performance (even if he or she can demonstrate a winning record), the respective coach's tenure can be very short.

Contracts involving men's college basketball and football are increasingly lucrative, not only in situations where these sports generate large revenues, but also because of the importance of these sports in the identity of these institutions. In fact, the amounts paid in salary and other compensation for coaches have increased dramatically. In 2009, at least twenty-five college head football coaches drew annual compensation of at least $2 million. According to a study in *USA Today*, the average pay for a head coach in the NCAA's top-level, 120-school Football Bowl Subdivision (FBS) increased 28 percent from 2007 and an astounding 46 percent from 2006, to an average of $1.36 million. Many earn more than their college presidents (Wieberg, Upton, Perez, & Berkowitz, 2009). In 2014, at least fifty head football coaches drew annual compensation of at least $2 million. These increases were 35 percent from 2009 with an average of approximately $1.84 million (Berkowitz, Upton, Schnaars & Dougherty, 2014).

Contracts for coaches of less popular sports and women's sports are more straightforward employment agreements. Coaches' contracts from public institutions are generally available under state disclosure laws. Also, football coaches' compensation from NCAA Division I-A schools are available at http://usatoday30.usatoday.com/sports/graphics/coaches_contracts/flash.htm.

Top-level college coaches routinely sign multiyear, seven-figure contracts laden with bonus provisions and income potential outside of coaching. In addition to base salary, a successful college coach can derive income from TV and radio shows, endorsement contracts with shoe companies, speaking engagements and summer camps (Greenberg & Gray, 1998). College coaches must adhere to NCAA rules, and their failure to do so may result in suspension without pay or outright termination (NCAA Division I Manual—August Version, 2014, sec. 11.2.1). Among the prohibitions, coaches cannot give remuneration or compensation to student-athletes or pay assistant coaches extra money (NCAA Division I Manual—August Version, 2014, sec. 11.1.3).

The following are some key sections found in college coaches' contracts.

Term

Much like athletes' contracts, the term of a coach's contract is dictated by the past successes attained. A successful coach will often have a multiyear contract. Sometimes, a "rollover" provision will be included, which works as an extension of the contract if the university is "satisfied" with the coach's performance after a particular season. For example, Coach X has a five-year contract and, after the first year, the university is satisfied with his performance; the contract term then increases to five more years from four. Who benefits from this rollover clause? Of course, the coach does because his employment extends another year (or more, if the clause is activated more often). However, a persuasive argument can be made that the university benefits even more because (a) the school triggers the clause at its discretion and (b) the clause serves to "lock in" this coach for a longer period of time and prevents other schools from recruiting that person without inducing a breach of contract.

Reassignment

This clause, unique to a college coach's agreement, permits the university to remove the person as head coach, but not to terminate the contract. Instead, "reassignment" to another job commensurate with the person's skill and duties occurs. The disadvantage of a reassignment clause for a top-flight coach is obvious: it serves as a way to keep the talented person from going elsewhere. This form of "golden handcuffs" often stipulates that the failure of the coach to accept the alternative employment constitutes a breach of contract, possibly subjecting him or her to an injunction barring the coach from working elsewhere.

Base Salary, Fringe Benefits and Bonuses

Every coach's contract will provide for some base salary. However, top-flight collegiate coaching agreements are filled with fringe benefits, such as free automobiles, free housing (or a down payment toward a house) and moving expenses. The bonus provisions may turn out to be more lucrative than the base salary. They include a signing bonus and bonuses for participation in postseason tournaments, attaining a certain win–loss record, victories in postseason tournaments, graduation rates for students and increases in attendance (Greenberg & Gray, 1998).

Termination

As in the case of an athlete's contract, the termination clauses are especially important. There are basically two types of terminations: "just cause" and "without cause." The key difference has to do with compensation. A coach who suffered a just-cause termination loses the right to compensation; one fired without cause can keep earning a paycheck under the guaranteed payment provisions (frequently found in big-time coaching contracts). The contract will define the parameters of just cause and state that particular transgressions justify just-cause termination. Often just cause includes specific illegal conduct or violation of NCAA rules. At the very least, a coach's contract should identify "major" NCAA violations that are the basis for just-cause termination. However, just cause could also cover certain types of conduct deemed to be against the social mores or that would "shock the conscience" of the particular institution.

Ethical Issue: What Is "Just Cause"?

Coach Z signed a three-year contract to coach the women's basketball team at Ames College. The school has a strict no-alcohol policy in accordance with the religious policy of the college. It is not a public institution, but one owned and run by a particular church which espouses temperance. His contract stipulated that if the coach engages in acts that "contradict the religious traditions of Ames College" or "shocks the conscience of the Ames College community," which includes administrators, faculty, students or alumni, his contract can be terminated for cause and compensation will cease. The decision to terminate will be made solely by the President of Ames College.

The coach is very successful, leading its conference and receiving an invitation to the NCAA Division I women's basketball tournament for the first two years of his contract. For that achievement, the coach is given a five-year extension, as per the contract. Two months later, he was caught drinking beer with several members of the student body in his home. Each of the students was over the legal drinking age, and there was no indication that any of the three were legally intoxicated. However, the students admitted that they were drinking beer.

Do you think there is a basis for termination for just cause? Do you think there are any arguments the coach can make to keep his compensation? Or, if you were the president, would you try to find another method of resolving this issue and, if so, what would you propose?

In our example, the coach's action had no bearing on the individual's ability as a coach. And no crime was involved. Clearly, however, the institution suffered embarrassment, potentially negative media coverage and potentially frayed relations between the school, its students, faculty, religious leaders and (not significantly) alumni.

A frequency cited example involved former men's basketball coach Bob Knight and Texas Tech University. Knight came to Texas Tech with a track record of success (both on the basketball court and in student graduation rates), but also controversy over his coaching methods when he led the men's basketball team at the University of Indiana. Because Texas Tech is a public institution, this contract is publicly available. Signed on

March 23, 2001, the original agreement's five-year term was extended for three additional years in 2004. Knight and the school structured the agreement to give Knight a base compensation of $250,000 per year (a low figure for someone of Knight's caliber).

Other details of this contract merit interest. Knight's term of employment was ten months per year, giving him two "free" months to earn extra income. Furthermore, the agreement permitted him to run private "summer camps" on school facilities. A key section, entitled "Guarantee of Outside Athletics Related Income," stated that if Knight's income outside of his base did not add up to $500,000 annually, the university guaranteed any of the shortfall. That outside income included endorsement agreements for clothing, shoes, TV and radio shows, sports camps and some speaking engagements. Excluded were book contracts and TV advertisement contracts. This means the school could guarantee Knight three-quarters of a million dollars per season. Knight's contract also included a deferred compensation plan, deferring certain percentages of his income, and two free automobiles.

The contract specified that Knight risked termination if he violated any NCAA, Big 12 Conference or university rules. As noted, such a "morals clause" is a highly important provision in such contracts. For example, the University of Texas–El Paso negotiated such a clause in Mike Price's five-year contract, which required that Price

> conduct himself with due regard to public convention and morals, shall not do any act that will tend to degrade him in society or bring him into public hatred, contempt, scorn or ridicule, or that will tend to shock or insult the community or offend public morals or decency.

It was the first time the school ever included such a section in a coach's contract (Moore, 2004).

Liquidated Damages

More and more coaches' contracts contain a clause that specifies monetary damages in the event that the coach and/or the school breaches the contract. A specific declaration of the damage amount is an effective way to impose a sanction because it avoids the difficulty of proving damages for the loss, a vexing problem in personal services contracts. For example, the former West Virginia football coach Rich Rodriguez had to pay $4 million in liquidated damages when he left that school to accept the head coaching position at the University of Michigan (although, as part of the settlement, Michigan paid $2.5 million of that amount) (Finder, 2008).

Ethical Issue: The College Coach and His Breach of Contract

In the last decade, contract breaches by some top-level college football or men's basketball coaches in order to accept an offer at a more highly regarded program or a one-time highly regarded program in need of rejuvenation have occurred with some frequency. Because colleges are not part of sports leagues and colleges from other conferences are not subject to no-tampering rules, there is no way to ban such a practice outright. For example, in 2009, Marist College sued its former basketball coach, Matt Brady, and his new employer, James Madison University, for breach of contract after Brady accepted the new head coach position without the written consent of Marist (Fitzgerald, 2009). Similarly, in 2011, Kent State University initiated a suit against Geno Ford and Bradley University, asserting that Ford, the former head coach of the men's basketball team at Kent State, breached his contract by terminating his employment with Kent State four years before the contract's expiration and commencing employment with Bradley University (Norlander, 2013). In each case, the defendants were found liable for breach of contract and were required to pay significant damages to the former employers. However, they did coach for their new institutions.

So, the only way to punish a breaching party is by subjecting that coach—and the institution that poaches that coach—to financial penalties for breach of contract. Because calculating the value of such a breach is difficult, more and more coaches' contracts contain the aforementioned liquidated damages clause. Additionally, the victim can sue the new institution for damages under a doctrine known as a third-party interference with contract.

Although this remedy attempts to make the victimized school "whole," does it really do so? What about the effect on the morale of the team, composed of student-athletes who, in many cases, came to the school because of that coach? What kind of an example does that set for young athletes? And is it an act of bad faith for the coach to engage in such an act?

Are there other remedies to this issue? Should the student-athletes have more rights than simply being able to transfer out of the program?

Professional Coaching

As in the case of their collegiate counterparts, professional coach and manager contracts are personal services contracts with the duties and responsibilities of the parties vested in the terms of the contract. Because coaches are not unionized, no labor law or collective bargaining requirements exist. Also, player salary limitations due to "salary caps" do not apply. Finally, professional coaches can be dismissed at the will of the owner or general manager, and, as in the case of college coaches, their continued compensation is dependent on whether the termination was based on just cause or was without cause. For inexperienced or minor league coaches just-cause termination is presumed and they will no longer be paid. For elite coaches, that standard is often limited to particular situations, such as engaging in illegal activity. Because professional coaches work for private organizations, no legal requirement of public disclosure exists. An exception occurs if a coach or his or her team is in litigation because court documents are public records.

Often a professional coach's contract will have a base salary, coupled with bonuses for on-the-field success. Team owners may further sweeten the deal by adding housing allowances, radio and television opportunities and public speaking. In 1994, in his first year at the helm of the NHL's New York Rangers, Mike Keenan coached the team to its first Stanley Cup championship in fifty-four years. Keenan's contract consisted of the following provisions:

- Term: five years
- Compensation: base salary of $750,000 (year 1), increasing to $850,000, $900,000, $950,000 and $1,000,000 annually for the ensuing four years
- Signing bonus: $660,875
- Loan to purchase residence: $400,000 (or 75 percent of the purchase price) at an interest rate of 5 percent per year
- Incentive clauses: if the team attained these goals, Keenan would be paid the following:
  - Best overall regular season record in the NHL—$50,000
  - Second best overall regular season record—$25,000
  - First in the conference—$40,000
  - First in the division—$25,000
- Postseason bonuses: if the team participated in the NHL postseason playoffs the bonuses would be as follows: winning first round, $50,000; winning second round, $75,000; winning third round, $100,000; winning Stanley Cup, $200,000
- Coach of the Year:
  - If Keenan received the "Coach of the Year" award—$25,000
  - If he was second in the voting—$12,500
  - If he was third—$7,000
- Miscellaneous: the club was willing to provide an annuity of $50,000 per year commencing when he reached the age of fifty-five years and continuing until his death (assuming he fulfilled the contract)

(Conrad, 1995)

Keenan's contract specified that his bonus payments were to be sent within thirty days after the conclusion of the NHL season.

In return, Keenan was required to devote "substantially all of his time, attention, skills and energies to coaching the team, in consultation and subject to the prior approval of the General Manager of the club." He warranted "extraordinary and unique" skills and ability with regard to the sport of professional hockey. His services were therefore exclusive and irreplaceable to the club. Because of Keenan's stature, the contract specified that any loss or breach could not be adequately compensated with money damages, thereby granting the team injunctive relief to stop the questionable activities. The contract specifically forbade any services and duties for any other professional hockey team or any business venture competing with the Rangers or the team's corporate parent at the time, Paramount Communications.

Because the team wanted Keenan's services, he negotiated some important protections. He could be discharged only for "cause"—which was defined as a material (major) breach of obligations or unreasonable neglect. If such cause was involved, the contract gave him 20 days to cure the problem. If no cure occurred, the team's obligations would cease. He could also be terminated for cause under the contract's "morals clause" but the parameter was quite limited. The contract stated that Keenan's dismissal was justifiable only due to conviction of a felony or a plea of *nolo contendere* (no contest) with respect to a felony charge. Convictions for misdemeanors then would not be grounds for termination for cause. The agreement also provided that if the team discharged Keenan "without cause," Keenan would receive a lump sum of 75 or 50 percent of his remaining base salary, depending on the date of notice.

One month after the team won the Stanley Cup, Keenan abruptly terminated his relationship with the Rangers, despite the fact that he had four years left on his contract. He claimed that the team breached the contract because his performance bonus check arrived one day later than prescribed in the contract. The Rangers sued Keenan in U.S. District Court in New York, but the case was settled through the intervention of the NHL commissioner's office (Swift, 1997).

The bonus check was considerable, but do you think that a one-day delay would constitute a major breach by the team, justifying Keenan's attempt to terminate the contract? Or do you think that it was Keenan who breached the contract unjustifiably? Finally, what if Keenan was able to show that the team intentionally sent the check late to try to induce him to quit?

Contract Negotiations

From a business point of view, any contract negotiation involves "give and take" between the parties. But the amount of compromise depends on the bargaining power of each party, an obvious but salient point for those involved in the contract process or those covering contract negotiations. A journeyman player often accepts whatever a team offers. On the other hand, a marquee player has the upper hand because the team needs that player more. The same can be said of a coach, general manager or broadcaster.

The athlete's representative must have familiarity with the league constitution, the terms of the CBA, the salary cap rules (if applicable), the value of the player and how that athlete compares with others. The prominent sports agent Leigh Steinberg noted the following:

> Once you understand the collective bargaining agreement and the trends, the second step is to try to understand the client's negotiation position. Aside from preparation, this is perhaps the most important step because it is not simply a function of what the name of your client is or what number he is picked. Rather, it is really a question of how much leverage you have. Leverage is the bottom line in my business. Leverage encompasses several concepts, some obvious, others less so. The first is simply talent. A top draft pick has more leverage than lower picks. Then there is a record of performance. For veteran players, evidence of prior success (as compared with other players playing a similar position) is crucial. However, leverage also involves more intangible concepts, such as fan popularity. If the athlete has developed a public persona that attracts fans to games, that counts as an important advantage at the bargaining table, even if the athlete is not necessarily an All-Star. Finally, team leadership—the impact that the athlete has in the locker room with other members of the team— comes into play. Often this involves a veteran player whose statistics may not be first rate, but whose years of experience and presence motivate the rest of the team. Conversely, attitude problems weaken leverage. A talented but spoiled player causing dissension in the team is a negative. Additionally, players who do not perform well in "big" games suffer from a weakened bargaining position.
>
> (Falk, 1992)

Many make the mistake of thinking that the only result of leverage is a high-salary contract. Of course high salary is very important, but a good negotiator looks at other key negotiating points. One is termination. A four-year, $5 million per year guaranteed contract that limits or prohibits termination by the team may be more valuable than a three-year, $10 million per year contract with a broader right to terminate.

In the NFL, the leverage focuses around the signing bonus. Because NFL contracts are often not guaranteed and teams can "cut" players with relative ease, these bonus monies serve as the only "guaranteed" portion of the contract. Essentially a trade-off, the system fosters fewer guarantees for more bonuses. Another trade-off is current cash dollars versus deferred money. David Falk, another well-known agent, stated, "Deferred money is one of the most abused areas in professional sports contracts. That is why I like to call it 'funny money'" (Falk, 1992). He felt that the devaluation of money due to inflation makes the deferred amount worth considerably less than it would be if paid up front. However, deferred income may be an area of compromise, as a team may be willing to pay more in deferred income than in upfront money.

Leigh Steinberg echoes this strategy regarding incentive bonuses: "When you are negotiating a contract and you are apart in your positions, one area available to you to close the deal is incentive bonuses" (Falk, 1992). Although it is best to maximize guaranteed money, incentives can be used to close gaps. However, a contract loaded with incentives may put undue pressure on the athlete to succeed because so much of his income is based on surpassing the stipulated goals.

Insurance

Given the lucrative contracts that star athletes sign, player disability insurance policies serve as a very important vehicle to protect the team from long-term injuries. These policies may be issued to athletes in all major sports, but the sport where insurance issues have been particularly important has been Major League Baseball, in which many player contracts are guaranteed. The following scenario provides the reason: Say that player X has a five-year guaranteed contract and gets a career-ending injury during a game or in practice after the first week of the first year. That player is entitled to the rest of his compensation—for the entire five years. With so much money at stake, it behooves the team to carry insurance.

Relatively little has been written about the costs of disability insurance contracts on overall team finances. One report put the total cost of insurance premiums paid by baseball teams in 2002 at $55 million (Chass, 2002). Generally, the cost of these premiums can vary depending on which athletes the team chooses to insure. For their largest contracts, major league teams purchase policies that will cover them if a star player misses extended time. However, not all teams insure their most expensive players. And those that do insure against the risks of a season-ending or career-ending injury often hedge their bets with less coverage in exchange for a lower premium (Kilgore, 2012).

Insurance contracts generally cover 50 to 80 percent of the value of the player's contract (Kilgore, 2012). At one time, these contracts covered up to five years of a player's contract. More recently, however, the term has been reduced to three years. One reason cited is the case of Albert Belle. In 2002, Belle, an All-Star player who rarely missed games on account of injury, was diagnosed with a degenerative hip condition that forced his retirement. Belle was covered by an insurance policy that paid his team, the Baltimore Orioles, $27.3 million of his remaining $39 million salary. Belle was forced to retire after playing only two seasons of his five-year contract, valued at $65 million.

Brian D. Burns, the chairman and chief executive officer of Pro Financial Services, one of two companies that underwrite most professional sports contracts, said that Belle's injury "shook everybody." "He was the kind of guy you would always want to insure. [This injury] told insurance companies that the rates had to go up and they had to go up dramatically" (Quinn, 2001).

Endorsement Contracts

Athlete product endorsement agreements have become a very important source of income for the relatively few professional athletes who have the marketability and name recognition to be able to make such contracts. At one time, endorsements were limited to local products. Dean Chance, a former Cy Young winner who pitched for the Minnesota Twins, signed an endorsement agreement for an unlimited amount of juice (Reed, 2003). Although agreements to endorse a local supermarket or auto dealership still exist, superstar athletes such as LeBron James and Tiger Woods have exemplified the modern trend of high-priced endorsement agreements. These contracts have bolstered the image of the company by branding the merchandise with the persona of that athlete and help turn the athlete into a cultural icon with worldwide exposure. Two aspects make these deals different from past agreements: (a) the products endorsed are not niche products catering to a small class of enthusiasts, but products or brands that have general public appeal, such as Pepsi and Buick; and (b) even brands that are athletic in nature, such as Nike, are given a broader appeal because of the endorser. Such an agreement, although made with sports manufacturing companies, may include leisure clothing and eyewear. But this has to be put into perspective. Few athletes achieve endorsement heaven. Many, if not most, athletes who are able to endorse products still do so on the local level or work for sports firms marketing to an audience of devotees. The few like James—who signed a $93 million, seven-year deal in 2003 (which was extended in 2010)—hit the jackpot.

Any athlete (or coach) endorsing a product is bringing a level of public confidence and credibility to that product. Yet that can be destroyed quickly and easily by acts that are criminal, immoral or offensive. Endorsement contracts contain a "morals clause" terminating the relationship in the event of such actions. In 2007, Nike terminated its endorsement deal with the then–Atlanta Falcons quarterback Michael Vick, who was convicted and jailed for bankrolling a dog-fighting ring (Reuters, 2009). Tiger Woods lost AT&T, Accenture and Gatorade after it was revealed he had adulterous affairs with a number of women (NYPost.com, 2010). And, as will be discussed in more detail later in the chapter, in 2011, Rashard Mendenhall, then playing with the Pittsburgh Steelers, lost an endorsement with Champion (an athletic apparel company) when he said that the killing of Osama bin Laden should be not celebrated and questioned whether airplanes could have taken down the World Trade Center (Smith, 2011). Although these statements constituted opinion and were not tied to a criminal act, such statements can violate the morals clause if they "shock the conscience" of the community. More recently, cyclist Lance Armstrong lost all of his sponsors after the U.S. Anti-Doping Agency concluded that he had engaged in using banned performance-enhancing drugs while competing in cycling events. These actions cost him an estimated $150 million in future earnings (Rishe, 2012).

The Marketing Assessment

A firm seeking to engage an athlete to endorse its products must find a "marketable" athlete who projects a sellable image with a targeted group that the firm thinks is likely to buy its product. There is no magic formula to predict success. In an excellent primer to endorsement agreements, Pamela Lester noted:

> The athlete's desire for endorsements, willingness to make personal appearances in connection with those endorsements, his or her likes and dislikes, strengths and weaknesses should be considered. A successful advertising campaign promotes both the athlete and the endorsed product by matching the product to the athlete, and vice versa. [And] knowledge of all the athlete's past and present endorsements is critical.
>
> (Lester, 2002, ch. 27, sec. 10)

In choosing an athlete, firms will consider public image, reputation and personality. Just because an athlete is an All-Star does not make him or her a successful seller of the product. Conversely, just because someone is not the top player of his or her era does not preclude that person from consummating lucrative endorsement deals. Let's compare Serena Williams and Maria Sharapova. At end of 2014, Williams has won four times as many Grand Slam events as Sharapova, but Sharapova made twice as much in endorsements (Rishe, 2015). Sharapova's admission of taking a performance-enhancing substance in 2016 and her subsequent suspension from competitive tennis is discussed in more detail later in this chapter and in Chapter 12.

Team athletes have a more difficult time achieving international stature (especially for sports such as baseball and American football, which have less appeal abroad) than tennis players and golfers, who play in tournaments all over the world. Their names and faces may be as familiar to fans in Tokyo as in Tallahassee.

The economics of the particular firm or industry creates a certain "up-and-down" aspect to the endorsement market. Past economic prosperity expanded opportunities for endorsements, but more recent corporate downsizing has resulted in a diminution of opportunities. Changes in popular taste and social mores also have effects. Although "noncontroversial" white males were coveted in the past, that changed in the 1980s with the success of Michael Jordan and other African American stars in the NBA. And, as noted earlier, the ability of "bad boys" such as John McEnroe and, later, Alan Iverson to secure endorsements demonstrates a change.

Ethical Issue: A Double Standard for Endorsers?

As noted earlier, in 2012 Lance Armstrong lost his endorsements after the finding that he engaged in doping over a period of years. Four years later, Maria Sharapova lost many of her deals when she admitted to taking a forbidden drug after a positive test. Some have questioned the haste of Sharapova's endorsers, notably Nike, to suspend their deals with her, whereas Nike was more patient with Armstrong and other male athletes like Tiger Woods, Michael Vick and Oscar Pistorius during their "troubles," which in some cases involved criminal trials in the case of Vick and Pistorius. Although every case is unique, a fair question could be asked as to the motivations behind the decisions of large companies like Nike in seeking to terminate their contracts with athletes (Dobinson, 2016).

The Key Clauses

Endorsed Products

Exactly what is to be endorsed must be specified in the agreement, not only so that the parties know exactly what they have to do, but also to avoid the problem of conflicting products. For example, let's say that golfer X has an endorsement agreement with a company that makes "golf equipment." Does that include shoes? If so, just shoes worn at golf tournaments? If the golfer wants to endorse sneakers for another company, does that conflict with the obligations under the first agreement? That point has to be addressed. Some endorsement agreements—especially those with multinational firms that manufacture equipment, apparel and shoes—may be "head-to-toe" deals, covering every product manufactured (e.g., hats, shirts, pants, athletic shoes). This is the goal of the companies, who want to "lock in" the athlete to everything they make as part of the compensation paid. On the other hand, an athlete (or coach) may seek individual deals for, say, golf clubs, leisurewear and athletic shoes. If an athlete is relatively unknown at the time of the golf club agreement and becomes more successful and better known after that, that athlete's power to negotiate a more lucrative contract for the later deals remains intact.

Termination

In terms of negotiation, the athlete or coach wants more protection against termination and the company wants more power to terminate if certain stipulated events occur. If not taken seriously by both sides, the results can lead to acrimony and litigation.

Frequently, the company contracts the right to terminate if the athlete becomes disabled or retires from the sport. It may well be that certain athletes may develop a public relationship that continues after retirement, but most often, a sports-oriented business may not find much use in a "former" athlete endorsing its tennis racquets.

Then there is the "morals" clause noted earlier. We have already discussed the importance of the reputation of the endorser. This clause, in effect, makes the agreement dependent on continuation of that reputation. With so many news reports of athlete misconduct, the company does not want a "tarnished" endorser on its roster. Such an individual creates a public relations problem and does not inspire confidence in the company or its products by the public. And the company certainly does not want to continue paying the athlete after the athlete engages in particular transgressions.

Of course, the athlete (or coach) wants this clause to be limited, whereas the company wants broader enforcement. In any case, the scope of what is "immoral" is hard to define. A typical clause states that if the athlete commits acts:

> tending to bring himself/herself into public disrepute, contempt, scandal, or ridicule, or tending to shock, insult, or offend the people of this nation or any class or group thereof, or reflecting unfavorably upon Company's reputation or products, then Company shall have the right, upon oral or written notice, to immediately terminate this agreement.

This is far more than simple illegal conduct. And it should be. It includes noncriminal conduct such as obnoxious behavior, offensive public statements or even controversial political actions. An athlete who decided to travel to a country hostile to the United States and make public statements criticizing U.S. policies would not be endorsing the company's products (in the United States) for very long. A coach who made offensive statements directed at certain groups of people could very well suffer termination.

Also, drug or alcohol abuse by the athlete or coach can serve to violate the morals clause. And, unlike some guaranteed coaches' or athletes' services contracts, termination also means the end to compensation. Alternatively, the athlete or coach may have termination rights as well, usually in the event that the firm becomes insolvent or fails to pay the required compensation. Possibly (but not frequently) the athlete may insist on a "morals clause" granting a right of termination in the event the company engages in improper or exploitative labor practices.

Compensation

The compensation is usually divided into two categories: base compensation and bonuses. Think of base compensation as a floor. This payment is received based on the athlete's or coach's performance of the terms of the contract. The bonuses are based on specific achievement. In the case of an individual athlete, bonus payments often apply to victories or high placements in given tournaments. In the case of a team athlete, criteria include selection to an All-Star team, team championships or regular season division championships.

The breakdown between guaranteed money and bonus money depends on the nature of the negotiations and the strength of the parties. Especially for a younger athlete, focusing on larger base compensation is key, as no track record of achievement exists. For the company, limiting the base compensation (and the term) but basing the bulk of the potential monies on bonuses is a better strategy. It protects the firm from paying too much money in the event the athlete is a bust, either competitively or publicly.

A third method of compensation, known as a "royalty on products sold," is limited to what are known as "signature" products—products specifically carrying the athlete's name or likeness. An endorser may negotiate a provision creating such a "signature line," and a certain percentage of sales would be paid to the athlete. Usually, "signature-line" athletes are experienced, marquee performers.

Term

The time period of the agreement is always stated.

Territory

For an agreement with a national or multinational firm, the agreement is frequently worldwide in scope. It applies everywhere. If the deal is for a local firm, such as an auto dealership in Ames, it will cover Ames and its environs (as defined in the contract).

Duties

The agreement addresses the duties of the athlete or coach, which include personal appearances (the number and schedule to be specified or subsequently negotiated), and advertising in various media, notably print, broadcast, cable and new media (Internet). Often the athlete or coach will have some right to approve advertising before a launch. As part of this duty, the company licenses the name and likeness of the athlete or coach as part of its advertising and appearances. Also, the person must wear the clothing or use the equipment covered during tournaments and at other specified times.

Other Provisions

An endorsement contract should contain clauses dealing with options to renew or extend the term of the agreement. These clauses, often called "right of first refusal" or "right to exclusive negotiations" or "right to extend," are often drafted very carefully. A "choice of law" section, mandating what law applies in case of a dispute is also a must.

Protection of Athlete or Coach

Endorsement agreements may include protections to the athlete in the event there is a lawsuit claiming liability for a defect in the manufacture and design of the equipment or the goods.

Ethical Issue: Rashard Mendenhall's Termination

As noted earlier in this chapter, morals clauses in endorsement contracts are commonplace. These provisions generally proscribe certain behavior of parties to the contract. However, lawsuits seeking to enforce these provisions are rather uncommon and can be quite controversial. An example was Hanesbrands, Inc.'s attempt to terminate its endorsement deal with running back Rashard Mendenhall based on the NFL star's controversial tweets about 9/11 and the death of former Al-Qaeda leader Osama bin Laden. Mendenhall was released from his endorsement contract on May 5, 2011, after comments deemed unsympathetic and unpatriotic drew attention on Twitter. As grounds for termination, Hanesbrands' attorneys referenced the morals clause in Mendenhall's contract, which stated he would avoid any conduct that brought him "into public disrepute, contempt scandal or ridicule, or tending to shock, insult or offend a majority of the consuming public."

However, on July 18, 2011, Mendenhall filed suit, seeking to recover the more than $1 million that he claimed he was due to be paid if the contract remained in effect. Ultimately in early 2013, both sides reached a settlement. Financial terms were not disclosed (Edelman, 2013).

Do you think that Hanesbrands should have terminated Mendenhall? Or, do you think that Mendenhall should have apologized in an attempt to keep the contract in place? Lastly, do you think that the contract should have been performed, no matter what the player said?

Sponsorship Agreements

For an event presenter, whether it be a local tennis match or the Olympic Games, sponsors are essential to the commercial success of the event. For the event organizer, the infusion of funds paid by one or more sponsors helps to defray the costs of planning and presenting the event. Sponsorships may help in publicizing the event through advertising and cobranding. Akin to the endorsement agreement, there are clauses of particular importance that can make the difference between a well-drafted agreement and one that leads to litigation.

Sponsorship agreements have been particularly important for entities such as the National Association for Stock Car Racing (NASCAR) and the Olympics, as well as for tours, such as the Women's Tennis Association (WTA) and individual tournaments, such as a tennis or golf event. Various levels or categories of sponsorship include title or cotitle sponsorship, team or vehicle sponsorship, associate or supporting sponsorship, broadcast sponsorship or official supplier sponsorships. Beyond the fundamentals each provides, benefits can include on-site signage, on-court signage or other on-field exposure. Moreover, benefits may include control over the sale of media rights (Yakovee, 2007).

The salient provisions of a sponsorship agreement are as follows.

Product Categories

There is nothing more important than exclusivity or sole sponsorship of the event in a particular "product category." Because the costs of sponsorship generally prohibit a single company from sponsoring the entire event, it is more frequent to award exclusive sponsorships for a certain type of product, such as "non-alcoholic beverage" or "automobile." Although simple enough, the problem is in the creation of the category. For example, does an "official credit card" include "charge cards" such as American Express? If it does, is the event sponsor barred from obtaining a sponsorship from American Express if it signs on MasterCard? However, if "credit card" is defined as a credit instrument only, then it is possible to have both MasterCard and American Express as sponsors (with the latter being an official "charge card"). The latter benefits the event sponsor, whereas the former gives more power and marketing clout to MasterCard.

To avoid "product category creep" sponsors and sponsored organizations must create product terms that are precise. And they must think in marketing terms. For example, who are the competitors of the sponsor? Many sponsor deals use the term "financial services" to define a credit card since Visa and MasterCard function as lenders. Yet what if the event wishes to have an "official banking institution" as well as an "official financial services firm"? Problems may arise because both types of firms may perform some overlapping services.

The problem is exacerbated by the greater importance of digital technology. Creating product categories involving Internet service providers, web-based search services and social media services is terribly confusing and often involves considerable negotiations to craft the contours of these product categories.

Renewals

The process for renewing a sponsorship agreement poses some intricate issues. Is there an automatic right to renew? By which party? If not, what notice provisions are there to communicate the intention not to renew? Finally, what kinds of prerequisites must be fulfilled before a party decides to sign with a different sponsor?

The renewal provisions should be especially well drafted. If the agreement allows automatic renewal by one party based on certain conditions, then renewal is automatic if the conditions are fulfilled. For example, if a sponsorship agreement states that if ticket sales achieve a certain level then the sponsor must renew, extension of the contract occurs. More frequently, there are requirements of exclusive negotiations with the sponsor for a period of time before the athletic organization can negotiate with others. Or there can be a "right of first refusal" clause, which requires that any competing offers must be matched by the present sponsor.

This problem involving such renewals was the central issue in a dispute between FIFA, the international soccer federation, and MasterCard. MasterCard paid $100 million for the right to sponsor the World Cup tournament for sixteen years. The sponsorship included the right to put its name in stadium and broadcast ads around the world. The contract had a ninety-day "exclusive negotiating period" whereby FIFA could not enter negotiations with any other firm for those rights. It also had a "right of first refusal" if FIFA received an offer after that exclusive negotiating period concluded. It had to permit MasterCard to match it and if it did, the contract would be extended for eight years. It turned out that FIFA officials were actively negotiating with Visa during the right of first refusal period and did not inform MasterCard. Shortly after it was announced that Visa "won" the rights, MasterCard sued. This activity was not only a breach of contract by FIFA, but ethically dubious. It was treating a longtime sponsor with contempt in the attempt to sign a lucrative new deal with a direct competitor. Ultimately MasterCard and FIFA settled the case, whereby MasterCard received $90 million to drop any claims to sponsorship rights for future World Cups. Visa was the official credit card sponsor for the 2010 and 2014 World Cup tournaments (Lee, 2007).

Example: Chase's Sponsorship with Madison Square Garden

In September 2010, JPMorgan Chase agreed to pay $300 million over 10 years to become Madison Square Garden's (MSG's) first-ever marquee, multiplatform, multivenue and multimedia partner. The deal, one of the most expensive annual sponsorships in U.S. sports, included the main arena, other MSG-owned properties, its regional television networks and digital platforms.

In 2012, Madison Square Garden and Chase expanded their marketing partnership, making Chase its "Official Card." Upon completion of the renovation of Madison Square Garden in 2013, two "Chase Bridges" and a remodeled Chase Square 7th Avenue entrance were included (Ozanian, 2012).

A more technology-based sponsorship agreement was made in 2013, when the NBA entered into a three-year deal worth $100 million with Samsung Electronics, making the company the league's official supplier for handsets, tablets and television screens for the NBA, WNBA and D-League. The agreement had an international scope, since it involved the United States, Canada and Mexico. As part of the deal, the NBA also agreed to customize video content specifically for Samsung devices.

Example: Adidas and the IAAF

In 2016, Adidas decided to terminate its sponsorship agreement with the IAAF after reports of widespread doping by Russian athletes came to light, along with the allegations of corruption on the part of the organization to take appropriate actions to punish wrongdoers. Adidas took this action with four years left in its eleven-year contract. Adidas justified this action, citing its "anti-doping policy" as grounds to terminate the $3 million deal early.

Let's assume that the contract did not have a specific clause that permitted early termination due to allegations of doping. How could Adidas justify its action? Most likely, it would have to rely on standard morals clause language, such as actions that cause "disrepute" or "shock the conscience" of the firm.

Do you think that Adidas would be successful in terminating the contract? Do you think that IAAF, fearing that other sponsors would use the same justification to terminate their deals, would try to challenge that action in court (Speechlys, 2016)?

Example: Soccer Jersey Sponsorships

As of the time of this writing, most U.S. sports leagues and their teams do not engage in jersey sponsorships, where the sponsor's name is prominently displayed on a player's uniform. However, such sponsorships are common internationally, especially in soccer. Often these "jersey" deals are not a part of a general stadium naming rights arrangement, but are standalone clothing agreements. And in recent years, they have become very lucrative, adding to the coffers of some of the world's most prestigious and valuable soccer teams. For example, Emirates Airlines has jersey deals with three major teams—Real Madrid, Arsenal and PSG—worth a combined $105 million annually. In 2014, Manchester United signed a seven-year, $559 million contract with Chevrolet. That $80-million-per-year payout more than doubled what the team was getting from its prior jersey sponsorship and blew away the rest of the field (Smith, 2016).

With so much revenue, it may be a matter of time before this practice comes to the four major leagues in North America. However, there are risks. Traditionalists may wince at the idea of players hawking ads prominently on their uniforms. The products involved could cause controversy for, say, environmental or political issues. And finally, how would their sponsorships be placed? How large should they be?

If you were to design a jersey sponsorship agreement, what factor would you take into account?

Ethical Issue: The Best (or Worst) Sports Contract Ever?

When does a $1 million investment in a sports team morph into a $800 million payment? Consider the case of the Silnas brothers, whose clairvoyance produced what may be the most one-sided sports contract in history.

In 1974 Daniel and Ozzie Silnas, whose business experience was in the garment industry, bought a team in the now-defunct American Basketball Association that became known as the Spirits of St. Louis. The team played for only two seasons, and their record was hardly noteworthy. What happened afterward certainly was.

After the conclusion of the 1976 season, the league folded and four ABA teams joined the NBA (the Denver Nuggets, Indiana Pacers, New York Nets and San Antonio Spurs). The Spirits were one of the teams not chosen to join, and negotiations commenced for compensation to fold the franchise and to prevent any legal claims. Instead of a one-time payment, the Silnas brothers and the NBA came up with a novel agreement. The four ABA teams joining the NBA would make a one-time payment to the

Silnas totaling $2.23 million, and, in addition, would compensate them an additional amount constituting one-seventh of their shares of national broadcast revenues *in perpetuity* starting in 1980. Yes, in perpetuity.

Very few business contracts are made with a term of in perpetuity, but the thought was that media deals would not be a major revenue stream. However, the attorney for the Silnas inserted a broad definition of "broadcast revenues," a clause that could one day make the contract applicable to distribution channels unimaginable in 1976. "I was blunt during these discussions," the lawyer wrote in a 2012 legal declaration. "Rather than narrow the definition of TV revenues, I insisted instead that we add a new sentence [to] emphasize that this was a broad definition that could not be evaded or made obsolete" (Wertheim, 2014).

According to court documents obtained by *Sports Illustrated*, the brothers received a total of $521,749 in 1980, the first year the contract vested. Six years later, the annual payout surpassed $1 million. By 1999–2000 it was over $10 million. For 2010–11, the Silnas brothers made $17.5 million annually. After the 2013 season the payments resulted in a cumulative total of over $300 million.

Trying to push the envelope even more, the Silnas brothers filed suit in 2009 seeking to include digital and international broadcast rights as well as U.S. TV rights to the formula. With a new (and significantly increased) broadcast deal starting in 2016, the Silnas' share would be about $40 million per year.

Ultimately, in 2014, the two brothers settled for a lump-sum amount reported to be over $500 million to discharge the contract (Wertheim, 2014).

Chapter Assignment: Negotiating an Endorsement Deal

Sara Jones is an eighteen-year-old tennis phenomenon born and raised in Korea. Her mother is a fashion designer in that country. Her father is Ben Jones, an African American former professional tennis player. Her parents are now divorced, and Ben serves as her advisor on all tennis-related matters. Sara has won the five junior competitions in her native country, and last year she won the Women's Tennis Association's (WTA) Junior Competition for her age group during a competition in Tampa, Florida. She recently turned professional. Since 2015, Sara has lived in Canada, but remains a citizen of South Korea. Sara turned pro on her eighteenth birthday.

Sara is a tall, good-looking young woman, with a classic "multiracial look." Two years ago, after watching her play, Martina Navratilova was quoted as saying, "Sara can be the next great women's tennis player." Sara has a short temper and tends to fly off the handle when matches are not going her way. At one amateur contest in Taiwan, she threw her tennis racquet at a spectator, claiming that the spectator was disturbing her by repeatedly making noise when she was preparing for a serve. Although he was uninjured, Sara was disqualified from participating in that year's tournament. During this year's Japan Open (where she played as a pro), she shocked many in the crowd by arguing with another player over a serve she claimed touched the net. Nevertheless, her talent has led her to win more often than lose. In San Jose (her first pro tournament), Sara lost to the WTA No. 5-ranked player in the first round, 6–4, 6–4. At the WTA World Series Event in Scottsdale, Arizona, Sara defeated the No. 9-ranked player 6–3, 7–6, in the first round before losing to the then-number-1-ranked player in straight sets, 6–2, 6–2. At her third tournament, a WTA event in Quebec City, she reached the quarter finals before losing to the No. 6-ranked player. She won her first tournament, which took place in Hong Kong, stunning the number-15-ranked in straight sets. Six months after she turned pro, Sara is ranked No. 49 on the WTA's rankings.

Forehand, a U.S. publicly traded company, with its headquarters in San Diego, is a full-service tennis product manufacturer, but is generally perceived in the marketplace as a racquet company. Currently, Sara uses a Head racquet but is trying the new line of Forehand topspin-maximizing racquets, which have won over many pros. In the past Forehand has not placed a lot of emphasis on products other than racquets, but with the declining tennis marketplace, Forehand recently developed and rolled out a line of tennis clothing that can double as casual sportswear for every day. Forehand's stock is currently trading at $11, a five-year high, in recognition of its racquet innovations and the successful launch of a projected first segment of a broader clothing line.

At the time negotiations begin, rumors on Wall Street have circulated that Forehand may be a takeover target, possibly by a larger clothing manufacturer. Analysts have noted that Forehand's stock is still undervalued based on its price/earnings ratio and its successful marketing to younger people in Asia. Additionally, Forehand has one of the savviest social media marketing departments in the clothing and sports industry, and older, more venerable firms would like to acquire that skill and expertise to expand their online presence. In the past, Forehand has featured its lone male tennis endorser online, but since he left three years ago, they have used models or nondescript players on their online and social media. Yet, their "Tennis is a HOOOOOT!" video (done digitally) has hit 30 million views on YouTube.

Sara is committed to environmental causes. After the Japan Open, she was arrested in a demonstration organized by Greenpeace, a leading environmental activist organization, against Japan's policy of whaling. Because she was still a minor, she was released and there was no criminal record. Yet, she has said that she would continue "peaceful demonstrations" with Greenpeace in the future.

Forehand has had a somewhat checkered past. In 2012, Forehand was charged with violating Britain's Bribery Act of 2010, which forbids British firms from engaging in payments to foreign government officials. An employee of Forehand paid $5,000 to a charity run by a director of foreign business office of a foreign state. One week later, an import license for Forehand racquets was granted. Forehand pled guilty and paid a fine of 7,000 pounds ($10,000).

The most recent clothing/equipment deal for a women's tennis player was an exclusive contract signed between Nike and a more established top-35 player for an estimated $750,000 per year.

Sara and Forehand have begun preliminary negotiations for an endorsement deal. The key remaining issues to negotiate are (1) compensation; (2) contract duration and extensions; (3) personal appearances, both number and timing; (4) use of Forehand's clothing and equipment; (5) termination; (6) dispute resolution; and (7) remedies.

Participants in this exercise will work in groups of two or four. The goal is to draft a basic agreement focusing on the deal points mentioned earlier. For example, do the points of agreement comport with the facts presented in the hypothetical? Do they cover the "bases" to make for a comprehensive agreement? And are they comprehensible? Do they deal with all the major issues you may find in this hypothetical?

The contract should be between nine and thirteen pages double-spaced.

References

Badenhausen, K. (2015, January 23). Average MLB player salary nearly double NFL's, but still trails NBA's. *Forbes.* Retrieved May 14, 2016, from http://www.forbes.com/sites/kurtbadenhausen/2015/01/23/average-mlb-salary-nearly-double-nfls-but-trails-nba-players/#225459dd269e

Berkowitz, S., Upton, J., Schnaars, C., & Dougherty, S. (2014, November 19). NCAA salaries. *USA Today.* Retrieved February 7, 2015, from http://sports.usatoday.com/ncaa/salaries/

Blum, R. (2015, January 27). AP source: Yanks thinking of not making $6M payment to A-Rod. *Sports.yahoo.com.* Retrieved February 6, 2015, from http://sports.yahoo.com/mlb/news?slug=ap-yankees-rodriguez

Central New York Basketball v. Barnett, 181 N.E.2d 506 (Common Pleas Court, Cuyahoga City, OH, 1961).

Chass, M. (2002, December 1). Costs are dictating 3-year offers. *New York Times*, p. 5.

Compensation for Division I-A college football coaches (n.d.). *USA Today*. Retrieved December 28, 2015, from http://usatoday30.usatoday.com/sports/graphics/coaches_contracts/flash.htm

Conrad, M. (1995). Perspective: Mike Keenan's power play—A slap shot against the Rangers and a slap on the wrist by the NHL. *Seton Hall Journal of Sports Law, 5*, 637.

Dobinson, K. (2016, March 8). Brands have been quick to drop Maria Sharapova without trial—But they aren't so hasty with their male athletes. *The Independent*. Retrieved March 19, 2016, from http://www.independent.co.uk/voices/brands-have-been-quick-to-drop-maria-sharapova-without-trial-but-they-arent-so-hasty-with-their-male-a6919071.html

Edelman, M. (2013, January 17). Rashard Mendenhall settles lawsuit with Hanesbrands over morals clause. *Forbes.com*. Retrieved February 9, 2015, from www.forbes.com/sites/marcedelman/2013/01/17/rashard-mendenhall-settles-lawsuit-with-hanesbrands-over-morals-clause/

Falk, D. (1992). The art of contract negotiation. *Marquette Sports Law Journal, 3*(1), 7, 13.

Finder, C. (2008, July 9). Rodriguez, WVU reach $4 million buyout settlement. *Pittsburgh Post-Gazette*. Retrieved March 18, 2016, from http://www.post-gazette.com/breaking/2008/07/09/Rodriguez-WVU-reach-4-million-buyout-settlement/stories/200807090201

Fitzgerald, D. (2009, August 6). A more detailed look at Marist v. Brady. *Ctsportslaw.com*. Retrieved February 7, 2015, from ctsportslaw.com/2009/08/06/a-more-detailed-look-at-marist-v-brady/

Greenberg, M., & Gray, J. (1998). *Sports law practice* (vol. I, 2nd ed.). Charlottesville, VA: Lexis, pp. 264, 266, 523, 534, 591.

Kilgore, A. (2012, September 5). Stephen Strasburg's shutdown and how baseball teams insure contracts. *Washington Post*. Retrieved February 9, 2015, from www.washingtonpost.com/blogs/nationals-journal/wp/2012/09/05/stephen-strasburgs-shutdown-and-how-baseball-teams-insure-contracts/

Lee, K. (2007, June 21). MasterCard settles suit with FIFA, gets $90 million settlement. *USA Today*. Retrieved April 22, 2010, from http://www.usatoday.com/sports/soccer/2007–06–21–1058545345_x.htm

Lester, P. (2002). Marketing the athlete: Endorsement contracts. In *The law of professional and amateur sports* (ch. 27, sec. 10). St. Paul, MN: West Group.

Major League Baseball, 2012–2016 Basic Agreement (2012), Schedule A, sec. 7(b). Retrieved February 7, 2015, from http://mlbplayers.mlb.com/pa/pdf/cba_english.pdf

Moore, J. (2004, May 31). Price's deal contains morals clause. *Seattle Post-Intelligencer*, p. D2.

NBA Uniform Player Contract (2015), sec. 2, 5(e), 9, 16(a)(ii). NBA Collective Bargaining Agreement, Exhibit A. Retrieved February 7, 2015, from http://www.nbpa.org/cba/2005/exhibit-national-basketball-association-uniform-player-contract

NCAA Division I Manual—August Version (2014). Bylaws, various sections. Retrieved February 7, 2015, from http://www.ncaapublications.com/product-downloads/D115.pdf

Norlander, M. (2013, July 17). Kent State wins $1.2 million lawsuit against former coach Geno Ford. *CBSsports.com*. Retrieved February 7, 2015, from www.cbssports.com/collegebasketball/eye-on-college-basketball/22794453/kent-state-wins-12-million-lawsuit-against-former-coach-geno-ford

NYPost.com (2010, February 27). Tiger just can't hold his drink. Retrieved March 25, 2010, from http://www.nypost.com/p/news/national/tiger_just_can_hold_his_drink_TDojJjNyGFPq2VNA0N5KrI

Ozanian, M. (2012, February 17). Jeremy Lin a gift for MSG sponsor JPMorgan Chase. *Forbes.com*. Retreived February 9, 2015, from www.forbes.com/sites/mikeozanian/2012/02/17/jeremy-lin-a-gift-for-msg-sponsor-jpmorgan-chase/

Player Index (n.d.). Retrieved February 6, 2015, from http://stats.nba.com/players/?ls=iref:nba:gnav

Quinn, T. J. (2001, November 25). Paying for it. Injuries to stars increasing insurance costs for teams. *New York Daily News*, p. 80.

Reed, T. (2003, May 25). Show me the money; It's much more of late. *Akron Beacon Journal*, p. A18.

Reuters (2009, October 1). Nike denies endorsement deal with NFL player Michael Vick. Retrieved November 4, 2009, from http://www.reuters.com/article/sportsNews/idUSTRE5903SW20091001

Rishe, P. (2015, June 6). Does appeal or corporate bias explain endorsement gap between Serena Williams and Maria Sharapova? *Forbes.com*. Retrived March 5, 2016, from http://www.forbes.com/sites/prishe/2015/06/06/does-appeal-or-corporate-bias-explain-endorsement-gap-between-serena-williams-and-maria-sharapova/#3d8d5d62706f

Rishe, P. (2012, October 18). Armstrong will lose $150 million in future earnings after Nike and other sponsors dump him. *Forbes*. Retrieved March 16, 2016, from http://www.forbes.com/sites/prishe/2012/10/18/nike-proves-deadlier-than-cancer-as-armstrong-will-lose-150-million-in-future-earnings/#253c4b2f59e2

Roberts, D. (2014). Fortunate 50 2014. *Fortune*. Retrieved February 6, 2015, from http://fortune.com/fortunate50/

Sando, M. (2013, March 7). How do contracts work? Glad you asked. *ESPN.com*. Retrieved February 7, 2015, from espn.go.com/blog/nflnation/post/_/id/73449/how-do-contracts-work-glad-you-asked

Smith, C. (2016, May 11). The most valuable sponsorship deals in soccer. *Forbes.com*. Retrieved May 15, 2016, from http://www.forbes.com/sites/chrissmith/2016/05/11/the-most-valuable-sponsorship-deals-in-soccer/#2e722aa2705f

Smith, M. (2011, May 5). Rashard Mendenhall loses endorsement deal with Champion. *NBCSports.com*. Retrieved May 15, 2015, from http://profootballtalk.nbcsports.com/2011/05/05/rashard-mendenhall-loses-endorsement-deal-with-champion/

Speechlys, C. (2016, January 27). Adidas termination of sports sponsorship highlights need to carefully draft termination clauses. *Lexology.com*. Retrieved January 30, 2016, from http://www.lexology.com/library/detail.aspx?g=5682344c-c1b3–499d-93d5-a353dcc79853

Swift, E. (1997, October 13). Odd man out: Mike Keenan, a proven big winner, is seen as prickly and power hungry. Those traits have kept him from getting another NHL coaching job. *SIVault*. Retrieved May 12, 2010, from http://sportsillustrated.cnn.com/vault/article/magazine/MAG1011117/index.htm

Wertheim, J. (2014, January 7). Best sports deal ever? How the Silnas outsmarted the NBA. *SI.com*. Retrieved December 29, 2015, at http://www.si.com/nba/2014/04/09/silna-brothers-nba

Wieberg, S., Upton, J., Perez, A. J., & Berkowitz, S. (2009, November 11). College football coaches see salaries rise in down economy. Retrieved November 11, 2009, from http://www.usatoday.com/sports/college/football/2009–11–09-coaches-salary-analysis_N.htm

Yakovee, V. (2007, Summer). Legal aspects of big sports event management—Part II—Sponsorships. *Entertainment and Sports Lawyer*, 25(1), 1.

6 Labor Relations in Sports

Labor relations between sports leagues and athletes present some of the most complicated and contentious issues in professional sports. In the last four decades, the intricacies of union–management relations and the tensions arising from disputes involving salaries and other working conditions have been frequently discussed on the sports pages and increasingly on the business pages as well. This chapter reviews the history of labor relations in professional sports and discusses the current collective bargaining agreements in place (as of 2016) in the major professional leagues.

The Labor Laws

For the last eighty years, the National Labor Relations Act (NLRA), a comprehensive law passed in 1935, structures labor relations in the United States. The NLRA grants workers the right to form unions and engage in collective bargaining. It also permits workers to strike (known in legal parlance as a "concerted activity") in order to achieve their goals of improved benefits and working conditions. In 1947, additions to the NLRA, known as the Taft–Hartley amendments, expanded employer rights during the collective bargaining process.

Not surprisingly, the bases of labor disputes are grievances over "wages, hours and working conditions" (NLRA, 29 USC, sec. 151). The ways to accomplish a new collective bargaining agreement (CBA) are steeped in leverage and tactics.

Generally, a union represents employees in negotiation with their employers, and, under the NLRA, employees cannot be fired for participating in union-related activities. Once a union is formed and recognized, the law permits the use of a strike as a method to attain the union's goal of an improved CBA in the event that contract negotiations fail. Conversely, the labor law gives employers the right to "lock out" employees after the expiration of a CBA as a preemptive measure to show their leverage in attaining an agreement more to their liking.

The NLRA lists a series of activities known as "unfair labor practices." Violations result in sanctions by the National Labor Relations Board (NLRB), an administrative agency created under the statute. The most important of the unfair labor practices is the refusal of the parties to "bargain in good faith" with regard to wages, hours or working conditions—so-called "mandatory subjects of collective bargaining." Although seemingly straightforward at first glance, in reality, this requirement has been the subject of considerable discussion by courts and law professors.

One example of lack of "good faith" involves protracted delaying tactics by one or both sides. Another involves an employer who takes unilateral action regarding wages, hours and working conditions without consultation with the union (Cozzillio & Levinstein, 1998). An important exception to that rule occurs during an "impasse"—a situation where, after honest and hard-fought negotiation, the parties cannot agree to a new CBA. In such a case, an employer does have the right to unilaterally impose changes in the mandatory subjects such as wages and working conditions. An employer can impose a new minimum salary or a new overtime policy after an impasse occurs and the employer's actions would not violate labor law. The standards for determining an impasse are not always clear, and the issue has occurred in labor disputes in Major League Baseball and the National Football League (NFL).

Although the NLRA gives workers the power to strike, it permits an employer to hire replacement employees and even to fire the strikers (NLRB, n.d.). Although athletes have been spared the remedy of termination, replacement players were used in past labor disputes, notably during the 1987 NFL players' strike and for a short time during the 1994–95 baseball players' strike (Selig, 1995).

For the union, the strike—or the threat of one—is the most important way to achieve tactical leverage. For management, it is the lockout. Although the effect is the same—employees don't work and don't get paid—the strategic difference is great. Initiated by the union at any time after the expiration of the agreement, the union controls the timing of the strike. In 1992, the National Hockey League Players Association (NHLPA) authorized a strike just before the Stanley Cup playoffs, even though the players worked most of the season without a CBA. Tactically, this strike gave the union members leverage because they had been paid most of their salaries for the season. For the league, it meant the possible elimination of the playoffs (the source of a great amount of team revenue). The 1994 Major League Baseball strike displayed a similar strategy. The players stopped working in August, six weeks before the beginning of the playoffs, after they worked for well over half the season.

On the other hand, the lockout serves as the league's and owners' gambit. The optimal time is the beginning of the season, before the players receive the bulk of their salaries. The owners can save money, put pressure on the union for settlement and not pay out any salaries as the weeks go by. It could even hire replacement players. The 2011 National Basketball Association (NBA) lockout cost the league one-fifth of the season, and the union agreed to a new CBA to salvage the season (and their paychecks) (Lee, 2011). The 2004–05 NHL lockout cost the players and the league the entire season and a subsequent lockout in 2012 cost almost half the season (Fitzpatrick, n.d.).

One last point: traditionally, a union negotiated on behalf of employees for improvements in wages and working conditions, but more recently many unions seek maintenance of the status quo when management seeks changes. That scenario has been found in recent negotiations involving all of the major sports leagues.

The Leagues

Presently, all of the major leagues, including Major League Soccer (MLS) and certain smaller leagues such as the Women's National Basketball Association (WNBA), are unionized. This means that each league's management must negotiate with the players' unions for a CBA that outlines salaries, benefits and working conditions.

In comparison with most labor organizations, sports athlete unions are small in numbers, consisting of elite, skilled practitioners. To become professional players, these athletes had to excel, either through a minor league system or through high school and college. The competition is fierce. Hundreds of thousands of young people play the sport, yet there are over 800 players on the opening-day roster in Major League Baseball, about 1,700 in the NFL, about 450 in the NBA and about 800 in the NHL. In the event of a strike or lockout, their elite status makes the management's use of "replacement workers" more difficult than in other industries. Replacing striking factory workers with others may not result in a significant decrease in the quality of the goods produced, but using substitute players (presumably ones who did not make it into the top pro leagues to begin with) has a tremendous effect on the quality of the game.

Professional athletes, unlike most of their unionized counterparts, negotiate their own contracts, although within the guidelines of the CBA, which focuses on broader issues such as free agency, salary constraints, luxury taxes and minimum and maximum wage standards. Although the terms of the CBAs vary greatly among the various sports, in every case, players (often represented by their agents) have the right to make their own deals.

Despite the "elite" nature of professional athletes, considerable variation in the talent and salary of players exists even on a major league level. The differences in pay of many unionized workers are often measured in single dollars per hour. However, in professional sports, the differences are often measured in millions, even tens of millions, of dollars per season. This adds tension to a union's cohesion. With some players being paid the minimum salary and others commanding salaries many times that amount, the goals and priorities differ. The minimum- or near-minimum-wage player may be more inclined to go on strike, whereas a highly paid free-agent All-Star may not.

Presently, sports labor relations involve rich owners and rich players, but, at one time, neither sports franchise owners nor their teams exhibited great wealth. Players' salaries were artificially low, and the owners' revenue streams were limited. Today many owners are billionaires, sometimes a number of times over. The list includes Microsoft's Paul Allen (NFL's Seattle Seahawks, NBA's Portland Trail Blazers and MLS's Seattle Sounders FC), Philip Anschutz (NBA's Los Angeles Lakers and NHL's Kings) and, more recently, former Microsoft CEO Steve Ballmer (NBA's LA Clippers), all members of the Forbes list of the 400 wealthiest individuals (Forbes, 2014). Some owners are scions of family fortunes, such as Robert Wood (Woody) Johnson (NFL's New York Jets). Others are tycoons, such as Daniel Snyder (NFL's Washington Redskins), who founded a successful marketing firm, and Mark Cuban (NBA's Dallas Mavericks), who founded broadcast.com, a leading provider of multimedia and streaming on the Internet and later sold it to Yahoo!. The values of their franchises can be in the billions of dollars. In the mid-2010s, league revenues were well in the billions and included revenue from broadcasting, cablecasting, new media deals, sponsorships and advertising, a far cry from the days of mere gate receipts (Badenhausen, 2014a).

Players' associations began as "fraternal orders" not involved in negotiating on behalf of their players. Although the NLRA dates from the 1930s, it was only in the 1950s that the players of the major team sports unionized, and it was another two decades before their organizations developed negotiating clout. Their colleagues in blue-collar industries were decades ahead. Before CBAs limited its application, antitrust law was the weapon of choice of players' unions, most notably in the NFL.

The births of the unions representing the four major sports occurred at about the same time. The Major League Baseball Players' Association (MLBPA) and the National Basketball Players' Association (NBPA) were created in 1954. The National Football League Players' Association (NFLPA) and the NHLPA were founded in 1956 and 1957, respectively. The MLS Players' Association was founded in 2003 (MLS Players' Union, n.d.).

At first, these "unions" resembled trade associations of players because many member players were averse to using their unions as negotiating representatives. Because of this, the leagues quickly recognized and welcomed these unions. The first head of the MLBPA was the Cleveland Indians pitcher Bob Feller, who rejected the idea of negotiating with the owners. It was almost as if this organization assumed that a friendly roundtable discussion with management would redound to the collective benefit and assure contentment across the board (Dworkin, 1981).

Salary Control

From a management point of view, salary control serves as the chief goal of every sports league and its respective teams. The need is obvious: because the talent pool consists of many elite players, a "free market" results in a limitless range of compensation. Salary control is achieved by several different methods. Major League Baseball operates under a luxury tax in which owners are penalized for overspending, but the salaries of players, especially free-agent players, are not directly limited or capped. Although the luxury tax results in money flowing to poorer teams, it does not necessarily prevent teams such as the Los Angeles Dodgers or the New York Yankees from spending. The team's profitability ensures that the payment of the tax amounts to a cost of doing business, rather than a ceiling on spending.

The NFL's approach to controlling salaries from the early 1990s has been the utilization of a cap system. As explained later in this chapter, for most of those years, NFL teams have been unable to exceed a stipulated salary amount each season. The NBA also employs a salary cap system, with an important exception for players re-signed by their present teams. The NHL and MLS also have adopted a cap system. Another method of salary control involves the power of termination. In baseball, many player contracts are guaranteed, meaning a very limited right of termination. In the NFL, that has not been the case, so much greater discretion exists in terminating ("cutting") players.

Because the experience of each of the major sports differs, we examine the labor history of each separately. We also analyze the present collective bargaining agreements.

Major League Baseball

From 1972–95, Major League Baseball and its players' union have endured eight work stoppages. The sport's history of labor–management relations reveals an atmosphere rife with anger; fortunately, this has eased considerably in the last two decades.

In 1876 William Hulbert, owner of the National League Chicago team and one of the league elders, declared, "It is ridiculous to pay ball players $2,000 a year when the $800 boys do just as well" (Fennell, 1994). One hundred years later, owners were still lamenting about salaries (Voigt, n.d.).

The close of the nineteenth century marked an era of confusion. Owners complained about escalating salaries and sought to control them. The players, angry over such attempts, engaged in strikes. Contract disputes ended up in court. Fans, angry and frustrated, talked about boycotting the sport. Attendance slipped in many cities, and some teams teetered on the brink of financial collapse.

In the 1890s, players' frustrations over salary and working conditions resulted in an unsuccessful attempt to unionize and then to start a "players' league" which quickly folded (Lamb, n.d.). Until the middle of the twentieth century, the emergence of a rival league was the only way that players could secure better wages in a more open, competitive environment. With the arrival of the new American League in 1900, a number of baseball's best and brightest players left their National League teams because the American League promised "fairer contracts," including fringe benefits and no salary limitations, provisions unheard of in the National League. The American League President Byron Bancroft "Ban" Johnson also promised not to apply the dreaded "reserve clause" found in all National League player contracts for players who signed with teams in his league.

The "reserve clause," a standard contract option interpreted in an unusual way, arose from a secret agreement among the National League owners in 1879 as a means to control player salaries. The clause stated that if the player and the team could not agree to a new contract, "the [team] shall have the right to 'reserve' the [player] for the season next ensuing . . . provided that the [player] shall not be reserved at a salary of below [$]." Essentially, the player remained the "property" of the team for the following season. If the parties could not agree to a contract at the end of that option season, the "reservation" extended for the following year, year after year. This clause effectively barred players from negotiating with different teams to get the best deal. Additionally, in the 1890s, there was even a salary cap of $2,500 (Dworkin, 1981).

The only way a player could move to another team would be through a trade. When the American League joined the National League, the reserve clause applied to American League players as well as those of the National League. A part of all baseball contracts until 1975, it served as the greatest salary restraint the owners had.

One can only guess the kinds of salaries the Babe Ruths, Joe DiMaggios, Ted Williamses and Henry Aarons would have commanded in a free-market environment. Not surprisingly, many players resented the reserve clause, but the owners fought to keep it intact over the ensuing decades. Yet many in the press supported the system, concluding that it was needed to ensure economic stability of the sport. But even those in favor of the reserve clause acknowledged its draconian effect. In 1889, the St. Louis *Globe-Democrat* noted, "The reserve rule is, on paper, the most unfair and degrading measure . . . ever passed in a free country. Still . . . it is necessary for the safety and preservation of the national game." However, other journalists criticized the clause as "tyrannical" and "un-American" (Seymour, 1960).

The Antitrust Exemption

Before the players had an active union, they tried to challenge the reserve clause in the courts as a violation of antitrust law. Unsuccessful attempts were made in the late 1940s, the early 1950s and the early 1970s. In each case, the players argued that the reserve clause was unilaterally imposed on them by a group of employers (the baseball team owners) and that the concerted actions of the owners violated the Sherman Act of 1890 and the Clayton Act of 1914, the two most important antitrust laws.

Section One of the Sherman Act prohibits any person from making "a contract, combination or conspiracy to restrain trade" in interstate commerce. At first glance, it seems clear that the reserve clause violates this section of the Sherman Act. However, baseball owners got a lucky break from the Supreme Court. In 1922, the high court ruled the sport of baseball exempt from antitrust laws because baseball was not a "business [engaged] in interstate commerce" (*Federal Baseball Club v. National League of Professional Baseball Clubs*, 1922). The *Federal Baseball Club* ruling is often misunderstood and misquoted. The mere three-page decision did *not* say (as some think) that baseball was not a business; rather, it reasoned that the business was so localized that it did not rise to the level of systematic interstate commerce. In the words of Justice Holmes:

> The business is giving exhibitions of baseball. . . . It is true that, in order . . . for these exhibitions [to attain] the great popularity that they have achieved, competitions must be arranged between clubs from different cities and States. But the fact that in order to give the exhibitions the Leagues must induce . . . persons to cross state lines and must arrange and pay for their doing so is not enough to change the character of the business. . . . [T]he transport is a mere incident, not the essential thing. That to which it is incident, the exhibition, although made for money would not be called trade or commerce in the commonly accepted use of these words. . . . Personal effort, not related to production, is not a subject of commerce.
>
> (*Federal Baseball Club v. National League of Professional Baseball Clubs*, 1922)

Despite changes in the business caused by the increase in revenue streams from the advent of radio, television, cable and league-controlled merchandising and a more expansive judicial interpretation of what activities constitute interstate commerce by the Supreme Court after 1937, the *Federal Baseball* precedent remained. Subsequent court rulings in 1953 and 1972 upheld the antitrust exemption.

The 1972 case of *Flood v. Kuhn* is well known. Curt Flood, an All-Star center fielder with the St. Louis Cardinals, refused a trade to the

Philadelphia Phillies after an eleven-year All-Star career. His salary was $90,000 per year, one of the highest in the game in 1969. Flood challenged the reserve clause as an antitrust violation in the hopes of reversing the *Federal Baseball* ruling and thereby gaining him the right to play for whatever team he wished. Three years later, the Supreme Court, in a 5–3 vote, rejected his claim and concluded that, although the legal basis of the 1922 ruling was no longer sound and the exemption an "aberration" compared with other sports, the *Federal Baseball* precedent remained valid. The justices noted that Congress had ample opportunity to eliminate the exemption numerous times but chose not to. Curt Flood never became a free agent, and baseball kept its unique legal bonanza: near-absolute protection in the realm of labor relations.

The *Federal Baseball* case distinguished baseball from other professional sports because the courts did not extend the antitrust exemption to football, basketball or hockey. Ironically, the effect of the case was short lived; just three and a half years later baseball became the first sport to introduce modern free agency, and the effect of antitrust exemption on labor relations was eliminated.

Labor Agreements Make Headway

In 1966, the Major League Baseball Players' Association became a negotiating representative for the players. The need for an effective union with a dynamic leader became evident, as the players did not previously achieve any improvements in their bargaining rights. For decades, the negotiation of players' contracts had often been reduced to annual take-it-or-leave-it offers, and long-term contracts were rare and unnecessary because of the continued enforcement of the reserve clause. To make matters worse, salaries were not released so players could not compare their salaries with those of their peers.

Yet many owners claimed, with some legitimacy, that their profits were small and they lacked deep pockets for long-term contracts. For the first half of the last century, revenues derived almost exclusively from gate attendance, and the balance sheet depended exclusively on bringing fans into the ballpark—something that poorly performing teams often could not do. Therefore, organized baseball argued the necessity of the reserve clause. However, in the 1960s the revenue streams changed significantly. Radio and television broadcasting agreements and income from licensing the teams' trademarks and players' names and likenesses brought greater amounts of money to the teams. And the players, hamstrung by the reserve clause, received little of it.

Marvin Miller, a labor economist and negotiator for the United Steelworkers Union, became the executive director of the MLBPA in 1966. To this day, some writers and commentators (and maybe a few former baseball executives) think of him as an uncompromising partisan with little appreciation for the traditions of the game (Burk, 2015); others opine that he only looked out for the interests of star players (Seybold, 2012). In reality, he was more nuanced. During his career with the Steelworkers, Miller also helped companies gain in productivity and profit. At the time of his ascension, Miller was not a leftist radical unionist, but a tough labor negotiator respected by industry, government and Steelworkers Union members alike.

He called the labor–management relations "as lawless, in [their] own way, as Dodge City in 1876" and classified baseball players as "the most exploited group I had ever seen" (Ryan, 1991). In a 1981 interview, he said,

> It was comical. I discovered the three most important issues the players had brought before the owners in the previous negotiations were a faulty drinking fountain in St. Louis, a drain pipe in the outfield in Chicago and a splintered bench in the Fenway Park bullpen.

He added, "I concluded that the owners were having a carnival at the players' expense." As an example, he noted that the players had not had an increase in their minimum salary since the 1940s (Down, 1981). Miller's transformation of the MLBPA from a struggling and ineffective organization to the most powerful union in sports is a testament to his leadership and vision.

Of course, the reserve clause remained Miller's major concern. However, Miller, aware he lacked the power to negotiate with the owners on an issue so dear to them, started with less controversial issues to build respect from the players. Given the ambivalence of many baseball players to an active union, that was not an easy task. In a 1991 interview, he said, "I would go as far to say that the players were brainwashed. They were led to believe they were the luckiest men on earth simply to be allowed to wear that uniform."

In 1966, a major league player's average annual salary was $19,000. In December of that year, Miller and then-commissioner William Eckert negotiated the first CBA in professional sports. The agreement raised the minimum salary for the first time in nearly two decades and covered pensions and insurance.

The 1966 agreement lasted two years. The next CBA (with Bowie Kuhn as commissioner, appointed after Eckert resigned) raised the minimum salary from $10,000 to $15,000. Moreover, Miller secured a clause requiring "grievance arbitration" of certain player disputes. This clause weakened the commissioner's power and gave the players a powerful new tool and, it turned out, a major concession by Kuhn.

Miller had delivered benefits for the players, and by the early 1970s he had their confidence and backing. The MLBPA union became more assertive and sought the big prize—elimination or alteration of the reserve clause. In April 1972 the players walked out for two weeks, forcing the cancellation of eighty-six games. The elite players, in particular, sought greater freedoms to negotiate their value. The players achieved some success as the owners agreed to arbitrate salary disputes for players with two years or more of service.

One year later, after a short lockout by the owners during spring training, a three-year CBA was reached. This agreement maintained the salary arbitration system, but tweaked it. Under this arrangement, any player with two years or more of service could bring a salary dispute to arbitration before a three-person board. The board was made up of one arbitrator appointed by management, one by the union and a third "neutral" arbitrator. However, the board specifically lacked the power to consider the validity of the reserve clause.

Nevertheless, the reserve clause was doomed not by the courts (which, by crafting and upholding the antitrust exemption over a fifty-year period, gave judicial approval of the provision), but rather by a labor arbitrator named Peter Seitz. In 1974, Seitz ruled that Oakland A's owner Charlie Finley had breached a contractual obligation to defer half of pitcher Jim "Catfish" Hunter's salary into an annuity. As a consequence, Seitz freed Hunter from his contract and made him a "free agent." At the time, Hunter was making $100,000 per season. One of the top pitchers of the game, he was free to sign with any team, and he ultimately chose the New York Yankees, who offered him a five-year guaranteed contract for $750,000. It also included a then-unheard-of $1 million signing bonus, deferred compensation and insurance benefits, making it worth $3.75 million. Hunter went from making $100,000 a year with the A's to earning over $3 million in his years with the Yankees. This unprecedented contract was the first indication of what a ball player could earn on the open market.

Other players now understood what Miller had been saying: they were grossly underpaid due to the anticompetitive system which depressed salaries. The Hunter grievance provided the impetus for baseball players to become free agents. Two pitchers, Andy Messersmith of the Dodgers and Dave McNally of the Expos, decided to "hold out" for the 1975 season, playing under the option period in the reserve clause. Then they planned to take their dispute to arbitrator Seitz in the hopes of making them free agents. The owners, fearful, offered them increasingly lucrative contracts, which both players refused.

Seitz, the "neutral" pick of the three-member arbitration board, cast the deciding vote in the Messersmith and McNally dispute. Although barred from ruling on the validity of the reserve clause because of the prohibition in the 1973 CBA, he could interpret its scope. The key question was this: Was it a one-year option that concludes at the end of that one year, or does it serve as a recurring set of options to be exercised by the team? Using basic contract interpretation rules, Seitz determined the reserve clause as having a one-year limit. He concluded that a plain meaning of the key term "for the period of one year" could only mean that after the one-year "reserve" period, any player was free to contract with a team of his choice, as he was released from his contractual obligations with the prior club. The modern age of free agency was born (*National & American League Professional Baseball Clubs v. MLBPA*, 1976).

After the award was unsuccessfully challenged in the courts (*Kansas City Royal Baseball Corp. v. MLBPA*, 1976), the baseball owners had to recognize a very different economic reality. When the 1973 CBA expired in 1976, the union had a much stronger hand to play in the negotiations for a new agreement. Owners, fearful of the effects of unfettered free agency and unprepared for its potential alteration of the baseball landscape, did not know what to do.

In one sense, Miller saved them. Miller did not favor complete free agency, but not because of concern about the owners. He thought it was not in the best interests of players, as younger and/or nonstar players could be adversely affected. The owners had an incentive to negotiate short-term contracts and to cast off mediocre players after bad seasons. What the union wanted (and received) was a system that allowed only veteran players free agency. The union hoped that free-agent veterans receiving market-level salaries would create a ripple effect benefiting younger players.

The 1976 CBA set the framework that still exists to this day. During the first two years in the league (since extended to three years), a player had to accept his club's contract offers, without right to arbitration or free agency. From years three to six, salary disputes were referred to arbitration, where the independent third party determined the salary. After six years of service, players would become free agents. This new system produced a considerable increase in player compensation, as the average salary rose from $50,000 in 1976 to $370,000 in 1985 (Weiler & Roberts, 2004).

Player salaries continued to rise and, in 1985, Commissioner Peter Ueberroth encouraged owners to refrain from signing free agents from other teams. That "encouragement" occurred in a number of owners' meetings after the season. As a result, free-agent signings dropped dramatically. Only four of thirty-two free agents signed with other clubs. The other twenty-eight did not receive a single offer from another team. A similar pattern occurred in 1986. The lack of signings kept salary increases in check, but raised the union's suspicions of collusion by the owners.

If the owners in any other sports league tried the same tactic, a court would likely conclude an antitrust law violation. However, baseball's antitrust exemption protected the owners from that possibility. Therefore, the union relied on a clause shrewdly negotiated in the 1976 CBA that prohibited players and owners from negotiating contracts as a group. This had been proposed by the owners to avoid situations where players (such as Dodgers pitchers Sandy Koufax and Don Drysdale) tried to negotiate as one unit. The union agreed to the clause, but in return demanded a reciprocal prohibition on the part of the teams. An arbitration panel ruled that the owners' actions to shut out free agents violated this provision, and damages of $280 million were assessed (*Matter of Arbitration Between MLBPA and the 26 Major League Clubs* (1987), Grievance No. 86–2).

The 1994 Strike

The last strike by the players occurred in the summer of 1994. By that time, both the NBA and NFL CBAs had provisions limiting the amount of money a team could spend on players' salaries. Many baseball owners wanted a "salary cap" system as well, especially those from smaller-market teams, who claimed economic hardship due to the rising costs of free agents and arbitration rulings using free-agent signings as a basis for their conclusions. Acting commissioner Bud Selig (who owned a small-market team, the Milwaukee Brewers) led the owners in a push for major changes in the way that baseball did business with its players. They sought a salary cap and the elimination of arbitration. The union (led by Donald Fehr, who succeeded Marvin Miller) chafed at the proposals. The players decided that their best leverage was a strike in August, when the season is three-quarters complete. Despite efforts of members of Congress and President Bill Clinton and the intervention of federal mediators, the strike continued and ultimately resulted in the cancellation of the World Series. Ultimately, the courts intervened and the strike ended in April 1995.

The players claimed that the owners engaged in an unfair labor practice in violation of the National Labor Relations Act. As said earlier, management and the union must negotiate in good faith, and management can impose its proposed changes only when an impasse is reached and further negotiations would be fruitless. The owners claimed that point had been reached and unilaterally imposed their terms, which included a salary cap. The players claimed that there was no impasse and that the owners had engaged in an unfair labor practice.

The National Labor Relations Board agreed with the players, and ultimately, the board's conclusions were upheld by a federal appeals court (*Silverman v. Major League Baseball Player Relations Committee*, 1995), and with this victory, the players ended the strike and returned to work in April 1995. As a result of the strike, fan attendance dropped, as did salaries, but that drop was temporary. Although average salaries dropped 10 percent in 1995, they grew 8.5 and 14.2 percent in the following two seasons (*Baseball Archive*, 1998). The result was an increasing gap between "small-market" and "big-market" teams. The luxury tax did not work to restrain salary growth.

The 2011 Agreement

In the summer of 2002, Major League Baseball and the MLBPA signed a collective bargaining agreement that ran through the end of 2006 and was then extended to 2011 and then to 2016. The agreement, echoing the two previous CBAs, combines salary control and payroll parity in an attempt to eliminate the disparity between "richer" and "poorer" teams. In recent years, the increased revenue sharing has done that, at least in terms of the competitive balance. Since 2001, no team has won the World Series two consecutive years. The present CBA (known as the "Basic Agreement") includes the following.

Free Agency

A player with six years of accrued service in the major leagues is eligible for unrestricted free agency (unless he remains under contract). A league year is defined in "service days," and a player who completes 172 service days has completed one service year. A player earns one day of service time for every day he is on the twenty-five-man roster or the Major League disabled list during the regular season (Major League Baseball CBA, Article XXI(A)) (Fangraphs.com, n.d.).

Salary Arbitration

Players with between three and six seasons of Major League service are eligible for salary arbitration. The dispute is submitted for "binding" arbitration to a selected three-person panel. Each side proposes a salary, and the arbitrator chooses the figure based on "overall performance, special qualities of leadership and public appeal" during the last season. Also, arbitrators can compare the contracts of similarly successful players in determining the award (Major League Baseball CBA, Article VI(E)).

Revenue Sharing

The CBA provides that each team contributes 34 percent of its "net local revenue," after deductions for ballpark expenses, to a cash pool, a portion of which is redistributed equally to all thirty teams. This is known as the "Base Plan" (Major League Baseball CBA, Article XXIV). A second fund, the Central Fund Component, allocates another portion from that central fund from "richer" teams to "poorer" teams (Major League Baseball CBA, Article XXIV). It includes all of the centrally generated operating revenues of the Major League clubs, including revenues from national and international television, cable, radio, Internet agreements and merchandise (Major League Baseball CBA, Article XXIV(A)(4)).

A Commissioner's Discretionary Fund

A $15 million fund, with monies derived from equal contributions ($500,000), goes to the commissioner. The commissioner may make distributions from the fund to a club or clubs, in amounts and at times to be determined at the commissioner's discretion, as long as the amounts do not violate other terms of the CBA (Major League Baseball CBA, Article XXIV(A) (14)).

A Luxury Tax on Excess Team Payrolls

Officially known as the "Competitive Balance Tax," this is a central component of the agreement. Teams whose payrolls exceed set thresholds will be taxed on the portions above the thresholds. The bulk of that money is to be used to fund player benefits (Major League Baseball CBA, Article XXIII).

It works like this. There is a "tax threshold," the maximum payroll a team can have without triggering the tax. The threshold was $178 million in 2013 and $189 million in 2014–16. If a team's payroll reaches beyond the threshold, then the tax is computed based on two variables: (a) the year of the CBA and (b) the team's Competitive Balance Tax rate in the previous year. For example, for a club that has an actual club payroll above the tax threshold in the 2013, 2014, 2015 or 2016 contract year, the applicable Competitive Balance Tax rate shall be 17.5 percent if the club did not exceed the tax threshold in the preceding contract year; 30 percent if the club's Competitive Balance Tax rate in the preceding contract year was 17.5 percent ; 40 percent if the club's Competitive Balance Tax rate in the preceding contract year was 30 percent; and 50 percent if the club's Competitive Balance Tax rate in the preceding contract year was 40 percent (Major League Baseball CBA, Article XXIII(B)(2)).

These rates may not be as onerous as they appear. Note that the tax kicks in only for payroll amounts above the threshold. Anything below the threshold is not a basis for the tax calculations. For example, if a team has a $200 million payroll in 2014 and is a first-time violator, the team pays $1.925 million in taxes ($200 million – $189 million threshold) × 17.5 percent). If the tax were based on the entire payroll amount, then the tax would be $35 million (Major League Baseball CBA, Article XXIII). In 2016, the Los Angeles Dodgers paid a record $43 million in luxury taxes on a payroll around $300 million (Associated Press, 2015).

Limits on the Debt a Team May Carry

Also known as the "Debt Service Rule," this states that a team's debt cannot exceed eight times EBITDA (earnings before interest, taxes, depreciation and amortization—a commonly used financial formula determined by subtracting a company's operating expenses such as payroll, administrative costs, travel and other items from gross revenues). For teams that have incurred debt to finance the construction or renovation of a stadium, the figure is extended to twelve times EBITDA for the first ten years after that stadium's opening or reopening. The purpose is to ensure that a team's cash flow is sufficient to meet its present and future obligations (Major League Baseball CBA, Attachment 22).

Minimum Salaries

The annual minimum salary paid to players increased from $490,000 in 2013 to $500,000 in 2014 and $500,000 (plus a cost-of-living adjustment) in 2015 (Major League Baseball CBA, Article VI).

Random Testing for Performance-Enhancing Substances

Discussion of these rules is found in Chapter 12.

Competitive Balance Draft

The goal of the revenue-sharing system is to increase the competitive balance between traditionally "rich" and "poor" teams in baseball. In addition, the 2011 collective bargaining agreement created a "competitive balance draft." Started in the 2013 player draft, this lottery means that every team that is one of the ten smallest-market and/or the ten lowest-revenue franchises will be eligible to win an extra pick in the draft. The odds of winning the lottery are determined by each team's winning percentage from the previous year. A total of twelve picks will be awarded, with six coming at the end of the first round and six at the end of the second (Halverson, 2012).

The increasing revenue sharing, and the draft, may have achieved some success. Lower-revenue teams such as the Kansas City Royals won the World Series in 2015. However, the salary gaps between the "rich" and "poor" teams remain (Gaines, 2014).

The 2016 Agreement

As the book was going to press, MLB and the players' association reached a new five-year CBA at the end of 2016. It keeps the same framework as the expired agreement, but does make changes in the compensation given up by teams who sign "premium" free agents. Those teams no longer have to give up a first-round draft pick to the team that lost that player. However, such teams with will have to give up players in the second, third or fifth rounds, depending on whether their payrolls are higher than the luxury-tax threshold or not. The new CBA also imposes salary caps on bonuses paid to foreign-born international amateur players and increases the luxury tax thresholds to a range of $195 million in 2017 to $210 million in 2021. The tax rates would remain the same. Minimum wages would increase to a range from $507,500 to $555,000 in 2019 with cost of living increases for the last two years). The CBA also ends the practice that the winning league of the All-Star Game gets home field advantage in the World Series. Instead it goes to the pennant winner with the better regular-season record. Changes in the domestic violence and revisions to the revenue sharing regiment were agreed to, but not released (Stark, 2016).

National Football League

History

Although the NFLPA was formed in 1956, the NFL players began collective bargaining negotiation with the league only in the late 1960s. As in baseball, the major issue centered on changes in wage restrictions based on a "reserve" system. However, unlike baseball, the NFL did not have immunity from antitrust laws, and until 1993 many of the labor controversies were decided by the courts.

Although NFL player contracts did not contain a "reserve clause" per se, the league commissioner, Pete Rozelle, imposed a requirement that had the same effect. The "Rozelle Rule" required a team signing a free agent to provide "fair and equitable" compensation to the team losing that player. The compensation could be in the form of active players and/or draft choices. The rule, unilaterally imposed in 1963, ultimately found its way into the first CBA made between the NFL and the NFLPA in 1968.

Over the next quarter-century, the NFLPA attempted to change the rule, but was not as successful as its baseball counterpart in creating a more open market for players. A 1974 strike failed after the union realized it lacked the leverage to ease the restriction. The union then turned to the courts, and in 1976 a federal appeals court concluded that the Rozelle Rule was an antitrust violation (*Mackey v. NFL*, 1976). Because the rule had been not negotiated, but imposed, it was held to be illegal.

After the court negated the Rozelle Rule, the union and NFL attempted to negotiate a new CBA. The league made proposals regarding free agency. One proposal (called "Plan B") provided free agency to a limited number of players on each team without a requirement of compensation to the old team. In return, certain players received diminished benefits. When negotiations failed, the NFL imposed Plan B unilaterally. Ironically, this system was even more restrictive than the Rozelle Rule because it gave the prior team the right of first refusal for thirty-seven players on each team's roster, even if they were free agents. During the period from 1963 to 1974, 176 players became free agents, of whom thirty-four signed with other clubs. From 1977 to 1987, only one free-agent player was signed by a new team.

In 1987, the NFLPA wanted to remove free-agency restrictions and went on strike to force the owners to eliminate Plan B. The NFL employed replacement players, a move that hastened the end of the strike. The use of replacements served two purposes for the owners. First, they were able to continue the season, although the quality of the games suffered. Second, the owners weakened the union's resolve. Ultimately, enough NFL players crossed the picket line to force the NFLPA to capitulate (Staudohar, 1988).

From the late 1980s to early 1990s, the union went back to court, unsuccessfully seeking antitrust protection. It lost on account of a legal doctrine known as the "nonstatutory labor exemption" to the antitrust laws. This doctrine prevents the courts from applying antitrust laws for activities that occur during the collective bargaining process. So the negotiating approaches used by one or both parties supersede antitrust law. A series of court rulings concluded that the players lost the protection of the antitrust laws when they negotiated free-agency terms through the union (*Powell v. NFL*, 1989). The players then voted to "decertify" the union, thereby revoking its authority to represent them in contract negotiations. By doing so, the players believed their antitrust claims would be resurrected, and a federal court agreed (*McNeil v. NFL*, 1992), finding that once revocation of union authority occurred, antitrust law claims could be used as a basis of a lawsuit to eliminate the restrictive free-agent rules.

Ironically, the attempt to decertify brought the NFL and the NFLPA back to the bargaining table. The two sides, realizing the potential chaos that could result from decertification, negotiated a CBA in 1993, one so successful that it has been extended twice at the time of this writing. The result has been relative labor harmony until 2011.

In that year, negotiations became contentious as NFL owners attempted to limit the definition of the revenue pool for the players. After negotiations broke down, the owners locked out the players and then the players decided to "disclaim" the union, meaning that it would stop representing players in contract negotiations, and after doing so, a lawsuit was filed accusing the NFL of engaging in antitrust violations (Battista, 2011). After months of litigation, the courts ruled in favor of the NFL, and the parties quickly came to an agreement, salvaging the 2011–12 season. This agreement continues until the end of the 2020 season.

The Present Collective Bargaining Agreement

Aside from a salary cap, discussed in detail later in the chapter, the CBA contains the following.

Rookie Compensation

The collective bargaining agreement provides a formula that imposes salary controls for rookies. In addition to the general cap rules (explained later), a rookie compensation pool is utilized, which puts limitations on the total amount teams can spend on a rookie's first-year salary and the total contract (usually four years) (NFL CBA, Article VII, sec. 3). As of 2016, that pool was estimated at about $1 billion, which is divided equally among the league's thirty-two teams. Within that pool, players who are high draft picks command handsome compensation packages, but those who rank lower see far less in salaries and bonuses. For example, the top pick of the 2016 draft received almost $28 million in salary and bonus in a four-year contract; the lower pick in the first round received a package of $8.25 million over four years (NFL.com, 2016).

Non–Free Agents

Generally, free agency for players with fewer than three "accrued" seasons of NFL tenure does not exist. An accrued season means eligibility to play six or more regular season games. The only exception occurs when a team fails to give one of its players a contract offer for at least one season by March 1 following the expiration of the prior season. In such a case, the player is free to negotiate a contract with any team (NFL CBA, Article 8, sec. 2).

Restricted Free Agency

A veteran with more than three and fewer than four accrued seasons in any capped year (or five in an uncapped year) shall, at the expiration of his last player contract during such period, become a restricted free agent. If, prior to the signing period set by the NFL and the NFLPA, such a player receives a contract proposal (known as an "offer sheet") from a new club, his old club may exercise a right of first refusal and match the offer and retain him. If the old club does not match the offer, the player may sign with the new team, but in many cases that team must "compensate" the former team by offering draft choices. The number and quality of the draft choices depend on the amount of the offer (NFL CBA, Article 9, sec. 2). If the new team offers the player 110 percent of his previous year's salary, the current club has both "right of first refusal" and rights to a draft pick from the same round (or better) from the signing club (NFL CBA, Article 9, sec. 2).

Unrestricted Free Agency

A veteran with four years or more of accrued service (six years in the uncapped final year of the CBA) may, once his contract expires, negotiate and sign a contract with any club, with no compensation awarded to the former team. (NFL CBA, Article 9, sec. 1). Although players are eligible for unrestricted free agency sooner than their baseball counterparts (six years), one should keep in mind that the average playing time for an NFL player is about three and a half years (Bennett, 2011) and only about 20 percent of all NFL players become unrestricted free agents (spotrac.com, 2015).

The Franchise Player

In order to prevent a star player from leaving a team as a free agent, the CBA created a category known as a "franchise" player. Each team can designate one player, who would otherwise be an unrestricted free agent, as a franchise player per season. The player so designated may also be one who would otherwise be a restricted free agent. The player may negotiate only with his old club for that season, and the club must pay him based on one of two standards: either 120 percent of his prior year's salary or an average of the five highest league salaries for his position, whichever is greater (NFL CBA, Article 10, secs. 1 and 2(i)). For 2015, the franchise player compensation ranged from the highest levels: $18.5 million for a quarterback to almost $11 million for a running back to the two lowest positions: $9.6 million for a safety and $4.1 million for a placekicker (Bien, 2015).

Transition Players

Each NFL club is permitted to designate one unrestricted free agent as a "transition player." Additionally, the club can designate a transition player in lieu of a franchise player, giving that team two transition players for the same season. Transition players are free to negotiate with any club during the designated time period, but the old club retains the right of first refusal over any offer with a new club. A transition player must receive the greater of either 120 percent of his prior year's salary or the average of the top ten players in his position (NFL CBA, Article 10, secs. 3, 4 and 11).

Guarantees

An NFL contract is generally not "guaranteed." Of all the major pro sports leagues, the NFL offers teams the most flexibility in releasing players, particularly given that most of an NFL player's contract is nonguaranteed income. Teams can cut players for performance reasons, business reasons and if a player has "engaged in personal conduct reasonably judged by [the] Club to adversely affect or reflect on [the] Club" (NFL Standard Player's Contract, Paragraph 11, 2011).

In some cases, however, a contract may contain "skill" or "injury" guarantees. A skill guarantee obligates the club to continue paying under the contract even if the player has insufficient skill to make or remain with the club. An injury guarantee ensures full payment to the player in the event that he is unable to satisfy the team's physical exam requirements or becomes physically unable to perform as a result of on-field injuries suffered during the contract. The payment covers the present season and up to 50 percent of salary for the following year up to $1.1 million in the 2015–16 season, gradually rising to $1.2 million in the 2019–20 season, the final year of this agreement (NFL CBA, Article 45, sec. 2).

From the players' standpoint, one of the major weaknesses of the CBA is the nonguaranteed salary. Despite the fact that the NFL has the richest television contract in sports and the league makes billions in revenue, NFL players do not enjoy the same security as many players in the other major league sports. In fact, by signing a nonguaranteed contract, an NFL player takes a considerable risk, as he can be terminated (or "cut") at any time.

For example, if the player becomes "too expensive" to the team due to salary cap constraints (discussed shortly), the team can either force a renegotiation of the contract or terminate the player. Stanford University professor Roger Noll put it best when he said that "the absence of guaranteed contracts transfers the risk of injury or deterioration of skills from the team to the player" (Cunningham, 2004).

Yet average football salaries, as shown in the table at the conclusion of this chapter, lag behind those of other sports, in part because of the salary cap restrictions found in the CBA. However, it should be noted that more and more rookie contracts have a significant portion of their salaries guaranteed in the event of injuries (McFarland, 2016).

Commissioner's Disciplinary Powers

Probably the most controversial portion of the collective bargaining agreement is Article 46, which covers player discipline. It gives the commissioner sole authority to determine sanctions against players for certain transgressions, with little effective redress on the part of the player (NFL CBA, Article 46). Other major league sports have some independent grievance arbitration process for player discipline, but the National Football League Players Association decided not to press for a similar system. In retrospect, the failure to bargain for a neutral grievance arbitration standard resulted in contentious relations between the commissioner and the National Football League Players' Association, as noted in Chapter 1 and a "loss" for the union (Armour, 2015). Because of Article 46, Commissioner Goodell was able to launch a new "personal conduct" policy in December 2014, which gives him even greater power over player transgressions. More specifically, the updated policy (permitted by the collective bargaining agreement) provides for the appointment of a disciplinary officer responsible for investigating accusations directed at players and issuing initial discipline, and also grants the commissioner the option of creating a panel of independent experts to participate in deciding appeals for discipline levied against players. The new measures further require that the commissioner appoint a new league Conduct Committee to review policy annually and recommend appropriate changes with advice from outside experts (National Football League, 2014). In response, the NFLPA filed a grievance against the NFL to challenge the new policy on the grounds that it was adopted "without the consent, and over the objections, of the NFLPA" (Schefter, 2015). The next year, an arbitrator rejected the union's claim, concluding that the new policy does not conflict with the collective bargaining agreement (Werly, 2016).

The scope of this power was put to the test in disciplinary matters involving three players: Ray Rice, Adrian Peterson and Tom Brady. As noted in Chapter 1, the Brady and Peterson determinations were challenged in the courts, but in 2016, two federal appeals panels ultimately reinstated the punishments against Peterson and Brady.

The Salary Cap

In 1993, the NFL and its union agreed to implement a salary cap. The NFL is the second league in the major leagues to do so (the first was the NBA). The salary cap limits the amount of salary growth in a modified free-agency system. Basically, player costs are limited to a specific percentage of league-wide revenues divided equally by the number of franchises existing in the league. The result, at least theoretically, restricts the cumulative salary that a team can pay its athletes. Not only intended to control salary growth, the cap also promoted competitive balance among the teams in the league. With a cap, a "richer" team did not have an unfair advantage over a "poorer" team in signing marquee players.

At the outset, the two most important considerations when discussing a salary cap have been (a) how the cap is calculated and (b) its exceptions. Many call the NFL salary cap system a "hard cap," compared with the "soft cap" system operated by the NBA. The NFL cap is considered a "hard cap" in that it seems to establish a more definite predetermined limit on the amount a team may pay its players. However, the NFL system is filled with exceptions (NFL CBA, Article 13, sec. 6(b)(i)).

The NFL salary cap set a ceiling on the amount of money that any one team may spend on its players within a given season (known as a "league year," starting from March 10 and lasting to March 9 of the following year) and effectively limits the number of teams with which a player may negotiate. Since 2012, that ceiling was based on the "player cost amount" in a given year minus "projected benefits," divided by the number of teams playing in the NFL during such year (NFL CBA, Article 12, Section 6(c)(v)). The player cost amount consists of the sum of (1) 55 percent of projected league media revenues; (2) 45 percent of projected NFL ventures/postseason revenues; (3) 40 percent of projected local revenues; and (4) if applicable, 50 percent of the net revenues for new line-of-business projects minus (5) 47.5 percent of the joint contribution amount (set at $55 million in 2012 and growing by 5 percent annually) (NFL CBA, Article 12, sec. 6(c)(i)). The local revenues include regular season, preseason and postseason gate receipts, including ticket revenue from "luxury boxes," suites and premium seating among NFL clubs (NFL CBA, Article 12, sec. 1(a)(1). Projected benefits include, among other things, player pension funding, group insurance, supplemental disability, workers' compensation, unemployment compensation, Social Security taxes, postseason salary, practice squad salary and medical costs (NFL CBA, Article 12, sec. 2). In 2016, the team cap came to $155 million (Knoblauch, 2016).

To ensure that NFL owners did not pocket too much of their projected revenues, the CBA stated that, league-wide, the players were guaranteed to receive a *minimum* of 48.5 percent of "all projected revenue" between 2015 and 2020 in any capped season (NFL CBA, Article 12, sec. 6(c)(ii). If player costs for all NFL teams fall below 47 percent of projected revenue in a capped season, the player cost amount is increased to that amount (CBA, Article 12, sec. 6(c)(ii)). Such revenue includes ticket sales, revenue from luxury box suites and premium seating, local and national broadcasting (TV/radio/Internet) royalties, concessions, parking, local advertising, stadium leasing and merchandising (NFL CBA, Article 12, sec. 1). In addition to the league-wide salary cap, the current CBA mandates that individual teams pay their players a specified minimum percentage of the salary cap. Between 2013 and 2020 it was set at 89 percent of the salary cap (NFL CBA, Article 12, sec. 9(a)).

Even though the standard just described seems strict, the cap rules have been applied in a clever fashion. Some amounts, such as a player's base salary and certain types of bonus payments, were to be calculated only for the particular season in which they are paid under the player's contract (NFL CBA, Article 13, sec. 6). But certain payments were prorated over the life of the player's contract in order to get "salary cap relief" (NFL CBA, Article 13, sec. 6). This strategy can produce instant results by keeping high-quality players for an attempt at a Super Bowl championship. However, by using this accounting technique, teams mortgaged their future in favor of opening up salary room immediately.

Hypothetically, a highly touted first-round quarterback could receive a contract including (a) a signing bonus of $20 million; (b) a base salary of $8 million; (c) a roster bonus of $75,000; (d) a reporting bonus of $75,000; (e) $75,000 for playing in 80 percent of team games; (f) $100,000 for gaining 1,200 yards in a season; (g) $200,000 for making the All-Pro team and being the most valuable player; and (h) $300,000 if the team goes to the Super Bowl. As described next, some of this money is prorated and some is not.

These rules were complex but important in calculating salary cap room. A summary follows.

Signing Bonuses

The signing bonus is the amount of money received by a player for merely agreeing to a contract with the team. The player and his agent attempted to maximize the signing bonus because it was *not* based on the player's performance and was typically the only guaranteed payment the player received. Thus, if a player had insufficient skill or was injured and not able to remain with his NFL team, the signing bonus was not forfeited or diminished in value. The rest of the contract, however, was usually terminated (NFL CBA, Article 13, sec. 6(b)(iii)).

The signing bonus was the best-known and simplest method of circumventing the salary cap because it was prorated over the life of the contract with a maximum proration of five years for salary cap purposes (NFL CBA, Article 13, sec. 6(b)(i)). In other words, the total bonus amount is divided by the number of years in the player's contract and, under the terms of the CBA, only the prorated amount is applied toward a given year's salary cap calculation. In the hypothetical noted earlier, if player X signs a four-year contract with a $20 million signing bonus, $5 million will count toward the cap over those four seasons.

However, the use of prorated signing bonuses carries some risk. Releasing players with large signing bonuses early in their contracts penalizes the team under the salary cap. So, if a player left the team before his contract expired, the remaining prorated portion of the bonus was counted immediately, in a lump sum, against the cap. Taking our last example, the team will take a "cap hit" of $10 million if the player with a four-year contract and $20 million bonus is released by June 1 before the upcoming season after playing two years.

Other types of bonuses exist, such as the guaranteed roster bonuses (a payment made in the preseason) and reporting bonuses (an extra payment for simply reporting to training camp). As described next, teams used other deferred compensation techniques to skirt the salary cap.

Contract Renegotiation

In order to save salary room and keep star players, owners have renegotiated player contracts. There are basically two ways to do this. The first is by reducing a player's salary and spreading it over a longer period.

The reduction will create salary room in that given season. Also, money guaranteed in contract extensions and modifications is proratable (NFL CBA, Article 13, sec. 6(b)(iii)(3)).

A second approach involves "reworking" a player's existing contract to get salary cap relief. This serves to diminish salary. Taking our earlier example, say the player under contract for $8 million per season accepts a modification to a lower amount, $5 million. The team then has an extra $3 million in salary cap room for the season. In some cases, the renegotiation may result in the player's salary being paid over a longer period. Let's take the following case.

An expensive veteran quarterback, under a four-year contract, making $15 million per season, coupled with a $15 million signing bonus, has two years left. The backup quarterback, making far less, played more games last season and achieved better production. The team does not want to continue paying such a high sum to a declining player. It could do several things:

(a) Force a salary reduction and use this quarterback as either a starter or a backup. The result would be a lower salary and a restructuring, spreading the cap hit over future years.
(b) Release the player and take about a $7.5 million hit against its salary cap for the remaining prorated portion of his past signing bonuses.
(c) Renegotiate the signing bonus.

Option (a) would save some salary cap room next year, but cost the team out-of-pocket cash (notably the signing bonus, which was paid up front). However, option (b) would cost salary cap room because $7.5 million would have been charged to this coming year, but would not cost the team any cash, because it would not have to pay the player (Miller, 2003). Option (c) would involve renegotiating the signing bonus. Part of the player's base salary would be swapped into an added signing bonus. As a result, the player would receive more guaranteed cash, and the owner creates more cap room, as well as retaining the player's services for a longer period if the contract term was extended. Also, this added bonus would not affect the proration of the original signing bonus.

Incentive Clauses

Incentive clauses are performance-based awards found in many NFL contracts. The number of incentive clauses and their values are a function of various factors, including the individual club's talent pool, the player's leverage, his expected and past contributions to his club, his salary and the number of years the player has served. The base salary theoretically reflects contributions that were covered by previous incentive packages.

"Playtime" incentives reward a player for the amount of time on the field. Performance can be measured by dividing the player's total regular season plays (offensive or defensive) by the club's total regular season plays (NFL CBA, Article 7, sec. 6(a)).

"Individual incentives" reward a player's on-field performance within various statistical categories based on terms and conditions set forth in the contract for a particular year. The scope of these clauses was limited only by the creativity and ingenuity of the negotiators. For example, a wide receiver can be rewarded if he leads the NFL in receptions, or a quarterback may receive extra money if he ends the season with the highest quarterback rating in the league (NFL CBA, Article 13, Exhibit B). However, the types of individual incentives that can be offered are limited to those specifically enumerated in the CBA (NFL CBA, Article 13, sec. 6(c)(vi)).

"Honors or media" incentives reward a player for exceptional individual achievements. Such incentives are attractive to clubs because relatively few players, regardless of their ability, earn such incentives in any given season. Some of the awards include NFL Most Valuable Player, NFL Defensive Player of the Year, All-NFL First or Second Team, selection to the Pro-Bowl and Rookie of the Year (NFL CBA, Article 13, Exhibit C). Again, the types of honors or media incentives that can be offered are restricted to those mentioned in the CBA (NFL CBA, Article 13, sec. 6(c)(viii)).

Additionally, players often receive bonuses contingent on the performance and success of their team. Team performance incentives include bonuses based on the team's statistical performance or ranking. Examples of performance categories include the NFL's top-ranked offense or defense. Also, a team can reward each player with a progressively higher amount of money if the team advances into the playoffs or wins the division, conference championship or Super Bowl (NFL CBA, Article 13, Exhibit A). Like the types of incentives mentioned earlier, team incentives are limited to those mentioned in the CBA (NFL CBA, Article 13, sec. 6(c)(v)).

As we can see, NFL contracts use incentive clauses with considerable frequency. But how the extra compensation fits into the salary cap during the many years of its use presents an important question. The NFL–NFLPA collective bargaining agreement created two different categories: (a) incentives "likely to be earned" based on whether the player's or the team's performance could have satisfied during the prior year and (b) incentives "not likely to be earned." If the incentive was likely to be earned, it counted toward the team salary in the current year's salary cap. If it was not likely to be earned, it was *not* to be counted against the cap even if the player met the incentive and got paid (NFL CBA, Article 13, sec. 6(iv)). To interpret this very subjective standard, the CBA provided this example to help in determining whether an incentive clause is likely or not likely to be earned for salary cap purposes. Assume that player X receives an incentive bonus if he participates in 50 percent of the team's offensive plays this season. Assume further that last season the team had 1,000 offensive plays. Therefore, as soon as player X plays in 500 plays in the current season (or 50 percent of last year's 1,000 plays), the incentive will be considered "earned" for salary cap purposes. The same incentive is considered not earned if the same player in the current year participated in only one of the team's first 502 offensive plays. In this situation, it would be impossible for the player to achieve the 50 percent incentive based on last year's performance of 1,000 plays.

Therefore, if the player receives money for attaining the "likely to be earned" incentive and that amount puts the team over the cap, the amount paid above the salary cap in performance bonuses will be subtracted from the team's salary cap in the next year (NFL CBA, Article 13, sec. 6(c)(xxv)).

Deferred Compensation

The present CBA requires that base salary and bonuses that are deferred be counted in the year earned, not the year paid (NFL CBA, Article 13, sec. 6(a)(ii)). However, there are limits as to how much money can be deferred. The collective bargaining agreement stipulates "that no more than 50% of the player's Salary up to and including a total of the first $2 million, and no more than 75% of the player's Salary in excess of $2 million can be deferred" (NFL CBA, Article 26, sec. 6). The use of deferred compensation has its risks. It could free salary room in the beginning but take up space in later years.

Case Study: A Hypothetical Salary Cap Situation

Note that the salary cap calculations may be very complex, depending on the player and the contract and the examples given here are relatively basic.

Player Z for the Jacksonville Jaguars signs a two-year $3 million contact with a $500,000 signing bonus. There is also a bonus of $250,000 if he makes the team in the second year of the contract. The only portion of this contract that is guaranteed is the signing bonus.

For the first year, Player Z will receive $2 million in compensation, which includes his $500,000 bonus. However, for cap calculation, the team will be assessed $1.75 million. However, for the second year, he could receive $1.75 million (his salary and the bonus), but the cap hit will be $2 million, since the half of the signing bonus is applied to that year of the contract. Therefore, the team will be assessed a larger cap hit than the money it is actually paying.

In the event Player Z is cut from the team, that extra $250,000 is known as "dead money." Basically it is on the ledger even though the player is no longer playing for the team. Too much "dead money" can be detrimental to a team's payroll under this system.

National Basketball Association

History

The modern NBA arose from a merger of two rivals, the Basketball Association of America (BAA) and the National Basketball League (NBL), in 1949. Not surprisingly, in its early years, the NBA players worked under the same restricted salary arrangements as in other major sports leagues.

Like their football and baseball counterparts, NBA players slowly adapted to labor–management negotiation. Although formed in 1954, the National Basketball Players' Association (NBPA) and the NBA did not engage in collective bargaining negotiations for over a decade.

Similar to the other leagues, the NBA attempted to control salaries by a form of reserve system. And, like their NFLPA counterparts, the NBPA first challenged the limitation based on antitrust violations, rather than negotiation of a collective bargaining agreement. The lawsuit, known as the Oscar Robertson litigation (after the Hall of Fame player), was filed in 1970 and challenged the league's reserve clause that severely curtailed free agency and effectively limited salaries (*Robertson v. NBA*, 1970). The case was settled in 1976, and the reserve clause was eliminated and replaced with a compensation system whereby teams that lost free agents would be entitled to cash, players or draft choices determined by the NBA commissioner from the signing team. Additionally, the player's former team would hold the right of first refusal on any free-agent signings.

At the time of the settlement, the NBA absorbed four teams from the defunct American Basketball Association (ABA) (1967–76), depriving players of a competitor league that attracted NBA players by offering more lucrative contracts. The terms of the settlement were memorialized in a CBA concluded in 1980. In 1983, the NBA became the first professional sports league to establish a salary cap. At the time, many NBA teams experienced financial difficulties. Franchises in Cleveland, Denver, Indiana, Kansas City, San Diego and Utah reported serious losses, and some fell behind on deferred payments to former players (Bradley, n.d.). In this atmosphere, the NBA and the NBPA decided to develop a novel salary structure. They created a salary cap on the amount teams pay most players, regardless of whether they are free agents or rookies. This agreement resulted in considerable success in stabilizing the finances of the league and its teams. The blueprint remains effective to the present day.

The players were to be paid an aggregate amount of at least 53 percent of the league's "guaranteed share of revenues," known as the "defined gross revenues," which included gate receipts, local and national television and radio revenue and preseason and postseason revenues (Bradley, n.d.). However, free agency remained restricted.

The NBA and NBPA agreed to unrestricted free agency for veteran players in a six-year CBA in 1988. By 1991, the average salary for an NBA player was $1 million, up from $200,000 in 1976. New CBAs were negotiated in 1995 (after a three-month lockout), 1999 (after a six-month lockout), 2005 and 2011 (after a five-month lockout) (Stern, 2011).

The Present Collective Bargaining Agreement

In late 2011, the NBA and the NBPA negotiated a ten-year CBA. However, in late 2016, it was replaced with a new seven-year agreement that expires in 2024. In many respects, it keeps the prior system in place. This CBA also set maximum salaries for players based on their years of service and regulated the salaries for rookie players' contracts. It also created an "escrow and tax" system if league-wide salaries exceed a certain percentage. The NBA's salary structure offered, at least in theory, substantive control of salary growth. In return, the players received a minimum salary for veterans based on service, and methods to circumvent the cap, most notably by the continuation of the so-called "Larry Bird Exception."

The most important provisions of the current CBA are as follows.

Player Salary Maximums

This was an important concession by the union, because it put a drag on the salaries of the most elite players. The 2011 CBA computes the maximums based on a flat amount, or a percentage of the salary cap or a stipulated increase from the prior season's salary. For players with six or fewer years in the league, the annual maximum is the greater of (a) 25 percent of the salary cap in effect at the time the contract is executed or (b) 105 percent of the salary for the final season of the player's prior contract. For players in the league who have completed between seven and nine years, the maximum is the greater of (a) 30 percent of the salary cap in effect at the time the contract is executed or (b) 105 percent of the salary for the final season of the player's prior contract. For veterans with ten or more years in the NBA, the maximum is the greater of (a) 35 percent of the salary cap in effect at the time the contract is executed or (b) 105 percent of the salary for the final season of the player's prior contract (NBA CBA, Article II, sec. 7).

Player Salary Minimums

The parties agreed not only on salary ceilings but also to salary minimums for veteran players, as well as predetermined rookie salaries. According to this rookie salaries system, a player's salary was based not on his performance, but rather on the position at which he was selected in the draft (NBA CBA, Article VIII; NBA CBA, Exhibit B). Because a player's performance in college was not necessarily representative of his potential for success in the NBA, this system may have resulted in unfairness regarding a player's true market value. As of 2014–15 the breakdown was approximately as follows: rookies, $507,336; one-year veterans, $816,482; two-year veterans, $915,243; three-year veterans, $948,163; four-year veterans, $981,084; five-year veterans, $1,063,384; six-year veterans, $1,145,685; seven-year veterans, $1,227,985; eight-year veterans, $1,310,286; nine-year veterans, $1,316,809; 10 years and up, $1,448,490 (NBA CBA, Exhibit C).

The Salary Cap

The NBA salary cap system has not changed appreciably since it was first introduced in 1983. A team's salary cap for each year was determined by a formula based on "Basketball Related Income" (BRI). The cap amount was based on a figure of up to a stipulated percentage (which varies between 49 and 51 percent) of the projected BRI for the season, subtracting player benefits and dividing that amount by the number of teams in the league (thirty) (NBA CBA, Article VII, sec. 2(a)(1)).

Of crucial importance was how the BRI is computed. It includes aggregate operating revenues received by the NBA, such as gate receipts, broadcasting rights fees, proceeds from exhibition games and in-arena sales of concessions and novelties, parking, team sponsorships, 40 percent of fees from fixed arena signage and 40 percent of proceeds from luxury boxes (NBA CBA, Article VII, secs. 1(a)(1)(vi) and 1(a)(1)(vii)). The salary cap maximums have increased over the years as a consequence of the NBA's economic fortunes. For example, the 1983–84 season had a cap of $3.1 million per team. For the 2014–15 season, it was $70 million. During the same period, the average player salary rose from $250,000 to $3,941,907 in 2014 (basketball reference.com, n.d.). Under the 2016 agreement, salaries are expected to increase significantly due to the league's new media rights deals.

Free Agency

Restricted free agency, whereby the player's original team may match an offer by a prospective team, occurs after the fourth season for first-round picks and after the third season for most veterans. For longer periods of tenure, unrestricted free agency applies in most situations (NBA CBA,

Article XI, sec. 1). The cap amount grew significantly during 2016–17 due to the significant increases paid to the league under a new broadcast rights agreement.

Escrow

To protect teams against spiraling salaries (in part due to exceptions to the salary cap rules), the CBA limits aggregate player salaries to 57 percent of the previously defined BRI (NBA CBA, Article VII, sec. 12). To enforce this limitation, an "escrow and tax" system was established. Under this system, an amount not to exceed 10 percent of players' salaries was placed in escrow for the years after 2011. If aggregate player salaries exceeded that percentage, the league would be reimbursed (with interest) the amount of the overage by the escrow fund (NBA CBA, Article VII, sec. 12(c)). Any money remaining in the escrow fund would be returned to the players with interest.

Luxury Tax

In addition to the salary cap system, the NBA created another mechanism to control team spending. Known as the "tax" or "luxury tax," it is paid by teams whose payroll exceeds a predetermined tax level (calculated by taking 53.51 percent of projected "Basketball Related Income" subtracting projected benefits and dividing by the number of teams in the league). If the tax was triggered, all teams over the luxury tax threshold had to pay, dollar for dollar, the amount by which their team salary exceeded the tax threshold (NBA CBA, Article. VII, sec. 12). The luxury tax threshold on 2014–15 salaries was approximately $1.50 for every dollar that a team exceeded the tax rate, up to $5 million. (The tax rate was set at just over $63 million. For amounts $5 million and above, the rate increases to $1.75 for every dollar; over $10 million, $2.50; over $15 million, $3.25.) For example, in 2013–14, a team with a team salary that exceeds the tax level by $11 million would pay a tax of $18.75 million (i.e., $5 million times $1.50, plus $5 million times $1.75, plus $1 million times $2.50) (NBA CBA, Article VII, sec. 12(f)). Note that the tax has not prevented teams from exceeding the salary cap but has presented strong monetary incentives to avoid doing so, similar to the luxury tax found in the present Major League Baseball CBA.

Minimum Team Salary Threshold

Under the CBA, after the 2013 season a team could not have a team payroll lower than 90 percent of a team's salary cap. In the event this occurred, the league could force that team to pay the players the amount equal to the shortfall (NBA CBA, Article VII, sec. 2(b)). The minimum and maximum salary budgets could be spent by each team when signing new players, whether rookies or veterans. What constituted a "salary" was determined by rules regarding calculation of deferred compensation, signing bonuses, loans to players, incentive compensation, foreign player payments, one-year minimum contracts and existing contracts entered into before the agreement was made (NBA CBA, Article VII, sec. 3).

Maximum Contract Length

The maximum length of a contract for most NBA players is four years. For "Larry Bird Exception" players, it is five years (NBA CBA, Article IX, sec. 1). The 2016 agreement extends some veteran contracts to six years.

Suspensions and Fines for Player Misconduct

Players could be fined and/or suspended for noncompliance with the terms of their contracts. Fines range from $2,500 for the first practice missed within a season, to $5,000 for the second, $7,500 for the third and, finally, to "such discipline as is reasonable" for the fourth or additional violations (NBA CBA, Article VI, sec. 2(a)). Also, the penalized player's cash compensation could be reduced by 1/110th for each game that was missed (NBA CBA, Article VI, sec. 1). In addition, players could be fined $20,000 for each promotional appearance and mandatory program that was missed (NBA CBA, Article VI, secs. 3 and 4). The NBA also had the authority to suspend a player for up to ten games when a player was convicted or pleaded guilty or no contest to a violence felony (NBA CBA, Article VI, sec. 7).

Drug Testing

The CBA permits two categories of drug testing: testing based on "reasonable cause" and "random testing." If either the NBA or the NBPA has information that gives "reasonable cause" to believe that a player is engaged in the use, possession or distribution of a prohibited substance, an independent expert may order a drug test on the player (NBA CBA, Article XXXIII, sec. 5). The random testing regimen, on the other hand, requires all players to undergo testing at any time, without prior notice to the player, no more than four times each season (NBA CBA, Article XXXIII, sec. 6). The list of "prohibited substances" includes marijuana and performance-enhancing drugs such as steroids (NBA CBA, Article XXIII, secs. 8 and 9).

A positive test for illegal substances, other than marijuana and steroids, results in dismissal and disqualification from any association with the NBA, although that player has the right to apply for reinstatement at a later date (NBA CBA, Article XXXIII, secs. 11 and 12). However, if a player tested positive for either steroids or marijuana, he is required to enter a substance abuse treatment program for a first-time violation. However, for the second, third or additional violation, penalties of fines and suspensions occur, together with the requirement to enter the abuse treatment program (NBA CBA, Article XXXIII, secs. 8 and 9). More discussion on drug testing follows in Chapter 12.

Exceptions to the Salary Cap

The salary cap system has several important exceptions, most of which remain in effect in the present CBA. The following is a general description of each.

"Larry Bird" Exception

The most significant, known as the "Larry Bird Exception," allows a team to exceed the salary cap when it re-signs its own free agents. The exception covers up to the player's maximum salary. The player must have played at least three seasons without being waived or changing teams as a free agent (NBA CBA, Article VII, sec. 6(b)). The team can sign the player to a contract with annual raises of up to 7.5 percent. This exception thus permits the team's total payroll to exceed the salary cap in order to sign its own free agents. A new team signing such a player can also use the exception; however, it can only offer up to a 7.5 percent increase in the player's previous salary (NBA CBA Article VII, sec. 5(c)(2)). The exemption is named after the Boston Celtics great Larry Bird, because he was the first player allowed to exceed the cap.

"Early Bird" Exception

This is a weaker form of the "Larry Bird Exception." Players who qualify for this exception are called "early qualifying veteran free agents" in the CBA. A player qualifies for this exception after just two seasons without being waived or changing teams as a free agent. Using this exception, a team may re-sign its own free agent for (a) 175 percent of his regular salary plus 175 percent of any bonuses for the final salary cap year or (b) salary plus bonuses totaling 104.5 percent of the average player salary for the prior salary cap year, whichever is greater (NBA CBA, Article VII, sec. 6(b)(3)).

"Non-Bird" Exception

This applies to any free agent not in the first two categories. This exception allows a team to re-sign its own free agent to a salary starting at either (a) 120 percent of the player's salary in the previous season plus 120 percent of any bonuses for the final salary cap or (b) 120 percent of the minimum salary, whichever is greater, even if they are over the cap (NBA CBA, Article VII, sec. 6(b)(2)). Raises are limited to 4.5 percent, and contracts are limited to four years when this exception is used (NBA CBA, Article VII, sec. 5(c)(1)).

Midlevel Salary Exception

This exception allows a team to offer any player a contract equal to 108 percent of the average NBA salary in a prior capped year, even if the team exceeds the salary cap. The exception amount for the midlevel salary exception is tied to the average player salary in the league. Thus, as the average salary in the league increases, the exception amount correspondingly grows. Contracts signed pursuant to the new exception may be up to five years. Finally, a team may utilize the midlevel salary exception every year (NBA CBA, Article VII, sec. 6(e)). For 2014–15, it was about $5.3 million, if a team has no salary cap room but is not subject to a tax. For teams within the cap, it is $2.575 million, and for those subject to the tax, it is almost $3.3 million (realgm.com, n.d.).

The 2016 deal anticipates an increase of an average player's salary from about $5 to $9 million. Other changes in include the player's taking back their group licensing rights (Stein and Begley, 2016).

The National Hockey League

Over the last quarter-century, the National Hockey League has had the most contentious labor issues of all the major league sports. The result has been three lockouts, one of which resulted in the loss of an entire season. However, what seems to be a period of labor peace was reached in 2013 after the most recent collective bargaining agreement was concluded.

With only six teams (two in Canada and four in the United States) from the 1940s to 1967, ice hockey served as a niche sport, inaccessible to most areas in the United States. Since expansion started in 1967, its presence has grown considerably. In the early 1990s, Robert Goodenow assumed the leadership of the NHLPA and sought a more aggressive stand against management than his more malleable predecessor, Alan Eagleson. As a result, relations between the NHLPA and the NHL have become more contentious. The problems began during the 1991–92 season, when the players and owners reached an impasse over free agency and the compensation system for restricted free agents. This led to a ten-day work stoppage between April 1 and April 11, 1992.

However, the players and owners reached a new CBA and the season was completed.

Labor peace was short lived. In the fall of 1994, after no agreement was made on account of issues of salary control and free agency, the owners locked out the players, and the result was the cancellation of almost half the season, plus the All-Star game. On January 12, 1995, the parties came to an agreement, which became the governing CBA for the next nine years. That CBA expired after the 2004 season, which led to another lockout and the cancellation of the entire 2004–05 season.

The 1995 CBA permitted unrestricted free agency at age thirty-one for veterans with at least four years of NHL experience. A shared pool of draft choices compensated teams losing such free agents (Lapointe, 1995). It also contained a rookie salary cap and a restrictive free-agency system (rarely used) for players who met either the specific age or experience requirements but did not attain unrestricted free-agent status.

The 1995 CBA did not employ any general salary cap structure, except for the rookie cap. Because the league did not share revenues except for national broadcasting and cable contracts and merchandising, significant salary disparities occurred. A dramatic increase in player compensation resulted from signings by large-market teams in the United States. During the 1990–91 season, salaries averaged $271,000. Three years later the figure jumped to $572,161. In the 2000–01 season, the average salary was $1,434,884, which rose to $1.8 million in the 2003–04 season (Youngblood, 2004).

The 2013 Collective Bargaining Agreement

In 2004, the NHL locked out the players, resulting in the cancellation of the season. Reflecting the uncertain financial health of the league caused by a significant diminution of broadcast and cable revenues, as well as the financial difficulties of certain teams, the new agreement, concluded in July 2005, came about after the union agreed to the proposals sought by the NHL management.

Although the 2012–13 lockout did not result in the cancellation of an entire season, nearly 60 percent of the regular 2012–13 season was canceled, along with the All-Star Weekend and New Year's Day Winter Classic games. The major issues prompting the lockout were related to the owners' desire to reduce the players' then-guaranteed 57 percent share of hockey-related revenues, introduce term limits on contracts, eliminate salary arbitration and change free-agency rules. The 119-day lockout ended on January 2013 with the ratification of the present collective bargaining agreement.

The present ten-year collective bargaining agreement, which expires in 2022, provides for a league-wide salary cap, revenue sharing, a revised salary arbitration process and greater restrictions on entry-level salaries. It consists of the following.

Salary Cap

The NHL became the third of the four major sports leagues to embrace a cap system. For the 2015–16 league year, salaries were capped at a level of about $71.4 million per team (sportsnet.ca, 2015), with a minimum of $52.8 million (capfriendly.com, 2016), up from $51 million the year before (Canadian Press, 2014). The agreement specifically requires that 50 percent of "hockey-related revenue" be used for player salaries. That amount is calculated at the end of the season, and it is quite possible that teams may exceed that threshold, due in part to the fluctuating exchange rate of the U.S. and Canadian dollars. Hence, the escrow rules, noted later, take on considerable importance (Drance, 2015).

League Revenues

For 2014–15, player compensation was based on 50 percent of hockey-related revenues (HRRs) (NHL CBA, 2012–22, Article 50, sec. 50.4(b)). The cornerstone provision of the deal that ended the 119-day lockout was the 50–50 split of HRR. The owners were the clear winners in that it substantially reduced the players' previous share of 57 percent.

Maximum Player Compensation

No player may receive more than 20 percent of a team's revenue in a single season (NHL CBA 2012–22, Article 50 Section 50.6(a)). This is a way to control spiraling salaries paid by richer teams for star players. As of the 2014–15 season, the highest paid player's salary was $14 million (Badenhausen, 2014b).

Revenue Sharing

Subject to certain conditions, the league redistribution commitment amount is set at 6.055 percent of HRR (NHL CBA, 2012–22, Article 49, sec. 49.1(y)). Under the new CBA, there are three funding stages that contribute to the fund shared by the bottom fifteen teams. First, a maximum of 50 percent of the redistribution commitment is drawn from the top ten money-making teams based on preseason and regular season revenue. The second source of funding comes from 35 percent of playoff gate receipts of all clubs participating in the Stanley Cup playoffs (regardless of their earning power during the regular season). If, after those two phases, the redistribution commitment has not been reached, the third source of funding comes from centrally generated revenues (NHL CBA, 2012–22, Article 49, sec. 49.5).

Salary Arbitration

The present CBA states that restricted free-agency players who sign their first NHL contracts are eligible for salary arbitration after four years of service (it drops to three years if the player is twenty-one, two years if twenty-two or twenty-three and one year if the player is twenty-four) (NHL CBA, 2012–22, Article 12, sec. 12.1(a)). It requires an arbitrator to choose between the club's offer and the player's request. Also, teams may seek arbitration for an unsigned player in an attempt to roll back the salary of a player whose production has slipped. As in the prior agreement, a team may "walk away" from an arbitration ruling, rendering the player a free agent. The ability to reduce the salary of a perceived underachieving player may be a real bonus for the owners (NHL CBA, 2012–22, Article 12, secs. 12.3(b) and 12.10(a)).

Entry-Level Salaries

Although the prior CBA imposed a cap on rookie salaries, bonuses paid to top rookies circumvented the limitations and, according to the owners, resulted in increases in salaries to veterans through salary arbitration. The new agreement capped salaries at $925,000 for 2012–22 and tied bonus money to both team and individual success during a particular season. So, for example, bonuses could be awarded if the player's team plays in the Stanley Cup final round (NHL CBA, 2012–22, Article 9, sec. 9.3(a) and Article 50, sec. 50.2(b)).

Free Agency

Before 2007, players over thirty-one or with ten years' experience qualified for unrestricted free agency. The 2007 agreement reduced the age requirement to twenty-seven, phased in over the life of the old CBA. Under the new CBA, it is also age twenty-seven or seven years of experience (NHL CBA, 2012–22, Article 10, sec. 10.1(1)).

Escrow Account

Players are required to deposit a percentage of their salaries into an escrow account at the start of the season, where it remains until the league calculates revenues for that year. If league-wide salaries exceed a stated percentage of revenues, set at 50 percent of hockey-related revenue, the players will be obliged to set aside a predetermined portion of their incomes to the escrow account (NHL CBA, 2012–22, Article 50, sec. 50.4(b), (c), and (d)). This amount can be significant. In the 2014–15 season, it was

12 percent of every player's salary. Therefore, each NHL player made that much less than their contract amount, a point that did not receive much publicity. In the case of the Shea Weber, he who earned the league's highest salary, the Nashville Predators paid him roughly $12.3 million in the end, not the $14 million contracted salary (Drance, 2015).

Minimum Salary

This was raised from $525,000 in 2012 to $550,000 in both 2013 and 2014. For the 2015 and 2016 league years, it was set at $575,000, and for 2017 and 2018, it jumps to $650,000. For 2019 and 2020, it was set at $700,000, and for 2021, it will be $750,000 (NHL CBA, 2012–22, Article 11, sec 11.12).

Draft

The CBA imposes a weighted NHL draft lottery in favor of poorer-performing teams: the club with the fewest regular season points will have the greatest chance (20 percent) of winning the draft drawing. The only clubs with the opportunity to receive the first overall selection are the fourteen with the lowest regular season point totals (NHL.com, 2014).

Ordinary Course Buy-Outs and Compliance Buy-Outs

During a fifteen-day period between June 15 (or starting forty-eight hours after the conclusion of the season) and June 30, a team may buy a player out of his contract at two-thirds of its value (if the player is twenty-six or older) or one-third of its value (if the player is under twenty-six) to be paid out over twice the remaining term of the terminated contract (NHL Standard Players' Contract, 2013, sec. 13). Though a bought-out contract is effectively terminated, the cost of an "ordinary course buy-out" counts against the team's salary cap, whereas the cost of a "compliance buy-out" has no effect on the team's salary cap. As per the CBA, compliance buy-outs were only permitted after the 2012–13 and 2013–14 league years (NHL CBA, 2012–22, Article 50, sec. 50.9(i)).

Drug Testing

The agreement requires a minimum of two drug tests a year with no advance warning. A player will earn a twenty-game suspension for a first-time offense, a sixty-game ban for a second and a permanent suspension from the NHL after a third violation. Drug testing occurs between January 15 and the end of the regular season (NHL CBA, 2012–22, Article 47, secs. 47.6 and 47.7).

Finally, in a benefit to veterans, players with ten years of service and 600 games can request a single hotel room while on the road (NHL CBA, 2012–22, Article 16, sec. 16.9).

The Women's National Basketball Association (WNBA)

Because of its recent vintage and smaller cash flow, the WNBA utilizes a salary cap structure more universally, but employs some novel methods to enhance player compensation.

In 2014, the WNBA and the WNBA Players' Association agreed to an eight-year collective bargaining agreement, with an opt-out after six years by the union. Among key terms of the pact:

> Minimum salaries for players with three or more years of service were set at $55,275 in 2015, increasing to almost $57,000 by 2021. Those for players with less than 3 years of service were $38,913 for that year, increasing to $43.491 by the conclusion of the agreement.
> (WNBA CBA, Article V, sec. 7)

The salary cap structure is unique: cap systems encompass a "guaranteed" salary cap and a "growth factor." The guaranteed salary cap was locked in at $857,000 in 2014, and for each year of the CBA thereafter is calculated by adding $12,000 to the previous year's salary, adding in the growth factor value of 2 percent and subtracting $12,000. The growth factor may be increased depending on the number of teams with at least twelve players on their active list. More specifically, if at least one-quarter but fewer than one-half of the twelve teams have at least twelve players on their active list for at least one-half of the days immediately preceding a regular season, the growth factor is set at 3 percent. If at least one but fewer than one-quarter of the teams have twelve players on their active list, that figure is 3.5 percent. And if none of the teams have at least twelve players on their active list, the growth factor is set at 4 percent (WNBA CBA, Article VII, sec. 1).

Players with at least six years in the league became unrestricted free agents, and restrictive free agency extends to those who have played at least four years (WNBA CBA, Article VI, secs. 9 and 5).

If a restricted free agent receives an offer she wants to take from a new team, details of the contract proposal must be made to the player's old team, which has ten days to match the offer (WNBA CBA, Article VI, sec. 7).

Additional provisions include a new "Time Off Bonus" of up to $50,000 that players can earn for limiting their overseas play to three months or less during the offseason (WNBA CBA, Article VII, sec. 17) and a reduction in the number of times that a player can be designated as a "core" player from five to four (WNBA CBA, Article VI, sec. 7), which means that the designated player will sign a contract with the respective team for the maximum salary allowed.

Major League Soccer

Unionization came relatively late to MLS players. After years of unsuccessful antitrust litigation, in which the courts ruled that MLS's attempts to impose salary caps and other cost controls were not illegal (*Fraser v. MLS*, 2002), the players and the league produced three CBAs, the most recent concluded in March 2015. The five-year CBA provides or revises rules on salary allocations and creates a free-agency system.

A team's salary budget will increase from $3.1 million per club in 2014 to $3.49 million in 2015 (12.5 percent) and will increase by roughly 5 percent each year thereafter. As a result, the average salary of senior roster players who are not designated players will increase by roughly $60,000 over the course of the agreement and should be approaching $200,000 by 2019. Minimum salaries for senior players increased from $48,500 in 2015 to $60,000 in 2015 and in smaller increments until 2016.

The agreement requires that twenty-four players be subject to the noted minimum, but for players beyond those twenty-four-roster slots, the minimums are smaller. For those players, the minimum salary increases from $36,500 in 2014 to $50,000 in 2015, along with smaller increases to the conclusion of the agreement. The present agreement also includes an increase in the number of guaranteed contracts, bonuses for wins in MLS games and international tournaments and appearance fees for exhibition games.

The agreement creates a free-agency system for the first time in the league's history. Players who are twenty-eight years old with at least eight years of service and are below the maximum salary can sign with a team of their choice. However, the amount of salary increase is limited. Players earning less than $100,000 can negotiate a salary increase of up to 25 percent; for those earning between $100,000 and $200,000, the amount of increase is 20 percent; and for the players earning $200,000, it is 15 percent (MLSsoccer.com, 2015).

Miscellaneous Labor Issues

Player Drafts—Age Restrictions

The NFL, Major League Baseball, the NHL and the NBA take varying approaches regarding the minimum age of player eligibility for the leagues' entry drafts. Of the four major leagues, the NFL's policy is the most controversial.

Consisting of seven rounds, it requires a player to be three seasons removed from the graduation of his high school class. So if his class graduated in 2015, eligibility begins at the 2018 draft (note that the requirement does not mandate graduation from high school; NFL CBA, Article 6, sec. 2).

In Major League Baseball, the draft is held yearly in June. It consists of a multiple number of rounds, which can vary from year to year. Because the pool of potential players is large, the draft consists of many rounds. In 2014 and 2015, there were forty rounds. Eligible players include those who have graduated from high school and have not yet attended college or junior college; college players from four-year colleges, who either have completed their junior or senior years or are at least twenty-one years old; and junior college players, regardless of how many years of school they have completed. If the player doesn't sign with the team that drafted him and goes on to enroll in college, he cannot be drafted again until after his junior year. Generally, a player is eligible for selection if he is a resident of the United States or Canada and has never before signed a major league or minor league contract. This includes residents of Puerto Rico and other U.S. territories. Also eligible are residents who enroll in a high school or college in the United States, regardless of their place of citizenship (MLB. com, n.d.). At this time, all thirty Major League Baseball clubs draft in the order of finish, worst to first. Any team can sign players from countries not covered by the draft.

In the NBA, the draft is just two rounds. One notable difference in the NBA draft is that the National Collegiate Athletic Association allows college athletes to apply for early entry into the NBA draft by giving notice sixty days before the draft date without automatically forfeiting their remaining college eligibility. The rule permits athletes to declare for early entry, though they can opt out ten days after the NBA draft to return to collegiate competition (NBA CBA, Article X, sec. 8(c)). The NBA rule permits players who choose not to attend college to be eligible, because the league now requires a prospective player to be at least one year removed from the graduation of a player's high school class or at least nineteen years old at the time of the draft (NBA CBA, Article X, sec. 1). Players from outside the United States must be twenty-two years of age during the calendar year of the draft to be eligible (NBA CBA, Article X, sec. 1(g)). The rule seeks to limit players opting for the NBA right out of high school, like LeBron James, Carmelo Anthony and Amare Stoudamire, who either opted to go pro after high school or left college early to do so (Henderson, 2009).

In the NHL, to be selected in the June draft, players must turn eighteen on or before the following September 15.

Summary of Key Information

Average Player Salaries (2014–15)

- MLB: $4.2 million
- NBA: $5.0 million
- NFL: $2.1 million
- NHL: $2.6 million

Salary Cap

- MLB: No cap.
- NBA: A "soft cap" calculated annually based on 44.74 percent of "basketball-related league income" over the life of the agreement. Amount: $70 million per team (2015–16). Note that the amount has jumped to about $90 million for 2016–17. Also, individual player salary caps are based on years of experience.
- NFL: A "hard cap" is set at an amount equal to the sum of (1) 55 percent of projected league media revenues; (2) 45 percent of projected NFL ventures/postseason revenues; (3) 40 percent of projected local revenues; and (4) if applicable, 50 percent of the net revenues for new line-of-business projects, minus (5) 47.5 percent of the joint contribution amount (set at $55 million in 2012 and growing by 5 percent annually). Amount: $155 million (2016). Teams can exceed the cap, but have to allocate a percentage of certain contracts to future years (in the form of signing bonuses or back-loaded contracts) to do it.
- NHL: Set every year according to projected NHL revenues for the coming season, based on a 50/50 revenue split between players and teams, or $71.4 million per team (2015–16).

Average Team Payroll (2015)

- MLB: $124 million (twenty-five players)
- NBA: $71 million (fifteen players)
- NFL: $136 million (fifty-one players)
- NHL: $105 million (twenty-three players)

Player Share of Defined Gross Revenue or Equivalent (2015)

- MLB: 38 percent
- NBA: 44.74 percent (of basketball-related income)
- NFL: 48.5 percent of "all revenue" (average)
- NHL: 57 percent

Contracts

- MLB: Guaranteed unless stated otherwise.
- NBA: Guaranteed.
- NFL: Not guaranteed. Teams can cut players at any time with no future obligations except signing bonuses, which for salary cap purposes are prorated over the life of the contract even if the amounts are paid up front.
- NHL: Contracts are fully guaranteed and can be bought out at two-thirds of their value.

Free Agency

- MLB: Players with six or more seasons of major league services can be unrestricted free agents at the end of their contracts.
- NBA: Unrestricted free agency applies in most situations after three years, subject to a right-to-match option by the player's original team.
- NFL: Restricted free agency after three seasons and unrestricted after four. Teams designate transition players and franchise players, but must pay them from a stipulated standard.
- NHL: In 2015, players became unrestricted free agents at age twenty-seven or after seven years of experience.

Arbitration

- Major League Baseball: Players with at least three seasons and fewer than six are eligible.
- NBA: None.
- NFL: None.
- NHL: Restricted free-agency players eligible after service of one to four years, depending on their first standard contract signing age.

Chapter Assignment—Constructing a New Collective Bargaining Agreement

The assignment found at the conclusion of Chapter 1 required the creation of the governance structure of a new women's professional softball league. For this project, we are assuming that after three years, the league is still in business and the popularity of this sport has increased. Revenues have increased 15 percent from its first to second year and 25 percent from the second to the third. At the conclusion of the third year, the league signed contracts with Fox

Sports to broadcast and stream a "Game of the Week" for ten weeks and the two-round playoff for a total of $10 million per year for the next four years. At the time the agreement was signed league-wide revenues came to $12.5 million to be divided over the league's five teams. Assume that the revenues except ticket receipts are shared by teams equally. Also assume that teams consist of fifteen players and that the number of franchises has stayed the same.

The players, sensing the increased economic success of the league, decided to unionize. Their effort was successful, as 90 percent of the players voted affirmatively on the question of forming the union, to be called the WPSL Players Association.

The league and the union opened talks for a collective bargaining agreement. Groups of two or four will be selected. Half will represent the league and half the union. The groups are to draft an outline for the new agreement. Issues include minimum and maximum salaries, salary cap, free agency, salary arbitration, grievance arbitration and/or merchandising. The length of the agreement should be between seven and twelve pages, double-spaced.

References

Armour, N. (2015, January 29). Armour: Union lost this battle with NFL three years ago. *USAToday.com*. Retrieved March 19, 2015, from www.usatoday.com/story/sports/2015/01/29/union-should-have-held-tough-three-years-ago/22556937/

Associated Press (2015, December 18). Dodgers lead MLB with record $43.6 million paid in luxury tax. Retrieved July 8, 2016, from http://espn.go.com/mlb/story/_/id/14396649/los-angeles-dodgers-new-york-yankees-boston-red-sox-san-francisco-giants-pay-luxury-tax-most-major-league-baseball-history

Badenhausen, K. (2014a, July 16). The world's 50 most valuable sports teams 2014. *Forbes.com*. Retrieved March 17, 2015, from www.forbes.com/sites/kurtbadenhausen/2014/07/16/the-worlds-50-most-valuable-sports-teams-2014/

Badenhausen, K. (2014b, November 25). The NHL's highest-paid players 2014–15. *Forbes.com*. Retrieved March 28, 2015, from www.forbes.com/sites/kurtbadenhausen/2014/11/25/the-nhls-highest-paid-players-2014–15/

Baseball Archive (1998). Minimum and average player salaries 1967–1997. Retrieved April 22, 2010, from http://www.baseball1.com/bb-data/bbd-mas.html

basketballreference.com (n.d.). 2014–15 NBA player contracts. Retrieved March 20, 2015, from www.basketball-reference.com/contracts/players.html

Battista, J. (2011, March 12). As N.F.L. talks fail, '11 season seems in doubt. *New York Times*. Retrieved March 13, 2015, from http://www.nytimes.com/2011/03/12/sports/football/12nfl.html

Belzer, J. (2016, April 29). 2016 NFL Draft 1st round rookie salary projections. *Forbes.com*. Retrieved July 7, 2016, from http://www.forbes.com/sites/

jasonbelzer/2016/04/29/2016-nfl-draft-1st-round-rookie-salary-projections/#2afe17017036

Bennett, D. (2011, April 18). The NFL's official spin on average career length is a joke. *Businessinsider.com*. Retrieved March 18, 2015, from www.business insider.com/nfls-spin-average-career-length-2011–4

Bien, L. (2015, March 2). The NFL salary cap explain. *SBNationa.com*. Retrieved March 6, 2016, from http://www.sbnation.com/nfl/2015/3/2/8134891/nfl-salary-cap-2015-franchise-tag-explained

Bradley, R. (n.d.). Labor pains nothing new to NBA. *Association for Professional Basketball Research*. Retrieved April 22, 2010, from http://www.apbr.org/labor.html

Burk, R. (2015). *Marvin Miller: Baseball Revolutionary*. Champaign, IL: University of Illinois Press, pp. 250–251.

Canadian Press (2014, June 28). NHL sets 2014-'15 salary cap at $69 million, floor at $51 million. *NHL.com*. Retrieved March 28, 2015, from www.nhl.com/ice/news.htm?id=724192

Capfriendly.com (2016, June 10). Frequently asked questions. Retrieved July 9, 2016, from https://www.capfriendly.com/faq

Cozzillio, M. J., & Levinstein, M. S. (1998). *Sports law: Cases and materials*. Durham, NC: Carolina Academic Press, pp. 663, 776.

Cunningham, M. (2004, February 29). Players pay price for booming NFL; Union members lag behind their pro counterparts. *Sun-Sentinel*, p. 1C.

Down, F. (1981, May 30). Man in the news: Marvin Miller. *United Press International*, Sports Section.

Drance, T. (2015, February 1). Setting the salary cap: The zero-sum game and how to fix it. *NHLNumbers.com*. Retrieved December 31, 2015, from http://nhlnumbers.com/2015/2/5/setting-the-salary-cap-the-zero-sum-game-and-how-to-fix-it

Dworkin, J. (1981). *Owners versus players: Baseball and collective bargaining*. Boston: Auburn House.

Fangraphs.com (n.d.). Service time. Retrieved March 20, 2016, from http://www.fangraphs.com/library/principles/contract-details/service-time-super-two/

Federal Baseball Club v. National League of Professional Baseball Clubs, 259 US 200 (1922).

Fennell, T. (1994, October 3). Baseball's troubled history, edited by Tom Fennell. *Maclean's*, p. 8.

Fitzpatrick, J. (n.d.). NHL lockouts and strikes: A history. *Aboutsports.com*. Retrieved February 28, 2015, from http://proicehockey.about.com/od/history/a/Nhl-Lockouts-And-Strikes-A-History.htm

Flood v. Kuhn, 407 US 258 (1972).

Forbes (2014, September 12). Forbes 400. Retrieved February 28, 2015, from www.forbes.com/forbes-400/list/#tab:overall

Fraser v. MLS, *284 F.3d 47* (1st Cir. 2002).

Gaines, C. (2014, October 2). Payrolls for MLB playoff teams show the revenue gap is as bad as ever. *Business Inside*. Retrieved December 29, 2015, from http://www.businessinsider.com/chart-payroll-mlb-playoff-teams-2014–10

Halverson, J. (2012, July 14). Explaining the competitive balance lottery of the MLB draft. *Bleacher Report*. Retrieved December 29, 2015, from http://bleacherreport.com/articles/1258849-explaining-the-competitive-balance-lottery-of-the-mlb-draft

Henderson, L. (2009, April 15). History of players in the NBA draft. *Associated Content.* Retrieved April 22, 2010, from http://www.associatedcontent.com/article/1628384/history_of_high_school_players_in_the_pg3.html?cat=14

Kansas City Royal Baseball Corp. v. MLBPA, 532 F.2d 615 (8th Cir. 1976).

Knoblauch, A. (2016, Febraury 26). NFL salary cap set at $155.27 million for 2016. NFL.com. Retrieved July 9, 2016, from http://www.nfl.com/news/story/0ap3000000639226/article/nfl-salary-cap-set-at-15527-million-for-2016

Lamb, B. (n.d.). John Montgomery Ward. Society of American Baseball Research. Retrieved May 4, 2016, from http://sabr.org/bioproj/person/2de3f6ef

Lapointe, J. (1995, January 12). Pact reached for salvaging hockey season. *New York Times*, p. A1.

Lee, M. (2011, November 26). NBA lockout: Owners, players reach tentative agreement to start season on Christmas. *TheWashingtonPost.com.* Retrieved February 26, 2015, from www.washingtonpost.com/sports/wizards/owners-players-reach-tentative-agreement-to-end-lockout/2011/11/26/gIQA8p6tzN_story.html

Mackey v. NFL, 543 F.2d 606 (8th Cir. 1976).

Major League Baseball Collective Bargaining Agreement ("Basic Agreement"). Retrieved March 17, 2015, from http://mlb.mlb.com/pa/pdf/cba_english.pdf

Matter of Arbitration Between MLBPA and the 26 Major League Clubs, Grievance No. 86–2 (1987).

McFarland, R. (2016). NFL salary cap FAQs. Russell Street report. Retrieved March 6, 2015, from http://russellstreetreport.com/salarycap/nfl-salary-cap-faqs/

McNeil v. NFL, 790 F. Supp. 871 (D. Minn. 1992).

Miller, I. (2003, November 12). 49ers are in bind for 2004. *San Francisco Chronicle*, p. C1.

MLB.com (n.d.). First year player draft official rules. Retrieved April 5, 2015, from http://mlb.mlb.com/mlb/draftday/rules.jsp

MLS Players Union (n.d.). About the MLS players union. *MLSplayers.org.* Retrieved March 17, 2015, from www.mlsplayers.org/about_mlspu.html

MLSSoccer.com (2015, July 16). MLS players union announces that it has ratified collective bargaining agreement. Retrieved January 1, 2016, from http://www.mlssoccer.com/post/2015/07/16/mls-players-union-announces-it-has-ratified-collective-bargaining-agreement

National & American League Professional Baseball Clubs v. Major League Baseball Players Association, Labor Arbitration (1976), 66, 101.

National Football League (2014, December 10). NFL owners endorse new personal conduct policy. *NFL.com.* Retrieved March 19, 2015, from www.nfl.com/news/story/0ap3000000441758/article/nfl-owners-endorse-new-personal-conduct-policy

National Labor Relations Act, 29 USC, sec. 151 *et seq.* (2010).

NBA CBA (2011). Retrieved March 20, 2015, from http://www.nbpa.org/cba/2011NBA Salary cap history (n.d.). *RealGM.com.* Retrieved December 30, 2015, from http://basketball.realgm.com/nba/info/salary_cap

NFL.com (2016, June 26). 2016 NFL Draft first-round signing tracker. Retrieved October 14, 2016, from http://www.nfl.com/news/story/0ap3000000660182/article/2016-nfl-draft-firstround-signing-tracker

NFL CBA, various sections. Retrieved March 18, 2015, from https://nfllabor.files.wordpress.com/2010/01/collective-bargaining-agreement-2011–2020.pdf

NFL Standard Player's Contract (2011). NFL CBA, Appendix A. Retrieved December 29, 2015, from https://nfllabor.files.wordpress.com/2010/01/collective-bargaining-agreement-2011–2020.pdf

NHL Collective Bargaining Agreement (2012–22). Various sections. Retrieved March 28, 2015, from http://www.nhl.com/nhl/en/v3/ext/CBA2012/NHL_NHLPA_2013_CBA.pdf

NHL.com (2014, August 20). NHL announces changes to draft lottery format. Retrieved March 29, 2015, from www.nhl.com/ice/news.htm?id=728795 (NHL.com, 2014).

NHL Standard Players Contract (2013). Exhibit 1, NHL Collective Bargaining Agreement. Retrieved March 29, 2015, from http://www.nhl.com/nhl/en/v3/ext/CBA2012/NHL_NHLPA_2013_CBA.pdf

NLRB (n.d.). Discriminating against employees because of their union activities or sympathies (Section 8(a)(3)). Retrieved February 26, 2015, from www.nlrb.gov/rights-we-protect/whats-law/employers/discriminating-against-employees-because-their-union

Powell v. NFL, 930 F.2d 1293, 1303 (8th Cir. 1989), cert. denied, 498 U.S. 1040 (1991).

Robertson v. NBA, 389 F. Supp. 867 (SDNY, 1970).

Ryan, B. (1991, June 23). Miller labored to make major leagues a better place to play. *Boston Globe*, p. 51.

Schefter, A. (2015, January 23). NFLPA files grievance against NFL. *ESPN.com*. Retrieved March, 19, 2015, from espn.go.com/nfl/story/_/id/12216057/nflpa-files-grievance-nfl-challenges-personal-conduct-policy

Selig, B. (1995, April 9). Baseball hired temporary replacements. *New York Times*, sec. 4, p. 14 [letter to the editor].

Seybold, M. (2012. December 3). Labour relations in baseball: Not so fast. *The Economist*. Retrieved July 10, 2016, from http://www.economist.com/blogs/gametheory/2012/12/labour-relations-baseball

Seymour, H. (1960). *Baseball: The early years*. New York: Oxford University Press, pp. 111, 150, 232.

Silverman v. Major League Baseball Player Relations Committee, 67 F.3d 1054 (2d Cir. 1995).

Sportsnet.ca (2015, June 23). NHL, NHLPA sets 2015–16 salary cap at $71.4M. Retrieved July 11, 2016, from http://www.sportsnet.ca/hockey/nhl/nhl-nhlpa-sets-2015–16-salary-cap-at-71–4m/

spotrac.com (2015). 2015 NFL free agents. Retrieved March 18, 2015, from www.spotrac.com/nfl/free-agents/

Stark, J. (2016, December 1). Baseball comes to its senses, making peace and avoiding chaos. *ESPN.com*. Retrieved December 2, 2016, from http://www.espn.com/mlb/story/_/id/18177502/new-mlb-collective-bargaining-agreement-keeps-labor-peace-adds-soft-cap

Staudohar, P. (1988). The football strike of 1987; The question of free agency. Retrieved May 12, 2010, from http://www.bls.gov/opub/mlr/1988/08/rpt1full.pdf

Stein, M., and Begley, I. (2016, December 15). NBA, players' union reach tentative agreement on new 7-year CBA. *ESPN.com*. Retrieved December 17, 2016, from http://www.espn.com/nba/story/_/id/18280618/nba-players-union-reach-tentative-new-labor-agreement

Stern, D. (2011, November 11). The NBA lockout timeline. *grantland.com*. Retrieved March 20, 2015, from grantland.com/the-triangle/the-nba-lockout-timeline/

Voigt, D. (n.d.). Owner player conflict. *SABR.org*. Retrieved March 17, 2015, from research.sabr.org/journals/owner-player-conflict

Weiler, P. C., & Roberts, G. R. (2004). *Sports and the law* (3rd ed.). St. Paul, MN: West.

Werly, D. (2016, April 11). NFL wins arbitration against the players association, Goodell's discipline authority upheld. *The White Bronco.com*. Retrieved July 9, 2016, from http://thewhitebronco.com/2016/04/nfl-wins-arbitration-against-the-players-association-goodells-discipline-authority-upheld/

WNBA Collective Bargaining Agreement (2014). Various sections. Retrieved April 4, 2015, from http://wnbpa-uploads.s3.amazonaws.com/docs/WNBA%20CBA%202014–2021Final.pdf

Youngblood, K. (2004, January 20). Business of the NHL; Bucks beget blame; NHL salaries have risen fast, as the rate of finger-pointing about the cause. (Minneapolis) *Star Tribune*, p. 1C.

7 Sports Agents

Agents are among the most misunderstood stakeholders in the sports business. Often unfairly depicted as high-powered unethical deal makers who negotiate multimillion-dollar contracts for their clients and take large amounts of athletes' money to live a life almost as glamorous as those they represent, most agents are not wealthy, flamboyant or criminally suspect. Although high-powered agents exist, many struggle and have to earn a living by combining agency with other work. This chapter provides a basic description of an agent's duties, roles and ethical requirements.

Agents have a number of important roles, depending on the particular athlete, the sport and the nature of his or her representation. Some agents only negotiate player contracts; others specialize in endorsement deals; still others either manage the athlete's finances or work with associates who do. Agents also serve as confidants, advisors and even babysitters of their athletes. Often an agent, especially one representing a young and inexperienced athlete, serves as de facto guardian of the athlete's interests. Among their tasks are speaking to the press when their athlete's conduct results in criminal charges, finding legal representation for the athlete and counseling the athlete about his or her confidential personal issues.

In the past, the diverse roles of a sports agent made the position difficult to regulate, and the lack of uniform regulation and standards has resulted in a number of agents who lack the skills to do the job effectively and, even worse, a few who commit criminal acts against the athletes they represent. More recently, attempts to impose more standard regulations through federal law and, in particular, from players' unions have brought more consistency.

The Business

As noted earlier, most agents do not live a life of riches and glamour. Only a select few land the big athlete and the lucrative contract. Many more have to struggle to stay in business. Often their agency will be a side business of their law or accounting practices. The Baltimore-based agent

Tony Agnone gives a word of advice for anyone interested in entering the sports agency business: "Don't." He adds:

> I try to explain to them it's not the best thing in the world. It's a very competitive business. I try to convince them there are other things to do besides being an agent. . . . It's a situation that's very competitive, very time consuming. It's got to be done very meticulously, and there is some involvement of luck. If the planets are all aligned, it works.
>
> (Cohn, 2004)

Many enter the business with dreams of glory. But according to figures provided by the National Football League Players' Association (NFLPA), which regulates anyone who represents an NFL player in contract negotiations with the league, of the approximately 714 NFLPA-certified agents, almost 42 percent do not represent even one active player. Twenty-five percent of the agents represent seventy-eight percent of the players (Brandt, 2012).

No matter what kind of sport is involved, one common thread permeates this business: difficulty in landing and keeping talent. Some agents expend considerable costs in travel and great amounts of time hoping to sign talent. With the growing internationalization of sports, many find basketball players playing in Europe or Asia.

Qualifications, or lack thereof, have created more headaches. Although some of the players' associations, such as the NFLPA, require agents to pass a qualifying exam, no uniform educational standards exist. Although many agents possess law or accountancy degrees, others do not. Even for those with professional licenses, a sports agency has particular rules and issues not found in a traditional law or accounting practice. The salary cap structure in the NFL and NBA and various arbitration rules among each of the major leagues are two important examples. Often the rules are technical (as shown in the preceding chapter), so even a competent and responsible person may forget or be unaware. In one case, an agent's failure to submit the paperwork for an NFL player's contract restructure in time caused him to be released by the Denver Broncos (Garafolo, 2013).

Ethical issues permeate the business. First, agents compete against other agents for clients. Although traditional legal rules forbid "tortious interference with contract"—one person attempting to get another to break a contract—in practice it is difficult to apply this prohibition. Athletes often sign with one agent and then change their mind and sign with another. If these terminations—whether by the athlete alone or with the encouragement of another agent—occur before the player signs a professional contract, there is little the first agent can do. If he or she sues the former client for breach of contract, two major problems exist: (a) the damages collected would be minimal or nonexistent because that aggrieved agent did not negotiate a contract for the player and (b) the act would have serious business consequences. Other athletes could very well shy away from this agent, hurting the business. So in many cases, the former agent has to consider client defection a cost of doing business.

Rumors of agent payoffs to prospective clients abound, despite the prohibition of this practice under state and federal law. Agents may do this using several techniques: outright payoffs, giving "loans" to athletes with repayment after a contract is signed, giving payouts to coaches to "deliver" clients and the use of third parties—known as "runners"—to dispense money and gifts to players (Heitner, 2013).

Examples of payoffs to athletes include allegations that an agent made payments to University of North Carolina football players (Browder, 2013). Despite attempts to regulate their conduct, payoff allegations and other cases of egregious behavior occur and make headlines. One case involved agents pushing athletes to invest in Burger King franchises that turned out to be a sham operation (Davis, 2015). In November 2004, the former NBA star Scottie Pippen won an $11.8 million judgment against a prominent Chicago financial advisor who was entrusted with $17.5 million of his money and proceeded to lose $7 million of it in questionable investments (Roeder, 2004). "It's a situation that goes on every day," Pippen was quoted as saying in the *Chicago Tribune*. "There's always a crook out there" (Isaacson, 2004). The article quoted Ron Shapiro, an agent and former securities commissioner for the state of Maryland, as saying "A significant number of professional athletes are de facto bankrupt [because of poor investments], meaning their debts outstrip their assets." The former Los Angeles Laker star Kareem Abdul-Jabbar lost close to $5 million on failed hotel and restaurant ventures, as well as investments in Arabian horses, oil wells and gold coins in the 1980s. He, like other athletes, gave their agents a power of attorney, meaning a legal right to invest the athlete's money in whatever manner the agent wanted. Presently, the NBA and NFL, in conjunction with their players' associations, include financial planning advice as part of their mandatory rookie orientation (Grossi, 2003).

Mega-agencies

Although many agents either work alone or as part of a small group, consolidation or merger with entertainment agencies has occurred over the last decade. If an agency has a strong stable of clients, the talent can be marketed into other areas of the sports business, such as event production and marketing and licensing the intellectual property of their clients. However, as we will see later, the personal aspect of the agency services can create succession problems if the founder or leader dies or leaves the agency.

The first and most venerable mega-agency is IMG. Founded by the late Mark McCormack in the early 1960s, the firm grew from a small operation representing the interests of a few individual golfers to a behemoth, representing some of the top tennis and golf stars (IMGWorld.com, 2010). Just as important, IMG owns and operates professional tennis tournaments showcasing its talent pool. By owning these tournaments, IMG earns more money than just commissions from its athletes; it keeps the revenues from the tournament itself. More controversially, IMG operates "training academies" for young athletes. In 1987, it bought the Nick Bollettieri Tennis Academy (considered one of the premier training centers for talented professionals-to-be) and expanded it to include more sports and locations. However, a succession crisis occurred when Mark McCormack died of cardiac arrest in 2003. Upon his death, McCormack's controlling interest in IMG was transferred to his widow, Betsy Nagelson. In addition to estate tax liabilities, Nagelson had to deal with the IMG's significant debt because several months before McCormack's death IMG had financed an enormous expansion with loans from twelve different banks amounting to a reported $200 million. With no management experience, Nagelson had only one real option—to sell the company.

When the company finally went up for sale, Forstmann Little & Co. had the highest bid. As a leveraged buyout firm, Forstmann's major focus was on profits, not on building relationships (CMG, 2014). As such, Forstmann dismantled the personal service culture of IMG, and instead turned IMG into an international production-and-packaging powerhouse. However, upon Forstmann's death in 2011, Ari Emmanuel was able to acquire IMG in a merger in mid-2014. Yet again, this merger introduced a slew of new risks resulting from leveraging the company's assets (Cohan, 2015). In the long run, Mr. Emmanuel hopes to bring the company public, but only time will tell whether the new mega-agency can meet expectations and remain viable.

IMG is not the only mega-agency firm. Octagon also provides more services than contract negotiation, including marketing and endorsements, team relations, public relations and financial planning services. Its website includes event management, TV rights sales and new media planning (http://www.Octagon.com).

More recently, Creative Artists Agency (CAA) started a sports division in 2004, which has become the dominant sports agency in the United States for representing athletes in the four major team sports with total contract commissions at close to $206 million in 2014. In 2015, CAA represented elite NFL quarterbacks like Tony Romo, Drew Brees, Matt Ryan and Phillip Rivers, as well as Eli and Peyton Manning. CAA also operates the industry's second largest baseball practice and represents top athletic talent. CAA's basketball division represents an equally impressive roster of NBA stars such as Dwyane Wade, Chris Bosh, Carmelo Anthony, Chris

Paul and Tony Parker. CAA has negotiated almost $5.6 billion dollars of player contracts since its inception, making it one of the most powerful agencies in sports history (Belzer, 2014).

The line between sports and entertainment has been a fuzzy one, particularly with those select athletes who are able to transcend their sport and become cultural icons. Athletes or former athletes have become actors, television personalities and pitchmen for commercial products. Names like former NFL defensive end Michael Strahan (former co-host of the daily television show "Live with Kelly and Michael"), former NBA hall of famer Kareem Abdul-Jabbar (films) and former heavyweight champion George Foreman (whose advertisements for an outdoor grill bearing his name sold millions of units) are but a few. As a result, Hollywood talent agencies, which are traditionally separate from sports representation, have become major players in sports agency in recent years.

CAA, and more recently, William Morris Endeavor which bought IMG in 2013, not only represent top-tier athletes (such as NBA star Dwyane Wade and the soccer star Cristiano Ronaldo, both represented by CAA as well as sprinter Usain Bolt and the mixed martial arts star Ronda Rousey represented by William Morris Endeavor as of 2016), but also can sponsor and produce events (Cieply, M. & Barnes, B., 2015).

Duties of an Agent

Agency law governs the basic responsibilities of any sports agent (sometimes called an athlete agent). Simply put, an agent represents another person, known as a principal, and negotiates on behalf of that principal (in our case, an athlete or a coach) in order to secure a contract. Agents often possess considerable power (known as "authority") but remain a representative. An agent cannot overrule the wishes of the principal because the agent can only act within the authority given to him or her by the principal.

Ethical Issue: Ricky Williams

The nature and limitations of an agent's authority are illustrated by the circumstances surrounding the incentive-laden contract signed by the running back Ricky Williams after he was drafted by the New Orleans Saints in 1999 (Shropshire & Davis, 2003, p. 16). The New Orleans Saints traded to get a high draft pick so that they could pick Williams. That fact gave the player considerable leverage in the negotiations. But the ultimate contract seemed odd. Williams's contract included an $8.84 million signing bonus and base salaries that ranged from $175,000 to $400,000 over the course of the deal. Williams could earn another $500,000 each year if he reached at least ten of twenty-six goals worth $50,000 apiece (Mihoces, 2000).

Many criticized the deal, questioning agent Leland Hardy's judgment and competence and pointed to his lack of experience in negotiating football contracts (Burwell, 1999). Ultimately, Williams fired Hardy and sought a trade to the Miami Dolphins because of his unhappiness in New Orleans. Upon arriving in Miami, his contract was reworked to a more traditional one, with fewer incentives and more upfront money.

What did not get proper attention was the fact that the idea for this incentive-laden agreement came not from Hardy, but from Williams. Williams reportedly told Hardy to reject a $25.6 million offer over seven years and to go with the incentivized contract. Williams later admitted: "I'm first and last when it comes to my decisions . . . I don't work for my agent. My agent works for me. This was my decision and my decision alone" (Shropshire & Davis, 2003, p. 16). Williams's statement perfectly summarizes the agent–principal relationship. The agent must follow the instructions of the principal, even if it may be against the agent's better judgment.

Do you think that the agent should have been more aggressive in arguing that Williams's approach was counterproductive? Or did the agent act ethically in trying to fulfill the wishes of his client? Finally, is this a case of "sour grapes" because Williams did not successfully fulfill the terms of the contract?

An agent has some important obligations to the principal, known as fiduciary duties. A fiduciary possesses a very high degree of loyalty to the principal and cannot engage in conduct considered a conflict of interest or act in bad faith. Based on this definition, an agent *cannot* do the following: (a) take payments from third parties to secure an agreement; (b) direct the principal to sign a contract with an entity owned or partly owned by the agent or a relative or close friend of that agent without disclosure of that fact; or (c) fail to reveal relevant information to the principal. The same fiduciary duties occur when an agent (or financial advisor) has the power to invest the athlete's money. The agent must invest it as a "reasonably prudent investor" would and must keep the athlete informed of the nature of the investments. Under no circumstance can the athlete's money be used for personal reasons. As discussed later, the NFLPA has drafted separate rules governing financial advisors.

A notorious example of a breach of fiduciary duty involved an agent named Jerry Argovitz, who represented Billy Sims, an All-Pro with the Detroit Lions. In 1983, Sims sought a new contract with the Lions, and Argovitz tried to leverage more money because the Houston franchise of the new United States Football League (USFL) also sought Sims's services. Argovitz and the Lions were making progress in their negotiations. However, Argovitz gave the impression that the Lions were "dragging their feet" and brought Sims to Houston. The USFL team made an offer, which was accepted by Sims. However, Sims did not know that Argovitz owned 29 percent of the Houston team or that Argovitz never contacted the Lions with that offer so they could attempt to match it. He even asked Sims to sign a waiver stating that Sims could not sue Argovitz for breach of fiduciary duty (*Detroit Lions & Sims v. Argovitz*, 1984). Not surprisingly, the court ruled that Argovitz breached his fiduciary duty.

The Rise of Agents

Although sports agents date from the 1920s, their numbers and use were at first limited. Most contract negotiations occurred directly between the athlete and the owner or general manager of a team. In the case of individual sports, the prohibition of professionals from the elite tournaments effectively negated the need for representation. A few highly regarded athletes negotiated endorsement agreements. A famous example occurred when the makers of the Baby Ruth chocolate bar signed the New York Yankees slugger Babe Ruth to an endorsement contract. In the few cases where athletes sought agent representation, management was often contemptuous. An often-recited story involves the late Green Bay Packers coach Vince Lombardi and a player named Jim Ringo. Lombardi, seeing a gentleman with Ringo, asked who he was. Ringo replied that the man was to help in the contract negotiations for the upcoming season. Lombardi then excused himself, stepped into an adjoining room and made a telephone call. When he returned, Lombardi informed Ringo that he was negotiating with the wrong team because the Packers coach had just traded him to the Philadelphia Eagles (Shropshire & Davis, 2003, p. 10).

The then-existing salary structure presented a fundamental problem. Compressed salaries existed in all of the major league sports because of "reserve" clauses that prohibited outright or at best severely restricted free agency. In the 1960s and 1970s, the emergence of rival leagues such as the American Basketball Association (ABA), the World Hockey Association (WHA) and the American Football League (AFL) gave players more negotiating opportunities and increased their need for agent representation. To obtain credibility, these new leagues needed established stars and offered talented players more lucrative contracts than what they had. "Negotiations" in a true sense did occur, and agents represented these players. In time, the rival leagues either folded or merged with the more venerable league. Fortunately for the players, this coincided with the end of the reserve system and the rise of free agency either through arbitration or through collective bargaining. For the first time, bona fide arm's-length negotiations, often with several teams simultaneously, increased demand for agents. The creation of salary arbitration systems for non–free-agent athletes created yet another reason to obtain agent representation.

Off-field activities increased the demand for agents and increased the need for sophistication and expertise. The rise of endorsement opportunities required contract negotiations between agents representing individual professional athletes such as Arnold Palmer and nonsports entities. The greater incomes derived from player salaries and endorsements necessitated money management skills, something that many athletes lacked. Finally, the higher-income brackets of more and more athletes necessitated the need for effective tax planning, and athletes used the services of agents or financial planners to limit the tax bite of federal and state tax laws. As a result, the higher salaries earned by players translated to more income for agents. Agents then (and now) normally take a percentage of the amount negotiated, so the higher the contract, the greater the reward for the agent's work.

Agent Responsibilities

Securing Talent and Contracting with Teams and Endorsers

The first (and possibly most difficult) task for the agent is to secure talent. A newly minted agent often must pound the pavement, speaking, cajoling and charming a potential client. Unethical agents have offered money and goods to secure a representation contract for a talented athlete.

Often, the fiercest competition surrounds collegiate or even high school athletes entering the draft of the league. In too many cases (although not all), the athlete being solicited exhibits little experience in making a choice. His or her decision in choosing one particular agent over others may be based on many variables, such as personality and opinions of family members (who can have a major say). Without belittling the importance of these reasons, the major consideration in choosing an agent should be experience in contract negotiations and financial planning—in other words, a more hard-headed business decision. But, in many cases, a hotshot young athlete pampered since junior high school has developed a large ego and seeks a person who accedes to his or her every whim. Of course, more sophisticated and mature athletes (and their families) exist, especially among veteran players, who, by experience and perspective, have learned not to choose an agent just on personality and salesmanship.

A successful agent develops a reputation based on the satisfaction of clients. Negotiating a lucrative contract for a first-round draft pick in the NFL or a free agent in baseball may bring many more clients. But a lack of perceived success renders the opposite effect, as unhappy clients switch agents, often for subjective reasons, unfair reasons or no reason at all. In May 2005, the NBA superstar LeBron James fired his agents, Aaron and Eric Goodwin, after they negotiated $135 million in endorsement agreements with Nike, Upper Deck, Sprite and others, in addition to the $18.7 million he was guaranteed in his first four seasons under his player's contract. Instead, James decided to hire a former high school teammate to handle his affairs (Banks, 2005). To determine the "success" of an agent, one should determine both how many new clients he or she has signed and how many he or she has retained. An agent who signed three NFL first-round draft picks but lost five established NFL players in a given year may arouse suspicion as to his success with veteran players.

After securing and retaining talent, the agent's goal remains signing the athlete to a contract. Without a player's contract, the agreement made between the agent and the athlete becomes practically meaningless. The athlete has no obligation to pay the agent because agent fees are based on a percentage of the contract consummated between the athlete and the team or endorsement company. A highly drafted player or a top free agent generates a lucrative contract, with a good payday for the agent. If it is a long-term deal, the agent receives the percentage for as long as the athlete plays under the contract. However, an agent representing a journeyman player often incurs more legwork for less compensation. The agent may have to spend more out-of-pocket money to take the player to team try-outs or to shop him or her to teams in other countries. Ultimately, the time and effort may be for naught. The agent may spend thousands of dollars to no avail if the athlete is not picked and signed by a team.

Of course, the more money paid to the athlete, the more the agent receives in compensation. This is particularly important because most of the players' unions (except the Major League Baseball Players' Association) cap the fees agents may earn. In the NBA, the cap is 4 percent of the amount paid to the athlete. In the NFL, it is 3 percent (Heitner, 2014). Because of these limits, the real money is made on endorsements and financial management. There is no limit on the percentages an agent may earn from endorsement deals (which usually is 15 percent, but can be as high as 20 percent of the contract amount).

Understanding National Collegiate Athletic Association Rules

An agent who seeks student-athletes must understand the NCAA's restrictions. As described in Chapter 3, as of 2015, the NCAA still imposes a system of amateurism that restricts compensation for student-athletes based on their athletic skills (NCAA Division I Bylaws, sec. 12.1.2). The rules also prohibit the student-athlete from signing any contract with an agent or receiving payments from an agent (NCAA Division I Bylaws, sec. 12.1.2(g). However, securing advice from a lawyer concerning a proposed professional sports contract shall not be considered "contracting for representation by an agent" (NCAA Division I Bylaws, sec. 12.3.2). If an agent violates these rules, the student-athlete loses eligibility and scholarship support. However, before state and federal laws were enacted, the agent often went unpunished because the NCAA bylaws do not directly apply to agents.

Understanding the Appropriate Sport's Collective Bargaining Agreement

Often agents specialize in only one sport for financial and practical reasons. Working in only one sport permits development of an expertise in the issues unique in that sport, which, in particular, include a detailed knowledge of the league's salary caps. An agent representing NFL, NBA and NHL players must demonstrate knowledge of the salary cap system for these respective leagues and have the challenge of negotiating in an atmosphere of "capped money" or "free money." Those agents representing Major League Baseball players do not have those challenges, because MLB does not utilize a cap system.

Engaging in Damage Control

One agent classified his job as "agent, manager, social worker, family counselor, and psychologist. All under one hat" (Shropshire & Davis, 2003, p. 28). Indeed, the agent's duties often transcend deal making. Often, the agent maintains a close relationship with the athlete and is the person the athlete turns to in the event of an arrest, family emergency or general personal crisis. If the athlete is connected with an embarrassing event made public, the agent serves as the spokesman, hoping to deflect criticism and to polish the tarnished image.

Alternatives to Agents

Going Alone

Before the advent of free agency, players generally represented themselves. Although most athletes now employ agents, a few still decide to negotiate on their own. One may question the wisdom of such a strategy, but if the athlete feels confident and sophisticated enough to represent himself or herself, there is no rule requiring procurement of an agent. Two notable baseball free agents—the slugger Gary Sheffield and the pitcher Curt Schilling—negotiated their own deals in 2003. Sheffield negotiated a three-year, $39 million deal with the Yankees, and Schilling a $25.5 million contract with the Boston Red Sox (Hohler, 2003). More recently, NFL linebacker Osi Umenyiora fired his agent in 2012 and subsequently rehired him after signing a one-year $7 million dollar contract with the New York Giants (Rosenthal, 2012).

In addition to confidence and sophistication, an athlete negotiating alone must display intestinal fortitude. Often, the player (or representative) discusses the "great abilities" possessed, whereas the general manager points out the "weaknesses." If an athlete takes the negotiations personally and feels slighted by the team during the process, those bad feelings may linger, affecting the athlete's morale. Often it is best not to have the athlete in the negotiating room, but to delegate the sometimes ugly process to a representative.

Sometimes family members represent the athlete. A seeming middle ground between athletes negotiating their own contracts and employing an outside party, the family representative has advantages, but some particular pitfalls. A familial relationship between the athlete and the agent may result in a strong bond of trust and respect, as opposed to a nonfamily agent who represents other similarly talented athletes and may not have the same bond. However, family members may also take management tactics personally, which will result in the same kind of hard feelings as if the athlete negotiates. Or the family member agent may interfere with the operations of the team. One reason for the deterioration in relations between the Philadelphia Flyers and its then-captain Eric Lindros in the late 1990s was the acrimony between Lindros's agent (his father) and the team's general manager, Bobby Clarke. The tension between Clarke and Lindros became particularly acute when Carl Lindros began advising Clarke on whom his son should play with and how long he should be allowed to recover from injuries (Gormley, 2001).

Legal Representation

Although many agents are attorneys, their duties are different. An attorney retained to negotiate a contract has a more limited role, whereas the agent acts as a general representative and confidant for the athlete. A number of mature athletes—who do not need the wisdom and guidance of an agent but require the expertise of a competent negotiator—may utilize legal help.

Although rare, some agents charge an hourly rate. Lon Babby, formerly an attorney for the Washington, D.C., law firm of Williams & Connolly, served as an example of an attorney retained for the purpose of negotiating a contract. In return, the athlete paid an hourly rate for services, rather than giving a percentage of salary. When Babby negotiated Grant Hill's $45 million deal with the Detroit Pistons, Babby billed $100,000, based on his hourly rate. An agent charging the National Basketball Players' Association (NBPA) rate of 4 percent would receive $1.8 million. Babby's client list included the basketball player Tim Duncan (Ludden, 2000). (More recently, however, Babby left sports agency to become the director of basketball operations for the Phoenix Suns).

Standards and Regulations

SPARTA

Unlike professions such as law or public accounting, agents are not licensed by a governmental body. Congress, in an attempt to impose uniform standards, passed the first federal law regulating agents: the Sports Agent Responsibility and Trust Act (SPARTA) in 2004.

SPARTA makes it unlawful for sports agents to sign student-athletes into representational contracts with bribes or misleading information (Sports Agent Responsibility and Trust Act, 15 USC, 2004, sec. 7802). It permits prosecution of violators by the state where the misconduct occurred. Before SPARTA, thirteen states did not have any laws governing sports agents. Thus, sports agents could operate with relative impunity in those states. Specifically, SPARTA makes it unlawful for a sports agent to (a) entice a student-athlete into entering an agency contract by giving false or misleading information or making false or misleading promises or representations, (b) provide anything of value to the student-athlete or anyone associated with the athlete, (c) fail to disclose in writing to the student that he or she may lose NCAA eligibility after signing an agency contract or (d) predate or postdate contracts. In that sense, SPARTA mimics many state laws and NCAA rules (15 USC, 2004, sec. 7802). But SPARTA provides a uniform standard for prosecuting agents who choose to ignore NCAA rules and state law.

Under provisions of SPARTA, both the sports agent and the student-athlete are required to notify the school's athletic director within seventy-two hours of signing the contract or before the athlete's next sporting event (15 USC, 2004, sec. 7805). Additionally, SPARTA brings sports agents under the jurisdiction of the Federal Trade Commission (FTC) and considers sports agents who lure student-athletes with lies and gifts to enter into agency contracts in violation of the FTC's Unfair and Deceptive Businesses Act (15 USC, 2004, sec. 7803). It allows schools to seek civil remedies for any damages or expenses incurred through its violation (15 USC, 2004, sec. 7805).

Although already prohibited by the NCAA and many states, the behavior targeted by SPARTA had been difficult to prosecute because of jurisdictional issues. The passage of this federal law eliminates these issues by enacting nationwide standards. Before the passage of SPARTA, only non–agent-specific laws, such as the Racketeer Influenced and Corrupt Organizations Act (RICO) and federal mail fraud statutes, were used to criminally prosecute agents.

State Statutes

SPARTA supplements and standardizes states' involvement with agents. In 2000, the Uniform Athlete Agents Act (UAAA) was proposed, and it was ultimately adopted in a number of states (in 2015 that number was forty, plus the District of Columbia). It requires agents to register in a given state and requires specific contract language in agreements between an agent and an athlete, including the amount and method of calculating his or her fees, a description of the services to be provided, the duration of the contract and, significantly, a notice that the student-athlete may lose eligibility to compete in the given sport and a requirement that the university's athletic director be notified within seventy-two hours. The UAAA contains a fourteen-day cancellation provision (UAAA, 2000, sec. 10c). Violators are subject to civil and criminal penalties. Its provisions served as the basis for the later federal statute.

Players' Union Certification

The unions from the major sports certify the agents that represent their players, requiring that the agent abide by the union's rules and regulations in order to maintain their sports agent certification. In 1983, the National Football League Players' Association asserted its authority to regulate player agents. The National Basketball Players' Association did so in 1986, followed by the Major League Baseball Players' Association and the National Hockey League Players' Association.

National Football League Players' Association

In order to represent an NFL player, the agent must be certified with the NFLPA. The NFLPA refers to these agents as "contract advisors," and its regulations require agents to pass a proficiency exam. Also, they limit how much compensation the agent receives from the player. The NFLPA regulations prohibit agents from providing inducements to college athletes and their family members and friends in order to sign a player, negotiating a contract in violation of the collective bargaining agreement, engaging in unlawful conduct, engaging in acts involving fraud or dishonesty or violating the fee schedule. Penalties, including expulsion, exist for those who violate the rules. Unlike rules for agent counterparts in basketball and hockey, the NFLPA does permit an agent to represent both players and coaches (NFLPlayers.com, 2012).

The maximum an agent receives under the regulations is 3 percent of the amount paid to the player, except for players tagged as franchise or transition players. In those cases, the amount ranges from 1 to 2 percent (Bechta, 2014). Because NFL player contracts are not guaranteed and are often incentivized, the rules prohibit the agent from receiving the 3 percent of the entire contract amount "up front" (Brandt, 2012). Note that the compensation restrictions apply only to contracts negotiated with an NFL team. Other types of contracts, such as endorsements, have no fee restriction.

The NFLPA also regulates "financial advisors" based on a different set of standards. This program, the first of its kind, requires such advisors to have appropriate education and three years of experience as a broker-dealer, investment advisor, certified public accountant (CPA) or certified financial planner (NFLPlayers.com, 2012).

National Hockey League Players' Association

The NHL Players' Association (NHLPA) regulates the conduct of agents who represent players in individual contract negotiations with clubs. Anyone not designated by the NHLPA as being duly certified ("certified agent") cannot represent players. Each prospective agent must complete an application and background check and must pass an exam. As is the case with the other players' associations, prospective agents do not have to be accountants or lawyers; agents need not possess a college degree.

Major League Baseball Players' Association

The standards of the Major League Baseball Players' Association (MLBPA) for agent certification are similar to those of the NHLPA. However, agent fees lack any limitation, so an agent can charge as much as he or she wishes (Heitner, 2014). However, these regulations include a peculiar exception. No agent can charge a fee that drives the player's actual compensation below the minimum salary (MLBPA Regulations, 2015, sec. 6(I)).

National Basketball Players' Association

Athlete agents representing NBA players must be certified with the NBPA. A person pursuing certification must have a degree from an accredited four-year college or university. Once a player agent is certified with the NBPA, that agent is subject to the NBA's "standard of conduct" regulations (NBPA Regulations Governing Player Agents, 2015, sec. 3).

The regulations include several general requirements, mainly administrative provisions regarding fees (both to the NBPA and from the players), as well as several sections labeled "Prohibited Conduct Subject to Discipline" (NBPA Regulations, 2015, sec. 3). The prohibited acts mirror those prohibited by the other players' associations: providing inducements to college athletes, families and friends in order to sign a player; negotiating contracts in violation of the collective bargaining agreement; committing fraud or deceitful acts; breaching the maximum fee schedule; and violating any provision of the standard player agent contract. The NBPA administers a comprehensive program involving mandatory instructional seminars and testing to ensure competence in contract matters. Presently, the maximum fee collected by the NBPA-certified agent is 4 percent of the contract amount.

In recent years, the costs of becoming an NBA player agent increased. In 2015, the NBPA proposed increasing the annual dues set at $1,500 per year, a minimal amount considering the average NBA salary hovered around $5 million. With a 4 percent commission, an agent can earn $200,000/year for representing a player earning that salary.

Among the changes were increases in yearly dues, limitations on the use of third parties for recruiting purposes, disclosures on referrals to financial advisors and a new entrance exam for those hoping to represent NBA players. The new formula is a sliding scale, depending on the number of players the agent represents. If the agent represents zero to nine players, the agent would pay $2,500 annually; those with ten to nineteen players $5,000; and agents with more than twenty players, $7,500. Under the new rules, certification will expire if the agent hasn't represented an NBA player during the previous five years.

The new rules require agents to report the use of "runners" (noncertified third parties who work for agents in securing talent) to the NBPA or be subject to discipline. In addition, agents are required to advise the union whenever they refer a client to a financial advisor and must specify their process for selecting such advisors. If the NBPA deems the referral process to be "below the fiduciary standard expected" of agents, the agent can be disciplined (Kobritz, 2016). Another change expands the potential penalties for any violation of the regulations. As of 2016, the NBPA will be able to impose a fine up to a maximum of $100,000.

References

Banks, L. (2005, May 20). James' switcheroo a youthful mistake; While there is nothing illegal about the move, there is much that is illogical and immature about it. *Chicago Sun-Times*, p. 155.

Bechta, J. (2014, August 20). 5 myths of the NFL agent business. *NFPost.com*. Retrieved April 20, 2015, from www.nationalfootballpost.com/5-myths-of-the-nfl-agent-business/

Belzer, J. (2014, September 2). The world's most valuable sports agencies 2014. *Forbes.com*. Retrieved April 20, 2015, www.forbes.com/sites/jasonbelzer/2014/09/02/the-worlds-most-valuable-sports-agencies-2014/

Brandt, A. (2012, November 27). An agent's life isn't all glamour. *ESPN.com*. Retrieved April 20, 2015, from espn.go.com/nfl/story/_/id/8681968/nfl-agent-life-all-glamour

Bowder, T. (2013, March 11). Agent investigation names UNC football money man. Retrieved October 20, 2016, from http://www.wralsportsfan.com/agent-investigation-names-unc-football-money-man/12207565/?hpt=ju_bn4#WjBpF2cb5BxrmzEr.99

Burwell, B. (1999, October 11–17). Think Williams got bad deal? Don't try to tell him that. *Sports Business Journal*, p. 54.

Cieply, M., & Barnes, B. (2015, September 13). Rivalry builds off the field as talent agencies turn to sports. *The New York Times*. Retrieved January 30, 2016, from http://www.nytimes.com/2015/09/14/business/media/rivalry-builds-off-the-field-as-talent-agencies-turn-to-sports.html?emc=eta1&_r=0

CMG (2014, July). Mark McCormack and IMG: What could have been. Retrieved April 20, 2015, from issuu.com/cmgpartners/docs/mark_mccormack_and_img

Cohan, W. (2015, March). The inside story of Ari Emanuel's big, risky WME-IMG merger. *Vanity Fair*. Retrieved April 20, 2015, from www.vanityfair.com/news/2015/02/wme-img-merger-ari-emanuel

Cohn, B. (2004, May 4). Few Jerry Maguires; Aspiring sports agents find the clients scarce, the glamour nonexistent and the going tough. *Washington Post*, p. C01.

Davis, K. (2015, January 30). FBI: Sports agents tried to swindle clients. Retrieved April 20, 2015, from www.utsandiego.com/news/2015/jan/30/fbi-nfl-agents-player-burger-king-vaccaro/

Detroit Lions & Sims v. Argovitz, 580 F. Supp 542 (E.D. MI, 1984).

Garafolo, M. (2013, March 16). Late paperwork costs NFL agent a big client. *USA Today*. Retrieved April 20, 2015, from www.usatoday.com/story/sports/nfl/broncos/2013/03/16/elvis-dumervil-agent-fired-denver-broncos-late-paperwork/1993199/

Gormley, C. (2001, August 21). One question unanswered as Lindros leaves. *Cherry Hill* (NJ) *Courier-Post*, p. 3.

Grossi, T. (2003, July 13). Brown's health big factor in contract restructuring. *Cleveland Plain-Dealer*, p. C10.

Heitner, D. (2013, January 3). Despite NFLPA's efforts "runners" remain powerful in recruitment of NFL prospects. *Forbes.com*. Retrieved April 20, 2015, from www.forbes.com/sites/darrenheitner/2013/01/03/despite-nflpas-efforts-runners-remain-powerful-in-recruitment-of-nfl-prospects/

Heitner, D. (2014, August 7). Baseball agency blows up standard agent commission model. *Forbes.com*. Retrieved April 20, 2015, from www.forbes.com/sites/darrenheitner/2014/08/07/baseball-agency-blows-up-standard-agent-commission-model/

Hohler, B. (2003, November 29). Red Sox hit jackpot, land schilling; Boston signs Arizona ace to $25.5 million deal. *Boston Globe*, p. A1.

IMGWorld.com (2010). About IMG. Retrieved April 22, 2010, from http://www.imgworld.com/about/default.sps

Isaacson, M. (2004, December 19). Unscrupulous advisors, bad investments, lavish spending leave many athletes bankrupt. *Chicago Tribune*, p. 10.

Kobritz, J. (2016, March 2). Life of NBA agents changing, and costing more. *The Daily Courier* (Prescott, AZ). Retrieved March 20, 2016, from http://dcourier.com/news/2016/mar/02/column-life-nba-agents-changing-and-costing-more/

Ludden, J. (2000, July 26). NBA law; Babby wins clients by acting like an attorney. *San Antonio Express-News*, p. 1C.

Mihoces, G. (2000, November 14). Williams' loss doesn't deter Saints. *USA Today*, p. 1C.

MLBPA Regulations Governing Player Agents (2015). See sec. 6(I).

NBPA Regulations Governing Player Agents (2015). Retrieved April 20, 2015, from http://nbpa.com/nbpa-agent-application-package/

NCAA Division I Bylaws (2015). Retrieved April 15, 2015, from http://www. ncaapublications.com/productdownloads/D115JAN.pdf

NFLPlayers.com (2012). NFLPA regulations governing contract advisors, sample representation agreement. Retrieved April 20, 2015, from https://nflpaweb. blob.core.windows.net/media/Default/PDFs/Agents/2012_NFLPA_ Regulations_Governing_Contract_Advisors.pdf

Pound, E. T., Pasternak, D., Madden, M., & Hook, C. (2002, February 2). Money players. *U.S. News & World Report*, p. 30.

Roeder, D. (2004, December 1). Developer's dealings costly to ex-Bulls star. *Chicago Sun-Times*, p. 81.

Rosenthal, G. (2012, June 4). Osi Umenyiora will re-hire agent after signing deal. *NFL.com*. Retrieved April 20, 2015, from www.nfl.com/news/story/ 09000d5d82990335/article/osi-umenyiora-will-rehire-agent-after-signing-deal

Shropshire, K. L., & Davis, T. (2003). *The business of sports agents*. Philadelphia: University of Pennsylvania Press, pp. 10, 14, 15, 16, 26, 28, 51–52, 78.

Sports Agent Responsibility and Trust Act, 15 USC, secs. 7802, 7803, 7805 (2004).

Uniform Athlete Agents Act (2000). Retrieved April 20, 2015, from http://www. uniformlaws.org/shared/docs/athlete_agents/uaaa_finalact_2000.pdf

8 Team Relocation and Facility Issues

Throughout the history of professional sports leagues, franchises have moved, sometimes two or three times. Within a twenty-year time frame, the Boston Braves moved to Milwaukee and then to Atlanta, and the Philadelphia Athletics moved to Kansas City and then to Oakland. Such moves sometimes result in acrimony and anger. The immigration and emigration of the NFL Raiders from Oakland to Los Angeles and back to Oakland has been one of the most controversial, drawing the ire of fans and resulting in considerable litigation.

Why does a team move? Lack of financial success in its present market is one reason. For example, in 2002, the NBA's Charlotte Hornets relocated to New Orleans on account of lack of attendance, financial losses and the refusal of voters to approve the financing of a new facility. Similarly, a year earlier, another NBA franchise, the Vancouver Grizzlies, relocated to Memphis. In 2016, the NFL's St. Louis Rams relocated to Los Angeles, returning to its former home in a larger market.

The potential for greater opportunities in a larger and/or growing market serves as a second reason, the textbook example being the relocation of the Brooklyn Dodgers to Los Angeles in the late 1950s. However, in recent years, the availability of new markets has been limited by expansion, resulting in few locations to which teams can relocate. That leads to the third and most recent justification for team (or, more officially, franchise) relocation: the revenue stream from the facility.

As discussed later, the economics of having a first-class stadium or arena with opportunities to generate revenues by seat licenses, naming rights, signage, parking, concessions, luxury boxes and premium seating has resulted in attempts by cities to woo teams to different locations or to keep teams. Often, part of the cost of building the stadiums or arenas is borne by taxpayers, either directly through funding or indirectly from taxes and bond payments. Although the idea of public financing of facilities has caused controversy, the majority of stadiums and arenas have some public component to their funding. This chapter discusses these issues and analyzes a typical stadium lease agreement. The subject of stadium economics deserves more media coverage, and young journalists must learn the basics of one of the most important issues in the business of sports.

A Short History of Franchise Relocation

The first phase of the evolution of the major sports leagues demonstrates a gradual shift from smaller cities to larger ones as the league matures and becomes successful. Although all leagues commenced operations with some teams in larger cities, a surprising number of franchises hailed from the heartland. Teams from baseball's National League, the oldest continuous sports league of the four major sports, once hailed from Providence, Rhode Island; Syracuse, New York; and Worcester, Massachusetts. However, by 1899, the National League was ensconced in the eight largest U.S. cities. The rival American League started as a minor league but then decided to compete with the older league head on by moving its teams from smaller cities to some of the larger cities where National League franchises were housed, such as from Milwaukee to St. Louis and from Baltimore to New York (Seymour, 1960). St. Louis had double the population of Milwaukee, and New York had over six times the numbers of Baltimore.

The history of the National Football League (NFL) also evidences this movement. The original franchises were in cities such as Canton, Ohio; Hammond, Indiana; and Green Bay, Wisconsin (with the last being the only surviving original NFL franchise in its city of birth). Professional football, initially given second-class status in favor of the far more popular college version, had its roots in these working-class Midwestern cities and towns. Most of the major urban teams such as the New York Giants, Detroit Lions and Cleveland Browns were expansion teams.

The NBA, created after World War II, included teams from both large and smaller cities. In fact, teams from smaller cities such as Fort Wayne and Syracuse were more stable than their counterparts in larger cities, such as Detroit, Cleveland, Toronto and Pittsburgh, which folded. Eventually, Fort Wayne moved to Detroit (and became the Pistons) and Syracuse moved to Philadelphia (and became the 76ers).

For decades, the National Hockey League (NHL) contained only six teams, two in Canada and four in the United States. Each of the "original six" franchises—the Montreal Canadiens, Toronto Maple Leafs, Detroit Red Wings, Chicago Blackhawks, Boston Bruins and New York Rangers—was financially stable and there was little reason to expand outside those cold-weather areas. A major expansion did not come until the mid-1960s. By the 1990s, team relocations, often from Canadian cities to the southern and western portions of the United States, occurred. The Quebec Nordiques moved to Denver and became the Colorado Avalanche in 1995. The Winnipeg Jets moved to Phoenix and became the Coyotes the following year. In an interesting turn of events, the Atlanta Thrashers moved to Winnipeg in 2011 and changed its name to the Jets, the former name of the Coyotes.

Waves of Relocation

It is best to look at franchise relocations episodically. Although the early relocations focused on playing in the largest markets (then in the Northeast and Midwest), a second wave of franchise movement—generally to the southern and western United States—began in the post–World War II era. These regions experienced major population growth and created fertile markets for sports franchises to flourish. By 1950, Los Angeles had become the third largest city in the United States, but it had no Major League Baseball franchises, whereas Chicago and Philadelphia, numbers two and four, respectively, had two teams each. Five years later, the Philadelphia Athletics of the American League moved to Kansas City. Then came the New York Giants' move to San Francisco and the Dodgers' departure to Los Angeles. Until that time, St. Louis was the westernmost location for a Major League Baseball franchise.

This era of franchise movement mirrored the movement of the nation as a whole. At the time, a Rustbelt–Sunbelt population migration began. Older stadiums and arenas, often found in decaying portions of cities, were not car friendly. Fear of crime made fans less likely to come to night games. The facilities, often spartan and ancient, lacked modern amenities. New York's Polo Grounds dated from the nineteenth century and began as a facility for polo. Newer cities, such as Los Angeles, Phoenix and Dallas, were more car friendly and spread over a larger area with swaths of empty space. Modern facilities could be built in undeveloped areas with little difficulty in a city's metropolitan area, rather than in the city proper. The Dallas Cowboys and the Texas Rangers, for example, play in stadiums located between Dallas and Fort Worth.

The popularization of air travel enticed leagues to set up franchises in the south and the west. With teams no longer dependent on railroad travel, a New York team playing a California team as part of a road trip would not cause undue schedule disruption.

With the advent of television, "nationalizing" a sport by opening every region to franchises became a greater priority. Teams in virgin territories could attract fans to a live game event and to watching the sport on television. The television networks broadcast championship games nationwide, and the more interested the fans were in the sport, the higher the viewership.

The NFL and NBA were more amenable to setting up shop in the West. The San Francisco 49ers was born as an expansion franchise in

1949. In the NBA, the Minneapolis Lakers moved to Los Angeles in 1960 and the Philadelphia Warriors moved to San Francisco two years later. Although the movement of franchises south and west had exceptions (e.g., in 1970 the Major League Baseball Seattle Pilots moved to Milwaukee and became the Brewers), such movements were not the norm.

The first two phases of relocations—the pre–World War II exodus to the larger cities from the smaller ones and then the postwar moves from the Rustbelt to the Sunbelt—made economic sense in a time when gate attendance was the primary factor of financial success. Building a large and loyal fan base was crucial because, with the exception of the NFL, teams did not share local revenues.

Therefore, teams in growing markets with modern facilities could attract more fans and, later on, win more lucrative broadcasting rights for games. In 1953, the National League owners agreed to the first team relocation in Major League Baseball in fifty years when the Boston Braves moved to Milwaukee. The Braves agreed to play in County Stadium, a publicly owned facility, under a favorable lease agreement. Prior to that time, only one other team played in a publicly owned stadium. Every other facility was in private hands (Quirk & Fort, 1997).

New Stadiums and Arenas

Teams in each of the major leagues keep all or most of the gate receipts, the money spent by fans to see a live contest. Additionally, teams keep revenues from stadium amenities such as concessions, parking, advertising and luxury seating. These facilities may also include such attractions as angled seating (thus relieving postgame neck strains and giving excellent views of game action from all angles), walk-around open-air concourses that keep fans connected to the game, state-of-the-art video boards, Wi-Fi connectivity, social media access, breathtaking views, retractable roofs and shopping zones. Therefore, the type of home stadium and the type of stadium lease agreement consummated between the franchise and the stadium owner become very important for a team's balance sheet.

New stadium construction boomed in the 1990s. Fourteen of the thirty Major League Baseball teams and fourteen of the thirty-two NFL teams play in stadiums that were built after 2000. And in a departure from the past, all of the new facilities were constructed solely for the sports they were designed for. Another change was that many of these facilities were located "downtown" rather than in a suburban area.

The revenue-generating characteristics of the stadium or arena are a major, if not the main, reason why franchise relocation has occurred in the last fifteen years. This is not to say that stadiums or arenas were not important in past years, but the revenue potential of a state-of-the-art facility is a crucial component because franchises must find consistent revenue streams to earn income at a time of record-high player payrolls. A team may be enticed to a different locale based on a lucrative new stadium deal. Also, a new facility often serves to increase attendance, whether it is in a new city or an existing one.

In some cases, the stadium's ability to produce revenue trumped the size of the market. For example, the Los Angeles Rams moved to St. Louis, an open market, because its former team, the Cardinals, moved to Phoenix in 1987. The team went from residing in the second largest market to the twelfth largest. What enticed the Rams were the proposed stadium and its lease. The team received 100 percent of concession revenues, 100 percent of revenues from luxury boxes and club seats and 75 percent of stadium advertising sales revenues (Masteralexis, Barr, & Hums, 1998). It turned out that a provision of this lease came to haunt the city years later, permitting a move back to Los Angeles, a point examined later in this chapter.

The 1990s and 2000s produced a spate of new stadiums and arenas on both the major league and minor league levels because the often functional but drab facilities built in the 1960s outlived their usefulness, and leases between the teams and the stadium owners (often governmental agencies) expired. Once the old stadium's lease agreement expired, teams often demanded a new facility. If this was not forthcoming, sometimes the teams threatened to move. The Chicago White Sox almost relocated from its venerable location to Florida until a stadium replacing old Comiskey Park was built. As of 2015, because of the construction boom, there are not many major league cities where new stadiums or arenas need to be built. This construction activity has also worked its way to the minor leagues, as state-of-the-art facilities are being built to cultivate the growing popularity of minor league baseball (Hill, 2015).

Leagues' Control of Relocation

The rules codified in each of the major league sports constitutions limit the right of a franchise to move without the approval of three-quarters of the other owners. In theory, this standard seems onerous, but in reality, few owners have blocked relocations. However, this process demonstrates the inherent conflicts in the relationship between a team and the league. On the one hand, the four major leagues have independently owned teams with their own staffs and their own independent revenue streams. On the other hand, they participate in a cooperative joint venture where certain rights are curtailed by provisions in the league's constitution and bylaws. This system has produced its share of operational difficulties (as explained in more detail in Chapter 1) and legal controversies, especially in the area of antitrust law, but it remains the predominant form of team sports administration.

The main reason for prohibiting relocation to a market where another league team already plays is that no owner will want a rival team moving into the same territory served by the existing team. Direct and potential destructive competition may result in the loss of fans and revenues. Moreover, other owners and the league itself may not feel comfortable with a team's relocation—even one to a previously unserved market—because of the potentially bad publicity from fans of the departing market losing that team. That may hurt the reputation of the sport and cause resentment for years to come. Additionally, other owners and the league may fear that relocation may make that team either too valuable or not valuable enough. Although this seems counterintuitive, logic behind this reasoning exists. An unsuccessful relocation may result in a drop in league-wide revenues, affecting the other owners' bottom lines, especially in a league such as the NFL, where virtually the entire broadcasting/cable revenue is shared (Cozzillio & Levinstein, 1997). Conversely, a successful relocation can hurt other teams as well, especially in a league such as Major League Baseball, where owners keep much more of their revenue. That in turn may drive salaries up because the relocated team has more money to pay, increasing its market value. In a salary-capped labor structure, the extra revenue may serve to increase the salary cap, costing the other owners more with little benefit in return.

Some have argued that most league attempts to block franchise relocations were directed at specific owners of the teams that sought to move, such as Charlie Finley, Bill Veeck and Al Davis, who were perceived as mavericks (Mitten & Burton, 1997). But, at least in the NFL, NBA and NHL, the leagues with no antitrust exemptions, these actions carry risks. An owner who blocks another's relocation attempt may expect retribution aimed at his own team's attempts in the future. So the result has been relocations without much challenge from the other owners.

From 1950 through 1982, seventy-eight franchise movements occurred in the four major league professional sports. Eleven of those relocations occurred in baseball, forty in basketball, fourteen in hockey and thirteen in football. In the last fifteen years, franchise relocations occurred when the NBA's Seattle SuperSonics moved to Oklahoma City and became the Thunder. The Montreal Expos relocated to Washington, D.C., and became the Nationals.

In the 1980s, franchise relocation issues often resulted in litigation. No league wants a repeat of the Oakland Raiders case, in which a federal appeals court ruled that the NFL's relocation rules constituted an antitrust law violation (*Los Angeles Memorial Coliseum Commission v. National Football League*, 1984). The federal appeals court did not conclude that all relocation limitations are invalid, but it determined that even a league as centralized as the NFL may not "improperly" block relocation. From a business as well as legal standpoint, that standard is vague and difficult to implement. (Note that Major League Baseball was not affected by this ruling because of its long-standing antitrust exemption.)

Given the steep penalties for antitrust violations (three times the jury's damage award), the NFL, NBA and NHL did not block franchise relocations, thereby diminishing the risk of further litigation. Knowing that maverick owners such as Davis have not been bashful about using the courts to get their way, the leagues decided to pay it safe.

Facility Attempts to Stop Relocation

Although we have focused on attempts by other owners to block a relocation, a related issue has been attempts by facility owners to stop a move. Team moves have a substantial immediate effect on the owner of the facility (often a municipality or state or county authority) because it loses its major paying client. Legally, a facility owner cannot stop a team from moving once its lease expires. However, an owner attempts to protect interests by drafting certain contract provisions in the lease agreement to make it more difficult for a team to terminate the lease before its expiration.

One common way to do this is to use a "liquidated damages" clause that spells out specific monies paid in the event the team breaches its contract and moves either to a facility in the same metropolitan area or to a different city. The amounts can be a flat amount or a per-game rate. For example, the lease agreement between the Minnesota Timberwolves and the Minneapolis Community Development Agency (the owner of the Target Center) stated that total damages for a breach would be $60 million, reduced by $3 million for each of the first ten years during the lease (Greenberg & Gray, 1998). In one NFL team lease, the damages are stated as $50,000 per game (Greenberg & Gray, 1998). The arena lease between the NHL's Phoenix Coyotes and the Jobing.com Arena had a complex liquidated damages clause that started at over $794 million (*Dewey Ranch Hockey, LLC*, 2009).

Relocation and Cities

Much has been written about the effects of a franchise's relocation on the economy of the departed city and on the psyche of the team's fans. Probably the classic example was that of the Brooklyn Dodgers' relocation to Los Angeles in 1957. But the reasons for the move are probably more complex than the simple answer of "abandonment" of Brooklyn by the team. In reality, Los Angeles' generous offer of land for a new stadium, the economic opportunities of a growing Southern California market and the failure of New York to condemn land for a facility in downtown Brooklyn served as the bases for the team's decision (Shapiro, 2004).

A similar public outcry occurred when the Baltimore Colts moved to Indianapolis in 1984. To entice the team to relocate from its long-time home, the city guaranteed twelve years of annual ticket sales of more than 45,000, took out a ten-year, $12.5 million loan at an interest rate of 8 percent, and committed $4 million for a training facility (Leone, 1997). The Colts were negotiating with both Indianapolis and Baltimore, which wanted to keep the storied franchise. When word of the possibility of the team's move to Indianapolis was made public, the Maryland state legislature tried a novel approach: it considered a law authorizing Baltimore to condemn the team under the concept of "eminent domain," the seizure of private property by the federal or state government or governmental agency for a "public use."

After passage of the Maryland law, the Colts' owner, Robert Irsay, made his decision to move. Without consulting the NFL, Irsay accepted the Indianapolis offer and packed the Colts' property into moving vans in the middle of the night, one day before the Maryland law was to go into effect. Even though the city sued to enforce the law, the fact that the Colts' business, along with any property connected with it, were outside the state made the Maryland law ineffective.

Cities hoping to obtain franchises or keep them have often been generous with funds and construction. For example, in 2009, Miami-Dade County and the Miami City Commission agreed to finance over 75 percent of the construction costs for Marlins Park—the new stadium for the Miami Marlins. The Marlins contributed $155 million in private funds to the $634 million stadium deal, received revenue rights from the stadium itself and received $35 million for renting the stadium (which was included in the team's $155 million contribution). In other words, the city and county put up over three-quarters of the cost of the stadium, but the team would receive virtually all of the revenues generated by the stadium (deMause, 2009).

Both the city and county commissions approved the stadium deal after team owner Jeffrey Loria argued that he needed the additional funding in order to field a competitive team (deMause, 2012). For all that public money, Miami fans expected a winner, and on opening day in 2012 it looked like Loria had assembled one. However, the Marlins lost that day, and ninety-two more times in 2012, finishing in last place in their league (Boudway, 2015).

In 2009, the issue of league control over relocation came about in a dispute between the Phoenix Coyotes and the NHL over an attempt to sell the team and move it to Hamilton, Ontario. The Coyotes, losing millions of dollars due to lack of fan support and a long-term lease commitment, wanted to sell the team to Jim Balsillie, reportedly one of Canada's richest individuals (he was a co-owner of the firm that makes BlackBerry) and move it to Hamilton. The league and the city of Glendale, Arizona (which built the facility for the team), protested the proposed sale and the move. The NHL did not want Balsillie despite making a bid for the Coyotes that was considerably higher than any other because of previous attempts to buy and move teams (which were rejected by the league's board of governors). Critical statements about the league's owners may have been a major reason for the board's rejection of his ownership application. However, he made a bid considerably higher than any other bidders.

In an attempt to circumvent the NHL's rules, the Coyotes' owner filed for bankruptcy, seeking a judicial sale of the team to Balsillie. However, the bankruptcy judge, in deferring to the NHL's franchise procedures, rejected that bid, emphasizing the primacy of the league's ownership approval rules (*Dewey Ranch Hockey*, 2009). As of 2015, the team, previously under the control of the NHL, was sold to Philadelphia hedge fund manager Andrew Barroway (Peters, 2014).

Expansion

As in the case of relocation, each of the major leagues requires that an expansion team application be approved by three-quarters of the owners. Because of the league structure, a new team must go through an involved and often costly process before being selected as an expansion franchise. It has been argued that the limited number of teams entering a league stifles competition and may (except in the case of baseball) run afoul of the antitrust laws. Except for New York, Los Angeles and Chicago, each city is limited to one team—if not by rule, then in practice. However, the leagues can offer legitimate business reasons for requiring franchise owners to have a certain level of financial security and to not hold ownership interests in other clubs in the same league.

Because a considerable capital investment is necessary to support a competitive professional sports team, a viable sports league must have financially secure franchise owners. Initially the franchise owner must pay expensive expansion fees and operating expenses and must retain sufficient financial reserves to hire players and coaches, based on rules determined by the league. In all the major league constitutions, a clause limiting expansion and relocation in a "home territory" of an existing franchise exists. Usually that figure is between a fifty- and seventy-five-mile radius around a major metropolitan area (Kurlantzick, 1983). Although the very largest markets have more than one team, a new or relocating team often has to pay what is known as an "indemnity fee."

To obtain an expansion franchise, the applicant must not only be able to pay the expansion fee, but must go through a "due diligence" process to ensure the validity of the information that the potential expansion franchise owner releases. Essentially, this investigation process has not always received enough attention from journalists. Sometimes the leagues themselves have not done a proper investigation, which has led to embarrassing results. In 1997, the NHL approved the sale of the New York Islanders to a "businessman" named John Spano, who, despite practical insolvency, was able to obtain bank loans and to convince the league he had adequate financial resources. Spano ultimately pleaded guilty to fraud in connection with the attempted purchase (Valenti, 1997). In 2007, the NHL approved a purchase of a minority stake in the Nashville Predators by William "Boots" Del Biaggio, who secured loans to buy the team based on fraudulent financial statements. In so doing, he defrauded banks and investors of millions of dollars. Ultimately, Del Biaggio pleaded guilty to securities fraud and received an eight-year prison sentence (Mickle, 2009). In 2016, the NHL board of governors voted to add a new team in Las Vegas for an expansion fee of $500 million (Rosen, 2016).

Financing a Stadium

The costs of constructing a new sports facility have increased dramatically over the last forty years. As an example, let's compare the respective costs of Atlanta's oldest and newest facilities. Taking inflation into account, the cost of building Atlanta's Fulton County Stadium (which housed the Braves from 1965 to 1996) cost $135 million in 2014 dollars. Turner Field, the facility that replaced it, came to $314 million, and Sun Trust Park (scheduled to open in 2017) will double that amount—$622 million. For the city's football venues, the increases are even steeper. The Georgia Dome, built in 1992, cost $360 million in 2014 dollars. Mercedes-Benz Stadium, scheduled to open in 2017, will run at least $1.5 billion (Scott, 2015). These kinds of increases are reflected in the costs of other recent stadiums. AT&T Stadium (home of the Dallas Cowboys), MetLife Stadium (New York Giants and New York Jets) and Yankee Stadium cost over $1 billion each.

The reasons may vary from facility to facility, but they focus on larger space, more advantaged technology and greater amenities. The new stadiums—especially those for football—tend to be larger than their earlier counterparts. Also, they are sport specific. Most are football only, baseball only and more and more, soccer only. The scoreboards are more complex and sophisticated. New facilities provide improved lighting and Wi-Fi capabilities. And the construction of luxury box seating and related amenities add to the cost (Klepal & Tucker, 2015). Not surprisingly, the extra costs and amenities result in higher ticket prices and services that cater to well-heeled fans.

With contributions made by cities or states, or both ("public sector"), along with those made by the owner(s) of a franchise or private businesses ("private sector"), franchises have been able to finance and build new state-of-the-art stadiums that provide economic returns and enhancements not recognized in their old counterparts. Except for AT&T Park, the first privately financed ballpark in Major League Baseball since Dodger Stadium opened in 1962, most ballparks are financed with substantial public money (Keating, 2001) in the form of subsidies or tax credits.

Although most new state-of-the-art stadiums replace multipurpose facilities three to four decades old, new facilities have supplanted venues of more recent vintage. In Memphis, Tennessee, an arena known as the "Pyramid" opened in 1991. Because the 19,000-seat facility was "antiquated," in that it did not attract restaurants and lacked other revenue generators, the public—through taxes to pay the debt from bond issuances—subsidized the construction of a $250-million arena that houses the NBA Grizzlies. The same occurred in Charlotte, North Carolina, where the Time Warner Cable arena opened in 2005, replacing the sixteen-year-old Coliseum that previously housed the team.

The economic benefits to a franchise include revenue enhancements such as naming rights, advertising, luxury box leases, increased number of club seats, pouring rights (beverages), parking revenues, concessions and favorable lease terms. This is in addition to the general increased attendance that results when the new facility opens.

Funding Vehicles

In theory, the use of revenue enhancements mentioned in the preceding paragraph has provided a financial base that allows the franchise to secure funding for a new state-of-the-art stadium or arena. Today, most facilities are financed through a public–private partnership. At least thirty-eight major league sports venues were built or rebuilt using nearly $7 billion in tax-exempt financing from 1990 to 2003, according to a *Washington Post* review of more than forty professional baseball, football, hockey and basketball projects (Whoriskey, 2003).

The public sector contributes equity (cash), pledges and revenue from taxes and/or issues debt through the issuance of bonds (until recently tax exempt). The private sector contributes private equity (cash contribution/guarantee from owners), private debt (bank or institutional funds) and/or funds borrowed under a credit facility program run by a particular league (MLB or NFL in particular). Private debt is usually secured by guaranteed streams of revenue from naming rights, luxury suites, club seats and advertising.

Public Funding

The use of public funding for financing stadiums remains controversial, drawing criticism from a number of economists, who argue that the money spent on the facilities does not result in increased revenues for cities, but provides considerable benefits to team owners. Studies by Baade (1994) and Zimbalist and Noll (1997) concluded that such arrangements were money losers (Krueger, 2002). Others have commented that the resulting costs end up being a drain on the taxpayers with benefits that are tangential, at best (Dorfman, 2015).

However, others hold a contrary view. The essence of those arguments is that "the primary benefits provided by teams to the local communities are consumption benefits," such as the benefits provided by "parks, golf courses, swimming pools, zoos, concert halls" (Green, Klein, & Lebowitz, 1998). They argue that the mere presence of the team in the community confers additional benefits, including "identifying with the success of the team, following the team on television and radio, reading about the team in the newspapers, and talking with their friends about the team" (Dorocak, 1999). Another economist argued that "retro-style" facilities are "likely to attract visitors from a wider area . . . and [ ] likely to induce longer stays and greater ancillary spending" (Santo, 2005). Also, if the facility is a part of a revitalization of a previously depressed area, with shopping centers, theaters and other public works, the new facility can serve as a spearhead to an economic rebirth of that part of the city.

However, the majority of economic studies point to limited benefits resulting from the funding of sports facilities on the local economy. One survey concluded that 90 percent of economists strongly agreed or agreed with the statement that governments should eliminate subsidies for professional sports franchises (Coates & Humphreys, 2008).

Examining and analyzing the economic merits of a proposed new facility requires a basic knowledge of financial lending techniques. It also involves asking pointed questions about the source of the money, the control of the facility once it opens and the proposed lease terms. In financially troubled times, the monies spent on facility construction or even ancillary issues such as highway construction to and from the stadium or arena can siphon away funds from other governmental activities.

Although a municipality ("the public") owns many stadiums and arenas, the primary tenant team controls the majority of the revenue. Once the facility opens, the amount of money directly invested by NFL teams is quickly recouped, often within a few years—thanks to lucrative luxury boxes, club seats and considerably higher ticket prices. Taxpayers, however, typically are committed to up to thirty years of debt payments.

Certain public interest or ad hoc groups representing public funding opponents have attempted to stop such funding by utilizing lawsuits, often on the grounds that the government lacked the power to seize land for a private stadium under its eminent domain power. However, such claims have been unsuccessful, particularly after the U.S. Supreme Court utilized an expansive view of "public use," allowing the state to seize private land for a private development as long as there is economic development

(*Kelo v. City of New London*, 2005). Based on this ruling, the courts will not block seizure unless the scheme violates a specific law or regulation (environmental rules come to mind). Otherwise, the courts grant deference to governments to make such decisions (*Goldstein v. New York State Economic Development Corp.*, 2009).

However, the question of the tax deductibility of bonds used to finance sports facilities is complex and has been the subject of controversy. In October 2008, the Internal Revenue Service limited the scope of the tax exemption, which could affect the financing of future stadiums (Internal Revenue Service, 2008, Treasury Reg § 1.141–4(e)(3)). More recently, President Obama proposed the formal elimination of tax-exempt bonds for stadium financing (Povich, 2015).

Still, the economic benefits of granting generous stadium deals to lure or keep teams continue to be debated. An economic downturn, market saturation and questionable economic benefits lead to increased public criticism. State and local governments, often forced to reduce public services or raise taxes, may not have the money to pay for new stadium or arena construction. On the other hand, "losing" a team carries political risk, as fans of the team may help vote the particular politician who presided over this loss out of office.

Methods of Public Funding

Bonds

A bond is a loan, payable with interest, often issued by municipal governments. Purchased by individuals or organizations who serve as creditors, bonds are often secured (guaranteed) by a municipality or state's general taxing power.

Types of bonds include the following:

- *General obligation bonds:* These securities are to be repaid from general tax revenues of the particular government. Such bonds often require governmental approval and have become more and more difficult to use because of public opposition and the need for state and municipal governments to provide more basic projects in uncertain economic times.
- *Special tax bonds:* These securities are guaranteed from monies coming from a specific tax. The municipality, county or state may levy an additional tax to be specifically used to pay these obligations.
- *Revenue bonds:* These securities are more complex, as they are secured by revenues coming from the facility and/or special taxes passed to pay for them. Often a hotel-use or other tourist-related tax (which is politically safe because tourists do not vote) or on tickets to events

in the new stadium or arena, revenue bonds frequently serve as an effective funding vehicle.

- *Lease revenue bonds:* These securities are issued by a governmental authority distinct from the municipality, county or state, not the government itself. These authorities, sometimes known as public corporations, often have the power to issue bonds and collect tolls or taxes. An example is a bridge or tunnel construction authority. Bonds will be issued as part of a lease agreement between the authority and the government, which leases the facility from the authority and then subleases it back to that very authority. Any revenues collected by the government—and the franchise(s) using it—may be used to pay the authority (Greenberg & Gray, 1996). A number of states have created such authorities, such as the Washington State Public Stadium Authority, which has a seven-member board appointed by the governor, and the Aloha Stadium Authority in Hawaii, whose board consists of nine members.

Bonds are either taxable or, in some cases, tax exempt. Tax-exempt securities, meaning those exempt from federal (but not necessarily state) taxation, are preferred as being more attractive to investors. However, as noted earlier, federal tax regulations have limited the use of tax-exempt bonds to fund sports facilities, and the question is not entirely resolved as of this writing.

Bond issuances continue to play a part in stadium financing. For the construction of the Cowboys Stadium, the city of Arlington, Texas, issued $325 million in bonds for its share of construction, which is being paid with sales, hotel–motel and rental car taxes. It also separately issued another $147 million issuance to help with the team's financing. That debt is being paid off with ticket and parking taxes from the stadium (Klepal & Tucker, 2015).

Taxes

States, counties and municipalities have the power to use tax revenues or levy new taxes to fund the construction of facilities. The type of taxes created is often dictated by the political popularity of the project as well as the creditworthiness of the proposal. Examples of additional taxes would be tax surcharges, sales taxes (or a portion thereof), special taxes on alcohol and tobacco products, restaurant- and hotel-use taxes and car rental taxes. The laws creating the taxes may have a "sunset" provision that ends a tax at a certain date (i.e., completion of the facility, payment of the debt). The locality or the state may also enact a lottery to raise money either to pay for the facility or to guarantee payment of the bonds.

Governments may also issue certain tax abatements on the real estate taxes the facility would normally pay. And costs of additional road construction, such as special exits from a highway to the facility, are often borne by the local government (and, by extension, the taxpayers) as general expenditures.

Example: Falcon Stadium Bonds (Mercedes-Benz Stadium)—The Public Funding Portion

To help in the construction of a new stadium for the NFL's Atlanta Falcons stadium (to be named Mercedes-Benz Stadium), the city of Atlanta, through the Atlanta Development Authority, authorized a $227 million bond package. In so doing, it was very important to ensure that the bonds are related as "investment grade," meaning that the risk of default is relatively small. Without such a designation (usually done by one or more investment firms), such bonds would either not attract investors or would have to pay a high interest rate to find such investors because of the added risk (these bonds were deemed investment grade with a stable outlook by Moody's Investors Service in 2015).

The reason that Moody's granted this credit rating was the existence of a hotel/motel tax. The bonds were secured by over one-third of the 8 percent tax on hotel and motel stays within the city of Atlanta.

The bond package includes three separate bond issues. Two issuances will help pay for the stadium's construction. The third issuance will create a reserve fund that can be tapped to make payments to bond holders if there's a lag in collection of the hotel/motel tax. In all, that bond package consisted of $170 million plus an additional $17 million to help fund construction and $40 million for the reserve fund (Pendered, 2015).

Private Financing

Most stadium and arena financing involves some private sources. Usually banks play a central role, as they lend money outright with some secured source of repayment, such as revenue from luxury suites or concessions. Additionally, private financing includes guarantees by the team owner backed by personal assets or by bonds backed by personal seat license fees. Another method is the use of personal seat licenses (PSLs), explained later in the chapter.

Example: Falcons Stadium (Mercedes-Benz Stadium): The Private Funding

In addition to the publicly issued bonds, the team has arranged private financing to build the $1.5 billion stadium. It negotiated an $850 million construction loan. This sum is to be reduced during the next several years with proceeds from sponsorships, sale of luxury suites and other revenue streams. Mercedes-Benz became the naming rights holder for twenty-seven years. As of this writing, financial terms have not been disclosed.

Another private source of construction financing was a $200 million contribution from owners of the National Football League. The sum includes a $100 million loan that the NFL will repay through stadium revenues, a $50 million grant that doesn't have to be repaid and a $50 million loan the Falcons are to repay (Pendered, 2015).

The Stadium/Arena Lease

Often teams obtain stadium or arena leases on favorable terms, especially if a municipality or government agency owns the facility. It is rare (but not impossible) that a team owns a stadium outright; more frequently, the team will lease to play its games in the facility. Given the public interest in sports franchises, the lease between the team and the stadium or arena it plays in is a document that should receive far more scrutiny and coverage than it often does receive, especially if the public and/or bondholders are paying for the facility's construction. The following sections break down the basic terms of such an agreement.

Duration

To recoup the cost of construction and upkeep, the stadium or arena lease often includes a long initial term—up to forty years—and some options to extend. The option clauses give the team the opportunity to extend the lease, usually on similar terms. Some lease agreements require affirmative written communications if a team wishes to extend the lease under an option clause. Others do the opposite: they require that the team notify the facility owners or manager if they do not wish to extend.

Termination

All leases have termination clauses giving the team the right to terminate the lease before the expiration. A lease may permit termination if certain attendance minimums are not met. The Minnesota Twins were able to escape from their lease from their former home, the Metrodome, if the number of tickets sold for three consecutive baseball seasons was less than 80 percent of the American League average (Greenberg & Gray, 1996). The St. Louis Rams exercised their termination right and announced a move back to Los Angeles (Belson, 2016) because the facility was no longer "state of the art." A more common provision, known as a "force majeure" clause, allows termination after damage or destruction of the facility due to war, weather condition or fire.

Additionally, some leases give the franchise the option to terminate at a specified period. The lease for MetLife Stadium, the home of the NFL's New York Giants and New York Jets, has a term of twenty-five years, but it contains options that, if fully utilized, extend it to reach ninety-seven years. It also contains an unusual termination clause, which allows either team to opt out of the lease every five years after the fifteenth year as long as that team gives the owner (a state agency) twelve months' notice. However, if one team exercises that option and leaves, the other team must stay for the remainder of the initial twenty-five-year lease term (Sports Facility Reports, 2009).

Ethical Issue: The Easy Exit from Portland

Stadium or arena lease termination issues apply to minor league teams just as much as the major league franchises. An example would be the Portland (Maine) Pirates, an American Hockey League (AHL) team that played for twenty-three seasons in Maine's largest city. The team played under a lease with the county arena until 2016, when, under new ownership, it abruptly announced it would move to Springfield, Massachusetts, shocking the fans, the city and even team members. The Pirates' new management did not even inform the city of its move (the city first found out from reporters).

At the time of the announcement, the Pirates completed the second year of a five-year lease with the county. The lease had a provision, but that limited damages for a breach of the lease to $100,000. Although that amount is not puny, it pales in comparison with the $34 million the county paid to renovate the facility for its anchor tenant. "Tens of millions of dollars went into that facility," Portland Mayor Ethan Strimling said. "When taxpayers put that much money into a project we should have at least been called to the table" (Jordan, 2016).

Use

The centerpiece of a stadium lease is the right for the team to use the facility and a corresponding right to limit use by others. Of course, a stadium or arena has many uses, such as concerts, rallies and other sporting events. The way this section is negotiated evidences the scope of the control the franchise has.

A facility is very much like a commercial airline. It makes no money when it is not used. If an airplane sits in a hangar for one day, that one day of income is lost and never replicated. The airplane must fly with paying passengers taking up as many seats as possible. Similarly, an unused facility does not generate revenues. So for the owner, frequent use is imperative.

On the other hand, the principal or "anchor" tenant (the team) may want to have "exclusivity" and limit other types of uses as much as reasonably possible. Too much use may result in wear and tear on the field and in seating and requires the cumbersome job of putting away and taking out equipment. Although rare, the lease may give the primary team absolute exclusivity, giving the franchise a veto right over any other events potentially held in the facility. Clearly that gives the tenant the right to dictate what events can and cannot be held. More frequently, the exclusivity right is more limited. For a baseball team, it may give the team exclusivity or a priority as to events during the season. For example, it can state that no other event may occur on the day of a baseball game or that if the team is involved in any postseason events, a conflicting event scheduled must be canceled to permit the playoff game to be held. Regarding the off-season, the lease may give the team "input" regarding the use of the facility, but not a veto power. If the event results in a likelihood of damage to the field, the team may have the power to reject the event. For example, a baseball team may have the right to bar an auto race on the grounds of the facility because of the likelihood of damage to the property. Finally, the lease often allows certain special events, such as a public memorial event, in the facility within the exclusivity period. In one case, a wedding was performed at Yankee Stadium after the groom received permission from the Yankees, the city of New York and Major League Baseball to exchange vows with his fiancée on the same spot where Lou Gehrig made his famous farewell speech (Salamone, 2006).

Sometimes, a team will "reserve" event dates (meaning dates of potential home games). That may occur even before a final schedule of games is released by the league involved. Those dates are held exclusively for the team until the team specifically "releases" them (usually because of final schedule changes by the team or the league). Other leases may prohibit sporting events for a certain period before the team's games. As the principal tenant, the team does not want competition that may limit gate attendance. For example, one release gives the primary tenant (a minor league baseball team) the power to reject certain events (other than those deemed "community events") (Lease between Hagerstown Baseball and Economic Development Authority of County of Spotsylvania, Virginia, 2015).

Although most leases require the team to play all their home games at the facility, in some cases the lease may permit some games at another location within the home team's market. Before moving into the Staples Center, the Los Angeles Clippers played most of their games in the Los Angeles Memorial Sports Arena. However, their lease granted the team the right to play up to six home games at Arrowhead Pond in Anaheim

(Greenberg & Gray, 1996). Likewise, the Cincinnati Bengals' lease with Hamilton County gave the team permission to play two international games as the "home" team (Coolidge, 2014). The lease deal with the Vikings and its home, US Bank Stadium, states that the team has a right to play up to six international "home" games over the next thirty years without penalty or having to make up for lost revenue (USbankstadium. com, 2013).

Many stadium leases contain a provision permitting the team to have its offices in the facility, along with some training areas and places to store equipment. This is less common in arenas because of lack of space.

Use by Other Teams

Restrictions on the use of the facility by other professional teams are often limited. However, exceptions occur. In the 1970s, the New York Yankees played in Shea Stadium, then the home of the rival Mets, during the reconstruction of Yankee Stadium and, more recently, the NFL's New York Giants and New York Jets agreed to share the cost of building MetLife Stadium, which opened in 2010 next door to the teams' former facility in New Jersey.

MetLife Stadium has a unique and complex bi-team arrangement. It marks the first time in NFL history that two rival teams have entered into a partnership for the purposes of building and subsequently sharing a sports facility. The two teams received a total of $1.3 billion for the stadium construction through separate private financing. The result was that each team completed separate $650 million financing deals. Citi-Corp and the Royal Bank of Scotland financed the Jets' portion, whereas the investment banks Goldman Sachs and Lehman Brothers financed the Giants' deal. In addition, NFL owners approved $300 million in loans to help finance the stadium (Wolffe, 2007). The teams share the revenues generated at the new stadium.

Stadium Naming Rights

The idea of naming a sports facility after a bank, brewery or orange juice maker who pays for the privilege is relatively recent. Before the 1990s, facilities were named for their teams, present or past owners, historical figures or in honor of war veterans. Yankee Stadium, Dodger Stadium, the Nassau Veterans' Memorial Coliseum (Long Island, New York), Veterans Stadium (Philadelphia) and Memorial Stadium (Baltimore) served as examples. Older fans may remember the owners' names, with Shibe, Comiskey, Griffith, Crosley, Baker and Ebbets emblazoned on their teams' stadiums. In Pittsburgh, Forbes Field was named after a British general who helped found the city. In one interesting example, the Cincinnati Reds played at the "Palace of the Fans," probably the last time a team thought of the fans when naming a ballpark (Erardi, 1999). However, in the last two decades, naming rights have become an essential part of stadium and arena economics. As these facilities become more and more expensive, naming rights defray some of the costs of construction.

When the Los Angeles Forum was renamed the Great Western Forum in 1988, many callers hung up, thinking they had dialed a wrong number (Horovita, 1988). Since then, public acceptance of "named" stadiums has increased. In 1973, Rich Stadium in Buffalo became the first stadium in any major league to utilize naming rights. The rights fee was $1.5 million for twenty-five years. By 1988, there had been only three naming-rights deals, with a total contract value of $25 million. In 2015, there were almost 300 "named" facilities in all levels of professional and college sports. Also, in that year, the amount committed in new, extended and amended naming-rights deals in professional and college sports venues came to over $1.1 billion (Sports Business Journal, 2015). More than three-quarters of the arenas and stadiums in professional baseball, football and basketball bore corporate names (Schaul & Belson, 2013). Some firms even have naming rights in multiple facilities. For example, American Airlines obtained naming rights for arenas in Dallas and Miami.

The naming-rights trend has also extended to minor league and college stadiums and arenas. Examples are the State Farm Center at the University of Illinois (which paid $60 million for a thirty-year period) (Sports Business Journal, 2015) and the University of Houston's TDECO Stadium (ten years, $15 million) (Duarte, 2014) Although the economic recession of late 2008 and 2009 reduced the interest for expensive naming-rights deals, in more recent years, naming-rights deals have resumed. Examples include MetLife Stadium in New Jersey (football Giants and Jets), commenced in 2011 and valued at $400 million for twenty-five years, and Levi's Stadium (San Francisco 49ers), for $220 million over twenty years.

A long-term naming-rights deal provides an excellent funding device. Corporations wish to purchase naming rights for a number of reasons. The repeated use of the name countless times during broadcasts and in print article references constitutes a potentially cost-effective way to advertise. Often, broadcast contracts stipulate that team announcers use the corporate name in all references. Additionally, given that the naming rights are exclusive, competitor firms do not have many alternative facilities to obtain similar rights. The facility becomes attached to that corporation and that corporation only.

Naming rights help create a positive image and foster local goodwill toward a firm, especially if the teams using the facility are successful and popular. They make the business a part of the sports community in that city, especially in regions where the firm seeks to expand operations. A previously unknown financial institution can make a major impact in its new territory by buying naming rights. However, that notoriety has its risks. The Houston Astros' stadium was originally named Enron Field and kept that name for only two seasons. This proved embarrassing after Enron's downfall, with indictments of many of its top directors and officers. Because Enron filed for bankruptcy, the Astros were legally able to find another sponsor. The stadium was renamed Minute Maid Park in 2003 to the great relief of the team and stadium owner. Another issue is team performance. If a firm obtains naming rights for a team that is consistently unsuccessful, it may hinder rather than help the brand.

Naming rights facilitate cross-promotion and tie-ins. For example, TD Bank has the naming rights to the hockey and basketball arena in Boston. As part of its rights, automatic teller machines from the bank were installed for patrons to withdraw cash (TDGarden.com, n.d.). Chicago's United Center has an airline ticket booth. Also, the firm obtains a luxury box or other select seating, a marquee location for bringing prospective or potential clients. Finally, tax advantages exist. The costs incurred in the purchase of naming rights may be allowed as "advertising business expenses" under the Internal Revenue Code (Internal Revenue Code, sec. 162).

Naming-rights agreements generally last from ten to thirty years with options to renew. Annual payments are made by the firm to the team or to the local government or stadium authority in charge of building the stadium or arena. If a franchise decides to end its tenancy and move out of the stadium at any time during the term of the signage agreement, the firm usually has the right to terminate that agreement. If the stadium or arena is significantly damaged or destroyed by an unforeseen event, the firm may terminate the agreement. If the facility cannot be used for a relatively short time due to an act of God (force majeure) event, the agreement may call for a suspension of payments for that period, but not a termination right.

Signage placement serves as a centerpiece of any naming-rights deal. A standard agreement involves placing signs on the side of the facility (able to be seen from a highway), on the roof (if it is enclosed) and on certain "exit" signs on the highway leading to the facility. In the interior, the agreement specifies the number of signs inside the facility and their locations (e.g., left field wall, back of home plate). Additionally, a sign is usually posted on or near the scoreboard. The agreement often specifies that the facility may contract with other advertisers, but the other advertisers cannot be competitors of the naming-rights firm. Or it may specify that the firm may have the right to veto the selection of any other advertiser inside the facility.

The San Francisco 49ers' Levi's Stadium provides an example of a typical deal. Levi Strauss, the venerable clothing firm whose roots in San

Francisco go back over 150 years, obtained the rights. A summary of its terms is as follows:

> Term: 20 years (with the company's option to extend for five more years at a total of $75 million)
> Total price: $220 million
> Annual payments: $11 million per year (average)
> Signage: Four large signs around the stadium
> Access to facility: A pair of 50-yard line luxury suites; ability to host up to four events a year at the facility
> Additional benefits: Fifty-two club seats

Ability to tap star players to help the company attract customers and allow the coach of the same to "pump up" employees

The stadium's 23,000-square-foot loft club will be called either Club 501 or the Denim Lounge (Rosenberg, 2013).

Concessions

Although many think of concessions as overcrowded stands selling over-priced hot dogs, pretzels and sodas, the kinds of items sold and the agreements to sell them constitute important aspects of a stadium or arena deal. Successful concessions—based on variety and placement—can add significant revenues to both the stadium owner and the team.

In the past, some teams established "official" concessions. When the Philadelphia Eagles moved into Lincoln Financial Field in 2003, they marketed an official hot dog (Dietz & Watson), an official salty snack (Utz Quality Foods) and an official ice cream (Turkey Hill). The companies had their products sold exclusively at the new stadium, and often their logos are displayed on signs throughout the concourses. In addition, all three obtained the right to use the team logo and colors in Eagles-themed food products for sale to the general public and can do cross-promotions. Utz issued a limited-edition, one-pound Eagles commemorative bag of potato chips. Dietz & Watson sells "Eagles Beef Franks" in stores around Philadelphia, and Turkey Hill planned a new ice cream called "Eagles Touchdown Sundae."

A particular segment of the concession deal, known as "pouring rights," applies to beverages. Pepsi and Miller Brewing secured pouring deals. Pepsi bought the rights to sell its soft drink and bottled water brands and to put its name on a gate and an open area to be known as the Pepsi Zone. Miller gets its Lite beer served and sponsors a party tent in the plaza outside the north end of the stadium (Brockinton, 2002).

In some facility agreements, the team gets 100 percent of the concession revenues, whereas in others the team may get 100 percent of concessions on game days (Greenberg & Gray, 1996). In other agreements (usually in older facilities), the owner gets 100 percent of the revenues. One other approach involves splitting the fees between the owner and team based on total revenues or on products. For example, the owner may get 100 percent of revenues for food, whereas the team gets 100 percent for souvenirs and programs.

More recently, concessions have evolved to a more sophisticated offering. Among beverage trends, the popularity of craft beer and spirits continues to grow. There also have been efforts to make healthier fare more widely available and accessible to fans. Offerings for fans with special diets, food allergies and other dietary preferences have become more common (Broughton, 2015a). For example, the Barclay's Center in Brooklyn, New York (the home of the NBA Nets and the NHL Islanders), has a large kosher food section for fans who observe dietary rules (Kosher Eye, n.d.).

"Carve-outs," which create more and more specific product categories for sponsorships, have become a contentious issue in negotiations. Terms such as "beverages" "water" or photographs or videos have become more specific due to changing product lines and technology. One example may involve bottled water. Water is defined as "a transparent, odorless, tasteless liquid, a compound of hydrogen and oxygen, H_2O, freezing at 32°F or 0°C and boiling at 212°F or 100°C" (Dictionary.com, n.d.). One would think that "bottled water" would be this substance inserted in a bottle and available for purchase. However, in the world of sports sponsorships and concessions, there are several types of bottled water: there is "artesian" water, "purified" water, "mineral" water and "spring water," to name a few. Each has its own characteristics, and there are different kinds of products selling these different types of water. For example, artesian water is found underground in aquifers. Spring water emerges from the ground and flows naturally to the earth's surface. Mineral water is natural water produced from a well or spring that naturally contains dissolved solids. Sparkling water is produced from a spring or well that naturally contains dissolved carbon dioxide, meaning it is naturally carbonated. Purified water is water that has been mechanically filtered or processed to remove impurities and make it suitable for use (Geology.com, n.d.).

Why all this science? There are different bottled waters out there. Fiji brand water is artesian, Perrier is sparkled, Evian is from a spring, Gerolstein is mineral and Dasani is purified (10bestwater.com, 2016). If a sports team or facility is in a strong position of leverage, that team or facility could carve out sponsorship deals with more than one kind of bottled water based on its properties. Carving out is yet one more way to monetize the sports property.

Other trends in concessions involve more communal seating, venues that reflect the local traditions of the location and more localized partnerships with particular food vendors. Some venues have employed local chefs to create particular menus that are unique to the city or area. In any event, fans realize that these kinds of meals do not come cheap.

Stadiums and arenas have embraced mobile technology so that patrons can pay through their cell phones. Mobile ordering and more advanced payment methods are becoming a common feature in facilities. With the use of mobile technology, teams glean information about fans' buying practices and can target messages about concession offerings, which could be delivered to their respective location. The data can also be used to target particular fans for other promotions.

Concessions also involve merchandise, and the increase in the variety of merchandise in terms of audiences and in terms of variety have been a hallmark of concession planning in recent years. Clothing targeted for women, children and pets have become more of a presence, as well as more general leisure wear. Although the more traditional jerseys continue to sell, there is a more fashion-oriented approach among clothing (Broughton, 2015a).

Seat Licenses

For a team or governmental entity financing the costs of building a new stadium or arena, revenues derived from the sale of PSLs help defray the costs of construction of the new facility. These licenses consist of agreements by ticket holders to pay a fee for the *right* to purchase tickets at a specified location for a designated period. By purchasing a property right in their seats (which may or may not be transferred to others, depending on the particular PSL), the fans contribute to the success of the team in helping build the new facility.

The concept does have drawbacks. First, if fewer fans than expected pay for licenses, the construction financing may be in jeopardy. A municipality may have to guarantee the shortfall, which occurred when the city of Oakland agreed to refurbish the Oakland Coliseum (Miller, 2010). Also, the often considerable fees charged by licensors limit access to the stadium by fans of lesser means. And disputes have arisen over the "caliber" of the seating received by the license holder. In one case, a group of Pittsburgh Steelers season ticket holders who bought seating licenses for the team's new stadium sued because the seats they received were not comparable to what was promised (*Yocca v. Pittsburgh Steelers Sports*, 2004). Additionally, PSLs tend to reward wealth over loyalty (Hill, 2008).

Seating Organization/Pricing

At one time, the typical seating plan in a stadium or arena had a graduated sectional approach. The facility consisted of four or five distinct sections (box seats, loge, reserved grandstand and unreserved grandstand), with the best seats toward the front and the more affordable seating farther back and higher up. The revenue generated from this arrangement was often unpredictable, unless many season tickets were bought.

Even for those facilities with a strong season-ticket commitment, teams and facility owners create levels of premium seating to increase revenue. Luxury suites are the best known and most successful form of seating-based revenue. Although many older stadiums had some "private boxes" (the first being eighteen private boxes furnished with drapes and arm-chairs in the stadium for the Chicago White Stockings in 1883), modern luxury suites have become far more ubiquitous in the newest facilities. Not surprisingly, revenues derived from luxury box or club seating consti-tute a major revenue stream for professional sports franchises. With prices in the hundreds of thousands of dollars per season, these suites frequently include a kitchen, waiter service and comfortable seating in an enclosed, climate-controlled environment, somewhere toward the middle or top of the stadium or arena.

In considering the importance of such seating to the economics of a franchise, let's take the example of Citi Field, the present home of the New York Mets, which opened in April 2009. It contains fifty-four luxury suites of three levels (ten "Sterling Suites," thirty-nine "Empire Suites" and five "Party Suites"), available for prices ranging from $250,000 to $500,000 per season. This compares with only forty-five luxury suites located at one level in the team's prior venue, Shea Stadium, which cost only $4,000 for a fifteen-person suite and $8,000 for a thirty-person suite (mlb.com, n.d.; toptentopten.com, n.d.). In some cases, the luxury suite prices will reach seven figures. After a $1 billion renovation, Madison Square Garden has twenty "bunker" (or event-level) suites priced at over $1 million (Calder, 2013). Larger stadiums have more space to build premium seating. FedEx Field, the home of the Washington Redskins, includes over 240 suites; MetLife stadium has 220. As one expert said: "Luxury boxes should produce twice as much revenue as all regular seats in the stadium" (Klepal & Tucker, 2015). The revenues from luxury boxes may go to defray the costs of construction, to pay off debts or to the sta-dium owner and the franchise according to some formula found in the lease. Often the franchise takes the lion's share of the money.

Club seats constitute a second class of premium seating. This idea came from the late Joe Robbie, the owner of the Miami Dolphins. The biggest difference between club seats and luxury suites is that club seating mixes with the general seating layout of the facility, although with more perks. Far less costly than luxury suites, club seats cost tens of thousands of dollars per season, rather than the six- or seven-figure amounts for suites. No uniform location exists for club seats, although they are often found at choice loca-tions, such as center ice or the third-base dugout. Often club seat holders have waiter or waitress service and television monitors. Generally sold on an annual lease that can cover from one year to ten, the team usually keeps the bulk of the revenues from club seating, although facility agreements usually require that a small percentage go to the facility owner.

"Regular" seating generally follows the more traditional pricing model, although with higher prices than in the past. An increasing number of franchises, such as the San Francisco Giants and Phoenix Suns, have utilized "dynamic pricing" whereby certain matches with more competitive or popular opponents will feature higher prices for all (or part of) the seats than for those with less attractive rivals. The ticket costs vary based on real-time market conditions and consumer demand. Also, such pricing is designed to respond to changing conditions related to each individual game, such as the injuries to key players on an opposing team or the emergence of a traditionally weak opponent into a contender (Kaplan, 2015). The calculation of price is based on analytic programs. A related example of alternative pricing is known as "variable pricing," which allows teams to set fixed lower prices to their season tickets for less attractive games. Similarly, more attractive games carry higher face values.

Secondary Market

At one time, the idea of ticket holders selling their tickets to others was looked on with disfavor by leagues, teams and even the law. Known as an outlier in the sports business, many secondary market sellers were individuals, some with questionable veracity and quality control. Not surprisingly, teams and leagues did not want to deal with this market. Many states restricted so-called "scalping" of tickets, either by price or by location (New York Arts and Cultural Affairs Law, 2006). In the last ten years, there has been a major rethinking and institutionalizing of this practice with the ascension of firms like StubHub. Adding guarantees and an organized distribution system, such firms were able to secure sponsorship deals with teams and leagues to serve as a conduit for fans to buy tickets based on supply and demand variables. The teams often get a flat rate from the secondary seller, according to the sponsorship agreement (King, 2013). Also, the most restrictive states eased their laws to permit at least some kind of secondary ticket sales (New York Arts and Cultural Affairs Law, 2011).

Presently, purchasing tickets for sporting events through the secondary market has become commonplace, and it has served to create a freer market. Many teams have struck agreements with these firms or handle the secondary market themselves.

Advertising

As anyone who has attended a sporting match can attest, advertising is a ubiquitous component of the viewing experience. Often placed in conspicuous locations in the stadium or arena, the size and frequency (in the case of rotating advertisements) of the material vary, depending on the agreement made. A key point is product exclusivity. Rarely will advertisements for two products of a similar type occur in one facility.

The heart of facility advertising is signage. The company with the naming rights will often have the pick of the best location(s) for signs, which often means the scoreboard display. However, the team and/or facility owner may contract with other advertisers for signage and or advertisements outside the location of play, such as near concession stands or near the entrances and exits. Ads even grace bathrooms. Advertisement procurement and revenues are controlled by the lease agreement with the facility owner and the team. In some cases, the lessor (facility owner) retains advertising selection and revenues, whereas in others it is the team that controls both. In some cases, revenues are split between the team and the owner.

Parking

Fees from parking may be divided between the franchise and the stadium owner or kept by one of the parties. Additionally, the fees may include nonevent parking.

Other Revenue Generators

In addition to the options already described, a stadium or arena may include other devices designed to generate revenue. The facility may include one or more retail stores (with agreed-on amounts going to the team and/or the owners), sit-down restaurants open to the public on game and nongame days, paid public tours and even museums. The lease agreements will often divide the revenues in some proportion between the team and the facility owner.

Looking to the future, forms of gambling may be a huge generator. It may be possible for legalized betting firms to sponsor teams or facilities to permit on-game betting during a sports event. However, sports gambling would first have to be legalized to accomplish this result.

Renovation of Existing Facilities

If an established team cannot construct a new facility or get the stadium/ arena owner or a locality to build one, expansion or alteration remains a viable option. Often done by creating different seating tiers or adding more space for venders, renovation serves to modernize the facility and increase revenue potential. San Antonio's AT&T Center, the home of the Spurs, went through a $115 million renovation in 2015, which included new seats, new video boards inside and outside the arena and expanded lounges and dining areas. Renovations to collegiate facilities have been frequent in recent years for many of the same reasons as their professional facility counterparts: more amenities, technology and better fan experience. Also in 2015, the University of Florida announced a renovation of its O'Connoll Center, which will include a new concourse and entryway, premium upper deck seating, a state-of-the-art sound system and a separate entrance for the aquatic center (Schweers, 2015).

Terrorism and Facility Security Designation

In the wake of the 9/11 attacks on the World Trade Center and the Pentagon, Congress passed and President George W. Bush signed into law the Support Anti-terrorism by Fostering Effective Technologies Act (known as the "Safety Act") (6 USC secs 441–444, 2002). Enacted in 2002 in response to concerns that businesses would face liability if security equipment they made or used failed to stop a terrorist attack, the law grants to facilities that have been designed as "compliant" a limitation of liability (6 USC. Sec. 443, 2002).

Specifically, the designation guarantees that liability from claims resulting from terrorist acts is limited to the amount of liability insurance coverage already recommended by the Department of Homeland Security. Therefore, lawsuits for any extra amounts are not permitted.

As of 2016, all NFL stadiums received a "designation and certification" status, the highest level of protection, granting this the waiver. Yankee Stadium (New York) and Comerica Park (Michigan) also are so designated. Other Major League Baseball parks are working to achieve that level of protection. Standards to attain this designation include physical and electronic game-day policies, documents that spell out evacuation plans, cyber security and the hiring, vetting, training and management oversight of its employees and contractors (Broughton, 2015b).

Sustainability

The growing awareness of environmental sustainability has become an important aspect in both the construction and operation of sports facilities. Although "green" has become a common term involving environmental sensitivity, its beginnings go back almost four decades; it has become a more important factor in sports facility design and in implementation of environmentally friendly policies than in the past.

Collegiate facilities have served as a bellwether for sustainability, although professional stadiums and arenas have been catching up— especially ones that have been recently completed or are under construction. A 2013 report from the National Resources Defense Council (NRDC) sums up the benefits of "greening" facilities: cutting operational costs, educating and empowering students, enhancing the college's or university's athletics and institutional brand, attracting sponsors and partners, strengthening community ties and creating a healthier workout environment (Henly, 2013). With the rise of global warming, difficulties in solid waste disposal and increases in the use of fossil fuels, creating more environmentally friendly sports locales has taken on greater importance.

The NRDC cites a number of specific examples of facilities that reflect these goals. Folsom Field at the University of Colorado at Boulder was the first major collegiate sports stadium in the nation to adopt a "zero waste" goal. In 2012, this resulted in collection of about 70,000 pounds of recyclable and compostable materials. The university worked with vendors to switch virtually all packaging used in the stadium to refillable, recyclable or compostable materials and all public trash containers were replaced with thirty stations that have only recycling and composting containers. The University of North Texas's Apogee Stadium was the first sports venue in the United States to be awarded Leadership in Energy and Environmental Design (LEED) Platinum certification. The stadium is powered by wind energy and designed to optimize resource efficiency while minimizing environmental impact. The University of Florida's Heavener Football Complex installed dual-flush toilets and other low-flow plumbing fixtures that reduced water use by 40 percent and 100 percent of the wastewater is treated on site. The University of Arizona has installed photovoltaic cells to power its student athletic center (Henly, 2013).

On the professional side, Seattle's Safeco Field became one of the most successful "sustainable" facilities when it opened in 2006. Since then Atlanta's Mercedes-Benz Stadium may become a trendsetter for sports facilities when it opens. It will have an LED lighting system that may use up to 60 percent less electricity than the current lighting, a retractable roof that will utilize natural lighting (when opened), use of solar panels, a system for rainwater collection that will be used for irrigation and water for the cooling towers, high-efficiency condensing boilers that will provide heating and high-efficiency cooling, farm-to-table and organic food, with a landscape that will feature on-site edible gardens and a light rail stop (Blaustein, n.d.). Although there are certainly important societal goals in sustainable facilities, there are also direct economic aspects. Utilizing many of these practices can help save money for the facility owners and the teams.

A Final Word

Stadiums serve as major money machines for sports teams, and a state-of-the-art facility generates potentially more revenues than an older venue. Although the 1990s and 2000s were a boom period for new facilities, demands for new stadiums and arenas continue on the minor league and college levels. In 2015, $1.6 billion was spent on construction for college stadiums, the most ever in one year. One-third of that total came from Texas A&M's expansion of Kyle Field (Sports Business Journal, 2015). This kind of spending serves to continue the debate as to whether such facilities are worth cost, governmental aid and public support.

Ethical Issue: The State-of-the-Art Clause

As noted earlier in the chapter, the facility lease is a crucial component of stadium and arena usage. Although we discussed the basics of such a lease, a lease is basically a contract, and the terms negotiated in that contract will be enforceable, unless a court finds those terms illegal or against public policy.

When the city of St. Louis lured the NFL Rams from Los Angeles in the mid-1990s, their sports commission offered an abundance of riches: not only would the city, through its county sports commission, build the stadium, but the team would keep the bulk of revenues. In addition, although the lease term would be thirty years, it included an interesting opt-out provision: the so-called "state-of-the-art" clause, which permitted the team to terminate the lease every ten years if:

> the Facilities, taken as a whole, and each Component of the Facilities, respectively taken as a whole, must be among the "top" twenty-five percent (25%) of all NFL football stadia and NFL football facilities, if such stadia and facilities were to be rated or ranked according to the matter sought to be measured.
> (Lease between St. Louis Rams and Regional Convention and Visitors Commission, 1995)

Fifteen criteria were set to determine whether the top 25 percent standard was met:

> everything from luxury boxes to club seats, lighting, to scoreboards, . . . regular stadium seating, concession areas, common areas (such as concourses and restrooms), electronic and telecommunications equipment, locker and training rooms, and even the playing surface of the field itself.
> (Knauf, 2010)

Including such a broad provision opened up this lease to the possibility of termination in 2015, and that is exactly what happened. When an arbitrator ruled that the facility did not meet the standard, the lease was converted to a year-to-year lease, leaving the city with few options, paving the way for the team to move to Los Angeles the following season. St. Louis offered a very generous proposal for a new stadium in the hopes of keeping the team. It found a new site alongside the Mississippi River, offered to put up $400 million of the estimated $1 billion cost and asked owner Stan Kroenke to pay $250 million (in exchange for all revenues from naming rights) and asked the NFL to contribute $300 million.

Why did the convention and visitors' bureau negotiate such a one-sided clause? Was the city so desperate to have a football team that it lost its leverage? Was it worth so much to the city to have the Rams to take this risk? And if the team stayed in St. Louis with a new stadium (and the city having a twenty-year-old facility with no tenants), what would you do if you were the city to negotiate a less onerous clause?

Ultimately, the Rams will move into a state-of-the-art facility and accompanying entertainment complex in Inglewood, California, estimated to cost $3 billion and open in 2019.

Chapter Assignment—Stadium Lease between the Serpents and the Washington County Sports Authority

The following project involves drafting a lease between a sports team and a stadium owner/operator. You are to draft a document (page length can be specified by the professor/instructor) drafting provisions that you think would be salient to such an agreement. You are to consider the following facts, but do not make any other assumptions outside of what is stated in the facts. You may utilize whatever outside written sources you wish, but if you do, please note them in a bibliography at the conclusion of this agreement.

Washington County, in the state of Ames, has a population of 1 million. Its largest city, Lincoln City, has a population of 350,000; a 20-mile radius outside of that city raises the population to 500,000. Washington County is large, and it would take about two hours to get from the farthest end to Lincoln City by car. There is little public transportation access in the county, although a few bus lines in Lincoln City that only run on weekdays from 8 AM to 8 PM, and their routes are through the central parts of the city. There is no rail service in the city or from the suburbs to the city. Amtrak shut down the lone passenger station in 1976.

From 1940 to 2005, Lincoln City had a Triple-A minor league baseball team. That team first played in County Stadium, built in 1939. It was built by the county for a total of $2 million and seated about 35,000. The goal was to attract a minor league team. It did, but by the 1980s, it was clear that the stadium had outlived its usefulness. It lacked luxury box seating, there were too few concession areas, too many obstructed-view seats and it was deemed to be too cavernous for a minor league team. It was also used for high school football, rodeos, religious revival meetings and rented events by groups like the local chamber of commerce.

In 1994, that AAA team threatened to move out of the stadium upon the expiration of the lease in 1996. The mayor of Lincoln City, the Washington county council (the elected body) and the governor of the state proposed a new facility to be paid for entirely by the state and county and presented as a referendum to voters in the county. It was rejected, and the team moved.

In 2008, a new mayor of Lincoln City, sensing the civic and (potentially) economic loss of not having a new minor league baseball team, pressed the county council and lobbied the state legislature to reconsider building a new facility to lure another AAA team. After voters approved the construction in a referendum, the state legislature passed an authorization bill to build the facility, which was supported by the governor. The state sales tax would increase by 1 percent until construction is completed. A new state lottery was also proposed and approved by the voters in a separate referendum and then approved by the legislature. The Washington county council approved an additional 0.5 percent of sales tax on "sin items"—such as tobacco products and alcoholic beverages—to provide more funding. Such tax increases were within the power of the counties in the state.

Also, the state decided to issue bonds to provide for additional public transportation (light rail service before and after games which connect to downtown and to the Lincoln Shopping Mall, which has parking space for 10,000 vehicles) and a widening of the exit off the interstate highway to the new facility, which would be built at the site of the old one. The estimated costs would be allocated in the following manner: estimated revenues from a state-wide lottery (for a five-year period)—$50 million; estimated revenues from the 1 percent sales tax increase (for a five-year period)—$15 million; estimated revenues from sin taxes—$10 million. A new bond issue would generate up to $50 million (payable in fifteen years), with a provision that if more funds were needed due to overruns, then new bonds can be issued to cover those costs.

The final configuration of the stadium (which would go by the name of "County Stadium" until a naming-rights deal could be reached) has 20,000 seats, thirty-five luxury boxes and five rows of "privileged seating" in back of home plate. The facility is convertible for soccer, football (for high school games) and concerts. The parking area would hold 6,500 vehicles. A proposal for the construction of an auxiliary lot to hold another 3,000 vehicles was rejected by the county, because it wants to promote public transportation and even walking to the stadium.

After the stadium proposal passed the county and state legislature (and was signed by the county executive and governor) and the constitution was amended, construction began in 1996. After some delays, due to the Environmental Protection Agency's requirement of eliminating environmental waste in the ground under the stadium, which took a special hazardous waste team to dispose, the stadium was completed in 2015. The new facility attracted the attention of a number of AAA clubs who were playing in older facilities and explored the possibility of relocating to Lincoln City.

However, there are drawbacks. The stadium would not have a retractable roof, due to cost. Also, Lincoln City is a Rustbelt area, where it can snow even in mid-April. Tornados are not uncommon in the spring. Temperatures can range from 105 degrees (F) in the summer to −12 in the winter. However, until 2016, the energy economy has helped the economy and for the first time in 100 years, the populations of the county and the city have increased. Companies like Exxon have opened offices here. Unemployment is only 3 percent, and the median income in the county is the highest in the state and one of the highest in the region. Some high-tech companies like Intel and Adobe are planning to open back-end offices, but there is no indication as to when these projects will be completed.

The stadium opened in 2015 without an AAA team to call home. It has been used for college football games, country/western concerts and rodeos. It has also held religious events and political rallies. The most lucrative events have been the three religious meetings in 2015, but a federal court has issued an injunction prohibiting further religious events because the stadium is owned by a public entity. The case is on appeal.

Many in the community are becoming vocal about this "boondoggle," and the politicians are getting concerned. However, there is a possibility of a viable solution.

The Scranton (Pennsylvania) Serpents, an affiliate of the New York Towers of MLB, is looking for a new home. They play in an old facility, and their city and county would not fund a new one. Their old deal, which ended after a term of twenty-five years, included the following terms: annual rental fee: $10,000 (team paid to stadium owner, the county); some split of revenues from parking, but nothing from concessions. There were no luxury boxes or privileged seating at that Scranton stadium, so there was nothing to negotiate regarding revenues for this kind of seating. All revenues from ticket sales go to the team, but the team pays costs of upkeep. That stadium did not have a naming-rights deal.

The team is owned by Lance Toneham III and his family, including his wife and two children, Lance IV and Lucinda. Lance III has a controlling share of the ownership—75 percent. The ownership is in a close corporation, and no stock transfers can be made without his consent. Although the Towers have a following in Scranton, that has not translated to attendance success for the Serpents. They averaged about 10,000 per game over the last decade.

Except for the retractable roof, the facility has state of the art in amenities. It has a large entrance and "hall of fame" walk that has signage space and space for pictures honoring past great Lincoln City athletes. However, it could also have photos of great players for the baseball team that will play in it. Because of the weather conditions and relative lack of use, upkeep is about $150,000 a year.

Although rental fees are difficult to determine, note that a recent deal for a similar facility in a locale that had 25 percent less population than the Lincoln City metro area resulted in a rental fee of $2 million, but that was a straight rental with no other benefits or requirements. The team in question has publicly stated that the failure to tap into revenue streams such as parking and concessions was a "considerable mistake."

Groups of two or four will negotiate this lease. One or two students will take the side of the county sports authority and one or two will represent the Serpents. The lease should contain the following: (1) duration; (2) options and extensions; (3) rental fees (if any) the team would pay to the county; (4) nature of use; (5) what other entities could also use the facility; (6) responsibility for upkeep costs; (7) control or division of revenues from the various revenue-producers, such as concessions, parking, rentals and signage; (8) responsibility for security; (9) control in-stadium advertising and signage; (10) force majeure (unforeseen events that can cause the facility to be unusable); (11) responsibility for insurance; (12) indemnification in the event of liability to third parties; (13) renovation requirements and when they would apply; (14) grounds for termination; and (16) default.

Alternative/Additional Assignment

Assume that the Serpents moved to Lincoln City after negotiating a long-term lease deal in 2016. They would start play in the 2017 season. Shortly after the lease was signed, Handlebar Energy, an energy firm that develops alternative and sustainable energy in five states and has their headquarters near Lincoln City, is interested in a naming-rights deal with the county. What key terms should be found in such an agreement? The groups could focus on issues such as the term, renewals, fees and grounds for termination.

References

10Bestwater.com (2016, July). Ten best water brands. Retrieved July 15, 2016, from https://www.10bestwater.com/brands/

Abigael's at the Barclay's Center (n.d.). *Koshereye.com.* Retrieved January 3, 2016, from http://www.koshereye.com/koshereye-exchange/2885-abigaels-at-the-barclays-center.html#.Von1R1JBnnc

Baade, R. (1994). *Stadiums, professional sports and economic development: Assessing the reality.* Chicago: The Heartland Institute.

Belson, K. (2016, January 13). Rams moving to Los Angeles area, and Chargers could join them. *The New York Times.* Retrieved January 13, 2016, from http://www.nytimes.com/2016/01/13/sports/football/rams-moving-to-los-angeles-area-and-chargers-could-join-later.html?ref=sports&_r=0

Blaustein, L. (n.d.). Mercedes-Benz stadium: Super cool, super green future home of the Falcons and Atlanta FC. *GreenSports Blog.* Retrieved March 22, 2016, from http://greensportsblog.com/2015/11/13/mercedes-benz-stadium-super-cool-super-green-future-home-of-the-falcons-and-atlanta-fc/

Boudway, I. (2013, April 1). Why is the Marlins' Jeffrey Loria the most hated man in baseball? *Bloombergbusiness.com.* Retrieved August 13, 2015, from www.bloomberg.com/bw/articles/2013–03–29/why-is-the-marlins-jeffrey-loria-the-most-hated-man-in-baseball

Brockinton, L. (2002, September 9). Pepsi becomes Philly founder. *Street and Smith's Sports Business Journal,* p. 4.

Broughton, D. (2015a, February 23). What's trending with concessions? *Sports Business Journal.* Retrieved January 3, 2016, from http://www.sportsbusiness daily.com/Journal/Issues/2015/02/23/In-Depth/Roundtable.aspx?hl= concessions%20citi%20field%20food&sc=0

Broughton, D. (2015b, October 5). Comerica Park earns Safety Act designation. *Sports Business Journal.* Retrieved April 24, 2016, from http://www.sports businessdaily.com/Journal/Issues/2015/10/05/Facilities/Safety-Act-Comerica. aspx?hl=CoMerica%20Park&sc=0

Calder, R. (2013, April 26). It's a "suite" chance for MSG tickets. *NYPost.com.* Retrieved August 12, 2015, from nypost.com/2013/04/26/its-a-suite-chance-for-msg-tickets/

Coates, C., & Humphreys, B. (2008, August). Do economists reach a conclusion on subsidies for sports franchises, stadiums and mega-events? International Association of Sports Economists/North American Association of Sports Economists. Working Paper 08–18. Retrieved January 3, 2016, from http:// college.holycross.edu/RePEc/spe/CoatesHumphreys_LitReview.pdf

Coolidge, S. (2014, April 17). Bengals, county reach major deal on The Banks. Retrieved August 12, 2015, from www.cincinnati.com/story/news/politics/2014/04/17/bengals-county-reach-major-deal-banks/7833975/

Cozzillio, M., & Levinstein, M. (1997). *Sports law—Cases and materials.* Durham, NC: Carolina Academic Press, pp. 568–569.

deMause, N. (2009, March 24). Marlins win final stadium approval (kinda). Fieldofschemes.com. Retrieved August 13, 2015, from www.fieldofschemes. com/2009/03/24/2090/marlins-win-final-stadium-approval-kinda/

deMause, N. (2012, November 14). Miami taxpayers spent $500m on a Marlins stadium, and all they got were some lousy Jose Reyes t-shirts. *Fieldofschemes. com.* Retrieved August 13, 2015, from www.fieldofschemes.com/2012/ 11/14/4110/miami-taxpayers-spent-500m-on-marlins-stadium-and-all-they-got-were-some-lousy-jose-reyes-t-shirts/

Dewey Ranch Hockey, LLC. (2009) 414 B.R. 577.

Dictionary.com (n.d.). Definition of water. Retrieved July 15, 2016, from http:// www.dictionary.com/browse/water

Directory of college arena projects (2015, November 9). *Sports Business Journal.* Retrieved January 3, 2016, from http://www.sportsbusinessdaily.com/Journal/ Issues/2015/11/09/In-Depth/Arena-projects.aspx?hl=naming%20rights%20 college%20stadiums&sc=0

Dorfman, J. (2015, January 31). Publicly financed sports stadiums are a game that taxpayers lose. *Forbes.com.* Retrieved May 17, 2015, from www.forbes.com/ sites/jeffreydorfman/2015/01/31/publicly-financed-sports-stadiums-are-a-game-that-taxpayers-lose/

Dorocak, J. (1999). Tax advantages of sports franchises: Part I—The stadium. *Law Review of Michigan State University—Detroit College of Law,* 579.

Duarte, J. (2014, July 8). UH's stadium naming-rights deal among colleges' most lucrative. *Houston Chronicle.* Retrieved January 3, 2016, from http://www. houstonchronicle.com/sports/cougars/article/UH-s-stadium-naming-rights-deal-among-colleges-5608015.php

Eight Details You Need To Know About The New Vikings Stadium Agreement (2013, October 8). *US Bank Stadium.* Retrieved January 3, 2016, from http:// www.usbankstadium.com/8-details-you-need-to-know-about-the-new-vikings-stadium-agreement/

Erardi, J. (1999, April 5). A ballpark built for the fans. *Cincinnati Enquirer,* p. 8S.

Fostering Effective Technologies Act, 6 USC secs 441-444 (2002).

Geology.com (n.d.). Where does bottled water come from? Retrieved July 16, 2016, from http://geology.com/articles/bottled-water.shtml

Goldstein v. New York State Urban Development Corp., 13 NY3d 511 (2009).

Green, K., Klein, B., & Lebowitz, B. (1998). Using tax–exempt bonds to finance professional sports stadiums. *Tax Notes,* 78, 1663.

Greenberg, M., & Gray, J. (1996). *The stadium game.* Milwaukee, WI: National Sports Law Institute, Marquette University Law School, pp. 63, 71, 159, 161– 162, 185, 339, 349.

Greenberg, M., & Gray, J. (1998). *Sports law* (vol. 1, 2nd ed.). Gaithersburg, MD: Aspen, pp. 218, 225, 523.

Henly, A. (2013, August). Collegiate game changers: How campus sport is going green. *Natural Resources Defense Council.* Retrieved March 22, 2016, from http://www. nrdc.org/greenbusiness/guides/sports/files/collegiate-game-changers-report.pdf

Hill, B. (2015, February 20). P-Nats aim to build home with private funds. *MiLB. com.* Retrieved May 17, 2015, from www.milb.com/news/article.jsp?ymd= 20150220&content_id=109782348&fext=.jsp&vkey=min_bus&sid=milb

Hill, J. (2008, August 4). Personal seat licenses, rising ticket prices spell doom. Retrieved February 8, 2010, from http://sports.espn.go.com/espn/page2/story ?page=hill/080801&sportCat=nfl

Horovita, B. (1988, December 6). They are banking that it's a great advertising forum. *Los Angeles Times*, p. 2.

Internal Revenue Service, Treasury Reg, sec. 1.141–4(e)(3), 2008.

Jordan, G. (2016, May 4). Portland blindsided by Pirates' plan to leave for Spring-field after 23 seasons in Maine. *Portland Press Herald*. Retrieved July 15, 2016, from http://www.pressherald.com/2016/05/04/portland-pirates-leaving-maine/

Kaplan, D. (2015, October 26). Dynamic ticket pricing makes successful debut in NFL.*Sports Business Journal*. Retrieved January 4, 2016, from http://www.sportsbusinessdaily.com/Journal/Issues/2015/10/26/Leagues-and-Governing-Bodies/NFL-dynamic.aspx?hl=dynamic%20pricing&sc=1

Keating, R. (2001). Baseline welfare cases: Stadiums, subsidies and the dole. Retrieved June 20, 2005, from www.newcolonist.com/stadium.html

Kelo v. City of New London, 545 U.S. 469 (2005).

King, B. (2013, September 16). How StubHub built a home in sports. *Sportsbusiness Daily*. Retrieved January 4, 2016, from http://www.sportsbusinessdaily.com/Journal/Issues/2013/09/16/In-Depth/StubHub.aspx?hl=secondary%20market&sc=1

Klepal, D., & Tucker, T. (2015, February 21). Skyrocketing stadiums. *Atlanta Journal-Constitution*. Retrieved March 22, 2016, from http://www.ajc.com/news/news/local-govt-politics/skyrocketing-stadiums/nkFD7/

Knauf, K. (2010). If you build it, will they stay? An examination of state-of-the art clauses in NFL stadium leases. *Marquette Sports Law Review, 20*, 479.

Krueger, A. B. (2002, January 10). Take me out to the ballgame, but don't make taxpayers build the ballpark; The high cost and low benefit of sports subsidies. *New York Times*, sec. C, p. 2.

Kurlantzick, L. (1983). Thoughts on professional sports and the antitrust laws: *Los Angeles Memorial Coliseum Commission v. National Football League*. *Connecticut Law Review, 15*, 183, 203.

Lease between Hagerstown Baseball, LLC and Economic Development Authority of the County of Spotsylvania, Virginia, section 4(b) (2015, May 4). Retrieved March 21, 2016, from http://www.spotsylvania.va.us/filestorage/20925/20953/Stadium_Lease_5.4.15.pdf

Lease between St. Louis Rams and St. Louis County Convention and Visitors Bureau (1995), Annex 1).

Leone, K. C. (1997). No team, no peace: Franchise free agency in the National Football League. *Columbia Law Review, 97*, 473.

Los Angeles Memorial Coliseum Commission v. National Football League, 726 F. 2d 1381 (9th Cir. 1984).

Masteralexis, L. P., Barr, C., & Hums, M. (1998). *Principles and practice of sports management*. Gaithersburg, MD: Aspen, pp. 299–300.

Mickle, T. (2009, September 14). Del Biaggio gets 8-year sentence. *Sports Business Journal*, p. 6.

Miller, M. (2010, March 9). Owners v. fans: Owners win and it costs the fans, every time. *San Francisco Sports Business Examiner*. Retrieved May 14, 2010, from http://www.examiner.com/x-39410-SF-Sports-Business-Examiner~y2010m3d9-Owners-v-Fans—Owners-win-and-it-costs-the-fans-every-time

Mitten, M. J., & Burton, B. W. (1997). Professional sports franchise relocations from private and public law perspectives: Balancing marketplace competition, league autonomy, and the need for a level playing field. *Maryland Law Review, 56,* 57, 104.

mlb.com (n.d.). Citi Field vs. Shea Stadium. Retrieved February 12, 2010, from http://newyork.mets.mlb.com/nym/ballpark/comparison.jsp

New York Arts and Cultural Affairs Law, §, 25.30 .1.(c)) (2006).

New York Arts and Cultural Affairs Law, §, 25.30 .1.(c)) (2011).

Pendered, D. (2015, May 5). Atlanta's bonds for Falcons stadium rated investment grade, sale slated to close Tuesday. *Saporta Report.* Retrieved January 3, 2016, from http://saportareport.com/atlantas-bonds-for-falcons-stadium-rated-investment-grade-sale-to-close-tuesday/

Peters, C. (2014, December 31). NHL approves sale of majority stake in Coyotes to Andrew Barroway. Retrieved May 17, 2015, from www.cbssports.com/nhl/eye-on-hockey/24926736/nhl-approves-sale-of-majority-stake-in-coyotes-to-andrew-barroway

Povich, E. (2015, March 16). Is Obama proposal the end of taxpayer-subsidized sports stadiums? *USA Today.* Retrieved January 3, 2016, from http://www.usatoday.com/story/news/politics/2015/03/16/stateline-obama-proposal-taxpayer-subsidized-sports-stadiums/24845355/

Quirk, J., & Fort, R. (1997). *Pay dirt: The business of professional team sports.* Princeton, NJ: Princeton University Press, pp. 131–132.

Rosen, D. (2016, June 22). Las Vegas awarded NHL franchise. *NHL.com.* Retrieved July 12, 2016, from https://www.nhl.com/news/nhl-expands-to-las-vegas/c-281010682

Rosenberg, M. (2013, May 8). Levi's Stadium: 49ers' new Santa Clara home gets a name in $220 million deal. *San Jose Mercury News.* Retrieved January 3, 2016, from http://www.mercurynews.com/ci_23198944/levis-stadium-49ers-new-santa-clara-home-gets

Salamone, G. (2006, July 30). One of a kind weddings: Tie the knot at some of N.Y.'s most famous landmarks. *New York Daily News.* Retrieved August 31, 2010, from http://www.nydailynews.com/archives/entertainment/2006/07/30/2006-07-30__one_of_a_kind_weddings__tie.html

Santo, C. (2005). The economic impact of sports stadiums: Recasting the analysis in context. *Journal of Urban Affairs, 27*(2), 177–191.

Schaul, K., & Belson, K. (2013, July 31). Playing the stadium name game. *The New York Times.* Retrieved January 3, 2016, from http://www.nytimes.com/interactive/2013/07/31/sports/playing-the-stadium-name-game.html

Schweers, J. (2015, September 8). UF, contractor agree on $64.5M O'Dome renovation. Gainsville (FL) Sun. Retrieved March 22, 2016, from http://www.gainesville.com/article/20150908/ARTICLES/150909726?p=1&tc=pg

Scott, L. (2015, February 21). Skyrocketing stadiums, chart one. *Atlanta Journal-Constitution.* Retrieved March 22, 2016, from http://www.ajc.com/news/news/local-govt-politics/skyrocketing-stadiums/nkFD7/

Seymour, H. (1960). *Baseball: The early years.* New York: Oxford University Press, pp. 319–323.

Shapiro, M. (2004). *The last good season: Brooklyn, the Dodgers and their final pennant race together.* New York: Doubleday.

Sports Facility Reports (2009). Vol. 10, sec. 3B. National Sports Law Institute, Marquette University. Retrieved February 1, 2010, from http://law.marquette. edu/cgi-bin/site.pl?2130&pageID=4239

TDGarden A to Z Guide (n.d.). TDGarden.com. Retrieved March 20, 2016, from http://www.tdgarden.com/a-to-z-guide/toptentopten.com (n.d.). The top ten baseball's best skyboxes suites. Retrieved February 12, 2010, from http://www.toptentopten.com/topten/baseball_s+best+skyboxes+suites

Valenti, J. (1997, October 8). Spano cops plea; Admits he lied about wealth, could get 5 years in prison. *Newsday (New York)*, p. A05.

Whoriskey, P. (2003, July 28). Stadiums are built on federal tax break. *Washington Post*, p. A01.

Wolffe, D. (2007, August 29). Giants, Jets land $1.3b stadium financing deal. *Real Estate Weekly*. Retrieved February 17, 2010, from http://www.allbusiness. com/construction/nonresidential-building-construction/5519082–1.html

Year in sports business 2015 (2015, December 14). *Sports Business Journal*. Retrieved January 2, 2016, from http://www.sportsbusinessdaily.com/Journal/Issues/2015/12/14/Year-End/Numbers.aspx

Yocca v. Pittsburgh Steelers Sports, Inc., 854 A. 2d 425 (Pa. 2004).

Zimbalist, A., & Noll, R. (1997). *Sports, jobs and taxes: The economic impact of sports teams*. Washington, DC: Brookings Institute Press.

9 Sports Gambling

Gambling on sports events—whether legal or illegal—has been a constant in the sports landscape. Although permitted in much of the world, such wagering remains illegal in most of the United States. Despite the illegality, Americans have been betting on sports for years. The history of betting, the policy reasons behind its prohibition and the beginnings of a trend to legalize certain kinds of sports gambling will be examined in this chapter. Given the pace of potential changes, it is quite possible that by the time you are reading this, the legal and industry landscape may be different with a choice of legal, though regulated, forms of sports gaming.

The reasons for sports gambling restrictions are both moral and protectionist. Gambling has traditionally been considered a vice, one where people could and have lost much of their personal fortunes. The problem of gambling addiction has bolstered the argument that gambling poses a risk of health and safety. One estimate shows that 2.2 percent of Americans are considered "problem gamblers" (Williams, R. & Volberg, R., 2012), and organizations like Gamblers Anonymous were created to rid people of this addiction (Gamblers Anonymous, n.d.). If sports gambling is legalized, the argument follows, it will lead to more addiction and more economic loss. Yet those who argue for liberalized gambling laws point out that the illegality of gambling has not stopped those who bet from losing and losing big (Stock, 2007).

In the United States, it is estimated that between $80 and $380 billion was illegally wagered on sports events (National Gambling Impact Study Commission Final Report, 2012). That compares with $2.76 billion wagered legally on sports in Nevada during the same year (American Gaming Association, 2015). Globally, in the countries where sports betting is legal, it has been estimated that between $250 and $600 billion is bet annually (International Centre for Sport Security, 2014). As of 2016, countries with legalized sports gambling systems include China, Taiwan, Australia and the United Kingdom (onlinebetting.com, n.d.). It is safe to say that sports betting—legal and illegal—is not going to go away.

Another principal argument justifying a ban on sports betting derives from the deleterious effects gambling has had on the integrity of sport. Baseball and basketball, in particular, have histories of gambling scandals, where players and/or officials received bribes to "throw" a game or series of matches, most famously noted in the 1919 "Black Sox" scandal where a number of players from the Chicago White Sox took payoffs and lost the 1919 World Series to the Cincinnati Reds. The repercussions from that event led to the creation of the modern commissioner of a professional sport with virtually unlimited powers (Seymour, 1971). More recently, an NBA referee pleaded guilty to receiving cash payments from those involved in the business of sports betting in exchange for providing betting recommendations on NBA games that he officiated (*U.S. v. Donaghy*, 2008).

One popular type of gambling infraction involves a method of sports gambling that has been a system of paying players not to lose a game, but to win by fewer points than the gamblers' point spread (Goldstein, 2003). Point-shaving scandals involved a number of college basketball players over the last century, which included players from universities such as Northwestern (1998), Boston College (1978–79), Tulane (1985), Kentucky (1952) and the City College of New York (1950–51) (Singer, 2013).

As of 2015, all of the major professional sports have antigambling sanctions in their respective constitutions (Major League Baseball Rule 21(d)); (NHL Constitution, Article 3, sec. 3.9(b)). Even in an era of collective bargaining agreements which restrain league powers over players in various areas of discipline, the commissioners' powers to punish for gambling remain very broad (NBA CBA, Article XLI, sec. 5(a), 2011). Although some of the professional leagues such as the NBA softened their opposition to legalized sports betting (Silver, 2014), the NCAA remains adamant against this practice (*NCAA v. Christie*, 2015). Even in countries where sports gambling is legal, corruption has occurred. In 2015 and 2016, soccer, rugby and horse racing athletes, coaches or handicappers were caught betting on games in their respective sports, a practice that is prohibited by most local and national sports federations (Carpenter, 2016).

Legal sports gambling has evolved into a very sophisticated business. In the United Kingdom, for example, one can bet on events from sports enterprises that utilize the latest in analytic technology. For example, software exists to not only gauge the odds before a game, but also to determine how the odds can change during a match. If a soccer team's star player is forced out of the match due to injury or due to a red card, the betting program can change the odds (Taylor, 2014). Additionally, team and individual sports can be wagered, and the betting can continue while the match is played (Football Betting Basics, n.d.).

In the United States, the greater social acceptance of gambling, coupled with the staggering amounts of money that are wagered, have raised the possibility of reforming the law to legalize some form of gambling (known as "gaming"). Additionally, the rise of what has become known as "daily fantasy sports" may also be changing public attitudes.

What Is Gambling?

On the surface, crafting a definition of gambling is not difficult. Gambling occurs when one risks something of value upon the outcome of a contest of chance or a future contingent event not under his control or influence, upon an agreement or understanding that he will receive something of value in the event of a certain outcome (New York Penal Law sec. 225.00, n.d.). Theoretically, there is minimal skill involved, or whatever level of skill is involved, it is overtaken by a large element of luck in determining the outcome of the event. A lottery comes to mind. One chooses several numbers from a pool, and if those numbers are chosen, the bettor wins. This randomized choice involves little skill.

However, in the realm of sports betting, many, including those in law enforcement, have debated the respective levels of skill and luck to determine the appropriate level of randomness (Rodenberg, 2015). A former attorney general noted: "Sports betting . . . involves 'substantial [not slight] skill.'" Sports bettors can employ superior knowledge of the games, teams and players in order to exploit odds that do not reflect the true likelihoods of the possible outcomes (Rodenberg, 2015).

But even more dizzying is the subtle, but different definitions states utilize for gambling. Because the regulation of gambling was traditionally based on state law as much as federal law, the distinctions make a difference. The central question focuses on the term "contest of chance." New York describes a contest of chance as "any contest, game, gaming scheme or gaming device in which the outcome depends in a *material degree* (emphasis added) upon an element of chance, notwithstanding that skill of the contestants may also be a factor therein." (N.Y. Penal Code, sec. 225.00). This meaning may include a game where there is a considerable level of skill. On the other hand, Florida defines a game of chance somewhat differently, based on whether skills or chance is the *predominant* factor (emphasis added) (Wallach & Dunbar, 2015). The varying state-by-state definitions have a major effect on hybrid games that combine chance and skill, such as daily fantasy sports, which we will discuss later in the chapter.

Reasons to Restrict Sports Betting

As noted earlier, the major sports leagues and the NCAA have resisted any attempts to legalize sports betting, although the opposition by some of the professional leagues may be easing. The reasons center on the effect gambling would have on the integrity of the sport. A consistent argument made against legalized sports gambling is that it increases the potential for corrupting the game, as athletes and referees can be subject to payoffs from big-time gamblers to alter the result.

College athletes could be particularly vulnerable to payoffs because, as "student-athletes" they have not been compensated in the form of a salary. As noted earlier, a number of point-shaving scandals have occurred in college basketball where players were bribed by gamblers not to lose, but to win by a closer score than predicted. Therefore, the idea was seductive. The athletes (on the favored team) would be paid not to win above the predicted point spread for the game. For example, let's say that College Team X is favored to win over Team Y by 10 points. A gambler could pay the starting players of Team X to keep the victory at 10 points or below. Team X wins by 8 points, and the gamblers who bet on the weaker team (Team Y) get their winnings. In other words, they make a game of chance into a sure thing.

In addition to the social costs due to gambling addiction noted earlier, another argument against sports gambling is the difficulty in crafting a precise regulatory system. Traditionally, gambling was regulated state by state until the ban on sports gambling was federalized by the passage of nationwide bans by Congress in the early 1990s. Would Congress simply pass a new law revoking the old ban, effectively washing its hands of trying to enforce a ban and bringing the issue back to the states? Or would Congress pass a new law legalizing gambling nationwide, preempting the states from taking any action and creating a federal regulatory authority to police the sport? If the latter should occur, the kind of regulatory apparatus would cause considerable debate. Would, say, a federal gambling commission have the power to issue binding rules and regulations? Would it have enforcement powers? Would the president appoint the head of this authority? And would Congress have some kind of "veto power" over its actions? As of this writing, it is difficult to determine if, when and how such changes will occur.

Reasons to Permit Sports Betting

Advocates for legalizing sports betting argue that, with certain limits and regulations, it can reap large economic benefits. Because sports gambling is illegal in most of the United States, most of the gains received by successful bettors are not taxed. With legalized sports betting, the winnings would be taxed as income by the IRS and could also be taxed under state law. With many states seeking more revenues but reluctant to raise taxes for political reasons, income from sports betting could be a very attractive way to supplement state and federal coffers since presumably any legalization would create a systematic way to report gambling winnings to the

Internal Revenue Service and state tax agencies. For example, Nevada, with legal sports wagering, earned over $170 million in revenue in 2012, or about 5 percent of the more than $3.4 billion legally bet on sporting events (Americangaming.org, 2013).

Another justification for liberalizing gambling is that the activity is so pervasive that it may be better to regulate it than ban it. Government can exert more control by legalizing and regulating. The history of Prohibition, the federal government's attempt to ban the sale of intoxicating liquors, illustrates the point. The ban on alcohol created an underground economy for liquor and led to the creation of modern organized crime. Once Prohibition ended with the passage of the 21st Amendment in 1933, a more practical regulatory structure was created by states, and alcohol consumption did not increase to pre-Prohibition levels (Ogle, 2008).

Although sports leagues have traditionally opposed sports betting, that opposition has begun to erode in recent years. In 2014, NBA Commissioner Adam Silver signaled a change in NBA policy by advocating regulated sports gambling (Silver, 2014). Coincidence or not, the next day, the NBA partnered with FanDuel, the No. 1 daily fantasy sports company at that time. FanDuel offered prizes to successful competitors, making this deal the first of its kind involving a pro sports league (Zwerling, 2015).

In a computer- and analytics-driven age, the nature of sports betting has changed. In other countries, it is run by large firms based on sophisticated software that is heavily technology based. The rise of mobile telephony can be seen as a springboard for facilitating sports betting because of the ease of application and the ability to use this technology at any time. For example, Betfair, the largest online bookmaker, claimed in its annual report that 1.7 million customers bet online in 100 countries (Betfair Annual Report, 2015).

Where legal, an array of betting choices exists. Taking soccer as an example, one can bet simply on whether a team wins, loses or draws. Or, one can bet on various portions of the game, such as who "wins" the first half. The betting can be even more specialized as to the number of corner kicks, penalty kicks, how many goals will be scored in the match or even bets covering more than one possible outcome (10Bet, n.d.).

What has become known as "micro-betting" has become a central component of the analytics-based approach to gambling. The various betting possibilities are huge: betting on the number of points a player scores in an NBA game, wagering on the total number of points scored by both teams in a baseball game, determining whether a player scores a hat trick or combines in a certain number of goals and assists in a given game or predicting how many interceptions will a quarterback throw in a game. Even wagering on a fan sinking the half-court shot at halftime may be a micro-bet. As of this writing, the NBA is seriously considering investing and possibly sponsoring some of these tracking systems (Zwerling, 2015).

Legal betting firms emphasize their capability as "self-regulators" to track compulsive gambling. In their goal of providing "responsible" betting, these companies developed site tools to track betting patterns and to limit bets by customers. In some cases, these companies have become watchdogs for certain sports by concluding agreements with sports federations to track questionable betting patterns (Betfair annual report, 2015). One independent firm called Sportradar monitors potential fraud and match fixing by analyzing betting patterns worldwide to identify suspicious activities and then provides educational tools and services for leagues and teams to raise awareness for illegal betting practices.

How Betting Odds Work

Because it is very rare that the competing teams or individuals are evenly matched, mathematical odds must be factored to make it attractive to bet for the "weaker" or "less favored team." Several methods can be utilized to ensure equal chance for success. One method, often used in high-scoring sports like basketball, involves a "point spread."

The easiest way to describe a point spread is to define it as a number odds makers use as a median between two teams or sides in an effort to generate betting interest on both of them (oddshark.com, n.d.). The favorite team (also known as the "chalk") must not only win the match, but do so by a prescribed number of points. So, if Basketball Team X is favored by 4.5 points that team must win by at least 5 points for the bettor who bet on that time to collect his or her winnings. If the favored team wins by fewer than 5 points, the person who bet for the "losing" team wins the bet because the victory did not cover that spread.

Another method of computing odds is known as "moneylines." Many sports, especially those that are low scoring like ice hockey, utilize this method rather than point spreads. It involves a plus/minus system to compensate for the relative advantages or disadvantages of a particular team. So, let's say that Team A plays against Team B in a hypothetical baseball game. One may see odds such as "Team A –185/Team B +165. What that means is that A is favored to win the game, but the payoff is going to be lower than if B wins. For example, if one bets $185 on Team A, that person collects $100 if Team A wins. However, if the person bets on Team B, he or she would bet $100 to collect $165.

Because Team A is favored, the sportsbook needs you to risk more to bet on that team. So wagering on baseball favorites with moneylines calls for you to risk a certain number ($185 based on –185) in order to win $100. On the other side, the sportsbook is also willing to reward you for taking the underdog, so they give you an incentive to bet on the Team B. In this case, you would risk $100 in order to win $165 (+165) on Team B. The same principles and math apply with moneyline betting on hockey.

Say that Team Y may be −130 (that is 1.3 goal) favorites against the Team Z, which is a +130 underdog. You risk $130 to win $100 on the favored team and wager $100 to win $110 on the underdog team (Oddshark. com, n.d.).

The U.S. Legal Restraints

Defining what constitutes illegal gambling in the United States has resulted in an often inconsistent series of state laws, coupled with some broad federal legislation. Two federal laws essentially ban sports gambling: the 1992 law titled "Professional and Amateur Sports Protection Act" (known by the acronym "PASPA") (27 U.S.C. sec. 3702, 2006) and the 2006 Uniform Internet Gambling Enforcement Act (known as "UIGEA") (31 U.S.C. sec. 5362, 2006). However, both statutes leave it to states to define what illegal gambling is. Enacted with the blessing of the major sports leagues and the NCAA, PASPA prohibits governmental entities or individuals from promoting, advertising and licensing a scheme in which amateur or professional athletes participate (28 U.S.C. sec. 3702). However, because four states—Nevada, Delaware, Montana and New Jersey— had some form of legalized sports gambling at casinos or by lotteries before the passage of the law, PASPA "grandfathered" those states and those particular gambling schemes, exempting them from enforcement. For example, Nevada had legal sports betting as part of their gambling regimen, and it was not going to have the federal government ban a legal activity in that state, which provided for a considerable source of income. This is the reason why casino-based sports betting remains legal in Las Vegas and other Nevada cities and sports lotteries are legal in Delaware.

Courts have interpreted PASPA as a broad prohibition on expanding the gambling regimens in place in those states (*Office of Commissioner of Baseball v. Markell*, 2009). More recently, PASPA's scope and its constitutionality has been challenged by the state of New Jersey, which passed legislation legalizing sports gambling as a way to reinvigorate casino gambling in Atlantic City. New Jersey's attempts have been challenged by the NCAA, sports leagues and the U.S. Department of Justice, which has resulted in several court rulings, generally upholding PASPA's constitutionality and prohibiting the state from circumventing the law (*NCAA v. New Jersey*, 2013, 2015). It is possible that the case may ultimately reach the U.S. Supreme Court, but as of this writing, it is too early to say.

An additional, though less direct, restriction on online sports gambling is found in the Uniform Internet Gambling Enforcement Act (UIGEA), the 2006 law mentioned earlier. It bars U.S. residents from engaging in online gambling (not just sports related, but all gambling) run by firms located outside the country, and by extension it prohibits online betting on any activity that would constitute illegal gambling (31 U.S.C. sec. 5362,

2006). Practically, it is targeted to the payment systems, such as credit card companies, that would process those bets (Edelman, 2016). The passage and implementation of UIGEA was a major factor in ending online gambling regimens such as Internet poker.

It is possible that the U.S. restrictions on sports gambling and gambling generally may be eased by the courts or by legislation in the next few years. But as of 2016, the state and national bans on sports gambling in the United States are quite broad, with the exception of the limited exceptions under PASPA.

Ethical Question—How Different Is Gambling from Investing?

Isn't the stock market gambling and, if so, why is such investing legal when gambling is not? There is a legal answer to this question. Many things in life constitute activities of chance—only certain wagering actions are restricted as *illegal* gambling. That sounds simple enough, but the fine line between illegal games of chance and legal investment may be getting hazier. In 2015, Nevada enacted a law that allowed out-of-state business and investment groups to pool their money in funds managed by handicappers who can legally place bets in that state. In a sense, it's like a mutual fund for betting (Chen & Green, 2016). How does this differ from traditional investing? The fund managers claim they are investors, rather than gamblers, and use these funds to diversify assets for the investors. The wagering scheme is a long-term one; the investors do not know what teams or sports are bet on. They find out their financial performance in twelve or eighteen months. Is this a way to circumvent gambling laws? Is this the future of gambling—part of an evolution from a back-door cash business to a professionalized, numbers-driven investment vehicle?

Fantasy Sports

The rise of fantasy sports, notably the version known as "daily fantasy," has presented a major test of the applicability of gambling restrictions on an activity that may or may not be described as "gambling." As of 2016, these issues have not been settled, and they pose a major challenge to the viability of an industry that has exploded in both public awareness and in profitability and exposure.

The more traditional season-long fantasy sports gradually evolved in the 1960s and 1970s, when sport enthusiasts decided to create a system whereby players picked their own teams and based on the respective players' success for a given season. For example, those who created a fantasy baseball league would award winners based on players' batting averages, RBIs and ERAs. For a golf fantasy, players picked a team of golfers, and the winner would be the person with the lowest combined total of strokes by the tournament's end (Daily Fantasy Sports USA, 2016).

In the 1980s, "rotisserie" leagues were formed and the activity became more ubiquitous. What attracted players was the use of strategy to predict end-of-season results. So, players would try to pick players based on their performance in past seasons and by predicting expected performance in the upcoming season. In essence, a player was becoming a fictional general manager of the team. Rotisserie attracted a number of academics who were baseball fans and was considered more of a hobby than a vocation.

The commercial application of the Internet in the 1990s expanded the possibilities of fantasy, as fans were able to access far more information—such as real-time statistics, updated databases, message boards and updated box scores—and therefore create bigger and more expansive leagues with other online players (Daily Fantasy Sports USA, 2016). With many more "owners" the business opportunities of this industry grew. Both "free" and "premium" platform fantasy sports sites grew. Of the free sites, Yahoo!'s became one of the most popular. Premier sites, where players pay a fee to join, offer more information and potentially greater prizes.

The online expansion of fantasy sports has resulted in a boom in popularity. In 2010, it was estimated that about 32 million people played some version of fantasy sports; in 2015, that number increased to over 56 million (industry demographics, fsta.org, n.d.). The industry avoided a potential roadblock when UIGEA, the 2006 law passed to ban Internet gambling, created an exemption for fantasy sports as Congress concluded that fantasy sports did not constitute illegal gambling under federal law (31 U.S.C. § 5362(1)(E)(ix).

Daily Fantasy Sports

Without the flourishing and maturing of the Internet, there would be no daily fantasy sports. The Internet facilitated the playing of fantasy sports, not only among friends, but also among a wide group of participants from around the world. Because it is almost exclusively online, daily fantasy requires the utilization of third-party payment services to collect entry fees and pay prize winners (Edelman, 2016). Sensing the potential economic benefits of this newer version of fantasy sports, online firms such as FanDuel and DraftKings became major players in this endeavor. And the sports leagues have become financially involved. In 2014, the NBA and the NHL allowed individual teams to negotiate deals with daily fantasy providers. Major League Baseball made DraftKings its official daily fantasy game provider (Bales, 2014; Kaburakis, Rodenberg & Holden, 2015).

The basic rules for daily fantasy sports are similar to those for season-long fantasy sports: picking a roster of players from draft lists based on a salary cap, with participants competing against one another for prizes involving matches in the traditional team sports such as baseball, basketball, football and hockey. The real skill comes with the choosing of the players for a daily game based on probabilities determined from player statistics (FanDuel: How it works, n.d.; Edelman, 2011).

At first glance, it seems that daily fantasy is exempted from gambling enforcement because of the exemption crafted in UIGEA. However, it turned out that the federal law exemption did not necessary protect daily fantasy sports. State law gambling rules remained in effect and left open the possibility that individual states could consider the activity gambling under state-crafted definitions. Not surprisingly, some officials thought that daily fantasy would be subject to the gambling ban in their respective states.

Because daily fantasy contains elements of chance and elements of skill, it is difficult to determine exactly whether it is mainly in the ambit of illegal gambling or becomes a legally protected game of skill. Some commentators remain convinced that Daily Fantasy is gambling and does not employ the same level of skill set as season-long fantasy sport. As one expert noted:

> Daily fantasy games have a fundamentally different relationship to chance than season-long fantasy games. On a given day an injury, a hailstorm or a ball bouncing strangely could affect a result. In this regard, playing daily fantasy seems very similar to placing a bet with a bookmaker. It's tough to make an intellectually honest distinction between [daily fantasy and placing a bet].
>
> (Brustein, 2013)

What complicates this further is that states often define gambling— particularly the central term "game of chance"—differently, as noted earlier in the chapter, Most states use a "predominance test" stating that if the element of skill in a particular game predominates over chance, then the game is permitted (Rodenberg, 2016a). Others use a "materiality" test, meaning that chance must be a material element of activity. Still others prohibit all games and contests that involve any degree of chance no matter how slight (Apfel & Kim, 2015). The differences in the definitions have led to differences in enforcement. As of the middle of 2016, some states have legalized it by statute, others by opinion of state attorneys general and others have banned it (Rodenberg, 2016b). At the end of 2016, DraftKings and FanDuel announced a merger.

Chapter Assignment: How Would You Regulate Daily Fantasy Sports?

Given the uncertain legal landscape for daily fantasy sports, how would you create a system whereby the activity is legalized but regulated by the state? The assignment may be done individually or as a group. As part of the project, participant(s) should offer reasons why this activity should be legal and regulated and propose a sample bill to be submitted to the respective state legislature stating the standards to be used. The assignment can be four to six pages in length.

References

10Bet—Soccer (n.d.). General information. Retrieved March 26, 2016, from https://www.10bet.com/help/betting-rules/soccer/

Americangaming.org (2013). State of the States. The AGA survey on casino entertainment, P. 36. Retrieved May 22, 2016, from https://www.americangaming.org/sites/default/files/research_files/aga_sos2013_rev042014.pdf

Apfel, D., & Kim, A. (2015, April 6). Fantasy sports vs. illegal gambling: Where's the line? *CNBC.com*. Retrieved May 7, 2016, from http://www.cnbc.com/2015/04/06/fantasy-sports-vs-illegal-gambling-wheres-the-line-commentary.html

Bales, J. (2014, March 24). Daily fantasy game a new way to play for DraftKings. *MLB.COM*. Retrieved January 5, 2016, from http://m.mlb.com/news/article/70013300/daily-fantasy-baseball-a-new-easy-way-to-play-from-draftkings

Betfair annual report (2015). Retrieved January 4, 2016, from http://corporate.betfair.com/~/media/Files/B/Betfair-Corporate/pdf/annual-report-2015.pdf

Brustein, J. (2013, March 12). Fantasy sports and gambling: Line is blurred. *New York Times*. Retrieved January 5, 2016, from http://www.nytimes.com/2013/03/12/sports/web-sites-blur-line-between-fantasy-sports-and-gambling.html

Carpenter, K. (2016, April 22). No gambling permitted; How sports governing bodies regulate betting by athletes and "connected persons." *Law in Sport*. Retrieved April 23, 2016, from http://www.lawinsport.com/blog/kevin-carpenter/item/no-gambling-permitted-how-sports-governing-bodies-regulate-betting-by-athletes-and-connection-persons

Chen, A., & Green, W. (2016, June 27). Mutual attraction. *Sports Illustrated*, 49.

Country specific gambling laws (n.d.). *Onlinebetting.com*. Retrieved April 23, 2016, from http://www.onlinebetting.com/legal/

Daily Fantasy Sports USA (2016). *Playinglegal.com*. Retrieved October 21, 2016, from https://playinglegal.com/fantasy-sports

Edelman, M. (2011). A short treatise on fantasy sports and the law: How America regulates its new national pastime. *Harvard Journal of Sports & Entertainment Law*, *3*, 1, 12.

Edelman, M. (2016). Navigating the Legal Risks of Daily Fantasy Sports: A Detailed Primer in Federal and State Gambling Law. 2016 University of Illinois L. Rev. 117 (2016).

FanDuel: How it works (n.d.). *Fanduel.com*. Retrieved January 5, 2016, from https://www.fanduel.com/how-it-works

Football Betting Basics (n.d.). Online betting sites. Retrieved March 26, 2016, from http://www.onlinebettingsites.org.uk/football-betting-basics

Gamblers Anonymous (n.d.). History. Retrieved March 25, 2016, from http://www.gamblersanonymous.org/ga/content/history

Goldstein, J., 2003, November 15). Explosion: 1951 scandals threaten college hoops. Retrieved March 26, 2016, from http://espn.go.com/classic/s/basketball_scandals_explosion.html

Illegal Super Bowl Bets to total 38 billion this year (2015, January 22). American Gaming Association. Retrieved March 4, 2016, from http://www.americangaming.org/newsroom/press-releases/illegal-super-bowl-bets-to-total-38-billion-this-year

Industry Demographics, Fantasy Sports (n.d.). Fantasy Sports Trade Association (FSTA). Retrieved May 6, 2016, from http://fsta.org/research/industry-demographics/

Kaburakis, C., Rodenberg, R., & Holden, J. (2015). Inevitable sports gambling, state regulation, and the pursuit of revenue. *Harvard Business Law Review Online*. Reference, January 5, 2916, from http://www.hblr.org/wp-content/uploads/2015/01/Kaburakis-Rodenberg-Holden-Inevitable1.pdf

Major League Baseball Rule 21(d). Retrieved March 26, 2016, from http://seanlahman.com/files/rose/rule21.html

National Gambling Impact Study Commission Final Report (2012), sec. 2014. Retrieved May 21, 2016, from http://govinfo.library.unt.edu/ngisc/reports/2.pdf

NBA—NBPA Collective Bargaining Agreement, Article XLI, sec, 5(e) (2011). Retrieved April 24, 2016, from http://nbpa.com/cba/

NCAA v. Governor of New Jersey ("Christie I"), 730 F. 3d 208 (3d Cir. 2013).

NCAA v. Governor of New Jersey ("Christie II"), 799 F.3d 299 (3d Cir. 2015).

New York Penal Law, sec. 225.00

NHL Constitution, Article 3, sec. 3.9(b)). Retrieved March 2, 2016, from http://v1.theglobeandmail.com/v5/content/pdf/CoyotesDaly.pdf

Office of Comm'r of Baseball v. Markell, 579 F.3d 293, 295 (3d Cir. 2009).

Ogle, M. (2008, December 4). 75 years after the repeal of prohibition, we're still captives of the "dry" crusaders. *US News and World Report*. Retrieved April 24, 2016, from http://www.usnews.com/opinion/articles/2008/12/04/75-years-after-the-repeal-of-prohibition-were-still-captives-of-the-dry-crusaders

Professional and Amateur Sports Protection Act ("PASPA") 27 U.S.C. sec. 3702 *et seq.*

Professional and Amateur Sports Protection Act of 1992 ("PASPA") 28 USC sec. 3702 (2006).

Rodenberg, R. (2015, July 21). Documents show DOJ, NFL have argued that sports betting is skill-based. *ESPN.com*. Retrieved April 24, 2016, from http://

espn.go.com/chalk/story/_/id/13268458/documents-show-justice-department-nfl-argued-skill-sports-betting

Rodenberg, R. (2016a, February 18). Why do states define gambling differently? *ESPN.com*. Retrieved May 7, 2016, from http://espn.go.com/chalk/story/_/id/14799507/daily-fantasy-why-do-states-define-gambling-differently

Rodenberg, R. (2016b, April 16). Daily fantasy sports state-by-state tracker. *ESPN.com*. Retrieved May 7, 2016, from http://espn.go.com/chalk/story/_/id/14799449/daily-fantasy-dfs-legalization-tracker-all-50-states

Seymour, H. (1971). *Baseball: The golden age*. pp. 296–310. New York: Oxford University Press.

Silver, A. (2014, November 13). Legalize and regulate sports betting. *The New York Times*. Retrieved January 15, 2016, from http://www.nytimes.com/2014/11/14/opinion/nba-commissioner-adam-silver-legalize-sports-betting.html

Singer, M. (2013, May 2). Ranking the 10 most shocking scandals in college basketball history. *Bleacher Report*. Retrieved April 24, 2016, from http://bleacherreport.com/articles/1625497-ranking-the-10-most-shocking-scandals-in-college-basketball-history/page/10

Sports Odds. *Oddshark.com*. Retrieved April 10, 2016, from http://www.oddsshark.com/sports-betting/betting-money-line

Stock, C. (2007, February 19). Government addicted to gambling profits: Albertans bet more, lose more, but spend little to. Treat problem gamblers. *The Edmonton Journal*, p. 1.

Taylor, M. (2014, November 6). How to calculate live odds following a red card. *Pinnacle Sports*. Retrieved March 26, 2016, from http://www.pinnaclesports.com/en/betting-articles/soccer/how-to-calculate-live-odds-following-a-red-card

The threat to sport: The facts at a glance (2014). International Centre for Sports Security, pp. 1–4. Retrieved January 3, 2016, from http://www.theicss.org/wp-content/themes/icss-corp/pdf/SIF14/Sorbonne-ICSS%20Report%20-%20Infographic_WEB.pdf

United States v. Tim Donaghy, 570 F. Supp. 2d 411, 416 (SDNY, 2008).

Unlawful Internet Gambling Enforcement Act (UIGEA), 31 USC sec. 5362 (2006).

Wallach, D., & Dunbar, M. (2015, November 9). Florida's uncertain legal landscape for fantasy sports: A closer look. *644* (2015).

Williams, R., & Volberg, R., 2012. Population prevalence of problem gambling, Ontario Problem Gambling Research Center. Retrieved March 22, 2016, from https://www.uleth.ca/dspace/bitstream/handle/10133/3068/2012-PREVALENCE-OPGRC%20%282%29.pdf?sequence=3

Zwerling, J. (2015, May 5). Betting on the future: Imagining the NBA fan experience with regulated gambling. Bleacher Report. Accessed October 16, 2016, from http://bleacherreport.com/articles/2324874-betting-on-the-future-imagining-the-nba-fan-experience-with-regulated-gambling

10 Analytics in Sports

In the last decade, the use of data analytics has become a major source of personnel decisions and playing strategies in the world of sports. Although a complex subject, the concept is straightforward. Analytics involves the collection of large quantities of statistical data, identifying trends derived from that information and, ultimately, using the findings to derive conclusions. It has been the basis for predicting outcomes in finance, weather, sales and nearly every other industry, but this concept was not embraced in the sports business until recently. And its adoption has not been universally accepted, with many "purists" deriding the concept as taking the joy out of sports (Glockner, 2014). Analytics even grabbed popular culture attention with the release of the book (and later the film) *Moneyball*.

Analytics Defined

Analytics, generally speaking, is the study of data. The process begins by recording information, either in predetermined categories or through mass information mining, which becomes the data used in the study. This data is analyzed in a variety of ways in hopes of recognizing a pattern (businessdictionary.com, n.d.). These patterns can then be used as tools for predictions, decision making, problem solving and more. This is how your web browser is able to guess your next search or how your credit card company can detect fraudulent use—the latter case as a result of your spending behavior *not* aligning with your past actions.

Analytical predictions have been frequently used in the area of financial investments. Every second of the day, computers worldwide are collecting price changes for every stock, bond, commodity and any other financial instrument that exists. In addition, the state of external factors like exchange rates, inflation, interest rates, political climate, weather, seasonality and other stock prices are recorded at that same moment. Once the data is gathered, computers run analyses on this information to find any type of correlation between all of those factors and the movement of the financial instrument being studied. The information gathered is important to determining the confidence of investing in a particular stock or bond (Infosys.com, 2016).

There are generally two primary categories for data collection: *structured* and *unstructured*. Structured data is that which is gathered and organized in discrete, predefined categories. Structured data is used when an analyst knows what variables he wants to collect before the data collection begins. It is easy to organize and analyze because everything falls into its prearranged location as soon as it comes in (Sherpasoftware.com, n.d.).

Unstructured data, on the other hand, can be extremely complex and has very little organization to it. There are no predefined categories. Data is simply collected en masse on everything possible related to that which is being studied. This process is often referred to as data mining. A common use for this type of data is customer behavior analysis. A business will simply gather information about every action and characteristic it can related to a customer. It differs from structured data in that a numeric formula cannot simply be ascribed to specified information. The phrase "big data" is often used in reference to this type of data gathering and storage.

Analytics' Entry into Sports

Both methods of analytics have been utilized in many different industries, due to the highly valuable information it can provide. But one area where the scientific study of numbers was traditionally shunned was in sports. Until fairly recently, the prevalent notion was that the outcomes of athletic contests cannot be measured in numbers and that data analysts and business school graduates cannot possibly understand the game like those who play and coach in the respective sport (Silver, 2014). There still is tremendous weight placed on intangible characteristics like team chemistry, individual "heart" and desire and mental toughness. Although these are all valid concepts, it hindered the notion that a player's performance could be predicted with some degree of certainty.

Due to greater technological sophistication, there exists incredibly detailed statistical history of every action of every game. Many are familiar to casual fans: wins, losses, plus/minus ratings, on-base percentage, wins above replacement ("WAR") and save percentages are all statistical information. To data analysts, the question became whether or not to use this and more sophisticated information in a comprehensive manner to help assist teams and athletes in producing optimal results.

Analytics in Baseball

In 1977, Bill James self-published a book titled *The Baseball Abstract: Featuring 18 Categories of Statistical Information That You Just Can't Find Anywhere Else*, which was subsequently updated in 1985 and 2001

(James, 1985, 2001). Throughout the baseball season, James had compiled data from baseball box scores of each game and studied it to find new measures of performance and success. He used statistical calculations and ratios that had not been analyzed previously. He then made this book an annual release, offering his subscribers more of the same each year.

In the 1980s, it was very difficult for fans to obtain detailed statistics on games. Many people did so in a self-help manner: those viewing the game in the stands or at home liked to keep their own box scores. In response, James created a nonprofit organization called Project Scoresheet that worked as a fan network with members committed to logging info about every play of every game they had access to so that they could be published and released to the public. This process would collect all of the data needed to find meaningful knowledge about the performance of the players. Members of this network went on to form STATS, Inc., which quickly became the leading sports statistics database in the world and still continues to this day (Stats.com, 2016).

During this time of increased public awareness and desire for detailed statistics, James, along with others, was developing a new methodology of measuring performance in baseball called sabermetrics, which is derived from the acronym SABR (Society for American Baseball Research) (Sabr. org., 2016). It placed far less weight on the previously utilized measures, such as batting average, runs batted in (RBIs) and earned run average (ERA), in favor of a more statistical approach, similar to the work James had been doing for years. The purpose was to analyze a player's performance in a way that excluded extraneous factors, such as the performance of his teammates or the particular opposing pitcher and fielders. This would provide a true representation of that player's skill and ability, without putting it in the context of the particular situation he was playing in. For example, RBIs are mostly dependent on a teammate being on base when you get a hit. Simply because the teammates that bat ahead of you are not putting themselves in a position to score runs, your statistical measurement, and thus your *own* skill as a hitter, is deemed inferior.

One example of a sabermetric statistic is slugging percentage (SLG), which is used to measure the power of hitters. This is calculated by taking the total bases reached on your hits (one for a single, two for a double, etc.) divided by your total number of at-bats (smartfantasybaseball. com, 2014). Another measure is on-base percentage (OBP), which gives a numerical representation of how often a player gets on base purely through his own efforts (i.e., discounting plays resulting from the fielders' actions, such as fielding errors, fielder's choices and others). It is calculated by adding hits, walks and hit by pitches and dividing that number by the sum of at-bats, walks, hit by pitches and sacrifice flies (Fangraphs.com, 2016a). The equation is as follows: OBP = (H + BB + HBP) / (AB + BB + HBP + SF)].

Probably the most popular and widely used sabermetric statistic is On Base Plus Slugging (OPS), which is simply the sum of the previous two numbers (OBP + SLG). This statistic has become a favorite to compare the hitting abilities of players from different eras, as it helps remove the element of advancements in the game and skewed abilities of the average player over time (Grochowski, 2015). In particular, it applies to the pre-1947 (segregated) era before Jackie Robinson and the period after the breaking of racial barriers in the sport. For example, many felt it was unfair to compare a player from Babe Ruth's era to those in the modern era because Babe Ruth was facing limited competition with no black or Latino players allowed on the field—many of whom were exemplary players in the Negro leagues and would likely be All-Stars if they were allowed to play in the Major Leagues.

A popular sabermetric fielding statistic is fielding independent pitching (FIP), which, as the name implies, removes the variable of the defensive skills of the players behind the pitcher when evaluating that pitcher's ability. It is designed to represent a pitcher's ERA, had that pitcher had the league average defense and luck helping him (beyondtheboxscore.com, 2014). The calculation is somewhat complex:

$$FIP = \frac{13 * HR + 3 * (BB + HBP) - 2 * K}{IP} + C$$

HR represents home runs, BBs are walks, HBP is hit by pitch (number of times a player got on base this way), Ks are strikeouts, IPs are innings pitched and C is a constant that changes for each season and is based on statistical averages from that season. The constant is simply to make the resulting number look more representative to an ERA (fangraphs.com, n.d.).

Another important sabermetric tool to mention is Wins Above Replacement (WAR). It is meant to be the ultimate measure of a player's true value by calculating the number of wins that player provided his team compared to what a readily available replacement at his position would have provided (fangraphs.com, 2016b). In other words, if a second baseman's WAR is 6.3, it means his team would have won 6.3 *fewer* games that season were he to be replaced by an average free agent or minor league second baseman being paid the league minimum. This measure can be extremely valuable for general managers who have to decide how much a player is worth in dollars. But it should be noted that this is a fairly complex calculation and far from a precise measurement.

These relatively modern concepts were gaining traction among fans and some analysts, but they were still rejected by "purists," which encompassed all those working within the sport. The first person credited with not only embracing, but implementing, these measurements in baseball decision making is Sandy Alderson, while working as general manager of the Oakland Athletics. Alderson was an outsider from the start, having no prior professional baseball experience. He had graduated from Harvard Law School and was originally the general counsel for the team. In the mid-1990s, Alderson was given a minimal budget to work with, which made fielding a competitive team difficult. With no traditional bounds to restrain his thinking, he did not hesitate to look for advantages in other ways, which led him to hire Eric Walker, a former aerospace engineer and baseball writer who studied numerical analysis of the sport (Rubin, 2010).

Walker would become the bridge linking the new-age quantitative analysts with the inner circle of team management. Alderson would finally put these studies to practical use. It was taken even further by Alderson's successor, Billy Beane, whose widely publicized adoption brought sabermetrics and sports analytics to the general public when it yielded surprisingly successful results in the face of scrutiny. This became the basis of the book *Moneyball*. Today, numerical analysis in baseball is ubiquitous. Practically every baseball team in the league has incorporated it into their decision making.

Analytics in Basketball

After becoming widely accepted within baseball, the concept of analytics began to spread to other sports, but none have utilized it to quite the same extent. Baseball can be boiled down to a single batter vs. pitcher matchup broken down pitch by pitch, whereas most other team sports have far too many variables in play and other teammates involved in everything that occurs (Holmes, 2014). Of the remaining three major professional American sports, basketball is most conducive to isolating individual player actions throughout the game. That is why it makes sense that numerical analysis has made the most progress in that sport.

Traditional basketball box scores track the basic actions of a player that are easy to recognize and document. They are field goals attempted (FGA), field goals made (FGM), points (PTS), rebounds (REB), assists (AST), steals (STL), blocks (BLK), turnovers (TO) and personal fouls (PF). These numbers can offer a general picture of a player's abilities, but they do not take into account any variables such as teammates and game situations. As an example, a player who averages a lot of points per game is not likely to be as good as someone else averaging the same if one of those players has very high skilled teammates and the other has duds. The player with unskilled teammates is bound to score more because no one else on his team has the competence to do it. Similarly, a player who threads a pass behind the back through three defenders to a teammate he signaled to charge the basket will be credited with the same "1 assist" as a player who simply tossed the ball to the person standing next to him who then hits a shot. There is a lot more that contributes to a player scoring a basket than that player taking the shot. It makes sense that, just as in baseball, a certain subgroup of people looked for ways to account for things like these when comparing players' abilities.

Just like baseball comes down to scoring runs, everything that occurs on a basketball court is done so with the ultimate goal of scoring as many points as possible. Essentially, basketball analytics boils down to determining the average number of points a team will score when they possess the ball or the probability that the team scores any points at all in a given possession. One analytical measure that has been developed is the "expected possession value," or EPV (Goldsberry, 2014). This attempts to account for every possible variable in a given moment, such as which player is holding the ball, the arrangements of the other players on the court (as well as who those players are) and the time left on the shot clock. To quantify exactly how one player contributes to an increase in this number, his "EPV-added" or "points added" value is determined. In theory, this represents how a player affects the overall EPV compared with an average replacement player swapped into the identical situation. The resulting player's "points added" is a number representing how many more points are scored in a game simply by having that player on a team. For example, if a player has a "points added" rating of 2.1, theoretically, his team would average 2.1 more points per game by having him instead of an average replacement. Many players even produce negative points added, which means their teams would actually be better off without them. If accurate, this offers obvious advantages to teams valuing players for trades or for contract negotiations. Further, from a coach's perspective, with all of this data available, one could devise plays that put all of the players in the positions that maximize the EPV of his team on a given possession.

Another advanced statistic used to boil down a player's value to a single number is the Player Efficiency Rating (PER). This has become one of the more well-known of the new statistics, most likely due in part to its developer, John Hollinger, who worked at ESPN and used the PER in front of the mainstream audience. The statistic is designed to measure a player's per-minute performance, taking into account the traditional box score statistics, as well as deducting for negative accomplishments, like turnovers or fouls. There are some questions and criticisms of the process, but the resulting data does produce fairly accurate results (Hollinger, 2011).

Some other advanced basketball statistics are becoming more common. A team's offensive and defensive ratings are calculated by finding the average points scored or points allowed per possession. An "effective field goal percentage" (eFG%) is similar to a traditional measure of field goals made divided by field goals attempted, but it awards a bonus for 3-point shots made, because they are both more difficult and more valuable. The resulting equation is (FGM + 0.5 × 3FGM) / FGA. The player is receiving credit for an extra half FGM for each 3-point shot made. True Shooting Percentage is a similar measure, but one that also accounts for free throws made (sportingcharts.com, n.d.).

The first step to an analytics study—sports or otherwise—is to gather data, and modern-day technology has made this easier than ever. The NBA, for example, has facilitated the collection of data by installing stationary drones with cameras in the rafters of every arena (Lowe, 2013). These cameras capture and log information about every single movement made throughout the game—including the players, referees and the ball. The league gathers all of the data and sells it to the teams for an annual fee (which was about $100,000 as of 2014). Teams can also elect upgraded "add-ons," like software that can track a player's physical exertion, for an additional annual fee. Teams now have an almost overwhelming amount of data to pick through to find that trend that can give them the advantage they are looking for. However, without the manpower and resources to decipher it, the raw data does not offer much.

Just about every NBA team applies advanced statistical analysis in some way, be it through internal analytics professionals or utilizing statistical consultants. Helping propel this movement is the fact that current NBA Commissioner Adam Silver is himself an ardent backer (Lee, 2013).

Analytics in Football

As of 2016, data analytics is still in its early stages in the NFL, but the presence is growing (Fleming, 2013). Still others claim that football analytics has not kept pace with other sports (Causey, 2015). Analytics is growing in college football, although it has been largely limited to major programs that have the economic resources to utilize it (Myberg, 2014). Even if a college football team accumulated the massive amount of data necessary to produce meaningful information, more than likely it does not have the advanced computers or mathematic experts required to make sense of it.

However, high-level statistics and sabermetric-style data have been used to decide on the four teams that would participate in the College Football Playoff (Schlabach, 2014). The committee choosing the teams cannot simply look to the best record, because there are so many teams and there is an extremely wide range in competition talent. Instead the selections are made by subjectively choosing the four best teams, being as objective as possible. But instead of the typical Bowl Championship Series (BCS) methodology of ranking based mostly on record and strength of schedule, the committee was armed with every conceivable data point that may be considered when trying to decipher which team is better than another.

At the time of this writing, there are not many mainstream or standout advanced statistics in football as there are in baseball and basketball. The development of a play is so complex that it makes it difficult to whittle a player's contribution down to a single number. But we are still in the early stages, so it is inevitable that some measures will come to the forefront, much like they did in basketball.

Analytics in Hockey

More and more NHL teams have embraced analytics in determining which players to sign, how long players should be on ice, the quality of play during power play, penalty kills, overtime and types of zone entry (McIndoe, 2014). In the past, the most common data used to determine player effectiveness was the "plus/minus" rating, which simply measured a player's success by the noting if the player was on the ice for his team's goals more often than if that participant was when his team was scored against. Therefore, a player is awarded a "plus" each time he is on the ice when his club scores for an even-strength or shorthanded goal. The player receives a "minus" if he is on the ice for an even-strength or shorthanded goal scored by the opposing club. The difference in these numbers is considered the player's "plus-minus" statistic (NHL.com, n.d.).

The metrics for measuring success have expanded greatly in recent years. Teams utilize more sophisticated metrics, which include the major possession-oriented standards: (1) Corsi and (2) Fenwick (both named after their respective creators). Before discussing each one, it should be noted that they are not pure determinates of puck possession, but rather are proxies or indirect ways to do so. As one commentator stated: "In order to shoot the puck, you have to possess the puck. Since we do not have the technology or another practical way to measure time of possession in hockey, we must employ [Corsi or Fenwick as a] proxy." (JenLC, 2013).

Corsi's formula involves shots *directed* at the goal. It involves shots on goal, shots high, shots wide, shots that get saved and shots that go into the goal. A player who has a positive Corsi has more shots directed toward the opponent's net while he is on the ice at even strength than shots directed toward his own net under the same criteria. It is a far more in-depth version of the old plus/minus standard. For example, let's say that player A is on the ice for 10 shots on behalf of his team during a game. The opposing team takes 3 shots while Player A is on the ice during the game.

Corsi For (CF) = 10
Corsi Against (CA) = 3
Player A +7 Corsi (10 − 3 = 7) on this night

Under the Fenwick formula, the idea is the same, but as noted earlier, the blocked shots are omitted. So, taking our earlier example, let's say of the 10 shots Player A was on the ice for, 2 were blocked by players on the opposing team. The opposing team had 3 shots while Player A was on the ice, but 1 of those was blocked. Because Fenwick excludes blocked shots from the formula, Player A's numbers would look like this:

Fenwick For (FF) = 8
Fenwick Against (FA) = 2
Kane would be a +6 Fenwick (8 − 2 = 6) on this night

(JenLC, 2013)

These figures are often translated into percentages for easier comparison. So, in the first case, Player A would have a 70 percent Corsi and a 75 percent Fenwick rating. Proponents of these statistical standards believe these formulas are reliable metrics for possession because the more shots a team is able to direct toward the net, the longer it controls the puck. However, a high plus Corsi rate does not ensure victory. A team could have many more shots than its opponents and still lose if too many of these shots are wide or saved by a superb goaltender on a given night.

These formulas deal with the typical five skaters vs. five skaters situation in hockey (the goaltender is not included). However, penalties in hockey—more than other sports—affect the numbers of skaters on the ice. If Team A's center was caught engaging in a specified infraction, the team will be short one player on the ice because that player will have to sit for at least two minutes in the penalty box. This may affect the dynamics of the game—and is not reflected in the Corsi or Fenwick ratings.

So, how do we find analytic information for these situations? What players are more effective on the power play (for the team with the player advantage) or the penalty kill (for the team with the player deficit)? One method is to determine which player(s) "draw" the most penalties in a given season, meaning that the player is able—usually through his skills—to lure opposing players to commit penalties, forcing the power play advantage. So, Player A skates around Player B who is "forced" to trip Player A to prevent a goal-scoring opportunity. The players who are best at drawing penalties can give their teams an advantage. If one assumes that a team has an 18 percent chance of scoring a power play goal (which is about the NHL average), then these players can "add" a certain number of goals per season, helping their respective team's standings (Tulsky, 2013).

These are just a few samples of the kind of analytics research and practice that has been utilized in the period from 2010–16. More analytical standards are being developed and it is likely that this area will involve more sports, more data and more analysis in the years ahead.

References

Beyondtheboxscore.com (2014). Retrieved May 20, 2016, from http://www.beyondtheboxscore.com/2014/6/2/5758898/sabermetrics-stats-pitching-stats-learn-sabermetrics Businessdictionary.com (n.d.).

Causey, T. (2015, September 23). The sorry state of football analytics. *Thespread.com*. Retrieved May 23, 2016, from http://thespread.us/sorry-state.html

Definition of analytics. Retrieved May 1, 2016, from http://www.businessdictionary.com/definition/analytics.html

Fangraphs.com (2016a). Fielding independent pitching. Retrieved May 20, 2016, from http://www.fangraphs.com/library/pitching/fip/

Fangraphs.com (2016b). OPS and OPS+. Retrieved May 24, 2016, from http://www.fangraphs.com/library/offense/ops/

Fangraphs.com (2016c). What is war? Retrieved May 24, 2016, from http://www.fangraphs.com/library/misc/war/

Fleming, D. (2013, August 20). The geeks shall inherit the turf. *ESPN.com*. Retrieved May 23, 2016, from http://espn.go.com/nfl/story/_/id/9581177/new-jacksonville-jaguars-coach-gus-bradley-relies-analytics-espn-magazine

Glockner, A. (2014, March 3). Do analytics take the fun out of sports? A dispatch from Sloan. *The big lead*. Retrieved May 22, 2016, from http://thebiglead.com/2014/03/03/do-analytics-take-the-fun-out-of-sports-a-dispatch-from-sloan/

Goldsberry, K. (2014, February 6). Databall. *Grantland.com*. Retrieved May 24, 2016, from http://grantland.com/features/expected-value-possession-nba-analytics/

Grochowski, J. (2015, April 27). Baseball by the numbers: OPS+ not perfect, but it's a useful tool. *Chicago Sun-Times*. Retrieved May 24, 2016, from http://chicago.suntimes.com/sports/baseball-by-the-numbers-ops-not-perfect-but-its-a-useful-tool/

Hollinger, J. (2011, August 8). What is PER? *ESPN.com*. Retrieved May 24, 2016, from http://espn.go.com/nba/columns/story?columnist=hollinger_john&id=2850240

Holmes, B. (2014, March 30). New age of NBA analytics: Advantage or overload? *The Boston Globe*. Retrieved May 24, 2016, from https://www.bostonglobe.com/sports/2014/03/29/new-age-nba-analytics-advantage-overload/1gAim4yKYXGUQ2CTAe7iCO/story.html

Infosys.com (2016). Use of big data technologies in capital markets. Retrieved May 22, 2016, from https://www.infosys.com/industries/financial-services/white-papers/Documents/big-data-analytics.pdf

James, B. (1985). *The Bill James historical baseball abstract*. New York: Villard.

James, B. (2001). *The new Bill James historical baseball abstract*. New York: Free Press.

JenLC (2013, December 4). Stats made simple Part 1: Corsi & Fenwick. *SBNation*. Retrieved March 27, 2016, from http://www.secondcityhockey.com/2013/12/4/5167404/nhl-stats-made-simple-part-1-corsi-fenwick

Lee, M. (2013, October 27). NBA deputy commissioner Adam Silver backs the analytical movement. *The Washington Post*. Retrieved July 15, 2016, from https://www.washingtonpost.com/news/wizards-insider/wp/2013/10/27/nba-deputy-commissioner-adam-silver-backs-the-analytical-movement/

Lowe, Z. (2013, September 4). Seven ways the NBA's new camera system can change the future of basketball. *Grantland.com*. Retrieved May 24, 2016, from http://grantland.com/the-triangle/seven-ways-the-nbas-new-camera-system-can-change-the-future-of-basketball/

McIndoe, S. (2014, September 17). The NHL's analytics awakening. *Grantland*. Retrieved March 27, 2016, from http://grantland.com/the-triangle/the-nhls-analytics-awakening/

Myberg, P. (2014, August 24). Slowly but surely, college football teams embrace analytics. *USA Today*. Retrieved May 24, 2016, from http://www.usatoday.com/story/sports/ncaaf/2014/08/24/college-football-preview-revolution-analytics/14289989/

Plus/minus explained (n.d.). *NHL.com*. Retrieved March 26, 2016, from http://www.nhl.com/ice/page.htm?id=26374

Rubin, A. (2010, October 27). Original A's analyst discusses Alderson. *ESPN.com*. Retrieved May 24, 2016, from http://espn.go.com/blog/new-york/mets/post/_/id/11448/original-as-analyst-discusses-alderson

SABR.org (2016). SABR convention history. Retrieved May 22, 2016, from http://sabr.org/content/sabr-convention-history

Schlabach, M. (2014, August 21). The CFB Playoff's stats gurus. *ESPN.com*. Retrieved May 24, 2016, from http://espn.go.com/college-football/story/_/id/11382331/stats-company-sportsource-analytics-inform-college-football-playoff-selection-committee-decisions

Sherpasoftware.com (n.d.). What's the difference between structured and unstructured data. Retrieved May 23, 2016, from http://www.sherpasoftware.com/blog/structured-and-unstructured-data-what-is-it/

Silver, N. (2014, February 19). The search for intelligent life. *ESPN.com*. Retrieved May 22, 2016, from http://espn.go.com/espn/story/_/id/10476210/nba-mlb-embrace-analytics-nfl-reluctant-espn-magazine

Smartfantasybaseball.com (2014). How do I calculate SGP for slugging percentage? Retrieved May 24, 2016, from http://www.smartfantasybaseball.com/2014/02/how-do-i-calculate-sgp-for-slugging-percentage/

Sportingcharts.com (n.d.). Effective field goal percentage—eFG%. Retrieved May 24, 2016, from http://www.sportingcharts.com/dictionary/nba/effective-field-goal-percentage-efg.aspx

Stats.com (2016). About STATS. Retrieved May 22, 2016, from http://www.stats.com/about/

Tulsky, E. (2013, July 11). Hidden value: Penalty differential. *SBNation*. Retrieved March 28, 2016, from http://www.broadstreethockey.com/2013/7/11/4504236/hidden-value-penalty-differential

11 Sports Injuries

Whether one is a professional athlete or a weekend warrior, almost every participant in sports incurs physical injury at one time or another. Sports such as football and ice hockey pose a risk of injury due to the frequent physical contact between players. Auto racing displays particular danger because of the limited space between drivers racing around an oval track at high speeds. Activities not associated with physical contact also maintain a level of injury risk—recreational jogging and tennis come to mind. Even spectators at sporting events have suffered injuries.

In the majority of cases, sports injuries are minor, but serious, even fatal, accidents do take place. When a fatality results from a sports event, news coverage occurs (Odum, 2015). The same with the death of a fan during a game (Gregory, 2014).

In the past, the media covered an injury suffered by a professional or collegiate athlete that sidelines that athlete for a period of time and adversely affects the team's chances of success. Issues such as the causes and preventions of sports injuries have not been brought to the forefront of public attention until recently, when the effects of repeated concussions in football and hockey have generated attention, debate and litigation (Mihoces & Axon, 2015), in part due to lawsuits filed by retired NFL and NHL players, arguing that the respective leagues and teams did not adequately notify or protect players from these debilitating injuries. This issue will be explored in detail later in this chapter.

Another problem involves disclosure. Whereas the National Football League (NFL) makes its injury information public, other leagues, such as the NHL, do not. In college sports, disclosure of injuries may be limited because the Health Insurance Portability and Accountability Act (HIPAA) and its accompanying privacy regulations restrict the dissemination of individuals' health information. There remains a question as to the amount of protection the law imposes and whether coaches are subject to the privacy rules (Smith, 2014).

The majority of the total number of injuries involves the millions of recreational athletes who participate simply for fun and exercise

(Weisenberger, n.d.). Yet such injuries and deaths receive little coverage because these athletes are largely unknown. That is unfortunate because, statistically, 40 percent of deaths and serious injuries related to athletics occur in swimming, diving and boating, not team contact sports (Appenzeller, 2005, p. 40). Lack of training and lack of supervision are common threads that run through such cases—issues worth focusing on when reporting on the subject.

Despite the litigiousness of American society and the perception that plaintiffs have an easy time winning judgments from juries, difficult legal hurdles exist. Traditionally, the law often immunized liability of other participants, team owners, leagues and schools. The responsibility rested almost solely on the person suffering the injury because he or she assumed the risk of harm or consented to participating in an activity with an inherent risk of harmful bodily contact.

However, recent changes in law and society have made this issue less clear-cut. Although legal victory is far from guaranteed, stakeholders such as sponsors, municipalities, stadium/arena owners and insurance companies may incur liability, with the possibility of considerable damages awarded against one or all of them by juries. The most difficult and increasingly important issues involve not the responsibility of one athlete for injuring another, but lack of adequate protection, such as safety standards provided by third parties to prevent injuries from occurring. This concept, known as risk management, is discussed later in the chapter.

This chapter discusses several topics: (a) the key legal standards governing sports injuries, (b) the consequences of dangerous athletic activities, (c) how sports organizations attempt to minimize the risk of injury to participants and spectators and (d) facility safety in the post-9/11 environment.

Sports injury cases centers on the law of torts. A tort occurs when someone engages in conduct that violates a duty imposed by law resulting in damages to the victim and involves certain levels of *liability* (rather than *guilt* because guilt is a criminal law concept). When a jury hears a tort case, it determines (a) the defendant's liability and (b) the amount of monetary compensation awarded to the victim.

It is important not to confuse torts with criminal law. In tort cases, the injured party, not the state, brings claims. A jury determines liability and a monetary amount for the damages, not a prison term. The standard for proving the tort is less onerous than for a criminal case. Liability is based on a "preponderance of the evidence," whereas a criminal case requires guilt "beyond reasonable doubt"—a high level of certainty.

Who Can Be Liable?

Potentially, tort liability extends to many parties. And plaintiffs sue as many parties as practically possible in an attempt to collect damages from the defendant with the most assets (known as "deep pockets"). Defendants to such lawsuits may include the following parties:

Participants

Participants are those who take part in the event. When one participant commits an intentional, reckless or negligent act against another, liability accrues.

Service Personnel

Teachers, coaches, lifeguards, aerobics instructors and trainers are in this category. Each has a duty of care to the students or participants and may be liable for tortious acts. The liability of coaches and athletic personnel includes failure to provide competent personnel, adequate instruction or proper equipment; failure to warn; failure to supervise; and improperly treating injured athletes. Liability also occurs for violations of association or conference rules and injuries due to the improper design of a facility.

Spectators

Spectator injuries occur during sports events, and it is common to categorize fans as victims—one hit by a foul ball or a hockey puck—rather than producers of the injuries. However, cases where spectators instigate violence against other spectators, or even against athletes and officials, may result in liability against those aggressors. Nevertheless, as discussed later, owners, operators and administrators are also liable for such transgressions, as they have responsibility for the safety of patrons, athletes and officials.

Administrative/Supervisory Personnel

This category includes amateur league officials, school principals and the school districts, with liability based on their supervisory role, rather than participation in the act itself. If a plaintiff can prove that these defendants employed unfit personnel, failed to provide proper supervision, failed to have a supervisory plan, improperly directed an event or athletic program, failed to establish safety rules or comply with existing safety requirements or failed to remedy dangerous conditions, liability (usually negligence) occurs.

Employers

A doctrine known as "vicarious liability" results in employers having responsibility for the acts of employees. Even if the employer shows no fault of his or her own, the employer's liability occurs through the negligent acts of the employees. For example, if an employee of an arena fails to attach portions of the floor of the basketball court correctly and a spectator trips and breaks an ankle, that employer is vicariously liable. However, limitations exist. The employee causing the injury must have acted within the "scope of employment," meaning that the incident occurred during working hours and under the supervision and control of the employer. Courts have to determine how much control and supervision were present at the time of the injury (*Bailey v. Filco, Inc.*, 1996).

Liability

Torts are classified into four basic categories: intentional acts, recklessness, negligence and strict liability. These require different standards of proof. The following describes the basic requirements to determine liability and defenses for the following torts.

Intentional Torts

Intentional torts require the plaintiff to prove that the defendant displayed a desire to injure. Most frequently, intentional torts in sports involve assault and battery cases among participants. Assault is defined as the intent of one person to put another in fear of imminent, unauthorized bodily contact. The battery is that unauthorized contact. Assault and battery tend to occur in body contact sports such as football, ice hockey and soccer. However, considerable difficulties occur when applying these torts in an athletic context. A football tackle, for example, displays an intention to hit another player; the same applies to a body check in hockey.

Legal and practical reasons exist for the difficulty of proving assault and battery lawsuits in sports cases. An important defense known as "consent" applies in a great many situations. If the athletes voluntarily participate in a sport, have knowledge of the risks involved and have an awareness of potential injuries that may occur, consent occurs (van der Smissen, 2003). A football player who steps onto the field consents to being tackled, and a hockey player on the ice consents to bodily contact. For youth and amateur participation, this standard is supplemented with a contract that the participant (or parent) signs, outlining the nature of these risks. The consent defense covers activities within the reasonable contemplation of one who plays a particular sport. For example, an intentional high stick in a hockey game is not permitted and results in a penalty against the wrongdoer. But high sticking occurs in hockey, and the internal rules of the sport attempt to regulate this conduct. Therefore, an assault and battery lawsuit would likely be unsuccessful. When the act goes beyond those boundaries of reasonable activities—legal or illegal in the sport—then the consent defense fails.

Professional athletes are particularly reluctant to bring assault claims to court. Sports organizations, particularly professional leagues, frown on litigation and prefer to enforce penalties against transgressors by their own internal governance. Other players may ridicule the athlete for resorting to courts, rather than the league process (or, in some cases, for defending himself or herself on the field or in the rink). Then the reputation of the athlete and even of siblings entering the sport suffers. In one case, a hockey player for the NHL's Colorado Avalanche considered bringing a lawsuit against a Vancouver Canucks player whose improper body check rendered him unconscious, but decided not to because the victim's brother sought to play in the NHL (Berlet, 2004). Finally, the potential damage recovery may not be worth the effort. Those with guaranteed contracts will, in any event, be paid a salary for the rest of their contract terms.

Recklessness

Reckless conduct does not require intent to render a specific injury, but exists when a player "intends to commit the act but does not intend to harm an opponent." One commentator defined it as "highly unreasonable conduct where a high degree of danger is present" (Keeton, 1984). Recent case law provides that "recklessness exists where a person knows that the act is harmful but fails to realize that it will produce the extreme harm which it did produce" (*Archibald v. Kemble*, 2009).

The leading case defining this concept involved a professional football player who sued an opposing player and team for injuries suffered during an exhibition game in 1973. Dale Hackbart, a safety for the Denver Broncos, attempted to block Charles "Booby" Clark, a rookie running back for Cincinnati. Clark, "acting out of anger and frustration, but without a specific intent to injure," hit Hackbart on the back of the head and forearm. No penalty was called. After the game Hackbart was diagnosed as having a neck injury, ending his career. A federal appeals court concluded that Hackbart had a viable claim for recklessness, rejecting the view that the inherent danger of the sport precluded this action (*Hackbart v. Cincinnati Bengals*, 1979).

Negligence

Negligence, the most heavily utilized tort, is based not on intent, but rather on carelessness. Known as a "fault" standard, a plaintiff alleging negligence must prove that the defendant failed to act in a manner commensurate with a "reasonable person" in the same circumstances. To prove a case of negligence, the injured must show (a) that the defendant (the team, school, doctor) had a duty of care to the injured person, (b) that the duty of care was breached, (c) that the breach foreseeably caused the injury and

(d) that the injured person suffered damages (Goldberg & Zipursky, 2001). Although this standard seems easier than that of intent and recklessness, many claims involving sports injuries are precluded by dangers inherent in the given sport or by clauses in contracts prohibiting such claims.

As a prerequisite to a negligence claim, a duty of care must be present, meaning a legal responsibility of the defendant to the plaintiff. Although at first glance this may not seem difficult to establish, courts in sports injury cases often conclude that the facts fail to establish the duty, as in this example.

A member of a college rugby team broke his neck while participating in a tournament hosted by another college. The plaintiff sued both his school and the hosting school, claiming negligence. He claimed that the hosting school was responsible for the "negligent conduct" of its rugby team because the host school's team held a cocktail party the night before the tournament, even though two matches were scheduled on the next day. The court dismissed the lawsuit against the host school because no legal relationship was found between the parties (*Fox v. Board of Supervisors of Louisiana State University*, 1991).

Another issue involves a duty to warn of potential dangers. Many courts have noted that if the danger is so obvious there is no duty to warn. In 2004, a Massachusetts appeals court overturned a jury award of $486,909 in a lawsuit against the Red Sox filed by a spectator hit by a foul ball. The court concluded that

> even someone with scant knowledge of baseball should realize that a central feature of the game is that batters will forcefully hit balls that may go astray from their intended direction. . . . [The Red Sox] had no duty to warn the plaintiff of the obvious danger of a foul ball.
> (*Costa v. Boston Red Sox Baseball Club*, 2004)

State law may limit the scope of the duty. A majority of courts in the United States have adopted a specialized negligence standard for spectators at sporting events known as the "no duty" or "baseball rule." The rule requires that:

> the proprietor of a ball park need only reasonably provide screening for the area of the field behind home plate where the danger of being struck is greatest, and that such screening must be of sufficient extent to provide adequate protection for as many spectators as reasonably be expected to desire such seating in the course of an ordinary game (*Atkins v. Glen Falls City Sch. Dist.*, 1981). Some courts, however, have refused to adopt the baseball rule, preferring to determine the duty based on general negligence law requirements.
> (*Rountree v. Boise Baseball, LLC*, 2013)

Once it is determined that a duty exists, the focus shifts to the second element—a lack of reasonable care in the defendant's actions. A core concept in the law of negligence, this means that a court compares the defendant's actions with those of a fictitious "reasonable person" under the same circumstances to determine whether a breach of that duty occurred. For example: Would a reasonable trainer permit a player complaining of severe headaches to continue playing? Or would a reasonable physical education teacher permit a student to stand directly behind another who was practicing a golf swing, which might result in severe injury to that student?

The third portion of the negligence requirement concerns whether that breach of duty "caused" the injury. This is a complicated and abstract legal doctrine, and we do not have to engage in in-depth analysis here. For our purposes, causation means a direct or foreseeable connection between the act and the accompanying injury.

Let's take this example: D, a softball player, decides to take batting practice outside an area of the field designated for such practice. He disregards the signs posted in the locker room designating the area for batting practice. While taking practice swings, he hits P, another player, who was standing nearby. P suffers a concussion and a broken cheekbone. Analyzing this case based on the preceding standard, a legal duty existed between players D and P, and D acted below the standard of reasonable care by disregarding the sign and engaging in an activity involving a blunt instrument. Also, the injury to P was a direct result of D's improper activity. Even though D did not seek to hit P, the actions demonstrated negligence.

The preceding case is quite simple; however, negligence cases involving sports are often more complex and involve more than one defendant. A key issue surrounds the role of "supervisory" personnel, such as a coach, teacher, league, school district or, in some cases, sponsor.

The focus of the liability on the supervisory personnel differs from that of the person who committed the act. Here, the liability results from a lack of an adequate safety plan or proper training. For example, if a teacher acted negligently in failing to properly administer first aid to a student who suffered an injury, the principal, the school or the superintendent of the school district can be held liable if that teacher did not possess the requisite first-aid certification mandated by the state's law and that deficiency caused the injury.

The last element of a negligence case involves damages to the victim. This monetary award, normally up to a jury, permits the panel to factor in pain and suffering, lost earnings and earning power and costs of care (Owen, 2007). Punitive damages—a result intended to punish the wrongdoer for his or her actions—are also permitted.

Defenses to Negligence Claims

Defenses to negligence exist. One is contributory negligence, which results if the plaintiff also acted in a negligent manner, contributing to the injury. Contributory negligence traditionally served as a complete defense and resulted in a dismissal of the lawsuit no matter how egregious the defendant's negligence. Even if the plaintiff was slightly negligent, the defendant won the case (Restatement of Torts 2d, 1977, sec. 463).

The harsh results of contributory negligence prompted most states to eliminate that defense and replace it with "comparative negligence." Comparative negligence rules vary from state to state, but basically this concept apportions the damages between the negligent plaintiff and one or more defendants. If both a defendant and plaintiff are deemed negligent, the jury's damage award is reduced to the extent to which the plaintiff contributed to his or her own harm. In some states, negligence plaintiffs can recover some percentage from liable defendants, regardless of the extent of their own negligence, a concept known as "pure" comparative negligence (*Li v. Yellow Cab Co.*, 1975). In other states, in a modified version, plaintiffs are allowed a partial recovery unless the plaintiff is either *more* negligent (greater than 50 percent at fault) than the defendant(s) or equally as negligent as the defendant(s) (*McIntyre v. Balentine*, 1992).

Taking the last example, under a pure comparative negligence system, if a jury determines that the plaintiff was 70 percent at fault and the defendant 30 percent, and the jury awards $100,000 in damages, the plaintiff receives only $30,000. However, under the modified system, the plaintiff cannot recover any award.

The final defense, assumption of risk, ranks as the most important used in sports injury cases. A participant in an athletic activity, who voluntarily and knowingly assumes a risk of harm arising in that activity, cannot recover damages for a negligent act occurring during that activity. Assumption of risk is a defense only in negligence and strict liability cases. Intentional tort claims, as mentioned earlier, employ the defense of consent.

For example, fans attending a baseball game know that a ball may be hit foul and into the stands. They assume the risk of that injury. An amateur hockey player hit by a puck causing injury to his eye also will likely lose any lawsuit on that basis. (Note that professional athletes are barred from most injury lawsuits based on workers' compensation laws, discussed later.) In most states, assumption of risk requires that the risk be "foreseeable." This issue of foreseeability is a key point to ask a lawyer representing any party in a negligence case. The assumption of risk doctrine frequently involves contractual clauses in which participants agree before they can participate in an activity. Participants frequently contract to limit negligence liability arising from an injury in a sports event. Often explicit (known as an express assumption of risk), these limitations clauses are generally enforceable as to activity-related injuries.

Limitation of Liability Clauses

Most organizations that sponsor sports competitions require participants to sign event participation agreements. These contracts contain provisions limiting the liability of sponsors, owners, schools and other organizations in personal injury lawsuits. Known as "agreements to participate," they may include issues such as protective gear requirements, medical prerequisites and the types of care available in case of an emergency.

An example of a simple agreement to participate follows:

> The undersigned is voluntarily participating in the above event, and assumes all risks associated with participating in that event, including, but not limited to, falls, contact with other participants, spectators or others, the conditions on the location of the event and surrounding areas, and the effect of the weather, including heat and/ or humidity, all such risks being known and appreciated by me. Having read this Waiver and knowing these facts, and in consideration of your acceptance of this application, the undersigned, for him/herself, and anyone entitled to act on his/her behalf, waive and release New York Road Runners, Inc., New York Road Runners Foundation, Inc., Road Runners Club of America, USA Track & Field, the City of New York and its agencies and departments, the Metropolitan Athletics Congress, and all sponsors of the event, if any, and the representatives and successors of the foregoing persons and entities, from present and future claims and liabilities of any kind, known or unknown, arising out of the undersigned's participation in this event or related activities, even though such claim or liability may arise out of negligence or fault on the part of any of the foregoing persons or entities.
>
> (New York Road Runners, 2014)

For those participants under the age of eighteen years, a parent or guardian must sign; otherwise, the waiver may not be enforceable because the minor lacked the legal right to consummate the contract. Note that the agreement serves as evidence of notification of the risks involved.

Courts tend to scrutinize these agreements to ensure that they are not manifestly one-sided. If so determined, a court can strike them down as "unconscionable" and the injured person may sue based on traditional tort concepts. Most states do not enforce a clause that "limits all liability to the presenting organization, league, school, coach and other participants," even if signed with free will. Instead, the courts usually enforce a clause limiting liability for negligence, but not for intentional torts such as assault and battery (Connell & Savage, 2003). The language in such agreements must be clear and concise. If not, courts may refuse to enforce them on the basis of public policy.

Strict Product Liability

It is possible that the equipment utilized in participating in a sports event may be defective in some manner, and in the last half-century, the law expanded to protect the public from injury from such defective goods. Known as "strict product liability," it is an expansion from traditional negligence and the doctrine imposes liability for acts that lack intent or fault on the part of the defendant for products that are deemed "unreasonably dangerous." Product liability cases focus on defects in design, manufacture or warnings making the product unreasonably dangerous, rather than the actions of individual players, coaches or supervisory personnel. The reason or cause of the defect is not important—it's the dangerous defect that becomes central. Liability extends to both manufacturers and retailers, as long as a third party does not alter the product.

Note that the "no-fault" standard of product liability does not guarantee liability. Many of these lawsuits fail to make it to court because of the difficulties in determining "defect," "unreasonable dangerousness" and "cause." Also, the defense of assumption of risk may be applicable.

As a result of product liability litigation, manufacturers attempt to limit their liability by posting warnings on both the product and in the instructions. They should carefully craft the language in the advertising, marketing and promotion of the product. Clear and unambiguous warnings should mark the packaging as well. Product liability lawsuits center on athletic equipment. Frequent claims allege design defects in football helmets. Some plaintiffs have suffered tragic consequences, such as quadriplegia or head injury (*Arnold v. Riddell Sports*, 1994; *Rodriguez v. Riddell Sports*, 1999).

State Law Immunity

States and localities are favored defendants in personal injury lawsuits because of their "deep pockets"—considerable resources to pay legal judgments. A bar to unfettered lawsuits against these defendants is the use of "sovereign immunity," a traditional doctrine aimed to protect the state from lawsuits for its actions. Many jurisdictions retain laws limiting lawsuits; others have granted permission for parties to sue them. If a plaintiff sues a town for an injury sustained in a town park, claiming negligence due to inadequate supervision, the existence of an immunity law may prohibit the lawsuit. Even when lawsuits are allowed, states and localities can require "notice of claims" filed in an expedited manner or mandate that the trial be held before a judge, not a jury (New York General Municipal Law, sec. 50e; New York Court of Claims Act, sec. 12).

Medical Malpractice

The issue of the conduct of medical personnel in servicing athletes (and sometimes spectators) has two distinct components: the malpractice of the physician or emergency medical technician and the responsibility of the team or organization for that conduct. Often, the distinction between the two is blurred.

First, consider the malpractice of physicians, trainers and emergency medical technicians. Similar to negligence, medical professionals have a duty to the patient to exercise the level of care that a reasonable medical expert of their level of training would provide, given the circumstances. If the care falls below that standard and causes or exacerbates the injuries, liability accrues—for example, when a doctor performs duties below a general, competent standard, or when a trainer fails to promptly refer an injured athlete to a physician for evaluation and treatment (Mitten, 1999).

Over the last three decades, the rise of sports medicine as a distinct specialty and the increase in the quality of medical care in general has increased the standards of "reasonable care." Professional teams often employ sports physicians as consultants and, even if that is not the case, most franchises are located in cities with major medical centers. On the collegiate and high school level, presenters of sports events commonly have some emergency medical assistance on hand or nearby. The failure to do so may result in negligence. Courts appear to be most receptive to suits by athletes alleging that a physician or athletic trainer has improperly treated their injury, thereby causing "enhanced harm" to the athlete. In addition, courts have found that an athlete has a valid claim against a physician for improperly providing medical clearance to resume or continue playing a sport, or failing to fully inform the athlete of the material risks of athletic participation with his or her medical condition (Mitten, 1999).

However, courts have dismissed negligence suits by athletes against team physicians and athletic trainers employed by public educational institutions based on state immunity laws. On the professional side, many lawsuits against teams and team physicians have been dismissed under state workers' compensation laws prohibiting employees from suing employers or other employees for negligence. These laws provide back wages and compensation for medical costs to victims of work-related injuries. They do not require fault, but, in return, injured employees give up the right to sue their employers for damages. For one who is injured by falling on a loading dock and experiences a temporary backache, this system works reasonably well. But for athletes whose careers end prematurely or who experience permanent injury, workers' compensation is a difficult barrier. If the team doctor is an "employee" of the team, many states bar or limit suits against the employer and the doctor under workers' compensation (*McLeod v. Blase*, 2008).

Often the relationship between the team physician and the athlete differs from the typical doctor–patient relationship. In a typical scenario, the doctor serves the patient, not the employer. Communications are confidential, protected by the doctor–patient relationship. In the case of team doctors, the physician receives payment from the team and works for the team. The duty of reasonable care in skill and treatment remains, but questions of confidentiality, conflict of interest and loyalty surface, especially when the medical advice or treatment results in an incomplete recovery or, worse, in a permanent injury (DiCello, 2001).

Athletes who allege that they were "forced" to play despite their injuries include the former National Basketball Association (NBA) player Bill Walton. In order to play, Walton claimed he "reluctantly accepted" injections of cortisone and Novocain and ingested other medications for several years. Walton eventually settled a lawsuit filed against his former team, the Portland Trail Blazers (Habib, 2002).

In 2002, a New Jersey jury awarded the former Philadelphia Flyers defenseman Dave Babych $1.37 million for his claim against the Flyers' team doctor. Babych alleged that the doctor "deviated from standard medical practice" and "failed to inform Babych of the ramifications of playing with the injury" (Roberts & Conrad, 2002).

The traditional arrangements between a team and its medical professionals have been changing. Due to the increasingly competitive health-care market, hospitals and medical practices have sought to pay professional teams for the right to treat their players. In addition to the revenue, sports franchises get the services of the provider's physicians either free of charge or at substantially discounted rates. In return, the medical groups and the hospitals obtain the exclusive right to market themselves as the team's official hospital, health maintenance organization or orthopedic group.

Critics argue that such team doctors are "ethically compromised" because they are employed by an organization that prefers that their patients return to work as soon as possible. Doctors, understandably, are among the critics of hospital sponsorship deals. For example, former

Atlanta Falcons team doctor Andrew Bishop told the *New York Times* in 2004 he would resign if the team entered such a deal, arguing that

> [i]t compromises you as a physician. The perception is that if this individual was so eager to do this he's willing to pay to do it, then he's going to do whatever management wants to keep the job he paid for.
>
> (Eifling, 2013)

To be fair, professional athletes can opt out from this policy and see doctors of their choice, but for college and high school athletes with limited resources, that may not be an option.

Note that an imperfect result does not automatically make the doctor or the team liable. Athletes share responsibility. Often, the athlete pressures the physician for certification to play. Professional athletes realize their tenure is limited and do not want to end their careers prematurely because of being sidelined by an injury.

Risk Management

The bulk of the preceding text focused on remedies following a personal injury. This portion details attempts by leagues, teams and facility operators to *reduce* the risk of injury. This concept, known as *risk management*, involves the planning and logistics of a sports event, whether it is the Super Bowl or a local high school soccer game. The failure to adequately cover potential risk may result in injuries, bad publicity, the diminution of the reputation of the organization or team (or even sponsor) and, of course, litigation. The goal of risk management is first to minimize the amount of injury overall and second to ensure that, when injury does occur, someone else pays.

In a sports setting, risk management involves many stakeholders: players, coaches, managers, teams, facility owners, the equipment manufacturers, vendors, spectators and the media. A well-organized and safe event is the goal. The potential for mishaps is high, and it behooves the organizations sponsoring or running the event to attempt to limit the injuries that occur on their watch. Think of the possibilities: a riot in or outside the facility, people falling over slippery surfaces, inebriated fans, a natural disaster or a terrorist attack. Risk management procedures include planning to provide a prompt response to incidents. Organizers of an event should establish a response team and develop a well-defined strategy so that each member of that team knows what to do (Appenzeller, 2005, p. 44).

As noted earlier in the chapter, all sports club participants should be required to sign a waiver or release form prior to participating. But this only scratches the surface of risk management. Presenters, including sports clubs, leagues and stadium or arena owners or sponsors, should develop a disaster handbook, obtain insurance, provide equipment and facilities fit for that particular use (which they should inspect regularly) and develop an emergency medical plan (Appenzeller, 2005). Often, they consult with independent firms specializing in this kind of work. A good risk assessor sizes up the potential risk of the event or events. Journalists covering an incident should inquire about the level of risk prevention planning involved.

Common Risk Management Issues

Athlete Protection

The stabbing of women's tennis star Monica Seles in 1993 by a deranged fan and the assault on figure skater Nancy Kerrigan in 1994 resulted from security breakdowns. In the latter case, the only transportation provided by the organizing committee hosting the U.S. National Figure Skating Championship was a hotel shuttle van with no security protection (Graham, Neirotti, & Goldblatt, 2001). Event promoters, teams and leagues must have plans to protect the talent. First comes the identification of potential harms. Who had access to the dressing room areas? Did he or she enter from restricted entrances? What kind of security detail existed? What steps were taken to prevent fans from going on to the playing area? Were the athletes made aware of the security protections available to them? In the case of a team, did the coaches and general managers know the extent of the protection?

Financial Protection

During many sporting events, significant amounts of cash change hands. Purchases of food, beverages, souvenirs and payment of game-day tickets result in the need to store the money to prevent theft. Where was the money kept? And, in the case of credit card information, were the records secured in password-protected computers? Other questions include: How was the theft or loss discovered? What access did employees have to the information?

Crime Prevention

No organization guarantees spectator safety from criminal acts, such as thefts of wallets and pocketbooks. Frequently, the victims carelessly left these items in open pockets or simply hanging on a seat. But what if the facility gave access to non–ticket holders through an unguarded passage? In one example, at (now destroyed) R.F.K. Stadium in Washington, D.C., it was discovered that kids would sneak under the end of zone bleacher seats and steal bags and purses. To prevent this, fences with gates had to be constructed to close off the ends of the bleachers and ushers placed at every gate (Graham, Neirotti, & Goldblatt, 2001). After a number of fans, upset over a controversial boxing decision, threw chairs into the ring in Madison Square Garden, resulting in a number of injuries and arrests, it was reported that only seventy security guards and fifty ushers serviced the entire arena (Schultz, 1996). In the wake of greater needs for security, stadiums and arenas have had to increase their security.

Searches of Personal Belongings

Since the terrorist attacks on September 11, 2001, many sports facilities have limited what items can be brought into the facility, and many have implemented inspection checkpoints (Yankees.com, 2010). More recently, Major League Baseball instituted league-wide security measures for all its teams' ballparks, including mandatory metal detection security and bag checks (Associated Press, 2014). Many teams and leagues, notably the NFL, have worked with the Department of Homeland Security to establish a common protocol of safety procedures for their venues. In doing so, all of the NFL's stadiums and a number of baseball stadiums have earned a "Safety Act" designation, including Yankee Stadium, Citi Field (both in New York City) and Comerica Park (Detroit) (Broughton, 2015) These measures, designed to prevent terrorist acts in marquee sports events, have increased facilities' operating costs and burdened fans by delaying their entrance. Yet, if event planners did not take such action and a terrorist act occurred, questions would surely arise as to the adequacy of the precautions.

Terrorism

Terrorist attacks are not new to sports. Internationally, the most infamous attack occurred during the 1972 Munich Summer Games, when Palestinian terrorists killed twelve members of the Israeli Olympic team. However, the issue has become more acute in the United States and elsewhere since the September 11th attacks and the rise of terrorist acts in Europe, which has resulted in attacks in Madrid, London and, most recently, in Paris and Brussels in 2015 and 2016. The most serious terrorist attack during a U.S. sporting event occurred in Boston, during the running of its famed marathon in 2013. Two explosions on the finish line resulting in three deaths and 264 injuries brought renewed focus on the dangers of hosting large outdoor events. Since then sports organizations have spent more on security—both on personnel and on technology. More recently constructed facilities have an advantage because construction has incorporated improved security, such as advanced software that uses cameras and sensors to detect any security breaches and notify law enforcement agencies in real time of such threats (Roberts, 2015).

The federal government has classified sports events based on a rating level. A "level 1" constitutes a high threat level and has been reserved for events such as the Super Bowl. Level 4 denotes a minimum threat level. The higher the assessment level, the more involved the federal government's Department of Homeland Security becomes (Mihalek, 2014). And, for major events, the team, league and stadium facilities officials work with local police and the FBI to provide counterintelligence and security analysis. Additional security personnel remains the best option for improving security, but private security, coupled with improved technology and increased insurance costs, adds to the price of a ticket.

Credentialing

For the press, access to nonpublic areas of the facility requires credentials. Often, the sports organization or presenter issues the credentials, and a person without the proper credentials lacks the access needed to adequately cover the event. In the case of a team playing a number of games at "their" stadium or arena, the credential procedures are well known to editors and reporters. But for an individual event, such as a national competition, the organizers must specifically state the requirements and procedures for seeking credentials. It also helps to give the credential holder proper directions and rights. Often, the presenters will not "advertise" these areas to prevent the general public from seeking access.

Staffing

As noted earlier, for major events, private firms, working with local police, handle security matters. Hiring those employees involves a "reasonable" job search. In many cases, these firms do not advertise, but hire based on referrals. If a staff member embezzles money from an event, the question becomes whether the security firm failed to adequately check that employee's background. Or, if the security staff members carry weapons, what is the nature of their training? Note that laws regulating such training vary, so no uniform standard exists.

Ingress and Egress

How quick and easy is it to enter and exit the facility? Are the exits well marked and easy to find? In older or smaller venues, the issue deserves particular attention when a crowd control problem or riot occurs. Questions to ask include: How many exits exist? Are the exits well marked? How do disabled spectators exit in an emergency?

Pyrotechnics

As part of the entertainment, many sports events feature half-time, pre-game or postgame shows involving special effects, such as smoke and fireworks. If problems occur, questions should be asked about whether the producers of the show and the sports event complied with local fire code requirements.

Use of the Public Address System

What kinds of announcements are made on the facility's public address system? Often, announcements notifying fans of risk of injury from foul balls or hockey pucks are broadcast during sports events. But what announcements occur in the event of an emergency? Are they audible? Presenters should script such announcements in advance to ensure that announcers do not "ad lib" any statements.

Outside Climate and Indoor Climate Control

What is done in the event of inclement weather? If the weather forecast calls for snow or ice, this mandates the existence of procedures alerting the staff to clear passageways and stairways. Bad weather *before* an event requires greater steps. The clearance of snow and ice prevents injuries and ugly occurrences, such as the throwing of snowballs onto the field. Snowball incidents at a few NFL games caused injury to those on the field and raised questions about the organizational planning of the event (Freeman, 1995). For indoor events, the facility engineers should frequently test the climate control system.

Medical Emergencies

It has become standard to have some medical personnel on the premises in the event of an unanticipated need. Particular challenges occur in events that take place over a large area, such as a marathon, where water stations, medical technicians and transportation are spaced through the entire course. Because of its world-class medical facilities and medical schools, Boston was very well prepared for the 2013 marathon terrorist bombing (Gawande, 2013). But not every location has those kinds of facilities and trained personnel. Nevertheless, questions should focus around the training, accessibility and amount of the equipment and personnel. Even if one operates a park or gym used by the general public, questions regarding the first-aid training and other qualifications of personnel may exist.

Alcohol and Public Safety

In 1974 the Cleveland Indians hosted the Texas Rangers in a game at which over 25,000 fans consumed more than 65,000 cups of beer that night—thanks to the 10-cents-a-cup promotion. Not surprisingly, the crowd became unruly, and some fans ran onto the field and attacked players, who feared for their lives. The Indians were forced to forfeit the game (Johnson, 2008). In an article published shortly after the melée between fans and players at a 2004 game between the NBA's Indiana Pacers and Detroit Pistons, George Hacker, the alcohol policies project director at the Center for Science in the Public Interest, a nonprofit health advocacy group, summed up the source of the problem. "It's the beer talking," Hacker said. "Most people don't do that kind of stuff when they're sober. Who in their right mind wants to attack a big athlete? You've got to be nuts to do that" (McAllister, 2004).

As a result of the violence, the NBA created a "Fan Code of Conduct," which sets forth expected standards for all attendees of NBA games. It also restricts the size of drinks to twenty-four ounces and limits purchase to two drinks at a time. The guidelines prevent alcohol sales after the fourth quarter begins. Other leagues do not have a uniform policy, but many teams stop beer sales after a certain point in the event. However, prevention of dangerous incidents may involve greater measures. However, a complete ban on alcohol sales is highly unlikely, given the adverse fan reaction and the importance of beer advertising in sports.

Criminal Law and Sports

This text does not cover criminal law issues in sports in great detail, despite the seeming frequency of the connection between crimes and athletes. Highly publicized athlete-defendant trials such as those of O. J. Simpson, Kobe Bryant and Michael Vick received considerable media coverage. More recently, domestic abuse arrests of Ray Rice (Baltimore Ravens) and Adrian Peterson (Minnesota Vikings) have generated considerable discussion and debate. But the issues involving most criminal charges against athletes are not related to their sport or sports in general. And the laws and procedures utilized are the same as those against any defendant.

The notoriety of elite athletes cuts two ways. They are subject to public scrutiny because they are public figures and their actions could be targeted by ambitious prosecutors. Yet, they often have the financial wherewithal to afford high-price counsel and crisis management experts.

Athletes, especially star athletes, enjoy a great deal of press coverage, a fact well known to prosecutors, who ultimately have the discretion to bring charges (victims of crimes do not make the decision). The prosecutors' discretion, often based on strategic as well as legal reasons, is rarely second-guessed by courts. For prosecutors, conviction is the goal—and the favorable publicity resulting from the conviction of a high-profile athlete can lead to public acclaim for that prosecutor.

The Kobe Bryant sexual assault case in 2003 demonstrates a powerful interplay between a famous athlete with high-powered legal representation and an aggressive local district attorney. Ultimately, it turned out to be a fiasco for the district attorney, who was forced to drop the sexual assault charges because the victim chose not to proceed with the trial. Some of the mistakes included staff members of the trial judge inadvertently releasing *in camera* (closed hearing) transcripts with the name of the victim (a violation of Colorado's rape shield law) and then the judge demanding a "gag order" barring publication of those transcripts. The Colorado Supreme Court, in a 4–3 ruling, permitted their publication (*People v. Kobe Bryant,* 2004). Had a trial occurred, it is likely that the superior quality of Bryant's attorneys would have outshone those of a rural district attorney's office, especially in a case where the alleged victim's sexual activities could be an issue. Yet high-quality lawyers do not necessarily win in the court of public opinion. Although the tactics they utilize may work in a courtroom, the athlete may suffer a loss of reputation even if an acquittal results. Therefore, wealthy athletes often hire public relations experts to deal with the public fallout. In the case of Bryant, his reputation was saved by his success on the court. As one commentator wrote: "When the Lakers started hoisting the Larry O'Brian [championship] trophy multiple times, the perception of Kobe went from villain to hero very quickly" (Crouse, 2010).

Criminal charges against athletes are not a rare occurrence. This raises the question of whether there is more such activity today than in the past. Some have argued that professional athletes are held to a higher standard (Robinson, 1998), whereas others see the opposite (*Harvard Law Review*, 1996). Certain commentators have suggested that there is a greater incidence of off-the-field criminal activity, drug-related gambling and domestic violence by athletes for three reasons: (a) athletes are conditioned to believe that the rules do not apply to them, (b) the subculture of sports perpetuates violence and drug use and (c) the subculture of sports glorifies violence and denigrates women (Cart, 1995; Nack & Munson, 1995).

Examples of On-Field Criminal Activity

Although violent activity occurs at football fields, hockey rinks and basketball courts almost every day, participants rarely are charged with criminal conduct. District attorneys are reluctant to get involved in matters traditionally handled under the enforcement powers of a professional or amateur sports organization. What may constitute a criminal assault outside of sports could be within the rules of the game. However, egregious acts do occur, and in such cases players have been criminally charged.

In 2000, the chief prosecutor in Vancouver, British Columbia, charged the then-Boston Bruins player Marty McSorley with assault after he hit Vancouver Canuck Donald Brashear from behind with his stick. A quick two-handed swing of his stick clubbed Brashear on the side of his face. Brashear suffered a severe concussion and was hospitalized. McSorley was handed a one-year suspension from the NHL and was found guilty of assault with a weapon by a provincial court in British Columbia. The trial judge rejected McSorley's defense that the act occurred during the "heat of the game" (*Regina v. McSorley*, 2000).

A different result occurred in a 1969 NHL exhibition game. Ontario prosecutors charged Edward "Ted" Green and Wayne Maki with assault for a harrowing on-ice incident. It began when Green hit Maki in the face with his gloved hand and in the shoulder with his stick. A fight then erupted in which Maki ultimately fractured Green's skull. Both players were acquitted, however, based on their "consent" to play a violent sport (*Regina v. Green*, 1970; *Regina v. Maki*, 1970).

In 2004 another NHL player, Todd Bertuzzi, was charged with assault causing bodily harm over an on-ice incident in which he gave a behind-the-head punch to an opponent. Steve Moore, the injured player, was carried off the ice unconscious. He suffered two fractured vertebrae and concussion-related symptoms. He was not able to resume his career. The charge carried a maximum penalty of ten years in jail. The NHL suspended Bertuzzi indefinitely, causing him to miss the remaining thirteen games of the regular season and the playoffs with a corresponding loss of $500,000 in salary. However, in a plea bargain, the British Columbia court sentenced Bertuzzi to a conditional discharge that also included a $500 fine and eighty hours of community service (Joyce, 2004). In 2014, a civil lawsuit filed by Moore against Bertuzzi, the Canucks and the team's parent company was settled for an undisclosed amount (Peters, 2014). Both this incident and the McSorley case a few years earlier received heavy media attention. Because the actions were recorded, millions viewed the injury.

Many other examples of potentially criminal conduct occur that have not been prosecuted, such as the infamous choking of the then-Golden State Warriors coach P. J. Carlessimo by player Latrell Sprewell during a practice in 1997. Another instance was the 1977 mauling of NBA player Rudy Tomjanovich (of the Houston Rockets) by Kermit Washington of the Los Angeles Lakers. Tomjanovich suffered several bone fractures, a brain concussion and leakage of spinal fluid from the brain cavity; the blow ended Tomjanovich's career as a professional basketball player (*Newsweek*, 1977; Howard, 2003).

Criminal prosecution and civil injuries arising from injuries and deaths caused in the ring are nonexistent because the nature of the sport sanctions assault. In the history of boxing, deaths in the ring, though rare, have occurred. In 1930, Frankie Campbell died after a knockout by Max Baer. Four decades later, Emil Griffith knocked out Benny "Kid" Parente, and the brain damage was so severe that he died. On April 2, 2005, Becky Zerlentes became the first female boxer to die as a result of a punch, received during a Colorado Golden Gloves match. She died the next day from "blunt force trauma" to her head (Bianculli, 2005). More recently, super featherweight Davie Browne died one week after suffering brain injuries in the last minute of a fight in 2015 (Guardian, 2015).

Ethical Issue: Who Is Responsible for Player Concussions?

The condition of a number of former NFL players who have been incapacitated by head injuries deriving from their playing experience has been well reported in recent years (Crossman, 2007). The long-term effects of the concussions received from on-field hits and the lack of treatment for the cumulative effects of these injuries have resulted in dementia, early-onset Alzheimer's disease and depression. Not only serious, concussions are frequent. The NFL reports approximately one concussion every two games. Given that the NFL stages about 320 games per year that translates to about 160 reported concussions per season (Benjamin, 2009).

In recent years, greater awareness of the disabilities of retired NFL and NHL players has generated debate as to whether these and other leagues, teams, colleges and high schools have done enough to protect their players from concussions and their resulting effects. In 2011, seventy-three former NFL players filed suit in California against the NFL alleging that the league failed to take reasonable actions to protect players from the chronic risks created by concussive head injuries and fraudulently concealed those risks from players. Since then, about 5000 players filed similar lawsuits against the NFL, which were consolidated into a single class-action lawsuit (*In re National Football League Players' Concussion Injury Litigation*, 2015).

In their complaints, the NFL players alleged that the NFL failed to meet its duty to provide players with rules and information that protect players from short- and long-term health risks, including the risks of repetitive mild traumatic brain injury (*In re National Football League Players' Concussion Injury Litigation*, 2015). Instead, as concern about head injuries in contact sports grew in the medical community, the NFL chose to insert itself into the discussion regarding these dangers. For example, in 1994, the NFL created the Mild Traumatic Brain Injury Committee ("MTBI

Committee") to study the effects of concussions on players (Ezell, 2013). Over the next decade and a half, the MTBI Committee would publish several scientific papers denying a link between concussions and long-term effects on brain function (Mihoces, 2013). By contrast, research from multiple professional sources suggested otherwise—more specifically, that the "onset of dementia-related syndromes may be initiated by repetitive cerebral concussions in professional football players" and that "players with a history of three of more concussions are at a significantly greater risk for having depressive episodes later in life compared with those players with no history of concussion" (Ezell, 2013). However, in 2009, the NFL acknowledged for the first time the long-term effects presented by repeat concussions, giving credence to the cascade of litigation that would soon follow (Schwarz, 2009).

Rather than face protracted litigation, or worse, admission of wrong-doing, the NFL and the players' group reached a settlement. In 2015, U.S. District Judge Anita Brody issued final approval of the proposed settlement. It consists of the creation of a monetary award fund that has no cap (a revision from the original settlement proposal, which capped the amount at about $765 million); to provide compensation for retired players who submit sufficient proof of concussion-related brain injuries and a $75 million "baseline assessment program" providing eligible retired players with free examinations of their neurological functioning and medical monitoring for players to determine if they qualify for payment. Funds from this pool will be used to provide supplemental benefits, such as prescription drug benefits. Finally, the agreement provides for the establishment of a fund to educate the class of former players regarding the medical and disability benefits available for those eligible and to promote safety and injury prevention for football players of all ages. The maximum individual payment can be $5 million. A federal appeals court upheld the judge's determination, concluding that "although not perfect, it is fair" (*In re National Football League Players' Concussion Injury Litigation*, 2016).

The NFL insisted that all retired players—not just the 5000 who joined the class-action suit—be covered by the settlement as a way to prevent lawsuits in the future (Belson, 2015). Many players have criticized this landmark deal. Since the settlement was approved, nearly 90 plaintiffs have chosen to appeal the ruling and an additional 200 plaintiffs opted out of the settlement to preserve their right to continue fighting the league (Epstein, 2015). Critics of the settlement argue that the quantity and variety of diseases covered by the deal are too small and that the settlement needs to acknowledge more classes of plaintiffs, not only those with diagnosable diseases and those without them (Belson, 2015). For example, the settlement covers expenses for treatment of neurological disorders including Alzheimer's disease, Parkinson's disease and dementia, but does not cover chronic traumatic encephalopathy (CTE)—a debilitating condition that is believed to cause depression, aggression and loss of memory and motor skills. Notwithstanding the CTE-related deaths of prominent former players, such as Pittsburgh Steelers center Mike Webster and San Diego Chargers linebacker Junior Seau, Judge Brody challenged the legitimacy of clinical studies on CTE, questioning whether the disease progresses over time and whether it even causes various accompanying symptoms (Epstein, 2015). However, a new study has revealed that CTE may be even more prevalent among football players than previously thought. Of ninety-one former NFL players who donated their brains for research after death, eighty-seven tested positive for CTE (Barrabi, 2015).

In late 2013, a group of former NHL players filed suit against the NHL alleging concussion-related injuries (Harrison, 2015). At the time of writing, there has been no resolution to this case. The league has taken the position that there is no proven connection between concussions and CTE (Branch, 2016).

A point not often discussed has been whether the NFL players would have fared better in a jury trial than in this settlement. One element that must be proven in a personal injury case of this kind is whether the alleged inactions of the NFL directly caused the injuries. This question is not an easy one because the evidence has to be fairly conclusive (in legal parlance, foreseeable) that the NFL's actions caused the concussions that led to the subsequent injuries for the case to be successful. Given that football players may have received concussions in high school or college, it is hard to say whether the actions of the player while in the NFL caused these injuries. In the settlement, the NFL conceded the causation issue (*In re National Football League Players' Concussion Injury Litigation,* 2015). If a trial would occur, it would take more time, difficulty and expense for each athlete to prove the causal connection, even though the league did admit that possibility in 2016 (Belson & Schwarz, 2016).

There also has been litigation involving former college players. In 2016, a federal judge approved a $75 million settlement of a class-action concussions case against the NCAA. The money is to be used to set up a fifty-year, $70 million medical monitoring program for college athletes and a new $5 million program "to research the prevention, treatment, and/or effects of concussions." All current and former NCAA student-athletes are eligible (Berkowitz, 2016).

A number of ethical questions result: First, do you think that the NFL settlement adequately represented the interests of the players? Do you think that the settlement benefits players, who, despite their injuries, were paid (in some cases fairly well paid) for their services? Do you think that, despite the settlement with the NCAA, college players are shortchanged and whether the NFL should have established a broader trust fund to deal with claims of those students? What about the role of the colleges and high schools to engage in greater protection for football players?

Finally, the question becomes whether football, in its present form, should even be played by youngsters. Should the rules change to make it safer? And, if so, how would you change the rules? Do you think that recent studies showing more parental concern over the dangers of football could threaten the existence of the sport?

The problem is not limited to NFL players. High school football players alone suffer 43,000 to 67,000 concussions per year, though the true incidence is likely to be much higher, as more than 50 percent of concussed athletes are suspected of failing to report their symptoms (Gregory, 2010). For the players, the dangers are real, but, unlike professional players, interscholastic football involves young people who are, for the most part, minors. Should rules be changed to provide extra protection? Legally, should courts expand liability rules by limiting the effect of releases and waivers? Should the state scholastic associations mandate insurance and a no-fault payment system to avoid costly and time-consuming litigation?

Chapter Assignment: The Very Hot Marathon

After reading about the economic success of marathon races all over the United States, the Ames Road Runners Club, a not-for-profit entity not affiliated with any local or state government, agreed to create and host an annual marathon. To make it an attractive and unique event, the organizers created a course that utilized the geography of the city of Ames. The city and its environs are hilly. There is a portion of the course that requires runners to race over a dirt road for three miles because this portion displays a panoramic view of the surrounding mountains and glacial lakes that are associated with Ames and its surroundings. The rest of the course consists of paved roads. Miles 1 to 5 feature a gentle uphill, miles 6 to 9 a steep downhill, miles 10 to 14 a steep uphill and miles 15 to 17 the dirt road. The rest of the 26.2-mile course is a gradual downhill to the finish. At its height, the course goes to 4000 feet above sea level; at start and finish, it is 1500 feet above sea level. These differences are greater than found in 90 percent of competitive marathons in the United States, but within the guidelines of the American Runners' Association, the organization that sanctions such events.

The participation agreement, required to be signed by each participant states:

Participation Agreement and Liability Release

I acknowledge that this athletic activity is a test of a person's physical and mental limits and carries with it the potential for death, serious injury and property loss. The risks include, but are not limited to, those caused by terrain, facilities, temperature, weather, my personal health conditions, equipment, vehicular traffic, actions of other people, including but not limited to, participants, volunteers, spectators, trainers, event officials, and event monitors, and/or producers of the event, and lack of hydration. I hereby assume all risks of participating in this activity. I realize that I release the above-mentioned people from any and all liability, including liability for dangerous or defective equipment or property owned, from any improper and reckless and intentional conduct by medical personnel, including, but not limited to, physicians, trainers, emergency medical technicians, ambulance drivers, as well as hospitals, clinics and any other recovery facility in the City of Ames. The City of Ames is also released from any or all liability.

There are no standards or requirements to be eligible to run. Any person can enter, and selection is done by a lottery system.

The race was scheduled for the last Sunday in October. That is normally a cool weather period in Ames. Temperatures average a high of 53 degrees and a low of 38. Rainfall is minimal. Thunderstorms are rare. However, this year the weather pattern was markedly different. For ten days before the race, the region endured a series of warm and cold fronts resulting in temperature drops of 30 degrees from one day to the next and increases of 15 to 20 degrees the following day. The day before the race, the high temperature was 75 degrees with considerable humidity. On the morning of the race, the temperature at 6:00 AM was 66 degrees, and forecasts predicted a high of 87 degrees before a cold front would move in. Race organizers and the lead race sponsor Ferrier Water decided to increase the amount of water available by 10 percent. The water and Razorade (an energy drink produced by Ferrier) would be available every 3 miles, except for the 3-mile dirt road area (where no water stops were available due to logistical reasons). Originally, the distance between water stops was going to be 1.5 to 2.0 miles, but there were not enough volunteers to work the tables, so ten days before the race, the decision was made to extend the distance.

The race began at its appointed time of 7:30 AM. Fifteen thousand runners, 90 percent of them first-timers, participated. At 8:30 AM, the temperature reached 76 degrees, with 70 percent humidity. At 9:00 AM, the National Weather Service forecast the potential for tornados in the area and issued a tornado watch. That became a tornado warning at 10:00 AM when a funnel cloud was found 25 miles from Ames. By 10:30 AM, heavy rains descended upon the route with rainfall of about three inches during a ninety-minute period. The area never experienced such a weather event. Many runners were forced to stop. Others continued as best they could. Ultimately, five runners experienced heart attacks and needed transport to a hospital. However, three of those runners suffered the heart attacks in the dirt road area where ambulances were not able to come. When rescuers came to them—after having to walk in heavily muddied terrain for about half a mile from their ambulance—the runners were found dead. There were no volunteers present in that area at the time of their deaths. Others—about 300 runners—were taken to hospitals due to various injuries—sprains, stress fractures, pulled tendons. Because police and ambulances also had to contend with nonrunner injuries (mainly spectators) due to the heat before the torrential rain, there was a shortage of ambulances and hospital emergency rooms were at full capacity.

After four hours, race officials called the race off. Anyone who did not finish was asked to stop running. Most runners complied, but many were angry, especially those who were 1 or 2 miles from the finish.

1 What errors do you think that the organizers made in the planning and execution of the race?
2 Do you think that any of the injured runners could successfully sue the organizers of the race? Or Ames?
3 The organizers had a limited budget for this race. Let's assume that for next year, they will increase the entry fee to create a reserve fund to plan for further safety. That fund would be $1 million. Let's say that the following ideas have been proposed:

A More liquid stops (each mile). Estimated cost: $500,000
B More volunteers (up to 250). Estimated cost: 10,000—for thank-you gifts like bags and rain jackets.

C Contracting with a private ambulance company in Beta City (a much larger city 50 miles away) so ambulances could be located every 3 miles (the dirt road area would have an ambulance at the beginning and end of that portion of the course). Estimated cost: $500,000.

D Contracting with a marathon course consulting firm to design a "safer" course. $250,000.

E Increasing insurance for injuries from a $1 million maximum per occurrence (meaning that the total insurance payments would be $1 million no matter how many injuries) to $10 million: $250,000.

As noted, the budget is only $1 million. Decide which of these options you would want to utilize and why?

References

Appenzeller, H. (ed.). (2005). *Risk management in sport: Issues and strategies.* Durham, NC: Carolina Academic Press, pp. 40, 42–44.

Archibald v. Kemble, 971 A.2d 513 (Pa. 2009).

Arnold v. Riddell Sports, Inc., 853 F. Supp. 1488, 1489 (D. Kan. 1994).

Associated Press (2014, January 21). Major League Baseball stadiums to have mandatory metal detection security by 2015. Retrieved September 18, 2015, from www.nydailynews.com/sports/baseball/mlb-metal-detection-stadiums-2015-article-1.1587239

Atkins v. Glen Falls City School District, 53 NY2d 325 (1981).

Bailey v. Filco, Inc., 48 Cal.App.4th 1552 (Court of Appeal, Third District, California, 1996).

Barrabi, T. (2015, September 18). NFL concussion lawsuit settlement: What "frontline" CTE data means for the appeals process. Retrieved October 13, 2015, from www.ibtimes.com/nfl-concussion-lawsuit-settlement-what-frontline-cte-data-means-appeal-process-2104528

Belson, K. (2015, April 22). Judge approves deal in NFL concussion suit. Retrieved October 12, 2015, from www.nytimes.com/2015/04/23/sports/football/nfl-concussion-settlement-is-given-final-approval.html

Belson, K., & Schwarz, A. (2016, March 16). N.F.L. shifts on concussions, and game may never be the same. *The New York Times.* Retrieved March 26, 2016, from http://www.nytimes.com/2016/03/16/sports/nfl-concussions-cte-football-jeff-miller.html

Benjamin, J. (2009, June 22). League, union must redouble efforts to protect players' health. *Street and Smith's Sports Business Journal*, p. 21.

Berkowitz, S. (2016, July 14). Judge OKs $75M class-action concussions settlement against NCAA. *USA Today.* Retrieved July 20, 2016, from http://www.usatoday.com/story/sports/ncaaf/2016/07/14/college-football-concussions-lawsuit-ncaa/87097982/

Berlet, B. (2004, March 11). Pack's Moore focuses on job. *Hartford Courant*, p. C2.

Bianculli, D. (2005, April 19). A welter of emotions: Documentary looks back at fatal '62 fight. *New York Daily News*, p. 74.

Branch, J. (2016, July 26). N.H.L. commissioner Gary Bettman continues to deny C.T.E. link. *The New York Times*. Retreived July 31, 2016, from http://mobile. nytimes.com/2016/07/27/sports/nhl-commissioner-gary-bettman-denies-cte-link.html?smid=tw-nytsports&smtyp=cur&referer=&_r=1

Broughton, D. (2015, October 5). Comerica park earns safety act designation. *Sports Business Journal*. Retrieved January 6, 2016, from http://www. sportsbusinessdaily.com/Journal/Issues/2015/10/05/Facilities/Safety-Act-Comerica.aspx?hl=risk%20management%20safety&sc=0

Cart, J. (1995, December 27). Crime & sports '95: Sex & violence. *Los Angeles Times*, p. C4.

Connell, N.A. and Savage, F.G. (2003) Releases: Is there still a place for their use by colleges and universities? 29 J.C. & U. L. S79.

Costa v. Boston Red Sox Baseball Club, 61 Mass. App. Ct. 299 (2004).

Crossman, M. (2007, June 19). Concussions create living hell for former NFL players. *The Sporting News*. Retrieved April 10, 2010, from http://www. sportingnews.com/yourturn/viewtopic.php?t=224682

Crouse, D. (2010, November 23). Michael Vick, Ray Lewis and Kobe Bryant: Redemption through victory. *Bleacher Report*. Retrieved January 7, 2016, from http://bleacherreport.com/articles/525280-michael-vick-ray-lewis-kobe-bryant-redemption-through-winning

DiCello, N. (2001). No pain, no gain, no compensation: Exploiting professional athletes through substandard medical care administered by team physicians. *Cleveland State Law Review*, 49, 507.

Eifling, S. (2013, January 30). Why NFL team doctors are ethically compromised. Retrieved September 18, 2015, from www.slate.com/articles/sports/sports_nut/2013/01/nfl_team_doctors_the_problem_with_pro_football_s_medical_sponsorship_deals.html

Epstein, T. (2015, June 6). The next battleground for NFL concussion litigation. Retrieved October 13, 2015, from https://casetext.com/posts/the-next-battleground-for-nfl-concussion-litigation

Ezell, L. (2013, October 8). Timeline: The NFL's concussion crisis. Retrieved October 12, 2015, from www.pbs.org/wgbh/pages/frontline/sports/league-of-denial/timeline-the-nfls-concussion-crisis/

Fox v. Board of Supervisors of Louisiana State University, 76 So. Wd, 978 (La. 1991).

Freeman, M. (1995, December 28). Pro football: Giants express regret over snow-ball throwers. *New York Times*. Retrieved May 16, 2010, from http://www. nytimes.com/1995/12/28/sports/pro-football-giants-express-regrets-over-snowball-throwers.html

Gawande, A. (2013, April 17). Why Boston's hospitals were ready. *The New Yorker*. Retrieved October 2, 2015, from www.newyorker.com/news/news-desk/why-bostons-hospitals-were-ready

Goldberg, J., & Zipursky, B. (2001). The restatement (third) and the place of duty in negligence law. *Vanderbilt Law Review*, 54, 657, 658.

Graham, G., Neirotti, L. D., & Goldblatt, J. J. (2001). *Guide to sports marketing.* New York: McGraw-Hill, p. 119.

Gregory, S. (2010, January 28). The problem with football: How to make it safer. *Time.* Retrieved April 29, 2010, from http://www.time.com/time/nation/article/0,8599,1957046,00.html

Gregory, S. (2014, October 2). Another high school football player dies after injury. *Time.com.* Retrieved September 18, 2015, from time.com/3457700/another-high-school-football-player-dies-after-injury/

Habib, H. (2002, June 16). When injuries rob athletes, who's to blame? *Palm Beach Post*, p. 1C.

Hackbart v. Cincinnati Bengals, 601 F.2d 516 (10th Cir. 1979).

Harrison, S. (2015, May 24). NHL may follow football's lead on concussion lawsuits. Retrieved October 12, 2015, from www.businessinsurance.com/article/20150524/NEWS08/305249980/nhl-may-follow-footballs-lead-on-concussion-lawsuits?tags=%7C75%7C329%7C304

Harvard Law Review (1996). Out of bounds: Professional sports leagues and domestic violence. *109*, 1048.

Howard, J. (2003, December 24). Spree delivers words, deeds. *Newsday* (New York), p. A69.

In re Nat'l Football League Players' Concussion Injury Litigation (final order approving settlement). 307 F.R.D. 301 (E.D. Pa. 2015).

In re Nat'l Football League Players' Concussion Injury Litigation, 821 F. 3d 410 (3d Cir. 2016).

Johnson, P. (2008, June 4). The night beer and violence bubbled over in Cleveland. *ESPN.com.* Retrieved February 22, 2010, from http://sports.espn.go.com/espn/page2/story?page=beernight/080604

Joyce, G. (2004, December 23). Bertuzzi on probation one year; Plea bargain to conditional discharge carries chance of no criminal record. *Toronto Star*, p. A10.

Keeton, W. P. (1984). *Prosser and Keeton on the law of torts* (5th ed.). St. Paul, MN: West, p. 215.

Li v. Yellow Cab Co., 532 P.2d 1226 (Cal. 1975).

McAllister, M. (2004, November 24). Beer muscles; Fans take leave of senses when alcohol involved. Retrieved May 6, 2010, from http://sportsillustrated.cnn.com/2004/basketball/nba/11/23/alcohol/index.html

McIntyre v. Balentine, 833 S.W.2d 52 (Tenn. 1992).

McLeod v. Blase, 290 Ga.App. 337 (Court of Appeals of Georgia, 2008).

Mihalek, D. (2014, June 26). Super bowl security: Guarding America's biggest game. Retrieved October 2, 2015, from www.tactical-life.com/military-and-police/super-bowl-security-guarding-americas-biggest-game/

Mihoces, G. (2013, October 7). Documentary: For years, NFL ignored concussion evidence. *USA Today Sports.* Retrieved October 12, 2015, from www.usatoday.com/story/sports/nfl/2013/10/07/frontline-documentary-nfl-concussions/2939747/

Mihoces, G., & Axon, R. (2015, April 22). Judge approves settlement—at least $900M—to NFL concussion lawsuits. *USA Today Sports.* Retrieved September 18, 2015, from www.usatoday.com/story/sports/nfl/2015/04/22/concussion-related-lawsuits-judge-settlement-nfl/26199011/

Mitten, M. J. (1999). Medical malpractice liability of sports medicine care providers for injury to, or death of, athlete. *American Law Review, 33*, 619.

Nack, W., & Munson, L. (1995, July 31). Sports' dirty secret. *Sports Illustrated*, p. 62.

Newsweek (1977, December 26). In brief: Basketbrawl, p. 79.

New York Court of Claims Act, sec. 12 (2015).

New York General Municipal Law, sec. 50e (2015).

New York Road Runners, Inc. (2014). New York Road Runners (NYRR) Release Form. Retrieved September 18, 2015, from http://www.nyrr.org/sites/default/files/Tuesday%20Night%20Speed%20Series%20Waiver_7.8.14_0.pdf

New York Times Company (2005). Policy on ethics in journalism. Retrieved March 29, 2010, from http://www.nytco.com/press/ethics.html#A1

Odum, C. (2015, August 30). Fan dies in fall from Atlanta stadium. *Associated Press*. Retrieved September 18, 2015, from www.usnews.com/news/sports/articles/2015/08/29/fan-falls-from-upper-deck-in-atlanta-taken-to-hospital

Owen, D. (2007). The five elements of negligence. *Hofstra Law Review, 35*, 1671.

People v. Kobe Bryant, 2004, 94 P.3d 624 (Colo. 2004).

Peters, C. (2014, September 4). Steve Moore's settlement with Todd Bertuzzi, Canucks finally official. CBSSports.com. Retrieved October 16, 2016, from http://www.cbssports.com/nhl/news/steve-moores-settlement-with-todd-bertuzzi-canucks-finally-official/

Regina v. Green, 2 C.C.C.2d 442 (Ont. Provincial Ct. Sept. 3, 1970).

Regina v. Maki, 1 C.C.C.2d 333 (Ont. Provincial Ct. Mar. 4, 1970).

Regina v. McSorley, B.C.P.C. 0117 P 21 (2000).

Restatement of the Law of Torts, 2d (1977). The American Law Institute. Retrieved May 6, 2010, from http://cyber.law.harvard.edu/privacy/Privacy_R2d_Torts_Sections.htm

Roberts, G., & Conrad, M. (2002, November). Jury awards $1.3 million to former Flyers player against team doctor. *Sports Lawyers Association Newsletter*. Retrieved September 25, 2005, from www.sportslawyers.org

Roberts, M. (2015, September 29). State-of-the-art security technology at Levi's Stadium in time for Super Bowl 50. Retrieved October 2, 2015, from www.nbcbayarea.com/news/local/State-of-the-Art-Security-Technology-at-Levis-Stadium-in-Time-for-Super-Bowl-50–330016471.html

Robinson, L. N. (1998). Professional athletes—Held to a higher standard and above the law. *Indiana Law Journal, 73*, 1313, 1322–1323.

Rodriguez v. Riddell Sports, Inc., No. B-CV-96–177 (S.D. Tex. Mar. 16, 1999).

Rountree v. Boise Baseball, LLC, 154 Idaho 167 (Supreme Court of Idaho, 2013).

Schultz, J. (1996, July 13). Brawl another low blow for boxing; Officials point finger at "reckless individuals". *Atlanta Journal and Constitution*, p. 01G.

Schwarz, A. (2009, December 20). NFL acknowledges long-term concussion effects. Retrieved October 12, 2015, from www.nytimes.com/2009/12/21/sports/football/21concussions.html?pagewanted=all

Smith, H. (2014, May 14). Coaches, schools unsure about HIPAA rules when athletes are injured. *NWI Times*. Retrieved March 28, 2016, from http://www.nwitimes.com/sports/high-school/coaches-schools-unsure-about-hipaa-rules-when-athletes-are-injured/article_b56ced76–3f51–540a-a4e8–41d4754d695d.html

Sydney Boxer Davey Browne Jr dies in hospital after title fight (2015, September 14). *The Guardian.* Retrieved March 27, 2016, from http://www.theguardian.com/sport/2015/sep/15/sydney-boxer-davey-browne-jr-dies-in-hospital-after-title-fight

van der Smissen, B. (2003). Symposium: General aspects of recreation law: Legal concepts related to youth responsibility. *Journal of Legal Aspects of Sport, 13,* 323.

Weisenberger, L. (n.d.). Youth sports injuries statistics. Retrieved September 18, 2015, from www.stopsportsinjuries.org/media/statistics.aspx

Yankees.com (2010). Stadium A to Z guide. Retrieved May 15, 2010, from http://newyork.yankees.mlb.com/nyy/ballpark/guide.jsp#Entry Guidelines

12 Performance-Enhancing Drugs in Sports

One of the most complex issues in sports involves the scope and the legitimacy of drug use by professional and amateur athletes. The use of performance-enhancing drugs (PEDs), testing standards and punishments involving competitive athletes has generated debate among fans, players, sports executives and politicians. With all this in mind, this chapter serves as a basic primer of the drug-testing standards in various sports organizations. As of 2016, implementation of the enforcement standards varies among the U.S. professional leagues, which contrasts with the almost uniform enforcement standards for international sports organizations and their national governing bodies.

Drug use in sports has changed over the last thirty years. At one time, drug use—at least in the United States—constituted *illegal* "recreational" drugs, such as smoking marijuana, popping amphetamines or snorting cocaine. In the 1980s, Major League Baseball, stunned by the convictions of four Kansas City Royals players on cocaine possession charges, suspended them for one year.

Note the word *illegal*. For the leagues and other sports organizations, little difficulty occurs in drafting a policy against illegal drug use. Such activities violate criminal laws, and those involved are subject to prosecution by the state. Both the unions and leagues recognized the problem and drafted sections in their collective bargaining agreements (CBAs) to address illegal drug use.

Athletes used legal substances (particularly alcohol) for years with little consequence and little publicity from the media. Often occurring after a game, alcohol use was within accepted standards of conduct at the time, and sports writers, not wanting to reveal the dark side of star athletes, refrained from such coverage (Sprattling, 2010).

More recently, a different type of drug abuse has evolved: of substances, some legal, many not, that boost performance, giving the athlete a competitive edge. Leagues and sports organizations have grasped for ways to control these drugs, often "designer" compounds created specifically to boost athlete performance. Although athletic federations have banned "stimulating substances," the lack of a comprehensive testing program has made these rules almost useless.

Early drug tests were first introduced in the 1960s. Nevertheless, the use of the first-generation class of drugs, known as *anabolic steroids*, continued. Anabolic steroids enhance muscle development and allow athletes to train harder and recover more quickly from strenuous workouts. In the 1970s, athletes from East Germany were given these drugs in a government-ordered quest for athletic glory. The policy worked. In a short time, that nation's athletes won a striking number of medals at the Olympics. At the 1976 Olympics at Montreal, East German women won eleven of the thirteen swimming events, an astounding achievement in a nation of only 16 million people (steroid-abuse.org, n.d.).

In non-Communist countries, some individual athletes started using these drugs. Yet, despite occasional mention, the issue did not generate much attention until two events propelled this issue into the public eye: the suspension of the Canadian sprinter Ben Johnson after testing positive for anabolic steroids, and the revelations of state-sponsored doping after the fall of Communism. Johnson won the gold medal in the 100-meter sprint at the Seoul Olympics in 1988, but afterward tested positive for the steroid stanozolol. Subjected to a torrent of negative publicity along with the ire of millions, he was forced to forfeit his medal. Shortly thereafter, the demise of East Germany revealed a state-run pattern of performance-enhancing drug abuse among its athletes. Some 10,000 East German athletes took steroids to boost their performance. The revelations resulted in criminal convictions and jail sentences for doctors and trainers (Ungerleider & Wadler, 2004). As noted later in the chapter, post-Communist Russia was caught in a massive doping scandal in 2015.

Performance-enhancing drugs pose different pharmacological issues from traditional illicit drugs, which serve as addicting agents. Unlike those drugs (or alcohol), which may adversely affect an athlete's performance, performance-enhancing drugs aid in performance and are taken solely for that purpose. And, as said earlier, many of them were *not* illegal, although in 1990 Congress passed the Anabolic Steroid Control Act, which categorized certain anabolic steroids (although not all) as *controlled substances* (Anabolic Steroids Control Act of 1990, 2003, 21 USC, sec. 802). The 1990 act was tightened by enactment of the Anabolic Steroids Act of 2004, which prohibits over-the-counter sales of "steroid precursors" such as androstenedione, which act like steroids once ingested (Iwata, 2004). Further, in 2006 President George W. Bush signed into law the Office of National Drug Control Policy Reauthorization Act, which prohibits the use of gene doping and bans from athletic competition anyone who uses genetic modification for performance enhancement. The law came three years after the World Anti-Doping Agency (WADA) banned gene doping for Olympic athletes (21 USC, secs. 2001 and 2007). More recently, in 2014, President Obama signed into law the United States Anti-Doping Agency Reauthorization Act, which authorized between $11.3 and $14.8 million in appropriations for USADA use for fiscal years 2014 through 2020 (United States Anti-Doping Agency Reauthorization Act, 21 USC 2014).

Still-legal performance-enhancing substances, classified as either prescription drugs or nutritional supplements (which escape the rigorous regulation of the Food and Drug Administration), are available for purchase at drug stores or laboratories. But, even with more regulation, detection is often difficult as athletes may take other substances, known as "masking agents," to hide the presence of those substances in the athlete's system, thus avoiding a positive urine sample test (the preferred method of drug testing).

When regulating the substances ingested by athletes, privacy issues mix into the debate. U.S. law and society value a right of privacy, and many argue that random drug testing, especially during nonwork time, is intrusive and a violation of individual rights (Ludd, 1991). Unless specific cause exists, testing should be limited in time and scope. In the past, certain players' unions have used this argument to forestall strict drug testing (Barker, 2004).

Ultimately, the professional leagues and, to a greater extent, the international and domestic athletic organizations tightened standards. But, as noted earlier, variations exist between the professional sports leagues and between the international athletic organizations (whose participants are not unionized) and professional league athletes, whose unions negotiate collective bargaining agreements detailing the drug-testing regimen and the rights of players who test positive.

When news stories of athlete use of performance-enhancing drugs first surfaced, many politicians and commentators demanded strict drug testing and punishment by professional sports. Many criticized "lax" standards utilized by the major leagues (Dvorchak, 2005). However, a counterargument also merits attention. If an athlete uses legal or even illegal drugs during the off season, is it his or her employer's business? And, if so, how invasive should the tests be? The drug-testing procedures governed by international and amateur athletic organizations are far more invasive than those in the pro leagues. They raise greater privacy concerns, and a system exists that many people find burdensome and intrusive.

Given that the rules and standards are changing rapidly, the rest of the chapter consists of a short summary of the drug-testing standards implemented in various organizations as of 2016.

National Collegiate Athletic Association

The National Collegiate Athletic Association (NCAA) executive committee has created a list of banned substances, updated yearly, for which they test athletes for use by urinary analysis. The listing is found at the NCAA's website (ncaa.org). The classes of drugs banned include stimulants and so-called "anabolic agents" (NCAA.org, 2014). Each student-athlete must sign a drug-testing consent form annually, in which the student-athlete agrees to be tested for prohibited drug use. Failure to complete and sign the consent form results in the student-athlete's ineligibility to participate in all intercollegiate athletics. Since 1999, NCAA drug-testing programs have been administered by the National Center for Drug Free Sport.

Essentially two plans exist, one for the season and another for postseason events. As far as the seasonal tests are concerned, the program, implemented by the NCAA in 1990, applies to about 10,000 student-athletes each year, and its focus was to deter the use of anabolic steroids (ESPN.com, 2007). During the regular season, the center randomly selects football and track and field programs for short-notice testing (less than forty-eight hours of notice to the schools). The center also randomly selects the individual athletes for testing based on the institutional squad lists. Every Division I and II football program conducts tests at least once each academic year. Selection is based on such criteria as player position, competitive ranking, athletics financial-aid status, playing time, an NCAA-approved random selection or any combination thereof. A student-athlete who tests positive cannot participate in at least one season of competition, which includes any postseason play.

The National Center for Drug Free Sport selects NCAA postseason events for testing and submits the confidential testing schedule to the NCAA president for approval on behalf of the NCAA executive committee. Each NCAA championship competition is tested at least once every five years. Approximately 1500 athletes are tested at those events each year, and any who test positive lose their collegiate eligibility for at least one year.

The NCAA list of banned drug classes is composed of substances that are generally considered to be performance enhancing and/or potentially harmful to the health and safety of the student-athlete. The NCAA recognizes that some banned substances are used for legitimate medical purposes. Accordingly, exceptions can be made for those student-athletes with a documented medical history demonstrating the need for regular use of such a drug. Exceptions may be granted for substances included in the following classes of banned drugs: stimulants, beta blockers, diuretics and peptide hormones (NCAA Division I Bylaw 31.2.3.2, 2015). The NCAA drug-testing program grants an appeals procedure by the institution for a student-athlete who tests positive for a banned drug or who violates NCAA drug-testing protocol. At least three members of the drug education and drug-testing subcommittee of the NCAA Committee on Competitive Safeguards and Medical Aspects of Sports hear appeals (NCAA Division I Bylaw 18.4.1.5.4, 2015).

The Olympic Movement

United States Anti-Doping Agency

Although the International Olympic Committee (IOC) has the ultimate drug-testing authority for Olympic sports, it assigns this duty to the individual national bodies such as the U.S. Olympic Committee (USOC). The USOC in turn created an independent organization to manage a comprehensive, independent drug-testing program. That organization is the United States Anti-Doping Agency (USADA). The USADA began operating on October 1, 2000, with full authority for testing, education, research and adjudication for U.S. Olympic, Pan-American and Paralympic athletes.

The USADA drafts principles, standards, policies and methods of enforcement in antidoping policy. In addition, the USADA is responsible for educating athletes about the rules governing the use of performance-enhancing substances and the harmful health effects of the use of such substances. As a requisite of recognition by the USOC, any national governing body or Paralympic sports organization must comply with the USADA procedures.

The USADA has authority to test any athlete who is a member of a national governing body, such as USA Track & Field, who participates in a USOC-sanctioned competition or who has given his or her consent to testing by the USADA. Generally, the prohibited substances fall in the following categories: anabolic agents, diuretics, masking agents and peptide hormones, stimulants and narcotics. Alcohol also may be tested in certain circumstances.

What makes this system comprehensive (or an egregious violation of privacy rights, depending on one's point of view) is the testing of individual athletes in an out-of-competition setting with little or no notice. Once athletes are identified by the national governing body and/or the USADA for inclusion in the program, the USADA will select athletes to test based on an automated draw that considers a number of factors, including ranking, risk of doping within each sport and test history (USADA Protocol for Olympic and Paralympic Movement Testing, 2014). A "doping control" officer may come to the athlete's home, school or training facility. The athlete's failure to cooperate may result in suspension.

The athlete submits urine samples to the USADA. After the USADA receives notification from the laboratory that a sample is positive, it notifies the athlete, the USOC and the particular national governing body. The test results are turned over to the USADA's Anti-Doping Review Board (a group of experts independent of USADA) for review, and the review board then presents its recommendation to the USADA. The USADA is then responsible for proceeding to an adjudication of the matter or closing the matter based on the review board's recommendation. The USADA will forward the review board's recommendation to the athlete, the national governing body, the USOC, the relevant international federation and the WADA (USADA Protocol for Olympic and Paralympic Movement Testing, 2014). The athlete has the right to a hearing if USADA proceeds with adjudication as a result of a positive or elevated test. He or she may choose between two separate hearing procedures:

1 The athlete may elect to proceed to a hearing before the American Arbitration Association.
2 The athlete may elect to proceed directly to a final and binding hearing before the Court of Arbitration for Sport (CAS) held in the United States.

The second option may be more practical because it saves time.

In many cases, a proposed sanction is provided by the arbitrator or, if accepted by the athlete without a hearing, forwarded to the national governing body to impose. In some cases, the sanction may be determined by the national governing body or the USADA.

Under Travis Tygart's tenure as CEO of the USADA, the organization has shown a greater focus on enforcement of its antidoping rules and regulations. In August 2012, the USADA issued a lifetime ban to Lance Armstrong, an American professional cyclist and seven-time winner of the Tour de France, for his use of performance-enhancing drugs.

World Anti-Doping Agency

The creation of WADA, an international version of the USADA, resulted from a doping scandal at the 1998 Tour de France bicycle race. In a police raid during the race, a large number of prohibited medical substances were discovered. The amount seized and the accompanying bad publicity and embarrassment suffered encouraged a coordinated effort to stop doping in all sports. Before WADA's establishment, the IOC and other international federations suffered the same problems as their domestic counterparts: these governing bodies adopted their own standards and procedures, resulting in confusion and inconsistency.

In 1999, the World Anti-Doping Agency was established, headquartered in Montreal. Shortly afterward, WADA proposed a World Anti-Doping Code, which has since been adopted by an impressive array of national Olympic committees, international federations, national governing bodies and national antidoping organizations (such as the United States Anti-Doping Agency). The great majority of the international sports bodies have adopted the code and its procedures. But, as noted earlier, the major professional sports leagues in the United States have not.

The code has imposed a strict liability standard involving the use of banned performance-enhancing substances. Whether one takes the drug intentionally or accidentally does not matter. It states:

> It is each *Athlete's* personal duty to ensure that no *Prohibited Substance* enters his or her body. Athletes are responsible for any Prohibited Substance . . . found to be present in their Samples. Accordingly, it is not necessary that intent, Fault, negligence or knowing Use on the *Athlete's* part be demonstrated in order to establish an anti-doping violation.
>
> (World Anti-Doping Code, Article 2.1.1, 2015,
> original emphasis)

The code calls for a two-year ban for a first offense and a lifetime ban for a second, barring mitigating circumstances. However, it allows for the use of certain prohibited substances for "therapeutic" purposes on a case-by-case basis (World Anti-Doping Code, 2015, Article 4.4).

In 2015 the WADA Code was revised. A number of procedural and substantive amendments were made, and some of the important changes included a four-year ban from competition for a first offense for the use or possession of a substance. That penalty also applies to any athlete who refuses to participate in, evades or tampers with the sample collection process (known as an "intentional cheater") (WADA Code, 2015, Appendix 2).

At the same time, the revised code eases the strict liability standard with regard to the length of sanctions. If the athlete can prove "no significant fault" for a positive PED test, the athlete's period of ineligibility may range from a reprimand to a two-year sanction. This eases the stricter two-year ban utilized in past codes (WADA.org).

In 2016, a major doping scandal involving Russian track and field athletes came to light, which threatened Russia's participation in the Rio Olympics. After a German television channel aired a documentary that alleged the existence of a system of state-sponsored doping within Russia's recognized sports governing body that implicated Russian athletes, coaches, sports federations, the Russian Anti-Doping Agency (RUSADA) and the Moscow WADA-accredited laboratory, a commission was appointed to investigate these claims, which centered on evidence of an alleged "high level" of collusion to systematically provide Russian athletes PEDs (procon.org, 2015).

The report concluded that "a deeply rooted culture of cheating" existed due to a "win at all costs mentality" that, in effect, forced athletes to participate or leave them without access to top with medical personnel. As a result, an open and accepted series of unethical behaviors and practices became the norm.

This report concluded that some Russian doctors and/or laboratory personnel enabled the doping. It noted that 1400 testing samples were destroyed by testing laboratory officials in Moscow. It also identified corruption and bribery practices at the IAAF, the international track and field federation.

The three-person panel authorizing the report made a number of recommendations, including the revocation of the accreditation of the Moscow lab, the monitoring of the Russian doping agency by the World Anti-Doping Agency and the sanctioning of coaches who interfered with testing procedures. It also recommended that the WADA promptly investigate suspicious test results and tighten procedures for ensuring compliance (procon.org, 2015).

With weeks to go before the Rio Olympics, the IAAF banned Russian track and field athletes from the Rio Olympics, an action that survived a legal challenge (Ruiz, 2016). The International Olympic Committee, in response to the widespread system of doping and an elaborate attempt to cover it up by Russian sports officials, considered banning the entire Russian team. However, in a decision made less than two weeks before the games opened, the IOC decided to defer such a decision to the appropriate sports federation, a move that was widely criticized (Axin, 2016). Although the IOC presumed that Russian athletes were tainted unless proven otherwise, critics noted that many federations were unable to deal with so many appeals just before the opening of the Rio Olympics and that a likelihood of inconsistent standards may be applied, especially by federations that were opposed to the proposed blanket ban in the first place (Axin, 2016). By the time the Olympics opened, a significant number of Russian athletes were able to compete.

Professional Sports

Before we examine the drug-testing policies of the individual professional sports leagues, some major differences between the NCAA, the Olympic movement and professional leagues deserve mention. As noted earlier, unlike the collegiate and international sports, pro sports involve a core relationship between employers and employees. Because the players in each of the major leagues are represented by unions, labor law principles must apply. Drug-testing standards—a mandatory subject of collective bargaining—must be negotiated between those parties and memorialized in the CBA between the union and management. Therefore, unlike collegiate or international sports, implementing or changing a drug-testing regimen must be done by agreement. It cannot be mandated by one party. With this in mind, we will examine the policies of the major sports leagues.

National Football League

The illegal use of drugs and the abuse of prescription drugs, over-the-counter drugs and alcohol are prohibited for NFL players. Moreover, the use of alcohol may be prohibited for individual players in certain situations, such as following a charge for driving under the influence. The NFL and the NFL Players' Association (NFLPA) have maintained policies and programs regarding substance abuse. They can be found in Article 39, section 7(a) of the NFL CBA (NFL CBA, 2011, Article 39, sec. 7).

The NFL has separate drug-testing policies for "substances of abuse" and steroids. The so-called "Intervention Program" serves as the cornerstone of the substance abuse policy. Under the Intervention Program, players are tested, evaluated, treated and monitored for substance abuse. The NFL tests for illegal use of drugs and the abuse of prescription drugs and alcohol every year on a specified date between April 20 and August 9, with notice given to players far in advance. If a player fails the first test, he gets a second test before any disciplinary action (suspension) is taken.

Players who fail a drug test are placed in the Intervention Program, with the goal of treatment and rehabilitation. Only players who do not comply with the requirements of the Intervention Program are subject to disciplinary fines and without-pay game suspensions. If a player has been suspended indefinitely under the substance abuse program, he is eligible to apply for reinstatement no sooner than sixty days prior to the one-year anniversary of the suspension notification. The commissioner then determines whether or not to accept the reinstatement (National Football League, Policy and Program for Substances of Abuse, 2014a). The NFL also, and more strictly, tests for steroids and performance-enhancing drugs, giving random tests for steroids to players. A computer randomly selects ten players on each team each week to be tested. On the first positive test result for a performance-enhancing drug, a player is suspended for four games without pay. A ten-game suspension follows a second positive test, and a third positive test results in at least a two-season suspension. The league also tests for masking agents. If a player tries to pass a test by using masking agents, a player will face a two-game suspension even if a steroid is not detected and a six-game suspension if both a prohibited substance and masking agent is found in his system (National Football League, Policy on Performance-Enhancing Substances, 2014b). All disciplinary action provided under the policy is imposed through the authority of the NFL commissioner, who maintains the ability to impose other sanctions as he deems necessary, and, significantly, a player's right to a due process appeal is strictly limited to specific circumstances.

National Basketball Association

The National Basketball Association (NBA) policy on drug testing and drug use was considered a bellwether when first adopted in 1983. The players and the owners agreed to a drug-detecting system administered by an independent expert. However, it did not provide for mandatory testing, but only required testing based on "reasonable cause." For non–performance-enhancing drugs, the regimen remains essentially the same today. Actual drug testing does not occur unless confidential evidence brought to that expert demonstrates a drug abuse problem. Only then can "authorization for testing" occur. The policy also encourages players to come forward and admit their problems. If they do, then treatment is available without the threat of disciplinary sanction.

In the present CBA, the illegal addictive drugs and performance-enhancing drugs are covered, including amphetamines, cocaine, LSD, opiates (heroin, codeine and morphine), PCP, MDMA (popularly known as "Ecstasy"), marijuana and steroids (NBA CBA, 2011, Article XXXIII, sec. 4(c)).

Notably, the league, the team and the union are prohibited from publicly disclosing information regarding the testing or treatment of any NBA player in the program, except as required by the suspension or dismissal of a player who tested positive for performance-enhancing drugs. This differs from the approach of the WADA and USADA.

A player may come forward voluntarily regarding his use of a prohibited substance and seek treatment in the program. There is no penalty the first time a player comes forward voluntarily. A player may not come forward voluntarily when he is subject to an authorization for reasonable cause testing or when he is subject to in-patient or aftercare treatment in the program (NBA CBA, 2011, Article XXXIII, sec. 7(a)).

A player tests positive for a prohibited substance at the concentration levels set forth in the CBA. The player is also deemed to have tested positive if he fails or refuses to submit to a drug test, or if the player attempts to mask, substitute, dilute or adulterate his urine sample. A player notified of a positive result has five business days to request a retest from the NBA and National Basketball Players' Association (NBPA). The retest will be performed at a laboratory different from the laboratory used for the first test (NBA CBA, 2011, Article XXXIII, sec. 4(e)). If the NBA or NBPA receives information that provides "reasonable cause" of a player's use, possession or distribution of a prohibited substance, the NBA or NBPA will request a hearing with the other party and the independent expert within twenty-four hours of the receipt of that information. If the independent expert decides that "reasonable cause" exists, an authorization for testing is granted, and the NBA arranges for testing of the player no more than four times during the next six weeks (NBA CBA, 2011, Article XXXIII, sec. 5). If, after the test, the NBA or NBPA believes that there is sufficient evidence to show use, possession or distribution of a prohibited substance, the matter may be taken directly to the league's grievance arbitrator. If the grievance arbitrator determines that the player has used or possessed amphetamine or one of its analogs, cocaine, LSD, opiates or PCP or has distributed any prohibited substance, the player will be dismissed and disqualified from the NBA (NBA CBA, 2011, Article XXIII, sec. 5(e)).

Presently, all rookies and veteran players are subject to no more than four random tests during the regular season and no more than two tests during the off-season (Abbott, 2013). All random tests are at the discretion of the NBA and without prior notice to the player. As noted earlier, when a player tests positive for illegal substances other than marijuana and steroids, he is dismissed and disqualified from any association with the NBA and can apply for reinstatement at a later date. However, if a player tests positive for either steroids or marijuana, he is required to enter a substance abuse program.

If a player tests positive for amphetamines or one of their analogs, cocaine, LSD, opiates or PCP during reasonable cause testing, first-year testing or veteran testing, he will be dismissed and disqualified from the NBA. However, veterans can seek reinstatement after two years and rookies after one. Reinstatement occurs only with the approval of both the NBA and the NBPA, and such approval may be conditional on random testing and other terms (NBA CBA, 2011, Article XXXIII, sec. 12(a)).

These rules do not apply to performance-enhancing drugs or to marijuana possession. For a first offense, a player will be suspended for twenty games and will be required to enter the SPED (Steroids, Performance-Enhancing Drugs and Masking Agents) Program. A second positive test for steroids will result in a suspension of forty-five games and the player's reentry into the program. A third (or any subsequent) positive test for steroids will result in the player's immediate dismissal and disqualification from any association with the NBA (NBA CBA, 2011, Article XXXIII, sec. 9(c).

If a player tests positive for marijuana for the first time during reasonable cause testing, first-year testing or veteran testing or if he is convicted of the use or possession of marijuana in violation of the law, he will be required to enter the Marijuana Program. A second such violation will result in a $25,000 fine and the player's reentry into the program. A third (or any subsequent) such violation will result in a five-game suspension and the player's reentry into the program (NBA CBA, 2011, Article XXXIII, sec. 8(c)). A player will also be dismissed and disqualified from the NBA if he is convicted of a crime involving the use, possession or distribution of any prohibited substance other than marijuana (NBA CBA, 2011, Article XXXIII, sec. 11(b)).

Major League Baseball

In the wake of allegations of the use of performance-enhancing drugs by a number of star players and resulting pressure from politicians, commentators and the public, Major League Baseball and the Major League Baseball Players' Association twice amended their CBA to tighten their drug-testing procedures.

The first change, announced in early 2005, increased the penalties for violators and expanded the list of illegal performance-enhancing drugs (Fisher, 2005). It provided that every player will undergo at least one random test during the playing season and included random testing during the off-season, irrespective of a player's country of residence. It also provided for additional tests for an unspecified number of randomly selected players. In addition, testing would occur during the off-season for the first time.

The agreement also revised disciplinary penalties for positive test results, with first-time offenders suspended for ten days. Second-time offenders would be suspended for thirty days. Third-time offenders would be suspended for sixty days. Fourth-time offenders would be suspended for one year. All suspensions would be without pay. Significantly, offending players would be publicly identified, a departure from the prior policy of keeping the names of first-time offenders secret (Bodley, 2005).

This revised policy expanded the list of banned substances to include diuretics, masking agents, human growth hormone and steroid precursors. The penalties fell far short of those stated in WADA's code, which calls for a two-year ban for first-time offenders unless there are mitigating circumstances.

Yet, the changes did not mollify critics and, after months of continuing criticism and congressional pressure, Major League Baseball players and owners agreed to significantly tighten the Joint Drug Treatment and Prevention Program. This policy, effective from the 2006 season, sharply increased penalties for steroid use to a fifty-game suspension for a first offense, 100 games for a second offense and a lifetime ban for a third. It also established mandatory random testing for amphetamines, a first for any of the major professional leagues. First-time amphetamine offenders will be subject to mandatory follow-up testing. Second-time offenders will be suspended for twenty-five games and third-time offenders for eighty games. Players could be banned for life for a fourth offense. Any player banned for life has a right to seek reinstatement after two years (Hohler, 2005).

These changes were a significant improvement upon the previous agreement; however, critics still urged for stricter regulations and testing procedures. In March 2014, then-Commissioner Bud Selig and Tony Clark, the executive director of the Major League Baseball Players Association, announced amendments to the Joint Drug Prevention and Treatment Program (Snyder, 2014). Effective until December 1, 2016, the latest policy further increased penalties for performance-enhancing drug use to an 80-game unpaid suspension for a first offense and 162 games for a second offense. Players suspended for steroid use would also be subject to six additional unannounced urine collections and three unannounced blood collections during the twelve months post-violation and every subsequent year of their career (Major League Baseball, Joint Drug Prevention and Treatment Program, 2014, section 3(d)). It is possible that this policy may extend after 2016, but at this writing, the parties have not agreed on a new collective bargaining agreement.

Regarding illegal drugs, Major League Baseball players who possess, sell or use such controlled substances risk disciplinary action by their individual clubs or by the commissioner. This prohibition also applies to agreed-upon steroids or prescription drugs. The treatment board, a group composed of doctors and lawyers representing the league, the players and the office of the commissioner, is responsible for administering and overseeing the antidrug program. Once a player tests positive, he enters a treatment program under a "clinical track." The medical representatives will help tailor a treatment and counseling program for the player. However, if the player fails to comply by continuing to use or sell banned drugs, the player is put on an "administrative track" and is subject to immediate discipline with a fifteen-game minimum suspension for the first additional violation (Major League Baseball Joint Drug Prevention and Treatment Program, 2014).

In the summer of 2004, Major League Baseball and the players' association banned the use of androstenedione, the substance used by Mark McGwire when he hit seventy home runs six years earlier. However, this was done after the Food and Drug Administration banned its sale. Other leagues and organizations had banned "andro" years earlier.

In recent years, Major League Baseball has since issued lengthy suspensions to numerous players for performance-enhancing drug use and other violations of the Joint Drug Agreement. Major League Baseball suspended a total of thirteen players, including Alex Rodriguez, on August 5, 2013, for their connection to Biogenesis, a South Florida anti-aging clinic that provided athletes with prohibited substances (Axisa, 2013). Rodriguez missed the entire 2014 season. In 2015, New York Mets relief pitcher Jenrry Mejia received a 162-game suspension for his second positive performance-enhancing drug test result, effectively tying him with Rodriguez for the longest PED-related suspension in baseball history (DiComo, 2015).

National Hockey League

Before 2005, the National Hockey League did not randomly test for steroids, stimulants or any other performance-enhancing drugs; instead, it offered education and counseling (Wilstein, 2004). The present agreement, which dates from 2013 and runs until 2022, requires that each club will be subject to team-wide "no-notice" testing once during training camp and once during the regular season. Individual players will also be randomly selected to participate in the no-notice drug screenings throughout the regular season and playoffs (NHL CBA, 2013, Article 47.6).

If a player tests positive for a banned performance-enhancing substance, he is subject to a twenty-game suspension without pay and mandatory referral to the NHL Players' Association (NHLPA)/NHL Substance Abuse & Behavioral Health Program for evaluation, education and possible treatment. A second positive test results in a sixty-game suspension without pay, and a third positive test results in permanent suspension (although he is eligible to apply for reinstatement after two years). The NHL utilizes the WADA list of prohibited substances (NHL CBA, 2013, Article 47.2 (d) and 47.3).

Ethical Issue: Lance Armstrong

Lance Armstrong began his professional cycling career in 1992. A few months after a twelfth-place finish in the 1996 Summer Olympics in Atlanta, Armstrong revealed that he had been diagnosed with testicular cancer and would have to undergo a year of chemotherapy treatment. Armstrong overcame his unlikely survival odds, and upon his return to cycling in 1997, was nationally regarded as an inspirational athlete. He advocated for cancer research and provided support services to cancer survivors through his Livestrong Foundation. A year after his return, Lance Armstrong joined the United States Postal Service Pro Cycling Team and won an unprecedented seven consecutive Tour de France titles from 1999 to 2005, before retiring from the sport.

Armstrong's accomplishments became clouded by increasing suspicions of his and his U.S. Postal Service teammates' doping use. Former teammates Stephen Swart and Tyler Hamilton claimed that they saw Armstrong using and promoting the use of banned substances. In 2012, the USADA accused Armstrong of doping, trafficking and administering performance-enhancing drugs to others—including cortisone, erythropoietin (EPO), blood transfusion and testosterone—months after federal prosecutors dropped its investigation into Armstrong's alleged doping. Armstrong was provided the opportunity to challenge the USADA's allegations, but chose not to pursue an arbitration process to contest the evidence against him. As a result, the USADA issued a lifetime ban from the sport and immediate disqualification of his competitive results beginning from August 1, 1998 (Usada.org, 2012).

After years of adamant denials, Lance Armstrong finally admitted to using performance-enhancing drugs, including testosterone and EPO, in an interview with Oprah Winfrey in January 2013 (Albergotti & O'Connell,

2013). Armstrong acknowledged that his doping helped him win his seven Tour de France titles; however, he expressed his beliefs that his use did not provide him with an unfair advantage—arguing his doping only leveled the playing field as other cyclists also used banned substances—and did not consider himself to be a cheater. Lance Armstrong's lifetime suspension by the USADA from the sport of cycling proved to the cycling world that the USADA was a champion of enforcing and punishing those who violated the World Anti-Doping Code in order to protect the integrity of the sport. The Cycling Independent Reform Commission (CIRC), in a 2015 report, found that the doping culture originated in the 1990s by former Union Cycliste Internationale (UCI) presidents and still remained prevalent in cycling two years after Armstrong's ban (Cary, 2015). The report found that riders' manipulations of doping results have evolved through the practice of micro-dosing, and that therapeutic use exemptions (TUEs), such as those for insulin and corticoids, have been greatly abused, allowing cyclists to circumvent antidrug regulations.

What kinds of protocols do you think should be imposed? Do you think that the UCI (the international cycling federation) is at fault as well for allowing these practices to continue? What about the argument that "most riders" have used PEDs? Does that exonerate Armstrong? Is it a defense?

Ethical Issue: Maria Sharapova

In 2016, Maria Sharapova revealed that she tested positive for the banned drug meldonium after the Australian Open. Although she took the substance for about ten years, it was only added to WADA's banned substance list one month before she was tested. Sharapova admitted that she was not aware of the addition of meldonium. She received a two-year ban by the International Tennis Federation, but appealed it to the Court of Arbitration for Sport which reduced the penalty to 15 months. The panel noted that while she still bore responsibility for taking the banned substance, she received no specific notice from her agent of WADA's actions (ITFtennis. com, 2016). Do you think that such a penalty is excessive for failing to check to see if a previously allowed substance was banned?

Ethical Issue: The Barry Bonds Prosecution

Barry Bonds, San Francisco Giants' left fielder from 1993–2007, set several Major League Baseball records throughout his twenty-two-season career including the most career and single season home runs (762 and 73, respectively). Bonds's reputation and accomplishments were, however, tarnished by his involvement in the Bay Area Laboratory Co-Operative (BALCO) scandal and subsequent investigations into charges he committed perjury. Barry Bonds had hired Greg Anderson of BALCO as his personal strength trainer in 1998, and in 2003, a federal grand jury began to investigate Anderson and three other men connected to BALCO for supplying anabolic steroids to athletes (ESPN.com, 2007). In 2003, Bonds testified that he did in fact use "clear" and "cream" substances provided by Anderson during the 2003 Major League Baseball season, but believed they were flaxseed oil and arthritis rubbing balm.

Suspicions surrounding Bonds's alleged steroid use led a federal grand jury to begin investigating whether or not the baseball star committed perjury when testifying under oath that he had never knowingly taken performance-enhancing drugs. Two months after his final career game, in November 2007, Bonds was indicted on four felony charges of perjury and one count of obstruction of justice for lying during his 2003 testimony, as federal investigators found evidence that Bonds had allegedly tested positive for steroids (CNN.com, 2007). In 2010, the Ninth Circuit U.S. Court of Appeals determined that the positive steroid test results were inadmissible in court because there was no proof that the results were indeed that of Bonds (*United States v. Bonds*, 2010). The following year, a federal grand jury found Bonds guilty of obstruction of justice for providing an evasive answer regarding receiving injectable drugs from Anderson, and Bonds was sentenced to two years' probation and 250 hours of community service (ESPN.com, 2011). A three-judge panel from the U.S. Court of Appeals upheld the 2011 conviction two years later (*United States v. Bonds*, 2013).

However, in 2015, the entire eleven-judge panel of the Ninth Circuit U.S. Court of Appeals overturned Bonds's conviction and cited that there was insufficient evidence that the statement in question was material to the government's investigation into BALCO (*United States v. Bonds*, 2015; Branch, 2015). The U.S. Department of Justice then dropped the case against Bonds after it announced it would not ask the Supreme Court to consider an appeal of the reversal.

Ethical questions about the Bonds case abound. Was it proper for the U.S. government to get involved in what was essentially a case of taking substances that are not illegal? Although anabolic steroids are illegal, the kind of "cream" allegedly used by Bonds is not. If that is the case, why should the government even investigate such a matter, spending taxpayers' money in the process? The trial cost an estimated $6 million, and the investigation ran up to $50 million (Hruby, 2011).

A more fundamental question is whether PED use should be permitted. Although that may sound heretical, given the fair play, health and economic factors involved, some commentators have argued that competitors in other pursuits can and probably have used certain drugs without sanction. What is the difference between a PED in sports and a drug for attention deficit hyperactivity disorder (ADHD) taken by millions, in some cases to help high school students sharpen their focus before an exam? Or a competitor in a music competition who may take a drug for increased stamina (Savulescu, Foddy, & Clayton, 2004)?

The issues of drugs and drug testing will continue to be a major concern in the sports landscape. See Table 10.1 for a summary of sanctions in the four major team sports and the Olympics.

Ethical Issue: Gene Alteration

The establishment of WADA and the performance-enhancing drug testing regimen in the U.S. professional leagues have created a more systematic approach to controlling the use of PEDs in sports. But as medicine advances, what about the possibility of gene alteration to improve performance?

Let's say that gene enhancements will be developed with an honest and important purpose: to regenerate the body after cartilage damage, tears and fractures. Such a substance would be a boon for many recreational athletes who have these muscles break down after years of activity. It could revolutionize the way we preserve our bodies. However, they can also be used for competitive advantage.

Simply put, is it ethical, for example, for an athlete who has injured herself after super-aggressive training to use genetic therapy to repair her body—and gain an advantage over a competitor who was more judicious in her training program? Or, what about athletes who use genetic editing to avoid a debilitating disease—and also realize a side benefit of improved performance? Should they be banned from competition? Or only some kinds of competition (Entine, 2015)? These scenarios are quite plausible.

Even without ingesting such substances, certain humans have unusual biological features. Eero Mantyranta was phenomenally successful: he won seven skiing medals over three Olympiads. However, there were rumors of blood doping—adding red blood cells before the race to increase his oxygen and stamina, a not-uncommon practice of cheats of his era. Ultimately, he was tested and shown to have 15 percent more blood cells than normal. However, no evidence of doping was proven. By 1993, researchers came up with the answer: Mantyranta and his family carried a rare genetic mutation that produced the EPO hormone and loaded his blood cells with 50 percent more red cells than the average man's. In other words, he was a freak of nature (Entine, 2015). Should that disqualify him from competition?

What about surgical procedures that may enhance one's ability to compete longer? For example, should someone who had "Tommy John" surgery for a pitching arm be disqualified? Or what about advanced knee replacements that are more resilient than natural-born knees? Although this question is still more hypothetical than real and we do not know the risks involved in such treatments, important ethical issues are present in the next generation of performance enhancement.

Chapter Assignment

Compare the approaches to performance-enhancing drug testing and sanction found in international sports through the adoption of the WADA Code and the approach utilized by the U.S. sports leagues. What are the advantages and disadvantages of the two different models? Do you think that the professional sports leagues should adopt the WADA system? Why or why not?

Table 10.1 A Comparison of Penalties for Performance-Enhancing Drug (PED) Test Violations Among Sports Organizations

Organization	1st Violation	2nd Violation	3rd Violation
NFL (as of 2014)	4 games (min.)	10 games	2 years
NBA (as of 2011)	20 games	45 games	dismissal
NHL (as of 2013)	20 games	60 games	lifetime ban
MLB (as of 2014)	80 games	162 games	permanent ban
Olympics/Int'l Federations	2 years	lifetime ban	

References

Abbott, H. (2013, January 11). The gaps in NBA drug testing. *ESPN.com*. Retrieved March 30, 2016, from http://espn.go.com/blog/truehoop/post/_/id/51305/gaps-in-nba-drug-testing

Albergotti, R. and O'Connell, V. (2013, October 21). 'Wheelmen' Exposes Doping Culture And The Armstrong 'Conspiracy'. NPR.org. Retrieved October 21, 2016, from http://www.npr.org/2013/10/21/239081497/wheelmen-exposes-doping-culture-and-the-armstrong-conspiracy

Anabolic Steroids Control Act of 1990, 21 USC, sec. 802 (2003).

Axin, R. (2016, July 24). IOC declines to issue blanket ban of Russian athletes. *USA Today*. Retrieved July 31, 2016, from http://www.usatoday.com/story/sports/olympics/rio-2016/2016/07/24/ioc-declines-issue-blanket-ban-russian-athletes/87498940/

Axisa, M. (2013, August 5). A-Rod and Cruz among 13 players suspended for ties to Biogenesis. *CBS Sports*. Retrieved October 16, 2015, from http://www.cbssports.com/mlb/eye-on-baseball/23024816/arod-and-cruz-among-13-players-suspended-for-ties-to-biogenesis

Barker, J. (2004, December 9). White House pushes MLB to crack down on ste-roids; North Dakota senator says players union must put end to "stonewall-ing." *Baltimore Sun*, p. 3C.

Bodley, D. (2005, January 12). Baseball officials announce tougher steroids pol-icy. *USA Today*. Retrieved September 2, 2010, from http://www.usatoday.com/sports/baseball/2005–01–12-steroid-policy_x.htm

Bonds convicted of obstruction (2011, April 14). *ESPN.com*. Retrieved January 10, 2015, from http://espn.go.com/mlb/news/story?id=6347014

Branch, J. (2015, April 22). Appeals Court overturns Barry Bonds's only convic-tion. *NY Times*. Retrieved October 17, 2015, from http://www.nytimes.com/2015/04/23/sports/baseball/barry-bonds-obstruction-of-justice-conviction-is-overturned.html?_r=2

Cary, T. (2015, March 9). Cycling doping report: Drug taking remains wide-spread. *Telegraph*. Retrieved October 19, 2015, from http://www.telegraph.co.uk/sport/othersports/cycling/11458133/Cycling-doping-report-Drug-taking-remains-widespread.html

CNN.com (2007). Home run king Barry Bonds indicted on perjury charges. Retrieved October 17, 2015, from http://www.cnn.com/2007/US/law/11/15/bonds.indicted/

DiComo, A. (2015, July 28). Mejia suspended 162 games for positive test. *MLB.com*. Retrieved October 15, 2015, from http://m.mlb.com/news/article/139273272/mets-reliever-jenrry-mejia-suspended-162-games

Dvorchak, R. (2005, May 19). Congress remains skeptical; Grills, prods sports czars on steroids. *Pittsburgh Post-Gazette*, p. C-1.

Entine, J. (2015, June 23). Will genetic cyber-athletes come to dominate sports? *Genetic Literary Project*. Retrieved January 10, 2016, from https://www.geneticliteracyproject.org/2015/06/23/will-genetic-cyber-athletes-come-to-dominate-sports/

ESPN.com (2007, June 27). NCAA committee rejects proposal to test for street drugs. Retrieved May 10, 2010, from http://sports.espn.go.com/ncaa/news/story?id=2918911

Fisher, E. (2005, January 13). Baseball beefs up steroid penalties. *Washington Times*, p. C01.

Hohler, B. (2005, November 16). Baseball gets tough about doping. *The Boston Globe*, p. A1.

Hruby, P. (2011, April 14). The Barry Bonds trial: Was it worth it? *The Atlantic*. Retrieved January 10, 2016, from http://www.theatlantic.com/entertainment/archive/2011/04/the-barry-bonds-trial-was-it-worth-it/237313/

ITFTennis.com (2016, October 4). CAS decision in the case of Maria Sharapova. Retrieved November 20, 2016, from http://www.itftennis.com/news/243888.aspx

Iwata, E. (2004, December 21). Andro users, sellers push to beat ban. *USA Today*, p. 1A.

Ludd, S. O. (1991). Athletics, drug testing and the right to privacy: A question of balance. *Howard Law Journal, 34*, 599.

Major League Baseball (2014). Major League Baseball's joint drug prevention and treatment program. Retrieved October 16, 2015, from http://mlb.mlb.com/pa/pdf/jda.pdf

National Football League (2014a). Policy and program for substances of abuse. Retrieved October 11, 2015, from https://nflpaweb.blob.core.windows.net/media/Default/PDFs/Active%20Players/Drug_SOA_Policy_9-29-14.pdf

National Football League (2014b). Policy on performance-enhancing substances. Retrieved October 11, 2015, from https://nflpaweb.blob.core.windows.net/media/Default/PDFs/Active%20Players/PES_Policy_2014.pdf

NBA CBA, Article XXXIII, sec. 4(c) et al. (2011). Retrieved October 11, 2015, from http://nbpa.com/cba/

NCAA Division I Manual (2015). Bylaws, secs. 18.4.1.5.4 and 31.2.3.2. Retrieved October 9, 2015, from http://www.ncaapublications.com/productdownloads/D116.pdf

NCAA.org (2014). 2014–2015 *NCAA Drug-Testing Program Handbook* (chapter 1). Retrieved October 9, 2015, from http://www.ncaa.org/sites/default/files/DT%20Book%202014-15.pdf

NFL CBA, Article 39, sec. 7 (2011). Retrieved October 11, 2015, from https://nflpaweb.blob.core.windows.net/media/Default/PDFs/General/2011_Final_CBA_Searchable_Bookmarked.pdf

NHL CBA, Article 47.2 (d) et al (2013). Retrieved October 16, 2015, from http://www.nhl.com/nhl/en/v3/ext/CBA2012/NHL_NHLPA_2013_CBA.pdf

Procon.org (2015, November 9). The independent commission report no 1. Final report (executive summary). Retrieved May 25, 2016, from http://sportsanddrugs.procon.org/sourcefiles/world-anti-doping-agency-report-on-russian-doping.pdf

Ruiz, R. (2016, July 21). Sports court upholds ban on Russian track and field athletes. *The New York Times*. Retrieved July 21, 2016, from http://www.nytimes.com/2016/07/22/sports/olympics/russia-olympics-ban-doping-track-and-field.html

Savulescu. J., Foddy, B., & Clayton, M. (2004). Why we should allow performance enhancing drugs in sport. *British Journal of Sports Medicine, 38,* 666–670. Retrieved January 10, 2016, from http://bjsm.bmj.com/content/38/6/666.full

Snyder, M. (2014, March 28). MLB, MLBPA announce "upgrades" to Joint Drug Agreement. *CBS Sports.* Retrieved October 16, 2015, from http://www.cbssports.com/mlb/eye-on-baseball/24504793/mlb-mlbpa-announce-upgrades-to-joint-drug-agreement

Sprattling, S. (2010). Tiger's transgressions: A look at how sports coverage has changed. *USCAnnenberg.org.* Retrieved May 15, 2010, from http://blogs.uscannenberg.org/neontommy/2010/01/tigers-transgressions-werent-a.html

Steroid-abuse.org (n.d.). Women and steroids—The wonder girls. Retrieved May 6, 2010, from http://www.steroid-abuse.org/the-wonder-girls-women.htm

Ungerleider, S., & Wadler, G. I. (2004, June 20). A new world order in elite sports. *New York Times*, sec. 8, p. 12.

United States Anti-Doping Agency Reauthorization Act, 21 USC, S. 2338 (2014). Retrieved October 9, 2015, from https://www.congress.gov/113/plaws/publ280/PLAW-113publ280.pdf

United States v. Bonds, 608 F. 3d 495 (9th Cir. 2010).

United States v. Bonds, 730 F. 2d 390 (9th Cir. 2013).

United States v. Bonds, 784 F.3d 582 (9th Cir. 2015) (en banc).

USADA Protocol for Olympic and Paralympic Movement Testing (2014). Sections 3, 4, 9, 11, 13. Retrieved October 9, 2015, from http://www.usada.org/wp-content/uploads/USADA_protocol.pdf

Usada.org (2012). Lance Armstrong receives lifetime ban and disqualification of competitive results for doping violations stemming from his involvement in the United States Postal Service Pro-Cycling Team doping conspiracy. Retrieved October 19, 2015, from http://www.usada.org/lance-armstrong-receives-lifetime-ban-and-disqualification-of-competitive-results-for-doping-violations-stemming-from-his-involvement-in-the-united-states-postal-service-pro-cycling-team-doping-conspi/

Wilstein, S. (2004). NHL can't afford to be aloof about drug testing. Retrieved July 16, 2004, from http://msnbc.msn.com/id/4569409

World Anti-Doping Code (2015). Retrieved October 9, 2015, from https://wada-main-prod.s3.amazonaws.com/resources/files/wada-2015-world-anti-doping-code.pdf

13 Discrimination in Sports

Discrimination based on one's race, gender, ethnicity or sexual orientation constitutes one of the most controversial subjects in sports. Although there is no question that a legacy of discrimination in the world of sports (and in society at large) existed and continues to exist, the methods and remedies utilized to combat this discrimination have been widely debated.

Note the distinction between *illegal* discrimination and policies that, although not illegal, result in the lack of representation of certain groups of people. Witness the case of the Augusta National Golf Club, the home of the prestigious Masters' competition. Protests against the all-male club were launched during the 2003 tournament. William "Hootie" Johnson, the chair of the club, said, "There never will be a female member, six months after the Masters, a year, 10 years, or ever" (Bisher, 2003). Although controversial and possibly unethical, the action of the club and the statement was not illegal. The club has the right to exclude women because a private facility has the discretion to select the members it wishes, no matter what sex (or race) they are. However, since then, women were given membership at the club in 2012, and by 2015, there were a total of three female members in the club, one of whom is former Secretary of State Condoleezza Rice (Strege, 2015).

Although not applicable in private association membership, antidiscrimination laws do apply in the employment relationship, and these laws—state and federal—prohibit discrimination based on race, ethnicity, religion, age and, more recently in some cases, sexual orientation by private employers. And, suffice it to say, employment discrimination issues can exist in sports (Das, 2016).

In addition to employment, antidiscrimination laws apply to actions by government entities and private organizations that receive government funding. In particular, gender-based discrimination has received a great deal of coverage and discussion, due to the considerable litigation resulting from the interpretation of Title IX of the Education Amendments of 1972 (20 USC sec. 1681 et seq., 1972), the statute governing equity in federally funded institutions. The standards have produced intense debate about the nature of the enforcement of the law and the resulting claims by certain male athletes of "reverse discrimination." Discrimination against those with disabilities has also resulted in discussion and lawsuits, notably in high school and collegiate sports.

In 1964, the passage of Title VII of the Civil Rights Act barred discrimination in employment based on race, color, religion, sex or national origin. Since then, outright, intentional discrimination has been illegal (42 USC sec. 2000e et seq., 1964). Essentially, Title VII prohibits intentional discrimination in hiring, promotions and termination. A basic question arises of how to prove such acts. It is safe to say that most employers and their managerial and supervisory employees (even in the sports industry) refrain from making openly racist statements regarding employment standards. Therefore, limiting discrimination laws to purely intentional statements would result in few successful cases. Instead, a system based on "disparate impact" or statistical underrepresentation has been devised by the courts. Simply put, if such a statistical imbalance can be shown between the number, rank or termination of employees as compared with a general population, a basic presumption of employment discrimination occurs. For example, if only two of the NFL's thirty-two head coaches are black compared with the percentage of players or even the percentage of African Americans in the United States (which is far higher), it can merit a disparate impact claim by those eligible black candidates denied head coaching positions. However, the employer has a defense of "business necessity," and if the team or the league proves that the disparity is based on success (meaning victories) and that a full and fair job search yields candidates who are qualified, then the employer wins (*Griggs v. Duke Power*, 1971).

With this in mind, let us tackle some of the major issues.

Race Discrimination

If one thinks of an example of an egregious discriminatory policy in sports, the lack of African Americans in professional baseball ranks at the top. From the late nineteenth century to 1947, Major League Baseball enforced a ban on "Negro" ball players. The policy was never formalized, but the effect was pernicious. During the reign of commissioner Kenesaw Mountain Landis, not one black person played in the major leagues. As reportedly noted by Landis's successor, Albert "Happy" Chandler, "so long as Landis remained commissioner, . . . there wasn't going to be any black boys in the league" (Rogosin, 1995).

Certainly, talent existed. Marvelous players from Negro Leagues toured the country and even competed against white major leaguers in exhibitions (Weiler & Roberts, 2004). The foolishness and outrageousness of this policy resulted in a great talent pool of players being excluded from the major leagues. The segregation policy also violated good business sense. A greater number of players for owners to pick from would exist and owners' leverage over their players in a pre–free-agency era would increase, keeping salaries low, possibly even lower than was the case.

After Landis died in 1944, the color barrier was broken with the entry of Jackie Robinson (Brooklyn Dodgers) and Larry Doby (Cleveland Indians). It took another decade to integrate all major league teams. But changing attitudes about minority players, unfortunately, took years longer.

In 1987, the issue of race in sports became national news when Al Campanis, a vice-president for the Los Angeles Dodgers, made inopportune remarks on an ABC News *Nightline* broadcast when asked about the lack of Black managers and front-office personnel in the sport. He said, "I don't think it is prejudice. I truly believe that they may not have some of the necessities to be, let's say, a field manager or perhaps a general manager" (Johnson, 2007). Campanis was fired after that broadcast, and Major League Baseball instituted an affirmative-action program to expand opportunities for minorities on the coaching and managerial level. A few years before that, the National Football League and National Basketball Association instituted such programs. The NFL hired its first black head coach in the modern era, Art Shell of the Los Angeles Raiders, in 1989.

Another example of offensive comments occurred a few years later. In the early 1990s, the principal owner of the Cincinnati Reds, Marge Schott, made anti-Semitic and racist comments that received wide publicity. Ultimately, she accepted a one-year suspension from day-to-day control of the team's operations and a fine. Although her opinions constitute protected free speech under the First Amendment, that immunity does not apply to a private organization such as Major League Baseball, which was well within its rights to enact sanctions against her for those comments. In 2003, the conservative radio talk show host Rush Limbaugh stated that the Philadelphia Eagles quarterback Donovan McNabb was overrated by the media and the NFL because of their interest in seeing Black quarterbacks and coaches do well. The resulting criticism forced Limbaugh's resignation from his role on ESPN's *Sunday NFL Countdown* (Siemaszko, 2003). And in 2014, Donald Sterling, then-owner of the NBA's Los Angeles Clippers, was recorded making racially insensitive statements to a companion. The league reacted by suspending him and forcing a sale of the team (Berger, 2015). This matter was discussed in detail in Chapter 1. That same year, it was reported that an email written by then-Atlanta Hawks owner Bruce Levinson included racist remarks. In the email, Levinson posited that the team's struggle to fill the arena was because the "blacks scared away the whites, and there are simply not enough affluent black fans to build a significant season-ticket base." Levinson self-reported the email and, instead of dealing with protracted investigatory proceedings, decided to sell his controlling interest in the team (Lapchik, 2014).

Players have joined in this chorus of ill-timed statements. The Atlanta Braves relief pitcher John Rocker made insulting comments about various minority groups and gays in an interview in *Sports Illustrated* in 1999. In it, he ranted against the kinds of people who took the subway to Shea Stadium (then the home of the New York Mets) and then stated: "The biggest thing I don't like about New York are the foreigners . . . Asians and Koreans and Vietnamese and Indians and Russians and Spanish people and everything there. How did they get into this country?" (Pearlman, 2000). Commissioner Bud Selig suspended Rocker for the spring training and the first twenty-eight days of the 2000 regular season. Unlike the situation with Schott, Rocker, a unionized employee subject to the collective bargaining agreement, pursued arbitration. The arbitrator reduced the fine to $500 and the suspension to fourteen days during the season (Standora, 2001).

The Rocker case presents an important question when dealing with insensitive racial, ethnic or religious comments. Rocker made them during the off-season in a nonbaseball setting. Should his employer sanction him for his opinions, as odious as they are? If Rocker got along with his teammates and did not engage in any racial or ethnic insults while engaged in his job, should the league mete out punishment?

A number of athletes have made homophobic statements. In 2011, Kobe Bryant called a game official a gay slur during a game in 2011. He was fined $100,000 for the incident and issued an apology (Langton, 2015). In 2012, Voula Papachristou, a Greek track star, was kicked off the Olympic team for tweeting that "With so many Africans in Greece, the West Nile Mosquitos will be able to eat homemade food" (Turner, 2013).

An underlying ethical issue involves double standards in punishment. The rap group led by the then-Philadelphia 76ers Alan Iverson made a CD replete with comments about those with "faggot tendencies" and "fucking bitches." Then NBA commissioner David Stern criticized the lyrics as "repugnant" but did not take any disciplinary action (Smith, 2000). Given Rocker's statements and punishment, do these comments deserve equal sanction?

Underrepresentation of Minorities

Although underrepresentation of African Americans exists on the management level, with the exception of ice hockey the problem is not as acute among players. In 2015, 8.3 percent of baseball players, 68.7 percent of NFL players and 74.4 percent of NBA players were African American. What has become striking, however, is the increase in percentage of other minorities in professional sports. In 2015, 29.3 percent of baseball players were Latino, up from 14 percent in 1991, and 1.2 percent were Asian, an increase from 0 percent in 1991 (Lapchick, 2015a, 2015b, 2015c). Whereas the NFL and NBA stayed about the same, the percentage dropped in baseball, from 10.2 in 2008. The selection, cultivation and compensation of these athletes are commensurate with their abilities and the likelihood of illegal discrimination is scant, because professional athletics is the ultimate meritocracy, as only the very best make it to the major league level.

In terms of sports league and team management in 2015, the survey found that baseball had four general managers who are people of color—the fewest among the big three leagues. One person of color and nine women were majority owners of MLB teams, whereas 27.7 percent of MLB's central office employees were people of color, second only to the NBA's 35.4 percent. Further, 20 percent of MLB senior administrators were people of color and 24 percent were women. (Lapchick, 2015a, 2015b, 2015c).

The Institute for Diversity and Ethics in Sport gave the NBA the best racial and gender diversity rating in 2015. The NBA led all men's pro leagues for people of color among players (76.7 percent), vice-presidents (15.3 percent), league office professional staff (35.45 percent), head coaches (33.3 percent), chief executive officers/presidents (8.8 percent), general managers (19.4 percent) and professional administration (26.4 percent). The NBA was best for women in men's pro leagues in league chief executive officers/presidents (7 percent), assistant coaches (0.5 percent) and league office professional administration (36.1 percent) (Lapchick, 2015b).

Although frustration exists regarding the slow pace of recruitment of African Americans, Hispanics and women to head coaching, general manager and other executive positions, litigation is rare in the professional leagues. The time, cost, uncertainty of success and, possibly most importantly, limited prospect of employment after bringing such a lawsuit serve as disincentives to undertake such a strategy.

Title IX

Title IX of the Education Amendments of 1972 has become the signature law banning gender discrimination in interscholastic and college sports. Title IX merits recognition by many in the general public, something few laws achieve. However, public recognition is not always synonymous with accuracy, and some of the reporting and commentary about Title IX lack substantive knowledge about the language, history and enforcement of this important statute. The law's controversy lies in the enforcement issues created by regulatory bodies and the courts, rather than the actual text.

Although the main interpretation issues have been settled for at least twenty years, the social ramifications of Title IX continue, resulting in much debate and, at times, rancor. Explaining, rather than advocating, is the goal in this chapter.

Let us dispel several myths: (a) Title IX applies only to gender equity in sports, (b) the law constitutes a government-mandated affirmative action program and (c) the law applies only to women. None of these assertions is true. Title IX, enacted by Congress with the signature of President Richard Nixon, is an educational rights law, pertaining to *all* educational programs receiving federal assistance. It states: "No person in the United States shall, on the basis of sex, be excluded from participation in, be denied the benefits of, or be subjected to discrimination under any educational program or activity receiving federal financial assistance" (Civil Rights Restoration Act of 1987, 2000, 20 USC 1681(a)). That means that if university X has a biology program that limits participation to men and receives a federal grant of $1 million, the institution is in violation of Title IX. Note that the law applies to both public and private institutions. Federal funding is the key, and many private institutions receive such funding.

Affirmative action involves a voluntary or court-ordered remedy for past discrimination. Title IX, however, is a statute barring discrimination, not a judicial remedy to ameliorate the effects of past discrimination. Also, Title IX deals with opportunities for a historically "underrepresented sex." Although the great majority of cases involve females, it is at least theoretically possible for males to sue if they meet the statute's threshold requirements.

Yet the enforcement questions belie the outward simplicity of the law. The seemingly broad language of the statute led to years of interpretation questions. Although Congress passed the law, it empowered the Office of Civil Rights (OCR), a federal administrative agency, to craft the particular regulations needed to implement and interpret the law. As was the case with the Americans with Disabilities Act (discussed later in this chapter), the regulations caused the most controversy and required judicial intervention to ensure a uniform interpretation.

It took three years of input and drafting for the issuance of the first set of regulations by the Department of Health, Education, and Welfare in 1975. When the regulations were criticized as vague, the Office of Civil Rights (the successor agency in charge of implementing Title IX) reconsidered and came up with more specific recommendations in 1979. Although the 1975 regulations addressed broad terms such as admissions and employment of students, the 1979 rules for the first time specifically applied the statute to issues of gender equity in intercollegiate sports. These standards, despite criticism from certain quarters, remain in effect.

At the same time, a debate developed concerning the scope of Title IX's application. Is it institution-wide or merely applicable to the particular program funded by federal monies? If it is the latter, virtually no athletic programs fall within its ambit, because few, if any, athletic departments receive federal funding. Institution-wide application, however, results in school-wide enforcement. So if the college or university accepts $100,000 for its biology lab or its cyclotron, athletics must comply with Title IX and its regulations. The Supreme Court concluded that the more limited standard applied in *Grove City College v. Bell* (1984). Four years later, Congress overturned *Grove City* when it passed the Civil Rights Restoration Act (1987), which explicitly extended Title IX coverage to all programs of an institution that receive federal money.

By the late 1980s and early 1990s, Title IX litigation regarding athletic programs began in earnest. In addition to the federal government, the courts allowed individual lawsuits for money damages for violations of Title IX. Most cases have arisen from private litigants, and the plaintiffs emerged victorious in the great majority of these cases (Weiler & Roberts, 2004).

Unequal treatment in the participation, funding and scholarship opportunities in athletic programs served as the basis of these lawsuits. Because of these disparities, the argument went, colleges and universities lacked compliance with Title IX. The courts had to determine whether a violation of Title IX existed, and, in answering that question, they looked to the 1979 OCR guidelines. These important—and controversial—rules serve as the basis for Title IX interpretation.

To ensure compliance in *participation* of athletic programs, the college or university must prove one of three alternatives (or "prongs"):

1 Demonstrating that intercollegiate athletic participation is "substantially proportionate" to the respective enrollments of each sex in the particular institution; or if not
2 Demonstrating that the institution has a history of and continuing practice of expanding participation opportunities for the underrepresented sex; or if not
3 Demonstrating that the institution fully and effectively accommodates the abilities and the interests of the underrepresented sex in the current program
   (Title IX, Policy Interpretation, 44 Fed. Reg. 71, 418, 1979)

Revenue-producing sports such as men's football must be included in the calculation, despite the lack of women's football teams.

The rules cover not just participation, but also scholarships. Many schools grant athletic scholarships based on National Collegiate Athletic Association rules. The Office of Civil Rights guidelines require that male and female student-athletes receive such scholarships proportionally to their participation. The OCR policy outlines "nondiscriminatory factors" such as equipment and supplies, scheduling of goods and practice times, travel and daily allowances, access to tutoring, coaching, locker rooms and competitive facilities and other support services. Violation of the rules may result in monetary damages and judicial remedies to rectify the situation.

It is best for an institution to show prong one, the "proportionality" ratio. If an institution shows "substantial proportionality" in the numbers of male and female athletes, compliance occurs. Let's take an example: College X has 5000 students, 53 percent female and 47 percent male. Two hundred and fifty students participate in intercollegiate athletics. Of those 250, 100 are female and 150 are male (including a number of men's football players) or a breakdown of 40 percent female and 60 percent male. Because these numbers do not fit the proportionality of the student body, noncompliance occurs (unless one of the two other prongs is fulfilled). However, the regulations did not specify the parameters of "substantial proportionality." What if the student body is 53 percent female and athletic participation is 49 percent female? Does that result in compliance? That question is left up to the courts. One court concluded that an 11 percent discrepancy is not substantial proportionality (*Cohen v. Brown University*, 1993). Many, if not most, college and university athletic programs lack substantial proportionality (Department of Education, 2002).

The second prong, a demonstration of the institution's current and historical practice of program expansion, means that, although a disparity remains between the ratio of male to female students and the proportion of those engaged in intercollegiate athletics, the institution has a history of expanding opportunities for the underrepresented sex and a plan for continuing that practice. Applicable in the case of an institution seeking to remedy past practices, this prong requires greater resources to expand the numbers of athletes of the underrepresented sex.

Proving compliance under prong two involves considerable factual data. A court must examine the past practice of the institution. How many years has the college or university attempted to correct the disparity by adding programs for the underrepresented sex? Have new teams been created? Have club teams "graduated" to varsity teams? Have those teams been created or expanded to meet the interests of that gender? Simply creating new teams does not ensure compliance if little demand exists for them. Louisiana State University learned that lesson when a court concluded that its decision to add women's softball and soccer did not constitute an adequate response to student interest (*Pederson v. LSU*, 1996).

Once the history of program expansion is adequately demonstrated, the institution must then demonstrate a continuation of that practice. The regulations do not specify a particular timeline but do require the demonstration of consistency. An example of the difficulty of fulfilling prong two occurred in a lawsuit against Colgate University. Colgate added eleven women's varsity sports in the 1970s and 1980s, but did not add any women's sports from 1989 to 1993, when the lawsuit was filed. Afterward the court refused to rule in favor of the university and did not dismiss the case. Basically, the court determined that factual questions still existed as to whether the second prong's requirements were met (*Bryan v. Colgate University*, 1996). The parties settled the case shortly afterward.

The second prong benefits wealthier schools, those possessing the resources to invest in larger athletic activities. Many less affluent institutions lack this ability. The question becomes: What can these schools do to eliminate the disparity? That is the role of the third (and by far the most difficult) prong.

This last alternative allows an institution that maintains a disparity between men's and women's programs to determine that, despite the disparity, the interests and abilities of student athletes are "fully accommodated." In making this determination, the OCR regulations consider these factors: "(a) whether there is unmet interest in a particular sport, (b) sufficient ability to sustain a team in the sport, and (c) a reasonable expectation of competition for the team."

To show that the underrepresented sex's interest is met, the regulations require proof by such methodologies as surveys of students in the institution and potential students in the community. In addition, personal interviews may be utilized. If the institution so proves, then compliance occurs. If not, then a court considers the "ability to sustain an intercollegiate team," a particularly subjective and questionable consideration. The institution must show, through the opinions of coaches, administrators and athletes, whether it possesses the ability to field a particular team. What makes this ludicrous is that "a school may ask the women's softball, basketball and swimming coaches whether the school has the potential to sustain a varsity bowling team" (Bentley, 2004). If, somehow, the institution can show a lack of ability to sustain new teams, then compliance occurs. As noted, this standard is a very difficult one to prove compliance with.

Before the passage of Title IX, women constituted only 15 percent of the total number of athletic participants in college. By 2015, the figure had increased to 43.4 percent (1981–82–2014–15 NCAA Sports Sponsorship and Participation Rates Report, 2015).

Although many Title IX controversies centered on collegiate athletes, the law also applies to primary and high schools. In 1972, when Title IX was enacted, there were 295,000 girls participating in high school sports, or roughly one in twenty-seven. In the 2014–15 school year, there were more than 3,287,735 girls and 4,519,312 boys participating in high school sports (National Federation of High School Athletic Associations, 2015).

Title IX does not only involve numbers, but also requires equality in playing conditions and treatment. Therefore, the statute also applies to gender discrimination due to poorer playing fields, equipment and locker rooms (Women's Sports Foundation, 2008).

In researching a Title IX issue, considerably more information is available regarding collegiate athletic programs than those of primary and secondary schools. Under the Equity in Athletics Disclosure Act, a federal law enacted in 1994, colleges and universities must disclose all pertinent data on the financial support and numbers of male and female athletes (Equity in Athletics Disclosure Act, 20 USC, sec. 1092, 1999). In primary and secondary public schools, no such federal requirement exists, and much of the enforcement is sectionalized among local school districts or states.

Criticisms of Title IX

Title IX greatly helped create the boom in women's athletics in the United States. However, Title IX enforcement comes at a cost, and some have criticized the method by which it is enforced. In June 2002, the secretary of education created a fifteen-member commission to study Title IX and possibly recommend changes in its enforcement. Its conclusions, published eight months later, showed that although the panel agreed on many issues, sharp differences existed on others, prompting a dissenting report. The majority reaffirmed the ideal of Title IX but called for modification and "clarification" of the three-prong test. For example, it called for elimination of the category of "non-traditional" students (meaning older students) from the calculation of proportionality and permitting the Department of Education to allow for a "reasonable variance" from equality if proportionality is retained as a way of complying with Title IX (The Secretary of Education's Commission on Opportunity in Athletics, 2002).

Although the commission's recommendations did not translate into legislation, they demonstrated a discomfort with the proportionality standard (prong one of the three-part test) and the adverse consequences of Title IX for male teams. In certain situations, male athletics suffered in the quest for proportionality. The argument that men's teams had to "suffer" unfairly to ensure compliance with Title IX resonates strongly in sports such as men's wrestling that have seen reductions and eliminations in a number of schools. The impetus for the establishment of the commission was a lawsuit filed by the National Wrestling Coaches Association claiming "reverse discrimination." The organization alleged that Title IX discriminated against male athletes with respect to participation opportunities because sports programs had been eliminated at many schools as a result of the regulations. Neither the lower federal court nor the federal appeals court decided the merits of the case. The federal appeals court, in a 2–1 ruling, dismissed it on procedural grounds (*Nat'l Wrestling Coaches Ass'n v. U.S. Dept. of Education*, 2004). The following year, the Supreme Court rejected an appeal of the ruling (*Nat'l Wrestling Coaches Ass'n v. U.S. Dept. of Education*, 2005).

Ethical Issue: Should Title IX Enforcement Standards Be Changed?

Some men's programs have been eliminated or reduced to satisfy compliance (McEldowney, 2009). This raises a question as to whether alternatives approaches can be utilized to reduce the possibility of reduction of male programs. One example proposes changes in the numbers and scholarships in a school's football program, which is almost exclusively male and quite large in many institutions. Because women generally do not have football teams and men's teams contain high numbers of players (with high numbers of scholarships in some cases), this creates difficulties for other men's programs. Men's wrestling or swimming lacks the constituency and alumni interest that football has, so diminution or elimination of football, especially in an institution with a "football tradition," is less likely. Do you think that men's football numbers should be excluded from the formula? Or included in a less than one-to-one manner (such as one male football player is one-half for calculation purposes?

Another critique of Title IX enforcement focuses on primary and secondary schools. It concludes that such enforcement provides a disincentive to engage in any improvements because of the costs of compliance. If new training facilities are built, the argument posits, those facilities have to accommodate women's as well as men's teams. In other words, why commit to new men's facilities unless one can ensure that they are used by women as well?

These costs have become more acute in the face of the belt tightening by many states and localities. With many school districts forced to cut funding, is it always practical to construct or upgrade facilities? Or should there be a demonstrated commitment to participate in the sport before a school district takes such an action? Consider this example. Let's say that twenty girls wish to compete in interscholastic swimming, but their high school lacks a swimming pool and cannot afford to build one. Therefore, the girls are denied an opportunity to compete and, after parents complain, the Office of Civil Rights investigates. Ideally, the OCR would require the school to build a competition-sized pool (which would benefit boys as well), but the prohibitive costs prevent this. The school settles (as opposed to being drawn into time-consuming litigation with the government), and the settlement provides that the school rent the only competition-sized pool in the area (located fifteen miles from the school) and provide transportation to and from that pool for the girls after school for practice sessions for the next two years at a cost of tens of thousands of dollars.

If the settlement spurs momentum for girls' swimming, then the settlement helps ensure the goal of increased participation. However, if fewer girls—and more boys than expected—decide to participate, then the settlement raises difficult questions about priorities and economics. The result is that the school district committed resources that helped only a few students at a considerable cost.

This example raises unpleasant questions, but ones that must be addressed in such a circumstance. Like any law designed to remedy past social inequities, the results may not always be ideal.

Finally, Title IX poses a conflict of race and class. Many of the beneficiaries of Title IX have been women of middle- or upper-middle-class means. Does the proportionality test benefit such women over minority men from underprivileged backgrounds? A sensitive point rarely argued publicly, it was summarized in a 1997 speech given by the Rev. Jesse Jackson in Sacramento, California. In it, Jackson stated:

> There are those who say affirmative action is hurting whites. Let's look at that reasoning. The primary beneficiaries are the white family. The majority of beneficiaries under Title IX are white women who with education, as they join the work force, and get contracts, help stabilize the white family and expand the economy.
>
> (Jackson, 1997)

Like the prior example, this argument, if true, raises a difficult moral and ethical dilemma. For example, say that a university must spend a proportionate amount of money on athletic scholarships between men and women but, in doing so, disproportionately affects poorer or minority male students. In many cases, an athletic scholarship is the only opportunity for many of these male students to attend college.

Disability

Disabled people have attained legal protections through legislation passed in 1973 and 1990. Some of the protections mirror those for other groups with a history of discrimination. However, unlike race or sex discrimination, the disabled have unique obstacles in terms of athletic participation.

First, the central focus of disabled athletics rests in the secondary schools and colleges, rather than the professional sports. Given that professional athletes must rank at the pinnacle of those playing the sport, it is difficult, albeit unlikely, for someone without an arm or leg to perform competitively with others. And, in the rare event that someone with a life-altering disability makes it to the pros, that person should understand the risks involved in participation.

Discrimination laws protecting the disabled in public education have been in effect for over forty years, and a body of jurisprudence has developed from the many lawsuits that have been filed against school districts. The first of the two major disability protection laws, section 504 of the Rehabilitation Act of 1973, prohibits the exclusion of participation from any program or activity receiving federal financial assistance (29 USC, sec. 794, 2010). The second, the Americans with Disabilities Act of 1990 (ADA) (42 USC, sec. 12101 et seq., 2009), expanded this mandate. Enacted to protect disabled people from discrimination in the workplace, by private entities offering public accommodations and services and by the government, it ensures that disabled Americans are offered the same opportunities as all others in society. The ADA incorporated section 504 of the 1973 act and has been utilized by student-athletes when faced with exclusion from participation in a sport.

In order for an athlete (or just about anyone else) to bring an ADA claim, the person must demonstrate a "disability" and, despite that disability, the person must be "otherwise qualified" to obtain the benefit sought. The ADA defines disability as "a physical or mental impairment that substantially limits one or more of the major life activities of such individual" (42 USC, sec. 12132, 2009). An athlete has a claim when he or she proves that, if not for his or her disability, the person qualifies to engage in the activity. Once shown, the burden shifts to the defendant to show that the eligibility requirements are essential and neutral and that the proposed accommodations for the disabled athlete fundamentally alter the nature of the athletic program.

Under Title II of the ADA, which applies only to state or local governments or agencies, the individual must show that the defendant is a public entity, that he or she is a qualified individual with a disability and that this person has been excluded from participation or denied benefits offered by the entity because of the disability. Public educational institutions or state public school athletic associations fit into this definition. Typical disability claims under this title involve denials of student requests for waivers of certain eligibility requirements. More specifically, in the sports context, maximum age requirements, the eight-semester rule (which prohibits a student from participating in interscholastic sports if he or she has spent more than eight semesters completing grades 9–12) and physical requirements are frequently litigated. The following examples illustrate the point: a nineteen-year-old in a special education program seeks the right to try out for the football team but is barred because of an eighteen-year-old maximum age ceiling, a student in his ninth semester because of a neurological condition seeks the tryout for the track team or a student blind in one eye seeks a spot on the school's hockey team.

Cases against private entities offering public accommodations or services are brought under Title III of the ADA. The accompanying regulations define a place of public accommodation as "a facility operated by a private entity whose operations affect commerce and come within at least one of twelve enumerated categories." Under a Title III action, a plaintiff must show a disability, that the claim is against a private-entity defendant operating a "place of public accommodation," that the athlete was denied the opportunity to participate or benefit from services or accommodations on the basis of his disability and that reasonable accommodations could have been made without fundamentally altering the nature of the entity.

The intricacies of disability laws in the sports contexts under Title III were found in the Supreme Court decision in *PGA Tour, Inc. v. Casey Martin* (2001). Martin, a professional golfer, suffered from a circulatory disorder that causes severe pain and that had already atrophied his right leg, making it virtually impossible for him to walk an eighteen-hole golf game. Despite this condition, Martin progressed to the point where he sought qualification to the PGA Tour, the top professional level for men's golf. Unlike the PGA's other levels of competition, the PGA Tour rules stated that no participant may use a golf cart. Martin applied for a waiver from that rule but was denied. The PGA claimed that the use of the cart gives one participant an advantage over other players who have to walk a course.

Leaving aside the issue of poor public relations caused by the PGA's act, Martin's case brought forth a slew of comments, many of them off point. The key issues were (a) whether a private golf course (where most PGA tournaments are staged) becomes a "place of public accommodation" under the ADA because it hosts a golf tournament and, if so, (b) whether Martin fitted the definition of someone disabled. The majority opinion of the U.S. Supreme Court concluded that a golf course was indeed a place of public accommodation, for the players as well as the audience, thus bringing the dispute within the jurisdiction of the ADA. This key point received far too little coverage. Then the court had to determine whether Martin fit the definition of "disabled," which he did because his impairment substantially limited one or more major life activities.

Some mistakenly compared Martin's case to that of Ken Venturi, who suffered through heat stroke while competing in a golf tournament in the 1960s, to show the importance of this "walking only" rule. But that also missed the point. Venturi was not disabled because it was the weather conditions that caused his serious heat stroke, not a life-limiting physical condition. In rejecting the views of many golfers, the court noted that access to a cart would not fundamentally alter the competition because other levels of PGA competition permitted a cart. Therefore, a denial to accommodate Martin's disability was a violation of the ADA. The court reasoned that walking between holes was not an "essential attribute of the game itself." Even if it were to alter the game, Martin endures much more fatigue even with the use of the cart than his able-bodied competitors.

Ethical Issue—Player Compensation

In 2016, five members of the World Cup Champion U.S. National Women's Soccer Team filed a complaint with the Equal Employment Opportunity Commission, alleging that U.S. Soccer, the governing body of the sport, engaged in wage discrimination against the women's team. They claimed they received significantly less compensation on bonuses, appearance fees and per diem compensation compared with the U.S. men's team, despite the fact that the U.S. men have been far less successful in their sport (Das, 2016). They sought the right to strike over those terms.

According to the U.S. Soccer Federation's financial report, a men's team player, for example, receives $5000 for a loss in a friendly match but as much as $17,625 for a win against a top opponent. A women's player receives $1350 for a similar match, but only if the United States wins; women's players receive no bonuses for losses or ties.

The U.S. Soccer Federation argued that men's soccer generates more revenue than women's soccer, and in most of the world it is safe to say that is true. However, the members who brought the lawsuit argued that the U.S. Women's team generated almost $20 million more in revenue in 2015 than the U.S. men's teams.

This lawsuit was part of a long-standing dispute between the U.S. Soccer Federation and the women's team over a collective bargaining agreement. As there was no women's league in 2016, U.S. Soccer employed the women's team.

However, a court effectively dismissed the claim, concluding that the no-strike provisions of the prior collective bargaining agreement were in effect at the time of the lawsuit and therefore ruled that the players did not have the right to strike (*U.S. Soccer Federation v. U.S. Women's National Soccer Team Players' Association*, 2016).

References

1981–82–2014–15 NCAA Sports Sponsorship and Participation Rates Report (2015, October). Retrieved November 2, 2015, from http://www.ncaa.org/sites/default/files/Participation%20Rates%20Final.pdf

Americans with Disabilities Act, 42 USC, sec. 12101 et seq. (2009).

Bentley, E. (2004). Title IX: How Title IX should be interpreted to afford women the opportunities they deserve in intercollegiate athletics. *Sports Lawyers Journal*, 11, 89.

Berger, K. (2014, August 12). Sale of clippers to Steve Ballmer closes; Donald Sterling out. Retrieved October 30, 2015, from www.cbssports.com/nba/

writer/ken-berger/24657297/sale-of-clippers-to-steve-ballmer-closes-donald-sterling-out

Bisher, F. (2003, April 16). Johnson: Club will never have female member. *Atlanta Journal-Constitution*, p. C1.

Bryan v. Colgate University, 1996 WL 328446 (N.D.N.Y. 1996).

Civil Rights Restoration Act of 1987 (20 USC, sec. 1681, 2000).

Cohen v. Brown University, 991 F. 2d 888 (1st Cir. 1993).

Das, A. (2016, March 31). Top female players accuse U.S. soccer of wage discrimination. *The New York Times*. Retrieved April 3, 2016, from http://www.nytimes.com/2016/04/01/sports/soccer/uswnt-us-women-carli-lloyd-alex-morgan-hope-solo-complain.html?ref=soccer

Department of Education (2002). Equal opportunity in intercollegiate athletics: Requirements under Title IX of the Education Amendments of 1972. Retrieved August 25, 2010, from http://www2.ed.gov/about/offices/list/ocr/docs/interath.html

Equity in Athletics Disclosure Act (20 USC, sec. 1092, 1999).

Griggs v. Duke Power Co., 401 U.S. 424 (1971).

Grove City College v. Bell 465 U.S. 555 (1984).

Jackson, J. L., Sr. (1997, October 27). Save the dream: March on the Capital, speech delivered October 27, 1997, Sacramento, CA. Retrieved January 17, 2005, from http://www.inmotionmagazine.com/jjsave.html

Johnson, E. (2007, April 12). "Nightline" Classic: Al Campanis. *ABCNews.com*. Retrieved August 25, 2010, from http://abcnews.go.com/Nightline/ESPNSports/story?id=3034914

Langton, C. (2015, September 15). 20 Athletes who have been openly homophonic. *Thesportster.com*. Retrieved May 24, 2016, from http://www.thesportster.com/entertainment/20-athletes-who-have-been-openly-homophobic/?view=all

Lapchik, R. (2014, December 30). Racism still evident in sports world. *ESPN.com*. Retrieved October 21, 2016, from http://www.espn.com/espn/story/_/id/12093538/the-year-racism-sport

Lapchick, R. (2015a, September 10). Racial and gender report card: National Football League (Appendix I). Retrieved October 30, 2015, from http://nebula.wsimg.com/91f862c7e055dd1842f9ceb52428ae2c?AccessKeyId=DAC3A56D8FB782449D2A&disposition=0&alloworigin=1

Lapchick, R. (2015b, April 15). Racial and gender report card: Major League Baseball (Appendix I). Retrieved October 30, 2015, from http://nebula.wsimg.com/35d775f4b01264c377a96da7f616a3b8?AccessKeyId=DAC3A56D8FB782449D2A&disposition=0&alloworigin=1

Lapchick, R. (2015c, July 1). Racial and gender report card: National Basketball Association (Appendix I). Retrieved October 30, 2015, from http://nebula.wsimg.com/6e1489cc3560e1e1a2fa88e3030f5149?AccessKeyId=DAC3A56D8FB782449D2A&disposition=0&alloworigin=1

McEldowney, H. (2009, August 9). As colleges cut athletics, Title IX creates an injustice to men. *The Washington Post*. Retrieved May 10, 2010, from http://www.washingtonpost.com/wp-dyn/content/article/2009/08/05/AR2009080503089.html

National Federation of High School Athletic Associations (2015). 2014–15 high school athletics participation survey. Retrieved November 2, 2015, from http://www.nfhs.org/ParticipationStatics/PDF/2014–15_Participation_Survey_ Results.pdf

Nat'l Wrestling Coaches Ass'n v. U.S. Dep't of Education, 126 S. Ct. 12 (2005).

Nat'l Wrestling Coaches Ass'n v. U.S. Dept. of Education, 366 F.3d 930 (D.C. Cir. 2004), aff'g, Nat'l Wrestling Coaches Ass'n v. U.S. Dep't. of Education, 263 F.Supp.2d 82 (D.D.C. 2003).

Pearlman, J. (2000). At full blast. *Sports Illustrated, 91*(25), 60.

Pederson v. LSU, 912 F. Supp. 892 (La. 1996).

PGA Tour, Inc. v. Casey Martin, 532 U.S. 661 (2001).

Rehabilitation Act of 1973, Nondiscrimination under federal grants and programs, 29 USC sec 794 (2010).

Rogosin, D. (1995). *Invisible men: Life in baseball's minor leagues*. Lincoln: University of Nebraska Press, p. 192.

The Secretary of Education's Commission on Opportunity in Athletics (2002). *Open to All: Title IX at 30*. Retrieved June 10, 2005, from http://www. gpoaccess.gov/eric/200405/ed480939.pdf

Siemaszko, C. (2003, October 2). He quits ESPN gig over race remark. *New York Daily News*, p. 4.

Smith, S. (2000, October 13). Iverson's rap? NBA will take the rap. *Chicago Tribune*, p. 9.

Standora, L. (2001, June 23). Now, Rocker is headed to the Bronx, instead of Queens. *New York Daily News*, p. 4.

Strege, J. (2015, April 12). "111 rich and powerful" members of Augusta National. Retrieved October 30, 2015, from www.golfdigest.com/ story/111-rich-and-powerful-members

Title VII, Civil Rights Act (1964), 42 USC sec. 2000e et seq.

Title IX of the Education Amendments (1972), 20 USC sec. 1681 et seq.

Title IX, Policy Interpretation (1979) 44. Fed. Reg. 71, 418.

Turner, G. (2013, October 17). The most racist sports statements of the last 25 years. *Complex.com*. Retrieved May 25, 2016, from http://www.complex. com/sports/2013/10/racist-sports-statements-25-years/

U.S. Soccer Federation v. U.S. Women's National Soccer Team Players' Association, 2016 WL 3125008 (W.D. Ill. 2016).

Weiler, P., & Roberts, G. (2004). *Sports and the law—Text and cases* (3rd ed.). St. Paul, MN: West, p. 85.

Women's Sports Foundation (2008). Understanding Title IX and Athletics 101. Retrieved May 15, 2010, from http://www.womenssportsfoundation.org/ Content/Articles/Issues/Title-IX/U/Understanding-Title-IX-and-Athletics-101. aspx

14 Intellectual Property and Sports

Unlike a business that produces machinery or apparel, a league, team owner, college or individual athlete does not need an engineering plant, heavy equipment or a fleet of trucks to manufacture or transport its product. Instead, the leagues, teams, athletes, colleges, conferences and independent tournaments possess rights to "intangible" property—their names, logo designs and general rights to license and reproduce those items for merchandising purposes. Over the last quarter-century, the marketing and sale of the team names, designs, uniforms and player images have grown and now constitute a lucrative revenue base.

The licensing and merchandising of sports properties has been transformed from a relatively small and fragmented sideline into a $26 billion global industry. Licensed sports merchandise account for 11 percent of worldwide retail sales of licensed merchandise (Licensing Book Online, 2015). Owners of the intellectual property enter into licensing agreements that account for the bulk of the revenue. In 2014, the National Football League led the major leagues, earning $3.29 billion, followed by Major League Baseball ($3.289 billion) and the National Basketball Association ($2.32 billion) (The Licensing Letter, 2015). The list continues with the National Hockey League (NHL) receiving $995 million, the National Association for Stock Car Auto Racing (NASCAR) $761 million and Major League Soccer (MLS) $558 million.

What is licensed? Merchandise carrying the names, logos and designs associated with a particular sport, league, team, college, athletic conference or other governing body. The licensee, often a firm manufacturing clothing, shoes or sports equipment, contracts with the intellectual property owner or licensing firm for the use of its names, logos and designs on items sold to the public. The licensor often receives a stated percentage of the sales and, even more importantly, has control over the production, design and overall quality of the product. The major aspects of these agreements are discussed later in this chapter.

Trademarks

Intellectual property contains a broad category of rights; the most important for sports purposes is trademark protection and licensing. All too often, trademarks and copyrights are confused. They are quite different. Defined as "any word, name, symbol or device used to identify and distinguish goods from those manufactured or sold by others" (Trademarks, 2010), a trademark is a brand name, design, symbol, shape, color scheme, slogan or even smell for use in commerce. For example, the brand name Coca-Cola identifies a particular soft drink. The name *Coca-Cola* is trademarked—a rival cannot use that name without permission. If the rival does, it faces severe penalties, including civil fines, injunctions, even criminal prosecution (Trademarks, 2010). The law requires that a trademark owner use the mark. An unused mark loses protection after a certain period of time, opening it up for use by another entity.

Most U.S.-based trademarks are registered with the U.S. Patent and Trademark Office in Alexandria, Virginia. In order to obtain trademark protection, the mark has to be "distinctive." Examples of distinctiveness involving sports-related marks include "arbitrary" titles—common words applied in an unfamiliar way. The Detroit Tigers and the Carolina Panthers come to mind. In the context of their sport, these words connect a fan's mind to the particular team. There are also "suggestive" marks—those requiring imagination, thought and perception, such as the New York Yankees. Another basis for distinctiveness comes from "fanciful" marks—made-up names with no dictionary meaning. "Super Bowl" is a trademark of the NFL (although it did not coin the term and was hesitant to use it at first). A generic term cannot be trademarked, as it lacks distinctiveness. The terms *football* and *baseball* themselves have no protection, so, if anyone wanted to design a sweatshirt with those terms, no trademark infringement would result. Once a trademark is registered, the owner uses a circled R (®) as evidence of the existence of the mark.

A protected trademark cannot be used for a commercial purpose without the owner's permission. Trademark infringement occurs when one improperly uses another's protected trademarks or uses a mark "likely to cause confusion about the source of a product or service." The focus of trademark infringement analysis is on the confusion of actual or potential customers. Accordingly, an infringer's products or services need only be sufficiently related to the trademark owner's products or services so that it is likely that both are promoted to and/or used by common customers (inta.org, 2015). This rule protects consumers from being misled by the use of infringing marks and protects producers from unfair practices by an imitating competitor. Infringement involves one of two situations. The first involves creation of a design similar or substantially similar to an existing trademark, creating a "likelihood of confusion." Courts consider the following factors to determine whether confusion exists: the degree of similarity between the plaintiff's and defendant's mark, the proximity of the products or services and the existence of actual confusion (Trademarks, 2010). No one factor is necessarily controlling, and in general infringement is evaluated on a case-by-case basis, based on the totality of the circumstances.

It is incumbent on a sports organization to consider the trademark ramifications of a name or logo seriously. That requires due diligence, a legal term meaning a comprehensive search to see if the name or design is used by someone else or is sufficiently similar to the other mark. The failure to do so may not only lead to infringement claims. After the NFL's Colts left Baltimore for Indianapolis, that city was awarded a Canadian Football League (CFL) franchise, under the name "Baltimore Colts." The NFL and the Indianapolis Colts sued, and a federal appeals court enjoined the CFL team from using the "Colts" name *(Indianapolis Colts v. Metropolitan Baltimore Football Club*, 1994).

In another example, the (now-defunct) Atlanta Thrashers of the NHL received their name in an expeditious but risky manner. After the NHL awarded the franchise to Ted Turner, Turner, asked about the name of the team by a reporter, blurted out "Thrashers . . . I like the name Thrashers." (The brown thrasher is the state bird of Georgia.) A California team owned the mark, and Turner paid a settlement to avoid a lawsuit (Unger, 1998).

The second basis for infringement is clear-cut counterfeiting of goods, known as "knock-offs." Known as "unfair competition," such acts are prohibited by the Lanham Act (Trademarks, 2010), which is the most important law protecting trademarks. The act provides the courts with the right to enjoin the manufacture of knock-off merchandise, coupled with monetary penalties. Fake goods costs sports organizations sizable amounts of money, and, because these counterfeit goods are often made cheaply, such items hurt the image of the trademark holder. Seizure of the fake goods by the FBI and local police occurs, but, despite that power, it is often difficult to catch infringers because it is easy for them to make knock-offs and they are able to work quickly and sell their fake goods in locations such as street fairs and small shops. Larger and more reputable stores usually won't carry them.

More recently, a third method of trademark infringement, known as dilution, was created. Although dilution does not involve a likelihood of confusion, it applies when a similar, though not identical, mark "blurs" or "tarnishes" that trademark. The necessary elements to a claim of dilution by blurring require that (a) the first mark must be distinctive and (b) the second user attempts to capitalize on the first mark's status. Dilution by tarnishing occurs when a new trademark's similarity to a famous mark causes consumers mistakenly to associate the famous mark with the second user's inferior or offensive product (Kimpflen, 2004). A hypothetical example of blurring exists when a minor league lacrosse team calls itself the New York Yanquis; in the case of tarnishing, it would be a strip club called the New York Spankees. Whereas every nation has its own trademark laws, an international treaty known as the Madrid Protocol enables a person or entity from a member state to simultaneously register a trademark with all member states at the time of original filing in the home country. Adoption of this treaty means that trademark applicants do not have to file separately in every member country, making it easier and more cost efficient to obtain international trademark protection. Since the adoption of the treaty by the United States in 2003, domestic sports organizations have expanded their trademark applications to countries all over the world (wipo.int, n .d.).

Ethical Issue: Ambush Marketing

In recent years, ambush marketing has increasingly become a concern for major sporting event organizers, as this practice threatens to devalue its partnership marketing deals with their official sponsors. Ambush marketing is a controversial strategy that companies who are not official sponsors employ in an attempt to monetarily capitalize on an event's popularity and reputation through various marketing and promotional campaigns. By implementing ambush marketing tactics, these companies look to engage consumers and increase their brand awareness without experiencing the financial obligations and incurring activation duties that official sponsors are responsible for (Nufer, 2013). Many event attendees are often misled by carefully crafted advertising campaigns to believe that the ambush marketers are officially affiliated with the specific event.

One of the most common ambush marketing tactics used by unofficial sponsors is to strategically place advertisements within a close geographic proximity to the event, especially in locations where rights have not been secured through the official sponsorship (Fortunato, 2013). For example, Heineken had been the exclusive beer sponsor of America's Grand Slam tennis tournament, the U.S. Open, since 1992. Stella Artois, a rival brand owned by Anheuser-Busch InBev, had placed fifteen advertisements with tennis-themed slogans, including "A Perfect Match" and "Your Trophy Awaits," along the platform of a commuter railroad station near the U.S. Tennis Center. Officials from the United States Tennis Association, the national governing body of tennis and organizer of the three-week tennis tournament, asked Stella Artois to remove the advertisements; however, the Belgian beverage company declined. Stella Artois was not under any legal obligation to adhere to the USTA's requests, as the company did not feature any of the USTA's trademarked logos on its advertisements, and thus, technically did not infringe on any trademark protections. Also, Stella Artois was not in violation of any geographic restrictions since the tournament's sponsorship rules only covered the immediate geographic area of the USTA's Billie Jean King National Tennis Center, the surrounding parkland and the boardwalk used by fans to reach the tennis center from the subway station (Kaplan, 2011).

Ambush marketers have also caused global sporting event organizers, including the International Olympic Committee and FIFA, to implement measures to protect its official sponsors from ambush marketing. The IOC provides host cities and its organizing committees with the *Olympic Marks and Imagery Usage Handbook* as a guideline to the measures the host city must take to control ambush marketing in order to protect Olympic intellectual property and the rights of Olympic official marketing partners (Smith, 2012). In preparation for the 2012 Summer Olympic Games, the British government enacted the London Olympic Games and Paralympic Games Act, which created Olympic enforcement officers, employed by the London Olympic Organizing Committee, to conduct patrols around Olympic venues to ensure that local businesses were in compliance with the advertising regulations. Official Olympic sponsors were also given strict guidelines for properly implementing the Olympic rings into their marketing campaigns, including background and color reproduction restrictions (legislation.gov.uk, 2006).

Is there anything unethical about ambush marketing? It may comply with the letter of the law, but does its effect dilute the efforts of rights holders to get the proper brand value for what they paid for? Or is ambush marketing an attempt to stifle the right of a firm to advertise its wares, stifling competition?

Copyright

As noted earlier, the concepts of trademarks and copyrights are frequently confused. Although trademark law protects names, designs and logos, copyright protects "original words of authorship in any tangible medium of expression" (Copyright Act, 2010). Examples include books, music, recordings, broadcasts, films, theatrical presentations and choreography Changes in the late 1990s have expanded protection to the life of the author plus seventy years, whether the work is performed or not (Copyright Term Extension Act, 17 USC sec. 302 (1998).

The right to broadcast and rebroadcast sporting events has been a central topic involving copyrights. In copyright law, infringement can be direct (done by volition of the infringer), contributory (occurring when one, with knowledge of the infringing activity, induces, causes or materially contributes to the infringing conduct of another) or vicarious (when one has the right and ability to control the infringer's conduct and receives a direct financial benefit from the infringement) (*Fonovisa v. Cherry Auction*, 1996). Newer media such as YouTube have been accused of copyright infringement due to the posting of portions of copyrighted sports events. The claim centered on whether YouTube engaged in copyright infringement for individual uploads of copyrighted materials and, if so, what kind of infringement occurs. After protracted litigation, the parties settled the case in 2014 (Stempel, 2014).

Athletes' Right of Publicity

In addition to trademark protection, which concerns designs and logos used in commerce to identify products, there is an intellectual property right in one's name, likeness and voice. Known as the right of publicity, this concept allows an individual to protect and control the use of his or her identity for commercial purposes. Laws recognized by most states cover the unauthorized use of all recognizable aspects of a person, including image, name or nickname, biographical data and a distinctive feature such as voice or walk, all of which are often referred to as a celebrity's *persona* (*ETW Corporation v. Jireh Publishing, Inc.*, 2003). Unlike copyright or trademark law, which are based on federal statutes, the right of publicity is a creature of state law, and states vary on the amount and length of protection for this right (Cal. Civ. Code, 2009, sec. 3344; N.Y. Civ. Rights Law, 2009, secs. 50 and 51).

In addition, tension exists between the scope of publicity rights and the constitutional protection of free speech under the First Amendment, which has vexed courts and commentators and resulted in inconsistent rulings. Two cases demonstrate this problem. The first involved a painting entitled "Masters of Augusta," which commemorated Tiger Woods's victory at the 1997 Masters' tournament. The painting shows Woods in three different poses. Also featured are the Augusta National Clubhouse and likenesses of Arnold Palmer, Sam Snead, Ben Hogan, Walter Hagen, Bobby Jones and Jack Nicklaus looking down at Woods.

The artist, Rick Rush, sold "limited-edition prints" of the work. When Woods discovered this, he (or, to be more precise, his corporation, ETW, Inc.) brought suit, claiming a violation of his right of publicity. A divided federal appeals court concluded that Woods's right of publicity was outweighed by the First Amendment. Noting that the painting constitutes a "creative" work of art, not simply an illustration or photograph of Woods, it was protected expression and not an infringement of Woods's rights. The majority of the court noted that Rush's work consisted of a "collage of images" that in combination described a historic sports event and conveyed the significance of Woods's achievement in that event (*ETW Corporation v. Jireh Publishing, Inc.*, 2003).

Other courts, however, have ruled in favor of the athlete. Tony Twist, a former NHL player known as an "enforcer," filed suit claiming that a comic book producer misappropriated his likeness. After learning of the existence of a comic book that contained a villainous character named "Tony Twistelli," Twist sued the creators, publishers and marketers of the comic book. Twistelli engaged in activities such as multiple murders, abduction of children and sex with prostitutes. The fictional Twistelli and the real Twist bore no physical resemblance and, aside from the common nickname, were similar only in the sense that each had an "enforcer" or tough-guy persona, according to the court. Unlike the ruling in the Woods case, the Supreme Court of Missouri concluded that the comic book creators and publishers intended to gain commercial advantage by using Twist's name to attract consumer attention to the comic books and that they marketed the comics and the character to hockey fans who knew Twist and his reputation. This, according to the court, outweighed First Amendment protections (*Doe v. TCI Cablevision*, 2003). More recently, the courts have tilted toward greater protection for athletes' name and image rights (*Hart v. EA Sports*, 2013; *In re NCAA Student-Athlete Likeness Litigation*, 2014). Like holders of trademarks, athletes protect their image for economic and personal reasons. The more celebrity status an athlete has, the more leverage he or she has to enter into endorsement and marketing deals. Using that athlete's name or likeness without permission undercuts control of his or her reputation and results in damages for lost business opportunity. For example, if someone uses an athlete's name in connection with a tawdry business, the athlete will stop this use (usually by a court order) to protect the athlete's image. The failure to take action could create public perception that the athlete assents to the representation.

The public's interest in particular athletes based on their success and personality has resulted in the achievement of celebrity or near-celebrity status. Athletes such as Babe Ruth, Michael Jordan, Wayne Gretzky, George Foreman, Venus and Serena Williams, Derek Jeter and LeBron James have a protected property right in their personas. They can license their names or likenesses in posters, apparel, toys and video games, generating fees often based on a percentage of each item sold.

Licensing Agreements

Merchandising encompasses the practice of companies selling products with the trademark of a league, conference, team, college or other organization on those products. The theory behind sports merchandising is that the market power of that organization as a brand attracts fans of the sport to buy the merchandise and therefore enhances the value of the product sold. Although licensing agreements can involve individual names and likenesses, for our purposes we will focus on trademark licensing, as agreements are more frequent and standardized. A licensor (usually a league) and licensee sign a "trademark license agreement" granting permission from the licensor trademark owner for the licensee to use a trademark for a defined purpose. An agreement using the name of an athlete often results in a similar agreement (even if the name was not trademarked). The agreement specifies the scope of the license. In addition to identifying the parties to the agreement and the specific trademarks licensed, the agreement states what rights are licensed and, particularly in the case of goods manufactured bearing the trademark, the standards and quality control mechanisms.

The major segments of a license agreement involve the following.

Quality Control

In almost every license agreement, the licensor exercises quality control over a licensee's goods and services. The importance of this power cannot be overstated. Because a trademark represents the trademark owner's brand name and reputation, the owner wants to ensure that the goods and services possess a high level of quality, as consumers tend to rely on this reputation in making purchasing decisions. A licensed product of inferior quality hurts the reputation of the licensor.

For example, say that the Winnetka Wombats licensed their trademark to X Clothiers, Inc., to make apparel bearing the team's logo. If X Clothiers makes poor-quality goods, customers are apt to complain and, although the team did not make the goods, the image and brand of the team will be damaged by adverse reaction from buyers. That could translate to lower sales in the future and even to a diminishing interest in the team.

Specific Use of the Trademark

The licensor often specifies the manner in which a trademark will be used on or in connection with the goods and services of the licensee and on advertising and promotional materials. Often, the agreement requires that the licensee obtain the licensor's permission before using any new presentation of the trademark.

Term

The trademark license usually states a fixed term for the license and the conditions under which the license may be renewed for an additional period. In 2015, Major League Baseball Properties (MLBP) extended its contract with Majestic Athletics, its manufacturer for on-field uniforms and replica jerseys, through 2019, potentially doubling the previously guaranteed income (Sports Business Daily, 2015). The same year, MLBP extended its licensing agreements with New Era (for caps), Nike ("performance wear") and '47 brand for caps, uniforms and leisure clothing, respectively, through 2019 (Brown, 2015).

Exclusivity

An agreement almost always gives the licensee an exclusive right to use that trademark in connection with the manufacture of a certain line of products. If a shoe company obtains a license, it should have the exclusive right to use the name and logo owned by the licensor. If the licensor could negotiate with another shoe company, this would severely compromise the branding of the first shoe company.

Royalties

The royalty payments—usually a percentage of sales—are stated and defined to ensure that both parties understand the calculation.

In recent years, the four major professional sports leagues have reduced the number of licensees, seeking long-term exclusive agreements. In 2010, the NFL signed an exclusive five-year contract with Nike to provide all on-field and sideline apparel for all thirty-two teams, which began in the 2012 season (Belson, 2010). It was extended in 2015 for three additional years (Lefton, 2015). Also in 2015, the NBA and Nike announced an eight-year deal that would make Nike the official on-court apparel provider and first NBA apparel partner to have its logo appear on NBA uniforms beginning with the 2017–18 season (NBA.com, 2015). With this partnership, Nike will also expand its presence at WNBA events and become a marketing partner of the NBA Development League.

An exclusive deal makes sense. A few major licensing agreements with marquee firms outweigh a multiplicity of deals, which cheapens the brand and generates public confusion. However, such deals are not without the threat of litigation, as was the case when the apparel manufacturer American Needle brought an antitrust action against the NFL (discussed in Chapter 1) claiming that the exclusivity violated its rights (*American Needle v. NFL*, 2010).

Professional Leagues and Group Licensing

Each of the four major sports leagues has created separate corporations in charge of licensing the uses of the names, logos, symbols, emblems, signs, uniforms and identification of the league and its member clubs. Note that the individual teams no longer control such licenses (with a few exceptions), but the leagues brought this power "in-house." Specifically, NBA Properties, NFL Properties, NHL Enterprises and MLB Properties hold the exclusive trademark and licensing rights for each of the leagues and oversee the marketing and protection of individual trademarks and products. Revenues in the form of royalties deriving from these agreements are shared by all the teams in the respective league. The royalties are generally calculated based on a rate averaging 12 percent of sales among the major leagues (Silcox, 2012).

The unions representing major league players often act as agents for the licensing of athletes' names and likenesses and have, in some cases, made separate agreements with licensees from those of the league. These licenses focus around the athletes, not the team-owned property. Such agreements contain a royalty formula for the sharing of licensing revenues.

Both the leagues' and players' associations' licensing systems are group-wide and do not apply to deals negotiated by athletes individually (Ferber, 2005). For the NFL players, it is any program involving six or more players. For Major League Baseball players, the minimum is three.

The vast majority of league athletes participate in these arrangements by signing annual contracts with their union, allowing the leagues to market various items bearing their likeness (Players Choice Group Licensing Program, n.d.). The licensed items—T-shirts, trading cards and video games—are often controlled by the licensing division of the league. Revenues derived from the licensing are distributed among the athletes. Licensing agreements are made by a firm with both the league and union to ensure uniformity.

Players may opt out of the group licensing agreements, and on occasion some do in the hope of negotiating more lucrative marketing deals. One of the first players—and probably the most famous—to opt out of a group licensing agreement was Michael Jordan. He withdrew the use of his name and likeness for licensed NBA products. Jordan's superstar status and economic impact to the league afforded him the opportunity to go solo. However, most players remain a part of the agreement because they lack that kind of economic and marketing leverage.

A summary of the licensing systems in each of the four major sports leagues follows.

National Basketball Association

NBA Properties, Inc. (NBAP), the marketing and licensing arm of the NBA, owns and exclusively licenses all trademarks, service marks, trade names and logos of the NBA and its member teams. NBA Properties has complete control over all the league's trademarks and logos outside of each team's own arena. In addition, NBA Properties possesses the right to market the trademarks and logos internationally. All income that is generated from such intellectual property is split evenly among all the teams. NBAP acts as the exclusive licensor for NBA teams and controls all merchandising contracts. Regarding players' rights, the NBA and the players' union, the National Basketball Players' Association (NBPA), negotiated a group license agreement in their collective bargaining agreement. That agreement allows the league to retain the right to license a player's name, number and likeness for uniforms, trading cards, posters, video games and other products. It granted a license to Reebok (as the NBA's current apparel licensee) and to Nike (to replace Reebok beginning with the 2017 season) to manufacture player jerseys; revenues from sales of these jerseys are split between the league and the team. Retired NBA players also share in this agreement, whereby revenue from sales is split among the league, the National Basketball Retired Player's Association (NBRPA), and in some cases the retired player (NBA CBA, Article XXXVII, sec. 1, 2011).

In 2014, sales of NBA-licensed merchandise came to $2.3 billion (The Licensing Letter, 2015). Unlike the other major sports leagues' unions, the NBPA does not distribute licensing revenue or enter into group licensing agreements on behalf of the players. NBAP has the sole authority to enter into such licensing agreements (NBA CBA, 2011, Article XXXVII Sec. 1).

National Football League

The NFL teams created NFL Properties (NFLP) in 1981 to act as the exclusive agent for negotiating and entering into merchandise licensing and sponsorship agreements. The NFLP is equally owned by the franchises of the NFL, and its role consists primarily of holding the team and league trademarks and the receipt and distribution of any income derived from the licensing efforts of NFLP.

The income derived from these licensing deals passes to the NFL Trust, which controls these revenues before passing it to the teams on an equal share basis, regardless of the amount earned by any particular team's "club marks," which include a team's name, helmet design, uniform design and identifying slogans (*NFLP v. Dallas Cowboys*, 1996). In March 2004, team owners voted in favor of a fifteen-year extension of the NFL Trust. The NFL's licensees sold $3.29 billion worth of goods in 2014 (The Licensing Letter, 2015). In 2011, the NFL and Anheuser-Busch InBev entered into a six-year deal, including rights fees, marketing, media and team spending commitments. The rights fees for the beer category averaged $50 million over the life of the deal (Lefton, 2010). In 2015, Anheuser-Bush extended its sponsorship deal, reportedly worth over $1.4 billion, with the NFL through the 2022 Super Bowl (Roberts, 2015).

Unlike the other leagues, the NFL Players' Association (NFLPA) has its own marketing and licensing subsidiary, known as NFL Players, Inc., which represents 1800 active and 2700 retired players. Although a player may opt out of the arrangement, NFL Players, Inc., represents the overwhelming majority of NFL players.

NFL Players, Inc., negotiates the licensing of player names and images in trading cards and collectibles (such as bobble heads, figurines and pennants), video games, fantasy football, apparel and novelties and other retail licensed products. NFL Players, Inc., grants licensees the rights to use players' names, numbers, likenesses and images. It handles group licensing agreements involving six or more players. NFL Players, Inc., receives a royalty percentage for the licensing, which after administrative costs is distributed among the players. Licensing and sponsorship revenue totaled $117.2 million in the fiscal year ending in February 2015 (Kaplan, 2015). Sports trading card sales constituted a significant revenue source, totaling $36.3 million among two of the largest companies in the category: Panini America and Topps. During that year, Nike paid the NFLPA $10 million, and Electronic Arts paid $2.8 million (Kaplan, 2015). Retired players are now a part of the royalty pool.

Major League Baseball

Major League Baseball Properties (MLBP), established in 1966, controls the marketing and licensing of all league-wide and team trademarks. Individual teams retain some exclusive control of their trademarks within a specified radius of their home stadiums (*New York Yankees & Adidas v. MLBP*, 1997). All domestic promotional and retail licensing royalty income is shared among the teams in equal amounts, regardless of the actual income generated from a single team. MLBP obtains a percentage of fees based on their gross income. The royalty revenue derived from licensed merchandise is placed in a general fund, but the individual teams can increase their revenue by selling game souvenirs, such as bats and baseballs used during games. In 1997, team owners granted the Major League Baseball commissioner authority to distribute the shared sources of revenue unevenly, so that "poorer" teams (generally those playing in smaller markets) receive a larger share to make up for their losses or disproportionately low amount of local revenue. MLBA licensed merchandise amounted to $3.289 billion in sales and range from 11 to 14 percent (Silcox, 2012), or about $400 million in royalties in 2014 (The Licensing Letter, 2015)

For the past five decades, Major League Baseball players have signed annual contracts with the Major League Baseball Players' Association (MLBPA) to market their names and likenesses on merchandise. Any firm seeking to use the names or likenesses of more than two Major League

Baseball players in connection with a commercial product, product line or promotion must sign a licensing agreement with the MLBPA. The most recent agreement includes interactive rights, including group rights to player likenesses. The license grants the use of the players' names and/or likenesses only, not the use of any Major League Baseball team logos or marks. Examples of products licensed by the MLBPA include trading cards, video games, T-shirts and uniforms. Players receive a pro rata share of licensing revenue, regardless of popularity or stature. Each player's share is determined by his actual days of Major League Baseball service in a given season (Peters, 2004). Players can opt out of the agreement, but that rarely occurs. One example was Barry Bonds (Raine, 2003).

National Association for Stock Car Auto Racing

In the past, NASCAR teams managed their licensing rights in-house—each team operated as an independent contractor, separate from the sanctioning body. That model was considered cumbersome and confusing for licensees because they had to negotiate five different contracts to get the licensing rights to five different drivers. In 2010, NASCAR created NASCAR Teams Licensing Trust—now known as NASCAR Team Properties (NTP)—a group that serves as a centralized licensing agency. Under this system, NASCAR Team Properties controls the licensing for drivers, teams and NASCAR marks. Revenue will be distributed to the race teams based on sales rather than by an equal revenue-share agreement. Participation in the program is voluntary. The participating team, driver and NASCAR trademarks are available under the umbrella of the licensing arm, creating a "one-stop shopping" business model (Nascar.com, 2011). As of 2015, the royalty rate was about 10 percent (The Licensing Letter, 2015).

Olympics

The International Olympic Committee (IOC) owns the name and controls the trademarks to the Olympic Games, including the Olympic symbol (the five rings), the Olympic flag, the Olympic motto (Citius, Altius, Fortius), the Olympic flame and the Olympic torch (Olympic Charter, 2015, Chapter 1, rules 7–2 and 7–4). The IOC obtains legal protection both domestically and internationally to protect against trademark infringement of the previously mentioned trademarks. In cases where the national law or a trademark registration grants to a national Olympic committee (NOC) the protection of the Olympic symbol, the NOC may use the ensuing rights only in accordance with instructions received from the IOC executive board (Olympic Charter, 2015, Chapter 1, bylaw to rule 7–14).

Each NOC shall take the necessary steps to prohibit any unauthorized use of the Olympic trademarks. In the United States, Olympic trademarks are given automatic protection under the Amateur Sports Act and its amendments, meaning that the United States Olympic Committee (USOC) does not even have to show "likelihood of confusion" to successfully prosecute an infringement case (36 USC, sec. 220506(a)). In one notable case, the USOC successfully sued an organization not affiliated with the USOC to stop it using the term *Gay Olympics*. After lengthy litigation, the Supreme Court upheld the USOC's rights (*San Francisco Arts & Athletics, Inc. v. USOC*, 1987).

Corporations wishing to use any Olympic trademarks must first pay the IOC a rights fee and sign a general sponsorship agreement. For the 2016 Rio Summer Olympics, eleven multinationals such as Coca-Cola, McDonald's and Samsung paid as much as $100 million each to be global sponsors of the Summer Games (Grohmann, 2014).

There have also been sponsorship disputes between athletes and NOCs concerning apparel sponsors. In the 1992 Barcelona Games, Michael Jordan and other players under contract to Nike draped a U.S. flag over the Reebok logo of their basketball warm-up suits. Kim Clijsters, then the number two-ranked player in women's tennis, withdrew from the 2004 Athens Olympics because she could not wear apparel from her own sponsor. For all licensing agreements, the conditions set forth under the Olympic Charter state that NOCs will receive half of all net income from "exploitations derived from use of the Olympic symbol and Olympic emblems, after the deduction of all taxes and out-of-pocket costs relating thereto" (Olympic Charter, 2015, bylaw to rule 7–14).

Since its inception, the International Olympic Committee's Rule 40 became one of the Olympic Charter's most controversial provisions. Rule 40 bars athletes participating in the Olympic Games from promoting their own sponsors during the three-week Olympic period if that sponsor is not an official Olympic partner (Olympic Charter, 2015, By-law to Rule 40). Violators could lose their medals. Rule 40 was designed to protect Olympic official sponsors from ambush marketing by prohibiting athletes from engaging in any advertising campaigns during the Olympics that did not involve an official Olympic sponsor. Many athletes strongly opposed the strict limitations of Rule 40 and even launched a Twitter campaign during the 2012 Summer Olympics in London to urge an end to the provision (The Associated Press, 2015). One year before the Rio games, the IOC amended Rule 40 to "allow generic [non-Olympic] advertising during the period of the games." The relaxation of Rule 40 provides athletes "increased commercial opportunities to promote their individual sponsorships as part of sharing their Olympic story" (Grady, 2015). The Rio Olympics marked the first time athletes could continue relationships with their individual sponsors, provided that Olympic trademarks are not used in any traditional and social media advertising campaigns. For example, if an athlete had a sponsorship agreement with a watch company that was not an Olympic partner, that athlete could still have his or her image used in an advertisement during the time of the games (Associated Press, 2015).

National Collegiate Athletic Association

As of 2015, the bylaws of the National Collegiate Athletic Association (NCAA) provided that institutions may give third parties permission to use a student-athlete's name and as long as all money is paid to the member institution and not to the student (NCAA Division I Manual, 2015, sec. 12.5.1.1). Student-athletes are also prohibited from accepting compensation from any non-NCAA institution as an award for their athletic performance. But no restriction exists on the colleges themselves profiting from using the player's likeness for promotional purposes, and suffice it to say, many universities have done so.

Many universities are now getting into the trading card business, a practice deemed by the NCAA as a permissible promotional activity. Because NCAA players consent to the use of their likeness, they give up any right to sue for compensation. Additionally, players are not entitled to compensation when their coach or university contracts with a company to endorse their product, such as having the players wear Nike sneakers or other apparel (NCAA Division I Manual, 2015, sec. 12.5.2.1). The Collegiate Licensing Company (CLC), a for-profit firm licensed by the NCAA and about 200 schools, is the organization's official licensing representative. In 2014, collegiate-licensed merchandise generated about $600 million (Licensing Book Online, 2015), of which about 8 to 14 percent goes to the respective institution, depending on the kind of license (Silcox, 2012).

As noted in Chapter 4, the class action antitrust case involving the former UCLA basketball player Ed O'Bannon may change the present licensing system and may result in student-athletes having rights to their names and likeness for merchandising purposes. As of 2016, the case is still being litigated. A federal trial judge concluded that the restrictions signed by players barring the exercise of these rights violate antitrust law and proposed an easing of these rules (*O'Bannon v. NCAA*, 2014), but a federal appeals court has partially reversed that ruling (*O'Bannon v. NCAA*, 2015). As one commentator noted at the very beginning of this lawsuit:

> The stakes of *O'Bannon v. NCAA* are enormous. If O'Bannon and former student-athletes prevail or receive a favorable settlement, the NCAA, along with its member conferences and schools, could be required to pay tens of millions, if not hundreds of millions, of dollars in damages . . . The marketplace for goods may change as well, with potentially more competition over the identities and likenesses of former college stars.
>
> (McCann, 2009)

Chapter Assignment

After a two-year process, the Associated Curling League (ACL)has decided to welcome your proposed team as the league's twelfth and newest franchise. The team would be based in Cleveland, but has yet to have a name and logo. Your personal preference is the "Lakes" because Cleveland is located near Lake Erie. You have the logo in mind—a big letter C with a geographic image of Lake Erie in the background. None of the eleven other teams in the ALL have this name.

This project involves online research to determine whether the proposed name would likely be similar to other names of sports-related teams or entertainment firms and whether the logo could also cause confusion. If you conclude that the proposed name would not cause any such problem, please state your reasons. If you think it would, please propose another name that you think would be less likely to be challenged.

This project should involve an oral presentation as well as a paper between four and six pages. The presentation could show trademarks and logos that you think could conflict with "Lakes" or why you think that they would not.

References

American Needle v. NFL, 130 S. Ct. 2201 (2010).

The Associated Press (2015, February 26). IOC relaxes rule on athletes, sponsors at Olympics. *USA Today*. Retrieved November 10, 2015, from http://www. usatoday.com/story/sports/olympics/2015/02/26/ioc-relaxes-rule-on-athletes-and-sponsors-during-olympics/24084119/

Belson, K. (2010, October 12). Nike to replace Reebok as NFL's licensed-apparel maker. *The New York Times*. Retrieved October 25, 2015, from http://www. nytimes.com/2010/10/13/sports/football/13nike.html?_r=0

Brown, M. (2015, April 3). MLB Properties extends agreements with New Era, Nike and '47 Brand till 2019. *Forbes*. Retrieved October 25, 2015, from http:// www.forbes.com/sites/maurybrown/2015/04/03/mlb-properties-extends-agreements-with-new-era-nike-and-47-brand-till-2019/

California Civil Code (2009). Sec. 3344.

Copyright Act of 1976, 17 USC, sec. 102 (2010).

Copyright Term Extension Act, 17 USC sec. 103 (2010).

Doe v. TCI Cablevision, 110 S.W.3d 363 (Mo. 2003).

ETW Corporation v. Jireh Publishing Inc., 332 F.3d 915 (6th Cir. 2003).

Feldman, G. (2008, November 10). Retired NFL players win suit against NFLPA. *Sports Law Blog*. Retrieved March 31, 2010, from http://sports-law.blogspot. com/search?q=Retired+Players+Win+Suit+Against+NFLPA

Ferber, T. (2005). Symposium: Trademark and publicity rights of athletes. *Fordham Intellectual Property, Media & Entertainment Law Journal, 15*, 449, 488.

Fonovisa v. Cherry Auction, 76 F.3d 259 (9th Cir. 1996).

Fortunato, J. (2013). *Sports sponsorship: Principles and practices.* Jefferson, NC: McFarland & Company, Inc., Publishers, pp. 127–128.

Grady, J. (2015, May 18). The IOC's Rule 40 changes and the forecast for Rio 2016. *Street and Smith's Sports Business Journal.* Retrieved November 10, 2015, from http://www.sportsbusinessdaily.com/Journal/Issues/2015/05/18/Opinion/Grady-McKelvey.aspx

Grohmann, K. (2014, August 17). Samsung extends deal as Olympics top sponsor to 2020. *Reuters.* Retrieved November 9, 2015, from http://www.reuters.com/article/2014/08/17/us-olympics-samsung-deal-idUSKBN0GH04T20140817#hcZzFuVMUHZLWeUu.97

Hart v. EA Sports, 717 F.3d 141 (3rd Cir. 2013).

Indianapolis Colts v. Metropolitan Baltimore Football Club, 34 F.3d 410 (7th Cir. 1994).

In re NCAA Student-Athlete Name and Likeness Litigation 724 F. 3d 1268 (9th Cir. 2014).

inta.org (2015). Protecting a Trademark: Trademark Infringement—Must an infringer be a competitor? Retrieved October 23, 2015, from http://www.inta.org/TrademarkBasics/FactSheets/Pages/TrademarkInfringement.aspx

IP and Sports - Background Brief (n.d.). WIPO.int. Retrieved October 20, 2016, from http://www.wipo.int/pressroom/en/briefs/ip_sports.html

Kaplan, D. (2011, September 5). U.S. Open mad as ale over ads. *Street and Smith's Sports Business Journal.* Retrieved October 25, 2015, from http://www.sportsbusinessdaily.com/Journal/Issues/2011/09/05/Marketing-and-Sponsorship/US-Open-ambush.aspx

Kaplan, D. (2015, June 8). Licensing revenue up for NFLPA. *Street and Smith's Sports Business Journal.* Retrieved November 7, 2015, from http://www.sportsbusinessdaily.com/Journal/Issues/2015/06/08/Labor-and-Agents/NFLPA.aspx

Kimpflen, J. (2004). Trademarks and tradenames. In *American jurisprudence* (2nd ed., sec. 116). St. Paul, MN: West.

Lefton, T. (2010, May 10). Strong brew. *Street and Smith's Sports Business Journal*, p. 01.

Lefton, T. (2015, March 16). Nike extends on-field deal with the NFL. *Street and Smith's Sports Business Journal.* Retrieved October 25, 2015, from http://www.sportsbusinessdaily.com/Journal/Issues/2015/03/16/Marketing-and-Sponsorship/NFL-Consumer-Products-Summit.aspx

The Licensing Book Online (2015, June 9). LIMA study shows global retail sales of licensed goods hit $241.5 billion in 2014. Retrieved October 25, 2015, from http://licensingbook.com/lima-study-shows-global-retail-sales-of-licensed-goods-hit-241-5-billion-in-2014

The Licensing Letter (2015, May 4). Pro sports licensed retail sales score 5% increase in 2014: Most leagues grow, driven by apparel. *The Licensing Letter, 34*, p. 03. Retrieved October 25, 2015, from http://www.thelicensingletter.com/wp-content/newsletters/2015/TLL-05-04-15.pdf

London Olympic Games and Paralympic Games Act, sec. 23 (2006). *Legislation. gov.uk*. Retrieved May 24, 2016, from http://www.legislation.gov.uk/ ukpga/2006/12/crossheading/advertising

Madridprotocol.info (n.d.). Retrieved May 24, 2016, from http://ladas.com/ madrid-protocol-general-discussion/

McCann, M. (2009, July 21). NCAA faces unspecified damages, changes in latest anti-trust case. SI.com. Retrieved April 16, 2010, from http://sportsillustrated. cnn.com/2009/writers/michael_mccann/07/21/ncaa/index.html

Nascar.com (2011, June 15). Spin master eyes youth market with toys. Retrieved November 7, 2015, from http://www.nascar.com/en_us/news-media/ articles/2011/06/15/spin-master-youth-market-toys.html

National Football League Properties, Inc. v. Dallas Cowboys, 922 F. Supp. 849, 851 (S.D.N.Y. 1996).

NBA CBA, Article XXXVIII, Section 1 (2011). Retrieved November 8, 2015, from http://mediacentral.nba.com/media/mediacentral/2011-Collective-Bargaining-Agreement.pdf

NBA.com (2015, June 10). Nike to become uniform, apparel provider for NBA. Retrieved October 25, 2015, from http://www.nba.com/2015/news/06/10/ nike-nba-uniform-partnership/

NCAA Division I Manual (2015). Retrieved November 7, 2015, from http:// www.ncaapublications.com/productdownloads/D116.pdf

New York Civil Rights Law (2009). Secs. 50 and 51.

New York Yankees & Adidas v. Major League Baseball Properties (1997). No. 97–1153-civ-T-25B (Complaint for injunction and jury trial). Retrieved May 11, 2010, from http://www.ncbusinesscourt.net/FAQ/plaintiff/COMPLAINT.htm

Nufer, G. (2013). *Ambush marketing in sports: Theory and practice*. New York: Routledge, p. xiii.

O'Bannon v. NCAA, 7 F. Supp. 3d 955 (N.D. Ca. 2014).

O'Bannon v. NCAA, 802 F. 3d 849 (9th Cir. 2015).

Olympic Charter (2015, August). Retrieved November 10, 2015, from http:// www.olympic.org/Documents/olympic_charter_en.pdf

Peters, S. (2004, May 15). Phone conversation regarding MLBPA licensing, May 15.

The Players Choice Group Licensing Program (n.d.). MLBPA.com. Retrieved August 25, 2010, from http://mlb.mlb.com/pa/info/licensing.jsp

Raine, G. (2003, November 21). Giant's slugger to negotiate his own merchandise deals. *San Francisco Chronicle*, p. B1.

Roberts, D. (2015, November 4). Bud Light will remain NFL's official beer until 2022. *Fortune.com*. Retrieved November 7, 2015, from http://fortune.com/ 2015/11/04/bud-light-nfl-deal/

San Francisco Arts & Athletics, Inc. v. United States Olympic Comm., 483 U.S. 522 (1987).

Silcox, S. (2012, March 1). An insider's guide to the world of licensed sports products: Royalty rates—Is 12% the norm and when 12% isn't enough. *Licensed Sports*. Retrieved January 18, 2016, from http://licensedsports. blogspot.com/2012/03/insiders-guide-to-world-of-licensed_2802.html

Smith, J. (2012, July 24). Olympic hurdles for advertisers: The Games' unique rules and restrictions. *Forbes.com*. Retrieved October 25, 2015, from http://

www.forbes.com/sites/jacquelynsmith/2012/07/24/olympic-hurdles-for-advertisers-the-games-unique-rules-and-restrictions/

Sports Business Daily (2015, March 20). You wear it well: Majestic Athletic, MLB renew apparel partnership through '19. Retrieved October 25, 2015, from http://www.sportsbusinessdaily.com/Daily/Issues/2015/03/20/Marketing-and-Sponsorship/Majestic.aspx

Stempel, J. (2014, March 18). Google, Viacom settle landmark YouTube lawsuit. *Reuters.* Retrieved October 25, 2015, from http://www.reuters.com/article/2014/03/18/us-google-viacom-lawsuit-idUSBREA2H11220140318

Trademarks (Lanham Act of 1946), 15 USC, sec. 1114 (2010).

Unger, H. (1998, January 7). Thrashers' name at heart of federal lawsuit. *Atlanta Journal & Constitution*, p. C.01.

US Olympic Committee: Exclusive right to name, seals, emblems and badges, 36 USC, sec. 220506 (2002).

15 Traditional and New Media in Sports

Dissemination of sporting events through any one of various media outlets constitutes the single most important source of revenue for professional and amateur sports organizations. For sports leagues and individual events, fees earned from media rights bring in billions of dollars per year. This symbiotic relationship between media and sports benefits both. Sports entities can earn significant revenues, and media obtain an important source of programming. Print and digital media attract readers and viewers, and all-sports radio stations have become components of AM (and increasingly FM) broadcasting. Marquee sports events such as the Super Bowl draw large numbers of viewers or listeners, resulting in premium fees charged to advertisers.

This chapter examines the basics of the business of sports broadcasting, both involving the "traditional" media (defined for our purposes as radio, broadcast television, cable television and satellite) and new technologies (Internet, broadband, social media, mobile telephone communications and virtual reality). It outlines the history, the nature and variety of sports broadcast deals and concludes with some thoughts on the future of sports and media.

The Property Right

Think of a sports broadcast as a form of property. That team has the right to license a right to broadcast the event to others. Usually, this right involves licensing to a particular broadcaster, who receives the permission to disseminate the event through a particular communications platform (television, radio, cable, Internet) but *not* the right to own the product. When, for example, the National Football League (NFL) licenses broadcast rights, it permits the broadcasters, under prescribed conditions, to broadcast games. The radio, television and cable licensees are, in essence, delivery tools. They usually produce the event and pay a sum to the owner (the league) to broadcast it. More recently, Internet streaming has become a part of this mix. Initially, with the exception of boxing, organized sports were reluctant to license broadcasting rights. In particular, many in baseball felt that broadcasting games on the radio would siphon off fans coming to the ballpark. Boxing, however, took to licensing early on. As a dominant sport in the early decades of the twentieth century, boxing matches were filmed and distributed to theaters (Ward, 2004).

Today, sports events remain one of the last bastions of live programming. For broadcasters, cablecasters and, increasingly, Internet providers, this has advantages and poses challenges. Live broadcasts offer excitement and unpredictability that few other programs match. However, the economic value of the event diminishes sharply once the event concludes. Whereas broadcasters and cable network owners rerun successful entertainment programs—often for years—sports broadcasts do not command high audiences—or value—when rebroadcast, because the result is already known.

In part to add value to the event, broadcasters have added news programs, features, documentaries and sports talk shows to their package. Pregame and postgame analyses of the games, including press conferences, expert opinion and highlights, add to the fan's interest.

The Key Audience

Radio and over-the-air television earn their revenues through advertising. Advertisers choose particular types of programs to target certain audiences, based on demographics such as gender, age, race, ethnicity and income. Sports broadcasts have traditionally appealed to a male demographic. For all four major sports leagues, over two-thirds of the viewers are male (The Nielsen Company, 2014). Producers of items of interest to males found such events to be an excellent way to reach that audience. Hence, broadcasters paid fees to broadcast such events to earn money from advertisers. The more popular the event, the more the outlet charges for ads. Cablecasting differs in certain respects. Cable providers derive revenues from advertising, but in addition, there is another revenue stream—subscriber fees from local cable operators. For carrying a particular cable network, the operators pay a negotiated fee.

Radio

Once Major League Baseball teams discovered that radio (and eventually television) created new revenue streams by rights fees and by publicizing their teams and attracting more fans, they became more amenable to allowing game broadcasts. Even though it is sometimes dismissed as an antiquated medium, local radio broadcasts remain an important part of baseball coverage. Presently, ESPN Radio has exclusive national radio broadcast rights with Major League Baseball (through 2021 as a part of the total $5.6 billion broadcasting package). Included in the Major League Baseball package is a full schedule of Monday, Wednesday and Sunday night baseball games each season; opening day and national holiday games; select All-Star Week events; and one of the two Wild Card Games (Newman, 2012). Major League Baseball has a long-term contract with SiriusXM Satellite Radio, which includes streaming of games on the company's website and mobile phone app (Smith, 2013). SiriusXM paid the league $650 million over eleven years. In 2013, the agreement was extended through 2021. Financial terms of the extension were not disclosed.

The National Basketball Association also has a national radio deal (through the 2024–25 season, as part of the total $24 billion broadcasting package). ESPN is entitled to broadcast Wednesday and Friday night games, Sunday afternoon games, select playoff games and doubleheaders, all conference and NBA final games and the NBA draft until 2025 (NBA.com, 2014). In 2015, the National Football League signed a six-year rights agreement with SiriusXM to broadcast all professional games, extending its current deal through 2022. As in the case of Major League Baseball's deal, financial terms of the extension were not disclosed. Although these deals produce revenue for the respective league, they are secondary to the exposure and the monies derived from television and cable broadcasts.

The major leagues permit their franchises to negotiate local radio broadcasting license agreements, and just about every team has concluded such agreements with individual radio stations serving their markets. These teams—in all the professional leagues—keep the revenue earned. For example, the New York Yankees and WFAN-AM and FM have a ten-year deal that gives those stations the rights to broadcast all home and away regular season Yankees games and postseason games, pregame and postgame shows and select Yankees spring training games for a reported $15 to $20 million per season (Raissman, 2013).

Broadcast Television

Even in an age of newer technologies, television remains the primary economic and technical engine for sports broadcasting. Although introduced at the 1939 New York World's Fair, television broadcasting as we know it developed after World War II. As part of its programming, sports events—especially those in confined areas such as boxing—were standard fare.

Sports television—which at the time included the World Series, boxing matches and college football games—received increased interest and, by 1950, 10.5 million receivers rested in U.S. homes (Kumar, 2008).

Although it is hard to fathom, early sports broadcasts did not help the bottom line for many teams. Home attendance dropped precipitously in many instances. For example, after the Boston Red Sox started televising home games in 1950, attendance dropped from 1.45 million in 1948 to fewer than 300,000 in 1952. The Los Angeles Rams' gate receipts dropped 50 percent in the first year of home broadcasts. Ultimately, most teams adopted some kind of "blackout" policy for their home games. By the end of the decade, teams and leagues became more sophisticated in parceling out broadcast rights, making adept use of the blackout rules to focus on road games, which would result in fan interest without any diminution of attendance (MacCambridge, 2004).

In the 1950s, sports broadcasting became a province of weekend afternoons, rather than prime time. Entire shows sponsored by one company became the economic model for both entertainment and sports. By the mid-1960s, the amount and costs of broadcasting sports increased to a point that individual advertisers found it increasingly difficult to pay for sponsorship of major events by themselves. The modern approach of "spot advertising" took over. Advertisers would pay for one or more placed advertisements during a sports event, with payment negotiated between the broadcaster and the advertisers based on ratings measurements. This system created a bonanza for both sports leagues and the broadcast networks (and local stations as well).

Network Broadcast and Cable Television

The number of hours of sports on network television increased as the audiences grew and the multiplying ranks of spot-buying advertisers coveted these valuable minutes. This mutually beneficial situation persisted well into the 1980s. As technology improved, so did the quality and sophistication of the broadcast. Television networks and local stations began to pay ever-increasing rights fees, which increased the revenues of the rights holder, whether it was a league or an individual team. The experience of baseball is illustrative. In 1950, Major League Baseball earned $1.2 million from national broadcasts. By 1960, that amount had tripled to $3.3 million. Note the exponential increase since then: over $16 million in 1970, $47.5 million in 1980, $365 million in 1990 and $570 million in 2000 (Schaaf, 2004). Since 2014, the rights fees have averaged $1.5 billion per year (Settimi, 2012). The increasing revenue to team owners from television was one reason for the increased demands of the Major League Baseball Players' Association and the resulting increase in player compensation.

The experience of the NFL is even more striking. Baseball was "America's national pastime" well before the advent of television, but the NFL became the dominant spectator sport in large part due to television. Because the NFL had less public exposure than baseball, the league should have embraced television as a vehicle to gain exposure for the sport. Early attempts by the Los Angeles Rams and Philadelphia Eagles to televise home games met with resistance from the league, which imposed strict rules prohibiting the broadcast of NFL games in any city where there was a home game. A federal court concluded that these rules violated the antitrust laws (*U.S. v. National Football League*, 1953), resulting in a prohibition of league-wide contracts until the Sports Broadcasting Act of 1961 (15 USC, sec. 1291) created an antitrust exemption permitting such agreements. The Sports Broadcasting Act protects teams in smaller television markets by pooling broadcasting rights with teams located in larger, more lucrative television markets in order to assure small-market teams equal shares of television revenues and coverage (15 USC, sec. 1291, 2016). It created the present environment for network television rights agreements with the leagues. Besides the NFL, the other major sports leagues signed on to this legislation, but the legislation exempted college sports (15 USC, sec. 1293, 2016). Therefore, the antitrust exemption does not apply to the National Collegiate Athletic Association (NCAA). This omission hurt the NCAA years later when the Supreme Court concluded that its football package was an unreasonable restraint of trade under the antitrust laws (*NCAA v. Board of Regents of the University of Oklahoma*, 1984).

After the passage of the Sports Broadcasting Act, the NFL teams agreed to sell their television rights as a single package and to share broadcast revenues equally among all franchises. This revenue-sharing idea originated from the new commissioner, Pete Rozelle, and a number of the venerable NFL owners. It turned out to be a brilliant move. Rozelle argued that the league's competitive balance on the field would be compromised if teams in major television markets continued to sell their broadcast rights individually. The inequity would diminish the overall attractiveness of the NFL's product. Another reason for the single rights arrangement was that the rival American Football League had signed a similar television package with ABC one year earlier.

Television Deals

For the NFL, NBA, NHL and Major League Baseball, television agreements follow a "traditional" model. The network pays a specified rights fee for a one-time exclusive broadcast right. To recoup its investment, the network sells commercial airtime and keeps the revenue derived from that airtime. Production costs are covered by the network. This approach also applies to national cable networks, such as ESPN.

Why do broadcast and (more recently) cable networks spend large sums of money on major sporting events? The first reason is to draw a large audience in order to justify large advertiser fees. The Super Bowl is a prime example. In 1967, a thirty-second advertisement during the Super Bowl cost $42,000, whereas in 2016 the same ad would cost up to $5 million (Groden, 2015). Throughout much of the 1960s and 1970s, the networks earned profits on such deals. But there came a point where the rights fees became so high that profitability was necessarily guaranteed. That leads to the second, and more likely, reason for the hefty fees: prestige. Broadcasting a product such as the NFL or Major League Baseball gains or maintains credibility for the broadcaster (especially if it is an up-and-coming network) and serves as a lead-in to other programming. In other words, it adds to the reputation of the broadcaster. It also provides one of the few sources of live, must-see programming.

The NFL

The Fox Network's successful bid for the rights to broadcast NFL games in 1994 serves as a case study. Fox's agreement to pay an astounding $1.58 billion annually, well ahead of the previous contract price paid by CBS, resulted in great publicity for the then-fledgling operation. Although Fox wrote off $350 million in losses that year, the network as a whole showed an increase in profits of almost $100 million (Noland & Hoffarth, 1997). On the other hand, the loss cost CBS, the prior rights holder, prestige for many years and a few affiliated stations, which jumped to Fox upon the news that the upstart had won the broadcasting rights for National Football Conference (NFC) games.

In 2014, Fox, CBS and NBC paid the NFL a total of $27 billion (roughly $3 billion per year) over nine years, and ESPN is to pay $15 billion ($1.9 billion per year) and DirecTV is to pay $12 billion ($1.5 billion per year) over eight years for a cumulative total of $54 billion until their expiration in 2022 and 2021, respectively (Katzowitz, 2014). More recently, in 2016, the NFL reached a two-year, $450 million agreement with CBS and NBC to broadcast five Thursday Night Football games each in 2016 and 2017 (Deitsch, 2016). This does not count the NFL Network, the league's in-house broadcast entity, which provides coverage of events such as the draft and eight exclusive Thursday night games per season.

From 1973 to 2014, the NFL has had a "blackout rule," which mandates that a game cannot be broadcast in a seventy-five-mile radius of its local market if it did not sell 85 percent of "nonpremium" tickets within seventy-two hours of kickoff. For most of its tenure, the rule has not been frequently invoked, as most NFL games are sold out. For example, in 2013, only two games were blacked out (Wyatt, 2014). In 2014, the Federal Communications Commission (FCC) eliminated the NFL's blackout policy, citing that these regulations were "unnecessary and outdated" because television revenues have replaced ticket sales as the league's primary source of revenue (FCC.gov, 2014). Although the FCC allowed the NFL to maintain its blackout policy through its existing broadcast contracts, the league announced that team owners voted to enact a one-year suspension of the blackout policy for the 2015–16 season, and the NFL may consider extending the suspension after evaluating its impact during the off-season (Espn.com, 2015).

Major League Baseball

Major League Baseball's present television agreement, which expires in 2021, is divided into broadcast and cable segments. Fox retains the exclusive rights to broadcast selected Saturday games throughout the season: the All-Star Game, the World Series and two Division Series and one League Championship series alternating yearly between the National and American League (the other league's postseason games air on TBS). Fox pays a total of $4.2 billion, or $525 million per year for the eight-year term (Lee, 2012).

On the cable side, in 2012, in-season cable television rights were secured by ESPN for $5.6 billion ($700 million annually) and by Turner Broadcasting for $2.6 billion ($325 million annually) over eight years through 2021. Under this arrangement, ESPN broadcasts up to 90 games per season, on Sunday, Monday and Wednesday nights (Newman, 2012). Turner also broadcasts a Sunday afternoon game of the week and one Wild Card Game alternating yearly between the two leagues with the other game airing on ESPN.

NBA

The NBA renegotiated a 2007 deal with ESPN/ABC and Turner Broadcasting in 2014, two years before its scheduled expiration, creating a nine-year contract lasting through the 2024–25 season. An integrated broadcast and cable package, Disney (the owner of the network and cablecaster) pays a rights fee of $12.6 billion over the life of the contract. With Turner's fee, the deal totals $24 billion, or $2.66 billion per year, a huge 186 percent increase over the 2007 agreement of $930 million per year (Lukas, 2014).

Telecasts are divided among the ABC, ESPN and ESPN2 platforms. ABC broadcasts at least fifteen regular season games and fifteen postseason games, including the NBA finals. ESPN and ESPN2 broadcast eighty-five regular season games, mostly on Wednesdays and Friday nights, and can broadcast as many as thirty playoff games, including the conference semifinals and one conference final (NBA.com, 2014). The agreement also grants ESPN/ABC the rights to simulcast full games live on ESPN.com and WatchESPN.

NHL

In 2011, the NHL and NBC concluded a $2 billion, ten-year broadcast rights agreement, which involve televising games either on the television network or on NBC Sports Network, its cable arm. The agreement covers all playoff games and an average of three regular season games per week.

The league's television rights deal in Canada is even more lucrative, even though the viewing population of the country is about 10 percent of that of its southern neighbor. In 2013, Rogers Communications secured a twelve-year, $5.2 billion deal for the right to broadcast NHL games across Canada. Starting in 2014 and ending in 2026, Rogers made an up-front payment of $150 million and then annual payments starting at $300 million, which will escalate to $500 million in the final year of the deal (CBC News, 2013). Part of the deal involves a sublicense to the Canadian Broadcasting Corporation (CBC) to air 320 hours' worth of *Hockey Night in Canada* content.

MLS

In 2014, Major League Soccer (MLS) announced an eight-year, $720 million agreement with ESPN, Fox and Univision through the 2021–22 season. ESPN and Fox pay a combined $75 million annually for English-language rights to broadcast a minimum of thirty-four regular season matches per network, respectively, and to share all U.S. National Soccer Team matches (Ourand, 2014). Additionally, Fox and ESPN share rights to all playoff matches outside of two Univision-exclusive games and will alternate airing MLS Cup and the league's All-Star Game each year.

College Sports

Unlike the package of postseason college football bowl games, which is controlled by the respective athletic conferences, the NCAA controls the rights to postseason men's basketball games through its tournaments, whereas the various athletic conferences sell the regular season games. As noted in Chapter 4, the NCAA lost control of top-level football after the Supreme Court's 1984 ruling concluded their broadcast rules were illegal under the antitrust laws. However, the association adroitly kept its hands on the basketball tournament—and has reaped great financial rewards. Starting in 2011, CBS and Turner Broadcasting have broadcast rights for the men's tournament under a fourteen-year, $10.8 billion agreement, whereby the annual fees paid to the NCAA average $771 million. In 2016, that deal was extended for another eight years to 2032 for the men's basketball tournament. The additional eight years were valued at $8.8 billion total, or $1.1 billion per year (NCAA, 2016).

ESPN and the NCAA reached an agreement in 2011 to extend its partnership with the NCAA through the 2023–24 season, costing $500 million, which includes twenty-four championship games in women's basketball and the men's and women's College World Series, World Cup, fencing and indoor and outdoor track and field (NCAA.com, 2011).

Rights to broadcast games from various conferences also command impressive sums. Presently, the respective rights deals are as follows:

- The Southeastern Conference (SEC), fifteen years, $2.25 billion (ESPN/ABC) and $825 million (CBS), expires 2023.
- The Big Ten football, ten years, $1 billion (ESPN/ABC), expires 2017; Big Ten basketball, six years, $72 million (CBS). In 2016, it signed a new six-year agreement with Fox Sports paying up to $250 million per season for the rights to broadcast half of the scheduled football and men's basketball games. At the time of this writing, the "other half" has not been determined.
- Bowl Championship Series, twelve years, $5.6 billion, expires 2025 (ESPN/ABC).
- Big 12 football/basketball, thirteen years, joint $2.6 billion deal with Fox and ESPN/ABC (ESPN/ABC exclusively airs Big 12 basketball), expires 2025.
- Rose Bowl (ESPN/ABC), twelve years, $960 million, expires 2026.
- Atlantic Coast Conference (ESPN/ABC) football/basketball, fifteen years, $3.6 billion, expires 2027.
- Pac-12 football (ESPN/ABC and Fox), twelve years, joint $3 billion with Fox, expires 2024.

The Olympics and Other International Sports Events

The most lucrative single-event broadcasting contract involves the Olympic Games. Approximately 3.6 billion global viewers (out of a potential television audience of 4.8 billion) globally saw at least a small portion of the London Summer Games in 2012 (International Olympic Committee, 2012). For the 2010 Winter Games in Vancouver, the corresponding estimates were 1.8 billion (of an estimated reach of 3.5 billion) worldwide (Kantar, 2014) and 190 million Americans (Reynolds, 2010). For the 2014 Sochi games, the corresponding figures were 2.1 billion (of a potential 4.4 billion) worldwide (Kantar, 2014) and 199 million Americans (International Olympic Committee, 2014).

U.S. television networks have paid enormous sums of money for the rights to broadcast the games. The fees paid for exclusive rights to broadcast the Games in the United States account for the great majority of the money earned by the International Olympic Committee (IOC) for broadcast rights. These rights fees have shown consistent growth over the last half-century.

In 1960, the total U.S. rights fee to broadcast the summer games was merely $400,000. In 1996, the Atlanta Summer Games cost NBC $456 million, and in 1998 the Nagano (Japan) Winter Olympics cost CBS $375 million. NBC has since purchased the broadcasting rights for the Summer and Winter Games, beginning with the Summer Olympics in 2000, up to and including the Summer Games of 2032. In 2011, NBC agreed to pay $4.38 billion. The rights fees break down as follows: Winter 2014 (Sochi, Russia), $775 million; Summer 2016 (Rio), $1.23 billion; Winter 2018 (Pyeongchang, South Korea), $963 million; Summer 2020 (Tokyo) $1.45 billion (Crupi, 2011). The agreement was extended in 2014, requiring NBC to pay $7.75 billion for six Olympic Games from 2022 to 2032, breaking down as follows: Winter 2022 (Beijing) and Summer 2024, $2.5 billion; Winter 2026 and Summer 2028, $2.55 billion; and Winter 2030 and Summer 2032, $2.6 billion (Associated Press, 2014). In addition to profiting from advertising, carrying the Olympics served as a platform to publicize its fall schedule (Albiniak, 2004).

In the past, broadcasting the Olympics has posed unique issues not found in other sports. Because the Games are often held in time zones well ahead of the United States, many, if not the majority of, events may be on tape-delay in North America. Recent Olympic broadcasts have included far more live coverage, both on broadcast and cable television and online, so this issue is becoming less relevant. For example, NBC's coverage of the 2014 Sochi Olympics included live streaming on the network's NBC Sports Live Extra app and feature video, photo and other interactive content on Facebook and Instagram (Steinberg, 2014). As of 2016, the mobile and digital rights are part of the NBC rights deal (Olympic.org, 2014). NBC and its cable partners broadcast 6755 hours of competition across all of its platforms (nbcolympics.com, 2016).

The International Olympic Committee launched the Olympic Channel after the conclusion of the Rio Games. Available online or via a mobile app, it contains content that is intended to keep viewers interested in the Winter and Summer Games during the two-year break before the 2018 Pyeongchang Olympics (Spangler, 2016).

Types of Media Deals

The Major League Baseball, NFL, NBA, NCAA and Olympics agreements follow the traditional licensing method. For the payment of a stipulated amount of money, the broadcasters, cablecasters and satellite operators obtain the right to broadcast the event and as a result, they retain advertising revenues derived from those broadcasts. Cablecasters have another income stream, the compensation paid to them by cable providers (known as "multichannel video programming distributors" or MVPDs), and satellite firms such as DirecTV obtain compensation directly from subscribers. DirecTV, which has an exclusive package for distributing out-of-market NFL games, also utilizes multiple revenue streams as monies derived from the subscription package and from advertisements.

However, alternative arrangements exist. One, known as the "revenue-sharing" model, involves a league, team or other organization negotiating a broadcast/cable or streaming deal but not receiving any specific rights fee. Rather, the sports organization and the media rights holder split the revenues derived from the distribution of the event. At one time, the NHL and the (now defunct) Arena Football League (AFL) utilized such arrangements. For example, these leagues sold their broadcast rights to a particular cable or broadcast network but did not receive rights fees, but instead required the network to split the advertising revenue with the leagues after the network has paid the associated costs. In dealing with a relatively new or untested sports organization, the network is able to obtain all of the broadcasting rights, yet avoid all financial risk associated with having to pay rights fees (Gross, 2004). This method is not ideal for the league because any payments are far more speculative than the traditional rights deals. However, it could be utilized in the case of a league of recent vintage negotiating a streaming deal. The exposure of the content and the building of a fan base could lead to a more favorable future deal. A third method of securing broadcast rights is simply buying airtime. The rights holder keeps advertising revenues generated from the event after paying the costs of buying the time and production. An example is NBC's agreement to broadcast professional boxing on network television in 2015 for the first time in years (Ourand, 2016).

Ethical Issue: Tennis and Cable Migration

For many decades, tennis fans were able to tune into one of the major broadcast television networks for coverage of at least two of the four Grand Slam tournaments. However, the more recent history of tennis broadcasts serves as a case study of "cable migration," a thirty-year trend away from over-the-air to cable-based broadcasts of sports. Because cable networks had two revenue streams, they outbid the traditional networks after a substantial number of homes became cable subscribers.

It is not a surprise that coverage of international tennis tournaments has transitioned to cable networks. In 2013, ESPN and the United States Tennis Association (USTA), the national governing body of tennis, announced an $825 million, eleven-year agreement, providing ESPN the exclusive rights to broadcast the U.S. Open through the 2025 tournament. Viewers can watch all matches live through ESPN, ESPN2 and ESPN3 (Sandomir, 2015b).

Two years earlier, NBC lost its rights to air coverage of Wimbledon, the venerable premiere event in the United Kingdom. The All England Lawn Tennis and Croquet Club announced a twelve-year agreement with ESPN, providing the cable network with the exclusive U.S. television rights to air live coverage of Wimbledon on its various platforms through 2023

(Espn.com, 2011). Prior to this multiyear deal, ESPN2 had aired coverage of the early rounds of the tournament and one match each of the men's and women's semifinals since 2003, with NBC airing the other semifinals matches and the finals. The 2012 Wimbledon marked the first time that NBC would not televise matches after forty-six consecutive years. ESPN's ability and commitment to airing all Wimbledon matches live heavily contributed to the cable network acquiring the rights for $500 million over NBC, as NBC's tape-delay coverage had previously angered many fans (Sandomir, 2011).

However, the growth of cable as the prime source for sports programming may be stalling. The total of U.S. homes that subscribe to cable television has been decreasing from 2010 to 2016. The reasons given are the increasing costs of monthly cable service and ascent of alternative delivery services. As a result, layoffs have been announced at ESPN in 2013 and 2015, which many industry analysts attributed to ESPN's increasing payments of rights fees as well as its declining subscriber reach, since the network lost 8.5 million households from 2010 to 2015 (Ourand, 2015).

With decreasing subscribers and increased competition from broadband, has the point been reached where ESPN and other broadcasters overpaid for these rights? Can ESPN find ways to monetize coverage of sports that traditionally had a niche audience? And does the migration of such venerable events alienate long-time fans who may not want or cannot afford cable, resulting in less viewer interest in the sport?

League-Owned Sports Networks

Over the last two decades, sports leagues have created their own cable networks offering selected games and other programming that relates to the particular sport, including significant games of the past and interviews with players and coaches. Often these networks are subscriber based and carry events not under exclusive contract to a particular network or local service. Many have been successful. As of 2014, MLB Network has 71.3 million subscribers and has broadcast a modest number of games, but has nongame programming, such as awards shows, draft coverage and fantasy sports. NBA TV broadcasts to 57.2 million homes and programs ninety-seven live, regular season games per season (Turner.com, 2014). The 37.4-million-subscriber NHL Network broadcasts seventy-eight games (NHL.com, 2013). The NFL Network has 73.6 million subscribers (Travis, 2015).

International Soccer

Until recently, international soccer events were rarely televised in the United States, with the exception of the quadrennial World Cup tournament. However, given the growth of popularity of the sport, networks have secured agreements to broadcast English Premier League games and European Championships, as well as the World Cup. NBC and its cable network, NBCSN, began broadcasting English Premier League in 2013 and paid $250 million for exclusive rights to air all 380 matches each season for three years through 2016. In August 2015, the Premier League extended its deal with NBC for an additional six years, for an estimated $1 billion (Sandomir, 2015a).

Another major broadcast network that has significantly invested in the rights to air international soccer matches is Fox. Fox secured broadcast rights in 2013 to matches played by Bundesliga, the top German league, for five years in the Americas and Asia beginning with the 2015–16 season for an undisclosed amount.

In the most prestigious and potentially lucrative deal, in 2011, Fox outbid ESPN for English-language broadcast rights for all FIFA events from 2015–22, including the 2018 and 2022 Men's World Cup tournaments. Fox extended the FIFA agreement in 2015 and acquired the rights to the 2023 Women's World Cup and 2026 men's World Cup. Financial figures for the most recent deal were not disclosed. Fox previously paid FIFA $425 million for the initial agreement (Associated Press, 2015).

Cable Television and Carriage Issues

As noted earlier, cable television has a distinct advantage over traditional broadcast television because it has two streams of revenue: advertisements and user fees. The costs for program services found on cable are derived from a fee-per-subscriber basis with a local cable operator (the MVPD), and the fees earned constitute a solid income base.

Almost every cable operator carries local over-the-air broadcast stations, yet the relationship between them may get contentious. Under the 1996 Telecommunications Act, over-the-air broadcasters have two options with regard to carriage: the first, known as the "must-carry" rules, requires the cable operator (the MVPD) to carry the station. If the broadcaster opts for must-carry, then it cannot charge the cable operator for the privilege of carrying the station (Signal carriage obligations, 2007). Traditionally, the majority of stations chose must-carry. However, the law provides a second option, known as "retransmission consent," whereby broadcasters seek fees from the cable operator for the inclusion of the broadcast signal. This option has forced the operators and broadcasters to negotiate and has sometimes led to threats of a local station being pulled off the cable service (Retransmission consent, 2001). Retransmission consent has become a contentious issue that has affected sports broadcasts, and by 2015, major network stations have earned over $1.00 per subscriber—far less than ESPN and other major cable programmers, but a potentially more lucrative second source of income for broadcasters (Marszalek, 2015).

That conflict is especially relevant for the over-the-air broadcast rights holders of sports programming. Without retransmission consent revenue, those traditional broadcasters would not be able to match ESPN's bids for most sports rights. More such disputes may occur in the future as broadcasters look to increase their revenues, which some industry analysts predict could go far higher (Marszalek, 2015).

Aside from the retransmission issues, sports programming puts financial pressure on cable operators (and, by extension, on satellite and mobile telephone companies) because it is very expensive. For example, ESPN charges almost four times more than any other services for carriage on cable. In 2016, it was estimated to be about $7.21 per subscriber; TNT was second at about $1.70 (Bi, 2015).

Local Broadcast Rights and Cable Television

Except for the NFL, local teams negotiate their own broadcasting, which covers most regular season games (unless preempted by network "games of the week" or playoffs). The traditional method remains similar to the network arrangement, in which a station or local cable programmer pays a rights fee to broadcast games but retains advertising revenue. This is most common in Major League Baseball, where each team negotiates a broadcasting and/or cable deal. In the past, a local, over-the-air broadcaster could air a number of games, but in recent years, the majority of baseball teams have cable-only deals. As of 2015, the only noncable games broadcast include:

> Baltimore Orioles (WJZ-TV—20 games)
> Chicago Cubs: WGN-TV (40), WLS-TV (25), WPWR-TV (5)
> Chicago White Sox: WGN-TV (35), WPWR-TV (25)
> Cleveland Indians: WKYC-TV (4)
> New York Mets: WPIX-TV (25)
> New York Yankees: WPIX-TV (21)
> Philadelphia Phillies: WCAU-TV (11)
> San Francisco Giants: KNTV (15)
> Washington Nationals: WUSA-TV (20)
>
> (radioinsight.com, 2015)

Sometimes the over-the-air broadcaster pays for the rights; at other times, it leases time from the cable rights holder.

Regional Sports Networks

Most local cable television rights center on regional sports networks (RSNs), notably those by Fox Sports, Cablevision and Comcast.

Sometimes teams have an ownership interest in their services; other times not. Because of the value of their programming, RSNs have achieved market power and are a desired part of the programming package offered by cable system operators. In some cases, as with Cablevision and Comcast, the RSNs own or are owned by the local cable operator (Mabin, 2006). These RSNs produce revenues from advertisements as well as the fees paid to them by the cable operators. However, there are risks in this model. For example, in 2013, Time Warner Cable signed a twenty-five-year agreement with the Los Angeles Dodgers to broadcast the team's games on a regional network titled "SportsNet LA" for $8.35 billion. Time Warner believed the astounding price would eventually pay for itself, given their assumptions that other television providers, such as DirecTV and Dish Network, would be willing to pay their asking price of $4.90 per subscriber to carry the channel. In June 2015, Charter Communications became the first major distributor to pay Time Warner to carry SportsNet LA on Charter Spectrum TV Select, which serves 300,000 subscribers in the Los Angeles area (Brown, 2015a). Prior to Charter, however, Time Warner was expected to lose $1 billion from the deal because they were unable to come to an agreement with large providers. As a result, 70 percent of Southern Californian households were unable to watch Dodgers games (Cwik, 2015).

Other RSN agreements have fetched high rights fees. In 2015, the Arizona Diamondbacks signed a twenty-year, $1 billion deal with Fox Sports Arizona. Additionally, some agreements include a provision of an equity interest. The San Diego Padres acquired a 20 percent interest in Fox Sports San Diego as part of a twenty-year deal negotiated in 2012. This pays the Padres an escalating amount, which began at $28 million, and could be as high as $75 million by the time it ends in 2031 (McLennan, 2015).

A number of NBA, NHL and Major League Baseball owners have started up their own local sports networks in an attempt to augment profitability and keep control of content. Probably the best-known example of a team-operated network is YES, launched by the New York Yankees in 2002. By 2007, its estimated value ranged between $2.8 billion and $3.5 billion (Sandomir, 2007). However, the team found it more prudent to sell its interest in the property. In 2012, Fox purchased a 49 percent ownership of YES Network, and two years later, it announced that it had acquired an 80 percent ownership interest.

There is a risk in a stand-alone, team-owned RSN. If the team does not do well or viewers simply do not watch, the team's network may fold, which happened with the Minnesota Twins, Kansas City Royals, Portland Trail Blazers and Houston Rockets. Ultimately, these teams signed with established sports networks (Grover & Lowry, 2004). More recently, CSN Houston, a partnership between the Astros, Rockets and Comcast/

NBC, debuted in 2012 and filed for bankruptcy one year later. Although its broadcast work was well regarded, it was unable to obtain carriage deals with satellite and many cable providers, so, as a result, only about 40 percent of greater Houston's 2.2 million TV households had access (Barron, 2013).

New Technologies and Sports

The dizzying pace of change involving the application of new technologies in sports means that platforms that did not even exist a few years ago have taken an increasingly prominent place in the sports media landscape. The utilization of digital streaming, broadband and cellular telephony, coupled with social media, will lead to a transformation of the way sports are disseminated to viewers in the next decade. Although traditional broadcasting and cable still lead in revenue production, the monies generated by newer media have filled the coffers of the various leagues.

Wireless Technology

Mobile telephones have achieved market penetration rapidly, to the point that over 90 percent of the U.S. population owns a cell phone (Pewinternet.org, 2014). Moreover, the cellular technology has evolved into far more than a simple telephone without a cord. In particular, "smartphone" technology through either the iPhone or Android systems and the apps that run on those systems display sports video capabilities that serve as a major media platform and a major new revenue stream.

Distribution agreements involving mobile carriers have been quite lucrative. The NFL signed an exclusive four-year agreement with Verizon, starting with the 2014 season. Valued at $1 billion, it gives fans access to live footage of NFL games on their Verizon smartphones. The agreement allows live streaming of home-market Sunday afternoon games, NBC's *Sunday Night Football*, ESPN's *Monday Night Football*, NFL Network's *Thursday Night Football* and all postseason games, including the Super Bowl (Futterman, 2013). Beginning with the 2015 season, Verizon's NFL Mobile app was free for all fans to download regardless of their wireless carrier; however, non-Verizon customers have limited access to league and team news, in-game highlights, scores and analysis (Spangler, 2015).

The other leagues and National Association for Stock Car Auto Racing (NASCAR) also have exclusive cellular deals. Sprint and NASCAR announced a three-year contract extension of its 2008 deal with Sprint in 2011, but as of 2015, NASCAR is seeking a new sponsor for the Cup Series after Sprint announced in December 2014 that it would not extend its sponsorship beyond 2016 (Stern, 2015). In 2010, Major League Baseball began to provide live baseball so subscribers can watch live games on an iPhone, Android or iPod touch. As of 2015, the features of the service include bilingual functionality with the addition of Spanish as a default language; news, live audio, schedules and interactive rosters and player stats for every team; a video library searchable by player or team; and classic game videos (Prnewswire.com, 2015a). The NBA made its "League Pass" service available for purchase to users of Verizon's go90 mobile video application in February 2016, a few months after the NBA announced its sponsorship deal with Verizon (Aycock, 2016). The agreement provides go90 users who purchased a subscription to NBA League Pass with daily highlights, exclusive original content, streaming access to live out-of-market games and the ability to utilize the Cut & Share function to post video highlights on social media (Prnewswire.com, 2015b).

Internet Streaming

Internet transmission of sporting events has blossomed with the ascent of broadband technology. Today, it is a given that about every amateur and professional team and league has its own website with information and articles and blogs about teams, players and league issues. Many independent websites and blogs cover sports. One is able to find important information about league collective bargaining agreements and/or governing information such as the NCAA manuals and the constitution and bylaws of such organizations as the International Olympic Committee. Athletes often have their own websites and blogs, and there are online journals devoted to athlete perspectives (theplayerstribune.com, 2016). But the most salient development since the previous edition of this book has been the expansion of streaming. Streaming has become an essential part of many media deals.

Streaming involves what has become known as "over-the-top," or OTT, delivery of content, which means it disseminates programming not tied to cable or satellite. OTT has been a central component of Internet streaming, especially in the powerful social media websites such as Twitter and Facebook. However, at this time of this writing, methods of monetizing such deals are just developing, in part due to the rising number of cable cord-cutters (Zagger, 2016).

In 2013, the NBA announced a three-year deal with Fox Sports to begin in-market game streaming for sixteen of its seventeen NBA teams in its portfolio through various distributors, including Time Warner (now Spectrum) Cable, Cablevision and Charter (Ourand, 2014). In 2015, Major League Baseball reached a three-year agreement with Fox Sports to begin in-market game streaming for fifteen clubs (Brown, 2015b). Beginning with the 2016–17 season, fans were able to watch in-market games exclusively on the Fox Sports Go app or the Fox Sports website after logging into their account with a participating TV carrier, such as Verizon FiOS and Optimum Online.

Yet, at the time of this writing, Internet streaming still is in its infancy. However, it is likely to be a significant content platform in the near future. In 2015, the NFL announced a partnership with Yahoo! Inc., to distribute a live stream of a single game featuring the Buffalo Bills and Jacksonville Jaguars in London, England (NFL.com, 2015). This first-ever free global stream had 15.2 million unique viewers, and its success has proven that there is a genuine market interest in watching NFL games digitally. In 2016, the NFL revealed that the league commenced negotiations with several digital companies to acquire domestic and international digital rights to Thursday Night Football games (Steinberg, 2016). Also in 2016, Twitter announced rights deals with the NBA, NHL and Major League Baseball to live-stream games and behind-the-scenes content to viewers of the 140-character message service (Frier, 2016). Although no specific rights have been negotiated at the time of this writing, Facebook has expressed interest in partnering with sports leagues to stream games and to create a "digital social experience" watching sports (Team, 2016).

The rise in streaming may have a long-term effect on cable television broadcasting of sports. From 2010 to 2015, nearly 3 million people in the United States have dropped cable service. ESPN's subscribers decreased by the same amount to 92 million from 2014's 95 million subscribers (Koll-meyer, 2015). Many viewers object to the "tiering" of channels found in cable and the rising monthly costs. If more and more sports events are streamed with viewers paying a flat monthly charge just for that service, it could have lost-lasting negative effects for the cable medium, which in the past has been a prime driver of increased rights fees received by sports organizations.

Social Networking

The advent and ascension of social networking has provided exposure to players and coaches. A case in point involves the Kentucky head basket-ball coach John Calipari, who had over 1 million followers on Twitter and 138,000 fans on Facebook in 2010. The advantages of utilizing such networks mean that he can connect to and interact with fans more directly and personally. It also aided his philanthropic ventures, raising $1.3 million for the victims of the earthquake that ravaged Haiti in early 2010.

However, professional leagues have attempted to control the time and content of tweets and other social website entries. In 2009, the NFL announced a policy to crack down on the use of Twitter by any players, coaches and staff. However, less than one month later, it amended the policy to allow "players, coaches and other team personnel [to] engage in social networking during the season"; however, they would not be allowed to use social media 90 minutes prior to kickoff and until tra-ditional postgame interviews with the media are completed (Reisinger,

2009). In August 2010, the NFL issued Chad Ochocinco, who at the time was a wide receiver for the Cincinnati Bengals, a $25,000 fine for violating the policy by posting two messages on Twitter during a preseason game against the Philadelphia Eagles (ESPN.com, 2010). In 2012, Major League Baseball released its own social media policy, which prohibits players from using any electronic devices thirty minutes prior to the first pitch until the conclusion of the game. Additionally, the policy lists ten other prohibitions, including restricting players from questioning the impartiality of Major League umpires and from "displaying or transmitting content that reasonably could be construed as condoning the use of any substance prohibited by Major League Baseball's Joint Drug Prevention and Treatment Program" (Baseball-almanac.com, 2012). Under this policy, the Boston Red Sox benched its third baseman, Pablo Sandoval, for one game during the 2015 season after he violated the team and the league's in-game cell phone usage policy by using Instagram during a regular season game against the Atlanta Braves (Edes, 2015). On the collegiate level, in 2015, Clemson and Florida State Universities banned their football players from Twitter during their respective season (Dosh, 2015).

Mobile Applications ("Apps")

With the rising dominance of mobile devices in the technology industry, professional sports leagues and teams have recently reached agreements with technology companies in an effort to enhance the fan experience. Many sports teams have sought deals with new providers in order to enhance its current in-stadium Wi-Fi capabilities. For example, in 2015, AmpThink and Aruba became the new Wi-Fi providers for the Carolina Panthers' Bank of America Stadium beginning with the 2016 season (Kapustka, 2015). Sports teams have also partnered with technology companies to provide mobile applications specifically designed to enhance the in-stadium experience. In 2012, the San Francisco 49ers developed an in-house team to fulfill its mission of building an all-purpose mobile application with features that would entice fans to attend games at Levi's Stadium (Evangelista, 2014). Features of the Levi's Stadium App—available on both Android and Apple operating systems—includes instant video replays; services to locate the shortest bathroom and concession lines; and in-seat delivery of food, beverages and merchandise. The success of the 49ers' mobile application has since sparked genuine interest among other sports and entertainment venues that are looking to further customize the fan experience (Muret, 2015).

The NFL created its Super Bowl 50 stadium mobile application so that fans who attended the game were able to use the app to watch instant replays and all commercials aired on CBS's broadcast and to view an exclusive camera feed of celebrities in attendance. Fans were also able to have drinks delivered to their seats and pick up their food and merchandise orders at express lines after prepurchasing on their mobile devices (Tibken, 2016).

Colleges have also implemented new mobile technologies into their recruiting processes. Collegiate football coaches have used mobile applications geared to compliance solutions that logs calls to prospects and warns of any potential NCAA violations. Collegiate athletic departments have also heavily invested in mobile applications to virtually tour campuses and athletic facilities from the convenience of their home (Schnell, 2015). Does the introduction of these mobile applications have the potential to revolutionize the college athletics recruiting process? Only time will tell.

Virtual Reality

At this time of this writing, the first generation of virtual reality (VR) players entered the market mainly for the purpose of training athletes. These headset systems employ a special camera and audio system for capturing complete on-field action and simulations of on-field opponents and practice drills (vrbeginnersguide.com, 2016). Additionally, universities and college may use virtual reality to enhance recruiting efforts.

On the consumer side, there is huge potential for this technology to be a significant addition to the sports viewing opportunity. In 2016, Goldman Sachs projected that the global virtual reality market will grow to $80 billion by 2025, and in the most optimistic scenario, $200 billion (Fisher, 2016). These devices are also beginning to shape fan experiences. Firms like EON, Oculus and Sony have planned or have released VR sets aimed at experiencing a more in-depth sports viewing experience. It is too early to say whether these products will gain market access and, if they do, a number of knotty issues will have to be addressed, such as crafting broadcast rights for virtual reality content. Although game broadcasting is likely not to be included in such rights, events such as pregame practices could be carved out.

Strapping on a headset for virtual reality may result in vision or neurological issues, but it is too early to say. By the time this book is published, we may have a better idea as to whether virtual reality is going to be a major player in the sports business.

E-gaming

By 2016, e-gaming has become a rapidly growing industry, attracting many young people who play video games. The industry dates back to the earliest days of computing, when games were created for computer consoles, like the Nintendo 64. With the advent of the personal computer, more games were created, and gaming programs increased in sophistication, graphics quality and number of players. By the beginning of the Internet era, such games could be played online, and the modern e-gaming industry was born. More recently, mobile phone gaming apps spawned more interest and popularity.

E-gaming has become a major spectator sport. By 2014, tournaments have sold out large arenas, and some attract at-home audiences larger than those of many traditional sporting events. Sponsors have included Coca-Cola and American Express, and prize money ranks in the millions of dollars. In 2014, more than 70 million people worldwide watched e-sports over the Internet or on TVs (Wingfield, 2014).

The Future

Increasing the sources and types of revenue-enhancing deals will be a primary goal of the sports industry, and over the next five to ten years the maturity of "new" avenues of distribution will likely have major effects on the dissemination of sports information. The evolution of mobile technology as an alternative programmer changes the way fans view their sports. Untethered from a computer or cable television, mobile users may become the primary audience in the next generation. In addition, the viewing public will utilize their PCs, MacBooks or mobile phones to watch what used to be called "television." Will this make broadcast television obsolete?

The more traditional forms of program dissemination such as network television and traditional radio remain viable. They provide a mass audience, and to maintain that audience, they need marquee programming. For the networks, the NFL and Major League Baseball still bring a sizeable male demographic that few other broadcasts attract. Cable will remain a major player as well. The multiplicity of channels on cable continues to offer more exposure to niche sports such as cycling or lacrosse. With the expansion of streaming and the decrease in cable viewing, one wonders if that will be the next frontier of television. Of course, pitfalls exist. Not every promising technology becomes a commercial success. And format wars cause public confusion.

Finally, has sports broadcasting/cablecasting/streaming reached a saturation point? Will the audience grow or will post-Millennials find interest in other forms of entertainment? Will users play their own online games and stop watching the NFL? The continuing increase in rights fees may hit a bubble one day. But that day has not arrived, at least for the major sports. But if it comes, resulting in decreases in rights fees among the networks, cable services, satellites and Internet providers, will the storybook marriage between media and sports end? It is possible, but it has not happened yet.

References

Albiniak, P. (2004, August 9). The name of Olympic promotion; NBC sets up gold-medal Olympics ad campaign to hype new season. *Broadcasting & Cable*, p. 4.

Associated Press (2014, May 7). NBC extends Olympic deal. Retrieved November 22, 2015, from http://espn.go.com/oly/story/_/id/10896350/nbc-extends-olympics-deal-2032–775-billion

Associated Press (2015, February 12). FIFA extends World Cup TV deal with Fox Sports through 2026. Retrieved November 23, 2015, from http://www.foxsports.com/soccer/story/fifa-extends-world-cup-tv-deal-rights-with-fox-sports-through-2026-telemundo-021215

Aycock, J. (2016, February 5). Verizon launches NBA League Pass on go90 service. *Seekingalpha.com*. Retrieved February 7, 2016, from http://seekingalpha.com/news/3087226-verizon-launches-nba-league-pass-go90-service

Barron, D. (2013, October 26). Just what went wrong with Comcast SportsNet? *Houston Chronicle*. Retrieved May 16, 2016, from http://www.houstonchronicle.com/sports/article/Just-what-went-wrong-with-Comcast-SportsNet-4929307.php

Baseball-almanac.com (2012, March 12). Major League Baseball's Social Media Policy. Retrieved December 18, 2015, from http://www.baseball-almanac.com/downloads/mlb_social_media_policy.pdf

Bi, F. (2016, January 8). ESPN leads all cable networks in affiliate fees. *Forbes.com*. Retrieved May 15, 2016, from http://www.forbes.com/sites/frankbi/2015/01/08/espn-leads-all-cable-networks-in-affiliate-fees/#4d5319fe60c9

Brown, M. (2015a, June 4). Dodgers games (finally) coming to LA area Charter subscribers beginning Tuesday. *Forbes.com*. Retrieved February 7, 2016, from http://www.forbes.com/sites/maurybrown/2015/06/04/dodger-games-finally-coming-to-la-area-charter-subscribers-beginning-tuesday/#4b7e1cb95465

Brown, M. (2015b, November 19). Manfred announces 3-year deal with Fox to have MLB games streamed in-market. *Forbes.com*. Retrieved December 10, 2015, from http://www.forbes.com/sites/maurybrown/2015/11/19/manfred-announces-3-year-deal-with-fox-to-have-mlb-games-streamed-in-market/

CBC News. (2013). Rogers scores national NHL TV rights for $5.2B. CBC News. Retrieved May 20, 2016, from http://www.cbc.ca/news/business/rogers-scores-national-nhl-tv-rights-for-5-2b-1.2440645

Crupi, A. (2011, June 7). NBC bids $4.38 billion for Olympic gold. *Adweek*. Retrieved November 22, 2015, from http://www.adweek.com/news/television/update-nbc-bids-438-billion-olympic-gold-132319

Cwik, C. (2015, March 26). Time Warner Cable expected to lose $1 billion in messy Dodgers TV deal. *Yahoo! Sports*. Retrieved February 7, 2016, from http://sports.yahoo.com/blogs/mlb-big-league-stew/time-warner-cable-to-lose—1-billion-over-dodgers-tv-deal-215515975.html

Deitsch, R. (2016, February 1). NBC, CBS to split two-year, $450 mil. *Thursday Night Football* package. *Sports Illustrated*. Retrieved February 8, 2016, from http://www.si.com/nfl/2016/02/01/nfl-thursday-night-football-rights-nbc-cbs

Dosh, K. (2015, August 11). Clemson and Florida State ban football teams from Twitter. *Foxsports.com*. Retrieved May 16, 2016, from http://www.foxsports.com/college-football/outkick-the-coverage/clemson-and-florida-state-ban-football-teams-from-twitter-081115

Edes, G. (2015, June 19). Red Sox bench Pablo Sandoval for using Instagram during game. Retrieved December 18, 2015, from http://espn.go.com/boston/mlb/story/_/id/13108912/pablo-sandoval-boston-red-sox-benched-using-instagram-game-progress

Espn.com (2010, August 25). Chad Ochocinco fined $25K. Retrieved December 18, 2015, from http://sports.espn.go.com/nfl/trainingcamp10/news/story?id=5493157

Espn.com (2011, July 5). ESPN acquires all rights to Wimbledon. Retrieved December 20, 2015, from http://espn.go.com/sports/tennis/news/story?id=6739076

Espn.com (2015, March 24). NFL to suspend TV blackout policy. Retrieved November 15, 2015, from http://espn.go.com/nfl/story/_/id/12545081/nfl-suspend-tv-blackout-policy-2015-owners-vote

Evangelista, B. (2014, September 20). Levi's Stadium app spawns 49ers-backed tech startup. *Sfgate.com*. Retrieved February 7, 2016, from http://www.sfgate.com/sports/article/Levi-s-Stadium-app-spawns-49ers-backed-tech-5765459.php

FCC.gov (2014, September 30). FCC eliminates sports blackout rules. Retrieved November 15, 2015, from https://www.fcc.gov/document/fcc-eliminates-sports-blackout-rules

Fisher, E. (2016, May 9). What's holding up virtual reality as a game changer? *Sports Business Journal*. Retrieved May 18, 2016, from http://www.sports-businessdaily.com/Journal/Issues/2016/05/09/In-Depth/Main.aspx?hl=virtual%20reality&sc=0

Frier, S. (2016, July 25). Twitter's new deals with MLB, NHL sharpen focus on live video. *Bloomberg.com*. Retrieved July 29, 2016, from http://www.bloomberg.com/news/articles/2016-07-25/twitter-s-new-deals-with-mlb-nhl-sharpen-focus-on-live-video

Futterman, M. (2013, June 4). Verizon Wireless pads NFL deal. *The Wall Street Journal*. Retrieved December 10, 2015, from http://www.wsj.com/articles/SB10001424127887324563004578525060861520512

Groden, C. (2015, August 6). This is how much a 2016 Super Bowl ad costs. *Fortune.com*. Retrieved November 14, 2015, from http://fortune.com/2015/08/06/super-bowl-ad-cost/

Gross, A. (2004, May 23). TV deal a step back. *Journal News* (Westchester County, NY), p. 8C.

Grover, R., & Lowry, T. (2004, November 22). Rumble in regional sports. *Businessweek.com*. Retrieved May 7, 2010, from http://www.businessweek.com/magazine/content/04_47/b3909143_mz016.htm

International Olympic Committee (2012, December). London 2012 Olympic Games: Global broadcast report, p. 4. Retrieved November 22, 2015, from http://www.olympic.org/Documents/IOC_Marketing/Broadcasting/London_2012_Global_%20Broadcast_Report.pdf

International Olympic Committee (2014). International Olympic Committee marketing report: Sochi 2014, p. 34. Retrieved November 22, 2015, from http://www.olympic.org/Documents/IOC_Marketing/Sochi_2014/LR_Mkt Report2014_all_Spreads.pdf

Kantar (2014). Sochi 2014: Global broadcast & audience report. Retrieved November 22, 2015, from http://www.olympic.org/Documents/IOC_ Marketing/Sochi_2014/sochi-2014-global-coverage-audience-summary-vaug14.pdf

Kapustka, P. (2015, December 10). AmpThink, Aruba win Wi-Fi deal for Carolina Panthers' Bank of America Stadium. *MobileSportsReport.com*. Retrieved February 7, 2016, from http://www.mobilesportsreport.com/2015/12/ ampthink-aruba-win-wi-fi-deal-for-carolina-panthers-bank-of-america-stadium/

Katzowitz, J. (2014, October 1). NFL, DirecTV sign deal reportedly worth $12 billion over 8 years. Retrieved January 20, 2016, from http://www.cbssports. com/nfl/eye-on-football/24733096/nfl-directv-sign-new-deal-reportedly-worth-12-billion-over-8-years

Kollmeyer, B. (2015, November 26). Disney loses 3 million ESPN subscribers in a year. Retrieved December 10, 2015, from http://www.marketwatch.com/ story/disney-loses-3-million-espn-subscribers-in-a-year-2015–11–26

Kumar, R. (2008). A project report on market research of color television. Retrieved May 16, 2010, from http://www.scribd.com/doc/12730665/-market-research-on-color-television

Lee, E. (2012, October 2). MLB said to get $6.8 billion from Fox, Turner for TV rights. Retrieved November 15, 2015, from http://www.bloomberg.com/news/ articles/2012–10–02/mlb-said-to-get-6–8-billion-from-fox-turner-to-renew-tv-rights

Lukas, P. (2014, October 6). NBA in unique position with TV deal. *NBA.com*. Retrieved November 15, 2015, from http://espn.go.com/nba/story/_/ id/11653435/new-tv-deal-shows-league-unique-position

Mabin, C. (2006, January 11). Growing numbers of professional sports teams start own TV networks. *Kentucky New Era*. Retrieved April 20, 2010, from http://news.google.com/newspapers?nid=266&dat=20060111&id=vwUxAA AAIBAJ&sjid=l-AFAAAAIBAJ&pg=3346,811396

MacCambridge, M. (2004). *American's game*. New York: Random House, pp. 67–70.

Marszalek, D. (2015, June 26). Nowhere to go but up for retrains fees. *TV News Check*. Retrieved May 16, 2016, from http://www.tvnewscheck.com/ article/86466/nowhere-to-go-but-up-for-retrans-fees

McLennan, J. (2015, February 23). Arizona Diamondbacks new TV deal: $1.5 billion plus. Retrieved May 16, 2016, from http://www.azsnakepit. com/2015/2/23/8097375/arizona-diamondbacks-tv-deal-1–5-billion

Muret, D. (2015, September 28). Magic selects VenueNext for app. *Street and Smith's Sports Business Journal*. Retrieved February 7, 2016, from http:// www.sportsbusinessdaily.com/Journal/Issues/2015/09/28/Facilities/Venue Next-Magic-app.aspx

NBA.com (2014, October 6). NBA extends partnership with Turner Broadcasting, Disney. Retrieved November 14, 2015, from http://www.nba.com/2014/ news/10/06/nba-media-deal-disney-turner-sports/

NBAOlympics.com (Feb. 2). How to watch the 2016 Rio Olympic games. Retrieved July 10, 2016, from http://www.nbcolympics.com/news/ how-watch-rio-2016-olympic-games

NCAA v. Board of Regents of the University of Oklahoma, 468 U.S. 85 (1984).

NCAA.com (2011). ESPN extends deal through 2023–24. Retrieved November 21, 2015, from http://www.ncaa.com/news/ncaa/article/2011–12–15/espn-extends-deal-through-2023–24

NCAA.com (2016). Turner, CBS and the NCAA Reach Long-Term Multimedia Rights Extension for NCAA Division I Men's Basketball Championship. Retrieved May 15, 2016, from http://www.ncaa.com/news/basketball-men/article/2016–04–12/turner-cbs-and-ncaa-reach-long-term-multimedia-rights

Newman, M. (2012, August 28). MLB, ESPN agree on record eight-year deal. *MLB.com*. Retrieved November 14, 2015, from http://m.mlb.com/news/article/37476712/

NFL.com (2015, June 3). NFL and Yahoo! partner to deliver first-ever global live stream. Retrieved February 7, 2016, from http://www.nfl.com/news/story/0ap3000000495384/article/nfl-and-yahoo-partner-to-deliver-firstever-global-live-stream

NHL.com (2013, January 12). NHLN-US to broadcast 78 regular season games. Retrieved February 5, 2016, from https://www.nhl.com/news/nhln-u-s-to-broadcast-78-regular-season-games/c-650061

The Nielsen Company (2014). 2013 Year in Sports Media Report. *Nielsen.com*. Retrieved November 14, 2015, from http://www.nielsen.com/us/en/insights/reports/2014/year-in-the-sports-media-report-2013.html

Noland, E., & Hoffarth, T. (1997, June 24). Murdoch plays to win; Fox sports; Major deals put Fox in forefront. *Los Angeles Daily News*, p. 1.

Olympic.org (2014). Agreement ensures the long-term financial security of the Olympic Movement. Retrieved November 22, 2015, from http://www.olympic.org/news/ioc-awards-olympic-games-broadcast-rights-to-nbcuniversal-through-to-2032/230995

Ourand, J. (2014, October 6). Season brings a flood of live local streaming from NBA teams. *Sports Business Journal*. Retrieved February 5, 2016, from http://www.sportsbusinessdaily.com/Journal/Issues/2014/10/06/Media/NBA-streaming.aspx

Ourand, J. (2015, October 26). The moves that forced ESPN's cuts. *Sports Business Journal*. Retrieved February 5, 2016, from http://www.sportsbusinessdaily.com/Journal/Issues/2015/10/26/Media/ESPN.aspx

Ourand, J. (2016, January 11). The eyes have it. *Sports Business Journal*. Retrieved May 15, 2016, from http://www.sportsbusinessdaily.com/Journal/Issues/2016/01/11/In-Depth/Media-main.aspx

Ourand, J., & Botta, C. (2014, May 12). MLS's big play. *Sports Business Journal*. Retrieved November 22, 2015, from http://www.sportsbusinessdaily.com/Journal/Issues/2014/05/12/Media/MLS-TV.aspx

PewInternet.org (2014, October). Mobile technology factsheet. *Pew Research Center*. Retrieved December 10, 2015, from http://www.pewinternet.org/fact-sheets/mobile-technology-fact-sheet/

Prnewswire.com (2015a, February 27). At bat updated for spring training '15. Retrieved February 7, 2016, from http://www.prnewswire.com/news-releases/at-bat-updated-for-spring-training-15–300042794.html

Prnewswire.com (2015b, November 4). Verizon and NBA announce major content and marketing partnership. Retrieved February 7, 2016, from http://www.

prnewswire.com/news-releases/verizon-and-nba-announce-major-content-and-marketing-partnership-300172109.html

Radioinsight.com (2015, April 12). Are MLB teams required to air some games on free over the air TV? Retrieved May 16, 2016, from https://radioinsight.com/community/topic/are-mlb-teams-required-to-air-some-games-on-free-over-the-air-tv/

Raissman, B. (2013, September 11). Yankees, WFAN deal now official. New York Daily News. Retrieved October 21, 2016, from http://www.nydailynews.com/sports/baseball/yankees/wfan-yankees-official-article-1.1453136

Reisinger, D. (2009, September 2). NFL bans tweeting before, during, after games. Retrieved December 18, 2015, from http://www.cnet.com/news/nfl-bans-tweeting-before-during-after-games/

Retransmission consent. 47 CFR 76.64 (2001).

Reynolds, M. (2010, March 1). NBC's final medal count: 190 million Olympic viewers. *Multichannel News*. Retrieved April 22, 2010, from http://www.multichannel.com/article/449441-NBC_s_Final_Medal_Count_190_Million_Olympic_Viewers.php

Sandomir, R. (2007, August 3). Yankees YES Network stake not for sale. *New York Times*. Retrieved May 4, 2010, from http://www.nytimes.com/2007/08/03/sports/baseball/03yes.html?_r=1

Sandomir, R. (2011, July 5). Enough with delays: Why Wimbledon switched to ESPN. *New York Times*. Retrieved December 20, 2015, from http://www.nytimes.com/2011/07/06/sports/tennis/why-wimbledon-switched-to-espn-from-nbc.html

Sandomir, R. (2015a, August 10). NBC retains rights to Premier League in six-year deal. *New York Times*. Retrieved November 22, 2015, from http://www.nytimes.com/2015/08/11/sports/soccer/nbc-retains-rights-to-premier-league-in-six-year-deal.html

Sandomir, R. (2015b, August 30). Supplanting CBS and Tennis Channel, ESPN Empire will show all U.S. Open matches. *New York Times*. Retrieved December 20, 2015, from http://www.nytimes.com/2015/08/31/sports/tennis/supplanting-cbs-and-tennis-channel-espn-empire-will-show-all-us-open-matches.html

Schaaf, P. (2004). *Sports, Inc.: 100 years of sports business*. Amherst, NY: Prometheus Books, p. 13.

Schnell, L. (2015, June 23). Technology in college football: How can mobile apps impact recruiting? *Sports Illustrated*. Retrieved February 5, 2016, from http://www.si.com/college-football/2015/06/22/college-football-technology-recruiting-apps

Settimi, C. (2012, October 2). Baseball scores $12 billion in television deals. *Forbes.com*. Retrieved November 14, 2015, from http://www.forbes.com/sites/christinasettimi/2012/10/02/baseball-scores-12-billion-in-television-deals/

Signal carriage obligations. 47 CFR 76.56 (2007).

Smith, R. (2013, August 19). Sirius XM Re-ups Major League Baseball contract. *The Motley Fool*. Retrieved January 18, 2016, from http://www.fool.com/investing/general/2013/08/19/sirius-xm-re-ups-major-league-baseball-contract.aspx

Spangler, T. (2015, September 3). Verizon Wireless drops $5 monthly fee to watch NFL live games for all customers. *Variety.com*. Retrieved December 10, 2015, from http://variety.com/2015/digital/news/verizon-wireless-nfl-mobile-free-streaming-1201585307/

Spangler, T. (2016, July 27). IOC sets post-Rio launch for Olympic channel free over-the-top video service. *Variety*. Retrieved July 27, 2016, from http://variety.com/2016/digital/news/ioc-launch-olympics-channel-ott-1201824707/

Sports Broadcasting Act of 1961. 15 USC, sec. 1291, 1293 (2016).

Steinberg, B. (2014, January 16). NBCUniversal to stream video on Facebook to promote Olympics. *Variety.com*. Retrieved November 22, 2015, http://variety.com/2014/tv/news/nbcuniversal-to-stream-video-on-facebook-to-promote-olympics-1201060863/

Steinberg, B. (2016, February 1). NFL plans to award global digital rights to Thursday games. *Variety.com*. Retrieved February 7, 2016, from http://variety.com/2016/digital/news/nfl-digital-rights-thursday-night-football-1201693990/

Stern, A. (2015, March 2). NASCAR asks $1B, 10 years. *Street and Smith's Sports Business Journal*. Retrieved February 7, 2016, from http://www.sportsbusinessdaily.com/Journal/Issues/2015/03/02/Marketing-and-Sponsorship/NASCAR-sponsor.aspx

Stevens, T. (2007, Nov. 14). 82% of Americans own cell phones. *Switched.com*. Retrieved May 1, 2010, from http://www.switched.com/2007/11/14/82-of-americans-own-cell-phones/

Team, T. (2016, March 15). Live sports on Facebook: Will this keep its users hooked? *Forbes.com*. Retrieved July 29, 2016, from http://www.forbes.com/sites/greatspeculations/2016/03/15/live-sports-on-facebook-will-this-keep-its-users-hooked/#13c18493abb2

Theplayerstribune.com. Retrieved May 16, 2016, from http://www.theplayerstribune.com/

Tibken, S. (2016, February 6). Think the Super Bowl is high tech? Come back for a regular 49ers game. *Cnet.com*. Retrieved February 7, 2016, from http://www.cnet.com/news/think-the-super-bowl-is-high-tech-come-back-for-a-regular-49ers-game/

Travis, C. (2015, November 25). ESPN has lost 7 million subscribers in the past two years. *Foxsports.com*. Retrieved February 5, 2016, from http://www.foxsports.com/college-football/outkick-the-coverage/espn-has-lost-7-million-subscribers-the-past-two-years-112515

Turner.com (2014, August 13). NBA TV to Televise 97 Games during 2014–15 regular season with multiple appearances by the Spurs, Cavaliers, Thunder, Bulls, Clippers, Lakers, Heat, Rockets and Warriors. Retrieved February 5, 2016, from https://www.turner.com/pressroom/nba-tv-televise-97-games-during-2014–15-regular-season-multiple-appearances-spurs

U.S. v. National Football League, 116 F.Supp. 319 (D.C.Pa. 1953).

Vrbeginnersguide.com (2016). How virtual reality will change sports as we know it. Retrieved May 18, 2016, from http://www.vrbeginnersguide.com/how-virtual-reality-will-change-sports-as-we-know-it/

Ward, G. C. (2004). *Unforgivable blackness: The rise and fall of Jack Johnson*. New York: Knopf, p. 229.

Wingfield, N. (2014, August 30). In e-sports, video gamers draw real crowds and big money. *The New York Times*. Retrieved May 18, 2016, from http://www. nytimes.com/2014/08/31/technology/esports-explosion-brings-opportunity-riches-for-video-gamers.html

Wyatt, E. (2014, September 29). F.C.C. appears poised to loosen sports blackout rule, despite protests by the N.F.L. *The New York Times*. Retrieved January 20, 2016, from http://www.nytimes.com/2014/09/30/business/media/fcc-appears-poised-to-loosen-nfl-blackout-rule-despite-league-protests.html?_r=0

Zagger, Z. (2016, March 14). Internet giants look to tackle changing sports audience. *Law360.com*. Retrieved July 31, 2016, from http://www.law360.com/articles/770917/internet-giants-look-to-tackle-changing-sports-audience

16 Taxation and Sports

Tax laws and policies are important issues for both team owners and players in professional sports. This derives, in part, from the complexity of U.S. tax laws and the nature of the government structure of the United States (Badenhausen, 2013). The nation has a two-tier tax system. On one level, a federal tax system with nationally uniform rules exists. However, in addition, a separate system of fifty different state tax codes coexists. Because professional athletes and team owners often derive substantial income from their services and businesses, their tax obligations have important implications for their respective bottom lines. The goal of this chapter is to give readers a cursory glance into a very intricate area, one that is often overlooked in sports business discussion. Note that tax laws are also subject to change so the possibility exists that by the time of publication, some of the rules discussed may be different.

Although athletes and owners are subject to the same tax rules and regulations as other employees and businesses, there are a few issues unique to sports. For example, at one time, tax-free bonds could be issued to help fund facilities construction. Additionally, there were depreciation rules (most frequently used for business equipment) that applied to players' contracts.

Professional athletes—both team and individual players—face tax issues similar to other high-income earners. Many major league athletes often pay a high rate of taxation due to their substantial incomes. They are also subject to state taxes based on where they play and where they reside (which may not be the same). Because they travel to compete against other teams or individuals, these athletes are subject to what become known as a "jock tax" for the time(s) athletes are in a given state to compete (Lowe, 2015). As will be discussed later this chapter, this jock tax has been controversial and has been subject to court challenges.

Federal Income Tax

The Leagues

At one time, the NFL, NHL and Major League Baseball were structured as nonprofit associations. Although most think nonprofit businesses are charities organized for religious, scientific or educational purposes (Internal Revenue Code, sec. 501(c)(3), 2016), there are also provisions in the federal tax code that permit "business associations" to form nonprofit organizations (Internal Revenue Code, sec. 501(c)(6), 2016). The goal is to benefit an entire industry or help a common business interest (Zagorsky, 2015). Such organizations are exempt from paying federal income tax.

As noted in Chapter 1, the leagues keep a relatively small amount of their revenues because monies earned are generally passed down to the member teams. Therefore, the leagues' taxable income may be relatively small. As an example, the NFL kept over $300 million in revenue in 2013, a paltry amount compared to the $6 billion distributed to the teams. The league therefore only earned a profit of $9 million (IRS Form 990, NFL, 2013). In 2015, the profit amount increased to over $36 million (IRS Form 990, NFL, 2015).

Let's examine the computation of this "profit." Normally, a profit of $9 million on $327 million in revenues in a given tax year is not particularly impressive or even noteworthy. However, the reasons for the low profit are more eye-opening. One-fifth of the revenues went to employee compensation, a very high figure. And the compensation was top-heavy. Commissioner Roger Goodell received $44 million in salary, bonuses and other compensation, whereas five other key employees took home $19 million (Zagorsky, 2015). Charitable contributions from that revenue amounted to $1.4 million.

Because of its nonprofit status, the NFL had to report this information annually, which became fodder for critics claiming that the NFL generates lots of money and paid nothing in taxes (Briggs, 2013). As a result, the league concluded that the resulting bad publicity derived from the reporting requirement was not worth the tax advantage (Sherman, 2015) and therefore changed its status in 2015. Other sports organizations, such as the PGA Tour, maintained their nonprofit status, despite what seemed to very high revenues. According to one report, the tour generated almost $2 billion in revenues and paid no federal or state taxes on its $998 million in investments (which included some $675 million in player retirement benefits). In 2011 the tour paid less than $800,000 in total taxes. The tour generated over $130 million for charity, "but nearly all of that money comes directly from the tour's sponsors and host organizations, the biggest grantee, the World Gold Foundation, supports the cause of promoting golf" (Burke, 2013).

However, the tour chair pointed out that if the IRS canceled tax-exempt status, the local organizations that benefit from the PGA Tour will likely go to the government for help, which will increase the financial burden to the government (Lavigne, 2013).

Team Owners

Until 2004, when one purchased a sports franchise, the Internal Revenue Service allowed the new owner to assign a portion of the purchase price to player contracts and then depreciate them. Known as the "roster allowance depreciation," the idea was conceived by Cleveland Indians' owner Bill Veeck when he was in the process of selling the team to a group headed by his friend (and Hall of Fame ballplayer) Hank Greenberg. Veeck argued to the IRS that professional athletes, once they've been paid for, "waste away" like livestock. Therefore a sports team's roster, like a farmer's cattle or an office copy machine or a new Volvo, is a depreciable asset (Craggs, 2011).

Between 1977 and 2004, owners could utilize the roster allowance depreciation to write off half the team's purchase price over five years. The rule encouraged the sale of a franchise after that period, since the tax benefit expired. However, in 2004, President George W. Bush (who at one time was a part-owner of the Texas Rangers baseball team) signed the American Job Creation Act, which liberalized these rules to permit sports owners to depreciate all tangible property acquired in connection with the franchise over a fifteen-year period (Internal Revenue Code, sec. 168, 2004). This includes the cost of the players' contracts, along with other costs, like equipment and facilities maintenance (although the player roster costs still can make up the bulk of the deduction). Under the revised law, sponsorship agreements, luxury box/club seating and even the entire team's purchase price are subject to these rules (Ozanian, 2012). This rule is a key tax break because owners get to deduct player salaries twice over: as an actual expense and as a depreciating asset. The result is that the ledgers show lower profit than the reality (Belsky, 2012). A simple example is as follows: The Golden State Warriors, purchased in 2010 for $450 million dollars, can claim a $450 million exemption over the next fifteen years. If we assume a 35 percent tax bracket, that translates to a reduction in money owed to the IRS of $157.5 million over that period (Galletti, 2011). This method of depreciation has saved professional team owners considerable tax liability over the years.

Athletes

Federal Income Tax

Although team owners have special deductibility rules, athletes are not as fortunate. Because team athletes are employees, they are required to pay federal income tax under standards similar to that of any taxpayer. The U.S. system is a graduated system requiring a higher rate of taxation for those who are high income earners. Because the average salaries for NBA, NFL, NHL and Major League Baseball players hover in the millions of dollars annually, the great majority of that income is taxed at the highest federal tax rate. In 2016, that rate was 39.6 percent of all income over $415,000 for single filers and $467,000 for married joint filers (Pomerleau, 2015). As is the case with all employees, the tax formula takes one's annual gross income subtracted by allowable deductions to produce "taxable" income, which then is multiplied by the appropriate tax rate to determine tax liability.

Although the standards are the same, professional athletes do have tax issues that most employees do not. Most employees do not earn income from merchandising, endorsements, high signing bonuses or personal appearance fees. In many respects, professional athletes' tax concerns mirror those of entertainers rather than engineers: potentially high incomes, from salaries, bonuses, merchandising compensation, who perform their work in different jurisdictions.

Signing bonuses, utilized frequently in the NFL, can be particularly vexing. The amount of the signing bonus is taxed in the year that it is paid. So, if player X has a $10 million signing bonus for a four-year contract, but the bonus is paid in year one, that $10 million is subject to tax in that year. If, however, that bonus payment is spread over two or more years, then the tax bite can be less severe.

As noted earlier, professional athletes, like other taxpayers, are entitled to certain tax deductions. Although there are not special deductions just for athletes, athletes often benefit from the deduction of agent fees (typically 3 percent of wages, higher for outside income, such as endorsements), union dues, training and gym fees, "body maintenance" expenses and training supplements. More typical deductions center on amounts withheld for state, city and local taxes (Pro Sports Tax, 2009).

State and Local Income Tax

Different states have different tax rules. Most states have some income tax requirement, but a few states—such as Alaska, Florida, Nevada, New Hampshire, South Dakota, Texas, Wyoming and Washington—do not impose income taxes. On the other hand, some states have high income tax requirements. California has a 13.3 percent income tax for annual incomes above $1 million (taxbrackets.org, 2015). Sometimes, cities impose income taxes above the state tax rates. For example, New York State has a top rate of 8.82 percent for those who earn over $1 million (single payer). In addition, New York City imposes an additional rate of 3.8 percent for those earning over $500,000, reaching an approximate total of 12.7 percent for both the state income and city income tax for its highest earners (Wallace, 2015).

The differences among the states affect the amount of net income that the athlete receives. Figure 16.1 illustrates the different state tax rates (for the highest income brackets) in the states where the NFL has teams:

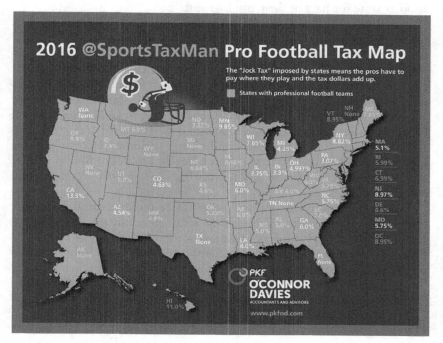

Figure 16.1

For example, a player for the Los Angeles Raiders or the San Francisco 49ers has to pay over 13.3 percent of the bulk of his income to the state of California. If that same player was on the Miami Dolphins' roster, he would pay no state income tax, resulting in a de facto increase of up to 13 percent in his compensation. When dealing with multimillion-dollar contracts, this amount of tax savings is not insignificant. Add to that any additional city taxes (not shown on this chart) and the figure becomes even larger. A point that is not often addressed is how this additional tax amount in "large tax" states affect contract negotiations for free agents.

In addition, professional athletes have to pay out-of-state "jock taxes" for visiting team athletes playing in a given state or city.

The "Jock Tax"

The idea of taxing out-of-state residents for income derived in a given state as part of their employment is not new. Commonly labeled "jock taxes" because the focus of enforcement has been on visiting athletes, these taxes have raised considerable sums for states and cities because of the high incomes that professional athletes command (taxaball.com, n.d.). These state tax principles are applicable to any employee who travels to another state for part of their employment.

Jock taxes can help states and governments generate a large amount of revenue without increasing tax rates to their own residents (Professional Athletes, 2013). Although the idea of taxing an out-of-state individual for in-state service is not new, the term "jock tax" was coined in 1991. After Michael Jordan and the Chicago Bulls defeated the Los Angeles Lakers in the NBA finals, California purportedly started the jock tax as "revenge" against Michael Jordan. In response to California's action, Chicago adopted a jock tax the following year (Ekmekjian, 1994). Subsequently, more and more states and cities—including Detroit, Kansas City and Philadelphia ((*Hillenmeyer v. Cleveland Board of Review*, 2015; *Saturday v. Cleveland Board of Review*, 2015))—followed in creating and enforcing the jock tax.

Jock taxes require athletes (and others in a similar position) to file tax returns in multiple states. Although the idea behind the tax is simple, the application is more complex. Most states use a "duty days" method to decide how much time and, consequently, how much tax an athlete has to pay in the "foreign state." The question involves whether a player "earns" income by just playing the games or by also practicing or engaging in off-season workouts in that state (taxaball.com, n.d.).

The formula is as follows:

$$Income\ Earned\ in\ State\ X = Yearly\ Salary * \left(\frac{Duty\ Days\ in\ State\ X}{Total\ Duty\ Days} \right)$$

In theory, this system does not substitute or take away from a player having to pay tax on his or her entire income in the state where he or she resides, although a state may have a reciprocal agreement between states not to tax each other's nonresidents or a tax treaty between two countries that essentially does the same, which is the case between the United States and Canada. Such agreements are rare among states regarding jock taxes (Random, 2010). Note that an athlete may play in one state and reside in another. As an example, let us assume that the athlete plays in Oakland, California, and is a resident of California. He will pay income tax on his entire income in California. In addition, he may pay taxes in other states based on income derived based on the number of days he played in that other state or city.

So, player X plays for the Oakland A's and earns $5 million a season. Given that the season is about six months, he would have 181 duty days. He would have to pay California's rate in addition to federal income tax. If his team plays a team from a state or city with a jock tax and spends a total of fourteen days during the season playing or practicing in that location (or just being there, if he is injured), the athlete would pay a percentage of the income he earned for those fourteen days to that locale, based on its tax rate. That amount would be based on the percentage of duty days as compared with the entire season.

For our next example, assume that the A's player does not reside in California, but rather in Florida, a state with no income tax. Then, the duty-days formula comes into greater focus. Let's start with spring training, which takes place either in Florida or Arizona, depending on where the team's facility is located. In either situation, the athlete ends up doing well. As we noted, Florida has no state income tax, and Arizona does not tax athletes until the start of their team's regular season (Packard & Baderhausen, 2015). Spring training is forty-five days, so that amount of the season is sheltered from taxes in those states.

As for the regular season, the 181 duty-days designation is not a coincidence, as it is just under the number of days most states require for "residency." So the number of days on the road is deducted from that time, as would be the All-Star break. So the Oakland A's player would be subject to California tax on his entire $5 million income if he lived in that state year-round (or for at least the minimum number of days required for residency).

To illustrate this point, the 2015 Dodgers spent more time than any other team in California. They had 107 games in the state, including a three-game spring training set with the Los Angeles Angels. At most their players were only in California for 128 days for work during 2015. But let us assume they went on to win the World Series and all playoff games took place in California. Their players still have only spent less than the residency requirement in California. This is a big tax deal. In 2015, the Dodgers' (and baseball's) highest-paid player was Clayton Kershaw, who earned $30 million. He reported to spring training on February 19 along with LA's other pitchers and catchers. Not including the playoffs, Kershaw worked a maximum of 228 days that year and earned $131,578.95 each day. As a resident of Texas, Kershaw did not pay state taxes, as Texas does not have a state income tax. If he was forced to claim California as his residence, he would have to pay about $5 million (Packard & Baderhausen, 2015).

Challenges to the Jock Tax

Computing the standard for tax liability has been questioned. Two former NFL players challenged the method by which Cleveland's municipal income tax was imposed during tax years 2004, 2005 and 2006. Cleveland has a "duty days" method, under which the taxable portion of a professional athlete's income is based on the number of games the athlete played in Cleveland in relation to the total number of games played that year. Given the relative paucity of NFL games in a season as compared with other sports, this was a significant percentage of income (*Hillenmeyer v. Cleveland Board of Review*, 2015).

Cleveland's definition of "game days" was a liberal one because it included earnings not only for the games he played, but also for the training, practices, strategy sessions and promotional activities he engaged in before the game even if these events took place *outside* of Cleveland. The Ohio Supreme Court concluded that this method of computation was unconstitutional. It required the city to calculate the taxable income by dividing the total amount of days a player *worked in Cleveland* by the total number of days a player worked in the taxable year. Hunter Hillenmeyer, a Chicago Bears' linebacker, worked a total of 157 days in 2004 and spent 2 of those days in Cleveland. Thus, Cleveland should be allocated approximately 1.27 percent of Hillenmeyer's income for 2004 (frostbrowntodd.com, 2015).

In a related case, that same court also concluded that Cleveland's assessment of taxes on Jeff Saturday, a center with the Indianapolis Colts who did not accompany the team to Cleveland, but rather trained in Indianapolis during that time, was "untenable" as Cleveland had no jurisdiction to tax over that player's activities in another state, even if his team was in Cleveland to play (*Saturday v. Cleveland Board of Review*, 2015).

Methods to Ease the Tax Burden

Because of the complexities and multiple tax returns, several methods can be used to relieve some of the tax burden. As noted earlier, one way is a reciprocal agreement between states, which agree not to tax each other's nonresidents. Virginia and Maryland have such an agreement (Wallace, 2015). The second one is tax credits: the state of resident grants a tax credit for taxes paid to another jurisdiction. The total tax bill that athletes pay will remain unchanged, but it will be paid to two separate tax collectors (Ekmekjian, 1994). Another way to reduce the burden is a universal one. State taxes are deducted from federal taxes, so those living and working in high-tax states can get a reduction in their federal taxes. Lastly, states and the federal government could simply reduce the tax rates for such high income earners.

Tax Benefits in Funding Facilities

As noted in Chapter 8, tax-free bonds were used to finance stadiums. The New York Yankees received over $1 billion in tax-exempt bonds issued by New York City (Holo & Talansky, 2008). Since then, the Internal Revenue Service (IRS) has changed its rules to limit the use of such tax breaks for facilities owned or operated by private owners.

International Taxes

Top-ranked individual athletes such as golf and tennis players, coupled with more and more team players, have competed in a number of different countries, and as a result, are called to pay taxes in the countries they work in. For example, a U.S. tennis player who wins prize money in a tournament in the United Kingdom or Australia must pay tax on those earnings under the respective laws of those countries.

Theoretically, a U.S.-based athlete who earns income in a foreign country is subject to double taxation. The income earned in the United Kingdom, for example, can be taxed in both the United Kingdom and the United States (Berry, 2002). To avoid this unfairness, the IRS has created a foreign tax credit to negate the double taxation. Generally, the foreign tax credit works by allowing U.S. resident taxpayers to credit their foreign taxes paid against their domestic tax liability (Dunlop, 2006). However, foreign tax credits do not always serve to completely nullify the foreign tax paid, so a more ideal approach is to utilize a tax treaty between the United States and a foreign country. Such a treaty deals with the double taxation issue broadly and more effectively than the foreign tax credit, which is a creation of domestic U.S. law. For example, the United States has tax treaties with Canada and Mexico. For NHL players, this is a very important factor in avoiding crippling tax liabilities.

References

Badenhausen, K. (2013, April 15). Pro athlete tax returns illustrate complexities of U.S. tax code. *Forbes*. Retrieved February 15, 2016, from http://www.forbes.com/sites/kurtbadenhausen/2013/04/15/pro-athlete-tax-returns-illustrate-complexities-of-u-s-tax-code/#2c201b4828b2

Belsky, G. (2012, March 9). Why $1.5 billion for the Dodgers might be a bargain. *Time: Business of Sports*. Retrieved February 15, 2016, from http://business.time.com/2012/03/09/why-1-5-billion-for-the-dodgers-might-turn-out-to-be-a-bargain/

Berry, C. (2002). Taxation of U.S. athletes playing in foreign countries. *Marquette Law Review*, 13, 1.

Briggs, B. (2013, October 27). Legal procedure: Critics cry foul as NFL defends nonprofit status. *NBCNews.com*. Retrieved July 30, 2016, from http://www.nbcnews.com/business/legal-procedure-critics-cry-foul-nfl-defends-nonprofit-status-8c11412804

Burke, M. (2013, May 8). The PGA Tour: A not-for-profit money machine. *Forbes*. Retrieved May 31, 2016, from http://www.forbes.com/sites/monteburke/2013/05/08/the-pga-tour-a-not-for-profit-money-machine/#5e59a1e82cec

Craggs, T. (2011, June 30). Exclusive: How an NBA team makes money disappear. *Deadspin*. Retrieved May 8, 2016, from http://deadspin.com/5816870/

exclusive-how-and-why-an-nba-team-makes-a-7-million-profit-look-like-a-28-million-loss

Dunlop, J. (2006). Taxing the international athlete: Working toward free trade in the Americas through a multilateral tax treaty. *Northwestern Journal of International Law and Business, 27*, 227.

Ekmekjian, E. C. (1994). The Jock tax: State and local income taxation of professional athletes. *Seton Hall Journal of Sport Law, 4*, 1.

Frostbrowntodd.com (2015, May 19). The city of Cleveland fumbles in applying municipal taxes to NFL players. *Frost, Brown & Todd*. Retrieved May 27, 2016, from http://www.frostbrowntodd.com/resources-1810.html

Galletti, A. (2011, July 7). Better angels. *The Wages of Wins Journal*. Retrieved May 26, 2016, from http://wagesofwins.com/2011/07/07/better-angels/

Hillenmeyer v. Cleveland Board of Review, 144 Ohio St.3d 165, 41 N.E.3d 1164 (Ohio, 2015).

Holo, R and Talansky, J. (2008). Taxing the professional athlete. 9 Fla. Tax Rev. 161.

Internal Revenue Code, sec. 168. 27 USC sec. 168 (2004).

Internal Revenue Code, secs. 501(c) (3), 501(c)(6). 27 USC sec. 501(c)(3) and 501(c)(6) (2016).

IRS Form 990, National Football League (2013). Retrieved October 21, 2016, from http://990s.foundationcenter.org/990_pdf_archive/131/131922622/1319 22622_201303_990O.pdf?_ga=1.126958217.507661570.1477234355

IRS Form 990, National Football League (2015). Retrieved October 21, 2016, from http://990s.foundationcenter.org/990_pdf_archive/131/131922622/1319 22622_201506_990O.pdf?_ga=1.152592061.507661570.1477234355

Lavigne, P. (2013, December 15). Tax breaks powers PGA Tour giving. *ESPN.com*. Retrieved April 2, 2016, from http://espn.go.com/espn/otl/story/_/id/10089803/pga-tour-tax-breaks-help-fuel-giving-which-falls-industry-standards

Lowe, M. (2015, June 28). Pro athletes pay a big price for their success in taxes. *Portland (Me.) Press Herald*. Retrieved February 18, 2016, from http://www.pressherald.com/2015/06/28/pro-athletes-pay-a-big-price-for-their-success-in-taxes/

Ozanian, M. (2012, April 6). New Dodgers' investors will get big tax breaks. *Forbes*. Retrieved May 26, 2016, from http://www.forbes.com/sites/mikeozanian/2012/04/06/new-dodgers-investors-will-get-big-tax-breaks/#2a 15b1d92392

Packard, K., & Baderhausen, K. (2015, April 6). MLB opening day: Tax planning for ballplayers. *Forbes.com*. Retrieved May 27, 2016, from http://www.forbes.com/sites/kurtbadenhausen/2015/04/06/opening-day-tax-planning-for-ballplayers/#18376d5e4c1b

Pomerleau, K. (2015, October 15). 2016 tax brackets. *The Tax Foundation*. Retrieved May 26, 2016, from http://taxfoundation.org/article/2016-tax-brackets

Professional Athletes (2015, February 12). Taxing to the mind, body and wallet. *AndersenTax*. Retrieved February 16, 2016, from http://www.andersentax.com/publications/newsletter/september-2013/professional-athletes-taxing-to-the-mind-body-and-wallet

Pro Sports Tax (2009). Tax information for the NFL rookie. Retrieved May 26, 2016, from http://www.prosportstax.com/Images/Attachments/rn4b61 f78e0a858.pdf

Random, A. (2010, June 28). The taxing impact of state taxes. *Heathoops.com*. Retrieved July 15, 2016, from http://heathoops.com/2010/06/the-taxing-impact-of-state-taxes/

Saturday v. Cleveland Board of Review, 142 Ohio St.3d 528, 33 N.E.3d 46 (Ohio, 2015).

Sherman, R. (2015, April 28). Why the NFL decided to start paying taxes. *SB Nation*. Retrieved May 8, 2016, from http://www.sbnation.com/2015/4/28/ 8508905/nfl-tax-exempt-nonprofit-roger-goodell-salary

Taxaball.com (n.d.). What is the jock tax? Retrieved May 26, 2016, from http:// www.taxaball.com/what-is-the-jock-tax.html

Taxbrackets.org (2015). California income tax brackets. Retrieved May 26, 2016, from http://www.tax-brackets.org/californiataxtable

Wallace, N. (2015, November 5). What do NFL players pay in taxes? *Smartasset*. Retrieved February 16, 2016, from https://smartasset.com/taxes/nfl-jock-taxes

Zagorsky, J. (2015, May 4). Why the NFL and other professional sports don't deserve nonprofit status. *Ohio State University/Jay Zagorsky's Research and Blog*. Retrieved May 8, 2016, from https://u.osu.edu/zagorsky.1/2015/05/04/ nfl-2/

Index